Communications
in Computer and Information Science 1367

More information about this series at http://www.springer.com/series/7899

Deepak Garg · Kit Wong ·
Jagannathan Sarangapani ·
Suneet Kumar Gupta (Eds.)

Advanced Computing

10th International Conference, IACC 2020
Panaji, Goa, India, December 5–6, 2020
Revised Selected Papers, Part I

 Springer

Editors
Deepak Garg
Bennett University
Greater Noida, Uttar Pradesh, India

Kit Wong
University College London
London, UK

Jagannathan Sarangapani
Missouri University of Science
and Technology
Rolla, MO, USA

Suneet Kumar Gupta
Bennett University
Greater Noida, Uttar Pradesh, India

ISSN 1865-0929   ISSN 1865-0937 (electronic)
Communications in Computer and Information Science
ISBN 978-981-16-0400-3   ISBN 978-981-16-0401-0 (eBook)
https://doi.org/10.1007/978-981-16-0401-0

This Springer imprint is published by the registered company Springer Nature Singapore Pte Ltd.
The registered company address is: 152 Beach Road, #21-01/04 Gateway East, Singapore 189721, Singapore

Preface

The 10th International Advanced Computing Conference (IACC 2020) was organized with the objective of bringing together researchers, developers, and practitioners from academia and industry working in the area of advanced computing. The conference consisted of keynote lectures, tutorials, workshops, and oral presentations on all aspects of advanced computing. It was organized specifically to help the computer industry to derive benefits from the advances of next-generation computer and communication technology. Researchers invited to speak presented the latest developments and technical solutions in the areas of High Performance Computing, Advances in Communication and Networks, Advanced Algorithms, Image and Multimedia Processing, Databases, Machine Learning, Deep Learning, Data Science, and Computing in Education.

IACC promotes fundamental and applied research which can help in enhancing the quality of life. The conference was held on 05th-06th December, 2020 to make it an ideal platform for people to share views and experiences in Futuristic Research Techniques in various related areas.

The conference has a track record of acceptance rates from 20% to 25% in the last 10 years. More than 10 IEEE/ACM Fellows hold key positions on the conference committee, giving it a quality edge. In the last 10 years the conference's citation score has been consistently increasing, moving it into the top 10% cited conferences globally. This has been possible due to adherence to quality parameters of review and acceptance rate without any exception, which allows us to make some of the best research available through this platform.

December 2020

Deepak Garg
Kit Wong
Jagannathan Sarangapani
Suneet Kumar Gupta

Organization

Honorary Co-chair

Sundaraja Sitharama Iyengar	Florida International University, USA
Sartaj Sahni	University of Florida, USA
Jagannathan Sarangapani	Missouri University of Science and Technology, USA

General Co-chair

Deepak Garg	Bennett University, India
Ajay Gupta	Western Michigan University, USA
M. A. Maluk Mohamed	M.A.M. College of Engineering and Technology, India

Program Co-chairs

Kit Wong	University College London, UK
George Ghinea	Brunel University London, UK
Carol Smidts	Ohio State University, USA
Ram D. Sriram	National Institute of Standards and Technology, USA
Kamisetty R. Rao	University of Texas at Arlington, USA
Sanjay Madria	Missouri University of Science and Technology, USA
Marques Oge	Florida Atlantic University, USA
Vijay Kumar	University of Missouri-Kansas City, USA

Publication Co-chair

Suneet K. Gupta	Bennett University, India

Technical Program Committee

Hari Mohan Pandey	Edge Hill University, UK
Sumeet Dua	Louisiana Tech University, USA
Jagannathan Sarangapani	Missouri University, USA
Roger Zimmermann	National University of Singapore, Singapore
Shivani Goel	Bennett University, India
Seeram Ramakrishna	National University of Singapore, Singapore
B. V. R. Chowdari	Nanyang Technological University, Singapore
Mun Han Bae	MIU/Mongolia International University, Mongolia
Selwyn Piramuthu	University of Florida, USA
Bharat Bhargava	Purdue University, USA
Omer F. Rana	Cardiff University, UK

Javed I. Khan	Kent State University, USA
Harpreet Singh	Wayne State University, USA
Rajeev Agrawal	North Carolina A&T State University, USA
P. Prabhakaran	St. Joseph University in Tanzania, Tanzania
Yuliya Averyanova	National Aviation University, Ukraine
Mohammed M. Banet	Jordan University of Science and Technology
Dawid Zydek	Idaho State University, USA
Wensheng Zhang	Iowa State University
Bal Virdee	London Metropolitan University, UK
S. Rao Chintalapudi	Pragati Engineering College, India
Qun Wu	Harbin Institute of Technology, China
Anh V. Dinh	University of Saskatchewan, Canada
Lakshman Tamil	University of Texas at Dallas, USA
P. D. D. Dominic	Universiti Teknologi Petronas, Malaysia
Muhammad Sabbir Rahman	North South University, Bangladesh
Zablon Akoko Mbero	University of Botswana, Botswana
V. L. Narasimhan	University of Botswana
Kin-Lu Wong	National Sun Yat-sen University, Taiwan
P. G. S. Velmurugan	Thiagarajar College of Engineering, India
N. B. Balamurugan	Thiagarajar College of Engineering, India
Pawan Lingras	Saint Mary's University, Canada
Mahesh Bundele	Poornima College of Engineering, India
N. Venkateswaran	Sri Sivasubramaniya Nadar College of Engineering, India
R. Venkatesan	National Institute of Ocean Technology, India
Manoranjan Sahoo	National Institute of Technology Trichy, India
Venkatakirthiga Murali	National Institute of Technology Trichy, India
Karthik Thirumala	National Institute of Technology Trichy, India
S. Sundaresh	IEEE Madras Section, India
S. Mageshwari	National Institute of Technology Trichy, India
Premanand V. Chandramani	SSN College of Engineering, India
Mini Vasudevan	Ericsson India Pvt. Ltd., India
P. Swarnalatha	School of CSE, VIT, India
P. Venkatesh	Thiagarajar College of Engineering, India
S. Mercy Shalinie	Thiagarajar College of Engineering, India
Dhanalakshmi K.	National Institute of Technology Tiruchirappalli, India
M. Marsalin Beno	St Xavier's Catholic College of Engineering, India
K. Porkumaran	Dr. N.G.P. Institute of Technology, India
D. Ezhilarasi	National Institute of Technology Tiruchirappalli, India
Ramya Vijay	SASTRA University, India
S. Rajaram	Thiagarajar College of Engineering, India
B. Yogameena	Thiagarajar College of Engineering, India
H. R. Mohan	IEEE India Council Newsletter, India
S. Joseph Gladwin	SSN College of Engineering, India
D. Nirmal	Karunya University, India
N. Mohankumar	SKP Institute of Technology, India

A. Jawahar	SSN College of Engineering, India
K. Dhayalini	K. Ramakrishnan College of Engineering, India
C. Jeyalakshmi	K. Ramakrishnan College of Engineering, India
B. Viswanathan	K. Ramakrishnan College of Engineering, India
V. Jayaprakasan	IEEE Madras Section, India
D. Venkata Vara Prasad	SSN College of Engineering, India
Jayakumari J.	Mar Baselios College of Engineering and Technology, India
P. A. Manoharan	IEEE Madras Section, India
S. Salivahanan	IEEE Madras Section, India
P. Santhi Thilagam	National Institute of Technology Karnataka, India
Umapada Pal	Indian Statistical Institute, Indian
A. Revathi	SASTRA Deemed University, India
K. Prabhu	National Institute of Technology Karnataka, India
B. Venkatalakshmi	Velammal Engineering College, India
S. Suresh	NIT Trichy, India
V. Mariappan	NIT Trichy, India
T. Senthilkumar	Anna University, India
S. Arul Daniel	NIT Trichy, India
N. Sivakumaran	NIT Trichy, India
N. Kumaresan	NIT Trichy, India
R. Gnanadass	Pondicherry Engineering College, India
S. Chandramohan	College of Engineering, Guindy, India
D. Devaraj	Kalasalingam Academy of Research and Education, India
Avani Vasant	Babaria Institute of Technology, India
S. Raghavan	National Institute of Technology Trichy, India
J. Williams	Agnel Institute of Technology & Design, India
R. Boopathi Rani	National Institute of Technology Puducherry, India
Anandan	Vellore Institute of Technology, India
R. Kalidoss	SSN College of Engineering, India
R. K. Mugelan	Vellore Institute of Technology, India
V. Vinod Kumar	Government College of Engineering Kannur, India
R. Saravanan	VIT, India
S. Sheik Aalam	iSENSE Intelligence Solutions, India
E. Srinivasan	Pondicherry Engineering College, India
M. Hariharan	NIT, Uttarakhand, India
L. Ganesan	A.C. Government College of Engineering and Technology, India
Varun P. Gopi	NIT Trichy, India
S. Mary Joans	Velammal Engineering College, India
V. Vijaya Chamundeeswari	Velammal Engineering College, India
T. Prabhakar	GMRIT, India
V. Kamakoti	IITM, India
D. Vaithiyanathan	NIT Delhi, India
N. Janakiraman	KLN College of Engineering, India

S. Suresh	Banaras Hindu University, India
R. Gobi	PRIST University, India
B. Janet	National Institute of Technology Tiruchirappalli, India
R. Sivashankar	Madanapalle Institute of Technology & Science, India
S. Moses Santhakumar	National Institute of Technology Trichy, India
G. Beulah Gnana Ananthi	Anna University, India
Bud Mishra	New York University, USA
S. Suresh Babu	Adhiyamaan College of Engineering, India
T. Ramesh	NIT Trichy, India
V. Anatha Krishanan	NIT Trichy, India
R. B. Patel	MMU Mullana, India
Adesh Kumar Sharma	NDRI, India
Gunamani Jena	JNTU, Andhra Pradesh, India
Maninder Singh	Thapar Institute of Engineering and Technology, India
Gurbinder Singh	GNDU, India
Manoj Manuja	Chitkara University, India
Ajay Sharma	NIT, New Delhi, India
Manjit Patterh	UIET, Punjabi University, India
Mayank Dave	NIT, Kurukshetra, India
A. L. Sangal	NIT Jalandhar, India
C. Suresh Thakur	Naval Research Board, India
L. M. Bhardwaj	Amity University Noida, India
Sh. Manu Goel	Infosys, India
Parvinder Singh	DCRUST, India
Gurpal Singh	PTU, Fatehgarh, India
M. Syamala	Punjab University Chandigarh, India
Lalit Awasthi	NIT Jalandhar, India
Ajay Bansal	NIT Jalandhur, India
Jyotsna Sengupta	Punjabi Univ, India
Ravi Aggarwal	Adobe, USA
V. R. Singh	New Delhi, India
Sigurd Meldal	San José State University, USA
M. Balakrishnan	IIT New Delhi, India
Renu Vig	University Institute of Engineering & Technology, Panjab University, India
Malay Pakhira	KGEC, India
Savita Gupta	University Institute of Engineering & Technology, Panjab University, India
Lakhwinder Kaur	University Institute of Engineering & Technology, Punjabi University, India
B. Ramadoss	NIT Trichy, India
Ashwani Kush	Kurukshetra University, India
Manas Ranjan Patra	Berhampur University, India
Sukhwinder Singh	University Institute of Engineering & Technology, Panjab University, India
Dharmendra Kumar	GJU, India

Chandan Singh	Punjabi University, India
Rajinder Nath	Kurukshetra University, India
Manjaiah D. H.	Mangalore University, India
Himanshu Aggarwal	Punjabi University, India
R. S. Kaler	Thapar Institute of Engineering and Technology, India
Pabitra Pal Chaudhary	Indian Statistical Institute, India
S. K. Pal	DRDO, India
G. S. Lehal	Punjabi University, India
Rajkumar Kannan	Bishop Heber College, India
Yogesh Chaba	GJU, India
Amardeep Singh	Punjabi Unversity, India
Hardeep Singh	GNDU, India
Ajay Rana	Amity University, India
Kanwaljeet Singh	Punjabi University, India
P. K. Bansal	MIMIT, India
C. K. Bhensdadia	DD University, India
Savina Bansal	GZSCET, India
Mohammad Asger	BGSB, India
Rajesh Bhatia	Punjab Engineering College, India
Stephen John Turner	NTU, Singapore
Om Vikas	Ministry of IT, India
Chiranjeev Kumar	IIT (ISM) Dhanbad, India
Bhim Singh	IEEE Delhi Section, India
Anandha Gopalan	Imperial College London, UK
Ram Gopal Gupta	IEEE India Council, India
A. K. Sharma	YMCA University of Science and Technology, India
Rob Reilly	MIT, USA
B. K. Murthy	C-DAC, Noida, India
Karmeshu	Jawaharlal Nehru University, India
K. K. Biswas	IIT Delhi, India
Sandeep Sen	IIT Delhi, India
Suneeta Aggarwal	MNNIT Allahabad, India
Satish Chand	NSIT, India
Savita Goel	IIT Delhi, India
Raghuraj Singh	HBTI Kanpur, India
Ajeet Kumar	Cognizant, India
Varun Dutt	IIT Mandi, India
D. K. Lobiyal	JNU, India
Ajay Rana	Amity University, India
R. S. Yadav	MNNIT Allahabad, India
N. Singh	NSUT, India
Bulusu Anand	IIT Roorkee, India
R. K. Singh	BTKIT Dwarahat, India
Sateesh Kumar Peddoju	IIT Roorkee, India
Divakar Yadav	JIIT, Noida, India
Naveen Kumar Singh	IGNOU, India

R. S. Raw	NSUT, India
Prabha Sharma	IIT Kanpur, India
Ela Kumar	GBU, India
Vidushi Sharma	GBU, India
Sumit Srivastava	Manipal University Jaipur, India
Manish K. Gupta	DA-IICT, India
Annappa B.	NIT Karnataka, India
Nikhil Pal	ISI, India
P. I. Basarkod	REVA ITM Bangalore, India
Anil Dahiya	Manipal University, India
Gautam Barua	IIT Guwahati, India
Anjana Gosain	GGSIP University, India
Saroja Devi	NMIT, India
P. K. Saxena	DRDO, India
B. K. Das	ITM University, India
Raghu Reddy	IIIT Hyderabad, India
B. Chandra	IIT Delhi, India
R. K. Agarwal	JNU, India
Basim Alhadidi	Al-Balqa' Applied University, Jordan
B. G. Krishna	Space Application Center, ISRO, India
Naveen Garg	IIT Delhi, India
K. S. Subramanian	IGNOU, India
Vijay Nadadur	Tationem, India
Biplab Sikdar	National University of Singapore, Singapore
Sreeram Ramakrishna	National University of Singapore, Singapore
Vikas Mathur	RightCloudz, India
B. V. R. Chaoudhari	NUS, Singapore
Hari Krishna Garg	Engineering National University of Singapore, Singapore
Raja Dutta	IIT Kharagpur, India
Y. V. S. Lakshmi	Center for Development of Telematics, India
Vishakha Vaidya	Adobe, USA
Sudipto Shankar Dasgupta	Infosys, India
R. Dattakumar	VTU, India
Atal Chaudhari	Jadavpur University, India
K. Rajinikanth	RR School of Architecture, India
Srikanta Murthy	PESCE, India
Ganga Boraiah	KIMS, India
Ananda Kumar K. R.	SJBIT, India
Champa H. N.	UVCE, India
S. N. Omkar	IISC, India
Bala Ji	C-DAC, India
Annapoorna Patil	Ramaiah Institute of Technology, India
Chandrashekhar S. N.	SJCIT, India
M. Misbahuddin	C-DAC, India
Roshini Charles	C-DAC, India

Saroj Meher	ISI, India
Jharna Majumdar	NMIT, India
Cauvery N. K.	RVCE, India
G. K. Patra	CSIR, India
Anandi J.	Oxford College of Engineering, India
K. V. Dinesha	IIIT Bangalore, India
Sunita K. R.	BIT, India
Shailaja	Ambedkar Institute of Technology, India
Andrzej Rucinski	University of New Hampshire, USA
K. R. Murali Mohan	DST, GOI, India
Ramesh Paturi	Microsoft, India
Chandra Sekharan K.	National Institute of Technology Karnataka, India
S. Viswanadha Raju	Jawaharlal Nehru Technological University, India
C. Krishna Mohan	Indian Institute of Technology Hyderabad, India
S. R. N. Reddy	Delhi University, India
R. T. Goswamy	Birla Institute of Technology, India
B. Surekha	KS Institute of Technology, India
P. Trinatha Rao	GITAM University, India
G. Varaprasad	BMS College of Engineering, India
M. Usha Rani	SPM University, India
Tanmay De	NIT Durgapur, India
P. V. Lakshmi	SPM University, India
K. A. Selvaradjou	Pondicherry University, India
Ch. Satyananda Reddy	Andhra University, India
Jeegar Trivedi	Sardar Vallabhai Patel University, India
S. V. Raoa	Indian Institute of Technology Guwahati, India
Suresh Varma	Adikavi Nannaya University, India
Y. Padma Sai	VNR Vignana Jyothi Institute of Engineering & Technology, India
T. Ranga Babu	RVR & JC College of Engineering, India
D. Venkat Rao	Narasaraopet Inst. of Technology, India
N. Sudhakar Reddy	SV College of Engineering, India
Dhiraj Sunehra	Jawaharlal Nehru Technological University, India
Madhavi Gudavalli	Jawaharlal Nehru Technological University, India
B. Hemantha Kumar	RVR & JC College of Engineering, India
N. Srinagesh	RVR & JC College of Engineering, India
Bipin Bihari Jayasingh	CVR College of Engineering, India
M. Ramesh	Jawaharlal Nehru Technological University, India
P. Rajeshwari	GITAM University, India
R. Kiran Kumar	Krishna University, India
M. Dhana Lakshmi	Jawaharlal Nehru Technological University, India
P. Raja Rajeswari	Andhra University, India
O. Srinivasa Rao	Jawaharlal Nehru Technological University, India
D. Ramesh	Jawaharlal Nehru Technological University, India
B. Kranthi Kiran	Jawaharlal Nehru Technological University, India
R. V. G. Anjaneyulu	National Remote Sensing Centre, NRSC, India

A. Nagesh	MGIT, India
P. Sammulal	Jawaharlal Nehru Technological University, India
G. Narasimha	Jawaharlal Nehru Technological University, India
B. V. Ram Naresh Yadav	Jawaharlal Nehru Technological University, India
B. N. Bhandari	JNTUH, India
O. B. V. Ramanaiah	VNRVJIET, India
M. Malini	Osmania University, India
Anil Kumar Vuppala	IIIT Hyderabad, India
Golla Vara Prasad	College of Engineering, India
M. Surya Kalavathi	JNTUH, India
Duggirala Srinivasa Rao	JNTUH, India
Makkena Madhavi Latha	JNTUH, India
L. Anjaneyulu	NIT Warangal, India
K. Anitha Sheela	JNTUH, India
B. Padmaja Rani	JNTUH College of Engineering Hyderabad, India
S. Mangai	Velalar College of Engg & Tech., India
P. Chandra Sekhar	Osmania University, India
Mrityunjoy Chakraborty	IIT Kharagpur, India
Manish Shrivastava	IIIT Hyderabad, India
Uttam Kumar Roy	Jadavpur University, India
Kalpana Naidu	IIT Kota, India
A. Swarnalatha	St. Joseph's College of Engineering, India
Aaditya Maheshwari	Techno India NJR Institute of Technology, India
Ajit Panda	National Institute of Science and Technology (NIST), India
Amit Kumar	Infosys Technologies, India
R. Anuradha	Sri Ramakrishna Engineering College, India
Anurag Goswami	Bennett University, India
B. G. Prasad	BMS College of Engineering, India
R. Balaji Ganesh	NIT Trichy, India
Chung	Trinity College Dublin, Ireland
D. Murali	VEMU Institute of Technology, India
Deepak Padmanabhan	Queen's University Belfast, UK
Dinesh G. Harkut	Ram Meghe Institute of Engineering and Management, Badnera, India
Dinesh Manocha	University of Maryland, USA
Firoz Alam	RMIT University, Australia
Frederic Andres	National Institute of Informatics, Japan
G. Kishor Kumar	RGMCET, India
G. L. Prajapati	Devi Ahilya University, India
Gaurav Varshney	IIT Jammu, India
Geeta Sikka	Dr B R Ambedkar National Institute of Technology, India
K. Giri Babu	VVIT, India
Gopal Sakarkar	GHRCE, India
Gudivada Venkat Naidu	East Carolina University, USA

Gurdeep Hura	University of Maryland, USA
G. V. Padma Raju	S.R.K.R., India
Yashodhara V. Haribhakta	Government College of Engineering Pune, India
Haritha Dasari	SRK Institute of Technology, India
Harsh Dev	PSIT Kanpur, India
Yashwantsinh Jadeja	Marwadi University, India
Jagdish Chand Bansal	South Asian University, India
Vinit Jakhetiya	Indian Institute of Technology (IIT) Jammu, India
Singaraju Jyothi	Sri Padmavati Mahila Visvavidyalayam, India
K. Subramanian	IIT Kanpur, India
Kalaiarasi Sonai Muthu Anbananthen	Multimedia University, Malaysia
Kalyana Saravanan Annathurai	Kongu Engineering College, India
K. Kotecha	Symbiosis Institute of Technology, India
K. K. Patel	Charotar University of Science & Technology (CHARUSAT) India
Kokou Yetongnon	University of Burgundy, France
Kuldeep Sharma	Jain University, India
Sumalatha Lingamgunta	JNTU Kakinada, India
Latika Duhan	Sushant University, India
Luca Saba	University of Cagliari, Italy
M. Arun	VIT University, India
M. G. Sumithra	KPR Institute of Engineering and Technology, India
M. Mary Shanthi Rani	Deemed University Gandhigram, India
Suneetha Manne	VR Siddhartha Engineering College, India
Milind Shah	Fr. C. Rodrigues Institute of Technology, India
Mohammed Asghar	Baba Ghulam Shah Badshah University, India
Nagesh Vadaparthi	MVGR College of Engineering, India
Navanath Saharia	IIIT Manipur, India
Neeraj Kumar	Thapar Institute of Engineering and Technology, India
Neeraj Mittal	University of Texas at Dallas, USA
Nikunj Tahilramani	Adani Institute of Infrastructure Engineering (AIIE), India
Nobel Xavier	Glassdoor, USA
Om Vikash	ABVIITM Gwalior, India
S. N. Omkar Subbaram	Indian Institute of Science, India
Laxmi Lydia	VIIT, India
P. Arul Sivanatham	Muscat College, Oman
P. K. Banssal	Quest Group of Institutions, India
Venkata Padmavati Metta	Bhilai Institute of Technology, India
Parteek Bhatia	Thapar Institute of Engineering & Technology, India
Pradeep Kumar	Indian Institute of Management Lucknow, India
Prashant Singh Rana	Thapar Institute of Engg. & Tech., India
Pushpender Sarao	Hyderabad Institute of Technology and Management, India

Krishnan Rangarajan	Dayananda Sagar College of Engineering, India
M. Naresh Babu	National Institute of Technology Silchar, India
R. Priya Vaijayanthi	GMR Institute of Technology, India
Saravanan R.	VIT University, India
Radhika K. R.	BMSCE, India
Rajkumar Buyya	University of Melbourne, Australia
Rajanikanth Aluvalu	Vardhaman College of Engineering, India
Ramakanth Kumar P.	R V College of Engineering, India
Roshani Raut	Vishwakarma Institute of Information Technology, India
Suresh Babu	Adhiyamaan College of Engineering, India
Sabu M. Thampi	Indian Institute of Information Tech & Mgt-Kerala, India
Sajal K. Das	Missouri Univ. of Science and Technology, USA
Samayveer Singh	Ambedkar National Institute of Technology, India
Sanjeevikumar Padmanaban	Aalborg University, Denmark
Sanjeev Pippal	GL Bajaj Institute of Management & Technology, India
Santosh Saraf	KLS Gogte Institute of Technolgy, India
Satyadhyan Chickerur	KLE Technological University, India
Saurabh Kumar Garg	University of Tasmania, Australia
Shachi Natu	TSE College, India
Shailendra Aswale	SRIEIT, India
Shirin Bhanu Koduri	Vasavi College of Engineering, India
Shom Das	Biju Patnaik University of Technology, India
Shreenivas Londhe	Vishwakarma Institute of Information Technology, India
Shweta Agrawal	SIRT, SAGE University, India
Shylaja S. S.	PES University, India
Srabanti Maji	DIT University, India
Sudipta Roy	Assam University, India
Suneet Gupta	Bennett University, India
Sunil Kumar Khatri	Amity University Tashkent, Uzbekistan
Tummala Ranga Babu	R.V.R. & J.C. College of Engineering, India
Tessy Mathew	MBCET, India
Anandakrishnan V.	National Institute of Technology Tiruchirappalli, India
V. Gomathi	National Engineering College, Kovilpatti, India
Vaibhav Gandhi	B H Gardi College of Engineering & Technology, India
Vaibhav Anu	Montclair State University, USA
Koppula Vijaya Kumar	CMR College of Engg. & Tech., India
Vikram Bambedkar	Cognizant Technology Solutions, Australia
Virendrakumar Bhavsar	Univ. of New Brunswick, Canada
Vishnu Pendyala	San José State University, USA
Vishnu Vardhan B.	JNTUH College of Engineering Manthani, India
M. Wilscy	Saintgits College of Engineering, Kottayam, India
Yamuna Prasad	IIT Jammu, India

Nishu Gupta	Vaagdevi College of Engineering (Autonomous), India
B. Surendiran	National Institute of Technology (NIT) Puducherry, India
Bhadri Raju M. S. V. S.	S.R.K.R. Engineering College, India
Deepak Poola	IBM India Private Limited, India
Edara Sreenivasa Reddy	Acharya Nagarjuna University, India
Seung Hwa Chung	Samsung, South Korea
Anila Rao	MLRIT, India
B. Raveendra Babu	RVR & JC College of Engineering, India
V. K. Jain	Mody University, India
Abhishek Shukla	R.D. Engineering College, India
Ajay Shiv Sharma	Melbourne Institute of Technology, Australia
G. Singaravel	K.S.R. College of Engineering, India
M. Nageswara Rao	KL University, India
K. Suvarna Vani	V R Siddhartha Engineering College, India
Amit Sinha	ABES Engg. College, India
Md. Dilshad Anasari	CMRCET, India
Mainak Biswas	JIS University, India
Abhinav Tomar	IIT(ISM) Dhanbad, India
A. Obulesu	Anurag University, India
Dattatraya V. Kodavade	D.K.T.E Society's Textile & Engineering Institute, India
Arpit Bhardwaj	Bennett University, India
Gaurav Singal	Bennett University, India
Madhushi Verma	Bennett University, India
Tanveer Ahmed	Bennett University, India
Vipul Kumar Mishra	Bennett University, India
Tapas Badal	Bennett University, India
Mayank Swankar	Bennett University, India
Hiren Thakkar	Bennett University, India
Shakti Sharma	Bennett University, India
Sanjeet Kumar Nayak	Bennett University, India
Shashidhar R.	Bennett University, India
Indrajeet Gupta	Bennett University, India
Kuldeep Chaurasia	Bennett University, India
Tanmay Bhowmik	Bennett University, India
Sridhar Swaminathan	Bennett University, India
Rohan Sharma	Bennett University, India
Suchi Kumari	Bennett University, India
Vijay Kumar Bohat	Bennett University, India
Simranjit Singh	Bennett University, India
Deepak Singh	Bennett University, India
Nidhi Chahal	Bennett University, India
Vijaypal Singh Rathor	Bennett University, India
Mohit Sajwan	Bennett University, India
Gunjan Rehani	Bennett University, India

Apeksha Agrawal   Bennett University, India
Samya Muhuri   Bennett University, India
Rahul Kumar Verma   Bennett University, India
Suman Bhattacharjee   Bennett University, India
Ankur Gupta   Bennett University, India

Contents – Part I

**Using Different Neural Network Architectures
for Interesting Applications**

Contents – Part II

New Approaches in Software Engineering

About the Editors

Dr. Deepak Garg is Director NVIDIA Bennett Research Center on AI, Director Leadingindia.ai and Chair, CSE, Bennett University with 30 SCI publications and 700 million INR funding in Grants He has ∼1000 citation count and h-index of 16 in Google Scholar. He has 60 Scopus papers and in total 130+ publications including IEEE Transactions, Springer and Elsevier Journals. Worked in national and international committees on ABET, NBA and NAAC accreditation. Known as algorithm and Deep Learning gurus in India and consulting algorithmguru.com. He is an active Blogger with Times of India with nickname as "Breaking Shackles". Homepage www.gdeepak.com

Kit Wong received the BEng, the MPhil, and the PhD degrees, all in Electrical and Electronic Engineering, from the Hong Kong University of Science and Technology, Hong Kong, in 1996, 1998, and 2001, respectively. Since August 2006, he has been with University College London.

Prof. Wong is Fellow of IEEE and IET. He is Area Editor for IEEE Transactions on Wireless Communications, and Senior Editor for the IEEE Communications Letters and IEEE Wireless Communications Letters.

Dr. Sarangapani Jagannathan is at the Missouri University of Science and Technology (former University of Missouri-Rolla) where he is a Rutledge-Emerson Distinguished Professor of Electrical and Computer Engineering and served as a Site Director for the NSF Industry/University Cooperative Research Center on Intelligent Maintenance Systems. His research interests include neural networks and learning, secure human-cyber-physical systems, prognostics, and autonomous systems/robotics. He has co-authored with his students 176 peer reviewed journal articles, 289 refereed IEEE conference articles, authored/co-edited 6 books, received 21 US patents and graduated 30 doctoral and 31

M.S thesis students. He received many awards including the 2020 best AE award from IEEE SMC Transactions, 2018 IEEE CSS Transition to Practice Award, 2007 Boeing Pride Achievement Award, 2000 NSF Career Award, 2001 Caterpillar Research Excellence Award, and many others. He is a Fellow of the IEEE, National Academy of Inventors, and Institute of Measurement and Control, UK and Institution of Engineering and Technology (IET), UK.

Suneet Kumar Gupta is a Asst. Professor in the Department of Computer Science Engineering at Bennett University, Gr. Noida. His current research interests are Wireless Sensor Network, Internet of Things, Natural Language Processing and Brain-Computer Interaction. Presently Dr. Gupta has completed a Wireless Sensor Network based project funded by Department of Science and Technology, Uttar Pradesh.

Dr. Gupta is also part of a project funded by the Royal Academy of Science London entitled with Leadingindia.ai. He has more than 45 research articles, authored 2 books and 2 book chapters in his account.

Application of Artificial Intelligence and Machine Learning in Healthcare

Epileptic Seizure Detection Using CNN

Divya Acharya[1]([⊠]), Anushna Gowreddygari[2], Richa Bhatia[3], Varsha Shaju[4], S. Aparna[5], and Arpit Bhardwaj[1]

[1] Bennett University, Greater Noida, India
{da9642,arpit.bhardwaj}@bennett.edu.in
[2] VNR Vignana Jyothi Institue of Engineering and Technology, Hyderabad, India
[3] VESIT College, Mumbai, Maharashtra, India
richa.bhatia@ves.ac.in
[4] Vidya Academy of Science and Technology, Thrissur, Kerala, India
[5] Saintgits College of Engineering, Kottayam, Kerala, India
aparnasanthosh1911@gmail.com

Abstract. Epilepsy is one of the most devastating diseases in the history of mankind. A neurological disorder in which irregular transmission of brain waves result in seizures and physical and emotional imbalance. This paper presents the study of effective use of Convolutional Neural Network (CNN) a deep learning algorithm for epileptic seizure detection. This innovative technology will help the real world to make diagnosis of the disease faster with greater accuracy. A binary class epilepsy dataset is considered with 179 feature extracted as the attributes. Binary and multiclass classification is performed by considering the class with epileptic activity against all non-epileptic class. For classification CNN model is proposed which achieved an accuracy of 98.32%. Then by applying a different multiclass data set having 4 classes, the degree of generalization of our model is also checked as the accuracy of end results was high. For 10-fold cross validation and 70–30 data splitting method our models for performance is evaluated using various performance metrics.

Keywords: Epilepsy · EEG · Deep learning · CNN · Machine learning

1 Introduction

Brain waves are electrical brain impulses. The behavior, emotions and thoughts of an individual within our brains are communicated between neurons. Brainwaves are produced by synchronized electric pulses from neuron masses that communicate with each other. Brainwaves happen at different frequencies [1]. Some are fast, and others are slow. Such EEG (Electroencephalogram) Bands are generally called delta, theta, alpha, and beta and gamma and are measured in cycles per second or hertz(Hz). Irregularity in these waves results in several problems ranging from irregular sleeping patterns to several neural diseases like epilepsy. An EEG (Electroencephalography) can be used to identify possible issues relevant to the irregularity in brainwaves [2].

Electroencephalography (EEG) is a method of electrophysiological monitoring to record activities of the brain [3]. It is a non-invasive method in which electrodes are

© Springer Nature Singapore Pte Ltd. 2021
D. Garg et al. (Eds.): IACC 2020, CCIS 1367, pp. 3–16, 2021.
https://doi.org/10.1007/978-981-16-0401-0_1

placed along the scalp. During EEG electrodes with wires are attached to one's head. This electrode detects the brain waves and the EEG machine amplifies it and later the wave pattern is recorded on screen or paper [4]. Most commonly used for evaluating the form and origin of seizure.

Epilepsy is a neurological disorder in which brain activity becomes abnormal resulting in the sensations, and loss of consciousness, exhibition of seizures, unusual behavior [5]. The two main types of seizures include focal and generalized seizures. The focal seizure is those which start at a particular part of the brain and are named after the origin. Generalized seizures are those in which the brain misfires and result in muscle spasms and blackouts.

Using new and emerging technologies like deep learning, this research paper is able to make a directional change in the field of medical science. This can be used as a prime tool in diagnosis, the most important phase in medical science. Epilepsy being one of the most complicated diseases, it needs accurate detection facilities. EEG signals recorded are analyzed by neuro physician and related specialists [6]. This detection and diagnosis method depends solely on the decision of humans are susceptible to human prone errors and is really time-consuming. Using deep learning algorithms, an automated alternative solution is found that is faster and less error-prone thereby increasing the patient's quality of life [7].

A detailed study of CNN (Convolutional Neural Network) for epileptic seizure detection is presented in this research paper. The network performance is tested using four approaches: a combination of a 10-fold cross-validation method and two databases (binary and multiclass). The results are presented using the confusion matrix and as well as by plotting accuracy-loss graphs. The overall performance of our model and the results obtained from this study prove that the superiority of our CNN based deep learning technique to effectively detect epileptic seizure.

2   Related Work

As deep learning is one of the most emerging and advanced technology now, there are numerous effective studies done in order to effectively incorporate it in different means of life. Like any other, epilepsy detection using deep learning have already undergone different assessment by scholars. Here some of the state-of-the-art work is described which were done earlier.

Sirwan Tofiq and Mokhtar Mohammad [8] mentioned how deep neural networks allow learning directly on the data can be useful. In almost all machine learning applications, this approach has been hugely successful. They created a new framework which also learns directly from the data, without extracting a set of functions. The EEG signal is segmented into 4 segments and used to train the memory network in the long and short term. The trained model is used to discriminate against the background of the EEG seizure. The Freiburg EEG data set is used. Approximately 97.75% accuracy is achieved.

Vikrant Doma and Martin pirouz [9] conducted an in-depth analysis of the EEG data set epoch and conducted a comparative study of multiple machine learning techniques like SVM, K-nearest neighbor, LDA, Decision trees. The accuracy was between 55–75%.

The study carried out by a group of researchers Mi Li, Hongpei Xu, Xingwang Liu, Shengfu Liu [10] used various EEG channel combinations and classified the emotional states into two dimensions mainly valence and arousal. Entropy and energy than measured as neighboring K-nearest characteristics. The accuracy was ranging from 89–95%.

Jong-Seob Yun and Jin Heon Kim [11] used the DEAP data set to classify emotions by modeling the artificial neural network, k-NN, and SVM models by selecting EEG training data based on the Valence as well as the Arousal values calculated using the SAM (Self-Assessment Manikin) process methods. Accuracy of 60–70% was shown.

Ramy Hussein, Hamid Palangi, Rabab Ward, Z. Jane Wang [12] used the LSTM network for the classification of their model. SoftMax functions were also found a handful in their research. But the approach was found noisy and robust in real-life situations.

3 Methodology

In this section proposed system architecture of detecting epilepsy using CNN and the architecture of proposed CNN is described next.

3.1 Proposed System Architecture

Data is the basis for any machine learning based classification problem. Data collection is a crucial task as data gathered will affect the model used for classification problem. Initially input data of epilepsy is taken. After the data is collected it is preprocessed as the real world data is noisy, incomplete, and inconsistent. To resolve such issues preprocessing is done on the data set. After collecting the data it is divide into training and testing data, where training data is large and testing data is smaller than the training data. Then an appropriate model which suits our data set and our requirements is selected. In our project, CNN model is taken for classifying the data into two groups. The model makes the prediction in two classes. Class 0 is for patients suffering from epileptic seizures and class 1 is patients not suffering.

3.2 Proposed Convolutional Neural Network Model (CNN)

The Convolutional Neural Network (CNN) is class of Deep Neural Network, most widely used for working with 2d image data, although it can be used to work with 1d and 3d data also. CNN was inspired from the biological process and its architecture is similar to the connections between the neurons in the human brain. The name CNN refers to the network using a mathematical operation called convolution.

A CNN usually consists of an input layer, an output layer and multiple hidden layers sometimes only one hidden layer is present. Typically, the hidden layers of a CNN consist of a series of convolutional layers which converge with a multiplication or other dot product (Fig. 1).

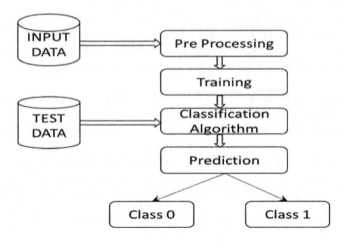

Fig. 1. System architecture of prediction algorithm

CNN model as the ability to learn the filters and these filters are usually smaller in size than the input and dot product is applied between the filter sized patch of the input and the filter which is added to get a value. Sometimes the size of the output data may be different from the input data so to retain the size and make it equal padding is done. Specifically, it is possible to inspect and visualize the two-dimensional filters learned by the model to discover the types of features that the model can detect, and it is possible to inspect the activation maps produced by convolutional layers to understand precisely what features were detected for a given input. Compared to other classification algorithms the pre-processing required for CNN is much lower.

CNN is a method of information processing which is influenced by the way information is processed by the biological neural network which is the human brain. The main goal is to build a system that performs specific computational tasks faster than the conventional systems. These tasks include the identification and classification of patterns, approximation, optimization and clustering of data. This includes a huge number of highly interconnected processing units that integrate to solve a particular problem. Messages passing through the network can influence the configuration of ANN when a neural network changes or learns depending on the I/O.

Figure 2 shows the architecture of our CNN model. The CNN model consists of an input layer and output layer and 4 hidden layers which has a dense layer. The data set is fed to the input layer and filters are applied which produce an output which are fed as input to the next layer.

Max pooling and dropout are applied on the 1d convolutional layers to avoid overfitting of the data and to reduce the computational costs. Max pooling will take the maximum value from the previous layer as the neuron in the next layer, and dropout reduces the number of neurons performing in the convolution to reduce computation cost. Relu activation function is used for the convolutional layers and SoftMax function is used on the output layer. The output layer classifies the data into seizure or not seizure.

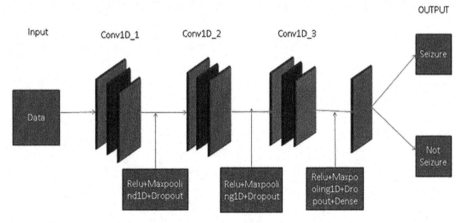

Fig. 2. Architecture of CNN Model

4 Experimental Results

This section contains the description of dataset used, implementation of proposed CNN model, and discussion and analysis on results obtained as follows:

4.1 Dataset

Figure 3 shows the dataset and is held by the UCI machine learning repository [13]. It is a preprocessed dataset. The sampling rate of the data was 173.61 Hz. It includes 11500 rows and 179 attributes with the closing attribute representing the class. The data set includes the recording of 500 people's brain activity. At a given time point, each data point represents the EEG recording value. So for 2.3.6 s, there are 500 individuals in total with 4097 data points. These 4097 statistical points were divided into 23 parts, each part containing 178 data factors, and each data point represents the EEG recording value at an exceptional time factor. Now the dataset have 23 * 500 = 11500 excerpts of facts (rows) and each record incorporates 178 data points. The last column shows the values of y that are 1, 2, 3, 4, 5. The dataset is converted into binary class problem having epilepsy and non-epilepsy for classification.

The values of y are given in 179 dimensional input vector column and the explanatory variables are referred to as X1, X2,...., X178. The label in y represents the EEG recordings of people taken from different states.

Class 2 to 5 are the records with people not having epileptic seizures and class 1 is for people suffering from epileptic seizure. In this research paper we have implemented a binary classification and multi class classification by means of thinking about class 1 as people who are epileptic and the rest of the classes are blended and made right into a class 0 that is taken into consideration to be the folks who are not epileptic for binary class.

FN	FO	FP	FQ	FR	FS	FT	FU	FV	FW	FX
X169	X170	X171	X172	X173	X174	X175	X176	X177	X178	y
8	-17	-15	-31	-77	-103	-127	-116	-83	-51	4
168	164	150	146	152	157	156	154	143	129	1
29	57	64	48	19	-12	-30	-35	-35	-36	5
-80	-82	-81	-80	-77	-85	-77	-72	-69	-65	5
10	4	2	-12	-32	-41	-65	-83	-89	-73	5
-6	-12	-31	-42	-54	-60	-64	-60	-56	-55	5
-137	-125	-99	-79	-62	-41	-26	11	67	128	4
-67	-79	-91	-97	-88	-76	-72	-66	-57	-39	2
-386	-400	-379	-336	-281	-226	-174	-125	-79	-40	1
65	49	31	11	-5	-17	-19	-15	-15	-11	4
-51	-38	-4	25	16	-16	-74	-101	-89	-49	5
415	423	434	416	374	319	268	215	165	103	1
-80	-56	-41	-40	-43	-32	-13	-1	-7	-44	3
-51	-88	-102	-97	-77	-45	-19	13	44	68	4
33	32	35	36	34	32	26	23	18	20	2
-57	-49	-39	-35	-29	-10	4	21	31	37	3
42	43	41	41	43	43	40	41	41	49	2
28	34	27	22	18	15	13	9	9	3	3
54	43	28	25	19	30	35	26	5	-13	4
2	3	5	10	19	31	36	40	43	36	2
409	415	428	463	510	562	607	667	748	763	1
-92	-81	-51	-38	-11	-12	4	5	-4	-3	2
-227	-231	-221	-248	-321	-444	-530	-548	-536	-486	1
-162	-189	-214	-226	-224	-203	-171	-129	-85	-40	1
271	312	360	421	445	413	310	177	41	-71	1
48	56	56	62	54	53	53	50	57	54	3
-12	-26	-45	-55	-55	-46	-45	-43	-42	-42	5
234	114	-39	-185	-293	-351	-379	-380	-350	-308	1

Fig. 3. Data set

4.2 Implementation of CNN Model

Our proposed CNN model is a 1 dimensional fully connected sequential model with an input layer an output layer and 4 hidden layers which has one dense layer. Implemented the model using two approaches one is by splitting the data set in 70–30 ratio and the other by 10 fold cross validation method. For the implementation of the CNN algorithm, Kera's API was used to develop the CNN model with input size as 178×1. The data set was divided into training and testing in the ratio 70:30. The input is fed into the CNN architecture with a sequence of convolutional and pooling layers. Max pooling and dropout is applied on the convolutional layers to avoid overfitting and to reduce the computational cost. Padding was applied for each layer and a stride of 2 was applied. SoftMax and ReLu were used as the activation functions and Adam as the optimizer. Compilation of the CNN model was done by specifying the loss function as "categorical cross-entropy" and evaluation metric as "accuracy". Training of the CNN model was done with batch-size equal to 16 for 200 epochs. When validated with the test set, an accuracy of 97.19% was obtained.

In the 10-fold cross validation model K-Fold was imported from sklearn.model_selection package and the number of folds were taken as 10. The same model was implemented within 10 folds each with batch size 20 and 200 epochs and accuracy was calculated for each fold and the mean accuracy of all the folds was taken, and the model achieved an accuracy of 98.32%. Using 10 fold cross validation, better accuracy is provide for both testing and training and it is also beneficial when the data set size is small.

Table 1. Hyperparameters for the proposed CNN Model

Parameters	Chosen values
Epoch	200
Batch size	16
Loss function	Categorical cross entropy
Optimizer	Adam
Metrics	Accuracy

To ensure that the results were valid and generalizable to make predictions from new data the detection was further tested on a different multiclass data set. For the new data set validation a splitting of the training and testing data in 70 and 30 ratio and 10 fold cross validation is done. When the dataset is divided into 70–30 ratio is it has obtained an accuracy of 77%. When 10 fold cross validation was implemented the obtained accuracy is 90.2%.

Convolutional Neural Networks are computationally efficient in terms of memory and time because of parameter sharing. They tend to perform better than regular neural networks. However, CNN has high computational cost and training is slow if you don't have a good GPU. In addition, they demand large training data in order to make accurate classifications.

Table 1 shows the hyper-parameters used for CNN model. A lot of hyper-parameter tuning was carried out while finalizing the Network parameters. In the CNN architecture, Conv1D layers are used because it is most suitable for time series data. Both Max pooling and average pooling was tried but, max pool gave better results as expected from the literature. Other parameters like the number of epochs, batch size, optimizer, loss function, activation functions and learning rates were finalized using the Grid Search. The epoch size finalized for the CNN architecture is 200 with batch size of 16. The models are trained on various train test splits like 80–20 and 75–25 and K-fold cross validation with 10 folds is also used for finding the most appropriate metrics-accuracy. The loss function used by them for updating the weights during back-propagation is categorical cross entropy and the optimizer used is Adam. Activation function for the last layers is SoftMax and ReLu.

4.3 Results and Analysis

Collected the multiclass data set to predict epileptic seizures and have preprocessed the data to fill in the missing values and performed binary classification on the data to predict if the patient has epileptic seizure or doesn't have epileptic seizure. Proposed CNN model is used as the classifier. The data was split into training and testing in the ratio 70–30 split and in 10-fold cross validation to check the performance of our model classifying epileptic or not epileptic data. The performance was evaluated using different performance metrics such as accuracy, recall, precision and f1 score.

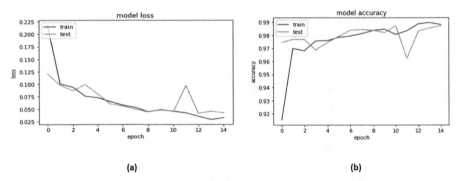

Fig. 4. (a) loss vs epoch performance graph of the proposed CNN model for 70–30 validation technique (**b**) accuracy vs epoch graph of the proposed CNN model for 70–30 validation technique

4.3.1 Results Obtained for Binary Classification of Proposed CNN Model

Results obtained by splitting the data set into training and testing in the ratio of 70–30 and 10-fold cross validation for the binary data set are described next:

Figure 4 shows the accuracy vs epoch and loss vs epoch graphs for the CNN model where the validation technique used is splitting the data in 70 and 30 ratios. Categorical Loss entropy function is used to calculate loss and accuracy is used as our metric. From the figure it's clear that our model is minimizing loss up to 0.032. The results show that the model has achieved higher accuracy and loss is low compared to the accuracy which means our model has got lower FP and FN values. Therefore, the model has achieved average accuracy up to 97.72% for 200 epochs.

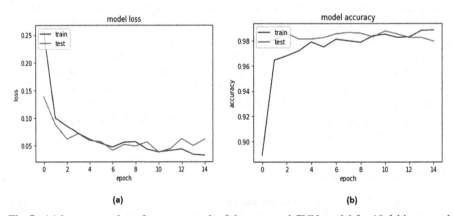

Fig. 5. (a) loss vs epoch performance graph of the proposed CNN model for 10-fold validation technique (**b**) accuracy vs epoch graph of the proposed CNN model for 10-fold cross validation

Figure 5 shows the accuracy vs epoch and loss vs epoch graphs for the CNN model where the validation technique used is 10-fold cross validation. From the Figure it's clear that our model is minimizing loss up to 0.02. The results show that CNN has achieved higher accuracy and loss is low compared to the accuracy. Therefore, achieved accuracy up to 98.32% for 200 epochs of the testing phase for the 10-fold cross validation. Also, here validation loss has deviated from training loss but the deviation is not too much which indicates our model is not over fitted and they are no overlapping, which indicates our model is neither under-fitted.

A confusion matrix is a table that compares the actual values to the predicted values, therefore evaluating the performance of the classifier on test data to which the true values are known. Fig. 6 and Fig. 7 show that our model is able to classify the classes correctly. The matrix shows high TP and TN values compared to the low FP and FN values therefore this can be stated that our model is able to predict correct samples correctly with higher accuracy.

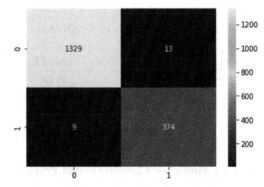

Fig. 6. Confusion matrix of the proposed CNN model for 70–30 validation technique

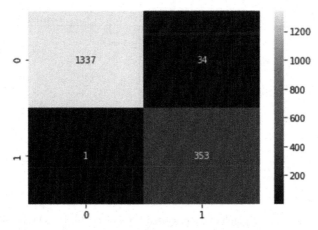

Fig. 7. Confusion matrix of the proposed CNN model for 10-fold cross validation technique

A binary classification was done to predict epileptic seizures. The data set was divided into training and testing with 70 and 30 ratio and the accuracy obtained was 97.72%. When the 10 fold cross validation was applied the model obtained a slightly better accuracy of 98.32% than the previous one as shown in Table 2. Therefore, it is stated that cross validation of the data set has given better accuracy. In the Table 2 various performance metrics were also evaluated such as precision, recall, f1 score.

The proposed CNN model has achieved recall of 97.65% and 99.71% for 70–30 and 10-fold cross validation data partition method. In terms of precision also our model has achieved 96.64% and 91.21% values for 70–30 and 10-fold cross validation data partition method.

Since the dataset was highly unbalanced as more samples of non-epileptic data was there so F1-score is also calculated for the proposed CNN model. For 70–30 and 10-fold cross validation data partition method F1-score obtained is 97.14% and 95.27% which proves that our proposed CNN based epilepsy classification model is able to handle and accurately classify unbalanced dataset too as shown in Table 2.

Table 2. Performance Metrics for CNN Model

Validation technique	Accuracy (%)	Precision (%)	Recal l(%)	F1-score (%)
70 and 30 ratio	97.72	96.64	97.65	97.14
Cross validation	98.32	91.21	99.71	95.27

4.3.2   Results Obtained for Multiclass Classification of Proposed CNN Model

Results obtained by splitting the data set into training and testing in the ratio of 70–30 and 10-fold cross validation for the multiclass data set are described next:

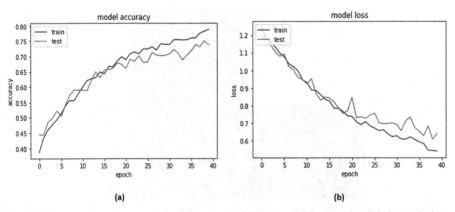

(a)   (b)

Fig. 8. (a) accuracy vs epoch graph of the proposed CNN model for 70–30 validation technique for multiclass dataset (b) loss vs epoch performance graph of the proposed CNN model for 70–30 validation technique for multiclass dataset

Figure 8 shows the accuracy vs epoch and loss vs epoch graphs for the CNN model where the validation technique used is splitting the data in 70–30 ratios. Categorical

Loss entropy function is used to calculate loss and accuracy is used as our metric. From the figure it's clear that our model is minimizing loss up to 0.5. The results show that our model has achieved higher accuracy and loss is low compared to the accuracy which means our model has got lower FP and FN values. It has achieved average accuracy of 78% for 200 epochs.

Figure 9 shows the accuracy vs epoch and loss vs epoch graphs for the CNN model where the validation technique used is 10-fold cross validation. From the figure it's clear that our model is minimizing loss up to 0.2. The results show that our CNN model has achieved higher accuracy and loss is low compared to the accuracy which means our model has got lower FP and FN values. Therefore, the proposed model has achieved accuracy of 89.40% for 200 epochs of the testing phase for the 10-fold cross validation. Also, here validation loss has deviated from training loss but the deviation is not too much which indicates our model is not overfitted and they are no overlapping, which indicates our model is neither underfitted.

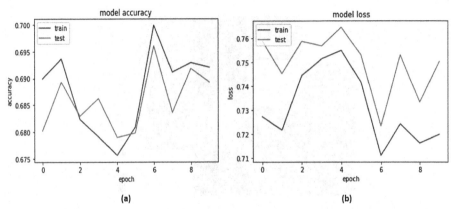

Fig. 9. (a) accuracy vs epoch graph of the proposed CNN model for 10-fold cross validation for multiclass data set (b) loss vs epoch performance graph of the proposed CNN model for 10-fold cross validation for multiclass data set

A confusion matrix is a table that compares the actual values to the predicted values, therefore evaluating the performance of the classifier on test data to which the true values are known. Fig. 10 and Fig. 11 show that our model is able to classify the classes correctly. The matrix shows high TP and TN values compared to the low FP and FN values therefore we can say that our model is able to predict correct samples correctly with a good accuracy.

In the Table 3, values for different performance metrics such as precision, recall, f1 score for 4 different classes is represented. In the data set class 0 is Sad, class 1 is Amusement, class 2 is Disgust and class 3 is Fear. The overall accuracy for the multiclass data set using the 70 and 30 ratios of splitting of data is 78.9% and a loss of 0.5. For the 10-fold cross validation the overall accuracy is 89.40% and a loss of 0.3. Therefore, 10-fold cross validation has given better results in terms of accuracy and loss and other performance metrics also.

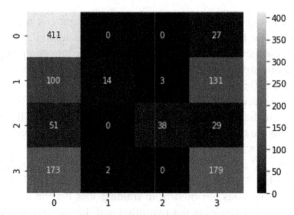

Fig. 10. Confusion matrix of the proposed CNN model for 70–30 validation technique having multiclass data set

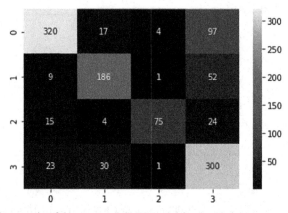

Fig. 11. Confusion matrix of the proposed CNN model for the 10-fold cross validation technique having multiclass data set

The proposed CNN model has achieved highest value of recall for multiclass classification as 0.94 in class 0 for 70–30 and 0.85 in class 3 for 10-fold cross validation data partition method. In terms of precision for multiclass classification also our model has achieved highest value as 0.93 and 0.94 by class 2 in both the dataset partition method i.e., 70–30 and 10-fold cross validation.

Since the dataset was highly unbalanced as more samples of non-epileptic data was there so F1-score is also calculated for the proposed CNN model. For 70–30 and 10-fold cross validation data partition method the highest F1-score obtained is 0.70 in class 0 and 0.80 in class 0 which proves that our proposed CNN based epilepsy classification model is able to handle and accurately classify unbalanced dataset too as shown in Table 3.

Table 3. Comparison of precision, Recall, F1-score of CNN model

Validation method	Classifier CNN			
	Class	Precision	Recall	F1 Score
70–30	0	0.56	0.94	0.70
	1	0.88	0.06	0.11
	2	0.93	0.32	0.48
	3	0.49	0.51	0.50
10-fold cross validation	Class	Precision	Recall	F1 Score
	0	0.87	0.73	0.80
	1	0.78	0.75	0.77
	2	0.94	0.64	0.75
	3	0.63	0.85	0.73

5   Conclusion and Future Scope

The first step in diagnosing a neurological disorder is always to assess if an EEG record indicates irregular or regular brain activity. Since manual EEG perception is a costly and time-consuming process, any classifier automating this first distinction will have the capability to minimize delays in treatment and alleviate the caregivers. In this research paper a new CNN model architecture is designed to be open and flexible and therefore suitable for analyzing EEG time series data and accurately diagnosing whether or not a person has Epilepsy. This novel CNN architecture outperforms the best accuracy previously reported and thus establishes a new benchmark. The performance of the proposed model was assessed using 70–30 and 10 fold cross-validation train-test split method. In both architectures, average of 95.02% accuracy is achieved.

In future we would implement other deep learning models like Recurrent Neural Network, cascaded-hybrid models to increase the accuracy of the automated epilepsy detection system.

Acknowledgment. This research work is performed under the nation wise initiative leadingindia.ai and Bennett University, India. They have supported us with lab and equipment during the experiments.

References

1. Bhardwaj, A., et al.: An analysis of integration of hill climbing in crossover and mutation operation for EEG signal classification. In: Proceedings of the 2015 Annual Conference on Genetic and Evolutionary Computation (2015)
2. Acharya, D., Goel, S., Bhardwaj, H., Sakalle, A., Bhardwaj, A.: A long short term memory deep learning network for the classification of negative emotions using EEG signals. In: 2020 International Joint Conference on Neural Networks (IJCNN), Glasgow, UK, pp. 1–8 (2020). https://doi.org/10.1109/IJCNN48605.2020.9207280.

3. Bhardwaj, H., et al.: Classification of electroencephalogram signal for the detection of epilepsy using innovative genetic programming. Expert Syst. **36**(1), e12338 (2019)
4. Acharya, D., et al.: An enhanced fitness function to recognize unbalanced human emotions data. Expert Syst. Appl. **166**, 114011 (2020)
5. Acharya, U.R., et al.: Application of entropies for automated diagnosis of epilepsy using EEG signals: a review. Knowl.-Based Syst. **88**, 85–96 (2015)
6. Acharya, D., et al.: Emotion recognition using fourier transform and genetic programming. Appl. Acoust. **164**, 107260 (2020)
7. Acharya, D., et al.: A novel fitness function in genetic programming to handle unbalanced emotion recognition data. Pattern Recogn. Lett. **133**, 272–279 (2020)
8. Jaafar, S.T., Mohammadi, M.: Epileptic Seizure Detection using Deep Learning Approach. UHD J. Sci. Technol. **3**(41), 41–50 (2019). https://doi.org/10.21928/uhdjst.v3n2y2019
9. Doma, V., Pirouz, M.: A comparative analysis of machine learning methods for emotion recognition using EEG and peripheral physiological signals. J. Big Data **7**(1), 1–21 (2020). https://doi.org/10.1186/s40537-020-00289-7
10. Li, M., Xu, H., Liu, X., Liu, S.: Emotion recognition from multichannel EEG signals using k-nearest neighbour classification. Technol. Health Care **26**(S1), 509–519 (2018). https://doi.org/10.3233/THC-174836
11. Yun, J.-S., Kim, J.H.: A Study on "training data selection method for EEG emotion analysis using machine learning algorithm." Int. J. Adv. Sci. Technol. **119**, 79–88 (2018). https://doi.org/10.14257/ijast.2018.119.07
12. Hussein, R., Palangi, H., Ward, R., Wang, Z.J.: Epileptic seizure detection: a deep learning approach, March 2018. arXiv:1803.09848 [eess.SP]
13. Andrzejak, R.G., Lehnertz, K., Rieke, C., Mormann, F., David, P., Elger, C.E.: Indications of nonlinear deterministic and finite dimensional structures in time series of brain electrical activity: dependence on recording region and brain state. Phys. Rev. E **64**, 061907 (2001)

Residual Dense U-Net for Segmentation of Lung CT Images Infected with Covid-19

Abhishek Srivastava[1], Nikhil Sharma[2], Shivansh Gupta[1], and Satish Chandra[1(✉)]

[1] Department of CSE and IT, Jaypee Institute of Information Technology Noida, Noida, India
satish.chandra@jiit.ac.in
[2] Department of Electronics and Communication Engineering, Jaypee Institute of Information Technology Noida, Noida, India

Abstract. The novel coronavirus disease 2019 (Covid-19) has been declared as a pandemic by the World Health Organization which in the current global scenario has brought everything from economy to education to a halt. Due to its rapid spread around the globe, even the most developed countries are facing difficulties in diagnosing Covid-19. For efficient treatment and quarantining of the exposed population it is important to analyse Lung CT Scans of the suspected Covid-19 patients. Computer aided segmentation of the suspicious Region of Interest can be used for better characterization of infected regions in Lung. In this work a deep learning-based U-Net architecture is proposed as a framework for automated segmentation of multiple suspicious regions in a CT scan of Covid-19 patient. Advantage of Dense Residual Connections has been taken to learn the global hierarchical features from all convolution's layers. So, a better trade-off in between efficiency and effectiveness in a U-Net can be maintained. To train the proposed U-Net system, publicly available data of Covid-19 CT scans and masks consisting of 838 CT slices has been used. The proposed method achieved an accurate and rapid segmentation with 97.2%, 99.1% and 99.3% as dice score, sensitivity and specificity respectively.

Keywords: Covid-19 · Deep learning · Dense residual networks · U-net · Segmentation

1 Introduction

SARS-COV-2 generally known as COVID-19 is a novel contagious virus whose first case was reported from Wuhan, China in late December 2019 [1] where a bunch of people were found suffering from pneumonia due to an unknown cause and since then the virus has spread almost all part of the globe. In micro genome study it was found that the strains of SARS-Cov-2 are highly similar to that of

D. Garg et al. (Eds.): IACC 2020, CCIS 1367, pp. 17–30, 2021.
https://doi.org/10.1007/978-981-16-0401-0_2

bat [1] whose primary sources were considered to be wet markets. High transmission rate of the novel COVID-19 is so threatening that it has forced humankind to take shelters for long lock down periods. It created a threatening situation of increasing clinical treatment forcing medical workers to work round the clock to help the infected beings risking their own life. It is observed that a COVID-19 positive will infect roughly three new susceptible (the reproductive number [2] is averaged to be 3.28) and the number increases even more if precautions are not taken. Symptoms in patients infected with Covid-19 vary from person to person based on immune response, with some patients remaining asymptomatic [3], but the common ones are fever, cough, fatigue and breathing problems. It was reported that [4] that 44% of the patients from China suffered from fever in the beginning whereas that 89% of them developed a fever while in hospital [5]. It was also revealed later that the patients had varying symptoms like cough (68%), fatigue (38%), sputum production (34%), and shortness of breath (19%) and some of them who already were suffering from other illness where more vulnerable to the impact of COVID-19. Not every community has sufficient infrastructure for dealing with outbreaks like this, so there is a need to do whatever we can to control.

A standard procedure is recommended by the World Health Organization (W.H.O.) to test the presence of pathogens in the suspected host known as Real-Time Fluorescence (RT-PCR) [6] for the in this procedure an oropharyngeal or a nasopharyngeal swab is used to collect the specimen of a suspected being to determine the nuclei acid in the sputum [7]. Still due to its high false positive rate, resampling of the suspected person is suggested by W.H.O. Computer Tomography (CT scan) imaging technique is one of the good options for the diagnosis of SARS- CoV2 virus [8]. With demand of finding a Vaccine for the COVID-19 (SARs-COV2) many laboratory and pharmaceutical industries are working to design vaccine based on immune response, targeting specific epitopes for binding sites. But part from these classic and important procedures and researches it was discovered that subjects infected COVID-19 form abnormalities such as bilateral, and unilateral pneumonia involves the lower lobes, pleural thickening, pleural effusion, and lymphadenopathy, which is then analyzed by experts for such characteristics features for diagnosis. Computer Aided Diagnosis (CAD) tools help in better diagnosis from the CT scans [9] are based on some application of machine learning algorithms. Moreover, CT scans improved false negative rate compared to RT-PCR. Several studies have exploited deep learning architectures for various applications in medical imaging viz. lesion segmentation, object/cell detection, tissue segmentation, image registration, anatomy localization etc. Dice similarity coefficient is widely used to validate the segmentation of white matter lesions in MRIs and CT scans [10]. In a recent work, Chen et al. [11] proposed a residual attention U-net for automatic quantification of lung infection in Covid-19 cases. They used aggregated residual transforms ResNet blocks on the encoder side followed by soft attention. It is focused on relative position of features on the decoder side in a U-Net like architecture evaluated for multi class segmentation on Covid-19 data from Italian Society of Medical and Interventional Radiology (SIRM). It contained 110 axial CT images of 60 patients. A DICE score of 0.83 was obtained without data augmentation compared to a DICE score of 0.75 with baseline U-net. Shan et al. [12] developed a deep learning based segmentation using VB-Net that is, a modified 3-D convolutional network V-net with bottleneck to make it faster to obtain volume, shape, point of interest (POI) alongside contours on data from 249 Covid-19 patients for training with a human in the loop strategy (HITL) and achieved a median DICE score of 0.922.

In another work, Wu et al. [13] proposed a joint classification and segmentation system using a Res2Net mode. A Res2Net model was used for classification with an attempt to explain the latent features by visualizing the spatial response regions from the final Convolution layer of the model and for segmentation. A VGG-16 model with deep supervisions was implemented to obtain the segmented image of the CT scans. This joint model was trained on 2794 CT images from 150 patients and achieved a DICE score of 0.783. Zhou et al. [14] proposed a segmentation scheme using res_dil blocks i.e. residue blocks with dilated convolution layers which caused the model to extract features at different granularities. The model also used attention blocks and deep supervision on the U-net architecture. CT scans can be used for the early detection of the Covid-19 and quarantining the active host in order to control the inexorable virus.

The work presented in this work is inspired by simple ladder U-net [15] which was designed especially for the segmentation of Bio-Medical Images bridging with Dense Residual Blocks [16] to enable the use of the hierarchical features from all the convolution layers along with the residual connections. Therefore, managing the features gradient explosion, without any explicit parameter optimization. Section 2 describes the materials and methods and the proposed deep learning architecture. In Sect. 3 experimental results are discussed followed by conclusions.

2 Materials and Methods

2.1 Dataset

Medical scans and data are usually private as they contain the information of patients making it hard to access publicly. But due to the rapid spread of Covid-19 many researches and organizations have released datasets which can be accessed publicly for CAD development. This research is based on two publicly available datasets described below.

COVID-CT. This CT- Scans based Covid-19 dataset [17][1] consists of 349 CT images containing clinical findings of Covid-19 and numerous Normal patients' slices.

---

[1] https://github.com/UCSD-AI4H/COVID-CT.

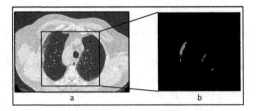

Fig. 1. Two different masks consolidation and pleural effusion for a Covid-19 patient which was the prime task as multi-class segmentation from CTSeg dataset [18].

CT-Seg. This CT-Scan COVID-19 segmentation-based dataset [18] was made publicly accessible on 13th April 2020, this dataset includes whole volumes of 9 patients, providing both positive i.e. 373 out of the total of 829 slices were label as COVID-positive with findings of consolidation (=1) and pleural effusion (=2) and rest were label as COVID-negative. Dataset included niftii CT volumes and niftii COVID-19 masks accessible free of costs through their online site (Fig. 1)[2].

2.2   Deep Learning Architecture

In this section the components of the proposed model viz. Dense Residual Blocks, U-Net and Residual Connections are described in length.

Residual Blocks. Residual blocks [19] are a special case of highway networks without any gates in their skip connections. Essentially, residual blocks allow the flow of memory from initial layers to last layers and avoiding training of some parameters for our output segmentation. Despite the absence of gates in their skip connections, residual networks perform as good as any other highway network in practice.

Residual Block ease the training of few layers due to its skip connection by producing an identity function which makes the model to learn the $F(x)$ part which is easier to learn than the $H(x)$ part as mentioned in Fig. 2. We deployed several residual blocks on the encoder decoder parts to avoid gradient vanishing during training.

U-Net. The U-net architecture is designed mainly for segmentation of Bio Medical images. The encoder part comprises of several Fully Connected Networks (FCN) [20] to extract the spatial features from the subject, similarly decoder is equipped with series of convolution, up-sample layers and skip connections between the two, to retain the features from each encoder levels. But range of interest of U-Net is very small, and do not have enough capability to distinguish those trivial difference.

---

[2] http://medicalsegmentation.com/covid19/.

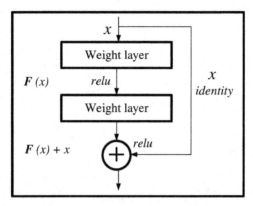

Fig. 2. Canonical form of ResNet Block. A skip connection allows reusing of activations from previous layer till current layer learns its weights hence avoiding vanishing gradient in the initial back propagation.

Dense Residual Connection. Dense Residual blocks [21] consists of densely connected structure where every Convolutional layer feed forward its learned representations to every succeeding layer in the block. Dense Residual Connection are designed to extract and adaptively fuse features from all hierarchical layers by exploiting these features efficiently, which are obtained from each level of convolutional layers. RDB as shown in the Fig. 4 uses the adaptive route mechanism for learning more effective features from current and preceding local feature in order to stabilize the training of encoder. RDB, can't only read a state from the preceding block via a contiguous memory (CM) mechanism, which avoid stacking up of numerous features all together to make it efficient in memory consumption. The accumulated features are then adaptively preserved by local feature fusion (LFF). These layers have relatively fewer channels (a.k.a growth rate) as higher number of channels affects the stability and due to such dense connections, it does not need to learn dispensable feature maps. Essential low-level feature maps are also sustained and the construction of the segmentation maps employ both high and low-level feature representations which improves the quality of the segmented image.

The continuous feed-forward from Local Residual Learning ensures restoration of the lost local features along with a deep and thorough extraction of relevant information in the foreground of the CT scans from shallow or initial convolution layers [23] with contiguous memory mechanism analogous to LSTM [24]. This memory, aids a vital role in maintaining a long-term relationship. The final concatenation in between RDB block and the Cth convolution layer produces the final output and makes a local residual block this deals with the issue of gradient vanishing by improving gradient flow due to the easy propagation of gradients through the network, eventually leading to a shorter pathway for an inadequate latent feature space. The RrDB block as shown in Fig. 5 is a collective unit of 3 RDB Blocks connected in sequence for the cohesive extraction of

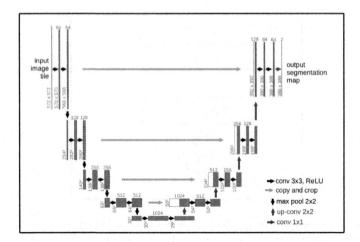

Fig. 3. U-network for segmentation of bio-medical imagesas proposed by Ronneberger et al.

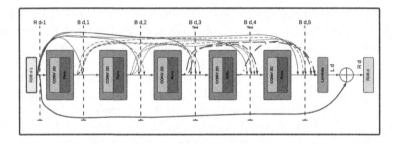

Fig. 4. Residual dense block consisting of dense connected layers, local residual learning through the Rd feature maps produced due to concatenation of feature map obtained through densely connected [Bd,1, Bd,2, Bd,3, Bd,4, Bd,5] and Rd-1, leading to a contiguous memory (CM) mechanism and improve the information flow.

all significant information from input low-resolution subject to high-resolution quality images as done with image restoration [25] through RrDB blocks without Batch Normalization [26] for restoring fine level of information for different textures within a CT Scan (Fig. 3).

3   Proposed Model

The proposed architecture shown in Fig. 6 is based on the U-Net architecture integrated with Dense Residual Network. Spatial features extracted from Encoder do not make full utilization of the hierarchical features which can help in focusing on the region and denoising any unwanted region that incorporates during CT scan acquisitions resulting in poor performance. In the Decoder part we included residual networks which are used for mapping the segmentation map from extracted spatial and hierarchical features from all convolution layers in encoder. Full description of the model layers s provided in the Table 1 along with the hyper parameters used during training process Table 2.

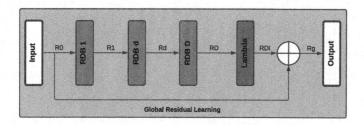

Fig. 5. 3-RrDB Network consisting of RDB block which is used in later stage for Encoder stem of U-Net through which information flow from input is processed through Global Residual Learning by concatenating the feature maps produced through Local Residual Learning of 3-RrDB blocks and feature maps produced by the Encoder of U-net. The extracted feature maps from the encoder branch are passed through 3-RrDB Network blocks and concatenated with feature maps of Encoder to give rise to Global Residual Pooling.

$$R_g = R_0 + [R_{dI}] \tag{1}$$

These feature maps obtained through 3-RrDB Network is fed into Decoder part of RrDB-U-Net. A skip connection is added from each filter level from encoder straight with decoder at every interval in order to get better precise locations. The traditional CNN used in the decoder often have limited receptive field which creates a shallow feature map of the encoder output. The dense blocks are a continuous memory mechanism preserves both the low dimensional features as well as high dimensional features of encoder output which is shown in Eq. (2 to 8).

$$X \rightarrow C_1 \rightarrow X_1 \tag{2}$$

$$(X, X_1) \rightarrow C_2 \rightarrow X_2 \tag{3}$$

$$(X, X_1, X_2) \rightarrow C_3 \rightarrow X_3 \tag{4}$$

$$(X, X_1, X_2, X_3) \rightarrow C_4 \rightarrow X_4 \tag{5}$$

$$(X, X_1, X_2, X_3, X_4, X_5) \rightarrow C_5 \rightarrow X_5 \tag{6}$$

$$X_5 = X_5 * \alpha \tag{7}$$

$$X = X + X_5 \tag{8}$$

Where X denotes the input to the decoder layer, C_1 is the first Convolution layer, C_2 is the second Convolution layer, C_3 is the third Convolution layer, C_4 is the fourth Convolution layer, C_5 is the fifth Convolution layer and α is a constant. The lower output channels of (X_1, X_2, X_3, X_4, X_5) ensures that the continuous mechanism of the dense blocks stay intact. At each level of dense

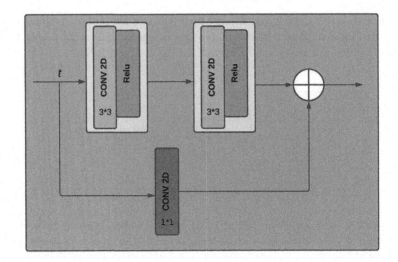

Fig. 6. ResNet block in encoder and decoder of U-net.

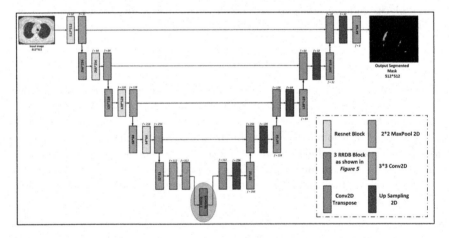

Fig. 7. Proposed residual dense U-net with residual connection and 3-RrDB network.

blocks only necessary higher as well as lower dimensional features are extracted and propagated for the decoder layers to allow better generation of mask.

Extraction of quality information is one of the tough tasks that need to be addressed before designing any model due to the presence of some proportion of SNR (Signal to Noise Ratio) in the CT scan during acquisition. This may result in poor performance of deep convolutional networks. To address this issue RrDB blocks were included in the U-Net. U-Net improves the flow of information, which leads to a dense fusion of features along with deep supervision, acting as a catalyst, to learn fine line features from and around the region of interest as the deep model has a strong representation capacity to capture semantic information.

Table 1. Dimension description of each layer incorporated within the proposed convolution model

Number of Layers	Type of Layer	Output Features	Output Size	Kernel Size
1	Input Layer	1	512*512	NA
2	ResNet Layer R1	32	512*512	(3*3), (3*3), (1*1)
3	Convolution C1	32	512*512	3*3
4	Maxpool M1	32	256*256	2*2
5	ResNet Layer R2	64	256*256	(3*3), (3*3), (1*1)
6	Convolution C2	64	256*256	3*3
7	Maxpool M2	64	128*128	2*2
8	ResNet Layer R3	128	128*128	(3*3), (3*3), (1*1)
9	Convolution C3	128	128*128	3*3
10	Maxpool M3	128	64*64	2*2
11	ResNet Layer R4	256	64*64	(3*3), (3*3), (1*1)
12	Convolution C4	256	64*64	3*3
13	Maxpool M4	256	32*32	2*2
14	Convolution C5	512	32*32	3*3
15	Convolution C6	512	32*32	3*3
16	Convolution a1	32	32*32	3*3
17	Leaky Relu l 1	32	32*32	Alpha = 0.25
18	Concatenate c1	544	32*32	NA
19	Convolution a2	32	32*32	3*3
20	Leaky Relu l 2	32	32*32	Alpha = 0.25
21	Concatenate c2	576	32*32	NA
22	Convolution a3	32	32*32	3*3
23	Leaky Relu l 3	32	32*32	Alpha = 0.25
24	Concatenate c3	608	32*32	NA
25	Convolution a4	32	32*32	3*3
26	Leaky Relu l 4	32	32*32	Alpha = 0.25
27	Concatenate c4	640	32*32	NA
28	Convolution a5	512	32*32	3*3
29	Leaky Relu l 5	512	32*32	Alpha = 0.25
30	Lambda 1	512	32*32	x * 0.4
31	Add 1	512	32*32	NA
32	Convolution a6	32	32*32	3*3
33	Leaky Relu l 6	32	32*32	Alpha = 0.25
34	Concatenate c5	544	32*32	NA
35	Convolution a6	32	32*32	3*3
36	Leaky Relu l 7	32	32*32	Alpha = 0.25
37	Concatenate c6	576	32*32	NA
38	Convolution a7	32	32*32	3*3
39	Leaky Relu l 8	32	32*32	Alpha = 0.25
40	Concatenate c7	604	32*32	NA

Number of Layers	Type of Layer	Output Features	Output Size	Kernel Size
41	Convolution a8	32	32*32	3*3
42	Leaky Relu l 9	32	32*32	Alpha = 0.25
43	Concatenate c8	640	32*32	NA
44	Convolution a9	512	32*32	3*3
45	Leaky Relu l 10	512	32*32	Alpha = 0.25
46	Lambda 2	512	32*32	x * 0.4
47	Add 2	512	32*32	NA
48	Convolution a10	32	32*32	3*3
49	Leaky Relu l 11	32	32*32	Alpha = 0.25
50	Concatenate c9	544	32*32	NA
51	Convolution a11	32	32*32	3*3
52	Leaky Relu l 12	32	32*32	Alpha = 0.25
53	Concatenate c10	576	32*32	NA
54	Convolution a12	32	32*32	3*3
55	Leaky Relu l 13	32	32*32	Alpha = 0.25
56	Concatenate c11	604	32*32	NA
57	Convolution a13	32	32*32	3*3
58	Leaky Relu l 14	32	32*32	Alpha = 0.25
59	Concatenate c14	640	32*32	NA
60	Convolution a14	512	32*32	3*3
61	Leaky Relu l 15	512	32*32	Alpha = 0.25
62	Lambda 3	512	32*32	x * 0.4
63	Add 3	512	32*32	NA
64	Lambda 4	512	32*32	x * 0.2
65	Add 4	512	32*32	NA
66	DropOut 1	512	32*32	NA
67	Up Sampling 1	512	64*64	2*2
68	Convolution C7	256	64*64	3*3
69	Convolution C8	256	64*64	3*3
70	Up Sampling 2	256	128*128	2*2
71	Convolution C9	128	128*128	3*3
72	Convolution C10	128	128*128	3*3
73	Up Sampling 3	128	256*256	2*2
74	Convolution C11	64	256*256	3*3
75	Convolution C12	64	256*256	3*3
76	Up Sampling 4	64	512*512	2*2
77	Convolution C13	32	512*512	3*3
78	Convolution C14	32	512*512	3*3
79	Convolution C15	32	512*512	3*3
80	Output Segmented Mask	1	512*512	NA

In contrast, to the fact that deeper model is hard to train, performance was facilitated with easy training and better performance.

4   Experiments and Results

4.1   Data Pre-processing

CT scans are collection of huge raw images that need meaningful pre-processing for unambiguous analysis and for a useful computer aided diagnosis. The scans were labeled by radiologists as: ground glass, consolidation and pleural diffusion. SegCT data includes 9 volumes, total 829 slices, where 373 slices have been evaluated and segmented by radiologists as Covid-19. Each suspicious slice was loaded and centre cropped in order to remove outer noise or unwanted regions. The resulting images obtained were of sizes 128 * 128 pixels each slice, as shown in the Fig. 9. The extracted image's intensity I is then scaled to Hounsfield [22] unit and linearly normalized before used as input for training the model in order

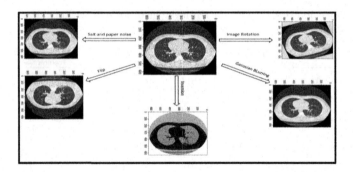

Fig. 8. Data Augmentation methods opted for our model.

Table 2. List of hyperparameters used for training the proposed network for COVID-19 CT scan segmentation

Hyperparameter values	
Epochs	150
Batch sizes	20
Activation function	Softmax, leaky relu, sigmoid [30,31]
Optimizers	Adam [29]
Loss	Categorical crossentropy
Learning rate	0.001
Performance matrices	Dice coefficient, accuracy

to prevent noises and black frame issues in raw data. The total of 838 images was split into training set (60%), validation set (20%), and test set (20%). Experiment was performed with 150 number of epochs on intel i5 8th Gen Intel® Core™ i5 9300H (2.4 GHz, up to 4.1 GHz, 8 MB cache, 4 cores) + NVIDIA® GeForce® GTX 1050 (3 GB) GPU.

4.2   Data Augmentation

It is known that Deep Learning performance depends heavily on the amount of data available to explore and exploit for the architecture. As the number of CT slices available for the experiment were less, we opted to increase the data through artificial method. This is done through domain specific techniques. Few data augmentation techniques can result into information loss around a suspicious region. To avoid such data from new training data is created with rotation, inversion, rescaling, blurring and contrast enhanced images from training data, with created data of the same class as that of the original data. CT Seg [18] provided with only 300+ CT Covid-19 slices which can result into overfitting [27]. Overfitting refers to the situation when network starts to memorize a function

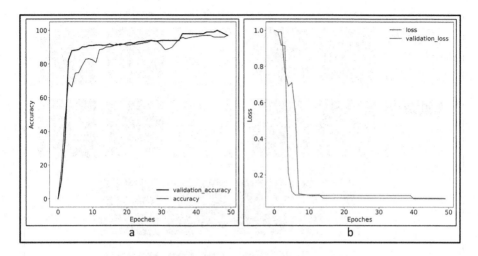

Fig. 9. Plot between training and validation data confirms that no over-fitting and under-fitting takes place and model converges nearly around 30–40 epochs.

with very high variance to perfectly model the training data hence, resulting poor performance on test/validation set.

4.3   Experiments and Performance Metrics

In multi-class image segmentation, the target area of interest may take a trivial part of the whole image. The performance measure metrics considered here for the segmentation task are DICE Score [28], accuracy, and precision, F1 score, sensitivity and specificity. The DICE score can be considered as validation metric to evaluate the performance of model's reproducibility of manual segmentations and the spatial overlap accuracy of automated generated mask.

From the above Table 1 it was found that the proposed architecture performed well from many of the other variations with U-net. It can be clearly observed that without increasing the much depth of our architecture model managed to learn complex relevant features while maintaining the efficiency and effectiveness. As deeper model requires large bunch of data and time to train, we noticed that by using RrDB blocks in U-Net leads towards better results and less training time.

As from above results we can conclude that our architecture performed well by focusing on the finest and smallest details around the suspicious region of interest. Our Model stabilize nearly around 30–40 epochs validating our use for including the RrDB blocks i.e. ease the training process without increasing the depth of model alongside with a quick convergence rate justifying our beliefs that U-Net performance can be enhanced significantly by focusing on tuning the model to focus on finer details rather than just increasing the model's depth as in our case RrDB blocks suitably deals with gradient explosion and over-fitting as can be validated from Fig. 10.

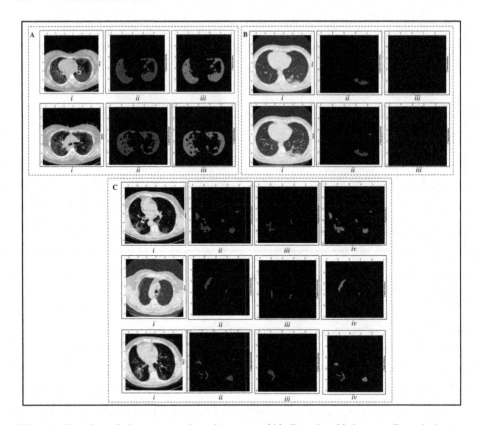

Fig. 10. Results of the proposed architecture (A) For the (i) lungs effected due to the COVID-19 labelled as from (ii) consolidation along with the generated segmented mask (in green) in (iii). (B) Similar to the above cases where (i) CT scan of human lungs labelled as (ii) pleural and its (iii) generated mask (in blue) (C) Atlast cases where both the consolidation and pleural cases were identified ((i), (ii), (iii)) and its (iv) segmented masks in green and blue for both the labels reprectively (Color figure online)

5   Conclusion

CT imaging is used for screening Covid-19 patients and for analyzing the severity of the disease. For Computer Aided Diagnosis, deep learning has played an important role. In this work, we explored the use of Residual Dense U-Net for segmentation of lung CT Images infected with Covid-19. The proposed approach can accurately and efficiently identify regions of interest within CT images of patients infected withCovid-19. As current clinical tests take relatively longer time, this approach of incorporating RrDB blocks in the standard encoder decoder structure of U-Net improves the quality of segmentations and proves as a useful component in COVIDs-19 analysis and testing through CT images. A superior performance was observed with dice coefficient of 97.6%. It was observed that by maintaining the hierarchal features a significant improvement in the Dice Coefficient was seen by just changing the baseline of U-Net. Availability of more data will lead to more findings in this area.

References

1. Zhou, P., et al.: A pneumonia outbreak associated with a new coronavirus of probable bat origin. Nature **579**, 270–273 (2020). https://doi.org/10.1038/s41586-020-2012-7
2. Liu, Y., Gayle, A., Annelies, W. S., Rocklöv, J.: The reproductive number of COVID-19 is higher compared to SARS coronavirus. J. Travel Med. **27** (2020). https://doi.org/10.1093/jtm/taaa021
3. Gao, Z., et al.: A Systematic Review of Asymptomatic Infections with COVID-19. J. Microbiol. Immunol. Infect. (2020). https://doi.org/10.1016/j.jmii.2020.05.001
4. Huang, C., et al.: Clinical features of patients infected with 2019 novel coronavirus in Wuhan, China. Lancet. **395**, 497–506 (2020). https://doi.org/10.1016/S0140-6736(20)30183-5
5. Guan, W.J., et al.: Clinical Characteristics of Coronavirus Disease 2019 in China (2020). https://doi.org/10.1056/NEJMoa2002032
6. Ai, T., et al.: Correlation of chest CT and RT-PCR testing for coronavirus disease 2019 (COVID-19) in China: a report of 1014 cases. Radiology. **296** (2020). https://doi.org/10.1148/radiol.2020200642
7. Di Gennaro, F., et al.: Coronavirus diseases (COVID-19) current status and future perspectives: a narrative review. Int. J. Environ. Res. Public Health **17**, 2690 (2020). https://doi.org/10.3390/ijerph17082690
8. Yang, W., Yan, F.: Patients with RT-PCR-confirmed COVID-19 and normal chest CT. Radiology. **295** (2020). https://doi.org/10.1148/radiol.2020200702
9. Lee, E., Ng, M.Y., Khong, P.: COVID-19 pneumonia: what has CT taught us? Lancet Infect. Dis. **20**, 384–385 (2020). https://doi.org/10.1016/S1473-3099(20)30134-1
10. Zijdenbos, A., Dawant, B., Margolin, R., Palmer, A.: Morphometric analysis of white matter lesions in MR images. IEEE Trans. Med. Imaging **13**, 716–24 (1994). https://doi.org/10.1109/42.363096
11. Chen, X., Yao, L., Zhang, Y.: Residual attention U-Net for automated multi-class segmentation of COVID-19 chest CT images (2020). arXiv:2004.05645
12. Shan, F., et al.: Lung infection quantification of Covid-19 in CT images with deep learning (2020). arXiv:2003.04655
13. Wu, Y.H., et al.: JCS: An explainable Covid-19 diagnosis system by classification and segmentation (2020). arXiv:2004.07054
14. Zhou, T., Canu, S., Ruan, S.: An automatic Covid-19 CT segmentation network using spatial and channel attention mechanism (2020). arXiv:2004.06673
15. Ronneberger, O., Fischer, P., Brox, T.: U-net: convolutional networks for biomedical image segmentation (2015). arXiv:1505.04597
16. He, K., Zhang, X., Ren, S., Sun, J.: Deep residual learning for image recognition (2015). arXiv:1512.03385
17. Zhao, J., Zhang, Y., He, X., Xie, P., Covid-CT (dataset): a CT scan dataset about Covid-19 (2020). arXiv:2003.13865
18. Jenssen, H.B., Covid-19 CT-segmentation (dataset). http://medicalsegmentation.com/covid19/. Accessed 13 April 2020

19. Zhang, Y., Tian, Y., Kong, Y., Zhong, B., Fu, Y.: Residual dense network for image super-resolution. In: Conference on Computer Vision and Pattern Recognition, pp. 2472–2481.IEEE/CVF (2018). https://doi.org/10.1109/CVPR.2018.00262
20. Basha, S.H.S., Dubey, S.R., Pulabaigari, V., Mukherjee, S.: Impact of fully connected layers on performance of convolutional neural networks for image classification. Neurocomputing (2019). https://doi.org/10.1016/j.neucom.2019.10.008
21. He, K., Zhang, X., Ren, S., Sun, J.: Delving deep into rectifiers: surpassing human-level performance on ImageNet classification (2015). arXiv:1502.01852
22. Freeman, T.G.: The Mathematics of Medical Imaging: A Beginner's Guide. Springer Undergraduate Texts in Mathematics and Technology. Springer, Heidelberg (2010)
23. Keiron, O.S., Nash, R.: An introduction to convolutional neural networks (2015). arXiv:1511.08458
24. Hochreiter, S., Schmidhuber, J.: Long Short-Term Memory, vol. 9 of Neural Computation. 8th edn. Cambridge, London (1997)
25. Wang, X., et al.: ESRGAN: enhanced super resolution generative adversarial networks (2018). arXiv:1809.00219
26. Ioffe, S., Szegedy, C.: Batch normalization: accelerating deep network training by reducing internal covariate shift (2015). arXiv:1502.03167
27. Salman, S., Xiuwen, L.: Overfitting mechanism and avoidance in deep neural networks (2019). arXiv:1901.06566
28. Shamir, R.R., Duchin, Y., Kim, J., Sapiro, G., Harel, N.: Continuous dice coefficient: a method for evaluating probabilistic segmentations. medRxiv and bioRxiv (2018). https://doi.org/10.1101/306977
29. Diederik, K., Jimmy, B.: Adam: A method for stochastic optimization (2014). arXiv:1412.6980
30. Maas, A. L., Hannun, A.Y., Ng, A.Y.: Rectifier nonlinearities improve neural network acoustic models. In: International Conference on Machine Learning (2013)
31. Nwankpa, C., Ijomah, W., Gachagan, A., Marshall, S.: Activation functions: comparison of trends in practice and research for deep learning (2018). arXiv:1811.03378

Leveraging Deep Learning and IoT for Monitoring COVID19 Safety Guidelines Within College Campus

Sahai Vedant[1]([⊠]), D'Costa Jason[1], Srivastava Mayank[1], Mehra Mahendra[1], and Kalbande Dhananjay[2]

[1] Fr. Conceicao Rodrigues College of Engineering, University of Mumbai, Mumbai, Maharashtra, India
vedantsahai18@gmail.com, jasondcosta99@gmail.com,
srivastavamayank679@gmail.com, mahendra.mehra@fragnel.edu.in
[2] Sardar Patel Institute of Technology, University of Mumbai, Mumbai, Maharashtra, India
drkalbande@spit.ac.in

Abstract. The widespread coronavirus pandemic 2019 (COVID-19) has brought global emergency with its deadly spread to roundabout 215 countries, and about 4,448,082 Active cases along with 535,098 deaths globally as on July 5, 2020 [1]. The non-availability of any vaccine and low immunity against COVID19 upsurges the exposure of human beings to this virus. In the absence of any vaccine, WHO guidelines like social distancing, wearing masks, washing hands and using sanitizers is the only solution against this pandemic. However, there is no idea when the pandemic situation that the world is going through will come to an end, we can take a breath of relief that someday we will surely go back to our colleges. Although having students wait in line to be screened for COVID19 symptoms may prove logistically challenging. Enthused by this belief, this paper proposes an IoT and deep learning-based framework for automating the task of verifying mask protection and measuring the body temperature of all the students entering the campus. This paper provides a human-less screening solution using a deep learning model to flag no facemasks on students entering the campus and non-contact temperature sensor MLX90614 to detect elevated body temperatures to reduce the risk of exposure to COVID19.

Keywords: WebApp · IoT · COVID19 · Deep learning

1 Introduction

Coronavirus 2019, since the day it originated in Wuhan city of Hubei Province of China in December 2019, was declared a pandemic on March 11, 2020. Globally, 14.6 Million confirmed cases had been reported with 610110 death cases by July 21, 2020. India registered its first COVID19 case of a student returned from Wuhan, China, in the state of Kerala, on January 30, 2020. Following this, numerous incidents were reported from

D. Garg et al. (Eds.): IACC 2020, CCIS 1367, pp. 31–53, 2021.
https://doi.org/10.1007/978-981-16-0401-0_3

different states of the country, mainly from travelers returning from abroad, and then local transmission led to widespread COVID19.

The graph depicts the severity of this pandemic and the rate at which it is spreading. The trajectory for all the affected countries started when 100 confirmed cases were reported within that country. This helps us in realizing how quickly the number of confirmed cases has grown worldwide. India recorded its 1 million cases on July 17, 2020 (Fig. 1).

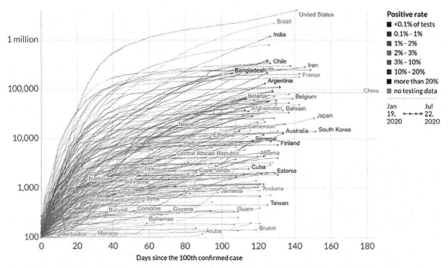

Fig. 1. Cumulative confirmed COVID 19 cases [2]

COVID-19 displays clinical symptoms varying from a state where symptoms are not seen to multiple organ dysfunction syndromes and acute respiratory distress syndrome. Conferring to the release of a recent study led by the World Health Organization based on confirmed laboratory cases, a majority showed clinical characteristics like fever being the most common symptom with 87.9%, dry cough with 67.7%, fatigue with 38.1% and sputum production was seen in 33.4%. Few cases had symptoms like a sore throat with 13.9%, headache with 13.6%, myalgia with 14.8%, and breathlessness in 18.6%, while symptoms such as nausea were seen in 5.04%, nasal congestion in 4.8%, hemoptysis in 0.9%, diarrhea in 3.7%, and conjunctival congestion in 0.8% were seen rarely [3].

At its inception, Coronavirus research was linked with the exposure of humans to suspected animals' species; the sudden outburst and quick spread have changed the direction of research to transmission due to human contacts. The study of COVID-19 cases has confirmed that the Coronavirus is principally transmitted amongst humans due to the spread of respiratory droplets via coughing and sneezing [4]. Respiratory droplets can cover a distance of up to 6 feet (1.8 m). Thus, any human being coming in close contact with another infected person is at high risk of getting exposed to these virus traces and can contract the Coronavirus. Touch in any form directly or indirectly with surfaces that are infected has been acknowledged as one of the likely reasons for Coronavirus spread. There is proof which reveals that coronavirus can live on metal and plastic surfaces for three days, on cardboard, it remains up to 24 h and on copper for nearly 4 h [5].

As the world struggles due to the COVID-19 pandemic, it is very much required to follow useful preventive guidelines to reduce the probability of being another fatality. Every Individual and group must adhere to the practices given below, and if these practices are strictly followed, the world may soon see a flattened Coronavirus curve. Curve Flattening indicates lowering the transmission of the Coronavirus to the level where available healthcare arrangements can adequately manage the effect of the disease.

1. Hands must be washed more often using an alcohol-based sanitizer or use soap and water to wash them thoroughly at regular intervals if you are away from home.
2. Practice social distancing – maintain a distance of 1 m from others
3. Make sure you don't touch your eyes, nose, and mouth with bare hands.
4. Spraying disinfectant on regularly touched surfaces is essential.
5. Try staying at home unless it's an emergency. Pregnant women's and old age people with any health conditions should avoid social interactions.
6. One should sneeze or cough in the open. Try covering your face with a cloth or use elbow pit.
7. One must wear a mask always if people surround them. However, care should be taken while disposing of the used masks [6].

The rate at which COVID19 is spreading across the world, the globe is facing issues of falling economies and increasing casualties. Regrettably, the human race is still under a persistent threat of contracting infection, with the condition getting worse every day. However, researchers worldwide are coming up with technological approaches to deal with Coronavirus pandemic's impacts. These technologies include AI, IoT, Blockchain, and the upcoming 5G Telecommunication networks, which have been at the forefront. [7]. As per the CDC and the WHO cutting edge technologies will play an important role in helping fight against Coronavirus Pandemic [8].

In this paper, we are focusing on the post lockdown scenarios where schools and colleges will reopen, pending examinations will be held. This reopening will lead to a lot of human movement and gathering at campuses. We are proposing a model where precautionary measures can be automated with the help of technology and alert the administration in the lapse of adequate precautionary measures or in the event of finding symptoms like high body temperature in the person entering the facility. Highlights of our research are the following:

Today, at the time of a severe crisis, screening of potential risk bearers is very crucial, wherein this must be done without human interaction, hence automation of this process must be done, such that a person can be identified uniquely and preventive measures can be taken after that if considered as a risk.

Machine Learning and Deep Learning models have been used to detect various kinds of objects and even faces. Wide range of applications have been using object detection techniques, yet no model uniquely identifies a person and if a mask is present or not at the same time. In the current scenario, there is a need for one such model, so that we can identify every person by their unique features and thus automate the facemask detection process along with identity verification. Just detecting whether a person is wearing a facemask is not enough. According to the World Health Organization, one of the primary symptoms of COVID-19 is the rise in body temperature. If fever patterns of a person can be monitored it will be easy to take preventive measures and break the chain of spread.

Due to advancement in the field of IoT, we are surrounded by various types of sensors. Infrared thermal sensors are the best way to scan and detect body temperatures. The speed of scanning is fast, measuring body temperature with an accuracy of ±0.5 °C. The speed of processing is fast making these sensors detect body temperatures even in larger groups of people. Another reliable method of scanning high temperature is using Thermal Imaging Cameras. They work by rendering the infrared radiations as visible light. Each College/University has a well-defined database of students studying in their facility. Using any programming language, we can access the database. If the model is running on the same server, where the database is present the computations and processing time will be very less. Migrating from Relational database to a NoSQL database will make the application scalable and easy to store data according to dates for the pattern checking. Accessing databases for the admin will also be easy to find out who are the potential risk bearers.

2   Literature Review

2.1   Object Detection

Various techniques exist for face detection with varying levels of accuracy and computation speed. The major deciding factor in determining the technique was a balance between accuracy and performance as the operation is run on a Raspberry Pi 3B+. Results from the paper "A comparison of CNN-based face and head detectors for real-time video surveillance applications" suggest that, although CNNs can accomplish a high level of precision in comparison to old-style detectors, they require high computational resources which are a constraint for several practical real-time applications [9]. The method of face recognition developed by P. Viola and M. Jones has appropriate accuracy for the purpose and can be run on a Raspberry Pi 3B+.

2.2   Facial Recognition

In facial landmark detection, relatively few of the techniques give the source code and rather simply give executable equals making the multiplication of codes on various training sets or using various landmark annotation plans problematic. Binaries simply permit certain pre-defined handiness and are routinely not cross-stage, making a continuous blend of the systems relying upon landmark detection insurmountable. Although there exist a couple of unique cases that give both getting training and testing code [10, 11], those philosophies don't consider landmark tracking on a real-time basis which is of utmost importance for an interactive system. The head pose estimation and AU affirmation point of view have not gotten a comparable proportion of energy as facial landmark detection. Watson structure is a committed head pose estimation, which is an execution of the Generalized Adaptive View-based Appearance Model [12]. Similarities exist between a couple of frameworks that contemplate head pose estimation using significance data [13], regardless, they can't go after webcams. While some facial landmark detection consolidates limits of estimating head pose [14, 15], most dismissal this issue. Even the Action Unit Recognition systems (FACET2, Affdex3, and OKAO4) have drawbacks related to prohibitive cost, dark estimations, and normally dark getting ready data. Looking at the eye-gaze estimation, contraptions and business systems require specialist hardware, for instance, infrared cameras or head-mounted cameras [16–18]. Even though there exist a few structures obtainable for eye-gaze estimation through webcam [19–21], they fight in authentic circumstances and some require blundering manual arrangement steps.

On the other hand, OpenFace gives both training and testing code considering the basic reproducibility of examinations. The model also shows top tier results on in-the-wild data and doesn't require any remarkable gear or individual express arrangement. Finally, the model runs dynamically with the total of the facial behaviour examination modules collaborating.

2.3 Mask Detection

CNN expects a critical activity in PC vision-related model affirmation endeavour's, considering its supervisor spatial component extraction capacity and less computation cost [22]. CNN uses convolution kernels to convolve with the principal pictures or feature advisers for independent progressively critical level features. In any case, how to arrange better convolutional neural framework structures remains an underlying request. The inception framework proposed in [23] grants the framework to get comfortable with the best mix of kernels. To set up a great deal of further neural frameworks, K. He et al. proposes the Residual Network (ResNet) [24], which can take in an identity mapping from the last layer. As object detectors are regularly passed on mobile or embedded devices, where the computational resources are incredibly confined MobileNet [25] is proposed. It uses significant adroit convolution to remove features and channel-wise convolutions to alter channel numbers, so the computational cost of MobileNet is a great deal lower than frameworks using standard convolutions.

2.4 IoT

We have based the embedded system design on systems already in use since it was not the primary objective of the paper. A fusion of the methods of temperature sensor interfacing [26] and the Pi camera library [27] was used to capture an image of the user's face and simultaneously record the user's temperature.

3 System Architecture and Implementation

(See Fig. 2).

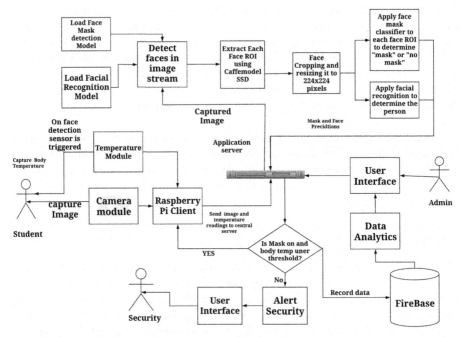

Fig. 2. Architecture diagram

4 Algorithm

The significant thought process behind the advancement of the Fig. 2 framework, was to make a strong framework which needn't bother with overwhelming registering necessities and hefty costing. But simultaneously doesn't settle on the precision part too. So, we propose such an architecture is very much cost-effective as well as makes sure that all the safety protocols are ensured by tracking every individual entering the college. When the students and the staff enter the college, they are required to go through the following process:

1. Get their image captured by the camera using the face detection model and temperature by the MLX90614 Infrared Temperature sensor once a face is detected.
2. This image and data are read and sent to the central server where the details of each student and staff members are present.
3. The machine learning models are applied to the captured image to identify the student and check if a mask is present or not.
4. For face recognition, we have used OpenFace.

5. For mask detection, we have prepared a model using Keras/Tensorflow.
6. On the classification of a student, we can extract information like Roll Number, Class to uniquely identify each student.
7. Similarly, on the classification of staff, we can extract information like Teacher Id, Department to uniquely identify each staff member.
8. The information along with the image and temperature is sent for checking and validation of data is done.
9. If the information is valid i.e. there are no null values and within the safety limits, then this data can be uploaded to the database. Once the database is updated, we inform the student that he can proceed.
10. Else if the Application server checks for null values, if exists it informs the Raspberry Pi to once again take the picture of the student or staff member present at the gate.
11. Else it checks the temperature value is higher than the prescribed normal body temperature or if a student or a staff member is wearing a mask or not. If safety protocols are broken by the predicted values which are not wearing a mask or higher body temperature or both, in that case, the applications server then notifies the administrator and the security personnel. Finally, admin and security personnel can take precautionary measures if required.
12. In any case, the data is always being uploaded to the database even if the data is within the safety protocols limits or not.
13. Once the data validation is completed the whole process is carried out again for the next person.
14. As all the value is being stored in database day and date wise, it makes it simpler for the administrator to apply various data analytics methods and generate charts in our UI to track those students who have flouted the safety protocols most of the time or students who have gradually shown any symptoms for COVID19. Hence making it possible for the administrator to take advance actions, thereby preventing the spread of such insidious virus to other students and staff present in the college. Also, at the same time help the individual by informing

Figure 3 shows the working of the system for a single individual when he/she approaches the entry point of the college. The process is repeated continuously in a loop for all the individuals entering the college.

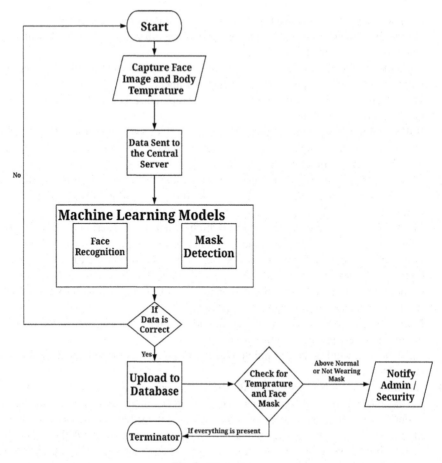

Fig. 3. Flow diagram

5 Software Design

Initially, the input is provided in the form of a captured image. The image is sent to the application server as soon as the face is detected. At the application server, its features are separated. Features are then contrasted with the authentic features for the face recognition part. Though the same features are likewise sent to the face mask classifier model to identify whether the student is wearing a mask or not. If the student's matches and different boundaries which include body temperature and mask detection are inside the permissible limits then the student is permitted to enter the school. On the off chance that the essence of the student is unrecognized or any of the boundaries like a face mask and the body temperature is off the breaking point, alert assistance will alarm the security about the sitting at a savvy social good way from the section/leave point. Beginning from coding language python to human-computer interaction through Face Detection, Mask Detection & Face Recognition model, and Firebase for the user interface. A detailed analysis has been done of the software stack used.

5.1 Face Detection

Face detection is performed to find the trigger to capture an image from the camera and simultaneously record the temperature at that instant. The entire procedure takes place on a Raspberry Pi 3B+. This necessitates an object detection algorithm which is robust, can run in real-time while not using too much processing power, since processing power is a limited resource on this platform. The limitations and demands of the algorithm are satisfied with the Viola-Jones Object Detection framework. When implemented on 384 × 288-pixel images, faces are detected at 15 frames per second on a 700 MHz Intel Pentium III, which is an x86 processor from 1999 [28]. The performance of the system and its accuracy suit the application perfectly.

The algorithm has four stages:

- Haar Feature Selection

  – Haar features are used to match human faces since all faces share some common characteristics like the upper cheeks are lighter than the eyes and the eyes are darker than the nose bridge.

- Integral Image creation

  – Integral Image Rectangle features are quick to compute using an intermediate representation for the image, which is known as an integral image. The integral image lets any rectangular sum be computed in four array references [28]. Thus, the integral image method reduces the number of calculations and thus can save a lot of time.

- Adaboost Training

  – The Viola-Jones detection framework employs an adaption of the algorithm 'AdaBoost' to both select the best features for face detection and to train classifiers that use them [28].

- Cascading Classifiers

  – Classifiers work in a sequence, with simpler classifiers first in line, which reject the majority of sub-windows before more complex classifiers are even necessary. This results in low false-positive rates. This detection process resembles a degenerate decision tree and is referred to as 'Cascading Classifiers' [28].

5.2 Face Recognition

For the motivation behind facial recognition, we have utilized OpenFace [29], which is an open face profound learning facial acknowledgement model. It is based upon the paper [30] developed by Google developers. OpenFace is actualized utilizing Python and Torch permitting the system to be executed smoothly on CPU as well as on a GPU acceleration which is CUDA. As we actualized the application in Keras (using TensorFlow [31] backend), and to do that we utilized a pre-prepared model known as Keras-OpenFace by Victor Sy Wangwhich [32] which is an open-source Keras execution of the OpenFace.

Applying CNN classifier to confront acknowledgement is certifiably not an extraordinary thought because, as a gathering of individuals (like representatives of an organization) increments or diminishes, one needs to change the SoftMax classifier work. here is a wide range of ways by which we can make a face recognition framework, and in this application, we utilized facial recognition along with one-shot learning by a profound neural system.

One-Shot Learning [33–35]

In one shot learning, just one picture for each individual is put away in the database, which is gone through the neural system to create an implanting vector. This installing vector is contrasted and the vector produced for the individual who must be perceived. If there exist similarities between the two vectors, at that point the framework perceives that individual, else that individual isn't there in the database. This can be comprehended in Fig. 4.

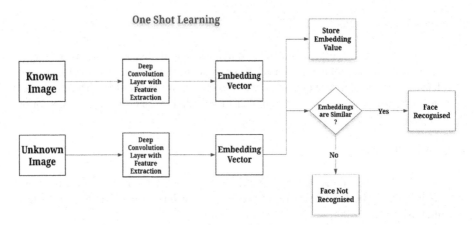

Fig. 4. OneShot [34] learning working

Triplet Loss Function [30]

Since we are utilizing the OpenFace pre-trained model for facial recognition. Preparing the neural system with the Triplet Loss Function limits the separation between similar pictures which have a similar personality, and amplifies the separation between the pictures of an alternate character. The function is appreciated beneath in Eq. 1.

$$Loss = \sum_{i=1}^{N}\left[||f_i^a - f_i^p||_2^2 - ||f_i^a - f_i^n||_2^2 + \alpha\right] \tag{1}$$

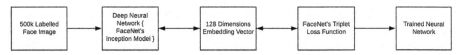

Fig. 5. OpenFace [29] model architecture

OpenFace Model [29]

The accompanying Fig. 5 shows the work process for a solitary info picture of Sylvester Stallone from the freely accessible LFW dataset [36].

1. Pre-trained models from libraries like OpenCV [37] or dlib are used to detect distinguished faces.
2. The faces are then fed into the neural network.
3. Utilize a deep neural system to implant the face on a 128-dimensional unit hyper-sphere. The embedding is a conventional portrayal of anyone's face. In contrast to other portrayals, inserting has a pleasant property: a bigger separation between two face embeddings implies that the appearances are likely not of a similar individual. Thereby making grouping, likeness discovery, & order assignments simpler than other face acknowledgement strategies where Euclidean separation betwixt highlights isn't significant.
4. Apply your preferred grouping or classifying methods to the highlights to finish your acknowledgement task.

Working

As we are utilizing the pre-trained model to compare the embedding vectors of the pictures put away in the file system with the embedding vector of the picture captured by the webcam. This can be clarified by underneath Fig. 6.

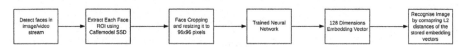

Fig. 6. Face recognition workflow

All the images stored in the file system are converted to a dictionary with names as key and embedding vectors as value. When handling an image, face recognition is done to discover bounding boxes around faces. We have used the same face detection code that is being executed at the Raspberry Pi end for extricating the face Region of Interest of the captured image. Before passing the picture to the neural system, it is resized to 96 × 96 pixels as the profound neural system expects the fixed (96 × 96) input picture size. When the picture is taken care of into the model, we produce the 128-measurement inserting vector for the obscure picture with the assistance of a pre-prepared model. Simultaneously, we likewise load the put away implanting vectors for the known datasets. To think about two pictures for likeness, we figure the separation between their embeddings. This should be possible by either computing Euclidean (L2) distance or Cosine separation between the 128-dimensional vectors. On the off chance that the separation is not exactly an edge (which is a hyperparameter), at that point the countenances in the two pictures are of a similar individual, if not, they are two distinct people.

5.3 Mask Detection

In the current situation due to Covid-19, there are no effective face mask detection applications that are presently popular for transportation implies thickly populated territories, private regions, huge scope producers, and different endeavours to guarantee security. Likewise, Also, the absence of large datasets of 'with_mask' images has made this task more cumbersome and challenging. The dataset used for the training of the mask detector comprises 10563 pictures having labels with two classes which are "with_mask: 7130 pictures" and "without_mask: 3433 images". The pictures utilized were genuine pictures of faces wearing covers. The pictures were gathered from Kaggle [38] and RMFD datasets [39].

To prepare a custom face mask detector, for accommodation, we have broken the entire procedure into two particular stages, each with its separate sub-ventures as appeared by Fig. 7.

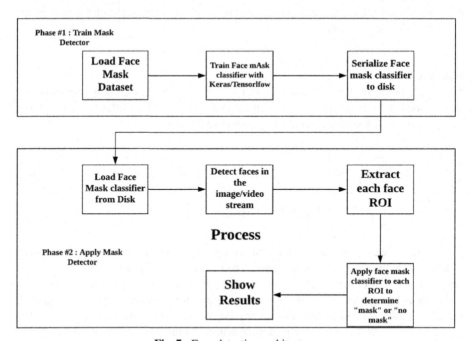

Fig. 7. Face detection architecture

Phase 1: Train Mask Detector

In the preparation stage, we concentrated on stacking our face mask recognition dataset from the hard drive, preparing a model (utilizing Keras/TensorFlow [31]) on the dataset, and afterwards stacking the face mask recognition in the file system. Utilizing Keras/TensorFlow [31] permits us to get to the CUDA computations of Nvidia GPUs which quickens our preparation procedure and permits a lot of functionalities while building the model. The procedure embraced while building the model for the face mask recognition involves:

1. Load the picture Datasets
2. Preprocessing steps incorporate scaling the dataset images to 224 × 224 pixels, transformation to exhibit configuration, and escalating the pixel forces in the image to the range [−1, 1].
3. Data augmentation steps incorporate applying on-the-fly transformations to the dataset to ameliorate speculation during the preparation procedure. Utilizing the scikit-learn technique, we section our images into 4:1 ratio for training and testing purposes respectively.
4. Loading MobilNetV2 [25] classifier which we fine-tune with the assistance of pre-prepared ImageNet [22] weights.
5. Building the completely associated (FC) head happens in three-advance:
6. Loading MobileNet [25] with pre-trained ImageNet [22] weights, excluding the head layers of the network.
7. We then construct another Fully Connected head layer and add this layer to the base layers instead of the original head layers.
8. Freezing the base layers of the neural network. As a result, the weights of these base layers are not updated during the process of backpropagation. On the other hand, the head layer weights will be tuned.
9. Compiling the model with the Adam optimizer, binary cross-entropy and a learning rate decay schedule. We have defined the hyperparameter constants which includes the underlying learning rate, batch size and the number of training epochs.

Phase 2: Apply Mask Detector

When the face mask classifier is prepared, we would then be able to proceed onward to loading the mask classifier model, performing face mask detection and afterwards characterizing each face as "without_mask" or "with_mask". When the face detection happens at the microcontroller end, the image captured is then sent to the application server which sends it further to the face classifier model. Before feeding the image directly into the model, we do pre-process on the captured image. Pre-processing is taken care of by OpenCV's [37] blobFromImage function, we resize the captured image to 300 × 300 pixels and perform mean deduction. After the preprocessing step, we at that point foresee the face guaranteeing that the threshold is met before finding the Region of Interest. Looping over the detections and extracting the confidence scores to measure against the confidence defined threshold. At that point, we compute the bounding boxes value for detected faces and guarantee that the bounding box falls inside the limits of the captured picture. In the wake of removing the facilitation of the bounding box of the face ROI, we feed it into our face classifier model and get the ideal forecasts for that face's ROI. At long last, we decide the classmark dependent on the probabilities score returned by the mask classifier model and thereby allocate the related class name which is "with_mask" and "without_mask" for that captured image of the understudy.

5.4 Firebase

Firebase Firestore is a horizontally scaling NoSQL cloud-based database service provided by Google Developers. Firestore is a serverless database hence it can be easily integrated with any platform very easily. The services of Firebase, being on the cloud is available for usage from anywhere. The cloud messaging service of Firebase gives a way to send notifications to the admin about a potential carrier of the virus. The Firebase Firestore being a horizontally scaling database is highly scalable. At any point in time, if we require new functionality, it can be integrated for the next versions of our database, hence increasing the scope of the project is possible.

The usage of firebase is happening as follows:

1. Firstly, the image is being captured and transferred to the central server along with the temperature.
2. Then, face recognition algorithms predict if a user is wearing a mask or not also assign the captured image identity of the person.
3. The complete data as a packet is checked for any vulnerabilities or Null values
4. If the checks are completed the data is stored on the Firebase firestore according to the current date. If the temperature readings are above normal or the student is not wearing a mask, in that scenario the admin/security personnel will be notified.

6 Hardware Design

We use the Raspberry Pi 3B+ as a platform to capture user images and temperature readings. The Raspberry Pi 3B+ has an ARMv8 64-bit SoC with Wi-Fi and Bluetooth support. Gigabit Ethernet is also supported over the USB 2.0 connection [40]. This allows the Raspberry Pi to perform basic face detection and communicate with the central server effectively. The camera used is the Raspberry Pi Camera v2, which interfaces over the Camera Serial Interface (CSI) port of the Raspberry Pi 3B+ [40]. It supports many video resolutions and has libraries to access the camera feed [41]. The MLX 90614 [42] (3.3 V) Infrared temperature sensor is used to measure user temperature. The sensor interfaces over i2c hardware bus through i2c_bcm2708 kernel module and the libi2c library [26]. The camera and temperature sensor have to be adjusted so that the Field of View of the sensor is aligned over the centre of the frame of the view of the camera (Fig. 8).

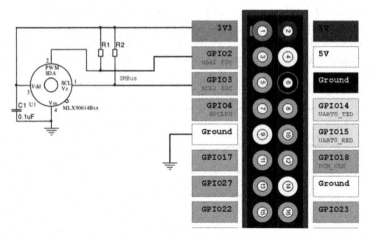

Fig. 8. Circuit diagram of raspberry Pi & MLX 90614 [26]

7   Results

The significant thought process behind the advancement of such a framework was to make a strong framework which needn't bother with overwhelming registering necessities and simultaneously doesn't settle on the precision part too. The models that we used should be computationally efficient and deployable to embedded systems (Raspberry Pi, Google Coral, etc.). This was the very explanation we have utilized the OpenFace [29] model for facial recognition, transfer learning on the MobileNet V2 [25] model for the face mask classifier and Viola Jones [24] for face detection.

Table 1. Time & memory consumption [9]

Detector	Time		Memory consumption (GB)
	GFLOPS	FPS	
Viola-Jones [43]	0.6	60	0.1
Head Hunter DPM [44]	5	1	2
SSD [45]	45.8	13.3	0.7
Faster R-CNN [46]	223.9	5.8	2.1
R-FCN 50 [47]	132.1	6	2.4
R-FCN 101 [47]	186.6	4.7	3.1
PVANEY [48]	40.1	9	2.6
Local RCNN [49]	1209.8	0.5	2.1
Yolo 9000 [50]	34.9	19.2	2.1

The Viola-Jones [43] framework has favorable performance in comparison to other object detection frameworks, especially when processing power and framerate are concerned. Table 1 and Fig. 9 show us a comparative study between the different detection frameworks present in the market along with their time taken and the memory consumption.

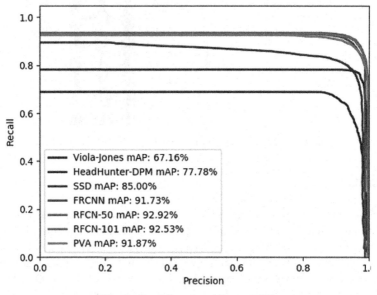

Fig. 9. Precision vs recall scores [9]

We can see that the training is done on LFW dataset [51] for the OpenFace [32] Keras model which gave us an exactness of around (93.80 ± 1.3) % alongside different measurements as according to the Table 2.

Table 2. OpenFace Keras metrics table [32]

Accuracy	0.938 ± 0.013
Alidation rate	0.47469 ± 0.04227@ FAR = 0.00134
Area Under Curve (AUC)	0.979
Equal Error Rate (EER)	0.062

Then again, the training is done on the custom dataset which incorporates around 10563 pictures downloaded from Kaggle [38] and RFID [39] for the face classifier model dependent on transfer learning based upon the MobileNetV2[25] gave us a precision of again 93% on normal conditions. Taking a gander at Fig. 11 we can see there are little indications of overfitting and the Fig. 10 shows the assessment measurements on the testing dataset per epoch which includes 20% of the all-out pictures present in the custom dataset.

```
[INFO] evaluating network...
                precision    recall  f1-score   support

   with_mask        0.95      0.96      0.95      1426
without_mask        0.91      0.89      0.90       687

    accuracy                            0.93      2113
   macro avg        0.93      0.92      0.92      2113
weighted avg        0.93      0.93      0.93      2113

[INFO] saving mask detector model...

(ai) D:\Vedant\Projects\COVID-Face-Mask-Detection>tensorflow
```

Fig. 10. Mask classifier metrics

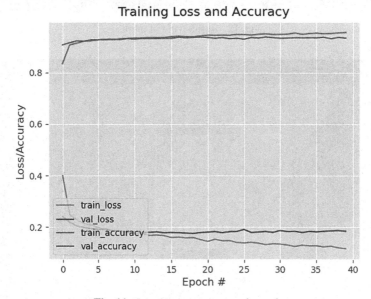

Fig. 11. Loss/accuracy per epoch graph

At the point when the image captured from the microcontroller is fed into the model by the application server after pre-preparing the image, the models return the probabilities of the expectations made and the name of the understudy perceived. For portrayal purposes, we have hued the bounding boxes showing up as red for an understudy without mask and green for an understudy with a cover. We at that point additionally print the class name {i.e. "with_mask" or "without_mask"}, likelihood, and the name perceived by the models on the head of the bounding enclosure as indicated in the underneath Fig. 12 and Fig. 13.

Fig. 12. Result without mask

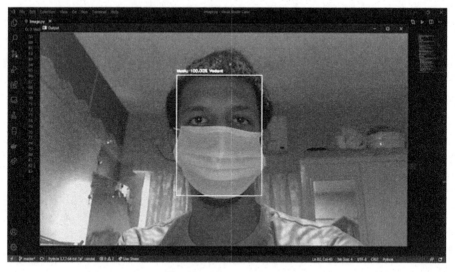

Fig. 13. Result with mask

For any great framework, UI is one of the most significant perspectives. It is through the UI that the individual interfaces with the framework get advantageous. Saving the accommodation for the administrator and the for the security staff, we have made such an interface, that would unravel the two fundamental purposes that are keeping up the record of the understudy with the name, timestamp, mask, and internal heat level just as keep any track in the abnormalities in the estimation of the mask-wearing and internal heat level of every single understudy entering the school. In the Firebase database, complete information is stored as a bundle of a packet of each understudy is embedded by the current date and day. This makes the framework progressively adaptable and the information from sorted out for playing out the data analysis by the administrator. To the extent the alert notification generation is considered, the alert notification is produced by the firebase itself as a message pop-up/email, which makes it considerably increasingly best for the framework. The accompanying Fig. 14 and Fig. 15 are of the UI and the firebase database respectively that we have utilized in our framework.

Fig. 14. User interface

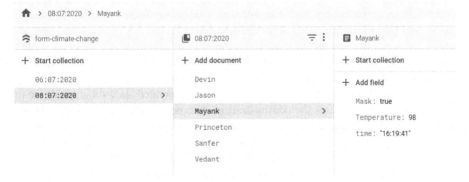

Fig. 15. Firebase database

8   Limitations

Our present strategy for recognizing whether an individual is wearing a mask or not is a two-advance procedure that performs face detection and afterwards applies a classification on faces to detect the mask. The issue with this methodology is that a mask darkens some portion of the face. If enough of the face is darkened, the face can't be distinguished, and hence, the face mask detector won't be applied.

Another issue is the reliability of the web relationship of the framework in which the system is being set up. The web relationship with the system must have low inaction and high transmission ability to send the alarm to the security as well as the image to the application server for further processing. The force flexibly of the framework must be steady as all the segments of the security framework run on power.

9   Future Work

We have entirely fair outcomes by simply contrasting the Euclidean separation with perceiving a face. Notwithstanding, if one needs proportional the framework to a creation framework, at that point, one ought to consider applying Affine changes additionally before taking care of the picture to the neural system.

Further to improve our face mask detection model, we need to assemble all the more genuine pictures of individuals wearing masks. Additionally, we have to assemble pictures of appearances that may "befuddle" our classifier into speculation the individual is wearing a mask when in truth they are not—potential models incorporate shirts folded over faces, a handkerchief over the mouth, and so forth. At long last, we ought to consider preparing a committed two-class object finder instead of a straightforward picture classifier.

10   Conclusion

Since the origin of Covid19, technological solutions have been worked out by researchers to combat the spread of Coronavirus pandemic. Few hot technologies like, IoT and Artificial Intelligence have been the front runners. Our paper discussed using IoT-based sensors and Deep learning-based algorithms to detect the breach of suggested precautionary measures like the use of masks in public places and to ensure no entry within the campus to individuals showing COVID19 symptoms in our case high body temperature. Our model also records every student's body temperature in a central database on a day-to-day basis and raises the alarm if the Pattern generated shows a gradual rise in body temperature also helps the administration in monitoring safety standards within the campus. This automated approach helps prevent the security personnel from coming in contact with every student or visitors and reduces the chances of human errors in identifying the person entering the facility with COVID19 symptoms.

References

1. WHO Homepage. https://www.who.int/health-topics/coronavirus#tab=tab_3. Accessed 16 July 2020
2. Ourworldindata Homepage. https://ourworldindata.org/. Accessed 14 July 2020
3. Report WHO-China Joint Mission Coronavirus Disease 2019 (COVID-19), February 2020. https://www.who.int/docs/default-source/coronaviruse/who-china-joint-mi%ssion-on-covid-19-final-report.pdf. Accessed 14 July 2020
4. Modes of Transmission of Virus Causing COVID-19: Implications for IPC Precaution Recommendations, April 2020. https://www.who.int/news-room/commentaries/detail/modes-of-transmission%-of-virus-causing-covid-19-implications-for-ipc-precaution-recommend ations. Accessed 14 July 2020
5. Study Suggests New Coronavirus May Remain on Surfaces for Days, March 2020. https://www.nih.gov/news-events/nih-research-matters/study-suggests-new%-corona virus-may-remain-surfaces-days. Accessed 15 July 2020
6. Coronavirus Disease (COVID-19) Advice for the Public: When and How to Use Masks, April 2020. https://www.who.int/emergencies/diseases/novel-coronavirus-2019/advice-%for-pub lic/when-and-how-to-use-masks. Accessed 15 July 2020
7. Ting, D.S.W., Carin, L., Dzau, V., Wong, T.Y.: Digital technology and COVID-19. Nat. Med. **26**(4), 459–461 (2020)
8. Digital Technology For Covid-19 Response, April 2020. https://www.who.int/news-room/det ail/03-04-2020-digital-technology-for-%covid-19-response. Accessed 16 July 2020
9. Nguyen-Meidine, L.T., Granger, E., Kiran, M., Blais-Morin, L.: A comparison of CNN-based face and head detectors for real-time video surveillance applications. In: 2017 Seventh International Conference on Image Processing Theory, Tools and Applications (IPTA), Montreal, QC, pp. 1–7 (2017). https://doi.org/10.1109/ipta.2017.8310113
10. Alabort-i-medina, J., Antonakos, E., Booth, J., Snape, P.: Menpo: a comprehensive platform for parametric image alignment and visual deformable models categories and subject descriptors, pp. 3–6 (2014)
11. Zhu, X., Ramanan, D.: Face detection, pose estimation, and landmark localization in the wild. In: CVPR (2012)
12. Morency, L.-P., Whitehill, J., Movellan, J.R.: Generalized adaptive view-based appearance model: integrated frame-work for monocular head pose estimation. In: FG (2008)
13. Fanelli, G., Gall, J., Gool, L.V.: Real time head pose estimation with random regression forests. In: CVPR, pp. 617–624 (2011)
14. Asthana, A., Zafeiriou, S., Cheng, S., Pantic, M.: Robust discriminative response map fitting with constrained local models. In: CVPR (2013)
15. Asthana, A., Zafeiriou, S., Cheng, S. Pantic, M.: Incremental face alignment in the wild. In: CVPR (2014)
16. Hansen, D.W., Ji, Q.: In the eye of the beholder: a survey of models for eyes and gaze. IEEE Trans. Pattern Anal. Mach. Intell. **32**, 478–500 (2010)
17. Lidegaard, M., Hansen, D.W., Krüger, N.: Head mounted device for point-of-gaze estimation in three dimensions. In: Proceedings of the Symposium on Eye Tracking Research and Applications - ETRA 2014 (2014)
18. Świrski, L., Bulling, A., Dodgson, N.A.: Robust real-time pupil tracking in highly off-axis images. In: Proceedings of ETRA (2012)
19. Ferhat, O., Vilarino, F.: A cheap portable eye–tracker solution for common setups. In: 3rd International Workshop on Pervasive Eye Tracking and Mobile Eye-Based Interaction (2013)
20. Wood, E., Bulling, A.: EyeTab: model-based gaze estimation on unmodified tablet computers. In: Proceedings of ETRA, March 2014

21. Zielinski, P.: Opengazer: open-source gaze tracker for ordinary webcams (2007)
22. Deng, J., Dong, W., Socher, R., Li, L., Li, K., Fei-Fei, L.: ImageNet: a large-scale hierarchical image database. In: 2009 IEEE Conference on Computer Vision and Pattern Recognition, Miami, FL, pp. 248–255 (2009). https://doi.org/10.1109/cvpr.2009.5206848
23. Szegedy, C., et al.: Going deeper with convolutions. In: Proceedings of the IEEE Conference on Computer Vision and Pattern Recognition, pp. 1–9 (2015)
24. He, K., Zhang, X., Ren, S., Sun, J.: Deep residual learning for image recognition. In: Proceedings of the IEEE Conference on computer Vision and Pattern Recognition, pp. 770–778 (2016)
25. Sandler, M., Howard, A., Zhu, M., Zhmoginov, A., Chen, L.: MobileNetV2: inverted residuals and linear bottlenecks. In: 2018 IEEE/CVF Conference on Computer Vision and Pattern Recognition, Salt Lake City, UT, pp. 4510–4520 (2018). https://doi.org/10.1109/cvpr.2018.00474
26. Sensor. https://olegkutkov.me/2017/08/10/mlx90614-raspberry/. Accessed 20 Apr 2020
27. GitHub Repository. https://github.com/waveform80/picamera. Accessed 05 June 2020
28. Viola, P., Jones, M.: Rapid object detection using a boosted cascade of simple features. In: Proceedings of the 2001 IEEE Computer Society Conference on Computer Vision and Pattern Recognition. CVPR 2001, Kauai, HI, USA, p. I-I (2001) https://doi.org/10.1109/cvpr.2001.990517
29. Amos, B., Ludwiczuk, B., Satyanarayanan, M.: OpenFace: a general-purpose face recognition library with mobile applications. CMU-CS-16-118, CMU School of Computer Science, Technical report (2016)
30. Schroff, F., Kalenichenko, D., Philbin, J.: FaceNet: a unified embedding for face recognition and clustering. In: 2015 IEEE Conference on Computer Vision and Pattern Recognition (CVPR), Boston, MA, pp. 815–823 (2015). https://doi.org/10.1109/cvpr.2015.7298682
31. TensorFlow Homepage. https://www.tensorflow.org/. Accessed 19 June 2020
32. GitHub Repository. https://github.com/iwantooxxoox/Keras-penFace/tree/master/weights. Accessed 16 Apr 2020
33. Lungu, I.A., Hu, Y., Liu, S.: Multi-resolution siamese networks for one-shot learning. In: 2020 2nd IEEE International Conference on Artificial Intelligence Circuits and Systems (AICAS), Genova, Italy, pp. 183–187 (2020). https://doi.org/10.1109/aicas48895.2020.9073996
34. Bromley, J., et al.: Signature verification using a siamese time delay neural network. Int. J. Pattern Recogn. Artif. Intell. 7(04), 669–688 (1993)
35. Koch, G.: Siamese neural networks for one-shot image recognition. In: ICML Deep Learning Workshop (2015)
36. LFW Dataset. http://vis-www.cs.umass.edu/lfw/person/Sylvester_Stallone.html. Accessed 02 May 2020
37. OpenCV Homepage. https://opencv.org/. Accessed 18 June 2020
38. Kaggle Datasets. https://www.kaggle.com/datasets. Accessed 28 June 2020
39. GitHub Repository. https://github.com/X-zhangyang/Real-World-Masked-Face-Dataset. Accessed 29 Apr 2020
40. Raspberry Pi Products. https://www.raspberrypi.org/products/raspberry-pi-3-model-b-plus/. Accessed 19 Apr 2020
41. Raspberry Pi Products. https://www.raspberrypi.org/products/camera-module-v2/. Accessed 19 Apr 2020
42. Sparkfun Sensors Datasheets. https://www.sparkfun.com/datasheets/Sensors/Temperature/MLX90614_rev001.pdf. Accessed 20 Apr 2020
43. Viola, P., Jones, M.J.: Robust real-time face detection. J. Comput. Vis. 57(2), 137–154 (2004)
44. Yan, J., Zhang, X., Lei, Z., Li, S.Z.: Real-time high-performance deformable model for face detection in the wild

45. Liu, W., et al.: SSD: single shot multibox detector. CoRR, abs/1512.02325 (2015)
46. Ren, S., et al.: Faster R-CNN: towards real-time object detection with region proposal networks. CoRR, abs/1506.01497 (2015)
47. Dai, J., Li, Y., He, K., Sun, J.: R-FCN: object detection via region-based fully convolutional networks. CoRR, abs/1605.06409 (2016)
48. Kim, K., Cheon, Y., Hong, S., Roh, B., Park, M.: PVANET: deep but lightweight neural networks for real-time object detection. CoRR, abs/1608.08021 (2016)
49. Vu, T., Osokin, A., Laptev, I.: Context-aware CNNs for person head detection. In: ICCV (2015)
50. Redmon, J., Farhadi, A.: YOLO9000: better, faster, stronger. CoRR,abs/1612.08242 (2016)
51. Huang, G.B., Ramesh, M., Berg, T., Learned-Miller, E.: Labeled faces in the wild: a database for studying face recognition in unconstrained environments. Technical Report 07-49, University of Massachusetts, Amherst, October 2007

A 2D ResU-Net Powered Segmentation of Thoracic Organs at Risk Using Computed Tomography Images

Mohit Asudani[1], Alarsh Tiwari[2], Harsh Kataria[2], Vipul Kumar Mishra[2(✉)], and Anurag Goswami[2]

[1] Indian Institute of Information Technology Senapati,
Imphal 795002, Manipur, India
mohitasudani20@gmail.com
[2] Bennett University, Greater Noida 201310, Uttar Pradesh, India
alarsh1309@gmail.com, hkataria99@gmail.com,
{vipul.mishra,anurag.goswami}@bennett.edu.in

Abstract. The recent advances in the field of computer vision have led to the wide use of Convolutional Neural Networks (CNNs) in organ segmentation of computed tomography (CT) images. Image-guided radiation therapy requires the accurate segmentation of organs at risk (OARs). In this paper, the proposed model is a 2D ResU-Net network to automatically segment thoracic organs at risk in computed tomography (CT) images. The architecture consists of a downsampling path for capturing features and a symmetric upsampling path for obtaining precise localization. The proposed approach achieves a 0.93 dice metric (DSC) and 0.26 hausdorff distance (HD) after using ImageNet stats for normalizing and using pre-trained weights.

Keywords: Convolutional Neural Networks · ResU-Net · Computed Tomography (CT) images · Organ segmentation

1 Introduction

Lung cancer is one of the leading cause of death in both males and females with a contribution of 26.8% of all cancer deaths [1]. There were approximately 3.05 million cancer survivors treated with radiation, accounting for around 29% of all the cancer survivors in 2016. The radiation-treated cancer survivors are projected to reach 4.17 million by 2030 [1]. The introduction of procedures like stereotactic body radiation therapy and intensity-modulated radiation therapy has led to the improvement of Radiation therapy techniques, therefore, protecting normal organs become a primary concern [2].

During the radiation treatment, it is necessary to segment organs at risk correctly to avoid a very high radiation dose from the computed tomography (CT). The segmentation of images has brought a significant impact on diagnosis and treatment. This segmentation helps the doctors in viewing the internal

© Springer Nature Singapore Pte Ltd. 2021
D. Garg et al. (Eds.): IACC 2020, CCIS 1367, pp. 54–65, 2021.
https://doi.org/10.1007/978-981-16-0401-0_4

anatomy. Many existing techniques include X-Ray like Computed Tomography (CT) and cross-section images, or Magnetic Resonance Imaging (MRI), or others like Positron Emission Tomography and Single Photon Emission Computed Tomography.

The CT images are complex, so the identification, including the localization of organs by using manual techniques, is time-consuming and challenging. In general, experts do segmentation manually by intensity levels and anatomical knowledge (e.g., the Esophagus is located behind the Heart, Trachea is above the Spinal cord, etc). In current medical practice, the fundamental method of OARs segmentation is contouring manually, due to large number of axial slices of images and scans it may take one to two hours for major thoracic organs [2]. Moreover, manual contouring also suffers not only from inter and intra-observer variability but institutional variability as well, where different varying sites adopt varying labeling criteria and contouring atlases [2]. For the development of fully or semi automated solutions for segmentation, a lot of effort has been invested. Atlas-based methods incorporate for consensus-based labeling [2]. The automation of the segmentation algorithms enabled the shorting of the segmentation duration as compared with the manual contouring, and adaptive therapy [2]. Due to segmentation availability and quality, the usage of these techniques are still limited. Our objective is to instinctively segment out the thoracic organs: heart, aorta, trachea, and esophagus in CT images. This is difficult because the medical images given are three dimensional; the separation of organs are hard to differentiate since they may be low contrast. There are significant variations in the shape, size, and location of these organs at risk between patients [3]. For some organs (e.g.-esophagus), the segmentation is the most challenging: position and shape vary significantly between varying patients; also, the contours in CT images have low contrast and may be absent [3].

In the paper, we proposed a 2D ResU-Net based deep network on segmenting the OARs and to identify tumors. The proposed network achieves a good accuracy, and speed as compared to previous approaches. The paper is organized in such a way to identify the problem, followed by understanding the dataset, which is then followed by pre-processing, training the model with different architectures, and post-processing.

2   Related Work

A few interesting work have been done in recent years using a deep neural network to segment the CT images. In [4] Olaf Ronneberger et al. introduced a model that was based on simple UNet architecture for biomedical image segmentation. Other modifications are also proposed like localization and organ-specific U-Net model, Pixel shuffle method on fully convolutional U-Net architecture like in the Two-stage encoder-decoder model with coarse and fine segmentation in [5]. The author in [6] Used multi-task learning on U-Net architecture. Another U-Net model with each layer containing a context pathway, a localization pathway, and 2D residual U-Net with dilation rate was proposed in [7]. Moreover, dilated

U-Net architecture is also used with convolution, dilation, ReLU, batch normalization, and average pooling in [7]. These architectures use 2D convolutions, but with more computational capabilities. In another research, 3D convolutions are also being used like Using two resolutions and applying the VB-Net for each with Single-Class Dice loss in [8]. These are modified by researchers with a 3D enhanced multi-scale network with residual V-Net and 3D dilated convolution in [9]. A Simple dens V-Net with post-processing is presented in [10]. In [11], the author used both 3D and 2D convolutions in a full convolution 3D network.

3   Proposed Methodology

3.1   Data Collection and Pre-processing

The experimental data was collected from the SegTHOR19 training and testing datasets. The training data set include 40 patients (7390 slices), and testing data contains 20 patients (3694 slices). By analyzing the provided training data, The data is in the Neuroimaging Informatics Technology Initiative (NifTI) .nii format. It was then converted into NumPy .npy format [13] and later to png format using the matplotlib and PIL. A sample training image is shown in Fig. 1a, and a masked image is shown in Fig. 1b.

Pre-processing, often overlooked, is a major concern in terms of performance. Generally, There are bright regions in the images as compared with the external objects which will have a key effect on the organ voxels when normalizing with the original intensity range. Due to the said reason, the key step was assumed to be normalization. The reduction in the variability in the size occurred due to the re-sampling of the images to the same voxel spacing. It also helped in bringing the testing case distribution near to the training case distribution [2]. The Computed Tomography scans have 512×512 pixels with its spatial variations varying from 0.90 to 1.37 mm. The most frequent spatial resolution is $0.98 \times 0.98 \times 2.5$ mm^3. The 3D CT scan was converted into 2.5D or 2D images formed by stacking the previous array and next array. They were also normalized to 256 range values. The 3D CT scan was cut into slices along the axial, sagittal, and coronal planes for visualization of the test data. The 3D visualization of the testing data is depicted in Fig. 2.

3.2   Data Augmentation

At the period of training, re-scaling was done. Images have arbitrarily rotated the images by flipping them horizontally [13]. The data augmentation was implemented on the png framework. The U-Net structure will not be affected by augmentation method used in the training period [4,7].

3.3   Evaluation Metrics

The Evaluation metrics used are Dice metric and Hausdorff distance in order to follow the metric evaluation of the competition Segthor'19. Moreover, they define

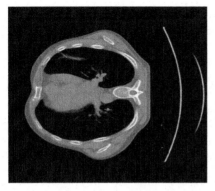

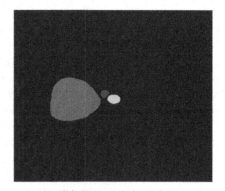

(a) CT-scan image in 2D for training   (b) Segmented mask

Fig. 1. A sample training and mask data

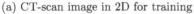

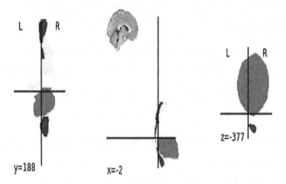

Fig. 2. 3D visualization of training data

similarity metrics and distinctions in pixels in accordance with the distance, which evaluates the segmentation models (especially medical ones) critically to gain better understanding about the practical working of the model.

The Overlap Dice Metric (DSC) has been used to find overlap between segmented area as result of proposed algorithm [3].

$$DSC(X,Y) = \frac{(2|X \cap Y|)}{(|X| + |Y|)} \tag{1}$$

The Hausdorff Distance (HD)

$$HD(X,Y) = max(h(X,Y), h(X,Y)) \tag{2}$$

HD is defined as max(d1; d2), where d1 and d2 are the maximum distance, to the closest manual contour point from automatic contour points, and manual contour points [3].

The model obtained the DSC and HD between two surfaces, G and S. The proposed model is trained on single class dice metric and modified accuracy metric. The modified accuracy metric defined only four classes that are to be segmented for accuracy metric calculation and didn't consider the void class.

In total, five classes (heart, esophagus, trachea, aorta, and void). Metric took into consideration the error of four main classes and did not include the void class. To get a better idea of performance of proposed model HD and DSC are used as their complementary nature.

3.4 Loss Function

The accuracy metric was utilized in our study. It was demonstrated by the research that for highly unbalanced segmentation dice loss yielded better results [15]. In this paper, the Dice loss has been used to rained the model [2]. The accuracy metric shows a high instability therefore, the localization neuralnet the more time to converge. We also used flattened loss of Cross-entropy loss function which gave nearly same results as compared with dice loss (Fig. 3).

$$DSC(X, Y) = \frac{(2|X \cap Y|)}{(|X| + |Y|)} \tag{3}$$

$$Diceloss = 1 - DSC(sum of all classes)/number of classes \tag{4}$$

3.5 Proposed 2D ResU-Net Network Architecture

We started our experiment from uniform U-net encoder-decoder segmentation architecture. The U-Net encoder-decoder architecture with long range connections has shown good performance in much of the segmentation tasks by effectively combining the spatial-information features of CT images with high level features with more global information to optimize classification. This model has symmetrical encoder and decoder parts. Here, the encoder has comparatively more non-linear mapping capability and learns by initializing parameters with the well-liked networks that have been trained on the classification of medical images. U-Net comprises of three sections, the contraction part, which is made of many contraction blocks. This is used for the extraction of high-level context information by convolutions and down-samplings. Each contraction block accepts an input that applies two 3×3 convolution layers. The convolution layers are followed by 2×2 max pooling. After each block, the number of feature maps or kernels doubles. Therefore, the architecture can effectively learn more complex structures. The bottleneck layer is the bottom-most layer that mediates

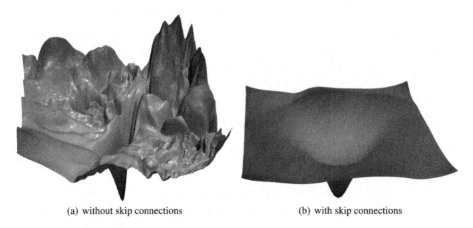

(a) without skip connections   (b) with skip connections

Fig. 3. The loss surfaces of ResNet-56 with/without skip connections. The proposed filter normalization scheme is used to enable comparisons of sharpness/flatness between the two figures.

between the contraction and the expansion layer of the U-net. This layer makes use of two 3×3 convolutional neural network (CNN) layers preceded by 2×2 up convolution layers. Same as the contraction layer on the left, the right expanding section is also formed by many expansion blocks. Each of these blocks gives input to two 3×3 convolution layers. To maintain the symmetry, Only half of the feature map will carry forward after each block. The number of expansion and contraction blocks on both sides is equal. The resulting mapping is fetched to another 3×3 CNN. In this CNN layer, the number of feature maps is the same as the number of segments desired.

The ResU-net model, as shown in Fig. 4, was implemented using the PyTorch framework. ResU-Net brings out appreciable segmentation accuracy compared with many other classical convolution networks. The residual connections provided the benefits in reducing the training difficulty [2]. Along with that, training a deep network required more memory and training time. A mix of residual connection with deeper network, as shown in Fig. 4 yields better or equal performances but takes a lot longer to train.

Utilization of dilated convolutions was another attempt as shown in Fig. 5 with more tunable parameters that includes dilation rates; the performances were alike and hence, no further investigate was carried out.

3.6 Training

For the training, the proposed model was trained with weight decay of $1e-2$ and a learning rate of $1e-4$ as shown in Fig. 6 learning rate and loss. Then slices were made for varying learning rates at different epochs. The model was trained for ten epochs. In the model, pixel shuffling and average pooling is used.

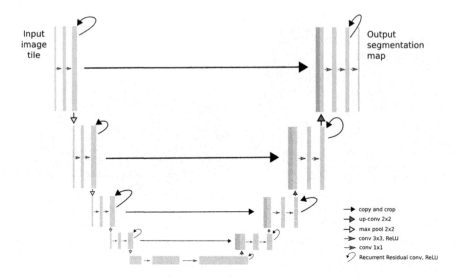

Fig. 4. The architecture of ResUnet

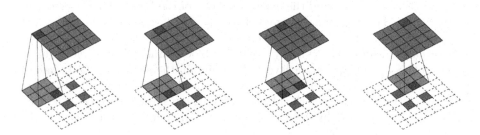

Fig. 5. The transposed convolution [21].

Total trainable parameters for our model are 19,946,396 and total non-trainable parameters are 11,166,912. ImageNet stats were used for normalizing the data.

For the task of image super-resolution, Shi et al. at [17] proposed to use pixel shuffle as an upsampling operator.

This operator rearranges input channels to produce a feature map with higher resolution, as shown in Fig. 7. Worth to mention, this technique solves the problem of checkerboard artifacts in the output image. Later, the same concept was employed for semantic segmentation tasks [18, 19]. The loss curve has been shown in Fig. 8 with respect to epoch.

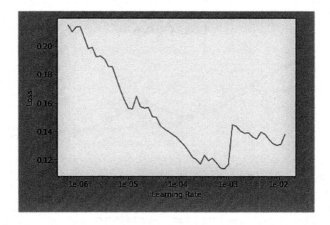

Fig. 6. Finding learning rate with respect to the loss graphically

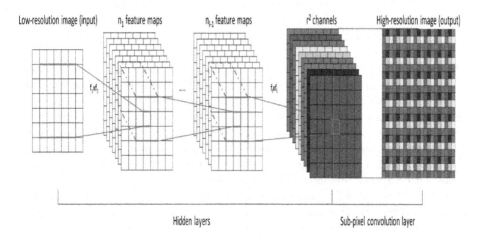

Fig. 7. The efficient sub-pixel CNN [20].

3.7 Data Post-processing

Due to conversion to 2.5D images, the number of total images formed is less by two images (i.e., first one and last one) as compared with the given training data. So, after the conversion of the results of 2.5D to 3D image again, void images are added to the 3D image by stacking all the 2.5D images depth-wise. It was noticed that the first and last images missing are void images in all the cases.

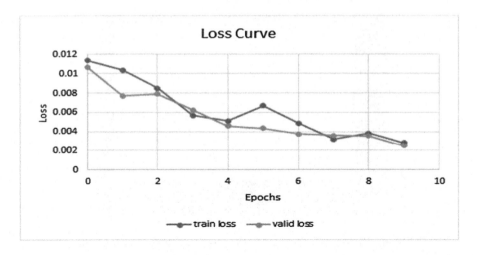

Fig. 8. Loss curve.

4   Experimental Results

The proposed algorithm has been implemented in Python 3.6, 64-bit Ubuntu
Linux platform in docker of Nvidia DGX-1 GPU. The proposed method was
validated on the 20 Computed Tomography scans of the given test data. No
external data was used, and our model was trained from scratch. The proposed
method uses the evaluation metrics, overlap Dice metric (DSC) Dice Similarity
Coefficient and the Hausdorff distance given in Eq. 2 and 1. The best result
obtained by the proposed algorithm shown in Fig. 9. Moreover, a comparative
result with a recent previous approach has been given in Table 1. It is evident
from Table 1 that the proposed approach is able to achieve better performance
in terms of DSC and HD both. Moreover, a sample predicted output and ground
truth is also shown in Fig. 10.

Rank		Dice				Hausdorff			
\<All\> ▲	\<Eusophagus\> ▲	Esophagus ▲	Heart ▲	Trachea ▲	Aorta ▲	Esophagus ▲	Heart ▲	Trachea ▲	Aorta ▲
1.00	1.00	0.8002 (1)	0.9349 (1)	0.9176 (1)	0.9257 (1)	0.5084 (1)	0.2365 (1)	0.3255 (1)	0.3110 (1)

Fig. 9. Dice and Hausdroff distance for all four classes

Table 1. Comparison with the previous approach

	Proposed		[13]		[10]	
	DSC	HD	DSC	HD	DSC	HD
Esophagus	0.80	0.5	0.81	0.68	0.77	1.68
Heart	0.934	0.23	0.93	0.26	0.93	0.20
Trachea	0.91	0.32	0.86	1.08	0.89	0.27
Aorta	0.93	0.31	0.92	0.52	0.92	0.30

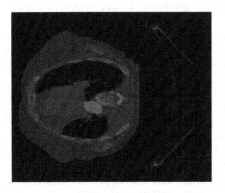 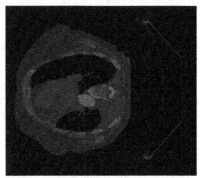

Fig. 10. Comparison between ground truth and predictions of masks and CT scans of the validation set

5   Discussion

The networks trained included U-net with ResNet34 and ResNet50, but the results and metrics were similar and approximately equal. This network used a 2D CNN for training, and then also it has similar or better results than using a 3D CNN network like V-nets or VB-net [8]. That's why the parameters to be trained are less, and the model is trained faster, cheaper, and with excellent efficiency in results. A few lessons on convolutional neural network implementation were learned, which are discussed below.

6   Conclusion

The images were converted to 3D CT scans from 2D to train our model. So, there is a loss in slicing. State of the art architecture was used, and that helped a lot with high accuracy. Without ResNet18, a single class dice metric was 0.39. Pre-trained weights were used for resnet18 downloaded from torchvision models.

After using ImageNet stats for normalizing and using pretrained weights, the accuracy graph got a high bump. This methodology gives accurate and more robust segmentation as compared to manual segmentation. The proposed model was applied to the test dataset and the results are depicted in Table 1.

Instead of training from scratch a better way that used in hospitals, is to fine-tune the general model with the same patient study before deploying to newer studies, which helps to incorporate the patient-specific features into the general model to provide much better results.

References

1. Cancer - World Health Organization. www.who.int
2. Feng, X., Qing, K., Tustison, N.J., Meyer, C.H., Chen, Q.: Deep convolutional neural network for segmentation of thoracicorgans-at-risk using cropped 3D images. Med. Phys. (2019)
3. Trullo, R., Petitjean, C., Ruan, S., Dubray, B., Nie, D., Shen, D.: Segmentation of organs at risk in thoracic CT images using a sharpmask architecture and conditional random fields. In: IEEE International Symposium on Biomedical Imaging (ISBI), pp. 1003–1006 (2017)
4. Ronneberger, O., Fischer, P., Brox, T.: U-Net: convolutional networks for biomedical image segmentation. In: Navab, N., Hornegger, J., Wells, W.M., Frangi, A.F. (eds.) MICCAI 2015. LNCS, vol. 9351, pp. 234–241. Springer, Cham (2015). https://doi.org/10.1007/978-3-319-24574-4_28
5. Zhang, L., Wang, L., Huang, Y., Chen, H.: Segmentation of thoracic organs at risk in CT images combining coarse and fine network. In: SegTHOR ISBI (2019)
6. He, T., Guo, J., Wang, J., Xu, X., Yi, Z.: Multi-task learning for the segmentation of thoracic organs at risk in CT images. In: SegTHOR ISBI (2019)
7. Vesal, S., Ravikumar, N., Maier, A.: A 2D dilated residual U-Net for multi-organ segmentation in thoracic CT. arXiv preprint arXiv:1905.07710 (2019)
8. Han, M., et al.: Segmentation of CT thoracic organs by multi-resolution VB-nets. In: SegTHOR ISBI (2019)
9. Wang, Q., et al.: 3D enhanced multi-scale network for thoracic organs segmentation. In: SegTHOR ISBI (2019)
10. Feng, M., Huang, W., Wang, Y., Xie, Y.: Multi-organ segmentation using simplified dense V-net with post-processing. In: SegTHOR ISBI (2019)
11. van Harten, L.D., Noothout, J.M., Verhoeff, J.J., Wolterink, J.M., Isgum, I.: Automatic segmentation of organs at risk in thoracic CT scans by combining 2D and 3D convolutional neural networks. In: SegTHOR ISBI (2019)
12. Badrinarayanan, V., Kendall, A., Cipolla, R.: SegNet: a deep convolutional encoder-decoder architecture for image segmentation. IEEE Trans. Pattern Anal. Mach. Intell. **39**(12), 2481–2495 (2017)
13. Gibson, E., et al.: Niftynet: a deep-learning platform for medical imaging. Comput. Methods Programs Biomed. **158**, 113–122 (2018)
14. Kim, S., Jang, Y., Han, K., Shim, H., Chang, H.J.: A cascaded two-step approach for segmentation of thoracic organs. In: CEUR Workshop Proceedings, vol. 2349. CEUR-WS (2019)
15. Sudre, C.H., Li, W., Vercauteren, T., Ourselin, S., Jorge Cardoso, M.: Generalised dice overlap as a deep learning loss function for highly unbalanced segmentations. In: Cardoso, M.J., et al. (eds.) DLMIA/ML-CDS -2017. LNCS, vol. 10553, pp. 240–248. Springer, Cham (2017). https://doi.org/10.1007/978-3-319-67558-9_28
16. Lambert, Z., Petitjean, C., Dubray, B., Ruan, S.: SegTHOR: Segmentation of Thoracic Organs at Risk in CT images. arXiv preprint arXiv:1912.05950 (2019)

17. Shi, W., et al.: Real-time single image and video super-resolution using an efficient sub-pixel convolutional neural network. In: Proceedings of the IEEE Conference on Computer Vision and Pattern Recognition, pp. 1874–1883 (2016)
18. Chen, K., Kun, F., Yan, M., Gao, X., Sun, X., Wei, X.: Semantic segmentation of aerial images with shuffling convolutional neural networks. IEEE Geosci. Remote Sens. Lett. **15**(2), 173–177 (2018)
19. Gao, H., Yuan, H., Wang, Z., Ji, S.: Pixel deconvolutional networks. arXiv preprint arXiv:1705.06820 (2017)
20. Wang, Z., Liu, D., Yang, J., Han, W., Huang, T.: Deeply Improved Sparse Coding for Image Super-Resolution, ArXiv 2015, abs/1507.08905
21. Boureau, Y., Ponce, J., LeCun, Y.: A theoretical analysis of feature pooling in vision algorithms. In: Proceedings of International Conference on Machine learning (ICML 2010), vol. 28 (2010)

A Compact Shape Descriptor Using Empirical Mode Decomposition to Detect Malignancy in Breast Tumour

Spandana Paramkusham[1(✉)], Manjula Sri Rayudu[2], and Puja S. Prasad[1]

[1] Geethanjali College of Engineering and Technology, Cheeryal Village, Kesara Mandal, Medchal, Hyderabad 501301, Telangana, India
spandanaparamkusham1@gmail.com

[2] Vallurupalli Nageswara Rao Vignana Jyothi Institute of Engineering and Technology, Vignana Jyothi Nagar, Pragathi Nagar, Nizampet (S.O), Hyderabad 500090, Telangana, India

Abstract. Breast cancer is the most common cancer in India and the world. Mammogram helps the radiologists to detect abnormalities in breast. Analysis of the lesions on breast helps doctors in the detection of cancer in early stages. Lesion contours of breast are characterized by their shape. Malignant lesion contours have speculated and ill-defined shapes and benign have circular and lobulated shape. In the present work, we proposed a method to classify breast contours into benign/malignant using empirical mode decomposition (EMD) technique. Initially, the two-dimension contours of breast lesions are compacted into 1D signature. Further, 1D signatures of lesions are decomposed into intrinsic mode functions (IMFs) by the EMD algorithm and statistical based features are calculated from these IMFs. This parameters form a input feature vector which are further fed to classifier.

Keywords: Breast cancer · Mammogram · Feature extraction · Empirical mode decomposition · Classification

1 Introduction

Breast cancer is the most common cancer in India and the world. According the WHO reports, 2.1 million women got affected with breast cancer each year, and resulted in highest mortality rate among women [1]. In 2018, nearly 627,000 women died due to breast cancer. Approximately 15% of death in women is due to breast cancer. Mammography plays prominent role in the detection of breast cancer in early stages. Computer aided diagnosis and detection of masses from mammograms helps radiologists in early indication of breast cancer. Mass is one of the abnormality in breast in which the radiologists look for diagnosis. Masses are characterized by their shape. Benign mass is circular or round with well defined boundary but where as malignant mass is spiculated with fuzzy boundary. Shape descriptors are very important tools to classify masses in breast. The goal of shape based descriptors is to measure spiculation in malignant masses based on their boundary. Complexity of 1D signature of mass contour is studied

© Springer Nature Singapore Pte Ltd. 2021
D. Garg et al. (Eds.): IACC 2020, CCIS 1367, pp. 66–74, 2021.
https://doi.org/10.1007/978-981-16-0401-0_5

using fractal analysis and achieved accuracy of 89% using ruler method [2]. Several studies have been carried out to classify masses as benign and malignant. Shape features such as compactness (C), fractional concavity (Fcc), spiculation index (SI), and a Fourier-descriptor-based factor (FF) are calculated to discriminate benign and malignant contours [3, 4]. Pohlman et al. [5] applied fractal analysis to benign and malignant contours of breast masses and achieved accuracy of 80%. Rangayan et al. [6] employed fractal analysis based on power spectral analysis to classify breast contour 1D signatures. Texture features can also be extracted from mammograms to classify masses as benign masses are homogeneous in nature and malignant masses have heterogeneous textures. Many researchers have contributed papers on classification of masses using texture features. Yang et al. [7], applied wave atom transform to extract features and classified the masses using random forest classifiers. Prathibha et al. [8] employed a method of bandlet and orthogonal ripplet type II transforms to extract features and applied KNN classifier to distinguish normal-benign, normal-malignant and malignant-benign images. Dhahbi et al. [9] used curvelet moment to classify masses. However, the use of texture features results in high dimensional feature vector and increases computational cost of the classification model [7]. Regardless, many researches have shown that shape based descriptors are more useful compared to any other descriptors such as texture, color, etc., [10]. In the work proposed we have implemented EMD algorithm to extract features from 1D signature of 2D mass contours to classify masses. Empirical mode decomposition algorithm is developed by Huang et al. [11] to analyse nonstationary or nonlinear signals. Djemili et al. [12] applied EMD algorithm and artificial neural networks to classify 1D EEG signals. Orosco et al. [13] employed EMD for epileptic seizure detection.

In this work we focus on extraction of compact shape feature vector from 2D mass contours. This work is proposed in three steps. In the first step, the 2D contour is mapped into a compact 1D signature using Eucleidian distance. In the second step the 1D signature is further compressed using empirical mode decomposition algorithm to extract statistical based features from IMFs of 1D signature and in the third step the extracted features are given to classifier to discriminate benign and malignant masses. The proposed model to classify breast masees is shown in Fig. 1.

2 Materials and Methods

2.1 Data Set

The mammography images used in this work are taken from publically available database "Digital Database for Screening Mammography" (DDSM) [14]. Each mammogram image containing massThe information related to particular patient is provided in overlay file. The overlay file consist information about type of abnormalities and its location present in mammogram. The description of abnormalities such as lesion type, subtlety, assessment and its outline is given in overlay file. The outline of mass contour is given as chain code in overlay file. The information related to contours in overlay file is given by expert radiologists. The database contains normal, benign and cancer volumes. For our research, we require benign and malignant mass contours. So, we have chosen 147 mammography images set from DDSM database which has only mass contours. These set include 73 malignant and 74 benign contours.

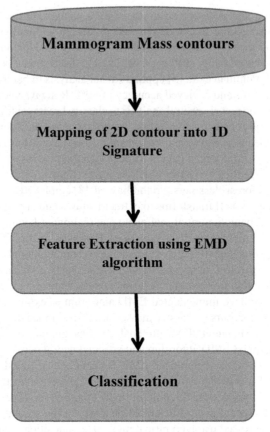

Fig. 1. Flow chart of the proposed model

2.2 Mapping of 2D Contour into 1D Signature

Benign masses are almost circular and well defined which gives smooth signature and malignant masses have speculated and rugged boundary. 1D signature curve of mass contours is an important component for diagnosis of benign and malignant tumors or masses due to its invariant properties in Euclidean space and the signature curve does not changes with the orientation of mass contours [14] in mammogram. Mapping od 2D contour into 1D signature is performed by centralized distance function method and it is discussed below.

Centralized Distance Function
1-D signatures, defined as the plot of Euclidean distance from centroid of mass to the each contour point vs a function of the index of the contour point. The contours and signatures of both malignant and benign masses are shown in Fig. 2a, b, c and d.

2.3 Compression of 1D Signature Using Empirical Mode Decomposition

EMD method is used to decompose the nonlinear or non-stationary 1D signal proposed by Huang et al. [11]. It decomposes the 1D signal into intrinsic mode function (IMFs) on two conditions. First condition is the difference between number of extremas and zeros for IMFs must be 0 or 1 and the second condition is the mean of envelopes of local maxima and local minima must be zero.

Let us consider the 1D signature of mass contour is $x(t)$, where t indicates contour index. The 1D signature $x(t)$ can be decomposed into IMFs as

$$x(t) = \sum_{m=1}^{M} x_m(t) + r_m(t) \tag{1}$$

The procedure to obtain IMFs from 1D signature is summarized in steps given below [12]

Step1: Intialize m = 0, and r(t) = x(t)

Step2: local minima and the local maxima of x(t) are to be computed

Step 3: Get the local minima and maxima envelopes using cubic spline interpolation and they are represented as $E_l(t)$ *(lowerenvelope)* and $E(t)(t)$ *(upperenvelope)*

Step 4: Calculate mean of the envelopes and it is given as

$$M(t) = \frac{E_l(t) + E_u(t)}{2}$$

Step 5: Compute mode 1 IMF represented as h(t)

$$h(t) = x(t) - M(t)$$

Step 6: h(t) is IMF1 $(imf_m(t) = h(t))$

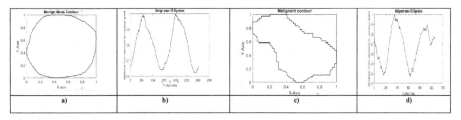

Fig. 2. a) Benign contour b) 1D signature of 2a c) Malignant contour d) 1D signature of 2c

If it satisfies the two condition specified above. Then increment m = m + 1 and go to step 7

else

$x(t) = h(t)$ and repeat step 1 to 5

Step 7: compute residual r(t) = r(t) − $imf_m(t)$ and go to step1

IMFs and residual 1D signature of Fig. 2c is shown in Fig. 3

Feature Extraction

Features are extracted from IMFs of 1D signature obtained by the EMD algorithm.
The features extracted from IMFs are given as follows

- Root mean square value of IMF1
- First order diff of IMF1
- Ratio of mean to standard deviation of IMF1
- Entropies of IMF1, IMF2, IMF3

Along with above features, we also calculated length of the 1D signature, area, solidity and eccentricity of 2D contour. We computed ten features for each contour considered in the dataset. These features are further given to different classifiers for further validation.

2.4 Classification

Classification is an important step to validate the efficacy of the proposed method. The features extracted from the procedure discussed above are given to different classifiers such as K-Nearest-neighbor (KNN), support vector machine (SVM), Adaboost decision tree classifier and artificial neural network (ANN) are used to discriminate benign and malignant mass contours.

Performance analysis of different classification model is achieved by computing different parameters such as accuracy, sensitivity, specificity and Area under the curve (AUC).

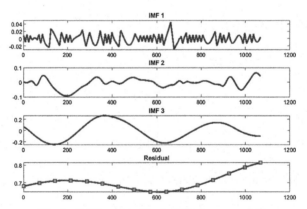

Fig. 3. IMF's and residual of 1D signature of 2d

3 Results and Discussion

The proposed method has been carried out on 97 contours out of which 67 are benign contours and 30 are malignant contours. Among 97 mass contours we have considered 19 images for testing 78 images for training. The proposed method for feature extraction from EMD algorithm is validated using different old-out technology. The simulations were carried using MATLAB 2018a.

To analyze the performance of classifiers we have evaluated accuracy, sensitivity, specificity and positive prediction value. Most of the features in the proposed method are extracted from IMF1 because it contains high frequency components.

Table 1. Accuracy (%) with different classifiers

Classifiers	IMF1 features	Entropies of IMFs	2D features	All ten features
SVM	81.8	78	80	94.7
KNN	68.2	77	78	86.1
Decision Tree	50	72.7	70	77.3

In the proposed work, ten features have been extracted and fed to SVM (Support Vector Machine), KNN (K-Nearest Neighborhood) and Decision tree classifier. Table 1 shows the accuracies computed with different classifiers. Among them SVM classifier achieved accuracy of 94.7%. Intially, the classifiers are fed with different feature set such as only IMF1 features, entropies of IMF1, IMF2 and IMF3 and 2D contour features and computed accuracies as shown in Table 1.

Table 2. Accuracies with different training to testing ration with classifiers

Training: testing ratio	SVM	KNN	Decision tree
80:20	94.7	86.1	77.3
75:25	83.3	66.7	79.2
50:50	75	72.9	75

Different sets of training to testing ratio of mass contours have been considered for classification. First, we used 20% of mass contours for testing and 80% for training and achieved accuracy of 94.7%, 86.1% and 77.3% with all three classifiers. The Area under curve (AUC) is 0.85 with SVM classifier and 80:20 testing to training ratio as shown in Fig. 4. In the same way the Fig. 5 shows the confusion matrix for testing images with SVM kernel. Secondly, we used 25% for testing and 75% for training and obtained accuracy of 83.3%, 66.7% and 79.2% with SVM, KNN and Decision Tree. Finally, we used 50% for testing and 50% for training and obtained accuracy of 75%,

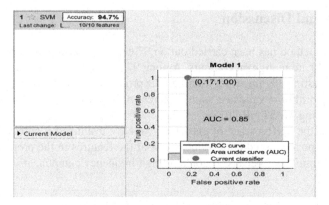

Fig. 4. AUC with SVM (linear kernel)

72.9% and 75%. Therefore, from Table 2 we can conclude that the accuracies obtained with different number of testing images is above 75%.

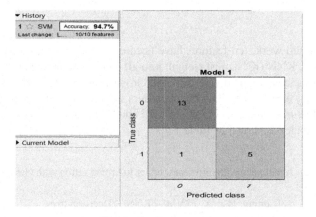

Fig. 5. Confusion matrix

Table 3 gives comparison of our proposed method with the existing methods. Our proposed model has given all assessment parameters such as accuracy, sensitivity, specificity and AUC which is not specified for other methods. Our method also achieved highest accuracy of 94.7%. The drawback of our model is we have tested with less number of mass contours when compared to other methods.

Table 3. Comparison of accuracies, specificity, sensitivity and AUC with our proposed method

Feature extraction method	Images	Acc (%)	Sens (%)	Spec (%)	AUC
GaborPCA [15]	114	80	–	–	–
Fractional concavity and spiculation index [3]	111	82			0.79
Fractal dimension using ruler method and fractional concavity [2]	111	–	–	–	0.82
Proposed method	97	94.7	100	83	0.85

4   Conclusion

In this paper, we proposed a compact shape descriptor with empirical mode decomposition algorithm from 1D signature of 2D mass contour for the classification of benign and malignant masses. This proposed method can help radiologists in classification of breast masses. The proposed methos is validated using different classifiers and achieved maximum accuracy of 94.7%. The experimental results show that our proposed method achieved accuracy of 94.7%, sensitivity of 100% specificity of 83% to classify benign and malignant masses.

References

1. https://www.who.int/cancer/prevention/diagnosis-sscreening/breast-cancer/en
2. Rangayyan, R.M., Nguyen, T.M.: Fractal analysis of contours of breast masses in mammograms. J. Digit. Imaging (2006). https://doi.org/10.1007/s10278-006-0860-9
3. Rangayyan, R.M., El-Faramawy, N.M., Desautels, J.E.L., Alim, O.A.: Measures of acutance and shape for classification of breast tumors. IEEE Trans. Med. Imag. 16(6), 799–810 (1997)
4. Rangayyan, R.M., Mudigonda, N.R., Desautels, J.E.L.: Boundary modelling and shape analysis methods for classification of mammographic masses. Med BiolEngComput 38, 487–496 (2000)
5. Pohlman, S., Powell, K.A., Obuchowski, N.A., Chilcote, W.A., Grundfest-Broniatowski, S.: Quantitative classification of breast tumors in digitized mammograms. Med. Phys. 23(8), 1337–1345 (1996)
6. Rangayyan, R.M., Oloumi, F.: Fractal analysis and classification of breast masses using the power spectra of signatures of contours. J. Electron. Imaging 21(2), 023018 (2012)
7. Yang, W., Tianhui, L.: A robust feature vector based on waveatom transform for mammographic mass detection. In: Proceedings of the 4th International Conference on Virtual Reality (2018)
8. Prathibha, G., Mohan, B.C.: Classification of benign and malignant masses using bandelet and orthogonal ripplet type II transforms. Comput. Methods Biomech. Biomed. Eng. Imaging Vis. 6(6), 704–717 (2018)
9. Dhahbi, S., Barhoumi, W., Zagrouba, E.: Breast cancer diagnosis in digitized mammograms using curvelet moments. Comput. Biol. Med. 64, 79–90 (2015)
10. Rojas-Domínguez, A., Nandi, A.K.: Development of tolerant features for characterization of masses in mammograms. Comput. Biol. Med. 39(8), 678–688 (2009)

11. Huang, N.E., Shen, Z., Long, S.R., et al.: The empirical mode decomposition and the Hilbert spectrum for nonlinear and non-stationary time series analysis. Proc. R. Soc. London **454**, 903–995 (1998)
12. Orosco, L., Laciar, E., Correa, A.G., Torres, A., Graffigna, J.P.: An epileptic seizures detection algorithm based on the empirical mode decomposition of EEG. In: Conference on Proceedings of IEEE Engineering in Medicine and Biology Society (2009)
13. Djemili, R., Bourouba, H., Korba, M.C.A.: Application of empirical mode decomposition and artificial neural network for the classification of normal and epileptic EEG signals. Biocybern. Biomed. Eng. **36**(1), 285–291 (2016)
14. Arica, N., Yarman-Vural, F.T.: A compact shape descriptor based on the beam angle statistics. In: Bakker, E.M., Lew, Michael S., Huang, T.S., Sebe, N., Zhou, X.S. (eds.) CIVR 2003. LNCS, vol. 2728, pp. 152–162. Springer, Heidelberg (2003). https://doi.org/10.1007/3-540-45113-7_16
15. Görgel, P., Sertbas, A., Ucan, O.N.: Mammographical mass detection and classification using local seed region growing–spherical wavelet transform (LSRG–SWT) hybrid scheme. Comput. Biol. Med. **43**(6), 765–774 (2013)

An Intelligent Sign Communication Machine for People Impaired with Hearing and Speaking Abilities

Ashish Sharma[1]([⊠]), Tapas Badal[2], Akshat Gupta[1], Arpit Gupta[1], and Aman Anand[3]

[1] Computer Science Engineering Department,
Indian Institute of Information Technology, Kota, Kota, India
`ashishsharma.fitt@gmail.com`
[2] Department of CSE, Bennett University, Noida, India
[3] Electronics and Communication Department,
Indian Institute of Information Technology, Kota, Kota, India

Abstract. People who are impaired with speaking and hearing abilities use sign language for communication between them, but it is a tough task for them to communicate with the outside world. Through this paper, we are proposing a system to convert Indian Sigh Language (ISL), American Sign Language (ISL) and British Sign Language (BSL) hand gestures to a textual format of the respective language as well as convert text in to their preferable Sign language. In this paper, we are capturing ISL, ASL, BSL gestures through a web camera. The streaming video of hand gestures is then sliced to distinct images to match the finger orientation to the corresponding alphabets. Finger orientations as features of the hand gestures in terms of angles made by fingers, numbers of fingers completely open, semi-open, fully closed, finger axis verticals or horizontal and recognition of each finger are prepossessed and required for gesture recognition. Implementation is done for alphabets uses single hand and results are explained. After prepossessing the hand part of the sliced frame in the form of masked image is projected to the extraction of features from the image frame. To classify different gestures we used SVM (Support Vector Machine), CNN (Convolutional Neural Network) for further testing the probable gesture and recording the accuracies of each algorithm. Implementation is done over our own regular ISL, BSL, ASL data-set made by us only, using the web camera of our laptops. Our Experimental results depict that our proposed work and methodology can work on different backgrounds like a background consist of different objects or may have some sort of color background etc. For text to sign conversion we create a video which tells respective text into sign language.

Keywords: Indian Sign Language Recognition (ISL) · Text to sign conversion · Hand gesture recognition · Hand segmentation · Support Vector Machine (SVM) · Convolutional Neural Network (CNN)

© Springer Nature Singapore Pte Ltd. 2021
D. Garg et al. (Eds.): IACC 2020, CCIS 1367, pp. 75–86, 2021.
https://doi.org/10.1007/978-981-16-0401-0_6

1 Introduction

All non-vocal communication requires a particular action for a particular context like the movement of the face, flipping of hands or folding fingers or actions by any other body part is a form of gesture. Gesture recognition is a method to make a machine or a computer get to recognize these actions. Algorithms used by these methods act as a mediator between human and machine. This enables a computer to interact with humans naturally by their own without any physical contact, actually just by using cameras as their eyes. Deaf and dumb people use hand gestures in their community for communication under the name sign language. This leads to a kind of isolation between their community and ours due to language differentiation as a normal person do not want to learn such language. So if we can program our computers in such a way that they take input in sign language and process them to convert in their respective language or maybe other languages also either in speech or in the textual format then they can act as a noble inter mediator and can remove the language barrier, the difference between communities can be minimized and the most important, knowing a language will meet to its worthy result in this high-tech world as sign language can interact to English and vice versa. All these discussions lead to a need for a system which can act as a translator and converts sign language to the desired language in the desired format, so people with a different language background can have a possible conversation with the people who know only sign language due to some disabilities but literate.

Sign Language shares grammar syntax like the use of pauses, full stop, and simultaneity, hand postures, hand placement, orientation, motion of the head, face gestures with different sign languages. As a country like India is completely diverse in terms of culture, religion, beliefs, and majorly in languages, so there is not a standard sign language is adopted in India. Various social groups of Indian Sign Language with their native and historical variation are there in India in various parts of the country. But still, language skeleton is similar for the maximum gestures. Work relating to the system of contrast relationships among the speech sounds that constitute the fundamental components of ISL started in the 1970s. With the help from Woodward, National Science Foundation USA Vasishta and Wilson visit of India and collection of signs from different points in the country for language analytic.

The organization of the paper is as follows: 'Sect. 2' the methods related to different technologies available in the language. 'Section 3' explains the given Sign language recognition system the method which uses algorithms for skin cropping and SVM(Support Vector Machine). 'Section 4' concerns on the implementation results and 'Sect. 5' is description and conclusion.

2 Literature Survey

This paper [14] proposes HSI color model for segmentation of images instead of RGB model. HSI model works better for skin color recognition. The optimal H and S values for hand as specified in [14] is $H < 25$ or $H > 230$ and $S < 25$ or $S > 230$. After this they use euclidean distance formula to evaluate the distance between centroid of palm and fingers. Distance transform method is used to identify the centroid of the hand. The pixel with the maximum intensity becomes the centroid. To extract each finger tip they select farthest point from centroid. Every finger is identified by predefined sign gestures. To recognize semi opened finger they divide every finger into 3 parts. and angle between the centroid and the major axis of finger is calculated (Figs. 1, 2 and 3).

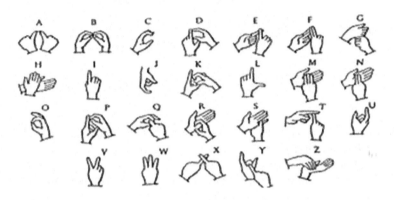

Fig. 1. Indian sign language alphabets [6]

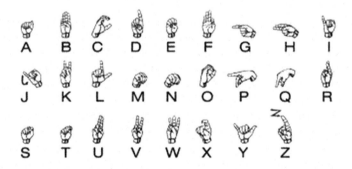

Fig. 2. American sign language alphabets [13]

In this paper [4] they used YCbCr color space, where Y channel represents brightness and (Cb, Cr) channels refer to chrominance. They use Cb, Cr channels to represent color and avoid Y since it is related to brightness only. There are some small regions near skin but not in skin so they use morphological operation. After that they select skin region and extract features to recognize hand gesture. They use three features velocity, orientation and location. They use orientation

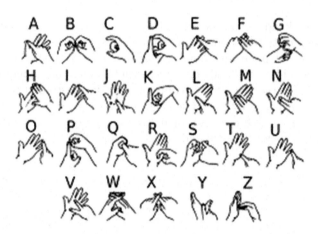

Fig. 3. British sign language alphabets [9]

feature as a main feature for their system. Then they classify features using Baum-Welch algorithm (BW). The gesture of hand motion is recognized using Left-Right Banded model with 9 stage.

In this paper [10] they used YCbCr color space. This color model is implemented by defining skin range in RGB model then convert these values into YCbCr model using conversion formula. They used support vector machine (SVM) algorithm. This algorithm use hyper plane to differentiate between two classes. Hyper plane is defined by the Support vectors which are nothing but the subset of training data. This algorithm also used to solved multi-class problem by demising it into two-class problem.

They [7] create data-set using an external camera having some specifications like 29 fps, 18 MP ans Canon EOS with 18–55mm lens. They eliminate background and extract hand region from left-out upper body part. They used RGB configuration of frame having dimensions of 640 * 480 then they extract key frames from video. They use orientation histogram to extract key frames. They used different distance metrics (Chess Board Distance, Euclidean distance etc) to recognise a gesture. After successful recognition of gesture they classified them for text formation.

They [8] use Fully convolution network algorithm. In particular they used 8 layers FCN model which achieves good performance and used for solving dense prediction problems. The output segmentation of this network is robust under various face conditions because it consider a large range of context information. After that they use CRF algorithm for image matting.

They [9] used Convolution neural network to generate their trained model. In this network they used 4 layers, in first stage they used five rectified linear units (ReLu), in second stage two stochastic pooling layers then one dense and one SoftMax output layer. They took frames of 640 * 480 dimensions then resize these frames into 128 * 128 * 3. They took 200 frames by 5 different people and at 5 different viewing angles. Their data-set size is of 5000 frames.

In this paper [13] they used CNN to recognize static sign gestures. They use American Sign Language (ASL) data-set to train their model which is provided by Pugeault and Bowden in 2011. There are around 60,000 RGB images they used for training and testing. They perform some operations on this data-set because not every is image has same depth according to their dimensions. They used V3 model to perform color features then for better accuracy they combined it with depth features. They use 50 epoch and 100 batch size to train their model using CNN.

Suharjito et al. [1] reviewed the different methods and techniques that researchers are using to develop better Sign Language.

Kakoty et al. [6] address the sign language number and alphabets recognition using hand kinematics with hand glove. They achieved the 97 % recognition rate of these alphabets and numbers.

In this article [11] the proposed system is translating the English text into Indian Sign Language (ISL). Authors have used human-computer interaction to implement it. The implemented system consists of the ISL parser, the Hamburg Notation System, the Signing Gesture Mark-up Language and generates the animation for ISL grammar.

Paras et al. [12] used the wordnet concept to extend and expansion of the dictionary and further construct the system to develop the Indian sign language system for dump and deaf peoples.

Matt et al. [5] address the video-based feedback information to students to learn the American Sign Language (ASL).

In this artical [3] authors address the deep learning based Gesture Images implementation for sign language. The validation accuracy obtained for this implementation using the different layers of deep learning is more than 90%.

3   Proposed Work

Flow Chart. The given flow chart explains the work flow of our project includes segmentation of video and then masking of image followed by canny edge detection which is used surf library and then features of images projected to clustering and comparisons between clusters of training and testing data is further done by svm library as described below flowchart.

Segmentation. As to recognize and classify each and every character of the input video it is required to apply image processing on it. For that purpose, the input video is converted into frames so that different image processing algorithm can be applied to them.

So for that in this step Input video is converted into frames, this step converts video into 30 frames per second (fps) which is default for the webcam used for making video but as we required less frames per second to recognize the each and every character in the video, so by giving delay to the function which is converting video to frame we are able to achieve the required output which is to get 5 frame per second of a input video.

Skin Masking. The reasoning behind a process such that to remove the extra noise in the segmented frame, after the masking there should be only the Region of Interest (ROI), which contains only useful information in the image. This is achieved via Skin Masking defining the threshold on RGB schema and then converting RGB colour space to grey scale image (Fig. 4).

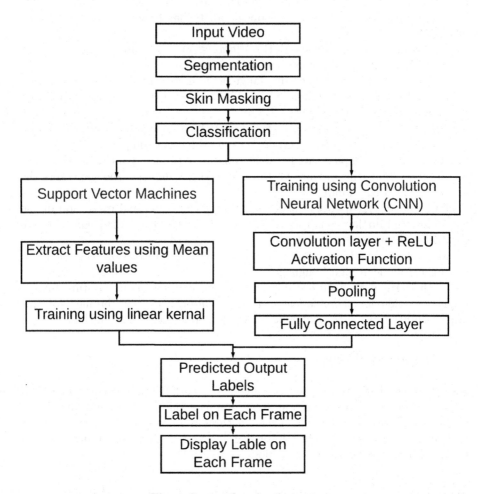

Fig. 4. Design flow for the project

So to achieve skin masking various image processing functions has been used. Firstly, the frame is convert into a gray schema. This output gray image will help us to convert it to HSV schema which will help us to detect the skin colour which is the main objective of ours so that we can identify the hand region. After identifying the hand region we have removed the noise from the image using blur function.

Classification. Sign classification is perform by using different techniques such as: a) Support Vector Machine (SVM) b) Convolution Neural Network (CNN).

Mainly we have use SVM for testing the accuracy of our system by dividing the 70% data as testing data and remaining as testing data where as we have used CNN mainly for live recognition of the sign of the alphabets.

Classification using SVM involves various steps as shown in figure. We convert saved masked image into 100 * 100 pixels then calculate its mean and variance oven 10 pixels.

$$\text{Mean } \mu = \frac{\sum_{i=1}^{n} x_i}{n}$$

$$\text{Variance} : \sigma^2 = \frac{\sum_{i=1}^{n} (x_i - \mu)^2}{n}$$

We use these parameters as classification features for SVM. We use linear regression as base kernel of our SVM algorithm. After creating model of these specifications (gamma = default and c = 1) we train our model with our data-set. To check accuracy of our model we use 30% data-set for testing purpose.

We use Convolution Neural Network as our second algorithm. To create CNN model we use Sequential Model in which three layers have been used:

1) Rectified linear unit (ReLU) Layer
2) pooling Layer
3) Fully connected layer for this we used Sigmoid activation function

After successful creation of this model we use our 70% data-set to train this model and remaining to test and validate our model.

We used CNN model for real time gesture recognition instead of SVM model because of its better performance (in terms of time).

Output Labels and Sentence Formation. Proposed System predict output labels using CNN model and show that label in real time on each frame. To form sentence system need to store that character into their words and provide space in between sentence. In this stage proposed system generate character from user input and arranged it into a word from dictionary, user can choose to provide space between words by pressing a key manually.

Text to Video. To convert text into sign video generation function is applied. We use sign of alphabets to convert text into sign language.

4   Experiment Setup

Data-Set. As we have searched on the internet and we found no resources from where we can get Indian Sign Language dataset. So after a long effort in searching and finding dataset from different resources, then we only made our own ISL dataset as in our lighting conditions and in other factors like own environmental setup. There we have $26 \times 150 = 3900$ static training images and $26 \times 30 = 60$ images which will use for testing. The actual resolution of the images is 640×480, which will be cropped and normalized into 120×120. The samples from the video are 320×260 in size and they are taken in a various lighting environment. Same process we used on two other sign languages American sign language and British sign language.

We have made one interface where we have given choice to the user in which language he/she wants to do operation i.e whether in ISL, BSL or ASL. After that another two other choices will come in which user have to tell whether he/she wants to do sig-text conversion or text-sign conversion. It makes our system user friendly and a normal people can easily use it for communication.

Algorithms

- Support Vector Machine Algorithm The support vector machine (SVM) is an algorithm which is used for two-class problems (Binary classification problems) in which the concerned data can be separated by a different plane like linear plane, parabolic plane etc depending upon the number of features of the sets. Hyper plane basically refers to a virtual plane that can be drawn in the 3D properties plot of the given data in order to separate them on the basis of some features. Different classes are separated using it which uses the training data to do the supervised learning of the system. Every feature in the training data set is send with the target value to do the learning of the system according to it. Support vector machine is mainly used to predict the targeted value of the given testing data set features according to the plane which is drawn by the algorithm for the distinguish of the different features in the training data set [2].
  Both Classification or regression function can be used for the mapping of function. When there are non-linear functions for the distinction non-linear plane is used according the features of it to convert it into n-d space distinction. Fig represents the plane which is drawn to separate the n-features in n-d plane. Then the creation of Maximum-margin hyper planes can be done. Proposed model works over only a subset of the training data set as per the class boundaries. Similarly, This model can also be produced by SVR (support vector regression).
  SVM uses different values of gamma and c to draw the hyper plane between the two clusters for distinct of them. Larger the value of gamma more it considered the points far from the hyper plane which will give the better result and c will tell how smoothly will the plane gonna be larger the value of c greater distinguish it will take in consideration.
- Convolution Neural Network The combination of neurons with biases and weights is known as Convolution Neural Network. The neurons which are there in the layer gets the input from the its parents layers. Computation of product between the weights and input is done, and posses an option to follow

the processes output with a non-linearity. Implementation of the properties in the CNN is done with the assumption that of taking all the inputs as images. The CNN architecture has been classified in to different layers, it contains many convolution layer along with the activation function layer called ReLU layer and Pooling step. Standard architecture of CNN is in the last layer. is plenary connected is a standard architecture of CNN.

The CNN architecture has been classified in to different layers: **(1) Convolution Layer:** We extract features from our frame in this convolution layer, Some parts of image is link to the upcoming layer convolution layer. Computation of the dot product is19 done in the receptive area and a kernel [3 * 3 filter] on all the image as shown in the image. The output of the dot product gives as the integer value which is known as features as shown in fig. After that feature extraction is done using filter or kernel of small matrix. **(2) Padding Process:** Padding means to do the summation of all the features which we got in the feature map and finally putting the summation in the middle of the 3×3 matrix. This is done to get the equal dimension of output which we have used in the input volume.

(3) Rectifier Activation Function (ReLU):
After the implementation of convolution layer on the image matrix, we will use ReLU layer to get the non-linearity to the system by applying ReLU (non-linear activation function) to the feature matrix. There are many activation function are present but here we are using ReLU as it does not which makes the network hard to train.

(4) Pooling Layer:
Controlling of over fitting and decreasing the dimension of the image is done in Pooling layer. It can be done in three ways first one is max, second one is average and third one is mean pooling, here we are using the max pooling, it is used to take maximum value from the input which we are convoling with features.

(5) Fully Connected Layer:
This one of the important layer of convolution layer as it gives the classified images according to the training data set. We have used the different sign images for the training set as discussed above.

(6) Epochs:
During the whole data set is going backward and forward propagation through networks is called epochs.

(7) Training Accuracy:
Training accuracy given by the model, when we are applying training on training data sets.

(8) Validation Accuracy:
After the successful training of the model then it is evaluated with help of test data sets then accuracy of model is predicted.

5   Experimental Result

We have performed the training on three different sign languages each having 45,500 training images and performed the testing on 20,800 images.

Accuracy. We have compare the performance of different languages using both the classification method below is the comparison table of that in terms of accuracy of each sign language (Tables 1 and 2).

Table 1. Performance of different languages using both the classification methods.

Language	CNN-accuracy	SVM-accuracy
Indian Sign Language (ISL)	0.9988209	0.9876898
American Sign Language (ASL)	0.98949781	0.9796472
British Sign Language (BSL)	0.98645851	0.97289481

Table 2. Accuracy table for different algorithms on ISL.

Algorithm	Accuracy
K-nearest neighbour	0.6628820960698
Logistic regression	0.7554585152838
Naive bayes	0.6283842794759

Fig. 5. Output of 'L' sign recognized by the system

Fig. 6. Output showing sentence formation using the system

Fig. 7. Output showing sentence formation in sign language

6 Conclusion

We have successfully perform different sign languages conversion into their respective alphabets as well as form sentences using these alphabets. We has used our webcam to capture gesture instead of some specified powerful camera like RGB-D. Our systems also work on text to sign conversion. So it is works like communication medium between who can communicate only in sign language and those who don't understand it (Fig. 5, 6 and 7).

- We have worked on the stationary hand gesture but sign language can have moving hands also. So, in future it can be done for both moving hands also.
- The major problem with the project is it is mainly depend on the lighting condition so in future the effect of lighting can be overcome.

References

1. Abraham, A., Rohini, V.: Real time conversion of sign language to speech and prediction of gestures using artificial neural network. Proc. Comput. Sci. **143**, 587–594 (2018). https://doi.org/10.1016/j.procs.2018.10.435. http://www.sciencedirect.com/science/article/pii/S1877050918321331. 8th International Conference on Advances in Computing & Communications (ICACC-2018)
2. Dai, H.: Research on svm improved algorithm for large data classification. In: 2018 IEEE 3rd International Conference on Big Data Analysis (ICBDA), pp. 181–185, March 2018. https://doi.org/10.1109/ICBDA.2018.8367673
3. Das, A., Gawde, S., Suratwala, K., Kalbande, D.: Sign language recognition using deep learning on custom processed static gesture images. In: 2018 International Conference on Smart City and Emerging Technology (ICSCET), pp. 1–6 (2018)
4. Elmezain, M., Al-Hamadi, A., Michaelis, B.: Real-time capable system for hand gesture recognition using hidden Markov models in stereo color image sequence. J. WSCG **16** (2008)
5. Huenerfauth, M., Gale, E., Penly, B., Pillutla, S., Willard, M., Hariharan, D.: Evaluation of language feedback methods for student videos of American sign language. ACM Trans. Access. Comput. (TACCESS) **10**(1), 1–30 (2017). https://doi.org/10.1145/3046788

6. Kakoty, N.M., Sharma, M.D.: Recognition of sign language alphabets and numbers based on hand kinematics using a data glove. Proc. Comput. Sci. **133**, 55–62 (2018). https://doi.org/10.1016/j.procs.2018.07.008. http://www.sciencedirect.com/science/article/pii/S1877050918309529. International Conference on Robotics and Smart Manufacturing (RoSMa2018)

7. Liu, L.: Research on logistic regression algorithm of breast cancer diagnose data by machine learning. In: 2018 International Conference on Robots Intelligent System (ICRIS), pp. 157–160, May 2018. https://doi.org/10.1109/ICRIS.2018.00049

8. Qin, S., Kim, S., Manduchi, R.: Automatic skin and hair masking using fully convolutional networks. In: 2017 IEEE International Conference on Multimedia and Expo (ICME), pp. 103–108, July 2017. https://doi.org/10.1109/ICME.2017.8019339

9. Rao, G.A., Syamala, K., Kishore, P.V.V., Sastry, A.S.C.S.: Deep convolutional neural networks for sign language recognition. In: 2018 Conference on Signal Processing And Communication Engineering Systems (SPACES), pp. 194–197, January 2018. https://doi.org/10.1109/SPACES.2018.8316344

10. Reshna, S., Jayaraju, M.: Spotting and recognition of hand gesture for Indian sign language recognition system with skin segmentation and SVM. In: 2017 International Conference on Wireless Communications, Signal Processing and Networking (WiSPNET), pp. 386–390, March 2017. https://doi.org/10.1109/WiSPNET.2017.8299784

11. Sugandhi, Kumar, P., Kaur, S.: Sign language generation system based on Indian sign language grammar. ACM Trans. Asian Low-Resour. Lang. Inf. Process. **19**(4), 1-26 (2020). https://doi.org/10.1145/3384202

12. Vij, P., Kumar, P.: Mapping Hindi text to Indian sign language with extension using WordNet. In: Association for Computing Machinery, New York, NY, USA (2016). https://doi.org/10.1145/2979779.2979817. https://doi.org/10.1145/2979779.2979817

13. Xie, B., He, X., Li, Y.: RGB-D static gesture recognition based on convolutional neural network. J. Eng. **2018**(16), 1515–1520 (2018). https://doi.org/10.1049/joe.2018.8327

14. Zhou, Q., Zhao, Z.: Substation equipment image recognition based on sift feature matching. In: 2012 5th International Congress on Image and Signal Processing, pp. 1344–1347, October 2012. https://doi.org/10.1109/CISP.2012.6469854

Features Explaining Malnutrition in India: A Machine Learning Approach to Demographic and Health Survey Data

Sunny Rajendrasingh Vasu[1], Sangita Khare[1]([⊠]), Deepa Gupta[1], and Amalendu Jyotishi[2]

[1] Department of Computer Science and Engineering, Amrita School of Engineering, Bengaluru, Amrita Vishwa Vidyapeetham, Bengaluru, India
`sunnyvasu8@gmail.com`, {`k_sangita,g_deepa`}`@blr.amrita.edu`
[2] School of Development, Azim Premji University, Bengaluru, Karnataka, India
`amalendu.jyotishi@apu.edu.in`

Abstract. India is one of the severely malnourished countries in the world. Under-nutrition is the reason for death among two-third of the 1.04 million deaths among the children under the age of five in the year 2019. Several strategies have been adopted by the Government of India and state governments to minimize the incidents of malnutrition. However, to make the policies effective, it is important to understand the key features explaining malnutrition. Analyzing the Indian Demographic Health Survey Data (IDHS) of the year 2015–2016, this paper attempts to identify causes of four dimensions of malnutrition namely, Height Age Z-score (HAZ), Weight Age Z-score (WAZ), Weight Height Z-score (WHZ) and Body Mass Index (BMI). Using machine learning approach of feature reduction, the paper identifies ten most important features out of available 1341 features in the database for each of the four anthropometric parameters of malnutrition. The features are reduced and ranked using WEKA tool. Results and finding of this research would provide key policy inputs to address malnutrition and related mortality among the children under the age five.

Keywords: Malnutrition · HAZ · WAZ · WHZ · BMI · Machine learning

1 Introduction

Under-nutrition refers to deficiencies, excess or imbalance of energy or nutrients in a person's daily diet. According to World Health Organization (WHO), malnutrition results from inability to absorb nutrients from food. Global Nutrition Report of 2018 has showed that India accommodates more than 46.6 million stunted children under 5 years of age which is approximately 33% of world's total, half of which are underweight. On contrary, a third of wealthiest children are over-nourished. Thus, India has the highest malnutrition rates followed by Nigeria (13.9 million) and Pakistan (10.7 million) [1]. Low socio-economic status of people leads to lack of diet in terms of quality and quantity.

© Springer Nature Singapore Pte Ltd. 2021
D. Garg et al. (Eds.): IACC 2020, CCIS 1367, pp. 87–99, 2021.
https://doi.org/10.1007/978-981-16-0401-0_7

Under-nourished women are most likely to have unhealthy babies. In addition, under-nourished individuals can do less productive work leading to low payments and poverty.

The Indian Government has started many programs such as midday meal scheme on 15th August 1995 in order to eradicate malnutrition. Under this scheme, fresh cooked meals are provided to millions of children in almost all government and government aided schools. Apart from this, the Government of India has also started Integrated Child Development Services in 1975 [2], which targets on improving health of mothers and children under age of 6 by providing health and nutrition education, health services, supplementary food, and pre-school education. But these programmes and many other such national as well as state level policies have not been designed considering the variation of factors responsible for malnutrition in children below five. This is the root cause of slower rate of decrease in number of deaths of children under age five caused due to undernutrition.

This paper is categorised into six sections. The literature review is the next section, IDHS dataset is explained in detail in the third section. Technique used in this analysis is described in the fourth section, results and findings are discussed in the fifth section of this paper followed by conclusion in the sixth section.

2   Literature Survey

Several studies on malnutrition have been carried out in past decades using different types of datasets and methodology amongst which most commonly used dataset is Demo-graphic Health Survey Data. Demographic Health Survey is conducted in every 10 years. Although, many studies have been done using this dataset in the past, but very few of them have used machine learning techniques for their analysis. Others have used either analytical or statistical approach. Following are some of the works carried out in the field of analysing increasing rate of malnutrition.

Nair et al. [3], has characterised malnutrition causes for states of India using IDHS 2005–2006 dataset. With the help of K-means clustering analysis states were divided according to different features. Synthetic Minority Oversampling Technique was used for pre-processing the dataset. For attribute selection Adaboost and Ranker algorithm were used. The analysis resulted in generating seven clusters of HAZ, four clusters of WAZ, six clusters of WHZ and five clusters of BMI which were the four anthropometric measures used. Later in the research, using Ranker algorithm, the features were ranked in which, the top rank features, those having highest variance amongst all four anthropometric parameters, were found to be mainly responsible for malnutrition. These features were considered important for policy makers as these would be helpful for improving and creating new policies for different regions of India to eradicate malnutrition from its root [4].

Many studies have used data mining techniques like decision tree and clustering. In this work [5], few patterns were found - like a child can be malnourished even if safe water source is used and there are 87% chances of malnutrition in the child if she acquires a major disease and does not use good toilet facility. Another research developed a model which can help policy designers and health care facilitators to identify children under risk. Factors which were found to be the major contributors in malnutrition were mother's education, child age, region, wealth index and residence [6].

Other studies were done using statistical analysis methods such as ANOVA, Case-based Reasoning (CBR), Euclidean distance, ID3 algorithm, Probabilistic Bayes theory and logistic regression [7–11]. To prove that malting technique produce phytase enzyme, least significant difference techniques on zinc, iron and phytic acid was used. Zinc is an essential metalloenzyme and it widely helps in reducing stunting, wasting and improves brain development in infants [12]. Using multivariate logistic regression on Bangladesh DHS dataset and environmental indicator, Normalized Difference Vegetation Index (NDVI), trends of nutrition security in foods of Ganges Brahmaputra Meghna Delta have been found for year 2007 and 2011. Results showed, with the increase of NDVI wasting probability decreases as the food consumption of medium income group varies with the variation in vegetation due to change in climate [13]. Results of statistical analysis on Pakistan DHS show secondary or higher education of parents, health facilities and rich children have less tendency of becoming stunted whereas, children of rural residence having no toilet facilities, smaller size during birth and older mother are more likely to be stunted [14].

Poverty have strong implications on malnutrition, this work [15] used Indian Health Development Survey (IHDS) of year 2012 to find the factors responsible for absconding and suffering from poverty. For this purpose, machine learning techniques have been applied such as info-gain and random forest classifier. The work found that livestock such as goat plays a vital role in explaining poverty. Also, caste, education and rural to urban migration are major factors in falling to poverty whereas, toilet and financial sector are features of escaping poverty. Another research was conducted on infant mortality rate by finding the influencing factors such as national income and fertility rate, etc. using data from indiastat.com [16]. Similarly, several machine learning techniques are deployed to identify probable causes of malnutrition [17–22].

From literature survey it is observed that, strategies deployed were based on country. There are many different techniques that were used to identify root cause of malnutrition and how it can be dealt effectively. Features themselves are divided into four classes of anthropometric parameters which are also recognized by WHO, they are HAZ, WAZ, WHZ and BMI. Identifying features for these anthropometric parameters is very important. Selecting most important features of all four anthropometric parameters HAZ, WAZ, WHZ and BMI from IDHS data, finding major impacting features using Principal Component Evaluator and ranking them with Ranker Algorithm are the main objectives of this paper. The features thus identified will help policy makers in improving the existing policies and address the important causes of malnutrition.

3   Data Source

Dataset used in this paper is IDHS data of year 2015–2016. The DHS program collects information on health and population in 90 developing countries, one of which is India. The data is categorized in fields like birth record, children's record, couples record, individual's record and men's record etc. Amongst all, birth record data set is employed for this purpose. Information of child such as age, sex, HAZ, WAZ, WHZ and BMI, etc. are recorded in this dataset [4]. The mother of the child is also interviewed to collect information about both mother and child health status such as type of place of residence, number of children under five in household, births in last five years, gave child pumpkin, carrots, squash, received polio vaccine, number of tetanus injections before pregnancy, during pregnancy, given or bought iron tablets, etc. Birth record of year 2015–2016 contains 1315617 instances of 1341 features of all states and union territories of India.

4   Methodology

Methodology used in this analysis is shown in the schematic diagram Fig. 1, which begins with data collection and cleaning of irrelevant information from the dataset, followed by selection of useful features of all four anthropometric parameters, determining the most important malnutrition impacting variables and ranking them using WEKA tool.

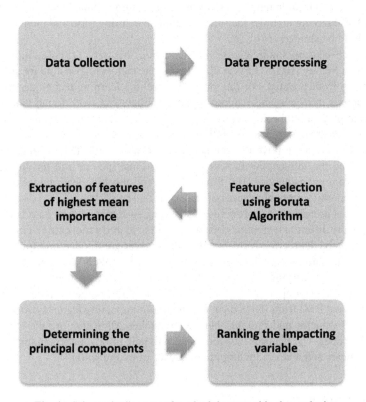

Fig. 1. Schematic diagram of methodology used in the analysis

4.1   Data Preprocessing

Before using the dataset for the analysis, it needs to be cleaned. Out of total 1341 features, some are not useful for the study. Few of them are repeated, few others have no value and instances of the remaining features have constant value. All these features are eliminated before analysis which reduced the variables to 745. On removing the duplicate instances using distinct method of dplyr package, total observations decrease to 639916. The remaining useful data, has both numeric as well as categorical data. For selection of features using Boruta Algorithm, the data need to be converted into numeric type. For this purpose, all the categorical variable instances are encoded based on factor levels of the feature whereas for numeric variables having NA values, the NA values are replaced by mean of the column.

4.2 Feature Selection

After cleaning the data, on the numeric birth record dataset, Boruta Algorithm is applied on all four dependent variables i.e. HAZ, WAZ, WHZ and BMI for selecting features having highest mean importance as this is most important processing step of Data mining. In Comparison to most of the traditional methods of feature selection, Boruta captures all the features relevant to the outcome variable, which are in same circumstances. The features captured are either strongly or weakly related to the decision variable unlike other random forest methods.

The Boruta algorithm is a wrapper around Random Forest Classification Algorithm. It generates shadow features by duplicating the dataset and shuffling values of each column thereafter training the random forest classifier with the duplicate dataset. After training, it compares the z-score of each original feature with that of its shadow feature. If the z-score (importance) of original feature is found to be much higher than its shadow, it implies that the feature is confirmed to be important else either left as decision pending or rejected. In the plot as shown in Fig. 2, red colour indicates those features which are rejected, green depicts confirmed features and features for which decision is left pending are depicted with yellow colour. Those attributes whose mismatch with shadow attributes is much higher than 50% and are close to 100% for HAZ, are confirmed as important such as M6. On the other hand, those attributes whose mismatch is much lower than 50% with its shadow attribute and are close to 0%, are rejected as they are unimportant such as V204. Remaining attributes with mismatch percentage nearby 50 are left as tentative such as M1. Similarly for WAZ, M19 is confirmed as important and M47 is left as decision pending as shown in Fig. 3. For WHZ, M6 is confirmed as important and M3A is kept tentative as shown in Fig. 4. For BMI, M19 is confirmed as important and M7 is left pending for decision as shown in Fig. 5. For all 3 remaining attributes V499E is rejected.

4.3 Feature Reduction

Boruta iterations reduced the dataset down to 153 as for HAZ 18 attributes were confirmed to be important, 80 pending for decision and all others rejected. Similarly, 47 attributes for WAZ, 43 attributes for WHZ and 45 attributes for BMI were selected. Applying the cut-off method on attribute stats of each anthropometric parameters i.e. HAZ, WAZ, WHZ and BMI generated by Boruta Algorithm, 10 attributes for each parameter are selected as the most important factors based on highest mean importance as described in Table 1, Table 2, Table 3, and Table 4 respectively. Features are not listed in the tables according to their ranking.

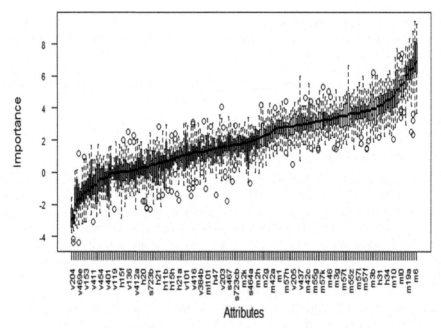

Fig. 2. Plot of Boruta algorithm result for HAZ (Color figure online)

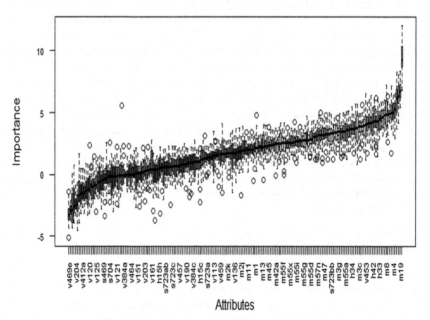

Fig. 3. Plot of Boruta algorithm result for WAZ

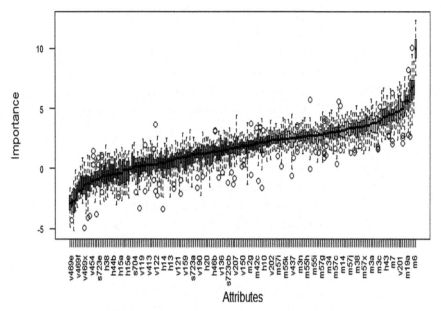

Fig. 4. Plot of Boruta algorithm result for WHZ

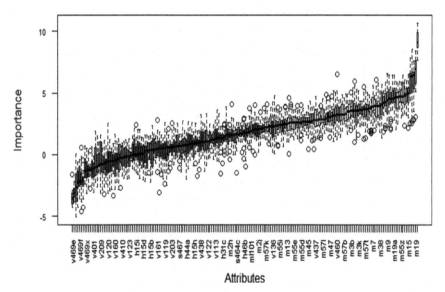

Fig. 5. Plot of Boruta algorithm result for BMI

The attributes which are found common in all the four anthropometric parameters are 'Had diarrhoea recently', 'Taking iron pills, sprinkles or syrup', 'Assistance: DAI/Traditional Birth Attendant', 'Place received most vaccinations', and 'Women's age in year'. Whereas, those which are unique are 'Daughters elsewhere', 'Delivery by

Table 1. Most important features of HAZ

Feature code	Features of HAZ
H11	Had diarrhoea recently
H42	Taking iron pills, sprinkles or syrup
M39A	Did eat any solid, semi-solid or soft foods yesterday
M3A	Assistance doctor
M3B	Assistance ANM/nurse/mid-wife/LHV
M3G	Assistance Dai/Traditional birth attendant
S515	Place received most vaccination
V137	Number of children five and under in household
V205	Daughters elsewhere
V477A	Women's age in years

Table 2. Most important features of WAZ

Feature code	Features of WAZ
H11	Had diarrhoea recently
H42	Taking iron pills, sprinkles or syrup
M39A	Did eat any solid, semi-solid or soft foods yesterday
M3A	Assistance doctor
M3G	Assistance Dai/Traditional birth attendant
S515	Place received most vaccination
V477A	Women's age in years
M10	Type of mosquito bed nets child slept under IPC
M38	Drank from bottle with nipple yesterday
M3H	Assistance friend/relative

caesarean section', and 'Haemoglobin level (g/dl - 1 decimal)'. The common attributes have higher probability of being the main cause of malnutrition as compared to the unique ones.

4.4 Determining Impacting Variables of Malnutrition

After finding the 10 most important features of all four anthropometric parameter, HAZ, WAZ, WHZ and BMI the next step is to find the ranking of the factors that are mainly responsible for malnutrition. For this purpose, WEKA tool is used in which, for attribute selection, Principal Component evaluator is used with Ranker algorithm to get ranking

Table 3. Most important features of WHZ

Feature code	Features of WHZ
H11	Had diarrhoea recently
H42	Taking iron pills, sprinkles or syrup
M3B	Assistance ANM/nurse/mid-wife/LHV
M3G	Assistance Dai/Traditional birth attendant
S515	Place received most vaccination
V137	Number of children five and under in household
V477A	Women's age in years
M10	Type of mosquito bed nets child slept under IPC
M38	Drank from bottle with nipple yesterday
M3H	Assistance friend/relative

Table 4. Most important features of BMI

Feature code	Features of BMI
H11	Had diarrhoea recently
H42	Taking iron pills, sprinkles or syrup
M3B	Assistance ANM/nurse/mid-wife/LHV
M3G	Assistance Dai/Traditional birth attendant
M38	Drank from bottle with nipple yesterday
S515	Place received most vaccination
V137	Number of children five and under in household
V477A	Women's age in years
M17	Delivery by caesarean section
V453	Haemoglobin level

of features. Former performs Principal Component Analysis (PCA) on data for dimensionality reduction by choosing enough eigen vectors to account for some percentage of variance in the original data whereas later rank the principal component features.

PCA reduces the dimensionality of the dataset having many interrelated variables, retaining the variation of data as much as possible. The data set then contains variables arranged according to decreasing variation amongst all. The first few of them which are ordered and uncorrelated are called principal component and all others as components. PCA finds the correlation pattern among the original variables thereafter substituting a new component in place of group of attributes which were correlated (Table 5).

Table 5. Ranking of features of all anthropometric parameters determined using WEKA tool

Rank	HAZ	WAZ	WHZ	BMI
1	H11	M10	M10	H11
2	H42	M38	H11	M38
3	M3A	H11	M38	H42
4	M3G	H42	H42	M3B
5	M3B	M3A	M3B	M3G
6	S515	M3G	M3G	M17
7	V447A	M3H	M3H	S515
8	V137	S515	S515	V137
9	M39A	V447A	V137	V447A
10	V205	M39A	V447A	V453

5 Discussion

Using Principal Component Analysis along with Ranker algorithm, features were selected and ranked based on their variance across all the four anthropometric parameters. The features having highest variation are identified as the most impactful features explaining malnutrition. Three highest ranking features of HAZ are had diarrhoea recently, taking iron pills, sprinkles or syrup and did eat any solid, semi-solid or soft food yesterday. Similarly, for WAZ type of mosquito bed nets child slept under IPC, drank from bottle with nipple yesterday and had diarrhoea recently are the most varying features of respective anthropometric parameter.

From the analysis on all four anthropometric parameters namely, HAZ, WAZ, WHZ, and BMI it was identified that 6 features are common across all the parameters. These are, "Had diarrhoea recently", "Taking Iron pills, sprinkles or syrup", "Assistance of Dai", "Received most vaccination", "Women's age" and "Type of mosquito bed nets child slept under IPC". These variables can be used for improving or making new policies. Three features are identified across three parameters, these are "Assistance from ANM", "Drank from bottle with nipple" and "Number of Children under five in the household". Besides, there are four features found across two parameters and there were only three features unique to any of the parameters. BMI did not have any unique feature.

Considering only the features which are present in all the four or at least three parameters different characteristics explaining malnutrition can be identified. These characteristics can be classified into broadly three categories. First category is related to 'availability and awareness' of safe drinking water and iron pills. It is irony of the country that even after seventy plus years of independence a large section of the society is deprived from availing safe drinking water. These problems are becoming even more acute in urban areas especially in the slums apart from remote terrains. It is not surprising that iron deficiency among the pregnant and lactating mother is one of the most important cause of malnutrition among the mothers and children. An effective reach out in rural as well as in urban areas to these mothers would be helpful in addressing such deficiencies. Easy availability and accessibility of iron rich food like fish, drumstick etc., would go a long way in addressing iron deficiency among mothers and children. It is equally important to invest and develop food products that can be easily stored, easily available at a very low price would go a long way in addressing iron deficiencies. A second category is "access to the services of ANM and trained Dais". Investment in public health and public health services especially creating a large pool of trained paramedical services would be effective in addressing not only malnutrition for children but also for mothers as well as general well-being of the mass in the need of healthcare services. Similarly access to free vaccinations in the vicinity is an important feature to address malnutrition. A third category is related to 'awareness and behavioural and social change'. Early marriage among the women and not having sufficient gap between the births are identified as two important features of malnutrition. Investing in education, creating awareness through the local governance structure as well as increasing income level of the households have been identified as important factors in the literature that can have positive impact on the behavioural as well as social change. These would require persistent investment and action at the ground.

6 Conclusion

Malnutrition is a serious problem everywhere in the world. Severity of this problem increases in developing countries like India due to lack of public health service support, infrastructure and investment. Despite implementation of several policies designed by Government of India, policy makes have failed to tackle malnutrition as these policies have not been appropriately and systematically targeted. In this work causes of malnutrition have been identified, using 2015–2016 IDHS dataset.

Further studies can go deeper into clustering the features similar across various states to target malnutrition effectively. Besides, comparison of different IDHS data over the years would reveal if there is any continuity or changes in the root causes of malnutrition in India over the years.

References

1. The Economic Times. https://economictimes.indiatimes.com/news/politics-and-nation/india-has-one-third-of-worlds-stunted-children-global-nutrition-report/articleshow/66865016.cms?from=mdr. Accessed 02 June 2020
2. Malnutrition in India. https://en.wikipedia.org/wiki/Malnutrition_in_India
3. Anilkumar, N.A., Gupta, D., Khare, S., Gopalkrishna, D. M., Jyotishi, A.: Characteristics and causes of malnutrition across Indian states: a cluster analysis based on Indian demographic and health survey data. In: 2017 International Conference on Advances in Computing, Communications and Informatics (ICACCI), Udupi, pp. 2115–2123 (2017). https://doi.org/10.1109/ICACCI.2017.8126158.
4. The DHS Program: Demographic and Health Surveys. https://dhsprogram.com. Accessed 23 June 2020

5. Ariyadasa, S.N., Munasinghe, L.K., Senanayake, S.H.D., Fernando, N.A.S.: Data mining approach to minimize child malnutrition in developing countries. In: International Conference on Advances in ICT for Emerging Regions (ICTer2012), Colombo, p. 225 (2012). https://doi.org/10.1109/ICTer.2012.6423030.

6. Markos, Z., Agide, F.: Predicting under nutrition status of under-five children using data mining techniques: the case of 2011 ethiopian demographic and health survey. J. Health Med. Inf. **5**, 152 (2014). https://doi.org/10.4172/2157-7420.1000152

7. Arun, C., Khare, S., Gupta, D., Jyotishi, A.: Influence of health service infrastructure on the infant mortality rate: an econometric analysis of indian states. In: Nagabhushan, T.N., Aradhya, V.N.M., Jagadeesh, P., Shukla, S., Chayadevi, M.L. (eds.) CCIP 2017. CCIS, vol. 801, pp. 81–92. Springer, Singapore (2018). https://doi.org/10.1007/978-981-10-9059-2_9

8. Jeyaseelan, L., Lakshman, M.: Risk factors for malnutrition in South Indian children. J. Biosoc. Sci. **29**(1), 93–100 (1997). https://doi.org/10.1017/S002193209700093X

9. Fenske, N., Kneib, T., Hothorn, T.: Identifying risk factors for severe childhood malnutrition by boosting additive quantile regression. J. Am. Stat. Assoc. **106**, 494–510 (2011). https://doi.org/10.1198/jasa.2011.ap09272

10. Mosley, W.H., Chen, L.C.: An analytical framework for the study of child survival in developing countries. Populat. Dev. Rev. **10**, 25–45 (1984). www.jstor.org/stable/2807954. Accessed 14 Aug 2020

11. Hanmer, L., Lensink, R., White, H.: Infant and child mortality in developing countries: analysing the data for robust determinants. J. Dev. Stud. **40**(1), 101–118 (2003). https://doi.org/10.1080/00220380412331293687

12. Ana, I.M., Udota, H.I.J., Udoakah, Y.N.: Malting technology in the development of safe and sustainable complementary composite food from cereals and legumes. In: IEEE Global Humanitarian Technology Conference (GHTC 2014), San Jose, CA, pp. 140–144 (2014). https://doi.org/10.1109/GHTC.2014.6970273.

13. Van Soesbergen, A., Nilsen, K., Burgess, N., Szabo, S., Matthews, Z.: Food and Nutrition Security Trends and Challenges in the Ganges Brahmaputra Meghna (GBM) Delta. Elem Sci Anth. **5**, 56 (2017). https://doi.org/10.1525/elementa.153

14. Abbasi, S., Mahmood, H., Zaman, A., Farooq, B., Malik, A., et al.: Indicators of malnutrition in under 5 Pakistani children: a DHS data secondary analysis. J. Med. Res. Health Educ. **2**(3), 12 (2018)

15. S. Narendranath, S. Khare, Gupta, D., Jyotishi, A.: Characteristics of 'escaping' and 'falling into' poverty in India: an analysis of IHDS panel data using machine learning approach. In: 2018 International Conference on Advances in Computing, Communications and Informatics (ICACCI), Bangalore, pp. 1391–1397 (2018). https://doi.org/10.1109/ICACCI.2018.8554571.

16. Suriyakala, V., Deepika, M.G., Amalendu, J., Deepa, G.: Factors affecting infant mortality rate in india: an analysis of Indian states. In: Corchado Rodriguez, J., Mitra, S., Thampi, S., El-Alfy, E.S. (eds.) Intelligent Systems Technologies and Applications 2016, ISTA 2016. Advances in Intelligent Systems and Computing, vol. 530, pp. 707–719. Springer, Cham (2016). https://doi.org/10.1007/978-3-319-47952-1_57

17. Shyam Sundar, K., Khare, S., Gupta, D., Jyotishi, A.: Analysis of fuel consumption characteristics: insights from the Indian human development survey using machine learning techniques. In: Raju, K.S., Govardhan, A., Rani, B.P., Sridevi, R., Murty, M.R. (eds.) Proceedings of the Third International Conference on Computational Intelligence and Informatics. AISC, vol. 1090, pp. 349–359. Springer, Singapore (2020). https://doi.org/10.1007/978-981-15-1480-7_30

18. Khare, S., Kavyashree, S., Gupta, D., Jyotishi, A.: Investigation of nutritional status of children based on machine learning techniques using Indian demographic and health survey data. Proc. Comput. Sci. **115**, 338–349 (2017). https://doi.org/10.1016/j.procs.2017.09.087

19. Khare, S., Gupta, D., Prabhavathi, K., Deepika, M.G., Jyotishi, A.: Health and nutritional status of children: survey, challenges and directions. In: Nagabhushan, T.N., Aradhya, V.N.M., Jagadeesh, P., Shukla, S., M. L., C. (eds.) CCIP 2017. CCIS, vol. 801, pp. 93–104. Springer, Singapore (2018). https://doi.org/10.1007/978-981-10-9059-2_10
20. Sharma, V., Sharma, V., Khan, A., et al.: Malnutrition, health and the role of machine learning in clinical setting. Front Nutr. 7, 44 (2020). https://doi.org/10.3389/fnut.2020.00044
21. Giabbanelli, P., Adams, J.: Identifying small groups of foods that can predict achievement of key dietary recommendations. Data mining of the UK national diet and nutrition survey. Public Health Nutr. 1, 1–9 (2016). https://doi.org/10.1017/S1368980016000185
22. Hearty, A., Gibney, M.: Analysis of meal patterns with the use of supervised data mining techniques - Artificial neural networks and decision trees. Am. J. Clin. Nutr. 88, 1632–1642 (2009). https://doi.org/10.3945/ajcn.2008.26619

Surveillance System for Monitoring Social Distance

Sahil Jethani[1] (ID), Ekansh Jain[2] (ID), Irene Serah Thomas[3], Harshitha Pechetti[4],
Bhavya Pareek[5] (ID), Priyanka Gupta[6]([✉]) (ID), Venkataramana Veeramsetty[7],
and Gaurav Singal[8] (ID)

[1] USICT, GGSIPU, New Delhi, India
`sahil.jethani@gmail.com`
[2] IIT, Kharagpur, Kharagpur, India
`jainekansh00@gmail.com`
[3] SCE, Thiruvananthapuram, Kerala, India
`thomasjessy2001@gmail.com`
[4] SVECW, Bhimavaram, Andhra Pradesh, India
`harshithashyam99@gmail.com`
[5] LNMIIT, Jaipur, India
`bhavya.ebooks@gmail.com`
[6] JECRC Foundation, Jaipur, India
`priyanka123gg@gmail.com`
[7] Center for Artificial Intelligence and Deep Learning, S R Engineering College,
Warangal, Telangana State, India
`dr.vvr.research@gmail.com`
[8] Bennett University, Greater Noida, India
`gauravsingal789@gmail.com`

Abstract. In the light of recent events, an epidemic - COVID-19 which
took the world by surprise and continues to grow day by day. This paper
describes an idea to control the spread of disease by monitoring Social
Distancing. As of now from where we stand, the only way to avoid further
spreading is to maintain proper social distance. Combining the advanced
detection algorithms such as SSD, YOLO v4, and Faster-RCNN along
with pedestrian datasets we reached the desired conclusion of calculating
the distance between two detected persons in a video and identifying
whether the social distancing norm is followed or not. This method can be
implemented in CCTV's, UAV's, and on any other surveillance system.
The rapid advancements in technologies led to more precise and accurate
values.

Keywords: Pedestrian detection · Distance calculation · UAV · Deep
learning · COVID19 · Surveillance

1   Introduction

Surveillance devices like drones are one of the most wonderful and precious
advancements of technology [16]. Science and technology are developing day by

day. A drone or UAV is an example of this. It can be remotely controlled or fly autonomously. In the unmanned apparatuses, lengthening of flight is a crucial factor [3]. It has a large number of applications like disaster management, wildfire tracking, cloud monitoring, and is also used for surveillance and monitoring. This paper is written to analyze and explore existing studies about drone monitoring so that a better and more reliable model can be obtained [7]. From where we stand UAVs and CCTVs are playing a significant role in not only offices, industries, homes, etc. but also in streets too. Their usage will also continue to grow in the nearby future.

Our world at present is alarmingly threatened by a deadly disease known as COVID-19. Even though science and technology have developed up to this extent, unfortunately, none can find a cure for this epidemic. For now, the most effective method to somehow prevent further spreading of this worldwide epidemic is by maintaining a certain distance between two individuals(say from 1 to 2 m) and this is termed as Social Distancing. So one of our main objectives should be to use UAVs, CCTVs, or any other surveillance mechanism to detect the real-time distance between two people.

In these incredulous times, it is not surprising that the COVID-19 pandemic and the rise of detection technologies are now intertwined, with the latter being harnessed as part of the fightback for the former. With the help of more efficient and advanced algorithms and freedom of customization of these systems, we can achieve the desired result. The effectiveness of this project lies where there is a chance of a large group of people gathering. In such cases, sometimes, it becomes difficult for an individual to maintain social distance between people. This situation is also true in bus stands, trains, streets, pilgrims, etc. These are the situations in which these surveillance systems come into action [10].

Person detection algorithms have developed rapidly for the past few years. These detection algorithms have been classified as two: One-stage approaches and Two-stage approaches. The two-stage approach shows good accuracy as compared to a one-stage approach, but more attraction is towards a one-stage approach because of its former computing efficiency. It consists of a single network of border boxes and class probabilities with an evaluation similar to RPN and SSD [7].

As we mentioned above, this kind of approach might help us in controlling the spread of COVID-19 to some extent. This is a challenging task because this disease can spread at any moment and in all sorts of places but with the advancement of technology and research, we can deal with this complex situation to a considerable extent [14]. There is a high risk where more humans might indulge in the case, so using surveillance devices can be a preferable choice in monitoring social distance [14].

In our research, we calculated the distance between two detected persons by converting the current perspective vision to bird's eye vision, if they are not maintaining the required threshold distance, a red bounding box along with a red line is displayed over them. Hence a graph can be made which shows the risk at a particular time in a given area. By doing so, vulnerable places can be identified and thereby giving out awareness to the public. To reduce human efforts and to make sure everyone follows the social distancing concept, this work may seem to be quite promising. Further paper is arranged as, in Sect. 2, the literature of related work is presented, in Sect. 3, the methodology of person detection technique and monitoring of distance is shown. In Sect. 4, performance evaluation is done and the final section gives the conclusion and future work of our work.

2   Literature Review

Surveillance devices such as UAV's have many real-world applications, including vision methods such as object detection. Surveillance Devices require memory capacity, computationally low cost, and fast solutions for Object detection [8]. Pedestrian identification has become an important task these days, especially in vision-based and aerial surveillance systems. Over the past few months, the role of computer vision in maintaining social distancing has been underlined to prevent COVID-19. Various methods are available for achieving the task of pedestrian detection in images and videos. Pedestrian detection is the process of localizing all objects considered to be individuals in the image or video stream.

The initial process of the pedestrian detection was to capture the area of interest from the image, describe the areas with descriptors, and then classify the areas as human or non-human [15]. Based on CNN, to solve this problem many methods pro-posed. These methods are classified into two groups, first is a two-stage approach [5,13,20], and second is one stage approaches [17,18]. Two parts are there in this two-stage approach. First, the candidate produces proposals for a set of objects, and the next part uses CNN to calculate the object region on stage. Good accuracy has been demonstrated in two-stage detection methods in MS COCO datasets [12]. Other than two-stage approaches, one stage approaches attract more attention, largely by the computational efficiency of the former. In an evaluation, the one-step approach consists of a single network that evaluates boundary boxes directly from the full image. To cover objects at different scales, this approach finds objects similar to RPNs and SSDs and with distinct resolutions use feature maps. YOLO calculates the feature map and to make predictions on a set of fixed areas uses an integrated layer. On the other hand, YOLO v2 includes batch normalization rather than integrated layers to assess border boxes to enhance accuracy. YOLO v3 for capturing characteristics and making predictions based on different feature maps uses deep networks. The main advantage of YOLO v3 is its high ability to detect objects and do calculations so that the detection speed can receive real-time estimates.

In the paper [21], the authors combined the DPPN architecture to improve the underlying class imbalance problem with the focal loss function embedded in the object detection model and also the ability to detect images with varying degrees. They considered both networks to be the backbone of their detection model, RESNET and MobileNet. Although their model combined with that provides better results with detection accuracy, the mobile-net combination comes with call time speed without recognition accuracy. Their model is compared with RetinNet RestNet50 and HAL-RetinNet.

In the paper [4], the authors demonstrate three collaborative-based DL applications for tracking and detecting objects and assessment of distance. The object edition is a developed method, it's high in accuracy and also the real-time imaginary limitations of identifying the object. They used SSD and YOLO V3 algorithms on object detection to know which algorithm is more suitable. YOLO V3 is higher when compared to SSD. The MonoDepth algorithm provides an asymmetric map as output. They verified policy with different datasets such as Citiescope and Kitty, also in the RSIG LBC vehicle on Row City Center Traffic Road in real-time. They confirmed under the railway dataset of the Tramway Rouen. The new method presented is based on SSD to analyze the behavior of objects such as pedestrians or vehicles. With the SSD modified algorithm, after identifying an object they assessed future status by including its direction of motion, for pedestrians willing to cross the road, for not willing to cross the road, etc. SSD and YOLO V3 algorithms are used for detecting and tracking objects. A large and appropriate dataset is very important to optimize their performance. Changing the detection classes does not yield a significant improvement.

In paper [1] provides a comparison based on time, accuracy, and parameter values of different algorithms for identifying and localizing objects with different dimensions of the input image. In this, they have identified a new method to improve speed for single stage models and for not losing accuracy. Final results declare that Tiny Yolo V3 improves detection speed, confirming the accurate result.

Speed and accuracy are important parameters for evaluating pedestrian detection performance. Performance is being squandered in different situations because the experiment does not always take place in the same condition [11]. Of course, many parameters can vary from one experience to another. By analyzing the characteristics for object detection three popular models are there, Single Shot Detection [13], YOLO [19] and F-RCNN [9]. F-RCNN is highly accurate compared to SSD and YOLO v3, but, it is slow. If high-quality accuracy needs to be achieved, RCNN is the fastest solution. But, it is not the fastest approach. If speed is important, then YOLO v3 is the best approach. If we want good accuracy and good speed at the same time, SSD is a good solution. At the same time, YOLO V4 is a good solution, as it is a fast approach, and accuracy is similar to faster-RCNN [22].

3   Methodology

The two major steps involved in monitoring social distancing are pedestrian detection and distance calculation. We get the video input from the surveillance system and convert the video input into image sequences. The model runs the detection on these images and then distance calculation is done. After we know the people breaking the social distancing threshold, we mark them with a red bounding box as shown in Fig. 1. This section is divided into two sub-sections. In the first subsection, we will discuss the models we used for pedestrian detection and in the other sub-section, we talk about the approaches we used to calculate the distance between each pedestrian.

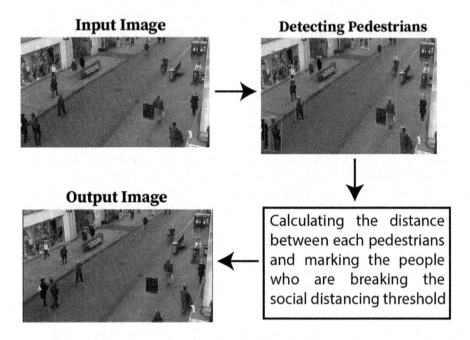

Fig. 1. The flow chart for the work flow of monitoring social distancing

3.1   Pedestrian Detection

There are various kinds of object detection models available. Since the models need to be deployed in surveillance systems like Unmanned Aerial Vehicle (UAV), CCTV Camera, etc. for pedestrian detection we had to select a model that does not require high processing power. Also, we need our model to be fast enough to do all the detection in real-time. Hence, we had to narrow down our selection of models based on the speed of detection and computational power required. The model which we selected are:

1. SSD (Single Shot Detector) + MobileNet (version 2)
2. SSD (Single Shot Detector) + Inception (version 2)
3. YOLO version 4 (You Only Look Once)
4. Tiny YOLO version 3
5. Faster RCNN
6. RFCN

All the above models were pre-trained on COCO Dataset and as per the requirements of our detection process, we filtered out the detection for only the class "person" from the COCO Dataset with 66808 samples. Further, we calculated various parameters such as confusion matrix, mAP, and the time required to do the detection for each model. These parameters give an understanding and help in differentiating and selection among the various pre-selected models. The hyper parameters used in training of SSD+Mobilenet(SSD+M), SSD+Inception(SSD+I), Faster RCNN(FRCNN), RFCN, YOLOv4 and Tiny YOLOv3 are listed in Table 1.

Table 1. Hyper parameters used in training of different models

Parameters	SSD+M	SSD+I	FRCNN	RFCN	YOLOv4	Tiny YOLOv3
Batch size	64	64	256	64	64	64
Momentum	0.9	0.9	0.9	0.89	0.949	0.9
Weight decay	0.0003	0.0004	0.0001	0.0003	0.0005	0.0005
Learning rate	0.004	0.004	0.001	0.003	0.0013	0.00261

3.2 Distance Calculation

Once we had the detection the next part was to calculate the distance between each person. To calculate the distance we used two approaches:

Using the Euclidean Distance Formula. (This approach is considered to calculate the relative error for the second approach) In this approach, we started by calculating the bottom centre coordinates of each of the bounding boxes. These coordinates are taken so that the height constraint is eliminated from detection as well as all the points can be considered to lie on the same plane in real life. We then had to calculate the distance between each of those coordinates. For that we used the Euclidean Distance formula:

$$D(p, q) = \sqrt{(p_x - q_x)^2 + (p_y - q_y)^2} \tag{1}$$

where $p(p_x, p_y)$ and $q(q_x, q_y)$ are the bottom centre point of two bounding boxes respectively and the unit of the distance will be "pixel". For conversion of units from pixel to centimetres (cm), we need to know how many pixels in the horizontal and vertical direction equates to certain ground truth distance. For that, we selected four points as shown in Fig. 2. Points 1 and 2 constitute a horizontal distance of 490 cm and Points 3 and 4 constitute vertical distance of 330 cm (the ground truth distance was calculated with the help of Google Maps [6]). We then calculated the distance(in pixels) between Point 1 and Point 2 and similarly for Point 3 and Point 4 using Euclidean Distance Formula in the given input frame. Let's name these distances as "distance_w" and "distance_h" respectively. Now we consider two coordinates on the image, say $P(P_x, P_y)$ and $Q(Q_x, Q_y)$ to calculate the distance between them in centimetres following process was done:

Fig. 2. Point 1 to Point 4 used for conversion of units from pixel to cm.

$$Height = \frac{(P_y - Q_y)}{Distance\_h} \times 490 \qquad (2)$$

$$Width = \frac{(P_x - Q_x)}{Distance\_w} \times 330 \qquad (3)$$

$$Distance = \sqrt{(Height)^2 + (Width)^2} \qquad (4)$$

The Distance Calculated here will have the units in centimetres.

The next step was to mark the people who were not following the social distancing protocols. As the social distancing guidelines suggest a minimum of 6 ft (182 cm) distance between two people, we set a threshold distance of 182 cm and whosoever falls below this distance threshold was marked by drawing a red bounding box around them. Also, we drew red lines between those people to show with whom they were at proximity.

Conversion from Perspective View to Bird's Eye View. The video input from CCTV, Drone or any other surveillance system can be in any random perspective view, we needed a method where we could calculate distance as accurately as possible in any view. In the method that we came up with, we converted the perspective view into a bird's eye view. The surveillance system has a monocular vision and it is not possible to calculate the distance between the detected persons from that view. By selecting four points from the image(Region of Interest) we can then map the entire image to a bird's eye view perspective using a perspective transformation matrix.

For the conversion and mapping from Perspective View to Bird's Eye View, we need to calculate transformation matrix (M_{sd}). Let's assume we have the point $P(x, y)$ in the perspective view image and want to locate the same point in the bird's eye view, say $Q(u, v)$ as shown in Fig. 3. If we have the transformation

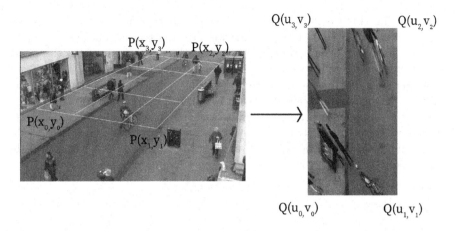

Fig. 3. The selected points from the perspective image and the four corners of the rectangle where we map the bird's eye view.

matrix (M_{sd}) we can find it easily using the following equation:

$$Q' = M_{sd}P' \Rightarrow \begin{bmatrix} u' \\ v' \\ q \end{bmatrix} = \begin{bmatrix} a & b & c \\ d & e & f \\ g & h & i \end{bmatrix} \begin{bmatrix} x' \\ y' \\ w \end{bmatrix} \tag{5}$$

Where $Q'(u', v', q)$ and $P'(x', y', w)$ are the homogeneous coordinates of the point P and Q, hence $Q(u, v) = (\frac{u'}{q}, \frac{v'}{q})$ and $P(x, y) = (\frac{x'}{w}, \frac{y'}{w})$. Now to find the transformation matrix we selected four points in the perspective image and also selected four corners of the rectangle where we wish to map the bird's eye view. Let points $P(x_k, y_k)$ and $Q(u_k, v_k)$ where $k = 0, 1, 2, 3$ be the selected points in the perspective and Bird's eye view respectively. We assume in the transformation matrix i to be equal to 1, then we need to find out elements from 'a' to 'h'. By solving the Eq. 5, we get the following:

$$u_k = \frac{(ax_k + by_k + c)}{(g_k + hy_k + 1)} \Rightarrow u_k = ax_k + by_k + c - g_k u_k - hy_k u_k$$

$$v_k = \frac{(dx_k + ey_k + f)}{(g_k + hy_k + 1)} \Rightarrow v_k = dx_k + ey_k + f - g_k u_k - hy_k u_k$$

For $k = 0, 1, 2, 3$ this can written as 8×8 system:

$$\begin{bmatrix} x_0 & y_0 & 1 & 0 & 0 & 0 & -x_0 u_0 & -y_0 u_0 \\ x_1 & y_1 & 1 & 0 & 0 & 0 & -x_1 u_1 & -y_1 u_1 \\ x_2 & y_2 & 1 & 0 & 0 & 0 & -x_2 u_2 & -y_2 u_2 \\ x_3 & y_0 3 & 1 & 0 & 0 & 0 & -x_3 u_3 & -y_3 u_3 \\ 0 & 0 & 0 & x_0 & y_0 & 1 & -x_0 v_0 & -y_0 v_0 \\ 0 & 0 & 0 & x_1 & y_1 & 1 & -x_1 v_1 & -y_1 v_1 \\ 0 & 0 & 0 & x_2 & y_2 & 1 & -x_2 v_2 & -y_2 v_2 \\ 0 & 0 & 0 & x_3 & y_3 & 1 & -x_3 v_3 & -y_3 v_3 \end{bmatrix} \begin{bmatrix} a \\ b \\ c \\ d \\ e \\ f \\ g \\ h \end{bmatrix} = \begin{bmatrix} u_0 \\ u_1 \\ u_2 \\ u_3 \\ v_0 \\ v_1 \\ v_2 \\ v_3 \end{bmatrix}$$

Computing this we can calculate all the elements from "a" to "h" and get the transformation matrix (M_{sd}). Once we have the transformation matrix we can apply it to the perspective image to map the entire image into the bird's eye view image. After this we follow the same steps as in the previous approach i.e, calculate the bottom point of each bounding box, convert those points into bird's eye view, Point 1 to Point 4 as shown in the Fig. 2 are also converted to bird's eye view and then the distance between them was calculated(in pixels). We then converted the distance from "pixels" to "centimetres" similarly as the previous method. Using the distance between the bounding box we marked the people who were in the proximity of less than 182 cm (6 ft).

4   Results

Evaluation of both the subtasks of this proposed work along with their inferences is discussed in this section. The models were trained on google colab which has the following configuration

GPU: 12GB NVIDIA Tesla K80
Python version: Python 3.6.9.

4.1   Evaluation of the Pedestrian Detection Models

For evaluating our selected models we have used the Oxford Town Center Data set [2]. It contains video from a CCTV camera located in the Cornmarket and Market St., Oxford, England. We calculated the Mean Average Precision (map) and the prediction time taken per image (in seconds). Following graphs were obtained after the evaluation.

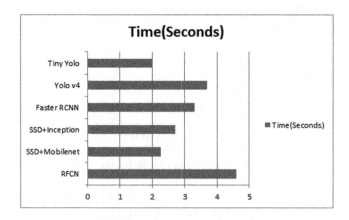

Fig. 4. Prediction time taken per image of all the selected models.

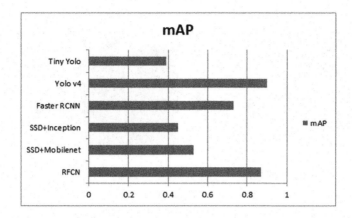

Fig. 5. Mean Average Precision of all the selected models

4.2 Evaluation of the Distance Calculations

We proposed two different distance calculation approaches, we will evaluate both of them with ground truth distance. We used the Oxford Town Centre Data set [2] for evaluation. We calculated the ground truth distance using Google Map [6] and compared it with the distance that we have calculated from both of our approaches. As seen in the Fig. 6 The mean error for the Euclidean Distance Approach is 2.84 m and for the Bird's eye view Approach is 1.05 m.

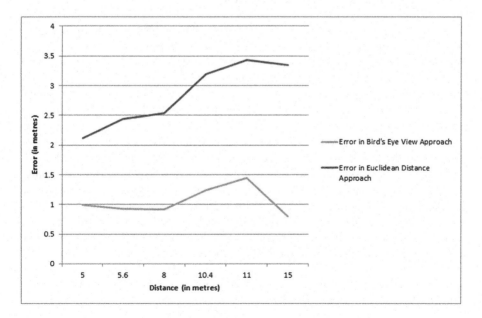

Fig. 6. Error in calculating the distance vs the ground truth distance for both proposed approaches

Using Euclidean Distance Formula   Conversion from Perspective View to Bird's Eye View

Fig. 7. Output Image from both the proposed approaches

From Fig. 4 and Fig. 5, we observed that YOLOv4 and RFCN had the highest mAP but took a long time for the detection while Tiny Yolo and SSD+Mobilenet took the least time but had low mAP. For the distance calculation, it is clear from Fig. 6 and from the mean scores of both the approaches, that the Bird's Eye View Approach is better than the Euclidean Distance approach. Also, from Fig. 6, it can be observed that as the distance increases the error also increases for the Euclidean Distance Approach but, the same does not happen for the other approach. Figure 7 shows the output for both of the proposed approaches of this work.

5   Conclusion and Future Work

Depending on the processing power of the surveillance device, we wish to deploy this social monitoring system, we can select a suitable model after seeing the results. It is possible that when deploying this system on a UAV that flies at a great height, mAP could be lower than mentioned since the model is not trained with aerial images taken at such height. Another limitation of our model is that for a given area we need to feed in the four points of Region of Interest for accurate distance calculation.

In the future, we could work upon the limitations to make this system more accurate in detecting pedestrians, from UAVs flying at great heights. Also, we could make this system in a way so that we won't have to enter the four points every time for the distance calculation. So far no ideal tool for monitoring social distancing has been implemented and this work is a small step that can be used to reach this goal. Furthermore, this model can be used in a way where the faces of people who are not maintaining proper social distancing will be sent to higher authorities so that effective action can be taken to avoid further violation.

Acknowledgment. A sincere thanks to LeadingIndia.ai who gave us this platform and opportunity.

References

1. Adarsh, P., Rathi, P., Kumar, M.: Yolo V3-Tiny: object detection and recognition using one stage improved model. In: 2020 6th International Conference on Advanced Computing and Communication Systems (ICACCS), pp. 687–694 (2020). https://doi.org/10.1109/ICACCS48705.2020.9074315

2. Benfold, B., Reid, I.: Stable multi-target tracking in real-time surveillance video. In: Proceedings of the 2011 IEEE Conference on Computer Vision and Pattern Recognition, CVPR 2011, pp. 3457–3464. IEEE Computer Society (2011). https://doi.org/10.1109/CVPR.2011.5995667

3. Cabreira, T., Brisolara, L., Ferreira Jr., P.: Survey on coverage path planning with unmanned aerial vehicles. Drones **3**, 4 (2019). https://doi.org/10.3390/drones3010004

4. Chen, Z., Khemmar, R., Decoux, B., Atahouet, A., Ertaud, J.: Real time object detection, tracking, and distance and motion estimation based on deep learning: application to smart mobility. In: 2019 Eighth International Conference on Emerging Security Technologies (EST), pp. 1–6 (2019). https://doi.org/10.1109/EST.2019.8806222

5. Girshick, R.: Fast R-CNN. In: Proceedings of the IEEE International Conference on Computer Vision (ICCV), December 2015. https://doi.org/10.1007/978-3-319-46493-0_22

6. Google: Google maps. https://www.google.com/maps/@28.5627323,77.1830238, 15z

7. Guo, Q., Li, Y., Wang, D.: Pedestrian detection in unmanned aerial vehicle scene. In: Lu, H. (ed.) ISAIR 2018. SCI, vol. 810, pp. 273–278. Springer, Cham (2020). https://doi.org/10.1007/978-3-030-04946-1_26

8. Gupta, S., Sangeeta, R., Mishra, R., Singal, G., Badal, T., Garg, D.: Corridor segmentation for automatic robot navigation in indoor environment using edge devices. Comput. Netw. **178**, 107374 (2020). https://doi.org/10.1016/j.comnet.2020.107374

9. He, K., Zhang, X., Ren, S., Sun, J.: Deep residual learning for image recognition. In: Proceedings of the IEEE Conference on Computer Vision and Pattern Recognition (CVPR), June 2016

10. Ministry of Health & Family Welfare, Government of India: Social distancing measure in view of spread of Covid-19 disease. https://www.mohfw.gov.in/pdf/SocialDistancingAdvisorybyMOHFW.pdf

11. Kushwaha, R., Singal, G., Nain, N.: A texture feature based approach for person verification using footprint bio-metric. Artif. Intell. Rev. 1–31 (2020). https://doi.org/10.1007/s10462-020-09887-6

12. Lin, T.-Y., et al.: Microsoft COCO: common objects in context. In: Fleet, D., Pajdla, T., Schiele, B., Tuytelaars, T. (eds.) ECCV 2014. LNCS, vol. 8693, pp. 740–755. Springer, Cham (2014). https://doi.org/10.1007/978-3-319-10602-1_48

13. Liu, W., et al.: SSD: single shot multibox detector. arXiv abs/1512.02325 (2016)

14. Lygouras, E., Santavas, N., Taitzoglou, A., Tarchanidis, K., Mitropoulos, A., Gasteratos, A.: Unsupervised human detection with an embedded vision system on a fully autonomous UAV for search and rescue operations. Sensors **19**(16), 3542 (2019). https://doi.org/10.3390/s19163542

15. Nguyen, D.T., Li, W., Ogunbona, P.: Human detection from images and videos: a survey. Pattern Recogn. **51** (2015). https://doi.org/10.1016/j.patcog.2015.08.027

16. Pareek, B., Gupta, P., Singal, G., Kushwaha, R.: Person identification using autonomous drone through resource constraint devices. In: 2019 Sixth International Conference on Internet of Things: Systems, Management and Security (IOTSMS), pp. 124–129 (2019). https://doi.org/10.1109/IOTSMS48152.2019.8939254
17. Redmon, J., Divvala, S., Girshick, R., Farhadi, A.: You only look once: unified, real-time object detection. In: Proceedings of the IEEE Conference on Computer Vision and Pattern Recognition (CVPR), June 2016
18. Redmon, J., Farhadi, A.: Yolo9000: better, faster, stronger. In: Proceedings of the IEEE Conference on Computer Vision and Pattern Recognition (CVPR), July 2017
19. Redmon, J., Farhadi, A.: Yolov3: an incremental improvement (2018)
20. Ren, S., He, K., Girshick, R., Sun, J.: Faster R-CNN: towards real-time object detection with region proposal networks. In: Cortes, C., Lawrence, N.D., Lee, D.D., Sugiyama, M., Garnett, R. (eds.) Advances in Neural Information Processing Systems 28, pp. 91–99. Curran Associates, Inc. (2015). http://papers.nips.cc/paper/5638-faster-r-cnn-towards-real-time-object-detection-with-region-proposal-networks.pdf
21. Vaddi, S., Kumar, C., Jannesari, A.: Efficient object detection model for real-time UAV applications. CoRR abs/1906.00786 (2019). http://arxiv.org/abs/1906.00786
22. Veeramsetty, V., Singal, G., Badal, T.: Coinnet: platform independent application to recognize Indian currency notes using deep learning techniques. Multimed. Tools Appl. **79**(31), 22569–22594 (2020). https://doi.org/10.1007/s11042-020-09031-0

Consumer Emotional State Evaluation Using EEG Based Emotion Recognition Using Deep Learning Approach

Rupali Gill[(✉)] and Jaiteg Singh

Chitkara University Institute of Engineering and Technology, Rajpura, India
{Rupali.gill,Jaiteg.singh}@chitkara.edu.in

Abstract. The standard methodologies for marketing (e.g., newspaper ads and tv commercials) are not effective in selling products as they do not excite the customers to buy any specific item. These methods of advertising try to ascertain their consumers' attitude towards any product, which might not represent the actual behavior. So, the customer behavior is misunderstood by the advertisers and start-ups because the mindsets do not represent the buying behaviors of the consumers. Previous studies reflect that there is lack of experimental work done on classification and the prediction of their consumer emotional states. In this research, a strategy has been adopted to discover the customer emotional states by simply thinking about attributes and the power spectral density using EEG-based signals. The results revealed that, though the deep neural network (DNN) higher recall, greater precision, and accuracy compared with support vector machine (SVM) and k-nearest neighbor (k-NN), but random forest(RF) reaches values that were like deep learning on precisely the similar dataset.

Keywords: Deep Neural Network · EEG · Support Vector Machine · K-nearest neighbor · Random forest

1 Introduction

As an emerging field, neuromarketing relates the full of feeling and psychological sides of consumer conduct by utilizing neuroscience. The field of neuromarketing is a rising field that individuals don't perceive what occurs in their minds that were oblivious. Furthermore, it has been exhibited that individuals are not satisfactory in their emotional s or objectives (Hammou 2013). The utilization of promoting and publicizing media, similar to reviews and meeting's needs, and purchasing purposes can cause making of ends (Telpaz et al. 2015; Barros et al. 2016). Similarly, oral communication about emotions can prompt biased decisions. It is hard to extricate the emotions of consumer straightaway through decisions, because of ethical issues associated with product purchase and delivery (Telpaz et al. 2015). These components accentuate a logical inconsistency in the shoppers' suppositions during the ease of use appraisals and their genuine assessments, sentiments, and observations with respect to an item's utilization (Barros et al. 2016). Hence, neuromarketing needs methodological choices that can check consumer

© Springer Nature Singapore Pte Ltd. 2021
D. Garg et al. (Eds.): IACC 2020, CCIS 1367, pp. 113–127, 2021.
https://doi.org/10.1007/978-981-16-0401-0_9

behavior successfully. A powerful way is given by novel neuroimaging methods. Techniques like these at last assistance advertisers to inspect the consumers cerebrums and secure understandings of the conscious and sub conscious strategies that contains fizzled or fruitful showcasing advertising messages. The data along these lines obtained in the wake of taking out the key issue in traditional advertising research, that is, confiding in people; explicitly, the consumer or employees must be believed, who report on how the shoppers get impacted by the particular area of any advertisement (Morin 2011).

The promising neuroimaging devices in neuromarketing is Brain-computer interfaces (BCIs). It permits frameworks and consumers to convey proficiently. To run and execute commands, BCI don't requires the utilization of any sort of device or muscle obstacle (Abdulkader 2015). Besides, to control a framework a BCI utilizes energetically created consumers' cerebrum action through signs, which offers the ability to associate or communicate with the nearby marketplace. To examine activity of the brain, Electroencephalography (EEG) is one of the main tools.

The rest of the paper is organized into sections. The next section provides the details of related work done by the various authors. The third section provides the details of methodology and proposed work done for the current experiment, followed by classification of DNN framework and discussion of results and last section of conclusion.

2   Background and Literature Review

BCIs help to communicate effectively between user brain and computer system. It does not involve in physiological interference and record signals through system generated commands (Ramadan et al. 2015). BCI have its application area in advertising, medical science, smart cities and neuroscience (Abdulkader 2015; Hwang 2013). BCI systems are working to aid the user. BCI systems are very challenging in the field of advertising and marketing.

The promising neuroimaging devices in neuromarketing is Brain-computer interfaces (BCIs). It permits frameworks and consumers to convey proficiently. To run and execute commands, BCI don't requires the utilization of any sort of device or muscle obstacle (Abdulkader 2015). Besides, to control a framework a BCI utilizes energetically created consumers' cerebrum action through signs, which offers the ability to associate or communicate with the nearby marketplace.

For the same various neuromarketing techniques which record the brain activity are used. The various techniques EEG, fNIRS, fMRI, MEG, SST, PET, TMS (Krampe 2018) are used for recording brain activity (Ohme 2009; Hakim 2019; Harris 2018). But from all the techniques EEG has best temporal resolution as shown in Table 1.

The study based on BCI based neuroimaging techniques indicate that there are three neuroimaging techniques – MEG, SST, EEG which have good scope for marketing research but due to limitations of MEG and SST these are not used for the current research. Because of the extensive advantages and varied features of EEG over SST and MEG (Cherubino et al. 2019), EEG is being used for the current research.

The EEG is the BCI to perform dreary, ongoing assessment of brains' associations in low temporal resolution (Ramadan 2017; Ramadan et al. 2015). Thus, in the experimental study, EEG was held onto as the info sign to get a BCI framework. BCIs might be

Table 1. BCI neuroimaging techniques

BCI technique	Characteristic					
	Temporal resolution	Spatial resolution	Cost	Portability	Training	Scope for marketing research
fMRI (function Magnetic Resonance	Low	High	Very high	No	Extensive	Limited
EEG (Electroencephalogram)	High	Low	Average	Yes	Moderate	High
fNIRS (Near Infrared Spectroscopy)	Low	High	Very high	No	Extensive	Limited
MEG (Magnetoencephalography)	High	Low	High	No	Extensive	High
SST (Steady State Topography)	High	Low	Average	Yes	Moderate	High
PET (Positron Emission Topography)	Low	High	High	No	Extensive	No
TMS (Transcranial Magnetic Stimulation)	Low	High	High	No	Extensive	Limited

utilized to make an interpretation of them advertisement to check the emotional strategies. The current research carried out an experiment using deep neural framework (DNN) framework and used a benchmark DEAP data set for performing the experimentation.

EEG is a tool which assesses brain action. By assessing the variants this electrical activity is logged on the scalp. These activities are logged utilizing electrodes placed over the cortex straight on the scalp. The electrodes are attached in a device (Agarwal 2015; Murugappan 2014). On the other hand, resolution and the ratio are limited in comparison with those of different practices. EEG is regarded as the BCI input to comprehend a real time brain evaluation (Lin 2018). EEG was chosen in this research as the input signal to the BCI. The space between the electrodes that are local is 10% or 20% of their entire scalp diameter as shown in Fig. 1.

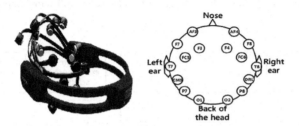

Fig. 1. EEG emotive headset placement

The previous studies on EEG based recognition systems for emotion state recognition are presented in this section. Emotional states can be defined as presentation of human behavioral state for recognition of pleasantness states which could help in making decisions (Ramsøy 2012).

The research by (Hwang 2013; Lotte and Bougrain 2018) stated that there is need of more than one classifier and classifier combinations to detect and define feature sets and improve the performance. The authors (Chew et al. 2016) stated that there is a great effect on buying decision due to aesthetics presentation. They used 3D EEG signals to record frequency bands and achieved good accuracy over liking scale. The extensive study and review by provided by authors (Lotte and Bougrain 2018; Teo 2018a, b) to study various deep learning and machine learning algorithms users to study consumer preferences. (Hakim 2019), provided in depth study of classifiers and prediction algorithms user for understanding consumer preference states and state that SVM with approximate accuracy of 60% is best classifier so far for preference prediction. As per the study, LDA, SVM are most studied algorithms for classifiers. The authors studied the various preferences using EEG based systems (Hakim 2019). The previous (Lin 2018; Alvino 2018; Yadava 2017; Teo 2018a, b; Boksem 2015) has done much work on EEG based emotional state detection.

With the emergence of neural networks and deep learning, EEG based studies have become popular for emotional state prediction. Deep neural network (DNN) is type of artificial neural network with various layers along with input and output layers. The most basic type is multi-layer perceptron (MLP). The author (Loke 2017) suggested use DNN for object identification. The authors (Teo 2018a, b; Roy 2019) have explores various deep learning frameworks and (Teo 2017; 2018a, b) proposed the methods for EEG based preference classification with compared with various machine learning classifiers.

The research has done considerable use of EEG in emotional state prediction to understand the consumer preferences.

3   Methodology and Proposed Work

The recognition system that uses EEG focuses on the use of feature extraction process along with the use of classification algorithm for decision making. In the experiment, we researched the prospects of utilizing two emotional states - unpleasant and pleasant and calculated of classifier accuracy through the EEG based recognition system (Ohme 2009).

Series of tasks involved in the paper are summarized as following steps (Ohme 2009) in Fig. 2:

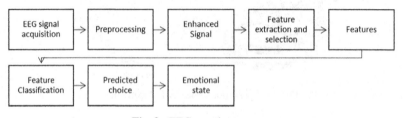

Fig. 2. EEG emotion process

1. Acquisition of Signal for the selected device: EEG-A DEAP dataset has been taken and pre-processed to remove the artifacts.

    EEG headset used in DEAP data set contain 32 channels. Table 2 provides the mapping of 14+2 EEG Emotive headset used for the current research work. The channels in bold are the mapped channels of EEG headset with DEAP dataset.

Table 2. Channel positioning according to 32 channel EEG headset used in DEAP dataset

Channel No	1	2	3	4	5	6	7	8	9	10	11	12	13	14	15	16
Channel	Fp1	**AF3**	**F3**	**F7**	**FC5**	FC1	C3	**T7**	CP5	CP1	P3	**P7**	PO3	**O1**	Oz	Pz
Channel No	17	18	19	20	21	22	23	24	25	26	27	28	29	30	31	32
Channel	Fp2	**AF4**	Fz	**F4**	**F8**	**FC6**	FC2	Cz	C4	T8	CP6	CP2	P4	**P8**	PO4	**O2**

2. The pre-processing techniques that have been used are Independent Component Analysis (IA). The data that has been pre-processed is fed into SVM, k-NN, RF and DNN classifiers
3. Features are extracted and selected for a chosen device using Power spectral density function. Features are selected where the most required optimum features have been identified
4. Classification of features based on machine learning and DNN algorithms: KNN, SVM, RF, DNN
5. Prediction of emotional states using classifiers by comparing the accuracy of each classifier

The selection and extraction of features are basic techniques which are used to evaluate the performance of EEG recognition systems. The current study aims to detect the emotional states-pleasant and unpleasant using classification algorithm through EEG Emotive headset (Hwang 2013; Pham and Tran 2012). An off-line analysis was conducted to evaluate the intelligence for the emotional detection and classification. The DEAP data set was used to explore the performance and computation of deep learning classification techniques. This might effectively replicate the emotional states of the consumers for advertisement prediction. To carry out the experiment, the authors intend to compare individuals' recordings of the k-nearest neighbor (k-NN) and random forest (RF), Support Vector Machine (SVM) classifiers and Deep Neural Network classifiers for evaluating the emotional states. The Scikit-Learn toolbox was used to develop the system learning suite, also used Python for EEG - artifact cleaning, filtering and pre-processing, Python library - MNE software suite which is an open-source library used to explore visualize and analyze cognitive and physiological signals, In addition Keras library is used on the top of tensorflow for understanding and managing the cognitive load.. This section discusses the methodology in conjunction with the experimentation details of the proposed experimental work for detection of emotional states. It starts with the outline of fact and, also the available prerecorded dataset of the emotional states.

Then the characteristic extraction is processed and eventually, the DNN classification model is illustrated.

DEAP Dataset
DEAP dataset is used for the experimentation (Koelstra 2013). This dataset can be divided into parts.

i.   Calculation of valence, arousal and dominance emotional ratings for 120 music videos of 1 min each.
ii. Calculation of participant ratings and recording of physiological and face video of 32 volunteers while watching 40 music videos mentioned in first parts. 22 participants frontal face video was also recorded as shown in Fig. 3.

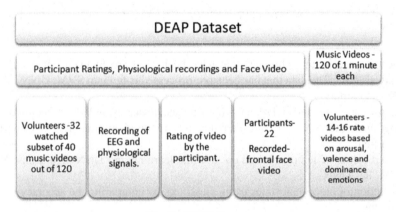

Fig. 3. DEAP dataset

Data Pre-processing
The experimental trial was done on the already pre-processed EEG based recordings from the DEAP database. The EEG signal recordings were down examined from 512 Hz to 128 Hz, utilizing a band pass frequency filter between 4.0 Hz to 45.0 Hz, and the EOG artifacts were eliminated from the epochs by using the dimensionality reduction method-independent component analysis (ICA) (Hadjidimitriou 2012). The ICA decompose the extracted features into independent signal by selecting a subset, by eliminating noisy and very high-dimensional data (Nezamfar 2016). The features which are useful features are retained and outliers are removed during the experimentation. Additionally, it reduces the experimentation cost of the consequent measures. Thus, only the mentioned channels were kept (Fz, F3, F4, AF3, and AF4) (Aldayel et al. 2020). Figure 4 shows the emotional state engagement in various regions of brain with channel with frequency band involved.

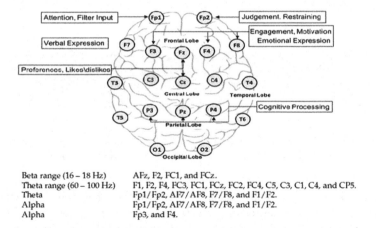

Beta range (16 – 18 Hz)	AFz, F2, FC1, and FCz.
Theta range (60 – 100 Hz)	F1, F2, F4, FC3, FC1, FCz, FC2, FC4, C5, C3, C1, C4, and CP5.
Theta	Fp1/Fp2, AF7/AF8, F7/F8, and F1/F2.
Alpha	Fp1/Fp2, AF7/AF8, F7/F8, and F1/F2.
Alpha	Fp3, and F4.

Fig. 4. EEG emotion detection with band detection for EEG Channel (Teo 2017)

Feature Extraction for EEG Based Emotional State Recognition

Feature extraction plays a vital role in implementation of EEG based emotional recognition system. Various feature extraction techniques are used by various researchers. The techniques can be classified into frequency domain, time domain and time frequency domain (Hwang 2013; Jenke et al. 2014; Roy 2019). The EEG features can also be extracted by applying signal processing methods; time domain signal analysis, frequency domain signal analysis, and/or time-frequency signal domain analysis. For the current experiment power spectral density (PSD) feature extraction method has been used to extract of the EEG frequency bands. PSD is a frequency domain technique. The frequency bands from the recorded through EEG Emotive signals were used for the calculation of valence.

Power Spectral Density - It is the contemporary feature extraction methods which uses the frequency domain for experiments. It is an emerging and robust feature extraction technique used for neuromarketing studies (Qin et al. 2019). The previous research (Ohme 2010; Ramsøy 2012; Khushaba 2013) has shown that the output of PSD obtained from the EEG-based data recordings functions well for determining understanding the consumer behaviors and emotional states. PSD is linear extraction method used to extract band power spectral features using either the parametric or non-parametric methods (Ameera et al. 2019). PSD uses the Fast Fourier Transform (FFT), discrete Fourier Transform (DFT) and FFT inverse for conversion of time domain signal into frequency domain and vice a versa. PSD technique used in this research divides each EEG based data recordings to four separate frequency bands: alpha (α), beta (β), gamma (γ), theta (θ), as shown in Fig. 5. The division of signals into frequency bands is done through Welch method or Burg method (Ameera et al. 2019). A thorough review by (Hwang 2013) says that PSD is being used in most of the researches for extracting features from EEG. Also, the Python open source suite (MNE) was used for calculation of PSD. The specific frequency band was computed to construct a feature using the MNE suite as shown in Fig. 5. The frequency bands are calculated with amplitude over y-axis and time over x-axis.

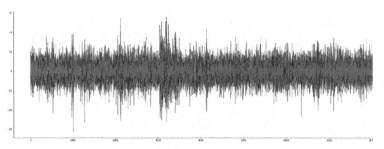

Fig. 5. Frequency domain EEG artifact with PSD computation

Valence - In the current study, valence was chosen as the rate of measure emotional states. The Likert scale values ranging from 0–9 was used to record the same. The value of activation for EEG frontal asymmetry (E) is directly proportion to valence (V), E ∝ V (Koelstra 2013). Also, DEAP dataset also reflects this association valence (V) and EEG frequency bands (αβγθ) (Koelstra 2011), shown in Fig. 6. The increase from valence, leads to increase in intensity value of frequency bands, which is in accordance with the results in a comparable study (Al-Nafjan et al. 2017a, b). The liking rating from the DEAP dataset is not used in the current experiment (Al-Nafjan et al. 2017a, b).

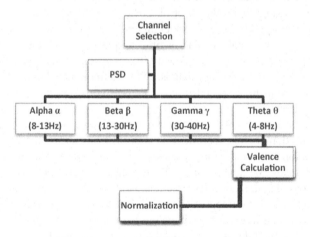

Fig. 6. Process of EEG feature extraction

Calculation of valence (V) is done using below equations (Eqs. 1–4) (Al-Nafjan et al. 2017a, b):

$$V = (\beta(AF3,\ F3))/\alpha(AF3,\ F3) - \beta(AF4,\ F4)/\alpha(AF4,\ F4) \tag{1}$$

$$V = \ln[\alpha(Fz, AF3, F3)] - \ln[\alpha(Fz, AF4, F4)] \tag{2}$$

$$V = \alpha(F4) - \beta(F3) \tag{3}$$

$$V = \alpha(F4)/\beta(F4) - (\alpha(F3))/(\beta(F3)) \tag{4}$$

4 DNN Classification

Deep Neural Networks are framework that contains layers of "neurons" combined with each other. Each layer of neuron performs a different linear transformation to the input information (Roy 2019; Aldayel et al. 2020). Then, every layer's transformation undergoes processing to the give an outcome through a nonlinear cost function. These cost functions are minimized to obtain the optimal outcome. The DNN functions in a single forward direction, by the input via the hidden ones (if accessible) into the output neurons in the forward directions. The neuron output from previous layer acts as activation of each neuron for the next layer.

For the current research, the DNN model using one input layer, three hidden layers, one batch normalization layer and one output layer. The hyperparameters used for DNN model training are learning rate calculated through Adam gradient, number of epochs, and ReLU activation function and output in the form of Softmax activation function. The trained DNN model was compared with accuracy results for classification algorithms - SVM, RF, k-NN. The DNN classifier's block structure is displayed in Fig. 7.

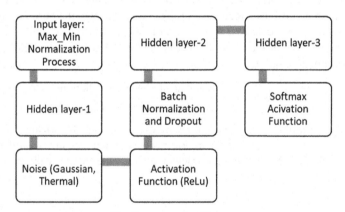

Fig. 7. DNN classification

The first step was to normalize the extracted features. There are two commonly used normalization techniques – min-max normalization and z-score. For the current experiment, min-max normalization (Eq. 5) was used and were fed to DNN classifiers. This is the most common way to normalize the data. The data is normalized in the range of 0 and 1. The minimum (min) value is converted to 0 and maximum (max) value is converted to 1, all other values (v) lies between decimals of 0 and 1.

$$v\_normalized = (v - min)/max - min \tag{5}$$

Adam gradient descent optimization strategy was used to train the DNN classifier. It is one of the most optimal strategy which uses an iterative algorithm in order to minimize a function to the local or global minima. For the current experiment, three reduction functions namely cross entropy functions - binary and categorical, and hinge cross function are used. The system was stopped when the machine started to over-fit and was stopped at 0.0001. With the acceptable defaults and proper setup: the starting experimentation learning rate was 0.001. The system consists of layers input layer, and 3 hidden layers 1700, 1200,700 respectively and an output layer. As per the experimental requirements the sample size for input layer was 2125 samples with decreasing the size to 75% after every filter operation in the hidden layers. The output measurements pertain to the amount of goal emotional states. The network was tested over the test data which comprised roughly 20% of DEAP data samples. Together with three hidden layers, that comprises components between rectified linear unit (ReLu). The output is DDN execution is obtained through soft-max activation function with a binary cross-entropy loss function. Soft-max activation function normalizes the outputs from various hidden layers.

5   Result and Discussion

The experiment was performed to predict the emotional states using different classification algorithms: Deep Neural Network, k-Nearest Neighbor, Random Forest and Support Vector Machine. The accuracy of emotional states was predicted using the machine learning classification algorithms. Accuracy is the measure through the performance of any system could be evaluated and same is used for EEG recognition system. The accuracy is defining the average of the accurate predictions over actual value availability in the proposed benchmark dataset.

$$\text{Accuracy}(A) = \frac{\text{Number of Correct Predictions}}{\text{Total Number of Cases}} \qquad (6)$$

Figure 8 presents the measured accuracy for experimented classification algorithms. The performance evaluation of these algorithms was done using cross validation technique. This technique helps the experimenter to train the model using subset of the

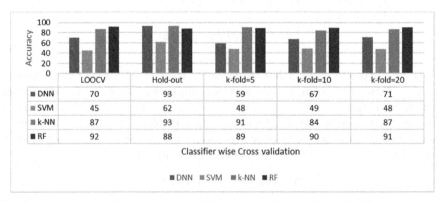

	LOOCV	Hold-out	k-fold=5	k-fold=10	k-fold=20
■ DNN	70	93	59	67	71
■ SVM	45	62	48	49	48
■ k-NN	87	93	91	84	87
■ RF	92	88	89	90	91

Classifier wise Cross validation

■ DNN   ■ SVM   ■ k-NN   ■ RF

Fig. 8. Accuracy prediction using cross validation method on various classifiers on proposed dataset

benchmark data set and then perform evaluation. For the current study three methods namely - holdout, k-fold cross validation, and leave-one-out cross validation (LOOCV) were used.

Hold out – Hold out (test/train splitting) method performs the training ay 50% of the data set and 50% for the test dataset. The results of DNN and k-NN are better than random forest (RF), support vector machine (SVM) as shown in Table 3:

Table 3. Outcome for the hold-out cross validation

DNN	RF	SVM	k-NN
93%	88%	62%	93%

LOOCV - This method performs training on the whole dataset leaving aside only one data-point and then iterates over each data point. This is very time-consuming process. The results of random forest (RF) outperformed other classifiers as shown in Table 4.

Table 4. Outcome for the leave one out cross validation

DNN	RF	SVM	k-NN
70%	92%	45%	87%

K-fold Cross Validation - The data set is spilt into number of subsets known as folds. This model uses k − 1 folds for training and 1 for testing and then iterated each time over every fold. The results of random forest and k-nearest neighbor is better than classifiers as shown in Table 5.

Table 5. Outcome for the k-fold cross validation

	DNN	RF	SVM	k-NN
K fold = 5	59%	89%	48%	91%
K fold = 10	67%	90%	49%	84%
K fold = 20	71%	91%	48%	87%

Since the very best results were achieved using the holdout validation from all the validation techniques, this technique was chosen to apply the loss function -hyper parameters for DNN framework. Figure 8 presents the summary of all the cross-validation techniques.

Figure 9 presents the results for accuracy calculation for SVM, RF, KNN, and DNN using three different loss functions: the cross-entropy function - binary and categorical, and hinge function. Categorical cross entropy loss is combination of softmax activation function and Cross - Entropy loss and is used for multi-class classification. Binary cross entropy is a combination Sigmoid activation and Cross-Entropy loss and is used for multi-label classification. The hinge loss is used for max-margin classification and shows best results with SVM classifiers.

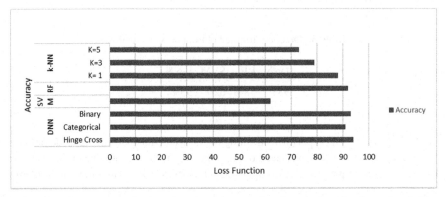

Fig. 9. Classifier accuracy for loss functions for emotional state classification using hold-out validation

The results demonstrate that the k-NN classifier highest accuracy of 88% when the cross validation of k = 1. Though, accuracy of 92% was achieved for RF, the DNN also reached the accuracy result of 91% which is the highest with hinge cross-entropy loss function as compared to the other studied algorithms.

Further the research work compared the work done in the using DNN model on EEG based emotion recognition. Table 6 provides summary of the results when compared with existing researches. Two studies were used which used PSD feature extraction on DEAP dataset and worked on detecting arousal. The comparative results show that proposed method gave comparative results when applied on DNN model.

Table 6. Comparison of EEG emotion analysis using DNN model

Ref	Data set	Feature extraction	Emotion classes	Result
(Al-Nafjan et al. 2017a, b)	DEAP	PSD	Valence and arousal	82% Accuracy for Hold out cross validation
(Aldayel et al. 2020)	DEAP	PSD	Arousal	94% Accuracy for Hinge Cross validation
Proposed DNN	DEAP	PSD	Arousal	93% Accuracy for Hold out cross validation

6   Conclusion

In this paper, a DNN based learning model has been proposed to detect consumer emotional states from EEG signals. The complete work is carried proposed dataset and DEAP dataset. Initially from EEG two types of signals are extracted i.e. PSD and valence. There are around 2125 different feature in each EEG activity. In this paper various evaluation parameters of accuracy are used. The parameters were used to test the classifier performance and validation using LOOCV, holdout and K-fold techniques. Total four different classifiers were used (DNN, SVM, KNN, RF), our proposed method achieves the accuracy of around 70%, 93%, 91%, 84% and 87% in all the validation parameters. Our proposed method had shown highest accuracy in contrast with all other methods. The research work results were compared with existing researches. The major limitations of the research if limited to only two emotional states and with evaluation using a smaller number of parameters. In future, DNN method can be further explored on certain parameters to improve the achieved accuracy for emotional state evaluation. The exploration of enhanced DNN model is proposed as future work for the valence arousal model. The authors recommend applying DNN model on multiple modalities used in order to understand consumer emotional states.

References

Abdulkader, S.N.: Brain computer interfacing: applications and challenges. Egypt. Inform. J. **16**(2), 213–230 (2015)

Agarwal, S.: Neuromarketing and consumer neuroscience: current understanding and the way forward. Decision 457–462 (2015)

Aldayel, M., Ykhlef, M., Al-Nafjan, A.: Deep learning for EEG-based preference classification in neuromarketing. Appl. Sci. **10**(4), 1525–1548 (2020)

Al-Nafjan, A., Hosny, M., Al-Ohali, Y., Al-Wabil, A.: Review and classification of emotion recognition based on EEG brain-computer interface system research: a systematic review. Appl. Sci. **7**(12), 1239 (2017a)

Al-Nafjan, A., Hosny, M., Al-Wabil, A., Al-Ohali, Y.: Classification of human emotions from electroencephalogram (EEG) signal using deep neural network. Int. J. Adv. Comput. Sci. Appl. **8**(9), 419–425 (2017b)

Alvino, L.C.: Towards a better understanding of consumer behavior: marginal utility as a parameter in neuromarketing research. Int. J. Mark. Stud. **10**(1), 90–106 (2018)

Ameera, A., Saidatul, A., Ibrahim, Z.: Analysis of EEG spectrum bands using power spectral density for pleasure and displeasure state. In: IOP Conference Series: Materials Science and Engineering, vol. 557, no. 1, pp. 012030–01203. IOP Publishing (2019)

Barros, R.Q., et al.: Analysis of product use by means of eye tracking and EEG: a study of neuroergonomics. In: Marcus, A. (ed.) DUXU 2016. LNCS, vol. 9747, pp. 539–548. Springer, Cham (2016). https://doi.org/10.1007/978-3-319-40355-7_51

Boksem, M.A.: Brain responses to movie trailers predict individual preferences for movies and their population-wide commercial success. J. Mark. Res. **52**(4), 482–492 (2015)

Chew, L., Teo, J., Mountstephens, J.: Aesthetic preference recognition of 3D shapes using EEG. Cogn. Neurodyn. **10**(2), 165–173 (2016)

Cherubino, P., et al.: Consumer behaviour through the eyes of neurophysiological measures: state-of-the-art and future trends. Comput. Intell. Neurosci. 1–41 (2019)

Hadjidimitriou, S.K.: Toward an EEG-based recognition of music liking using time-frequency analysis. IEEE Trans. Biomed. Eng. **59**(12), 3498–3510 (2012)

Hakim, A.: A gateway to consumers' minds: achievements, caveats, and prospects of electroencephalography-based prediction in neuromarketing. Wiley Interdisc. Rev. Cogn. Sci. **10**(2), e1485 (2019)

Hammou, K.A.: The contributions of neuromarketing in marketing research. J. Manag. Res. **5**(4), 20 (2013)

Harris, J.M.: Consumer neuroscience for marketing researchers. J. Consum. Behav. **17**(3), 239–252 (2018)

Hwang, H.J.: EEG-based brain-computer interfaces: a thorough literature survey. Int. J. Hum.-Comput. Interact. **29**(12), 814–826 (2013)

Jenke, R., Peer, A., Buss, M.: Feature extraction and selection for emotion recognition from EEG. IEEE Trans. Affect. Comput. **5**(3), 327–339 (2014)

Khushaba, R.N.: Consumer neuroscience: assessing the brain response to marketing stimuli using electroencephalogram (EEG) and eye tracking. Expert Syst. Appl. **40**(9) (2013)

Koelstra, S.M.: Deap: a database for emotion analysis; using physiological signals. IEEE Trans. Affect. Comput. **3**(1), 18–31 (2011)

Koelstra, S.P.: Fusion of facial expressions and EEG for implicit affective tagging. Image Vis. Comput. **31**(2), 164–174 (2013)

Krampe, C.G.: The application of mobile fNIRS in marketing research—detecting the "first-choice-brand" effect. Front. Hum. Neurosci. **12**, 433 (2018)

Lin, M.H.: Applying EEG in consumer neuroscience. Eur. J. Mark. **52**, 66–91 (2018)

Loke, K.S.: Object contour completion by combining object recognition and local edge cues. J. Inf. Commun. Technol. **16**(2), 224–242 (2017)

Lotte, F., Bougrain, L.: A review of classification algorithms for EEG-based brain–computer interfaces: a 10 year update. J. Neural Eng. **15**, 031005 (2018)

Morin, C.: Neuromarketing: the new science of consumer behavior. Society **48**(2), 131–136 (2011)

Murugappan, M.M.: Wireless EEG signals based neuromarketing system using Fast Fourier Transform (FFT). In: 2014 IEEE 10th International Colloquium on Signal Processing and its Applications, pp. 25–30. IEEE (2014)

Nezamfar, H.F.: A context-aware code-VEP based brain computer interface for daily life using EEG signals. Ph.D. Thesis, Northeastern University, Boston, MA, USA (2016)

Ohme, R.R.: Analysis of neurophysiological reactions to advertising stimuli by means of EEG and galvanic skin response measures. J. Neurosci. Psychol. Econ. **2**, 21–31 (2009)

Ohme, R.R.: Application of frontal EEG asymmetry to advertising research. J. Econ. Psychol. **31**(5), 785–793 (2010)

Pham, T.D., Tran, D.: Emotion recognition using the emotiv EPOC device. In: Huang, T., Zeng, Z., Li, C., Leung, C.S. (eds.) ICONIP 2012. LNCS, vol. 7667, pp. 394–399. Springer, Heidelberg (2012). https://doi.org/10.1007/978-3-642-34500-5_47

Ramadan, R.A., Refat, S., Elshahed, M.A., Ali, R.A.: Basics of brain computer interface. In: Hassanien, A.E., Azar, A.T. (eds.) Brain-Computer Interfaces. ISRL, vol. 74, pp. 31–50. Springer, Cham (2015). https://doi.org/10.1007/978-3-319-10978-7_2

Ramadan, R.A.: Brain computer interface: control signals review. Neurocomputing **223**, 26–44 (2017)

Ramsøy, T.Z.-O.: Effects of perceptual uncertainty on arousal and preference across different visual domains. J. Neurosci. Psychol. Econ. **5**(4), 212 (2012)

Roy, Y.B.: Deep learning-based electroencephalography analysis: a systematic review. J. Neural Eng. **16**(5), 051001 (2019)

Telpaz, A., Webb, R., Levy, D.: Using EEG to predict consumers' future choices. J. Mark. Res. **52**, 511–529 (2015)

Teo, J.C.: Classification of affective states via EEG and deep learning. Int. J. Adv. Comput. Sci. Appl. **9**(5), 132–142 (2018a)

Teo, J.H.: Deep learning for EEG-based preference classification. In: AIP Conference Proceedings, vol. 1891, p. 020141. AIP Publishing LLC (2017)

Teo, J.H.: Preference classification using electroencephalography (EEG) and deep learning. J. Telecommun. Electron. Comput. Eng. (JTEC), **10**(1–11), 87–91 (2018b)

Qin, X., Zheng, Y., Chen, B.: Extract EEG features by combining power spectral density and correntropy spectral density. In: 2019 Chinese Automation Congress (CAC), pp. 2455–2459. IEEE (2019)

Yadava, M.K.: Analysis of EEG signals and its application to neuromarketing. Multimed. Tools Appl. **76**(18), 19087–19111 (2017)

Covid Prediction from Chest X-Rays Using Transfer Learning

D. Haritha🆔 and M. Krishna Pranathi$^{(\boxtimes)}$🆔

SRK Institute of Technology, Vijayawada, India
harithadasari@rediffmail.com, pranathi.meegada@gmail.com

Abstract. The novel corona virus is a rapidly spreading viral infection that has became a pandemic causing destructive effects on public health and global economy. So, early detection and Covid-19 patient early quarantine is having the significant impact on curtailing it's transmission rate. But it has become a major challenge due to critical shortage of test kits. A new promising method that overcomes this challenge by predicting Covid-19 from patient X-rays using transfer learning, a deep learning technique is proposed in this paper. For this we used a dataset consisting of chest x-rays of Covid-19 infected and normal people. we used VGG, GoogleNet-Inception v1, ResNet, CheXNet models of transfer learning which is a deep learning technique for its benefit of decreasing the training time for a neural network model. Using these we show accuracies of 99.49%, 99%, 98.63%, 99.93% respectively in Covid-19 prediction from x-ray of suspected patient.

Keywords: Convolutional Neural Network · Covid-19 · Transfer learning

1 Introduction

In December 2019, Covid-19 caused by most recently discovered corona virus was first reported in Wuhan, China as a special case of pneumonia and later named as Covid-19 and the virus as SARS-CoV-2. It infects respiratory system at mild level common cold to most impacting MERS (Middle East Respiratory Syndrome) as well as SARS (Severe Acute Respiratory Syndrome). The clinical features of the disease include fewer, sore throat, headache, cough, mild respiratory symptoms even leading to pneumonia. The better accurate test techniques that are being currently used for Covid diagnosis are Polymerase Chain Reaction and Reverse Transcription PCR [1] tests and are laboratory methods that interact with other RNA and DNA to determine volume of specific RNA using fluorescence. This is done by collecting samples of nasal secretions. Due to limited availability of these test kits, early detection can not be done which in turn leads to increase in the spread of disease. Covid became a pandemic effecting globally and right now there is no vaccine available to cure this. In this epidemic situation Artificial Intelligence techniques are becoming vital. Some of the applications in this Covid pandemic scenario that show promising use of AI are AI techniques embedded in cameras to identify infected patients with their recent travel history using facial recognition techniques, using robot services to deliver food items and medicines for Covid infected patients, and

© Springer Nature Singapore Pte Ltd. 2021
D. Garg et al. (Eds.): IACC 2020, CCIS 1367, pp. 128–138, 2021.
https://doi.org/10.1007/978-981-16-0401-0_10

using drones to disinfect the surfaces in public places etc. [2]. Lot of research is being carried out in using AI for drug discovery for Covid cure and vaccine for Covid prevention by learning about the RNA of virus. Machine learning techniques are being used in medical disease diagnosis for reducing manual intervention and automatic diagnosis and are becoming supportive tool for clinicians. Deep learning techniques are successfully applied in several issues like carcinoma detection, carcinoma classification, and respiratory disorder detection from chest x-ray pictures. Day by day the Covid19 is growing at an exponential rate so, the usage of deep learning techniques for Covid prediction may help to increase testing rate and thereby reducing the transmission rate. Covid effects line up of respiratory track, shows preliminary symptoms like pneumonia and as doctors frequently use x-rays to test for pneumonia etc., identification of Covid using X-ray can play significant role in corona tests. So, to increase the Covid testing rate we can use X-ray test as preliminary test and if AI prediction test results in positive then patient can undergo medical test. In this paper, transfer learning, a machine learning technique is used that takes an approach of reserving knowledge gained in solving one problem and apply that knowledge for solving the other similar problems. A dataset consisting of x-rays of normal and Covid-19 patients is used for transfer learning. A deep neural network is build to be implemented with VGG, inception v1, ResNet and CheXNet models. We have chosen these models as they are CNNs and are trained with large ImageNet datasets. These are widely used in Image classification and disease prediction also. We selected in particular CheXNet as it was trained on Chest X-rays. Section 2 briefs some of the recent works done in Covid prediction using AI and Deep Learning (DL) techniques. Section 3 presents our methodology used for Covid prediction using Transfer learning. Section 4 discusses the results obtained in applying four VGG, GoogleNet-Inception v1, ResNet, CheXNet models. In Sect. 5 the use of Transfer Leaning in Covid prediction is concluded.

2 Related Work

Many researches are working rigorously on possibilities of early Covid-19 detection since Feb 2019. Both laboratory clinical testing methods and computer aided testing using Artificial Intelligence, machine learning and deep learning (DL) approaches are being developed. As this disease does not show symptoms immediately, early identification of infected person has become difficult. Artificial Intelligence can be aided for easy and rapid X-ray diagnosis using deep learning. The ideology of using x-ray images in prediction of covid19 came from the deep neural network approaches which were used in pneumonia detection using chest X-rays [3]. A deep learning based automated diagnosis system for X-ray mammograms was proposed by Al-Antari et al. [4]. They used YOLO, a regional deep learning approach which resulted in detection accuracy of 98.96%.

Bar et al., have detected chest pathology in chest radio-graphs using deep learning models [5]. The feasibility of detecting pathology based on non-medical learning using DL approaches is observed. Later many works for detection of lung abnormalities, tuberculosis patterns, vessel extraction using x-rays are developed [6, 7]. Covid-19 diagnosis using deep learning In recent days extensive work is being carried out in using deep learning and AI techniques in the Covid 19 prediction. More accurate and faster Covid-19 detection can be achieved by AI and DL using Chest X-rays with good accuracies. There were numerous previous works done in the application of transfer learning models based on Convolutional Neural Networks for different disease predictions. Apostolopoulos et al., have taken X-ray image dataset from patients with common microorganism respiratory disorder, Covid-19 positive, and normal diseases from public repositories for the automated detection of the Coronavirus sickness [8]. They used transfer learning models that uses CNN for detecting the varied abnormalities in little medical image datasets yielding outstanding results approximately 96%. Their promising results show that Deep Learning techniques from X-ray images extract important bio markers associated with the Covid-19 sickness. Three CNN based models ResNet50, InceptionV3 and Inception-ResNetV2 were applied for the detection of coronavirus using chest X-ray radiographs by Narin, Ceren, Pamuk [9]. They obtained 98%, 97% and 87% accuracies respectively. Salman, Fatima M., et al., used Convolutional Neural Network for Covid19 detection [10, 12]. As an alternate to build a model from scratch, Transfer Learning helps in reducing the computational overhead and is proved to be the most promising technique in many deep learning applications. In this paper we proposed covid-19 prediction from x-rays using transfer learning models with better accuracy.

3   Methodology

3.1   Dataset of Project

Collecting a good dataset is one of the most important requirements for getting better accuracy of any ML model. Since, in this project we are predicting covid19 from chest xrays we need a dataset consisting of chest X-ray images only. There is a collection of datasets available even on internet. The model is trained on chest X-rays of Covid-19 positive patients and normal patients. A balanced dataset comprising 1824 chest X-rays of both covid-19 and normal patients are considered [11] Fig. 1 shows sample chest x-rays of Covid-19 patient and normal patient. The hazy lung opacity that obscures the vessels and bronchial walls is a major feature that distinguishes Covid-19 positive x-rays from normal once.

3.2   Transfer Learning

Transfer Learning is one of the advanced deep learning approaches in which a model trained on similar problem is used as a starting point for the other similar problems. It decreases training time in neural network for optimization of tuning hyper parameters. One or more layers from the trained model are used in new model and some are freezed and fine tuning is applied to other output layers which are to be customized. Figure 2 shows the working of Transfer Learning technique. The popular methods of this approach are - VGG (VGG 16 or 19), GoogleNet (Inception v1 or v3), Residual Network (ResNet50), CheXNet. Keras provides access to a number of such pretrained models. In transfer learning initially Convolution Neural Networks (CNN) are trained on datasets and then they are employed to process new set of images and extract the features. In medical related tasks we use transfer learning to exploit CNN with these models and evaluate algorithms for image classification and object detection. In this section we discuss the architecture of four models VGG, GoogleNet, ResNet and CheXNet and explore their applicability using pretrained weights as part of transfer learning for Covid-19 prediction.

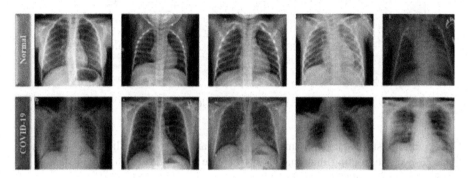

Fig. 1. Sample x-rays of Covid patient and normal patient.

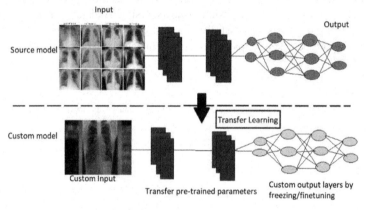

Fig. 2. Transfer learning

VGG: VGG is a CNN((Convolutional Neural Network), proposed by Karen and Andrew in 2014 [13]. The VGG 16 is deep network consisting of sixteen layers out of which thirteen layers are convolutional layers with 3 × 3 lters, and three fully connected layers. The fully-connected layers are of 4096 channels each. The stride of convolution is one pixel and padding is also one pixel value. All convolutional layers are managed as a group of three whose output is given to a max-pooling layer as shown in Fig. 3.

GoogleNet: GoogleNet was rst proposed by google research group in 2014 and is the winner of the ILSVRC 2014 Image Classification and detection competition from Google[14]. It attained a top-5 error rate of 6.67%. This model contains 22 layers deep

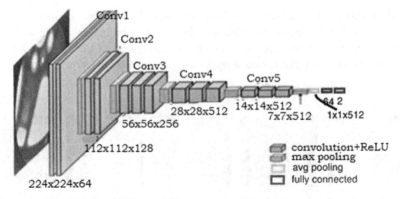

Fig. 3. Architecture of VGG16 model.

CNN and almost 12× less parameters. It uses variant strategies like 1 × 1 convolution and average pooling that enables it to create a deeper design. Fig. 4 depicts the architecture of GoogleNet model.

ResNet: ResNet abbreviation for Residual Neural Network proposed in 2015 as part of ImageNet challenge for computer vision task [15]. It was the winner of that challenge and is widely used for Computer Vision projects. Using Transfer learning concept we can train its 150 plus layers successfully. The last two or three layers that contain non linearity can be skipped. This helps to avoid gradient vanishing problem. It's architecture is shown in Fig. 5.

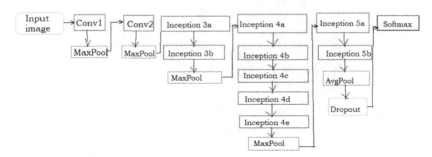

Fig. 4. Architecture of GoogleNet model.

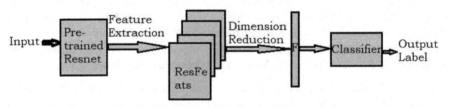

Fig. 5. Architecture of ResNet model.

CheXNet: CheXNet consists of 121 CNN layers. It produces heatmap comprising localized areas which can indicate the areas effected by the disease in the image along with the prediction probability [16]. This was developed to predict the pneumonia from chest x-rays. This model used chest X-ray14 dataset containing 14 different pathological X-ray images. It's architecture is shown below in Fig. 6. The test set labels were annotated by four reputed radiologists and was used for evaluating the performance of the model with reference to annotations given by radiologists.

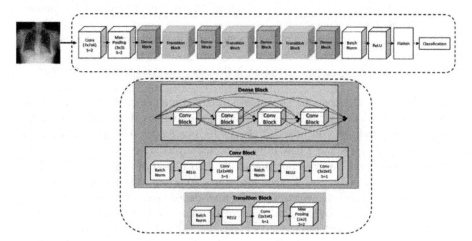

Fig. 6. Architecture of CheXNet model.

3.3 Implementation

In our paper, we performed of transfer learning models for Covid-19 prediction from x-rays. The deep architectures helped in predicting the results with good accuracies for VGG, GoogleNet, ResNet and CheXNet models. The Fig. 7 describes our proposed implementation model.

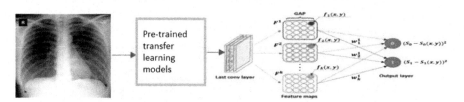

Fig. 7. Schematic representation depicting implementation of our model.

Algorithm

Step1: Load the dataset that contains 1824 images with 2 classes for binary classification.
Step 2: Resize the images in our dataset to 224 × 224, as the Transfer Learning CNN models takes input images of size 224 × 224
Step 3: Select pre trained layers from VGG/GoogleNet/ResNet/CheXNet and modify the output layers. The no of layers selected and modifications carried out are described below for each model individually.
Step 4: Fine tune the hyper parameters of each model individually and tuned parameters are indicated in Table 1
Step 5: Evaluate the performance of each model using the metrics explained in the next subsection.
Step 6: Pass a new X-ray image to detect whether the patient is having Covid-19 or not.

The VGG16 model contains 16 weight layers that include convolutional, pooling, fully connected and final dense layer. The final layer contains 1000 predictable output classes out of which we considered 2 classes for our model. This is done by freezing convolutional layers and 2 new fully connected layers are constructed. GoogleNet contains 22 layers with average pooling, all are trained and in output layer 2 softmax layers are taken for prediction. ResNet model has 50 layers with output layer capable of classifying 1000 objects. We freezed the final dense layer and added 2 layers for predicting our 2 classes covid-19 and non covid. Finally, for CheXNet we considered DenseNet121 network with pre trained weights and freezed the CONV weights. Then, new fully connected sigmoid layers are constructed and appended at top of DenseNet.

4   Results and Description

4.1   Dataset

We had given chest x-ray images as input to our model. This data is divided in 8:2 ratio in our model i.e. 80% for training the model and 20% for model validation. We also tested with other images. The resizing is done to a default image size (224, 224).

Table 1. Hyper parameters used in different models

Hyper parameters	Values			
	VGG	GoogleNet	ResNet	CheXNet
Epochs	30	50	30	10
Activation function	Softmax	ReLU	ReLU	Sigmoid
Batch size	5	20	5	5
Learning rate	1e−3	1e−1	1e−3	1e−3
Test size	0.2	0.2	0.2	0.2

4.2 Hyperparameter Tuning

The hyperparameters are tuned in order to obtain a highly performing model. We tuned around 5 different parameters which comprise of adjusting the learning rate, selection of optimizer, loss functions, changing number of epochs, batch size, test size, rotation range etc. Learning rate is given as parameter to the optimizer function. Working on different optimizer and loss function did not affected the working of the model much so we used Adam as optimizer function and binary cross entropy as loss function throughout the model. Batch size is the number of samples that will be propagated through the network and epochs is the number of times the model is implemented on training data. Dropout is a regularisation technique where some random neurons are ignored during training. Increasing dropout generally increases accuracy. Table 1 shows the values of hyperparameters that we used for different transfer learning models.

4.3 Performance Metrics

In a model the values like accuracy, precision, recall, and F1 score are considered as performance metrics since they are used to evaluate the model performance. Accuracy is the ratio of correctly classified to the total number of predictions. Precision is the ratio of true positives to the predicted positives.

Recall is the ratio of true positives predicted out of total positives.

F1-score It is the weighted average of precision and recall.

Precision and recall are useful when the dataset is imbalanced i.e. when there is large difference between the number of X rays with Covid and without Covid.

Table 2. Performance measures of different models

Model	Accuracy	F1-measure	Precision	Recall
VGG	99.49	99	99	100
GoogleNet	99.18	99	98.3	100
ResNet	98.63	97	100	99
CheXNet	99.93	100	100	100

4.4 Result

It ends up with a good accuracy of 99.49% and the values for sensitivity, specificity as 1.0000 and 0.9890 respectively using VGG 16 model, accuracy of 99% with values for sensitivity, specificity as 1.0000 and 0.9834 respectively using GoogleNet-inception v1 model, accuracy of 98.63% with values for sensitivity, specificity as 1.0000 and 0.9725 respectively using ResNet 50 model and 99.93% accuracy with values for sensitivity, specificity as 1.000 and 1.000 respectively using CheXNet model for Covid and normal classes in Covid prediction. The performance measures of all these models is shown below in Table 2.

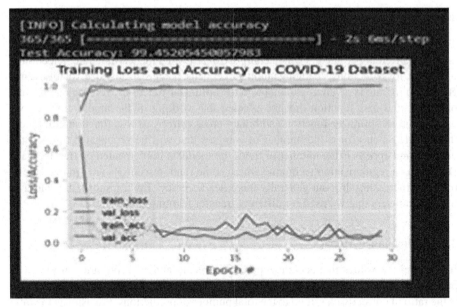

Fig. 8. Graph showing variations in different measures for VGG16 model.

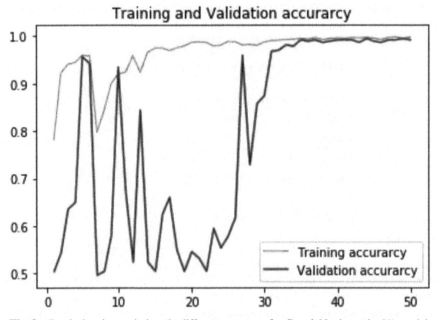

Fig. 9. Graph showing variations in different measures for GoogleNet inceptionV1 model.

Owing to the well performance of these proposed models, they can be incorporated in real-time testing which in turn increases the testing rate. The graphs in below figures, Fig. 8, 9, 10, 11 shows variation in different measures of accuracy and loss for VGG, GoogleNet, ResNet and CheXNet models.

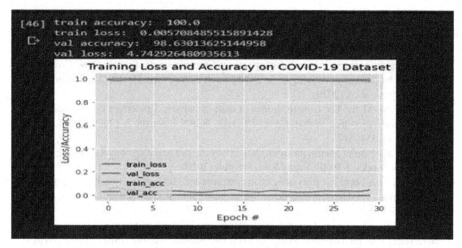

Fig. 10. Graph showing variations in different measures for ResNet50 model.

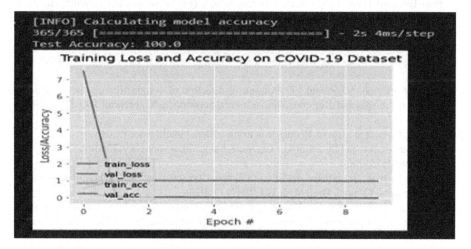

Fig. 11. Graph showing variations in different measures for CheXNet model.

5   Conclusion and Future Work

In this paper, we used transfer learning approach to train CNN using x-ray images to predict the novel Covid-19 disease. This idea can be implemented in real-time scenarios of Covid-19 detection with further developments. This can also be implemented using other transfer learning methods. Our work can be further extended to train with large datasets so that still better accuracy can be achieved even for the cases of unseen data. This can also be further enhanced to predict the possibility of survival of the covid affected patients. However the work carried in this paper can offer potential insight and will contribute towards further research regarding COVID-19 predictions.

References

1. World Health Organization: Laboratory testing for coronavirus disease 2019 (Covid-19) in suspected human cases: interim guidance, 2 March 2020. World Health Organization, World Health Organization (2020)
2. Ruiz Estrada, M.A.: The uses of drones in case of massive Epidemics contagious diseases relief humanitarian aid: Wuhan-Covid-19 crisis. SSRN Electron. J. (2020). https://doi.org/10.2139/ssrn.3546547
3. Wu, H., et al.: Predict pneumonia with chest X-ray images based on convolutional deep neural learning networks. J. Intell. Fuzzy Syst. Preprint (2020)
4. Al-Antari, M.A., et al.: A fully integrated computer-aided diagnosis system for digital X-ray mammograms via deep learning detection, segmentation, and classification. Int. J. Med. Inf. **117**, 44–54 (2018)
5. Bar, Y., et al.: Chest pathology detection using deep learning with non-medical training. In: 2015 IEEE 12th International Symposium on Biomedical Imaging (ISBI). IEEE (2015)
6. Bhandary, A., et al.: Deep-learning framework to detect lung abnormality-a study with chest X-ray and lung CT scan images. Pattern Recogn. Lett. **129**, 271–278 (2020)
7. Nasr-Esfahani, E., et al.: Vessel extraction in X-ray angiograms using deep learning. In: 2016 38th Annual International Conference of the IEEE Engineering in Medicine and Biology Society (EMBC). IEEE (2016)
8. Apostolopoulos, I.D., Mpesiana, T.A.: Covid-19: automatic detection from x-ray im-ages utilizing transfer learning with convolutional neural networks. Phys. Eng. Sci. Med. **6**, 1 (2020)
9. Narin, A., Ceren, K., Pamuk, Z.: Automatic detection of coronavirus disease (Covid-19) using x-ray images and deep convolutional neural networks. arXiv preprint arXiv:2003.10849 (2020)
10. Salman, F.M., et al.: Covid-19 detection using artificial intelligence (2020)
11. http://md-datasets-public-les-prod.s3.eu-west-1.amazonaws.com/bc9f750d-b663-48a7-844e-4e8246751706
12. Ozturk, T., et al.: Automated detection of Covid-19 cases using deep neural networks with X-ray images. Comput. Biol. Med. **121**, 103792 (2020)
13. Simonyan, K., Zisserman, A.: Very deep convolutional networks for large-scale image recog-nition. In: 3rd International Conference on Learning Representations, ICLR 2015, San Diego, 7–9 May 2015 (2015)
14. Szegedy, C., et al.: Going deeper with convolutions. In: Proceedings of IEEE Conference on Computer Vision and Pattern Recognition (2015)
15. He, K., Zhang, X., Ren, S., Sun, J.: Deep residual learning for image recognition. In: Proceedings of IEEE Conference on Computer Vision and Pattern Recognition (CVPR) (2016)
16. Rajpurkar, P., et al.: CheXNet: radiologist-level pneumonia detection on chest X-rays with deep learning. In: Proceedings of IEEE Conference on Computer Vision and Pattern Recognition (2017)

Machine Learning Based Prediction of H1N1 and Seasonal Flu Vaccination

Srividya Inampudi[1]([⊠]), Greshma Johnson[2], Jay Jhaveri[3], S. Niranjan[4], Kuldeep Chaurasia[5], and Mayank Dixit[5]

[1] Fr. Conceicao Rodrigues Institute of Technology, Vashi, Navi Mumbai, India
srivi2k@gmail.com
[2] Saintgits College of Engineering, Kottayam, India
[3] Vivekanand Education Society's Institute of Technology, Mumbai, India
[4] Sri Ramakrishna Engineering College, Coimbatore, India
[5] School of Engineering and Applied Sciences, Bennett University, Delhi, India

Abstract. The H1N1 Flu that came into existence in 2009 had a great impact on the lives of people around the world. It was a life-threatening season to hundreds of people mainly below 65 years old which eventually made the World Health Organization (WHO) to declare it as the greatest pandemic in more than 40 years. To find out the vaccination status National 2009 H1N1 Flu Survey (NHFS) was conducted in U.S. In this paper, the data from the above survey was used to develop a model that predicts how likely people got H1N1 and seasonal flu vaccine. For this purpose, various Machine Learning (ML) and Artificial Neural Network (ANN) models are used to determine the probability of person receiving H1N1 and Seasonal Flu vaccine.

Keywords: Machine learning · H1N1 · Seasonal flu · SVM

1 Introduction

H1N1 or swine flu virus first emerged in 2009, spring season in Mexico and then in the United States and quickly spread across the globe. A distinctive combination or integration of influenza genes was discovered in this novel H1N1 virus which was not identified prior in humans or animals [1]. This contagious novel virus had a very powerful impact on the whole world and spread across the world like a forest fire and as a result on June 11 2009 the World Health Organization (WHO) declared that a pandemic of 2009 H1N1 flu or swine flu had begun [2]. The effects of this novel H1N1 virus were more severe on people below the age of 65. There was significantly high pediatric mortality, and higher rate of hospitalizations for young adults and children [3].

According to Centres for Disease Control and Prevention (CDC) the first and foremost step in protecting oneself of this virus is a yearly flu vaccination [4]. There are various factors such as age, health perceptions of an individual and the similarities or "match" in the vaccine's virus structure and the virus structure which is affecting the community which affects the ability of the vaccination to provide protection to the person who is vaccinated [5]. Several activities were performed using various social media

D. Garg et al. (Eds.): IACC 2020, CCIS 1367, pp. 139–150, 2021.
https://doi.org/10.1007/978-981-16-0401-0_11

platforms and broadcasting networks such as Twitter was used to track the levels of disease activity and the concern of the public towards this pandemic [6]. The social media played an important role to assess the sentiments towards vaccination and the implications for disease dynamics and control [7] etc. The popular among them is the phone survey conducted by the U.S. where they asked respondents whether they had received the H1N1 and seasonal flu vaccines, in conjunction with questions about themselves.

In the present study, we used the data obtained from the National 2009 H1N1 Flu Survey (NHFS) to predict how likely people got H1N1 and seasonal flu vaccines. The NHFS data is used for estimating the probability of a person receiving H1N1 and Seasonal Flu vaccine using various Machine Learning (ML) and Artificial Neural Network (ANN) models. The performance of various ML and ANN techniques are also discussed. In Sect. 2 literature review is presented. Section 3 discusses the data resource i.e. NHFS survey and Sect. 4 presents the methodology used. Section 5 discusses the results obtained and Sects. 6 and 7 presents conclusion and future research scope.

2   Literature Review

Mabrouk et al. [8] "A chaotic study on pandemic and classical (H1N1) using EIIP sequence indicators", states that the methods such as moment invariants, correlation dimension, and largest Lyapunov exponent which were used to detect H1N1 indicated the differences between the pandemic and classical influenza virus. Chinh et al. [9] "A possible mutation that enables the H1N1 influenza A virus to escape antibody recognition" explained the methods such as phylogenetic analysis of pandemic strains, molecular docking for the predicted epitopes. Huang et al. [10], "Aptamer-modified CNTFET (Carbon NanoTube Field Effect Transistors) biosensor for detecting H1N1 virus in a droplet," suggested the combination immersed in nanotube which gives CNTFET and thus it acts as a biosensor which is used in the detection of H1N1 virus by droplet.

M. S. Ünlü [11], "Optical interference for multiplexed, label-free, and dynamic biosensing: Protein, DNA and single virus detection," described interferometric reflectance imaging sensor which can be used for label-free, high throughput, high sensitivity and dynamic detection and gives detection of H1N1 virus and nanoparticles and Kamikawa et al. [12] "Pandemic influenza detection by electrically active magnetic nanoparticles and surface plasmon resonance" indicated that the detection consists of several processes such as nanoparticle synthesis, glycans, polyaniline, and sensor modification by means to find H1N1 by nanoparticle and resonance. Jerald et al. [13], "Influenza virus vaccine efficacy based on conserved sequence alignment," spoke about the vital strain sequence used from National Center for Biotechnology Information (NCBI) and sequence alignment which helps vaccine efficiency for influenza.

Chrysostomou, et al. [14] "Signal-processing-based bioinformatics approach for the identification of influenza A virus subtypes in Neuraminidase genes" discussed the methods used for identification of influenza virus such as neuraminidase genes, signal processing, F-score, Support Vector Machines (SVM) and Wiriyachaiporn et al. [15] "Rapid influenza an antigen detection using carbon nano string as the label for lateral flow immune chromatographic assay," presented preparation of allantoic fluid infected with influenza A virus conjugation of Central Nervous System (CNS) to antibody and about the evaluation of CBNS-MAb using Lateral Flow Immunoassay (LFIA) and Ma et al. [16], "An integrated passive microfluidic device for rapid detection of influenza a (H1N1) virus by reverse transcription loop-mediated isothermal amplification (RT-LAMP)" demonstrated the loading of virus and magnetic beads and discussed about virus capture, collection of virus-magnetic beads complexes, removal of excessive wastes, virus particle lysis, RT-LAMP reaction and the coloration steps to detect H1N1 virus.

Nieto-Chaupis, Huber. [17]. "Face To Face with Next Flu Pandemic with a Wiener-Series-Based Machine Learning: Fast Decisions to Tackle Rapid Spread" explained about the Wiener model used in order to increase optimization, efficiency and performance to find the spread of seasonal flu and Stalder et al. [18] "Tracking the flu pandemic by monitoring the social web" related the retrieving data from Twitter and official health reports provides inexpensive and timely information about the epidemic and Motoyama et al. [19] "Predicting Flu Trends using Twitter Data" demonstrated the use of SNEFT model and twitter crawler methods for predicting the flu using twitter data.

Wong et al. [20] "Diagnosis of Response Behavioural Patterns Towards the Risk of Pandemic Flu Influenza A (H1N1) of Urban Community Based on Rasch Measurement Model" presented the source of data and data analysis methodology used for the response behavioral patterns towards H1N1 and Bao et al. [21] "Influenza-A Circulation in Vietnam through data analysis of Hemagglutinin entries" provided NCBI influenza virus resource datasets (2001–2012) which is used for the analysis of influenza virus and Hu et al. [22], "Computational Study of Interdependence Between Hemagglutinin and Neuraminidase of Pandemic 2009 H1N1" explained sequence data and informational spectrum model.

3 Data Resources

Data is one of the most important and vital aspect of any research study. The National Flue Survey (NFS) is being conducted since 2010–11 influenza season [23]. The data for our study is obtained from the National 2009 H1N1 Flu Survey (NHFS) which was carried out for Centres for Disease Control and Prevention (CDC). The main aim of the survey was to monitor and evaluate H1N1 flu vaccination efforts among adults and children. The survey was conducted through telephones, twitter and with the help of various other electronic media in all the 50 states. The survey consists of national random digit dialed telephone survey based on rolling weekly sample of landline and cellular telephone contacted to identify residential households. Various questions about flu related behaviors, opinions about flu vaccine's safety and effectiveness, medical history like recent respiratory illness and pneumococcal vaccination status were asked apart from the major question about H1N1 and seasonal flu vaccination status. The NHFS data was collected during Oct., 2009 to May, 2010. This data was obtained to get a fair idea about the knowledge of people on the effectiveness and safety of flu vaccines and to learn why some people refrained from getting vaccinated against the H1N1 flu and seasonal flu. Huge amount of data was gathered through this survey which is being commonly used for analysis and research purposes and the data also measures the number of children and adults nationwide who have received vaccinations.

4   Methodology

A methodology is proposed to determine the probability that a person will receive H1N1 and seasonal Flu vaccination based on many parameters. The data obtained from the National 2009 H1N1 Flu Survey (NHFS) contains 3 CSV files namely the training set features, the training set labels, and the test set features. The data has been obtained from over 53000 people from which around 26000 observations have been considered for the training set and the rest have been considered for the testing set.

We have considered various methodologies and compared different Machine Learning and Artificial Neural Network models to predict the probability. The Machine Learning algorithms such as Multiple Linear regression, Support Vector Regression, Random Forest Regression and Logistic Regression were used. The system architecture of Machine Learning model is presented in Fig. 1.

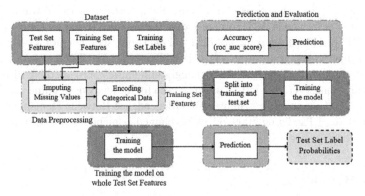

Fig. 1. System architecture of machine learning model

Artificial Neural Network (ANN) with different optimizers such as Adam, RMSprop, SGD were used to predict the probability of the test set features. The system architecture of ANN is presented in Fig. 2.

4.1   Taking Care of Missing Data

The missing data values in the dataset were imputed by univariate feature imputation using the most frequent strategy (statistics) with the help of the Simple Imputer class from the sklearn.impute module. This Simple Imputer class provides fundamental strategies for assigning some value for the missing values in the columns of the dataset [24, 25].

4.2   Encoding Categorical Data

For encoding categorical data the columns are transformed separately and then the features generated during this transformation of columns are concatenated to a single feature space and this process is carried out with the help of Column Transformer class of sklearn.compose module. Heterogeneous or columnar data is most benefited from this

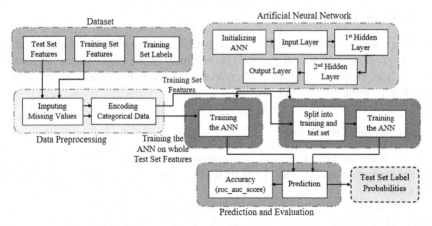

Fig. 2. System architecture of artificial neural network

method as several feature extraction mechanisms can be combined together or it gets transformed into a one transformer [24]. Then the categorical data is encoded using the One Hot Encoder class of the sklearn.preprocessing module. The features are encoded using an encoding scheme. A binary column is created in this method for every category. A sparse matrix or a dense array is returned depending on the sparse parameter [25].

4.3 Splitting the Dataset

The training set features and training set labels have been split into training set (80%) and testing set (20%) using train_test_split from sklearn.model_selection. This library splits the dataset into training and testing sets.

4.4 Hyperparameter Tuning

Hyperparameter tuning is done to find the most optimal parameter for the model on which the model gives the best results. We have used various Hyperparameter tuning methods such as GridseacrchCV, RandomSearchCV for our machine learning models to obtain better results. K fold cross Validation method has been used to tune hyperparameters for the Artificial Neural Network.

4.5 Training the Model on the Dataset

An open-source Python library scikit-learn is used which uses a unified interface to implement many machine learning, preprocessing, cross-validation, and visualization algorithms [26]. Scikit-learn can be used for both supervised and unsupervised learning, using a consistent, task-oriented interface [24].

In scikit-learn all supervised estimators implement a fit(X, y) method to fit the model i.e. to train a model and a predict(X) is a method that gives predicted labels y for given unlabelled observations X.

4.6 Predicting the Results

Given the training model, we have predicted the label output for the test set features using the predict function of the model. Probabilities of the labels of test set features have also been predicted using the predict_proba method. In this predict_proba method, the highest probability is returned [24, 27].

4.7 Evaluation of the Results

There are various evaluation methods available to measure the performance and the quality of the prediction made by the model such as roc_auc_score(), r2_score(), Confusion Matrix, etc.

In our implementation, we have used the roc_auc_score() method from the sklearn.metrics library. roc_auc_score metric is essentially defined for binary classification tasks. In this by default the positive class labeled is 1 and only the positive labelled class is evaluated. Then the roc_auc_socre function computes the area under the curve by this the curve information can be summarized in one number which is denoted as AUC or AUROC [24, 27].

5 Results and Discussion

5.1 H1N1 and Seasonal Flu Vaccination

In the default models the best performing method on the dataset has been the Artificial Neural Network method with 2 hidden layers and activation function being selu and the optimizer being Stochastic Gradient Descent (SGD) optimizer. The sigmoid function is used in the output layer for activation function. The accuracy obtained with ANN is shown in Table 1. Other Machine Learning algorithms have also yielded comparatively good results except logistic regression which has been the worst performing model with accuracy less than 70% in both H1N1 flu and seasonal flu vaccination prediction. Comparison of all the methods used during implementation are presented in Table 1.

The Results are also plotted using the ROC AUC curve. In Figs. 3, 4, 5 and 6 we can observe the performance of various models on the dataset and it can be concluded that Artificial Neural Network method has performed the best with accuracy over 82% in H1N1 flu vaccination prediction and 86% in Seasonal flu vaccination prediction.

5.2 H1N1 and Seasonal Flu Vaccination in ML Models with Hyperparameter Tuning

To obtain better results tuning of parameters has been carried out. Various methods such as GridSearchCV, RandomSearchCV, kfold method were used for hyperparameter tuning of the Machine Learning models. It is learnt that Support Vector Machine with Radial Basis Function (RBF) kernel and C:20 using the GridSearchCV method yields the best result for H1N1 vaccination prediction as shown in Table 2. The optimal parameters for

Table 1. Results for H1N1 flu and Seasonal flu vaccination prediction

Model	H1N1 score	Seasonal flu score	Parameters
svm	0.8085	0.8596	{'kernel':'rbf'}
random_forest	0.8154	0.8494	{'n_estimators': 100}
logistic_regression	0.6792	0.5949	{max_iter=1000}
ANN	0.8257	0.8601	{'1st hidden layer: 'units=60, activation='selu" '2nd hidden layer: 'units=30, activation='selu" output layer: 'units=1, activation='sigmoid" 'optimizer='SGD', loss='binary_crossentropy"}

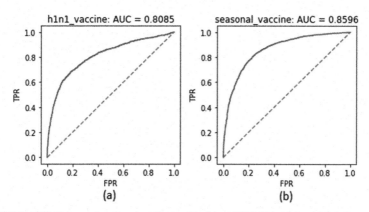

Fig. 3. ROC AUC Curve using Support Vector Machine: RBF Kernel for (a) h1n1 vaccine and (b) seasonal flu vaccine

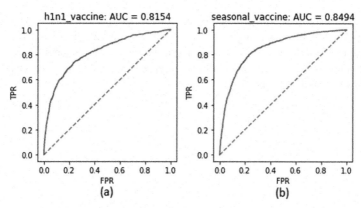

Fig. 4. ROC AUC Curve using Random Forest Regressor for (a) h1n1 vaccine and (b) seasonal flu vaccine

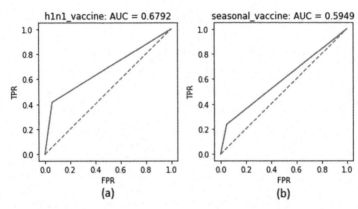

Fig. 5. ROC AUC Curve using Logistic Regression for (a) h1n1 vaccine and (b) seasonal flu vaccine

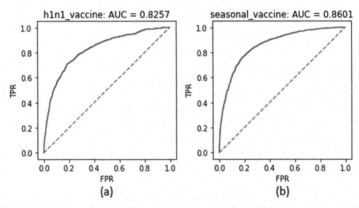

Fig. 6. ROC AUC Curve using Artificial Neural Network for (a) h1n1 vaccine and (b) seasonal flu vaccine

random forest regression are training the model with '10' n_estimators, and the optimal parameters for logistic regression is C:5. All these results are presented in tabulated form in Table 2 and Table 3. It is observed that the results of Seasonal flu vaccination prediction have not been upto the mark using hyperparameter tuning, they were better predicted using the default models.

Table 2. Results with Hyperparameter tuning (GridSearchCV) for H1N1 flu vaccination prediction

Model	H1N1 score	Seasonal flu score	Parameters
svm	0.8397	0.7836	{'C':20, 'Kernel': 'rbf'}
random_forest	0.8213	0.7504	{'n_estimators': 10}
logistic_regression	0.8363	0.7799	{'C': 5}

Table 3. Results with Hyperparameter tuning (RandomSearchCV) for H1N1 flu vaccination prediction

Model	H1N1 score	Seasonal flu score	Parameters
svm	0.8367	0.7836	{'Kernel': 'rbf', 'C':20}
random_forest	0.8205	0.7467	{'n_estimators': 10}
logistic_regression	0.8363	0.7799	{'C':5}

5.3 H1N1 and Seasonal Flu Vaccination in Artificial Neural Network with Hyperparameter Tuning

Kfold method is used to fine tune hyperparameters in the Artificial Neural Network method. The obtained results are more or less equal to the default method but a marginal increase in performance is noted which can be clearly seen in Table 4. The most optimal parameters obtained for ANN with kfold method are 1st hidden layer with selu as activation function and having 60 units, the 2nd hidden layer with selu as activation function and having 3 units, and the output layer with sigmoid as activation function and having 2 units. All the results are presented in Table 4.

Table 4. Results with Hyperparameter tuning (kfold method) for H1N1 flu and Seasonal vaccination prediction

Model	Best score	Parameters
ANN	0.8323	{'1st hidden layer: 'units=60, activation='selu'' '2nd hidden layer: 'units=3, activation='selu'' output layer: 'units=2, activation='sigmoid'' 'n_splits'=10, 'shuffle'='True', 'optimizer'='SGD', loss='binary_crossentropy''}

6   Conclusion

In this paper, prediction of H1N1 and seasonal flu vaccination are carried out using the data source given by the National 2009 H1N1 flu survey (NHFS) for Center of Disease Control and Prevention (CDC). Various ML and ANN models are used for predition of H1N1 and Seasonal Flu vaccination. The model studies are improved using several techniques such as taking care of missing data, encoding categorical data, hyperparameter tuning and splitting of data set for training and testing purposes. The results obtained from various models are compared and evaluated. The results indicated that prediction of H1N1 vaccination is done best by the help of SVM model with RBF kernel with the help of hyperparameter tuning using GridSearchCV which yielded an accuracy of 83.97% and seasonal flu vaccination prediction is done best with Artificial Neural Network which yielded an accuracy of 86.10%.

7   Future Research Scope

Although we have achieved promising results, our study has many limitations. Mainly, the use of Twitter for data collection is not uniform across time and geography. Due to this inconsistency in the data our model's performance may vary and suffer. The accuracy difference can be noticed among the regional level and national level pertaining to the fact that people of the same region usually tend to have the same behavioural aspects hence lack of proper data could tamper the implementation. In future with advancements in technology the quality and the quantity of data could increase which could result in better performance and analysis of the issue. More information about the seasons, especially non-pandemic seasons could be very helpful for analysis of this project. In future we also look forward to exploring more Machine Learning algorithms, methods and deep learning techniques to obtain more optimal results.

Acknowledgement. The work presented in this paper is carried out as part of Internship project at Bennett University, Noida, India. Success of our Internship Project involving such high technical proficiency requires patience and massive support of guides. We take this opportunity to express our gratitude to those who have been instrumental in the successful completion of this work. Big thanks to Dr. Madhushi Verma for all the encouragement, timely details and guidelines given to our team. We would also like to thank Dr. Deepak Garg, HOD of Computer Science Engineering Department and Dr. Sudhir Chandra, Dean, School of Engineering & Applied Sciences, Bennett University for giving us the opportunity and the environment to learn and grow.

References

1. CDC. https://www.cdc.gov/flu/pandemic-resources/2009-h1n1-pandemic.html. Accessed 21 June 2020
2. CDC. https://www.cdc.gov/h1n1flu/qa.htm. Accessed 22 May 2020
3. CDC. https://www.cdc.gov/mmwr/preview/mmwrhtml/mm5929a2.htm. Accessed 22 May 2020
4. CDC. https://www.cdc.gov/h1n1flu/. Accessed 22 May 2020

5. CDC. https://www.cdc.gov/flu/pastseasons/0910season.htm. Accessed 22 May 2020
6. Signorini, A., Segre, A.M., Polgreen, P.M.: The use of Twitter to track levels of disease activity and public concern in the U.S. during the influenza A H1N1 pandemic. PLoS ONE **6**(5), e19467 (2011)
7. Marcel, S., Khandelwal, S.: Assessing vaccination sentiments with online social media: implications for infectious disease dynamics and control. PLoS Comput. Biol. **7**(10), e1002199 (2011)
8. Mabrouk, M.S., Marzouk, S.Y.: A chaotic study on pandemic and classical (H1N1) using EIIP sequence indicators. In: Proceedings of 2nd International Conference on Computer Technology and Development, Cairo, pp. 218–221 (2010)
9. Chinh, T.T.S., Stephanus, D.S., Kwoh, C., Schönbach, C., Li, X.: A possible mutation that enables H1N1 influenza a virus to escape antibody recognition. In: Proceedings of IEEE International Conference on Bioinformatics and Biomedicine (BIBM), Hong Kong, pp. 81–84 (2010)
10. Huang, J., Lin, T., Chang, W., Hsieh, W: Aptamer-modified CNTFET biosensor for detecting H1N1 virus in droplet. In: Proceedings of 4th IEEE International NanoElectronics Conference, Tao-Yuan, pp. 1–2 (2011)
11. Ünlü, M.S.: Optical interference for multiplexed, label-free, and dynamic biosensing: Protein, DNA and single virus detection. In: Proceedings of XXXth URSI General Assembly and Scientific Symposium, Istanbul, pp. 1–2 (2011)
12. Kamikawa, T., et al.: Pandemic influenza detection by electrically active magnetic nanoparticles and surface plasmon resonance, nanotechnology. IEEE Trans. Nanotechnol. **11**, 88–96 (2012)
13. Baby Jerald, A., Gopalakrishnan Nair, T.R.: Influenza virus vaccine efficacy based on conserved sequence alignment. In: Proceedings of International Conference on Biomedical Engineering (ICoBE), Penang, pp. 327–329 (2012)
14. Chrysostomou, C., Seker, H.: Signal-processing-based bioinformatics approach for the identification of influenza A virus subtypes in Neuraminidase genes. In: Proceedings of 35th Annual International Conference of the IEEE Engineering in Medicine and Biology Society (EMBC), pp. 3066–3069 (2013)
15. Wiriyachaiporn, N., Sirikett, H., Dharakul, T.: Rapid influenza a antigen detection using carbon nanostrings as label for lateral flow immunochromatographic assay. In: Proceedings of 13th IEEE International Conference on Nanotechnology (IEEE-NANO 2013), Beijing, pp. 166–169 (2013)
16. Ma, Y., Chang, W., Wang, C., Ma, H., Huang P., Lee, G.: An integrated passive microfluidic device for rapid detection of influenza a (H1N1) virus by reverse transcription loop-mediated isothermal amplification (RT-LAMP). In: Proceedings of 19th International Conference on Solid-State Sensors, Actuators and Microsystems (TRANSDUCERS), Kaohsiung, pp. 722–725 (2017)
17. Nieto-Chaupis, H.: Face to face with next flu pandemic with a wiener-series-based machine learning: fast decisions to tackle rapid spread, pp. 0654–0658 (2019). https://doi.org/10.1109/CCWC.2019.8666474
18. Stalder, F., Hirsh, J.: Open source intelligence. First Monday **7**(6), 416 (2002)
19. Motoyama, M., Meeder, B., Levchenko, K., Voelker, G.M., Savage, S.: Measuring online service availability using Twitter. In: Proceedings of Workshop on online social networks, Boston, Massachusetts, USA (2010)
20. Wong, L.P., Sam, I.C.: Behavioral responses to the influenza A (H1N1) outbreak in Malaysia. J. Commun. Health **34**, 23–31 (2011)
21. Bao, Y., et al.: The influenza virus resource at the national center for biotechnology information. J. Virol. **82**(2), 596–601 (2008)

22. Hu, W.: Molecular features of highly pathogenic Avian and Human H5N1 Influenza a viruses in Asia. Comput. Mol. Biosci. **2**(2), 45–59 (2012)

23. Smith, P.J., Wood, D., Darden, P.M.: Highlights of historical events leading to national surveillance of vaccination coverage in the United States. Public Health Rep. **126**(Suppl 2), 3–12 (2011)

24. Pedregosa, F., et al.: Scikit-learn: machine learning in Python. J. Mach. Learn. Res. **12**, 2825–2830 (2012)

25. Buitinck, L., et al.: API design for machine learning software: experiences from the scikit-learn project (2013)

26. Dubosson, F., Bromuri, S., Schumacher, M.: A python framework for exhaustive machine learning algorithms and features evaluations. In: Proceedings of IEEE 30th International Conference on Advanced Information Networking and Applications (AINA), Crans-Montana, pp. 987–993 (2016)

27. Virtanen, P., Gommers, R., Oliphant, T.E., et al.: SciPy 1.0: fundamental algorithms for scientific computing in Python. Nat Methods **17**, 261–272 (2020)

A Model for Heart Disease Prediction Using Feature Selection with Deep Learning

Vaishali Baviskar[1], Madhushi Verma[2]([✉]), and Pradeep Chatterjee[3]

[1] GHRIET, Pune, India
vaishali.baviskar@raisoni.net
[2] Bennett University, Greater Noida, India
madhushi.verma@bennett.edu.in
[3] Tata Motors, Pune, India
pchats2000@yahoo.com

Abstract. The heart disease is considered as the most widespread disease. It is challenging for most of the physicians to diagnose at an early stage to avoid the risk of death rate. The main objective of this study involves the prediction of heart disease by using efficient techniques based on feature selection and classification. For feature selection, the enhanced genetic algorithm (GA) and particle swarm optimization (PSO) have been implemented. For classification, the recurrent neural network (RNN) and long short term memory (LSTM) has been implemented in this study. The data set used is the Cleveland heart disease data set available on UCI machine learning repository, and the performance of the proposed techniques has been evaluated by using various metrics like accuracy, precision, recall and f-measure. Finally, the results thus obtained have been compared with the existing models in terms of accuracy. It has been observed that LSTM when combined with PSO showed an accuracy of 93.5% whereas the best known existing model had an accuracy of 93.33%. Therefore, the proposed approach can be applied in the medical field for accurate heart disease prediction.

Keywords: Heart disease prediction · Deep neural network · Long short term memory · Recurrent neural network · Genetic algorithm · Particle swarm optimization

1 Introduction

In the research field, heart disease has created a lot of serious concerns, and the significant challenge is accurate detection or prediction at an early stage to minimize the risk of death. According to World Health Organization (WHO) [1], the medical professionals have predicted only 67% of heart diseases correctly and hence there exists a vast research scope in the area of heart disease prediction. A lot of technicalities and parameters are involved in predicting the diseases

© Springer Nature Singapore Pte Ltd. 2021
D. Garg et al. (Eds.): IACC 2020, CCIS 1367, pp. 151–168, 2021.
https://doi.org/10.1007/978-981-16-0401-0_12

accurately. Various machine learning, deep learning algorithms and several optimization techniques have been used to predict the heart-disease risk. All these techniques mainly focus on the higher accuracy which shows the importance of correct prediction of heart disease. It would be helpful for the doctors to predict the heart disease at an early stage and save millions of life from death [2]. For temporal sequenced data, the recurrent neural network (RNN) models are best suited and for sequenced features, several variants have been chosen. In various sequence based tasks like language modelling, handwriting recognition, and for other such as tasks, long short term memory (LSTM) has been used, which shows an impressive performance [3,4]. For better performance, evolutionary algorithms (EAs) are used for model optimization. The evolutionary algorithm related to self-adaptability based on population is very useful in case of feature selection and extraction. The EAs used in the recent year include ant colony optimization (ACO), particle swarm optimization (PSO) and genetic algorithm (GA). The GA is considered as a stochastic method for optimization and global search, which is very helpful in handling the medical data. The possible solutions are obtained from set of individuals using GA. GA which are generally used to create solutions with a better quality for global search and optimization are based on the mutation, crossover and selection operators. The PSO-a meta heuristic algorithm is considered in this study due to its simplicity and ease implementation. It uses only few parameters and required few numbers of parameters tuning. The PSO exhibits the information sharing mechanism and population-based methods, and hence it extended from single to multi-objective optimization. It has been successfully applied in the medical field for heart disease prediction and recorded good performances [5,6]. The main contribution of this study involves,

- Improve the accuracy of the prediction of heart disease in human using efficient feature selection and classification methods.
- Implementing the GA and PSO for efficient feature selection.
- Implementing the RNN and LSTM to improve an accuracy for heart disease prediction.
- Compared performance of the proposed method with the existing techniques in terms of an accuracy, precision, recall and f-measure.

The remaining organization of the paper is as follows: Sect. 2 includes the literature survey of the existing research work related to feature selection techniques and deep learning classification methods for heart disease prediction. Section 3 discusses the implementation process of the GA and PSO optimization algorithm and LSTM and RNN classification. Section 4 discusses the performance analysis of the proposed work. The conclusion has been presented in Sect. 5.

2   Related Work

In [7], researchers proved that optimization algorithms are necessary for an efficient heart disease diagnosis and also for their level estimation. They used support vector machine (SVM) and generated an optimization function using the GA for the selection of more substantial features to identify the heart disease. The data set used in this research is a Cleveland heart disease database. G. T. Reddy et al. developed an adaptive GA with fuzzy logic design (AGAFL) in [8], which in turn helps the medical practitioners for heart disease diagnose at an early stage. Using the hybrid AGAFL classifier, the heart disease has been predicted, and this research has been performed on UCI heart disease data sets. For diagnosing the coronary artery disease, usually angiography method is used, but it shows significant side effects and highly expensive. The alternative modalities have been found by using the data mining and machine learning techniques stated in [9], where the coronary artery disease diagnosis is done with the more accurate hybrid techniques with increased performance of neural network and used GA to enhance its accuracy. For this research work, Z-Alizadeh Sani data set is used and yields above 90% values in specificity, accuracy and sensitivity. In [10], researchers proposed trained recurrent fuzzy neural network (RFNN) based on GA for heart disease prediction. The data set named UCI Cleveland heart disease is used. From the testing set, 97.78% accuracy has been resulted. For large data related to health diagnosis, the machine learning has been considered as an effective support system. Generally to analyze this kind of massive data more execution time and resources have required. Effective feature selection algorithm has been proposed by J. Vijayashree et al. in [11] to identify the significant features which contribute more in disease diagnosis. Hence to identify the best solution in reduced time the PSO has been implemented. The PSO also removes the redundant and irrelevant features in addition to selecting the important features in the given data set. Novel fitness function for PSO has been designed in this work using the support vector machine (SVM) to solve the optimal weight selection issue for velocity and position of particle's updation. Finally, the optimization algorithms show the merit of handling the difficult non-linear problems with adaptability and flexibility. To improve the heart disease classification quality, the Fast correlation based feature selection namely (FCBF) method used in [12] by Y. Khourdifi et al. to enhance the classification of heart disease and also filter the redundant feature. The classification based on SVM, random forest, MLP, K-Nearest neighbor, the artificial neural network optimized using the PSO mixed with an ant colony optimization (ACO) techniques, have been applied on heart disease data set. It resulted in robustness and efficacy by processing the heart disease classification. By using data mining and artificial intelligence, the heart disease has been predicted but for lesser time and cost in [13], which focused on PSO and neural network feed forward back propagation method by using the feature ranking on the disease's effective factors presented in Cleveland clinical database. After evaluating the selected features, the result shows that the proposed classified methods resulted in best accuracy. In [14], for the risk prediction of diseases, machine learning algorithm plays a major role. The prediction accuracy influenced by attribute selection in the data set. The performance metric of Mathew's correlation co-efficient has been considered. For attribute selection performance, the altered PSO has been applied. N. S. R. Pillai et al. in [15] using the deep RNNs the language model like technique demonstrated to predict high-risk diagnosis patients (prognosis prediction) named as PP-RNNs. Several RNNs used by this proposed PP-RNN for learning from the patient's diagnosis code to predict the high risk disease existences and achieved a higher accuracy. In [16], M. S. Islam et al. suggested grey wolf optimization algorithm (GWO) combined with RNN, which has been used for predicting medical disease. The irrelevant and redundant attributes removed by feature selection using GWO. The feature dimensionality problem avoided by RNN classifier in which different diseases have been predicted. In this study, UCI data sets used and enhanced an accuracy in disease prediction obtained from Cleveland data set. From the structured and unstructured medical data, deep learning techniques exhibited the hidden data. In [17], researchers used the LSTM for predicting the cardio vascular disease (CVD) risk factors, and it generally yields better Mathew's correlation co-efficient (MCC) as 0.90 and accuracy as 95% compared with the existing methods. Compared with other statistical machine learning algorithms, the LSTM based proposed module shows best performance in the CVD risk factors' prediction. Based on novel LSTM deep learning method in [18], helped in predicting the heart failure at an early stage. Compared with general methods like SVM, logistic regression, MLP and KNN, the proposed LSTM method shows superior performance. Due to mental anxiety also CVD occurs, which may increase in COVID-19 lock down period. In [19], researchers proposed an automated tool which has used RNN for health care assistance system. From previous health records of patients for detecting the cardiac problems, the stacked bi-directional LSTM layer has been used. Cardiac troubles predicted with 93.22% accuracy from the obtained experimental results. In [21], Senthilkumar Mohan et al. proposed a hybrid machine learning technique for an effective prediction of heart disease. A new method which finds major features to improve the accuracy in the cardiovascular prediction with different feature's combinations and several known classification techniques. Machine learning techniques were used in this work to process raw data and provided a new and novel discernment towards heart disease. The challenges are seen in existing studies exhibited as,

- In the medical field, the challenging requirement is, training data in a large amount is necessary to avoid the over-fitting issue. Towards the majority samples, predictions are biased if the data set is imbalanced and hence over-fitting occurs.
- Through the tuning of hyper parameters such as activation functions, learning rates and network architecture, the deep learning algorithms are optimized. However, the hyper-parameters selection is a long process as several values are interdependent, and multiple trials are required.
- Significant memory and computational resources are required for timely completion assurance. Also, need to improve an accuracy of Cleveland heart disease data set using deep learning with feature selection techniques.

3   Methodology

The main purpose of this study is to predict the heart disease in human. The proposed workflow is shown in Fig. 1, which starts with the collection of dataset, data pre-processing, implementing the PSO and GA significantly for feature selection and for classification, RNN and LSTM classifiers used. At last, the proposed model is evaluated with respect to accuracy, precision, recall and f-measure. This section describes the workflow of the proposed study.

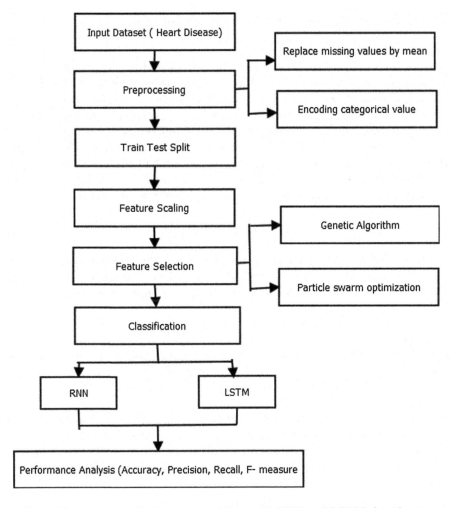

Fig. 1. Heart rate prediction proposed flow with RNN and LSTM classification

3.1 Preprocessing the Data

The data set contains 14 attributes and 303 records, where 8 are categorical and 6 are numeric attributes. Attribute of a class is zero for normal and one for having heart disease. Also, 6 records had been missing values. For pre-processing the two strategies is followed. By using features mean value; the missing values are replaced. Further the string values are changed into numerical categorical values. After filtering out such records, 297 were complete records available for the heart disease prediction.

3.2 Enhanced GA and PSO for Feature Selection

Genetic Algorithm (GA)

The GA is considered as the stochastic search algorithm that imitates natural evolutionary process using the operators which imposed upon the population. The GA algorithm used two major operators such as crossover operator and mutation operator. For individual's mating in parent population, the crossover operator is used whereas the characteristics of individual's randomly changed and diverse offspring resulted for the mutation operator. In the following algorithm 1, the offspring made systematic replacement of the generated parents. In nature the crossover of single point symmetric and through bit flipping the mutation is achieved. The expression of a minimization problem is,

$$fit = \alpha E(C) + \beta \frac{|sf|}{|Af|} \tag{1}$$

where, E(C) is the classifier's error rate, sf is the selected feature subset length and available features total count is the Af, the parameters used to control feature reduction and classification accuracy weights β is $1 - \alpha$ and $\alpha \in$ [0,1].

Selection

It selected a portion of population for next-generation breed. Based on the measured fitness values using Eq. (1) the selection is generated.

Crossover

For further breeding, randomly selected two parents from the previously selected pool. Until the suitable population size reached, the process is continued. At only one point, the crossover taken place and this is the parent solution's mid-point. The crossover probability parameter is $prob_c$ which controls the crossover frequency.

Mutation

Selected the random solutions from the chosen candidates for breeding and on these, the bit flipping has been carried out. A diverse group of solutions arise, which keeps various characteristics of their parents. The mutation probability parameter is $Prob_m$ which controls the mutation's frequency.

Table 1. Algorithm 1

1. Set the initial population-size value N, nsite, $Prob_c, Prob_m, max_{it}$
2. Initializing the population at random by $x_i = (x_{i1}, x_{i2}...x_{iD})$
3. Assess fitness of every solution using Eq. (1)
4. prevfit $\leftarrow$ fit
5. set counter=0
6. calculate fitness fitsort=sort(fit(x))
7. $x_{val} = \frac{N_{Top}}{2}(fitsort)$
8. for j in range(0,N/2)do
9. $ij = floor(\frac{N}{2} * random) + 1$
10. $ik = floor(\frac{N}{2} * random) + 1$
11. if $(Prob_c > random)$ then
12. $[x_{newval}(ij), x_{newval}(ik)] = crossover(x_{val}(ij), x_{val}(ik))$
13. Assess fitness functions for each of the new solutions using $f(x_i)$ Eq. (1)
14. if (fit < prevfit) then
15. $x = x_{newval}$
16. prevfit=fit
17. end if
18. end if
19. if $(Prob_m > random)$ then
20. select nsite no of random sites to mutate using
21. $il = floor(\frac{N}{2} * random) + 1$
22. $x_{newval}(il) = mutatex_{val}(il)$
23. Assess fitness of every solution
24. if (fit < prevfit) then
25. $x = x_{newval}$
26. prevfit=fit
27. end if
28. end if
29. x= Combine x_{val} and x_{newval}
30. end for
31. $[fit_{best}, i] = min(fit)$
32. $Sol_{best} = x(i)$
33. counter= counter+1
34. until(counter< max_{it})
35. Return Sol_{best}

GA algorithm 1 from Table 1 is described as, at first initialize the population size N, nsite, $Prob_c$, max_{it} values. Then for each solution, initialize the population randomly as $x_i = (x_{i1}, x_{i2}...x_{iD})$. The following calculations are repeated until the ending criteria is seen, i) evaluate the fitness value using $f(x_i)$ ii) breeding population selected as $x_{val} = N_{\frac{Top}{2}}(fitsort)$ iii) Taken random value and its higher than $Prob_c$, random sample mutation from x_{val} is taken iv) update the enhanced new solution with existing solution v) Taken random value and its higher than $Prob_m$, random sample mutation from x_{val} is taken vi) update the enhanced new solution with existing solution vii) combination of x_{val} and x_{newval} generated and it is considered a new solution and finally global best solution is produced considered as best found solution.

Particle Swarm Optimization (PSO)

The PSO is a population-based search technique derived from the exchange of information through birds. At first in PSO, initialize the particles' random population and based on their other particles interchange, these particles are moved with certain velocity in the population. At each iteration out of all particles, the personal, best and global best achieved and all the particles of velocity updated based on this information. To the personal, best and global, the weights are given by certain variables. The following algorithm 2 used specified transfer function type k is used for alteration of endless value to binary value, which is a substitute to basic hyperbolic tangent function. By the dimensional vector D, every particle is represented, and with every individual value, which is being binary are initialized randomly,

$$x_i = (x_{i1}, x_{i2}...x_{iD}) \in A_s \tag{2}$$

Where A_s is the search space which is available by dimensional vector D, the velocity v_i is represented and initialized to 0.

$$v_i = (v_{i1}, v_{i2}...v_{iD}) \in A_s \tag{3}$$

By each particle retained, the best personal position recorded as,

$$p_i = (p_{i1}, p_{i2}...p_{iD}) \tag{4}$$

From Table 2, the PSO algorithm described as, at first the swarm size values N, acceleration constant $A_{c1}, A_{c2}, w_{max}, w_{min}, v_{max}, max_{it}$ are initialized. As in Eq. (2) and Eq. (3), the population is randomly initialized and velocity vectors are initialized respectively. The following calculations are repeated until the ending criterion is seen, i) inertia weight value w is updated, ii) using $f(x_i)$ the each solution's fitness value is updated, iii) assigned the personal-best solution p_{best} and *gbest* as global test solution, iv) the velocity of each particle is formulated with respect to each iteration c, v) using the transfer function k, the continuous values are mapped into binary values and generate the new solutions. Finally, the global best is produced as best found solution.

LSTM and RNN for Classification

A classification technique to predict the heart disease using the RNN and LSTM model is developed. The LSTM model is proposed at first by Hochreiter et al. in 1997 considered as special RNN model [20]. The RNN is a catch up to the current

Table 2. Algorithm 2

1. Set the initial swarm-size value N, Acceleration constant A_{c1}, A_{c2},
2. $w_{max}, w_{min}, v_{max}, max_{it}$
3. Initialize population at random value x using Eq. (2) for every solution and v is the velocity vectors as dimensional D as 0 vectors as per in Eq. (3)
4. counter$\leftarrow$ c
5. set c=0
6. $w = w_{max} - c(\frac{w_{max}-w_{min}}{max_{it}})$
7. The fitness function for every solution is evaluated using $f(x_i)$ Eq. (1)
8. and assign the value for p_{best} and $gbest$
9. for i in range(1,N) do
10. $v_i^{c+1} = wv_i^{c+1} + A_{c1}rand_1(p_{best}(c) - x_i^c) + A_{c2}rand_2(gbest - x_i^c)$
11. end for
12. update velocity v of particles
13. for i in range(1,N) do
14. for j in range(1,D) do
15. If $v(Ij) > v_{max}$ then
16. $v(i,j) = v_{max}$
17. end if
18. If $(v(I,j) < -v_{max})$
19. $v(i,j) = -v_{max}$
20. end If
21. $k = v_{max}\frac{1}{1+e^{(-v(i,j)}}$
22. If $(rand < k)$ then
23. x (I,j)=1
24. Else
25. $x(I,j) = 0$
26. end If
27. end for
28. end for
29. c=c+1
30. Until $c < max_{it}$
31. return gbest

hidden layer state to previous n-level hidden layer state to obtain the long-term memory. Basis of RNN network, the LSTM layers are added to valve node, which overcomes the RNN long term memory evaluation problems. Generally, LSTM includes three gates to original RNN network such as an input gate, forget gate and an output gate. The LSTM design key vision is to integrate data-dependent controls and non-linear to RNN cell is trained and assures that the objective

Table 3. RNN and LSTM Specification

Simple RNN layer (100 units)
LSTM layer (100 units)
Activation Layer - Softmax
Optimizer - Adam
Epoch - 100
Batch Size - 4

function gradient does not vanish based on the state signal. The specification of RNN and LSTM shown in Table 3.

GA and PSO algorithms with LSTM deep learning model are shown in Fig. 2 and Fig. 3. Here, GA and PSO are used as feature selection algorithms and LSTM is used as classifier to classify the patients into normal and abnormal class. Selected features are given as an input to classifier. The details of features selected are given in Table 6.

4   Results and Discussion

4.1   Dataset Description

In this proposed study, the Cleveland heart disease data set described is available on the UCI machine learning repository. This data aset contains 303 instances, in which six instances exhibits missing attributes and 297 instances exhibit no missing data. In its original form, the data set contains 76 raw features. From Table 4, the experiments followed only 13 features. These instances have no missing values used in the proposed experiments.

Table 4. Dataset features description [22]

Feature no.	Feature description	Feature abbreviations	Features code
1	Age (Years) Numeric	AGE	F1
2	Sex	SEX	F2
3	Chest Pain Type	CPT	F3
4	Resting Blood Pressure	RBP	F4
5	Serum Cholesterol	SCH	F5
6	Fasting Blood Sugar	FBS	F6
7	Resting Electrcardiograpic Results	RES	F7
8	Maximum Heart Rate Achieved	MHR	F8
9	Exercise Indiced Angina	EIA	F9
10	Old Peak	OPK	F10
11	Peak Exercise Slope	PES	F11
12	Number of major vessels colored	VCA	F12
13	Thallium Scan	THA	F13

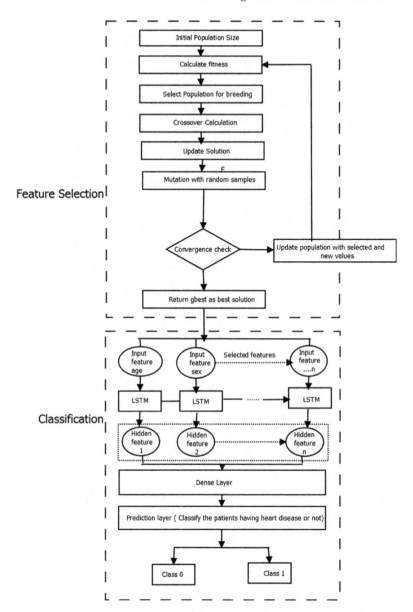

Fig. 2. GA with LSTM work flow

4.2 Performance Metrics

The proposed predictive model results are evaluated by performance metrics such as accuracy, precision, recall and f-measure. The formulations of all the metrics are,

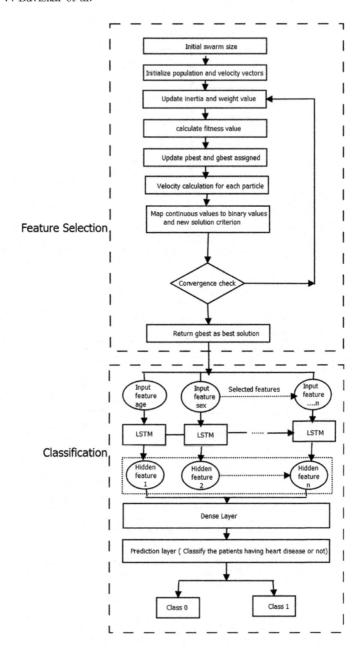

Fig. 3. PSO with LSTM work flow

Accuracy: The correctly classified in test data set shows in percentage values are termed as accuracy. The accuracy can be calculated based on the formula given in Eq. (5),

$$Accuracy = \frac{TP + TN}{TP + TN + FP + FN} \qquad (5)$$

Precision: While the correctly classified subjects showed by precision value. Precision is calculated by using the formula given in Eq. (6),

$$Precision = \frac{TP}{TP + FP} \qquad (6)$$

Recall: A recall is the proportion of related instances that have been recovered. Therefore, both accuracy and recall are based on an understanding of significance and measurement. It is estimated by the formula given in Eq. (7),

$$Recall = \frac{TP}{TP + FN} \qquad (7)$$

F-measure: The method of F1 score is referred to as the harmonious mean of accuracy and recall. This can be computed with the aid of the formula given in Eq. (8),

$$F1Score = \frac{2 * Precision * Reall}{Precision + Recall} \qquad (8)$$

4.3   Comparison of Results

The following figures representing the performance metrics of the proposed method with respect to feature selection by GA and PSO and classification using RNN and LSTM shown below. Here, data set is split into 30% testing and 70% training. Out of 303, randomly 212 records have taken for training, and 61 records have taken for testing and predicted for normal (class 0 - negative class having no heart disease) and abnormal (class 1 - positive class having heart disease) class of heart disease.

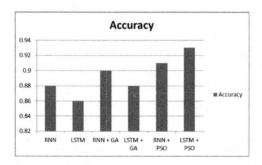

Fig. 4. Performance evaluation with an accuracy of model

From Fig. 4, it shows the results of the performance metric of accuracy of deep learning models, RNN and LSTM with and without feature selection algorithms of GA and PSO. Here, all six models are compared and LSTM + PSO shows better accuracy of 93.5%. Out of 61 records tested, 57 predicted accurately where 25 records are from normal class, and 32 records are from abnormal class. Also, LSTM gives an accuracy in less time compared to RNN as shown in Table 5.

Table 5. Performance in time

Methods	Accuracy	Time
RNN	88.52	3.4672741889953613 s
LSTM	86.88	1.3537867069244385 s

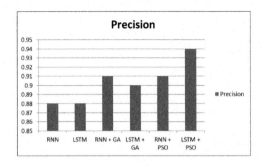

Fig. 5. Performance evaluation with precision of model

From Fig. 5, it shows the results of the performance metric of precision of deep learning models, RNN and LSTM with and without feature selection algorithms of GA and PSO. Correctly classified of positive class patients' percentage accuracy is shown. Here, all six models are compared and LSTM + PSO shows better performance of 94%. Out of 61 records tested, 34 records are predicted for abnormal class where 32 records are accurately predicted, and two records are from normal class but predicted wrongly as abnormal class.

From Fig. 6, it shows the results of the performance metric of recall of deep learning models, RNN and LSTM with and without feature selection algorithms of GA and PSO. Here, all six models are compared, and PSO shows better performance of 94% for RNN and LSTM classifier. Out of 61 records tested, 34 records are from abnormal class where 32 records are accurately predicted, and 2 are wrongly predicted as normal class.

From Fig. 7, it shows the results of the performance metric of f-measure of deep learning models, RNN and LSTM with and without feature selection algorithms of GA and PSO. Here, all six models are compared and LSTM + PSO shows better performance of 94%. It shows an average of precision and recall.

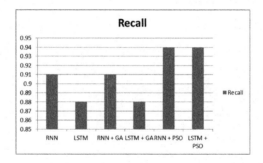

Fig. 6. Performance evaluation with recall of model

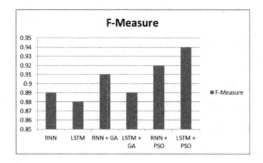

Fig. 7. Performance evaluation with F-measure of model

Table 6. Features accuracy

Methods	Selected feature	Feature count	Accuracy	Time
PSO	1110101011001	8	0.918033	92.51282
GA	1111111111010	11	0.901639	47.31271

From Table 6, the proposed method evaluation shows the PSO, and GA selected features. For PSO, the selected features' count is 8 and shows an accuracy level as 91% and takes more time. While the GA selected features' count is 11 and shows an accuracy level as 90% and takes lesser time compared with PSO. However, in terms of accuracy, the PSO shows better performance compared with GA.

From proposed Fig. 8, the evaluation performance for RNN is shown for GA and PSO features selected algorithms. It shows that, RNN with PSO shows the better performance compared to RNN with GA and without any feature selection. Also, accuracy is increased by 3% using PSO algorithm.

From proposed Fig. 9, the evaluation performance for LSTM is shown for GA and PSO features selected algorithms. It shows that, LSTM with PSO shows the better performance compared to LSTM with GA and without any feature selection. Also, accuracy is increased by 7% using PSO algorithm.

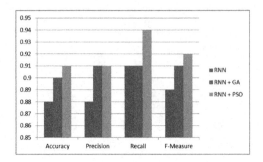

Fig. 8. Proposed method performance of RNN evaluation (With GA and PSO)

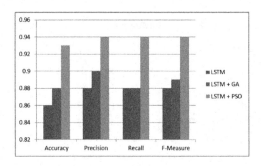

Fig. 9. Proposed method performance of LSTM evaluation (With GA and PSO)

Table 7. Comparison of Existing methods with Proposed method

Methods	Accuracy
DNN + χ^2 Statistical model [22]	(K-fold)91.57
DNN + χ^2 Statistical model [22]	(holdout) 93.33
RNN+GA (Proposed method)	90
RNN+ PSO (Proposed method)	92
LSTM+GA (Proposed method)	90
LSTM+ PSO (Proposed method)	93.5

From Table 7, it shows that by compared with the existing method the proposed method with LSTM + PSO shows higher accuracy for predicting the heart disease.

5   Conclusion

In this study, the efficient diagnosis approach has been developed for accurate prediction of heart disease. The proposed approach used enhanced GA and PSO for optimized feature selection from the heart disease data set. Further, the classification has been achieved by using deep learning models such as RNN and LSTM. The proposed model has been evaluated using the accuracy, precision, recall and f-measure performance metrics. The obtained results show that the proposed method which implements LSTM with PSO yields an accuracy of 93.5% and slightly higher computational time due to the feature selection phase but leads to an accurate prediction of heart disease as compared to the existing methods. For other performance metrics like precision, recall and f-measure also LSTM + PSO shows better performance. In the future, it may be considered for enhancing the performance of the proposed model.

References

1. Kirubha, V., Priya, S.M.: Survey on data mining algorithms in disease prediction. Int. J. Comput. Trends Tech. **38**, 124–128 (2016)
2. Sharma, H., Rizvi, M.: Prediction of heart disease using machine learning algorithms: a survey. Int. J. Recent Innov. Trends Comput. Commun. **5**, 99–104 (2017)
3. Choi, E., Schuetz, A., Stewart, W.F., Sun, J.: Using recurrent neural network models for early detection of heart failure onset. J. Am. Med. Inform. Assoc. **24**, 361–370 (2017)
4. Jin, B., Che, C., Liu, Z., Zhang, S., Yin, X., Wei, X.: Predicting the risk of heart failure with EHR sequential data modelling. IEEE Access **6**, 9256–9261 (2018)
5. Salem, T.: Study and analysis of prediction model for heart disease: an optimization approach using genetic algorithm. Int. J. Pure Appl. Math. **119**, 5323–5336 (2018)
6. Bobaoglu, I., Findik, O., Ulker, E.: A comparison of feature selection models utilizing binary particle swarm optimization and genetic algorithm in determining coronary artery disease using support vector. Expert Syst. Appl. **37**, 3177–3183 (2010)
7. Gokulnath, C.B., Shantharajah, S.: An optimized feature selection based on genetic approach and support vector machine for heart disease. Cluster Comput. **22**, 14777–14787 (2019). https://doi.org/10.1007/s10586-018-2416-4
8. Reddy, G.T., Reddy, M.P.K., Lakshmanna, K., Rajput, D.S., Kaluri, R., Srivastava, G.: Hybrid genetic algorithm and a fuzzy logic classifier for heart disease diagnosis. Evol. Intell. **13**, 185–196 (2020). https://doi.org/10.1007/s12065-019-00327-1
9. Arabasadi, Z., Alizadehsani, R., Roshanzamir, M., Moosaei, H., Yarifard, A.A.: Computer aided decision making for heart disease detection using hybrid neural network-Genetic algorithm. Comput. Methods Programs Biomed. **141**, 19–26 (2017)
10. Uyar, K., İlhan, A.: Diagnosis of heart disease using genetic algorithm based trained recurrent fuzzy neural networks. Proc. Comput. Sci. **120**, 588–593 (2017)
11. Vijayashree, J., Sultana, H.P.: A machine learning framework for feature selection in heart disease classification using improved particle swarm optimization with support vector machine classifier. Program. Comput. Softw. **44**, 388–397 (2018). https://doi.org/10.1134/S0361768818060129
12. Khourdifi, Y., Bahaj, M.: Heart disease prediction and classification using machine learning algorithms optimized by particle swarm optimization and ant colony optimization. Int. J. Intell. Eng. Syst. **12**, 242–252 (2019)

13. Feshki, M.G., Shijani, O.S.: Improving the heart disease diagnosis by evolutionary algorithm of PSO and Feed Forward Neural Network. In: Artificial Intelligence and Robotics (IRANOPEN) 2016, pp. 48–53 (2016)
14. Narasimhan, B., Malathi, A.: Altered particle swarm optimization based attribute selection strategy with improved fuzzy Artificial Neural Network classifier for coronary artery heart disease risk prediction. Int. J. Adv. Res. Ideas Innov. Technol. **5**, 1196–1203 (2019)
15. Pillai, N.S.R., Bee, K.K., Kiruthika, J.: Prediction of heart disease using RNN algorithm (2019)
16. Babu, S.B., Suneetha, A., Babu, G.C., Kumar, Y.J.N., Karuna, G.: Medical disease prediction using grey wolf optimization and auto encoder based recurrent neural network. Period. Eng. Nat. Sci. **6**, 229–240 (2018)
17. Islam, M.S., Umran, H.M., Umran, S.M., Karim, M.: Intelligent healthcare platform: cardiovascular disease risk factors prediction using attention module based LSTM. In: 2019 2nd International Conference on Artificial Intelligence and Big Data (ICAIBD), pp. 167–175 (2019)
18. Maragatham, G., Devi, S.: LSTM model for prediction of heart failure in big data. J. Med. Syst. **43**, 111 (2019). https://doi.org/10.1007/s10916-019-1243-3
19. Bandyopadhyay, S.K., Dutta, S.: Stacked bi-directional LSTM layer based model for prediction of possible heart disease during lockdown period of COVID-19: bidirectional LSTM. J. Adv. Res. Med. Sci. Technol. **7**, 10–14 (2020). ISSN 2394-6539
20. Sherstinsky, A.: Fundamentals of recurrent neural network (RNN) and long short-term memory (LSTM) network. Phys. D: Nonlinear Phenom. **404**, 132306 (2020)
21. Mohan, S., Thirumalai, C., Srivastava, G.: Effective heart disease prediction using hybrid machine learning techniques. IEEE Access **7**, 81542–81554 (2019). https://doi.org/10.1109/ACCESS.2019.2923707
22. Ali, L., Rahman, A., Khan, A., Zhou, M., Javeed, A., Khan, J.A.: An automated diagnostic system for heart disease prediction based on χ^2 statistical model and optimally configured deep neural network. IEEE Access **7**, 34938–34945 (2019)

CovidNet: A Light-Weight CNN for the Detection of COVID-19 Using Chest X-Ray Images

Tejalal Choudhary[1]([envelope]), Aditi Godbole[2], Vaibhav Gattyani[3], Aditya Gurnani[4], Aditi Verma[1], and Aditya Babar[5]

[1] Bennett University, Greater Noida, India
tejalal.choudhary@gmail.com, aditi.verma0015@gmail.com
[2] New Horizon Institute of Technology and Management, Thane, India
aditi.godbole.ag@gmail.com
[3] Sir Padampat Singhania University, Udaipur, India
vaibhavgattyani32@gmail.com
[4] Vivekananda Education Society's Institute of Technology, Mumbai, India
adityagurnani@gmail.com
[5] College of Engineering Pune, Pune, India
babaraditya07@gmail.com

Abstract. Corona virus more popularly known as COVID-19 is an extremely virulent strain from the Corona virus family of viruses and their origin is attributed to bats and civet cats. Currently, there is no cure for this virus nor are there any vaccines available to prevent this. Chest X-ray images are used for diagnosing the presence of this virus in the human body. Chest X-rays can be diagnosed only by expert radiotherapists for evaluation. Thus, the development of a system that would detect whether a person is infected by the Corona virus or not without any delay would be very helpful for people as well as doctors. In this research article, we proposed a novel deep learning model named CovidNet to detect the presence of Corona virus in a human body. We performed extensive experiments on the proposed model and pre-trained models, and the experiments show that the proposed model outperformed other pre-trained models. The proposed CovidNet model achieved best testing accuracy of 98.5%.

Keywords: Transfer learning · Deep learning · Image classification · Chest X-ray · COVID-19 · Convolutional Neural Network

1 Introduction

Corona virus has become a pandemic for the whole world. The virus spreads from people to people mostly during close contact, through small droplets. Identification of COVID-19 patients is one of the biggest challenges currently as the majority of the infected people remain asymptomatic and hence large scale testing is the only way to identify infected individuals. As of 12th September 2020,

© Springer Nature Singapore Pte Ltd. 2021
D. Garg et al. (Eds.): IACC 2020, CCIS 1367, pp. 169–179, 2021.
https://doi.org/10.1007/978-981-16-0401-0_13

there were 46,59,984 people infected with this virus in India and 77.77% had recovered while 1.66% of people had succumbed to the virus [2]. The computers and machines are performing activities in almost every sector known to us. The machines have proved to be a boon in the medical sector as well, and are used right from detecting the disease to the treatment of the disease. Machines have started performing operations which may be difficult even for humans to perform. Nowadays with the help of deep learning, machine learning, and AI technology, computers have been successful in detecting the diseases [4]. The use of machine learning algorithms for computing medical images was not useful earlier due to the lack of computing resources.

Deep learning methods, especially Convolutional Neural Networks (CNNs) has proven to be successful in image classification techniques [22]. Deep learning models have shown remarkable results in the analysis of medical images [19]. One of the popular variants of deep learning is the CNNs, and it has been used in various classification [12,15], detection [18], and generation [9] problems. There are various pre-trained CNN models like AlexNet, ResNet, Xception, MobileNet, etc. These models can be used with the help of transfer-learning to train our model as these models have already been trained on very huge datasets. The CNN models extract various peculiar features from the images and further help in classification of images according to the requirement. Figure 1 shows the deaths of people and the number of confirmed cases all across the world upto September 12, 2020 [1]. In today's situation with a population of 138.267 crores, the doctors cannot test every person for the detection of a virus. There is huge demand for self assisted systems through which the early detection of COVID infection can be identified [3].

Chest X-rays that are done for regular check-ups can be further used for detecting various diseases such as Pneumonia, Effusion, Cardiomegaly, with the latest application being Corona virus. Among all of these, Corona virus has become one of the deadliest and rampantly spreading diseases amongst humans. In the process of diagnosing the presence of Corona virus, chest X-rays have proved to be of great importance. With the help of image classification, we can extract even the granular features of the X-ray which is optimal for detection of the virus. Detection of such a virus is very difficult as it is a very hazy and blurred part in the X-ray which could be interpreted incorrectly as some other disease. Thus the task of developing an algorithm for detection of such a virus is difficult and complex. The use of deep learning models will be helpful for better performance and will enable faster, efficient and more accurate detection of diseases amongst humans. This technique will also facilitate the people in rural areas to get access to better medical facilities as it is not feasible for doctors to carry out various clinical processes in such remote regions.

Deep learning model are storage and computational intensive, require large computational power during training and inference [6]. We have proposed a CNN-based method for the classification of chest X-ray images to determine whether an individual is Corona infected or not. We worked with various CNN architectures and performed extensive experiments to test the effectiveness and usability of the models. In addition, we also proposed a new CNN model for the classification of the X-ray images. The main aim of this research is to find the suitability and applicability of the popular convolutional architectures in classifying chest X-ray images as COVID infected or not. The experimental results suggest that the CNN-based approach for the classification of X-rays as Corona infected or not is an effective approach for the early detection of Corona infection. For the part of this project, we used 9 different models to predict the output and get the accuracy. We have used proposed CovidNet, MobileNet, NasNetLarge, Xception, Densenet121, ResNet50, InceptionV3 and Inception-ResNetV2.

Total confirmed COVID-19 deaths and cases

The confirmed counts shown here are lower than the total counts. The main reason for this is limited testing and challenges in the attribution of the cause of death.

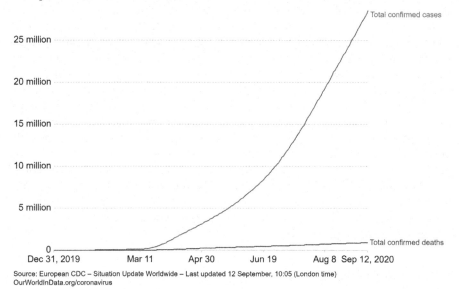

Source: European CDC – Situation Update Worldwide – Last updated 12 September, 10:05 (London time)
OurWorldInData.org/coronavirus

Fig. 1. Number of confirmed cases and deaths upto September 8, 2020.

This paper has been divided into various sections. Section 2 discusses the important contribution made by other researchers in the same field. In Sect. 3, we included the details of our methodology. Section 4, elucidated the experiments performed on various CNN architectures, discussion, and finally conclusion is given in Sect. 5.

2   Related Work

In this section, we have summarized the work done by the other researchers to detect the presence of COVID-19 from chest x-rays. The use of machine and deep learning methods is explored by many authors. We have included methods which are closely related to our work and are based on images.

In [5] the authors present a method for automatic detection of X-ray images with the help of transfer learning. The datasets were collected from the public medical repositories. Dataset 1 consisting of 1427 images and dataset 2 consisting of 1442 images. The authors have implemented pre-trained models VGG19, MobileNetV2, Inception, Xception and InceptionResNetV2. It was deduced that MobileNet-V2 model performed best for both the datasets in terms of sensitivity, accuracy, and specificity. In [10], the authors applied a deep learning method to classify COVID-19 from a small Chest X-ray dataset. The authors applied an ensemble of 3 classifiers (pre-trained models ResNet50, VGG16 and custom CNN model). The overall accuracy was 91.24%. In [11] the authors introduced a new deep learning framework called COVIDX-Net which automatically identifies the status of 2D X-ray images. The authors used 50 X-ray images to validate the model. Two models, VGG19 and DenseNet performed better.

In [16] the authors proposed a CNN model which consists of only one convolutional layer to accurately diagnose COVID-19. The convolutional layer has 16 filters and is followed by other kinds of layer namely batch-norm ReLU, two dense layers, and a final output layer. The authors worked on a total of 361 CT images and 170 X-ray images. Results of the model are 94% and 94.1% accuracy on X-ray and CT images respectively. The authors also proposed a pre-trained deep learning model i.e. AlexNet, which obtained 98% and 82% accuracy on X-ray images and CT images respectively. In [17] the authors performed the detection of COVID-19 with using pre-trained models. ResNet50 model gives highest performance with 98% accuracy among other models. [7] investigated how Bayesian CNN (BCNN) can estimate the uncertainty in the solutions provided by deep learning models to improve the diagnostic performance of human chest x-ray images. The uncertainty in prediction of x-rays is directly related to the accuracy given by the model.

3   Methodology

In this section, we have elucidated the details of our methodology. We proposed a light-weight CNN to detect whether the X-ray image is Corona infected or not. First, we have provided the details of the proposed convolutional architecture and followed by the dataset used while performing all the experiments. In addition, we also work with other pre-trained models and compare the results with CovidNet.

3.1   Dataset

Initially the model is trained and tested on the chest X-ray images dataset GitHub [8]. However, this dataset has very few images, so we combined images from the other dataset Kaggle [14]. It is very important for a deep learning model to have a reasonable images to better understand and analyse could help

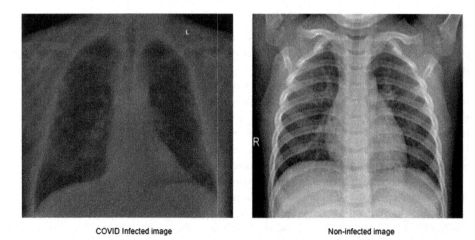

COVID Infected image   Non-infected image

Fig. 2. Infected and non-infected images from of the dataset.

us better understand the dynamics of the disease and better prepare treatments. The dataset is divided into 2 partitions i.e. training, and testing. Each of these parts are further divided into infected and normal sub-parts. The dataset consists of 689 images out of which 367 are normal, 322 are infected images. We use 593 images for training and 96 images are used for testing. Figure 2 show the infected and non-infected images present the dataset. Our main focus is to achieve the maximum accuracy with limited training and testing images. All the images are resized to 224*224*3. Before giving the images as input to the model, pre-processing is applied to all the images. Table 1 show the details of the dataset used in our experiments.

Table 1. Details of the dataset used in the experiments.

Image types	Training images	Testing images	Total images
Infected	296	26	322
Normal	297	70	367
Total	593	96	689

3.2 Convolutional Neural Networks

Convolutional neural networks popularly known as CNN are best known for their outstanding performances on images. CNNs have been used in a variety of applications area from image classification [20], object detection, image generation, to name a few. Image identification may include the detection of pedestrians on roads or moving cars etc. while those of image classification include classifying a image to a particular class. CNNs takes an image as input and assigns importance i.e weights and biases to them in order to differentiate them from one another. In CNN, convolution is nothing but a point-wise multiplication of two functions to produce a third function [15]. In convolution operation, the input image is multiplied with the feature detector to generate the feature map. CNN can have a variety of layers. The architecture of the basic CNN is shown in Fig. 3. Feature extraction is done by convolutional layers. After the convolution operation, pooling is applied to the image. The purpose of pooling is to reduce the spatial dimensions. A convolutional layer can optionally be followed by batch normalization [13] or dropout [21] layer. CNNs can also have fully connected layers. There are various popular pre-trained CNN architectures which are widely used for transfer learning namely VGG16, AlexNet, MobileNet, ResNet50, Inception-ResNet, NasNet, to name a few.

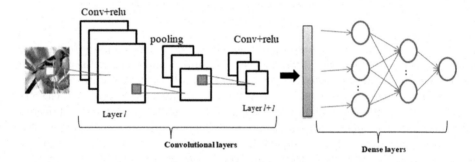

Fig. 3. Basic architecture of the CNN.

Table 2. Summary of the proposed CovidNet model

Layer	Filters, size	Input shape	Output shape	#Parameters
Conv1	80, 3*3	224*224*3	222*222*80	2240
Maxpool1	2*2	222*222*80	111*111*80	0
Conv2	32, 3*3	111*111*80	109*109*32	23072
Maxpool2	2*2	109*109*32	54*54*32	0
Conv3	32, 3*3	54*54*32	52*52*32	9248
Conv4	64, 3*3	52*52*32	50*50*64	18496
Maxpool3	2*2	50*50*64	25*25*64	0
Flatten	–	25*25*64	40,000	0
Dense1	64	40, 000	–	2560064
output	2	64	–	130
			Total	2,613,250

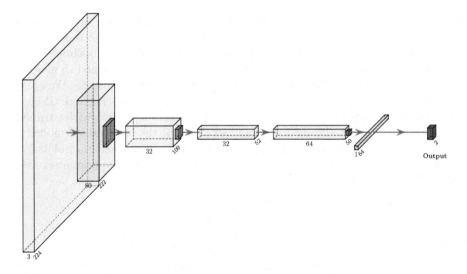

Fig. 4. Proposed CovidNet model architecture

3.3 Proposed Light-Weight CovidNet Model

In our experiments we have proposed a light-weight CNN to classify the Chest X-ray images. Our model is light-weight in terms of parameters, layers, filters and floating-point operations required compared to the existing standard models. The model has 4 convolutional layers. We do not use batch normalization [13] layer after convolutional layer. Figure 4 show the architecture of the proposed CovidNet model. In the first layer we applied 80 filters, and in the second layer it has 32, in the third layer it has 32, and in the fourth layer it has 64 filters. The size of the filters in all the convolutional is 3×3. We applied ReLU nonlinearity activation function in each convolutional layer to convert the linear operations into non-linearity. Layer 1, 2 and four 4 is followed by a max pooling of 2×2. Finally the output produced by the last convolutional layer is flattened and given as input to the first dense layer which has 64 nodes. Since the dataset is small and to avoid the issue of over-fitting, dropout [21] is used. At the end, the number of nodes are set to according to the number of classes to be classified. Sigmoid activation function is used in the last layer, as it is a binary classification problem. Table 2 shows the layer-wise details of the proposed architecture, it should be noted that the CovidNet has only 2.61M parameters.

4 Experiments and Results

All the experiments are performed on NVIDIA single GPU with 16 GB RAM. The proposed model is implemented in Keras deep learning framework with Tensorflow backend. Python programming language and other libraries such as Scikit-learn, Pandas, NumPy, and matplotlib are used for data pre-processing and plotting purposes. An Adam optimizer is selected, learning rate is initialized to 0.0001. The best accuracy is recorded while training the model using early stopping. We performed multiple experiment to tune the optimal values of hyper-parameters. Data augmentation techniques are also applied to increase the number of images as the dataset is comparatively smaller in size. We apply shearing, zooming, horizontal shifts, and rotation data augmentation. Table 3 show the details of the F1-score, precision, and recall for the CovidNet trained model. Figure 5 shows the accuracy and loss curve for the best trained model. It can be seen from Fig. 5 that the CovidNet has given maximum accuracy of 98.5%. Table 4 shows the details of the various experiments and hyper-parameters used while training and testing the proposed CovidNet.

Table 3. Precision, recall and F1-score

	Precision	Recall	F1-score
Infected	0.98	0.98	0.98
Normal	0.97	0.97	0.99

Table 4. Details of the various experiments performed and hyper-parameters used while training and testing CovidNet

Experiment	Training accuracy	Testing accuracy	Optimizer	Learning rate
1	53.7	52.8	Adam	3e−3
2	94.5	94.92	Adam	1e−3
3	**94.92**	**98.5**	**Adam**	**1e−4**
4	92.68	97.82	SGD	1e−3
5	94.75	97.10	RMSprop	1e−4

4.1   Pre-trained Models

To test the effectiveness of the CovidNe, we also performed experiments on the pre-trained models. All the pre-trained models that we use in our experiments have been trained on ImageNet dataset. Each model has different types of hidden layers, nodes, activation functions, batch normalization, filters, strides. Since the pre-trained models already have weights trained on the ImageNet dataset, we just need to put a few layers at the end and train those layers keeping the layers of the pre-trained models as it is. We reduce the number of nodes in the last output layers from 1000 to 2. As these models have been trained for 1000 different classes and we have only two classes to classify. We experimented with popular pre-trained models such as VGG16, MobileNet, NasNetLarge, Xception, Densenet121, ResNet50, InceptionV3, and Inception-ResNetV2. Table 5 shows the summary of the best results achieved with all pre-trained models along with

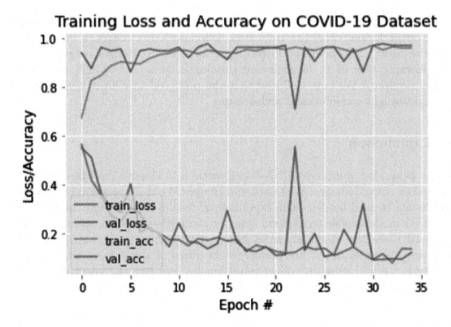

Fig. 5. Accuracy and loss curves for CovidNet model.

Table 5. Details of the results obtained with the pre-trained models

Exp	Model name	Training accuracy (%)	Testing accuracy (%)
1	VGG16	94.41	92.98
2	Inception-V3	94.04	98.1
3	ResNet50	88.99	96.49
5	NesNetLarge	96.33	97.2
6	DenseNet121	92.66	96.49
7	InceptionResNet-V2	93.12	94.74
8	Xception	96.79	97.8
9	**CovidNet**	**94.92**	**98.5**

the proposed CovidNet. From Table 5 it is visible that Inceptio-V3 and Xception performed best. However, it is important to note that CovidNet outperformed all other pre-trained models.

4.2   Discussion

We would like to mention that the analysis has been done on a limited dataset and the results are exploratory. Medical validations have not been done on the proposed approach. We plan to improve the model to increase the accuracy of model with more X-ray images so that the model can be generalized. We can concluded from the results that our proposed CovidNet COVID-19 detection model outperformed other pre-trained models chest X-ray images. It is concluded that the basic CNN model performed best for Adam optimizer over 35 epochs at a learning rate of 1e−4 achieving training accuracy of 94.92% and 98.5% testing accuracy. We have deduced that the proposed CovidNet is an effective and light-weight convolutional architecture.

5 Conclusion

In this paper, we proposed a CNN-based method to classify the Chest x-rays as infected or normal images. We tested and compared our proposed approach with various pre-trained models. The experimental results suggest that the proposed CovidNet model is able to perform superior than other pre-trained models. The proposed CovidNet model achieved best testing accuracy of 98.5%. The scale at which the experiments are performed in terms of the dataset size is small. In future, we will work to collect more images and test the effectiveness and generalization ability of the proposed light-weight CovidNet model.

References

1. Covid Cases. ourworldindata.org/grapher/total-deaths-and-cases-covid-19?year=latest&time=2019-12-31.latest
2. Ministry of Health and Family Welfare. https://www.mohfw.gov.in/
3. Population. https://www.worldometers.info/world-population/india-population/
4. US National Library of Medicine National Institutes of Health. https://www.ncbi.nlm.nih.gov/pmc/articles/PMC6616181/
5. Apostolopoulos, I.D., Mpesiana, T.A.: Covid-19: automatic detection from x-ray images utilizing transfer learning with convolutional neural networks. Phys. Eng. Sci. Med. **43**, 635–640 (2020). https://doi.org/10.1007/s13246-020-00865-4
6. Choudhary, T., Mishra, V., Goswami, A., Sarangapani, J.: A comprehensive survey on model compression and acceleration. Artif. Intell. Rev. **53**, 5113–5155 (2020). https://doi.org/10.1007/s10462-020-09816-7
7. Ghoshal, B., Tucker, A.: Estimating uncertainty and interpretability in deep learning for coronavirus (Covid-19) detection. arXiv preprint arXiv:2003.10769 (2020)
8. GitHub: Covid-19 chest Xray (2020). https://github.com/mdalmas/covid19_xray_detection?files=1/
9. Goodfellow, I., et al.: Generative adversarial nets. In: Advances in Neural Information Processing Systems, pp. 2672–2680 (2014)
10. Hall, L.O., Paul, R., Goldgof, D.B., Goldgof, G.M.: Finding Covid-19 from chest x-rays using deep learning on a small dataset. arXiv preprint arXiv:2004.02060 (2020)
11. Hemdan, E.E.D., Shouman, M.A., Karar, M.E.: COVIDX-Net: a framework of deep learning classifiers to diagnose Covid-19 in x-ray images. arXiv preprint arXiv:2003.11055 (2020)
12. Howard, A.G., et al.: MobileNets: efficient convolutional neural networks for mobile vision applications. arXiv preprint arXiv:1704.04861 (2017)

13. Ioffe, S., Szegedy, C.: Batch normalization: accelerating deep network training by reducing internal covariate shift. arXiv preprint arXiv:1502.03167 (2015)
14. Kaggle: Covid-19 chest xray. https://www.kaggle.com/bachrr/covid-chest-xray (2020)
15. Krizhevsky, A., Sutskever, I., Hinton, G.E.: ImageNet classification with deep convolutional neural networks. In: Advances in Neural Information Processing Systems, pp. 1097–1105 (2012)
16. Maghdid, H.S., Asaad, A.T., Ghafoor, K.Z., Sadiq, A.S., Khan, M.K.: Diagnosing Covid-19 pneumonia from x-ray and CT images using deep learning and transfer learning algorithms. arXiv preprint arXiv:2004.00038 (2020)
17. Narin, A., Kaya, C., Pamuk, Z.: Automatic detection of coronavirus disease (Covid-19) using x-ray images and deep convolutional neural networks. arXiv preprint arXiv:2003.10849 (2020)
18. Ren, S., He, K., Girshick, R., Sun, J.: Faster R-CNN: towards real-time object detection with region proposal networks. In: Advances in Neural Information processing Systems, pp. 91–99 (2015)
19. Shen, D., Wu, G., Suk, H.I.: Deep learning in medical image analysis. Ann. Rev. Biomed. Eng. **19**, 221–248 (2017)
20. Simonyan, K., Zisserman, A.: Very deep convolutional networks for large-scale image recognition. Published as a Conference Paper at ICLR (2015)
21. Srivastava, N., Hinton, G., Krizhevsky, A., Sutskever, I., Salakhutdinov, R.: Dropout: a simple way to prevent neural networks from overfitting. J. Mach. Learn. Res. **15**(1), 1929–1958 (2014)
22. Xin, M., Wang, Y.: Research on image classification model based on deep convolution neural network. EURASIP J. Image Video Process. **2019**, 40 (2019). https://doi.org/10.1186/s13640-019-0417-8

Using Natural Language Processing for Solving Text and Language related Applications

Analysis of Contextual and Non-contextual Word Embedding Models for Hindi NER with Web Application for Data Collection

Aindriya Barua[1]([✉]), S. Thara[1], B. Premjith[2], and K. P. Soman[2]

[1] Department of Computer Science Engineering,
Amrita Vishwa Vidyapeetham, Amritapuri, Kerala, India
barua.aindriya@gmail.com
[2] Center for Computational Engineering and Networking (CEN),
Amrita Vishwa Vidyapeetham, Coimbatore, Tamil Nadu, India

Abstract. Named Entity Recognition (NER) is the process of taking a string and identifying relevant proper nouns in it. In this paper (All codes and datasets used in this paper are available at: https://github.com/AindriyaBarua/Contextual-vs-Non-Contextual-Word-Embeddings-For-Hindi-NER-With-WebApp.) we report the development of the Hindi NER system, in Devanagari script, using various embedding models. We categorize embeddings as Contextual and Non-contextual, and further compare them inter and intra-category. Under non-contextual type embeddings, we experiment with Word2Vec and FastText, and under the contextual embedding category, we experiment with BERT and its variants, viz. RoBERTa, ELECTRA, CamemBERT, Distil-BERT, XLM-RoBERTa. For non-contextual embeddings, we use five machine learning algorithms namely Gaussian NB, Adaboost Classifier, Multi-layer Perceptron classifier, Random Forest Classifier, and Decision Tree Classifier for developing ten Hindi NER systems, each, once with Fast Text and once with Gensim Word2Vec word embedding models. These models are then compared with Transformers based contextual NER models, using BERT and its variants. A comparative study among all these NER models is made. Finally, the best of all these models is used and a web app is built, that takes a Hindi text of any length and returns NER tags for each word and takes feedback from the user about the correctness of tags. These feed-backs aid our further data collection.

Keywords: Gaussian NB · Adaboost Classifier · Multi-layer Perceptron Classifier · Random Forest Classifier · Decision Tree Classifier · Gensim Word2Vec · FastText · Transformer · BERT · RoBERTa · ELECTRA · CamemBERT · Distil-BERT · XLM-RoBERTa

---

A. Barua—Work done while interning at CEN.

D. Garg et al. (Eds.): IACC 2020, CCIS 1367, pp. 183–202, 2021.
https://doi.org/10.1007/978-981-16-0401-0_14

1   Introduction

Named Entity Recognition (NER) is an important sub-task of Natural language processing (NLP). It is often seen as the prior step to vital NLP problems of the modern-day, like question-answering systems, information retrieval, topic modeling, to name a few. An NER system identifies and categorizes the 'named entities', i.e, the proper nouns in a given text, for instance, person name, location, date, number, object, organization name, thing, etc. [1]. However, the majority of the advances made till now are in English and other resource-rich languages while research on Indian languages is still scarce. Though Hindi is the third most used language in the globe according to the 22nd edition of the World Language Database Ethnologue [2], very little work has been done to build state-of-the-art NER systems for the language. To make information more available to Indian users and to have more customized information about the Indian masses, NER in Hindi in its own Devanagari Script could be immensely beneficial. More Indian-user-oriented algorithms for content or product recommendations, customer support, etc. could be a game-changer for e-commerce companies, educational purposes, etc. If more cutting edge technological advancements are done in the Indian's mother tongue, language would no more be a barrier to knowledge or recent scientific developments for the masses.

1.1   Hurdles in Performing NER for Hindi Devanagari Script

The following linguistic features of Hindi language, or any Indian language for that matter, present certain hurdles to building a good NER system [3]:

- **Lack of capitalization:** A very useful feature in most European languages when it comes to recognizing proper nouns or named entities is capitalization. This can be evident from a simple example: "Radha works at the Microsoft headquarters located in Seattle." Since the proper nouns are capitalized, our job of identifying them just becomes manifold easier. Hindi, written in the Devanagari script, like most Indian languages, do not provide such leverage.
- **Vague names:** Hindi or Sanskrit names are often meaningful words, which are present in a dictionary as regular things, for example, *Varsha* (rain, common noun), *Pavan* (wind, common noun), *Sundar* (beautiful, adjective) this makes telling apart common nouns from proper nouns an extremely tedious errand.
- **Inadequacy of resources:** Although Indian languages have an extremely old and rich scholarly history, technological studies on them are still at their primary stages. It is often difficult to find abundant annotated corpus, big gazetteers, web or digital resources, etc.
- **Absence of standard spellings for proper nouns:** There are often different ways of spelling proper nouns in Hindi language. This expands the quantity of tokens to be learnt by the algorithm.

2   Related Works

In [4] Hindi and Bengali are recognized as resource-poor languages. It uses transliteration of English gazetteer to increase data availability, and performs NER task. It reports F1 scores of 69.59% for Bengali and 81.12% for Hindi. The paper [5] explores the importance of the quality of the embedding model in any NLP task and how they affect the outcomes. It uses data from [6–8].

The paper [9] proves that different contexts of a word lead to different embeddings since varied contexts cause different kinds of bias, which is the weighted mean of surrounding embeddings. This, in turn, proves the impact of context on the embedding and the quality of the model. They propose an extension of CBOW model which outperforms contemporary models as it is able to embed polysemous words, i.e. words with multiple possible meanings.

In [10] we find the classification of word embeddings into 3 families: Attention-based (BERT), Recurrent Neural Network (RNN) family-based (ELMo), and Bag of words based (Word2Vec). It specifies Attention-based models as contextual and Bag of words based models as Non-Contextual. This classification forms the basis of our research.

The paper [11] did a comparative study on performances in NER of 4 word-embedding techniques, Term Frequency and Inverse Document Frequency (TF-IDF), Global Vectors for Word Representation (GloVe), Skip gram, and CBOW on Code-mixed dataset [12], wherein English and Hindi languages are used together. It concludes that TF-IDF yields the best accuracy of 83%, outdoing GloVe whose accuracy is 82%, while GloVe outshines the other models in the pretext of fastest execution time, on a small dataset of 2700 tweets.

The work by [13] compared BiLSTM on Hindi, using data from [14], for BERT and FastText embeddings, and surprisingly found FastText outperformed BERT. The paper [15] did a comparative study of CNN, GRU, LSTM, RNN, on various NLP tasks and found that RNN performed well on a wide range of NLP tasks, except in key-phrase recognizing tasks, viz. question answering and sentiment detection.

The paper [16] extracts features of character-embedding on the basis of context to train its Support Vector Machine (SVM). It uses Tamil-English as well as Hindi-English code mixed corpus of tweets, where the tokenized words has BIO (Beginning, Inside, Outside) tags. It found that better results were achieved on Hindi-English code mixed data than the Tamil counterpart.

In another set of experiments, [17] compared conventional RNN techniques with the new Transformers technique on various automatic speech recognition, translation tasks, and text-to-speech tasks, and found that the transformers are superior to the former. In a recent study, [18] compares various Contextual Embedding pre-trained models based on LSTM architecture (ELMo) and Transformer architecture (BERT, and numerous BERT variants, XLNet, UniLM, ELECTRA, BART, etc.), it experiments with polyglottic and cross-lingual pre-training for downstream NLP tasks.

The paper [19] reports an overview of the 1st Shared-Task on information extraction for Indian Languages. Arknet in collaboration with FIRE 2018 developed datasets for Relation Extraction as well as NER in Tamil, Hindi, Telugu, Kannada and Malayalam. This paper evaluates solutions provided by ten teams, most of which are based on deep leaning techniques like LSTM, CNN, BiLSTM, etc. Our paper is based on the Hindi data taken from the same dataset. However, we have focused more on the performances of the word embedding models, unlike the previous works on this data. We performed a novel exhaustive comparative study on the efficiency of contextual embeddings against non-contextual embeddings on Hindi data, which has been hitherto unexplored, to the best of our knowledge.

3   Word Embedding

The machine cannot understand natural language or text the way humans can, so they need to be represented in form of real-valued vectors such that syntactically and semantically similar meaning word vectors lie close to each other in the vector space and mathematical relationships can be drawn between them. This technique is called word embedding. Designing an effective method of representing words and documents such that it is machine-understandable is a key to NLP and plays an important role in determining the quality of any NER model.

3.1   Classification Based on Context Dependency

We have classified the word embedding models into two broad classes: Contextual and Non-Contextual, based on [10]:

– **Non-Contextual Word Embedding Model:**
  Non-Contextual Word Embedding Model produces only one vector paying little heed to the position of the words in a sentence and disregards the various implications they may have. For example, "She walked by the river bank and went to the bank to deposit money.", where the word 'bank' has various implications dependent on the sentence setting, these models simply break them all down into one vector for 'bank' in their yield. Following are the two such models we will be analyzing:
  1. **Gensim Word2Vec:** Word2Vec is a prevalent method to embed words utilizing shallow neural networks [20]. It either uses Continuous Bag of Words (CBOW) or Skipgram.
     - **CBOW Model** takes the context of each word in a text sequence and predicts one word corresponding to the surrounding words i.e, given $w_{i-2}, w_{i-1}, w_{i+1}, w_{i+2}$, the CBOW model predicts w_i. The context is defined by the window size of neighbouring words. The input context words are given as one hot encoded vectors, in the process of finding the target word, the neural network gets trained.
     - **Skipgram** is similar to CBOW, the difference being that it learns by predicting the context words, for a given word, i.e, given w_i, the Skipgram model gives $w_{i-2}, w_{i-1}, w_{i+1}, w_{i+2}$.

2. **FastText:** A major loophole in Word2Vec is that it doesn't work for Out Of Vocabulary (OOV) words, while FastText does. FastText uses the same technique of Skipgram and CBOW, but instead of working on a whole word, it parts the word into n-grams, and then does the same process as Word2Vec, but on these character n-grams. A word is represented as the sum of vectors of character n-grams [21].

– **Contextual Word Embedding Model:**
Contextual Word Embedding Models can produce distinctive word embeddings for a word that catches the positioning of a word in a sentence, hence they are context-dependent. We will be analyzing Transformer based word embedding models which are contextual.

Transformer and Attention:
The concept of transformers is a major break-through from the previous sequence-to-sequence models (like RNN). Let us take an example:
"The artist <u>Rumi</u> reveals that <u>she</u> never pursued a formal degree in Art. A former engineer, the <u>youngster</u> had set <u>her</u> mind on doing an MS and pursuing a career in Data Science Research. The <u>all-rounder</u> excelled in academics and in various co-curricular activities. <u>She</u> admits that art and theatre came to <u>her</u> by chance!"
The underlined words refer to the same person - Rumi. As humans, we can easily relate all the underlined words to the same person, but for a machine, capturing these relationships over a long sequence of words in a sentence is very difficult. Transformers have brought many advancements in this context, by enabling "parallelization", unlike the "sequential" predecessors [22]. Transformer converts input sequences to output sequences, using "Attention". Attention is a mechanism that relates different positions of a sequence to compute its representation.

Following are such models we will be analyzing:
1. **BERT:** BERT is an acronym for Bidirectional Encoder Representations with Transformers. It is called bidirectional because it reads a sequence of text from both left and right simultaneously and captures both left and right context. For example,
"She walked by the river <u>bank</u>."
"She went to the <u>bank</u> to deposit money."
We can see the meaning of the word "bank" is completely different in the two sentences and depends on the left ad right context. BERT adopts bidirectionality to capture this. It uses multi-layer bidirectional encoders of Transformer. It is pre-trained on a huge dataset utilizing a combination of masked language modeling objectives and next text sequence predictions [23].
2. **RoBERTa:** RoBERTa is a modification of BERT and enhances the key hyper-parameters which trains with way bigger learning rates and mini-batches [24].

3. **XLM-RoBERTa:** XLM-RoBERTa is a huge multi-lingual model, pre-trained on a large amount of filtered data, that does not require special tensors to determine the language [25].

4. **CamemBERT:** CamemBERT is based on Facebook's RoBERTa, but trained on French language [26].

5. **DistilBERT:** DistilBERT is a comparatively very small, quick, less expensive, and light-weight Transformer model trained by distillation of Bert base [27].

6. **ELECTRA:** ELECTRA is a pre-training methodology that trains 2 transformers: generator and discriminator, proposed in [28]. The generator replaces tokens in a sequence, and is trained as a masked model. The discriminator identifies which tokens in the sequence were initially replaced by the generator.

The methodology for Word2Vec and FastText is similar, where we encode the words using either of the two algorithms and then pass them through various machine learning classifiers, while for BERT and other models using Transformers, we use respective pre-trained models.

4   Experimental Setup

4.1   Dataset Description

The dataset is taken from the first shared task on Information Extractor for Conversational Systems in Indian Languages (IECSIL) [19]. It consists of 15,48,570 Hindi words in Devanagari script and corresponding NER labels. Each sentence end is marked by "newline" tag. Figure 1 shows a snapshot of one sentence in the dataset. Our Dataset has nine classes, namely, Datenum, Event, Location, Name, Number, Occupation, Organization, Other, Things. Figure 2 represents a visualization of each class and its number of data points. Table 1 shows the distribution of data points per class.

Table 1. Classes and distribution of data-points

Classes	Number of data-points
Datenum	2672
Event	2932
Location	166547
Name	88887
Number	37754
Occupation	15732
Organization	12254
Other	1141207
Things	4048

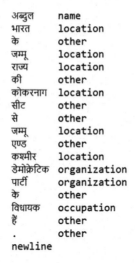

अब्दुल	name
भारत	location
के	other
जम्मू	location
राज्य	location
की	other
कोकरनाग	location
सीट	other
से	other
जम्मू	location
एण्ड	other
कश्मीर	location
डेमोक्रेटिक	organization
पार्टी	organization
के	other
विधायक	occupation
हैं	other
.	other
newline	

Fig. 1. Snapshot of one sentence in the dataset

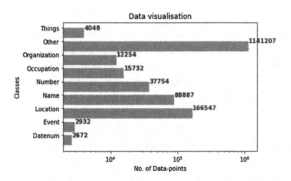

Fig. 2. Number of data-points in each class

4.2   Set-up for Non-contextual Embedding

Figure 3 shows the flow diagram of our set-up for experiments with non-contextualized embedding.

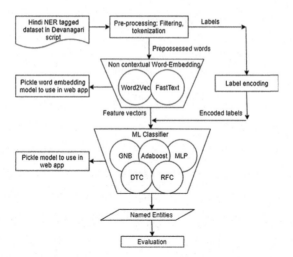

Fig. 3. Data flow diagram for proposed method using Non-Contextual Word Embedding methods

1. **Pre-Processing.** Pre-processing is the process of mining data that involves weeding out unnecessary data, wrong formatting, and overall standardization of the data. We used Python regular expression library Regex and Natural Language Tool Kit (NLTK package) to perform pre-processing.
2. **Word Embedding.** We use either Word2Vec or FastText, with Skipgram model. These word embeddings are non-contextualized models that yield only one vector for each word, consolidating all the various faculties of the meanings into one vector. CBOW performs better and faster on more frequent words, and hence works well on a large corpus [20]. We have used Skipgram in our experiments as it's better than CBOW in predicting for rare and infrequent words, and works well on a smaller corpus.
3. **Feature Vector Classification.** We divide the dataset into 80–20% ratios for training and testing respectively. We have experimented with six classical machine learning classifiers [32,33] for each of the two non-contextual word embedding models:
   (a) GaussianNB Classifier
   (b) Adaboost Classifier
   (c) Multi-Layer Perceptron Classifier
   (d) Decision Tree Classifier
   (e) Random Forest Classifier

After training the classifier model, with the various algorithms, it is sent forward for testing and evaluation. The Word embedding model and Classifier models are pickled and stored for later use, in making Web Application.

4.3   Set-up for Contextual Embedding Models: BERT and Variants

Figure 4 shows the flow diagram of our set-up for experiments with contextualized embedding models.

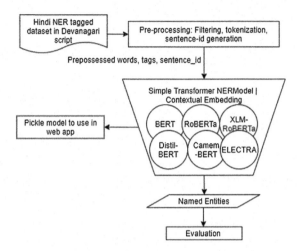

Fig. 4. Data flow diagram for proposed method using Contextual Word Embedding methods

1. **Pre-Processing and Sentence-ID Generation.** Pre-processing is similar to previous approach, with an addition that each word is given a sentence ID, so that the context sentence of each word can be preserved, unlike the previous methods. Figure 5 shows the sentence ID generation for each word in two consecutive sentences, at each 'newline', the sentence IDs are incremented by 1. So the input to the model is a list of lists of the form [[sentence_id, word, tag]].

2. **NERModel Creation and Training with Simple Transformers.** The NERModel is a pre-trained Simple Transformer model given at [29] which uses an embedding model and adds an extra layer to fine-tune it for NER task. In the creation of the model, we have to tweak two arguments: model_type and model_name, we specify model_type as one of six supported the model types: BERT, RoBERTa, ELECTRA, XLM-RoBERTa, Distil-BERT, CamemBERT. The model_name has to be specified to identify the exact architecture and trained weights that need to be used, which is to specify characteristics like 'uncased' and 'base'. After training, the model is sent out for evaluation. The NER model is pickled and stored for later use, in making Web Application.

Fig. 5. Processing and sentence ID generation of two sample sentences

5　Results and Discussion

We will be dealing with the following variables ahead: TP: True positives, TN: True negatives, FP: False positives, FN: False negatives. Let us understand and interpret the evaluation measures:

- **Accuracy:** It is a simple ratio of correct predictions to total number of predictions as shown in Eq. 1. Accuracy can be a reliable measure only if we have a symmetrical data-set, i.e, only when all classes in the data-set have almost equal number of data instances. Hence, we must consider the precision and recall.

$$Accuracy = (TP + TN)/(TP + FP + FN + TN) \tag{1}$$

- **Precision:** It is the ratio of correct predictions to total positive predictions. High precision indicates low number of false positives as shown in Eq. 2.

$$Precision = TP/(TP + FP) \tag{2}$$

- **Recall:** It is the ratio of predicted positives to actual positives in the class as shown in Eq. 3.

$$Recall = TP/(TP + FN) \tag{3}$$

- **F1 Score:** It is the weighted mean of precision and recall as shown in Eq. 4. Hence, it takes into consideration both false positive observations and false negative observations. In an unbalanced data distribution, F1 score gives a more reliable measure of goodness of the model.

$$F1score = (2 \times Recall \times Precision)/(Recall + Precision) \tag{4}$$

From Fig. 2 we can see that our data-set has a class imbalance, with a lot more data-points in the 'other' class, which is understandable because Named entities in a sentence will always be less than common nouns, verbs or other parts-of-speech. Hence, the accuracy score will be high due to the high accuracy in predicting 'other' class words, which is not our primary focus. Therefore, we will use the **F1-score** measure as the most reliable measure to judge how good the models are.

5.1   Intra-category Comparison: Non-contextual Embeddings

Table 2 compares the accuracy (1 being 100%), recall, precision, F1 score for various classifiers with Word2Vec and FastText.

Table 2. Performance evaluation of Non-Contextual Models for various classifiers

Classifier	Performance measure	Embedding	
		Word2Vec	FastText
RFC	Accuracy Score	0.9327	0.9359
	Precision	0.7029	0.6976
	Recall	0.8714	0.8826
	F1-score	0.7534	0.8335
DTC	Accuracy Score	0.9290	0.9629
	Precision	0.6701	0.6976
	Recall	0.9081	0.9094
	F1-score	0.7371	0.7593
MLP	Accuracy Score	0.8749	0.8913
	Precision	0.5991	0.7313
	Recall	0.2717	0.4017
	F1-score	0.3210	0.4831
Adaboost	Accuracy	0.7764	0.8710
	Precision	0.2852	0.2960
	Recall	0.1195	0.3258
	F1-score	0.1134	0.3023
Gaussian NB	Accuracy	0.4312	0.4743
	Precision	0.1839	0.1683
	Recall	0.3316	0.2683
	F1-score	0.1534	0.1400

From Table 2, we can see that RFC + Word embedding gives the highest F1 score, where, RFC+FastText does 10.63% better than RFC+Word2Vec. From Fig. 6a and Fig. 6b we can see that Fasttext provides better feature representation for classification than Word2vec for this task. This is expected as FastText

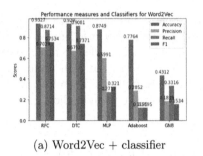

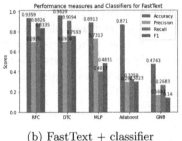

(a) Word2Vec + classifier   (b) FastText + classifier

Fig. 6. Performance Evaluation of Word2Vec and FastText with various classifiers

works better on morphologically rich languages like Indian languages. Hindi is morphologically rich and words are usually formed by a combination of sub-words called *'sandhi'*, which is intuitively similar to the act of breaking words into sub-words done by FastText [30]. Figure 7 shows some examples of *'sandhi-vichhed'*. For every word, FastText generates word embedding as the sum of the n-gram vectors. Therefore, when we train the model over a huge corpus, it is highly unlikely that the algorithm can't find the learned n-grams in OOV words. For OOV words, it sums up vectors for its component character n-grams, if at least one of the n-gram is present in the training data, it can speculate the representation of the new word with the help of that. Hence FastText is more successful in generating word embeddings for Hindi OOV words.

पुस्तक + आलय = पुस्तकालय
विद्या + अर्थी = विद्यार्थी
रवि + इंद्र = रविन्द्र
गिरी +ईश = गिरीश
मुनि + ईश = मुनीश
इति + आदि = इत्यादि
परी + आवरण = पर्यावरण
अनु + अय = अन्वय
सु + आगत = स्वागत
अभी + आगत = अभ्यागत

Fig. 7. Illustration of Hindi words made of sub-words

5.2   Intra-category Comparison: Contextual Embeddings

Table 3 shows the eval-loss (Cross entropy loss), precision, recall, F1-score for the various Contextual models. The lower the eval-loss, and higher the precision, recall, F1-score, the better the model.

From Fig. 8 it is evident that XLM-RoBERTa performs best and out-performs BERT by a good 23.78% (F1 measure) and RoBERTa by a 37.78%. It also has the lowest eval-loss. This is justified because XLM-RoBERTa is a multi-lingual model trained over 100 languages over a significantly larger data-set. The training corpus called CommonCrawl is as huge as 2.5 gigabytes, which is a manifold higher than its predecessors' training data- the Wiki-100 corpus. The other models are mono-lingual while XLM-RoBERTa is multi-lingual, hence it is more suited for our Hindi data. XLM-RoBERTa, in general, would do comparatively better on smaller and resource-poor data-set like that of ours. However, interestingly, BERT performs better than RoBERTa on Hindi NER by approximately 7%.

CamemBERT is trained on French monolingual data, and hence it is interesting to note its performance on Hindi data. It shows a 17% degradation from BERT's F1 score. DistilBERT is an extremely non-expensive and lighter model than its counterparts. The execution time is approximately four times less than that of BERT, but it did come with the trade-off of prediction metrics. It shows a massive 38% degradation on BERT in our training. Although [28] claims an improvement of ELECTRA Model on BERT, we find that it actually causes a degradation of 45% on our Hindi NER task.

Table 3. Performance evaluation of Contextual Models

NER model	Evaluation Measures			
	Eval loss	Precision	Recall	F1 score
XLM-RoBERTa	0.12416	0.89031	0.90850	0.908419
BERT	0.52152	0.76371	0.695395	0.73390
RoBERTa	0.401102	0.70591	0.605028	0.659321
Camem-BERT	0.44155	0.678628	0.545639	0.60911
ELECTRA	0.64112	0.522521	0.326321	0.3999
Distil-BERT	0.613491	0.571200	0.36401	0.45406

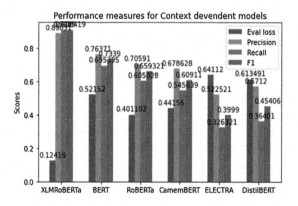

Fig. 8. Performance Evaluation of Contextual NER Models

5.3   Inter-category Comparison: Non-contextual vs. Contextual Embeddings

Let us examine the **Receiver Operation Characteristics (ROC) curves** for the two best performing models out of non-contextual and contextual models: FastText+RFC and XLM-RoBERTa NER Model. The 9 coloured lines'red', 'blue', 'green', 'pink', 'brown', 'aqua', 'black', 'orange', 'purple' represent the 9 NER tags, 'Datenum', 'Event', 'Location', 'Name', 'Number', 'Occupation', 'Organization', 'Other', 'Things' respectively. The true positives are plotted on the Y-axis and false positives are on the X-axis. Hence the top-left corner of the graph should have the lowest false positive rate. Hence steeper the graph, better the performance, as it implies fast maximization of true positive rate, and minimization of false negatives.

As we can see from Fig. 9a, even though the FastText+RFC model gives an accuracy of 93.59% (Table 2), the class-wise accuracy is not uniformly high. The ROC curves of lesser frequent classes are bad, but due to the almost perfect accuracies of the abundant classes, the overall accuracy is very high. This further strengthens the point that accuracy cannot be a reliable measure for our dataset.

On the other hand, Fig. 9b shows that the ROC curves of most classes in the XLM-RoBERTa model are steep and perform almost equally good. This difference is evident from the F1 scores of FastText+RFC and XLM-RoBERTa: 0.8335 and 0.9084 respectively. This clearly indicates that the contextual XLM-RoBERTa NER Model outperforms the best of Non-Contextual NER Models, i.e. FastText+RFC.

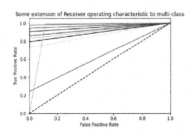
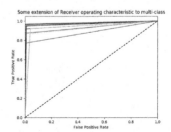

(a) ROC curve of Fast Text + RFC

(b) ROC curve of XLM-RoBERTa

Fig. 9. ROC curves of best of contextual and non-contextual models for class-wise performance visualization: 9 lines for 9 classes

Figure 10 compares the F1 scores of all the models. From a comparison of the scores, we can see that the contextual embedding models perform better than non-contextual models, as they can retain the positional, syntactical and semantical features of the words better because of their parallelized nature. Unlike former sequential models, they do not lose the relationships with words located far off in a long sentence. They are much more resource expensive and time-consuming, however, this comes with better performance.

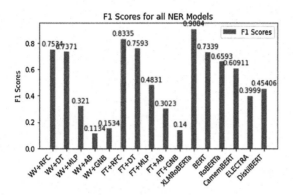

Fig. 10. F1 Score comparison of all NER Models for both Non-Contextual and Contextual Embeddings

6   Web App for NER Visualisation and Data Collection

After the successful completion of all the experiments, the best model was used to make the first of its kind interactive web application for NER in the Hindi Language in Devanagari script, which is deployed at http://3.7.28.233. We pickled and saved each word embedding and NER model so that we can use them in the web application back-end. Screenshots of web app are shown at Fig. 11, Fig. 12 and Fig. 13.

6.1   Web Application Building Methodology

Figure 14 shows the data flow diagram for the algorithm of the web app. Flask [31] was used to build the website which is a user-friendly python-based micro-framework.

NER Tagging

1. First the user is given an HTML form (Fig. 11) where she can enter the text to be tagged, and click the "Submit" button.
2. When the user clicks submit, the back-end receives the text input given by the user, and filters it to remove bad formatting, white spaces, non-Devanagari characters.
3. **In case of Non-Contextual embedding** we load/un-pickle the word embedding model and the classifier model, we tokenize each word, for each word, we use the word embedding model to embed the word, then pass it for prediction into the classifier model. The predictions made by the model are

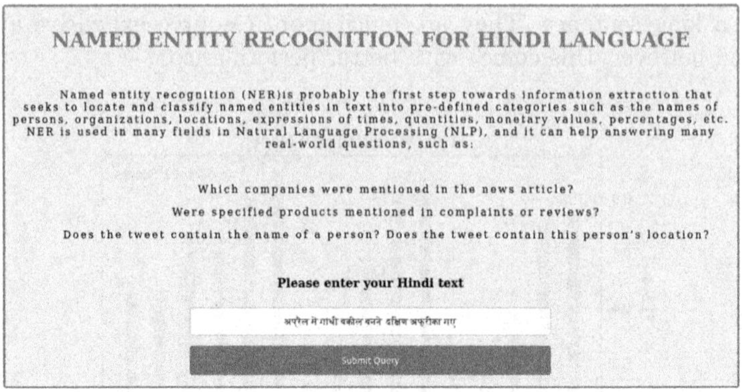

Fig. 11. Web App Screen 1: Input form

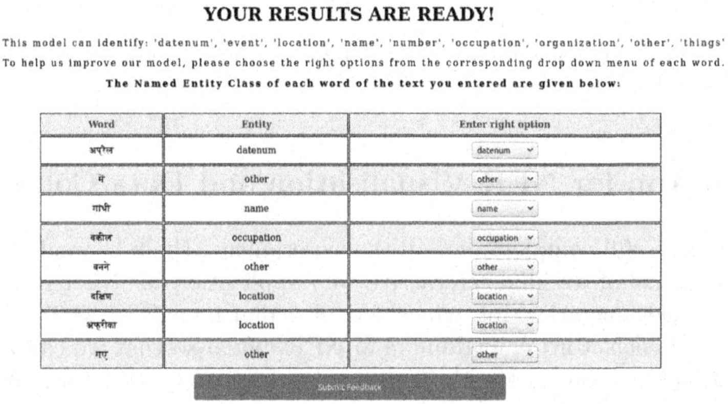

Fig. 12. Web App Screen 2: Results page and drop-down menus for feedback

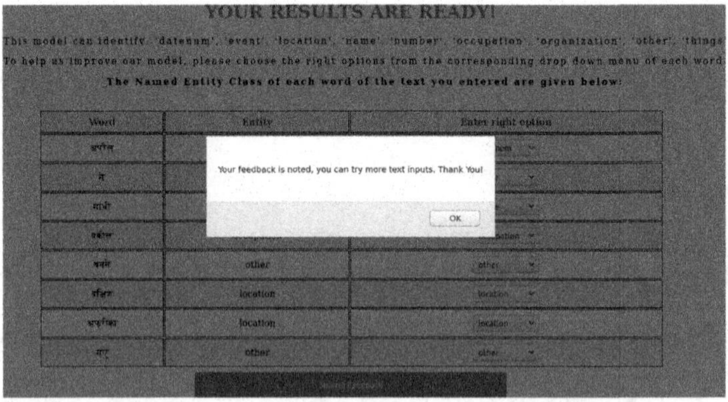

Fig. 13. Web App Screen 3: User feedback noted

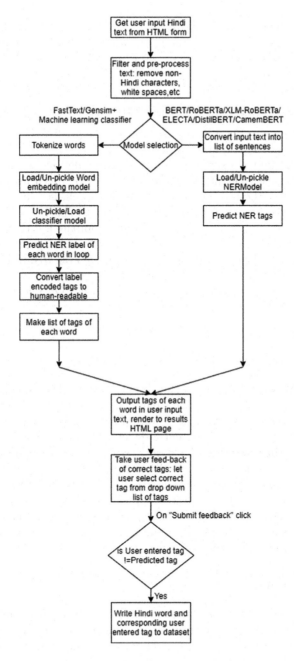

Fig. 14. Data-flow diagram of web app

label encoded, so we convert them to human-readable NER tags. After getting tags for each word, we concatenate those results to form the prediction for the whole text and render it to the results' HTML page (Fig. 12).

4. **In case of Contextual embedding** the input is split into a list of sentences. We un-pickle the NER Model, the list of whole sentences is input for prediction. The NER tags are output in the form of a list, which can be directly passed to be rendered to result's page (Fig. 12).

Dataset Collection and Enhancement from User Feedback

1. On the results page (Fig. 12), the user can see the predicted NER tags of each word in the text she had entered.
2. The user is prompted to help us improve the model by entering the correct NER tags, by selecting the correct tag from a drop-down list of tags beside each word. After the user gives the feedback and clicks "Submit Feedback", the back end receives a JSON dictionary of the feedback.
3. The user entered tag and the predicted tag is compared, if they are different, it means that she claims that the prediction is wrong. In that case, we write the Hindi word and the corresponding user-entered tag to our data-set, hence helping in further data collection (Fig. 13).
4. The user is prompted that the feedback is noted. On clicking 'Ok' she is redirected to first page to input more Hindi texts.

7   Conclusion

We experimented with various word embedding models, of contextualized and non-contextualized types, and established that contextual NER models work better than non-contextual ones, as their parallelised learning approach can retain syntax and positional information of words over longer sequences, unlike the sequential counterparts. Of all context-independent models, FastText with Random Forest Classifier achieves the best F1-score, but context-dependent outperforms it. Amongst all models, the XLM-RoBERTa excels the best, with the lowest eval loss, and highest precision, recall, and F1-score. We also used the best model to make an interactive web application that can be used for educational and experimental purposes, and help in collecting more data. This would particularly be beneficial keeping in mind the low availability of good data-sets in Hindi, written in pure Devanagari Script.

8   Future Work

All the results were obtained without any extensive hyper-parameter tuning. So it can be expected that better results can be obtained by making tweaks to the learning rates, batch sizes, etc. Adding a CRF-layer on top of the XLM-RoBERTa can also improve the NER task on Hindi, which can be looked upon as possible future work. Our dataset also has class imbalance as established during the experiments, hence, a cost sensitive learning approach could also yield better outcomes. Reinforcement learning can also be incorporated on the web application, to improve the models utilizing the user feedback that our website is designed to collect.

References

1. Nadeau, D., Sekine, S.: A survey of named entity recognition and classification. Lingvisticae Investigationes **30**(1), 3–26 (2007)
2. 22nd edition of the world language database Ethnologue. https://www.ethnologue.com/ethnoblog/gary-simons/welcome-22nd-edition
3. Srivastava, S., Sanglikar, M., Kothari, D.C.: Named entity recognition system for Hindi language: a hybrid approach. Int. J. Comput. Linguist. (IJCL) **2**(1), 10–23 (2011)
4. Kumar Saha, S., Sarathi Ghosh, P., Sarkar, S., Mitra, P.: Named entity recognition in Hindi using maximum entropy and transliteration. Polibits **38**, 33–41 (2008)
5. Chen, Y., Perozzi, B., Al-Rfou, R., Skiena, S.: The expressive power of word embeddings. arXiv preprint arXiv:1301.3226 (2013)
6. Godbole, N., Srinivasaiah, M., Skiena, S.: Large-scale sentiment analysis for news and blogs. ICWSM **7**(21), 219–222 (2007)
7. Bergsma, S., Lin, D.: Bootstrapping path-based pronoun resolution. In: Proceedings of the 21st International Conference on Computational Linguistics and the 44th Annual Meeting of the Association for Computational Linguistics, pp. 33–40. Association for Computational Linguistics, July 2006
8. Fellbaum, C.: WordNet. In: Poli, R., Healy, M., Kameas, A. (eds.) Theory and Applications of Ontology: Computer Applications. Springer, Dordrecht (2010). https://doi.org/10.1007/978-90-481-8847-5_10
9. Hu, W., Zhang, J., Zheng, N.: Different contexts lead to different word embeddings. In: Proceedings of COLING 2016, The 26th International Conference on Computational Linguistics: Technical Papers, pp. 762–771, December 2016
10. Rajasekharan, A.: Brief review of word embedding families (2019). https://mc.ai/brief-review-of-word-embedding-families-2019/
11. Sravani, L., Reddy, A.S., Thara, S.: A comparison study of word embedding for detecting named entities of code-mixed data in Indian language. In: 2018 International Conference on Advances in Computing, Communications and Informatics (ICACCI), pp. 2375–2381. IEEE, September 2018
12. Bhat, I.A., Shrivastava, M., Bhat, R.A.: Code mixed entity extraction in Indian languages using neural networks. In: FIRE (Working Notes), pp. 296–297 (2016)
13. Shah, B., Kopparapu, S.K.: A Deep Learning approach for Hindi Named Entity Recognition. arXiv preprint arXiv:1911.01421 (2019)
14. IITH. Workshop on NER for South and South East Asian Languages (2008)
15. Yin, W., Kann, K., Yu, M., Schütze, H.: Comparative study of CNN and RNN for natural language processing. arXiv preprint arXiv:1702.01923 (2017)
16. Srinidhi Skanda, V., Singh, S., Remmiya Devi, G., Veena, P.V., Kumar, M.A., Soman, K.P.: CEN@ Amrita FIRE 2016: context based character embeddings for entity extraction in code-mixed text. In: FIRE (Working Notes), pp. 321–324 (2016)
17. Karita, S., et al.: A comparative study on transformer vs RNN in speech applications. arXiv preprint arXiv:1909.06317 (2019)
18. Liu, Q., Kusner, M.J., Blunsom, P.: A Survey on Contextual Embeddings. arXiv preprint arXiv:2003.07278 (2020)
19. Barathi Ganesh H.B., et al.: Overview of Arnekt IECSIL at FIRE-2018 track on information extraction for conversational systems in Indian languages. In: FIRE (Working Notes), pp. 119–128 (2018)

20. Rong, X.: Word2Vec parameter learning explained. arXiv preprint arXiv:1411.2738 (2014)
21. Joulin, A., Grave, E., Bojanowski, P., Mikolov, T.: Bag of tricks for efficient text classification. arXiv preprint arXiv:1607.01759 (2016)
22. Vaswani, A., et al.: Attention is all you need. In: Advances in Neural Information Processing Systems, pp. 5998–6008 (2017)
23. Devlin, J., Chang, M.W., Lee, K., Toutanova, K.: Bert: pre-training of deep bidirectional transformers for language understanding. arXiv preprint arXiv:1810.04805 (2018)
24. Liu, Y., et al.: RoBERTa: a robustly optimized BERT pretraining approach. arXiv preprint arXiv:1907.11692 (2019)
25. Conneau, A., et al.: Unsupervised cross-lingual representation learning at scale. arXiv preprint arXiv:1911.02116 (2019)
26. Martin, L., et al.: CamemBERT: A Tasty French Language Model. arXiv preprint arXiv:1911.03894 (2019)
27. Sanh, V., Debut, L., Chaumond, J., Wolf, T.: DistilBERT, a distilled version of BERT: smaller, faster, cheaper and lighter. arXiv preprint arXiv:1910.01108 (2019)
28. Clark, K., Luong, M.T., Le, Q.V., Manning, C.D.: Electra: pre-training text encoders as discriminators rather than generators. arXiv preprint arXiv:2003.10555 (2020)
29. Simple Transformers. https://simpletransformers.ai/
30. Premjith, B., Soman, K.P., Kumar, M.A.: A deep learning approach for Malayalam morphological analysis at character level. Proc. Comput. Sci. **132**, 47–54 (2018)
31. Grinberg, M.: Flask Web Development: Developing Web Applications with Python. O'Reilly Media Inc., Newton (2018)
32. Soman, K.P., Diwakar, S., Ajay, V.: Data Mining: Theory and Practice [with CD]. PHI Learning Pvt. Ltd., New Delhi (2006)
33. Premjith, B., Soman, K.P., Anand Kumar, M., Jyothi Ratnam, D.: Embedding linguistic features in word embedding for preposition sense disambiguation in English—Malayalam machine translation context. In: Kumar, R., Wiil, U.K. (eds.) Recent Advances in Computational Intelligence. SCI, vol. 823, pp. 341–370. Springer, Cham (2019). https://doi.org/10.1007/978-3-030-12500-4_20

NEWS Article Summarization with Pretrained Transformer

Apar Garg[1]([✉]), Saiteja Adusumilli[1], Shanmukha Yenneti[1], Tapas Badal[1], Deepak Garg[1], Vivek Pandey[2], Abhishek Nigam[2], Yashu Kant Gupta[2], Gyan Mittal[2], and Rahul Agarwal[2]

[1] Computer Science and Engineering,
Bennett University, Greater Noida, India
ag1281@bennett.edu.in
[2] Times Internet Limited, Gurugram, India

Abstract. Pretrained language models have shown tremendous improvement in many NLP applications including text summarization. Text-to-Text transfer transformer (T5) and Bidirectional Encoder Representations from Transformers (BERT) are most recent pretrained language models applied most widely in NLP research domain. In this paper we have shown how T5 and BERT can be applied for text summarization task and can be use for both abstractive and extractive summary generation tool. Our hypothesis is that T5 performance outperform over BART and transformer developed from the scratch. To test our hypothesis used our dataset containing more than 80K news articles and their summaries. This dataset has been tested using BART, Text-to-Text transformer (T5), model generated using transfer learning over T5, and an encoder-decoder based model developed from scratch. The results show that T5 gives better result than other three models used for testing.

Keywords: Encoder-decoder model · Text summarization · Transfer learning · Text-to-text transformer

1 Introduction

Nowadays, news agencies across the world, face an inundation of stories flowing through their Content management system (CMS) on a daily basis. Many of them are written internally by internal editors while others come from external agencies and don't have a summary available with the content. Segregation of relevant articles from that of irrelevant can be a very tedious and time consuming task for the editorials, if the summaries are not present. Reading long articles one by one and then gaining insight into them is not a good idea. In order to gather way more information from articles in less time, it is beneficial for the agency to go through the summary of articles, while still gaining the essence or crux of the article.

Text summarization provides the user with only important details in a shortened version of text and thereby allows him/her to understand the text in a

D. Garg et al. (Eds.): IACC 2020, CCIS 1367, pp. 203–211, 2021.
https://doi.org/10.1007/978-981-16-0401-0_15

shorter period of time. The purpose of text summarization is to condense the content into a concise version while still retaining the relevant details.

Text Summarization methods can be classified into two types: (1) extractive and (2) abstractive summarization. Extractive approach pulls key phrases/ lines from the source document and combines them to make a summary. It doesn't make any changes to the text. On the contrary, abstractive text summarization algorithms, just like humans, create new phrases and sentences which contain useful information from the original text.

Primarily our task is not to proposed a new approach to generate summary of a given text, instead we want to explore and provide a state-of-art model used in NLP field for text summarization. We do the comprehensive study of text-to-text approaches. Our findings lead us to two transformer based model proposed by Facebook and Google that are BART and T5 respectively.

In this paper, we apply different language model suitable for text summarization. We find that T5 can be use as potential model which can generate the summary for news articles effectively. We evaluate the three different language model on news summarization dataset containing 8000 news articles and their summary. We achieve better result with pretrained model T5. Furthermore, we apply transfer learning over T5 model and we conclude that transfer learning may not necessarily increases the accuracy of pretrained model.

2   Related Work

Programmed summarization is the process of automatically producing a gist of the text that retains the most significant content of the original text document (Nenkova and McKeown, 2012) [11]. Conventionally, the summarization approaches can be classified into three classes: extraction-based, compression-based and abstraction-based methods. In fact, preceding research show that human-written summaries are more abstractive (Barzilay and McKeown, 2005; Bing et al., 2015) [12,13]. Abstraction-based approaches can produce new sentences based on the details from different source text documents. Barzilay and McKeown (2005) utilised sentence fusion to produce a new sentence from the original source sentences. Bing et al. (2015) put forward a more fine-grained fusion framework, where new sentences are produced by selecting and combining salient phrases. These approaches can be regarded as a kind of indirect abstractive summarization, and intricate constraints are used to promise the linguistic quality. Later, Miao and Blunsom (2016) [15] improved on the seq2seq framework and proposed a generative model to seize the latent summary info, the model has limited representation ability because they didn't consider the recurrent dependencies in their generative model.

Li et al. [1] introduced an extractive multimodal summary (MMS) method for asynchronous text, audio, image, and video collections. The summarization system produced textual summary from the sources.

Menéndez et al. [2] developed a summarization system to enhance the graph-based overview method by integrating genetic clustering and graph connectivity information. The various topics in a document were defined by genetic clustering, and connectivity information indicated the significance of the various topics.

The authors of [3] implemented a summarization system to retrieve the problem statement from a research paper and later used it to identify the related research papers. The output phrases made the search query succinct. This greatly decreased the amount of Internet searches and, at the same time, yielded a high efficiency.

This paper [4] discussed about one of the famous pretrained models "BART" which is an existing pretrained model which is an autoencoder based sequence to sequence model. It is a transformer based neural machine translation architecture which is trained with text corpus data including noise functions, aiming to reconstruct original text, text to text translation and text summarisation.

This paper [5] mainly discusses the concept of Transfer Learning, where the weights of a model which is fully trained on huge datasets are extracted and transferred into another network in order to tune the last the layers of the network according to our requirements based on our dataset. This kind of approach is implemented on various NLP and Deep learning models to give rise to different methodologies and practices to achieve state of the art results.

The authors of this paper [6] proposed a new abstractive based text summarisation based on deep recurrent generative decoder(DRGN). For improving the quality of summaries and address the intractable posterior inference recurrent latent summaries along with Neural variational inference is employed. These results achieves improvements over the state-of the-art methods.

In 2015, Fadl Mutaher Ba-Alwi et al. proposed a method [7] called as Latent semantic analysis for Arab text summarization. LSA or latent semantic analysis is a vectorial semantic form of analyzing connections and similarities between a collection of sentences. The root representative is empirically selected as the most effective word. In his research, he brought together the root representative with different weighting techniques and LSA then an optimal combination of them is used and proposed as the summarizer for Arabic text summarization. Only the root representative has an average ROGUE score of 48.5% and achieved an F1-score of 63%. While the LSA implemented technique has improved these numbers considerably when compared to human summarizer with an average ROGUE score of 59% and an F1-score of 68%.

3   Methodology

3.1   Dataset and Pre-processing

The dataset consists of 1093400 rows of articles that have been scraped from sites like Economic Times and Times of India. Seven columns make up the dataset including columns like – "articleid", article body", "synopsis" among other columns that describe the category of the article. The various categories of articles from the dataset are – News, Recos, Policy, Finance, Airlines/Aviation, Market News, Banking, Indicators, Earnings and Corporate Trends. The distribution of each kind of articles is shown in Fig. 1.

Label	No. of Rows
News	83634
Recos	59412
Policy	35605
Finance	17454
Airlines / Aviation	15207
Market News	14886
Banking	14571
Indicators	13953
Earnings	12488
Corporate Trends	12102

Fig. 1. The data distribution of dataset used in this paper.

Since the articles have been directly scraped from the websites, they consist of many HTML tags like <div>, <br> etc. A sample article from the "article body" column of the dataset is shown as below (Fig. 2):

"Extending its gain for the second consecutive trading session, shares of Anil Ambani-led Reliance Communications (RCom) on Monday surged over 5 per cent on the BSE to become the top gainer of the day.

After a strong opening on the Bombay Stock Exchange, the telecom giant continued its rally and zoomed 5.14 per cent to settle at Rs 175. During the day, the scrip had climbed 5.58 per cent to touch a month's high of Rs 175.75.

The scrip has gained 10.68 per cent in the last two trading sessions.
<br attributed the rise in the telecom stocks to renewed investor interest amid a spurt in telecom scrips globally.

On the National Stock Exchange, the stock ended with a gain of 5.25 per cent to close at Rs 175.50.

Most of the telecom counters nished the day in the green."

Fig. 2. The figure shows an article without preprocessing from the dataset used in this paper.

And the sample synopsis of the article is – "Extending its gain for the second consecutive trading session, shares of Anil Ambani-led Reliance Communications on Monday surged over 5% on BSE to become the top gainer of the day."

In addition to the HTML tags that are left behind in the article due to web scraping, there were many abnormal escape characters present in the article and synopsis as well which had to be cleared. A sample of the cleaned article is shown as below (Fig. 3):

"MUMBAI: Extending its gain for the second consecutive trading session, shares of Anil Ambani-led Reliance Communications (RCom) on Monday surged over 5 per cent on the BSE to become the top gainer of the day. After a strong opening on the Bombay Stock Exchange, the telecom giant continued its rally and zoomed 5.14 per cent to settle at Rs 175. During the day, the scrip had climbed 5.58 per cent to touch a month's high of Rs 175.75. The scrip has gained 10.68 per cent in the last two trading sessions. Analysts attributed the rise in the telecom stocks to renewed investor interest amid a spurt in telecom scrips globally. On the National Stock Exchange, the stock ended with a gain of 5.25 per cent to close at Rs 175.50. Most of the telecom counters nished the day in the green."

Fig. 3. The figure shows an article after preprocessing from the dataset used in this paper.

3.2 Transformers

Recent development has shifted the dependency to solve NLP task from recurrent neural networks to transformer-based models. The initial use of transfer was restricted to machine translation but now it is effectively applied to other text-to-text-based applications. The primary component of a Transformer is self-attention, self-attention mechanism uses the weighted-average method to generate a sequence from a given sequence [9].

The transformers use in this paper follow encoder-decoder architecture [10]. The text sequence is converted into tokens and then before passing into encoder these tokens are mapped to embedding vector. An encoder comprises self-attention layer and feed-forward module. The Fig. 4 shows the architecture of transformer.

A sequence to sequence denoising encoder model BART is used in this paper.

Another encoder-decoder model used for generating the summary is T5 [14]. It has given a unified method to convert all text-based language problem to be converted into a text-to-text problem. T5 has successfully shown the effectiveness of a single model in various text-based problems using same decoding and loss function.

Transfer learning has shown great success in various natural language processing applications. Transfer learning is effectively used in numerous text-based tasks as a state-of-the-art approach. The reason behind the success of transfer learning is that it is trained on an abundantly available dataset. This paper explores the possibilities of applying transfer learning by training the existing model with our dataset and check the performance of the updated system.

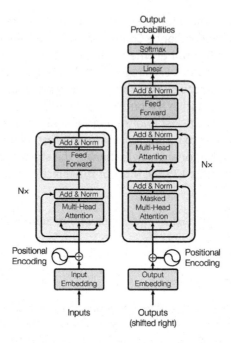

Fig. 4. The figure depicts the model architecture of transformer [10].

4   Experiments and Results

The experiments were conducted on different types of news articles related to politics, business, commodities etc. on all the models i.e. T5, BART and transfer learning models.

To compare the results and performance of the models we used ROUGE and BLEU score with standard options as evaluation metrics which basically compares the number of overlapping between the predicted summaries with original summaries based on N-grams, three types of Rouge Scales are used ROUGE-1 (R-1), ROUGE-L (R-L), ROUGE-L Sum (R-Ls).

Table 1 shows the results of both Rouge and BLEU scores obtained from Transfer Learning model based on T5 transformers where model predicted summaries are compared with the original Summaries.

Even though the model is not trained with much data and not much epoch/iterations the model was able to generate a decent summaries with a good score.

Table 2 depicts the results of both Rouge and BLEU scores obtained from T5 model where model predicted summaries are compared with the original Summaries.

The results generated by T5 pretrained model turned out to be very good and also the summaries generated by this model were accurate. Table 3 shows

Table 1. The Rouge and BLUE score obtained using transfer learning model based on T5.

S. No.	BLEU score	Rouge score (R-Ls)
1	0.353553	0.63157
2	0.329341	1.0
3	0.432802	0.67567
4	0.429694	0.16
5	0.488923	0.2

Table 2. BLEU and Rouge SCORE of T5 model.

S. No.	BLEU score	Rouge score (R-Ls)
1	0.429086	0.94
2	0.461736	1.0
3	0.445005	0.62
4	0.436683	0.19
5	0.436683	0.18

Table 3. BLEU and Rouge score of BART model.

S. No.	BLEU score	Rouge score (R-Ls)
1	0.35782	0.58
2	0.37239	0.12
3	0.35494	0.42
4	0.35782	0.21
5	0.42552	0.32

the results of both Rouge and BLEU scores obtained from BART model where model predicted summaries are compared with the original Summaries.

The results generated by BART pretrained model also turned out to be efficient and the summaries generated by this model were also delivering the message correctly from the article.

But by comparing all the obtained results as shown in Table 4 and Table 5, the pretrained T5 model results turned out to be high among all the models and also the summaries generated by T5 were more accurate and nearer to the original summaries.

Table 4. BLEU score of all models

S. No.	Transfer learning	BART	T5
1	0.353553	0.35782	0.429086
2	0.329341	0.37239	0.461736
3	0.432802	0.35494	0.445005
4	0.429694	0.35782	0.434720
5	0.488923	0.42552	0.436683

Table 5. ROUGE SCORE of all models

S. No.	Transfer learning	BART	T5
1	0.63	0.58	0.94
2	1.0	0.12	1.0
3	0.67	0.42	0.62
4	0.16	0.21	0.19
5	0.2	0.32	0.18

5   Conclusion

In several NLP applications, including text summarization, pre-trained language models have shown enormous progress. BART and T5 are two such state-of-the-art pre-trained models which have given excellent results for the task of text summarization. In this paper, we have tuned these models with the help of transfer learning to generate news article summaries. The results show that t5 gives better result than other two models used for testing.

References

1. Li, H., Zhu, J., Ma, C., Zhang, J., Zong, C.: Read, watch, listen and summarize: multi-modal summarization for asynchronous text, image, audio and video. IEEE Trans. Knowl. Data Eng. **31**, 996–1009 (2018)
2. Menéndez, H.D., Plaza, L., Camacho, D.: Combining graph connectivity and genetic clustering to improve biomedical summarization. Paper Presented at the 2014 IEEE Congress on Evolutionary Computation (CEC) (2014)
3. Alampalli Ramu, N.A., Bandarupalli, M.S., Nekkanti, M.S.S., Ramesh, G.: Summarization of research publications using automatic extraction. In: Hemanth, D., Shakya, S., Baig, Z. (eds.) Intelligent Data Communication Technologies and Internet of Things, ICICI 2019 (2020)
4. Lewis, M., et al.: BART Denoising Sequence-to-Sequence Pre-training for Natural Language Generation, Translation, and Comprehension. Facebook AI
5. Raffel, C., Shazeer, N., Roberts, A., Lee, K., Narang, S.: Exploring the Limits of Transfer Learning with a Unified Text-to-Text Transformer

6. Li, P., Lam, W., Bing, L., Wang, Z.: Deep recurrent generative decoder for abstractive text summarization. Key Laboratory on High Confidence Software Technologies (Sub-Lab, CUHK), Ministry of Education, China, Department of Systems Engineering and Engineering Management, The Chinese University of Hong Kong, AI Lab, Tencent Inc., Shenzhen, China

7. Ba-Alwi, F., Gaphari, G.H., Al-Duqaimi, F.: Arabic text summarization using latent semantic analysis. CJAST **10**(2), 1–14 (2015)

8. Liu, Y., Lapata, M.: Text summarization with pretrained encoders. arXiv preprint arXiv:1908.08345 (2019)

9. Cheng, J., Dong, L., Lapata, M.: Long short-term memory-networks for machine reading. arXiv preprint arXiv:1601.06733 (2016)

10. Vaswani, A., et al.: Attention is all you need. In: Advances in Neural Information Processing Systems, pp. 5998–6008 (2017)

11. Nenkova, A., McKeown, K.: A survey of text summarization techniques. In: Aggarwal, C., Zhai, C. (eds.) Mining Text Data. Springer, Boston (2012). https://doi.org/10.1007/978-1-4614-3223-4_3

12. Barzilay, R., McKeown, K.R.: Sentence fusion for multidocument news summarization. Comput. Linguist. **31**(3), 297–328 (2005)

13. Bing, L., Li, P., Liao, Y., Lam, W., Guo, W., Passonneau, R.: Abstractive multidocument summarization via phrase selection and merging. In: ACL, pp. 1587–1597 (2015)

14. Raffel, C., et al.: Exploring the limits of transfer learning with a unified text-to-text transformer. arXiv preprint arXiv:1910.10683 (2019)

15. Miao, Y., Blunsom, P.: Language as a latent variable: discrete generative models for sentence compression. In: EMNLP, pp. 319–328 (2016)

QA System: Business Intelligence in Healthcare

Apar Garg, Tapas Badal[(✉)] [ID], and Debajyoti Mukhopadhyay [ID]

Bennett University, Greater Noida, India
tapas.badal@bennett.edu.in

Abstract. Nowadays, Question Answering (QA) systems are used as an automated assistant system for resolving queries in various messaging applications. Accessing a database to get specific information can be stressful and time-consuming if one does not have the much needed technical skills. Designing a QA system/chatbot that can generate the result by accessing the database dynamically has linguistic and design challenges. In this work, we present a medical domain-specific QA system, which can provide real-time response to any employee's standard business queries in a healthcare company by removing unwanted dependencies on the analytics team. The QA system uses Natural Language Processing (NLP) and Deep Learning (DL) techniques for Named Entity Recognition and text pre-processing, etc. The higher precision value achieved during pilot evaluation has shown how effective our proposed system is for the medical domain question answering system.

Keywords: QA system · NER · Data engine · Bar plot

1 Introduction

A new study suggests that technology is turning individuals more and more impatient each day. In this age of information technology, Google has become the de-facto place to get instant answers to generic queries. However, these days a typical user wants a solution to his specific question. Users might have to query a vast database to get specific information they needs. A typical user is generally not comfortable using a database to retrieve the information he/she needs because it either requires the knowledge of complex programming languages or an inter-mediator, which can use the databases and tell the result to the user. However, using an intermediary or learning a programming language is very tiresome and taxing. People having a technical background could also find this task a bit difficult sometimes.

For solving these kinds of problems, Question Answering (QA) systems [1] were introduced. They are systems that take questions from the user in natural language as their input and send back answers. It indicates an advancement over regular IR frameworks. They integrate methods from the fields of Information Retrieval (IR), Information Extraction (IE), and, more broadly, Natural

© Springer Nature Singapore Pte Ltd. 2021
D. Garg et al. (Eds.): IACC 2020, CCIS 1367, pp. 212–223, 2021.
https://doi.org/10.1007/978-981-16-0401-0_16

Language Processing (NLP). A typical design for a QA system involves the query analysis, the detection of suitable keywords for retrieving results from an unstructured, semi-structured, or structured knowledge base.

A QA system manages natural language processing for interfacing the QA at the user side, who poses numerous questions. The first type of question that can be asked by a user is the factoid question. It is often asked about Named Entity (NE), utilizing, for example, the words: When, Where, How much/many, Who, and What, asking about the date/time, etc. The second type of question is the question raised about the meaning of a word or a concept. Such a question is generally asked using the words "Why" or "How".

QA systems can be open domain or closed domain [1]. Open domain systems answer any question and are not limited to domain and predefined knowledge. Such systems search for a substantial amount of data to answer. Whereas, in a closed domain system, domain knowledge plays a vital role. The answers to the queries are trained on domain-specific questions and answers. The other type of QA system is Knowledge-based QA (KBQA). The core idea of KBQA is to convert the natural language query into a structured database query.

This paper introduces a medical domain-specific knowledge-based QA system, which can answer the queries related to sales and marketing of drugs from a given database. This topic, though, to our knowledge, has not yet been explored. The QA system provides real-time response to the common business queries of any employee in a healthcare company by removing unwanted dependencies on the analytics team. This could bring significant time savings to both the analytics team and the employees having queries. We address factual questions expressed by WH pronouns. An answer can just be a table or a combination of table and bar plot(s). We focus on searching and extracting answers from our own database. However, the suggested solution can easily be extended to other resources as well.

There are four main contributions in this paper:

1. Design a QA system for Healthcare Domain: A Deep Learning based QA system is designed to understand healthcare queries. It extracts entities and establishes a correspondence between multiple instances of entities. Hence, we have proposed an end-to-end system to understand user queries and generate responses using a data engine.
2. Design an Interface to connect QA system with Data engine: An active real-time QA system is proposed, which replies to a user query by fetching the data in real-time from the data engine.
3. Collection of domain-specific data: No sample query data is available for healthcare QA system research. We have collected data for different types of sample questions, each with unique functionality for training and testing. We have also created a sample Data Engine to fetch results.
4. Customised training: We have custom trained spaCy[1] model for Named Entity Recognition [2].

---

[1] https://spacy.io/usage/training#ner.

The remainder of this paper is structured as follows. Section 2 introduces related work in QA systems with a focus on the medical domain. Section 3 describes the proposed methodology, comprises of five steps: User query, Query pre-processing, Named Entity Recognition(NER), Translation of Extracted Entities and Data Engine. Section 4 introduces the results. Finally, in Sect. 5, we discuss the Conclusion and Future Work.

2 Related Work

Recent developments in Deep Learning and Natural Language Processing have introduced domain-specific QA systems and chatbots as digital assisting technologies to answer user queries dynamically. In the following subsections, we summarize work done in the past related to medical domain-specific QA systems and chatbots.

2.1 Question Answering System

During early 1960s, when Artificial Intelligence was in a very rudimentary stage, various systems were created, which can understand variety of languages, with the help of a large database and dialogue system. The ideation of QA system was done by Turing, in 1950 by "Imitation Game", which was later known as the famous "Turing Test". This was the very first machine, which could communicate with a human with the help of a teletype.

Weizenbaum et al. [3] designed the first natural language database system called ELIZA for simulating a psychotherapist. It worked on identifying patterns and simple structural and syntactic structures in the database from the user inputs. In another research, Green et al. [4] proposed BASEBALL, which was another domain-specific question answering system for statistical queries regarding baseball games, played during the American league.

Woods et al. [5] proposed LUNAR, a QA system that gave information on soil samples taken from lunar exploration by Apollo. The system turned user questions into database queries by means of simple pattern matching rules and produce answers at last. In a similar research, Androutsopoulos et al. [6] proposed a NLIDB framework that facilitated the users to ask questions in their natural languages and later obtained data from databases.

Clarke et al. [7] looked to the web as a question answering asset. The framework provided by them performed complex parsing and extraction of entities for both queries and best-matching web pages.

Brill et al. [8] proposed the AskMSR QA system design and evaluated the contributions to accuracy from the various system components. They additionally discussed predictive approaches, where the answering question system would possibly throw an erroneous response. In a similar research, Zheng et al. [9] developed AnswerBus, which is an open-domain QA framework focused on retrieval of information at the sentence level. It addressed natural-language questions from users in various languages such as English and German and extract potential Web answers.

Abacha et al. [10] introduced MEANS, which combined NLP and semantic web technologies. The paper used Medical entity recognition, which could detect and eliminate the phrasal information referring to medical entities and classify the entities in predefined categories. The categories were problem, test, drug, etc.

Zhu et al. [11] gave a hierarchical attention retrieval model for question answering in the healthcare domain. The proposed model used two bi-directional RNN encoders to encode the inter-documents dependencies for a given query and document words. It also used cross attention between the query and the document. The system could answer binary answers, who, etc. But, it was mainly designed for "what" and "how" type of questions in the healthcare domain.

2.2   Chatbot

Question Answering (QA) is one of the tasks of a Chatbot. A Chatbot is a system, which interacts with humans in natural language. Besides answering, the questions of a user, it can be made to perform other tasks such as book tickets and order food.

Chatbots and QA systems are now prevalent everywhere, ranging from smartphones to domain-specific places. A chatbot comprises of, speech to text conversion and natural language processing, using dialogue act recognition and intent identification for information extraction. For intent identification, bag of words, latent semantic analysis, regular expressions, part of speech tagging, named entity recognition, etc. are used [12]. The basic components of nearly each chatbot system are chat engine, data engine, and interpreter program.

Previously, work has been done for chatbots in the medical domain. Ni et al. [13] proposed MANDY to facilitate the medical staff by automating the patient intake. The bot asked questions in natural language regarding symptoms of their illness. The previous reports and the symptoms of that person were then compiled together by the bot for the doctor. Another system was developed for giving medicines, by taking care of the age of the patients and side effects, by making disease predictions from the symptoms [14]. In another research, Liu et al. [15] developed a system for differentiating questions of consumers and professionals in the healthcare domain.

In 2018, Ahmad et al. [16] designed a chatbot containing mainly three functionalities. If the user is informed about any illness, then the bot suggested the type of medicine which can be consumed. Secondly, if the user asked about the medicine, then the bot gave the functions of the medicine. Lastly, the bot suggested how to consume that medicine. It also gave users an option for getting the delivery of the required medicine.

Cameron et al. [17] implemented iHelpr for mental healthcare which managed self-evaluation tools/scales and provided advice and information on welfare, all within a conversational platform.

Pereira et al. [18] conducted a survey in 2019 seeking answers to questions regarding chatbots in the medical domain. What illness chatbots are tackling, what are the competencies of patients the chatbot are aimed at, and what are the most popular technical enablers for a chatbot. They reached the conclusion that the most active health areas are mental and physical wellness. "Affect" and "cognition" are the most used human competencies to detect behavior change and "consumability" is the best enabler for the chatbot.

Ruf et al. [19] presented a travel chatbot companion for smartphones named Pharmabroad for medical assistance while traveling. It matched the medicine from the user's home market to the parallel product in the new surroundings. It used image recognition and OCR for text extraction from the user's medical box. It then mapped medicine name to molecule name and then inversed the mappings for the new medicine name in the new area. The new medicine image for the required drug was then presented to the user.

3   Methodology

In this paper, we have proposed a medical domain-specific knowledge-based QA system. A distinguishing feature of the proposed system is its ability to address dynamic queries using the data engine. Figure 1 presents the basic architecture of our QA system. Firstly, the user submits a query to the QA Engine. The submitted query is pre-processed and is sent to the NLP Engine. The NLP Engine extracts keywords or Named Entities, from the query. Then the extracted

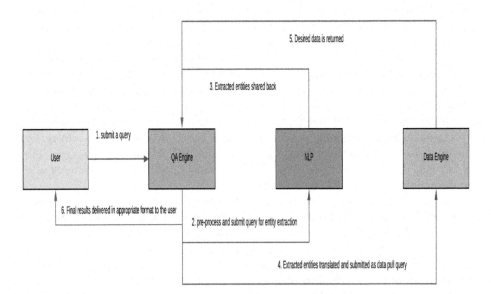

Fig. 1. Proposed QA system architecture. There AI enable QA system is used to resolve the queries and further it is connected with a data engine to perform the data analysis for response.

entities are forwarded to the Data Engine for retrieval of results. The retrieved results are formulated in the form of statistical figures if needed.

3.1 User Query

A user can submit multiple types of queries to the QA system, one at a time. The figure below shows some of the possible user queries with the type of functionality they are testing. Some of the queries are listed in Table 1 below.

Table 1. Sample queries

Type of functionality tested	Sample question
Singe value question	What is the total sales of Prolia in USA in quarter 1 of 2018?
Multiple value question	What is the total sales of Alendronate in Canada and France in Q2 2019?
Different KPIs	What is the QTD sales of Prolia and Alendronate?
Comparsion by time period	What is the sales of Xgeva in Q4 2016 vs last year same time period?

3.2 Query Pre-processing

Pre-processing of the user query is an important phase in our system. We have done pre-processing in three steps, as mentioned below:

Noise Removal. Punctuations and additional white spaces do not give significant information to the query. They are just noise in text. Therefore, we have removed all punctuations (except comma, a hyphen, and question-mark) and additional white spaces in the query.

Lowercasing. Lowercasing was done to simplify the task of normalization of the query. Hence, there is no need to map both 'United States' and 'united states' to 'US'. After lowercasing the query, 'United States' will also get converted to 'united states'. So mapping 'united states' to 'US' is sufficient. This task has saved a lot of space in our table of synonyms and acronyms.

Normalization. We have compiled a table of synonyms and acronyms from various sources on the web. The table consists of 200 synonyms and acronyms, which are mapped to their actual representation in the Data Engine. Table 2 given below shows some examples. This is helpful when for e.g. United Kingdom, England, Britain maps to only one country in the data engine i.e. UK.

Table 2. Synonyms and acronyms used in the dataset for QA system.

Representation in query	Representation in data engine
United Kingdom	UK
Year to date	YTD
United States	US
Quarter to date	QTD
England	UK

3.3 Named Entity Recognition (NER)

spaCy [2] is an open-source library for advanced NLP, in Python. spaCy provides an exceptionally efficient statistical system for NER in python, which can assign labels to groups of tokens, which are contiguous. The library is developed as a modular pipeline and offers a range of tools for rapid text processing. It parses content to construct a custom spaCy data structure which is later gone through structured pipeline components to be processed further. The pipeline components are highly customizable for optimal performance of NLP tasks such as NER etc. Additionally, these components can be changed separately to conform to different implementations. The NER component in the spaCy pipeline is a deep learning model utilizing CNN and LSTM architectures.

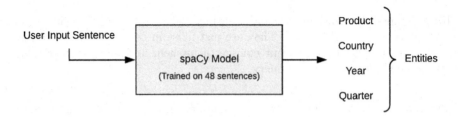

Fig. 2. spaCy model overview - black box

We have trained a blank spaCy model using annotated training data to recognize four custom entities from the user query: product, country, quarter, and year. For annotating data, a custom-built web browser-based tool called spaCy

NER Annotator[2] was used. These custom entity tags are also the attributes in the Data Engine.

The model was trained on 48 sentences. After training it for 20 epochs with dropout 0.2 and SGD optimizer, the model gave a training loss of 2.26^{-8}. Figure 2 presents black box of the model.

Our experimental set up included working with spaCy version 2.2.3 on an Anaconda Distribution, Python 3.8.1 environment running on a machine with Windows version 1903, Intel Core Processor i5 8th Gen with 8 GB RAM.

3.4   Translation of Extracted Entities

Edit distance [20] is a method for finding how dissimilar two strings are. It can also be viewed as the minimum number of editing required to transform a word into another word. For example, the edit distance between the words "ran" and "run" is 1. Three operations are allowed on a character: insert a character, delete a character, and replace a character. This problem is solved using dynamic programming.

We have used the edit distance technique, to rectify spelling errors in extracted entities. The entry in the Data Engine column (with corr. entity tag) having the minimum edit distance with the entity, is considered to be the right spelling of the entity. The minimum edit distance of an entity must be less than 2, for it to get transformed.

3.5   Data Engine

If the translated entities are not present in the Data Engine, then the QA system response is "Apologies... I don't understand your question". If there is any lack of information within the query, the QA system will request for more inputs from the user. After this, the translated entities are mapped to entries in the database to fetch "Total Sales" (represented by US\$ MNF in Data Engine) corresponding to those entries.

The retrieved results for sales could be a single row or it could be multiple rows. The QA system will accompany the result with a bar plot in case of multiple row output.

4   Results

We conducted a pilot evaluation task for the QA system that included a group of people who did not work on the QA system's design and implementation phases. We asked these people to manually construct 75 sample questions as per the 15 different functionality types (F1: five questions that are matched to the first functionality type; ...; F15: five questions that are adjusted to the

---

[2] https://manivannanmurugavel.github.io/annotating-tool/spacy-ner-annotator/.

fifteenth functionality type.). 5 sample questions were created for each functionality type. Table 3 shows the obtained results for each functionality type and
Table 4 presents the summarized results.

The pilot evaluation task aimed to check the robustness of the system with
respect to each functionality type by testing whether or not each of the 75
questions yielded the correct output. We apply the precision measure (P) as a
measure of evaluation specified as:

$$Precision measure(P) = \frac{No. \ of \ questions \ with \ correct \ output}{Total \ no. \ of \ questions \ in \ functionality \ type}$$

Table 3. Evaluation table showing functionality type of each question category and
precision achieved in this paper.

Functionality type	Questions	Correct	Precision
F1	5	5	1
F2	5	5	1
F3	5	5	1
F4	5	4	0.8
F5	5	5	1
F6	5	5	1
F7	5	5	1
F8	5	4	0.8
F9	5	5	1
F10	5	4	0.8
F11	5	5	1
F12	5	3	0.6
F13	5	5	1
F14	5	5	1
F15	5	4	0.8

Table 4. Summarized evaluation table gives overall result.

Functionality type	Questions	Correct	Overall precision
F1 to F15	75	69	0.92

Figure 3 presents some of the output bar plots for input user queries.

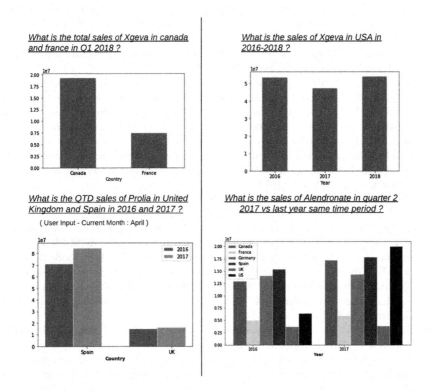

Fig. 3. Figure depicts the result after processing the query in the form of bar plots.

5   Conclusion and Future Work

The goal of this work was to build a Question Answering system in the medical domain which can provide real-time responses to the common business queries of any employee in a healthcare company by removing unwanted dependencies on the analytics teams. After applying our system to various sample queries made by a group of random individuals, it was found that our model showed promising results.

Our future goal is to work on boolean questions expecting a yes/no answer and other types of factual questions. Another future goal is to work on dependency parsing of a sentence, which will be helpful to determine the dependency of entities on one-another.

References

1. Terol, R.M., Martínez-Barco, P., Palomar, M.: A knowledge based method for the medical question answering problem. Comput. Biol. Med. **37**(10), 1511–1521 (2007)
2. Mansouri, A., Affendey, L.S., Mamat, A.: Named entity recognition approaches. Int. J. Comput. Sci. Netw. Secur. **8**(2), 339–344 (2008)
3. Weizenbaum, J.: ELIZA–a computer program for the study of natural language communication between man and machine. Commun. ACM **9**(1), 36–45 (1966)
4. Green Jr., B.F., Wolf, A.K., Chomsky, C., Laughery, K.: Baseball: an automatic question-answerer. Papers Presented at the May 9–11, 1961, Western Joint IRE-AIEE-ACM Computer Conference, pp. 219–224 (1961)
5. Woods, W.A.: Progress in natural language understanding: an application to lunar geology. In: Proceedings of the June 4–8, 1973, National Computer Conference and Exposition, pp. 441–450 (1973)
6. Androutsopoulos, I., Ritchie, G.D., Thanisch, P.: Natural language interfaces to databases-an introduction. Nat. Lang. Eng. **1**(1), 29–81 (1995)
7. Clarke, C.L.A., Cormack, G.V., Lynam, T.R.: Exploiting redundancy in question answering. In: Proceedings of the 24th Annual International ACM SIGIR Conference on Research and Development in Information Retrieval, pp. 358–365 (2001)
8. Brill, E., Dumais, S., Banko, M.: An analysis of the AskMSR question-answering system. In: Proceedings of the ACL-02 Conference on Empirical Methods in Natural Language Processing, vol. 10, pp. 257–264. Association for Computational Linguistics (2002)
9. Zheng, Z.: AnswerBus question answering system. In: Human Language Technology Conference (HLT 2002), vol. 27 (2002)
10. Abacha, A.B., Zweigenbaum, P.: MEANS: a medical question-answering system combining NLP techniques and semantic web technologies. Inf. Process. Manag. **51**(5), 570–594 (2015). University of Pennsylvania School of Engineering and Applied Science Department of Computer and Information Science (2017)
11. Zhu, M., Ahuja, A., Wei, W., Reddy, C.K.: A hierarchical attention retrieval model for healthcare question answering. In: The World Wide Web Conference, pp. 2472–2482 (2019)
12. Cahn, J.: CHATBOT: architecture, design, & development. University of Pennsylvania School of Engineering and Applied Science Department of Computer and Information Science (2017)
13. Ni, L., Lu, C., Liu, N., Liu, J.: MANDY: towards a smart primary care chatbot application. In: Chen, J., Theeramunkong, T., Supnithi, T., Tang, X. (eds.) KSS 2017. CCIS, vol. 780, pp. 38–52. Springer, Singapore (2017). https://doi.org/10.1007/978-981-10-6989-5_4
14. Madhu, D., Jain, C.N., Sebastain, E., Shaji, S., Ajayakumar, A.: A novel approach for medical assistance using trained chatbot. In: 2017 International Conference on Inventive Communication and Computational Technologies (ICICCT), pp. 243–246. IEEE (2017)
15. Liu, F., Antieau, L.D., Hong, Yu.: Toward automated consumer question answering: automatically separating consumer questions from professional questions in the healthcare domain. J. Biomed. Inform. **44**(6), 1032–1038 (2011)
16. Ahmad, N.S., Sanusi, M.H., Abd Wahab, M.H., Mustapha, A., Sayadi, Z.A., Saringat, M.Z.: Conversational bot for pharmacy: a natural language approach. In: 2018 IEEE Conference on Open Systems (ICOS), pp. 76–79. IEEE (2018)

17. Cameron, G., et al.: Best practices for designing chatbots in mental healthcare-a case study on iHelpr. In: Proceedings of the 32nd International BCS Human Computer Interaction Conference 32, pp. 1–5 (2018)
18. Pereira, J., Díaz, Ó.: Using health chatbots for behavior change: a mapping study. J. Med. Syst. **43**(5), 135 (2019)
19. Ruf, B., Sammarco, M., Aigrain, J., Detyniecki, M.: Pharmabroad: a companion chatbot for identifying pharmaceutical products when traveling abroad. In: Neidhardt, J., Wörndl, W. (eds.) Information and Communication Technologies in Tourism 2020, pp. 218–228. Springer, Cham (2020). https://doi.org/10.1007/978-3-030-36737-4_18
20. Ristad, E.S., Yianilos, P.N.: Learning string-edit distance. IEEE Trans. Pattern Anal. Mach. Intell. **20**(5), 522–532 (1998)

Multidomain Sentiment Lexicon Learning Using Genre-Seed Embeddings

Swati Sanagar[ID] and Deepa Gupta[✉][ID]

Department of Computer Science and Engineering, Amrita School of Engineering, Bengaluru, Amrita Vishwa Vidyapeetham, Bangalore, India
swatisanagar@yahoo.co.in, g_deepa@blr.amrita.edu

Abstract. Sentiment lexicon is widely used resource which plays an important role in sentiment analysis tasks. Sentiment lexicon learning using minimum labeled resources for multiple domains is a challenging task. Multiple domains with similar characteristics are considered as same genre domains in our work. We present an unsupervised sentiment lexicon learning model for same-genre multiple domains. The model uses pre-learned genre-based polarity seed words as only labeled input and explore sentiment lexicon learning using different unsupervised word-embedding approaches. The pretrained embedding provides generalized word vectors, so our approach explores it further by creating domain-based word-embeddings. The experimentation involves sentiment lexicon learning using Word2Vec, GloVe, and fastText word-embeddings. The experiments are conducted on 18 same genre domains. The different word-embedding sentiment lexicon learning model results are compared across genre-base domains using standard evaluation metrics. The proposed model performs good in comparison to the existing models from the literature.

Keywords: Sentiment Lexicon · Word2Vec · GloVe · fastText · Sentiment Analysis · Transfer Learning · Multiple domains · Word-embedding · Seed Words

1 Introduction

Sentiment analysis is a branch of natural language processing which deals with identifying and extracting sentiments/opinions from text data. In sentiment analysis, people's experiences are considered as public opinions gauge, which is used to monitor the brand status, to understand the product reputation, to analyze market, and in many other applications [1, 2]. Sentiment lexicon is a widely used resource which plays important role in sentiment analysis tasks. They are formed by putting together the sentiment words and their polarity/scores. Sentiment lexicons fall in two categories, general-purpose and domain based. The former is less effective in identifying sentiments in domain level tasks [3] as compared to the latter, which identifies domain-level sentiment words and domain-relevant polarity and intensity. One domain-level sentiment lexicon may differ from other domain in terms of sentiment word polarity, intensity, and domain-specific words. A domain-level learning process of sentiment lexicon is independent of

© Springer Nature Singapore Pte Ltd. 2021
D. Garg et al. (Eds.): IACC 2020, CCIS 1367, pp. 224–242, 2021.
https://doi.org/10.1007/978-981-16-0401-0_17

other domains. Sentiment lexicon learning is either a supervised or unsupervised/semi-supervised process [4, 5]. The supervised learning approaches need labeled data for every new domain, this leads to lacks in scalability as data labeling is costly and cumbersome work. Unsupervised/semi-supervised approaches, on the other hand, use seed words or a very few labeled data instances for sentiment lexicon learning [3]. Sentiment lexicon learning still remains a challenging task.

The general-purpose lexicons provide generalized polarity/scores for sentiment words, therefore domain-level lexicon learning approaches are important. Aiming at the unsupervised/semi-supervised sentiment lexicon learning, word-embeddings approaches can be promising based on their performance of sentiment analysis tasks [6]. Design and usage of distributed word-embedding has gained popularity and its applications are explored on multiple different tasks [7–9]. Word embeddings represent words as a continuous vector and their strength lies in the ability to capture similarities in word meaning. The popular and most explored word-embedding techniques includes Word2vec Skip-Gram and Continuous Bag-Of-Words (CBOW) [7], Global Vector (GloVe) [8], and fastText [9]. Word2Vec is a statistical word-embedding technique that efficiently captures syntactic and semantic regularities. It has two models CBOW that predicts target word from context words and Skip-Gram model that predicts context words from the given word. GloVe model is considered an extension of word2vec model that combines global statistics and local learning. fastText is as well considered as an extension of word2vec in different direction with granularity consideration using n-gram.

We propose an unsupervised solution to address the research gap in the learning process between general purpose lexicon and in-domain lexicon learning. Different sources of data are spread over multiple domains such as consumer reviews, blogs, news, twitter etc. Each of these data source is a genre which is characterized by style of writing, the text used beneath, content size, other unique, and general characteristics. We propose a genre-based multidomain sentiment lexicon leaning approach, where the model uses pre-learned genre-based polarity seed words [10] as only labeled input and explores sentiment lexicon learning using different existing unsupervised word-embedding models. The pretrained embeddings provide generalized word vectors, so our approach explores it further by creating domain-based word-embeddings. The model benefits from word-embedding characteristics which maps similar words closer. The genre-based polarity seed word and its domain-based embeddings play an important role in our genre-based domain sentiment lexicon learning approach.

The rest of this work is organized as follows. The related literature work is described in Sect. 2. The proposed genre-seed embedding model with different word-embedding creation process is described in Sect. 3. Data used in different experiments, the experimental setup, evaluation metrics and, baselines are described in Sect. 4. Experimental results in comparison with baselines are discussed in Sect. 5 and the analysis of results is discussed in Sect. 6. Section 7 presents conclusions and future directions.

2 Related Work

Lexicon learning from corpus is vastly studied in literature using different frameworks and approaches. In-domain sentiment lexicon learning, and domain transfer learning are the major frameworks. In-domain learning approaches learn and evaluate using domain corpora, while domain transfer learning approaches adapt/transfer learned knowledge from the source domain to the target domain.

One of the early in-domain learning approaches includes word polarity learning using Latent Semantic Analysis (LSA) and Pointwise Mutual Information (PMI) approaches [11]. A set of labeled words act as seed to calculate semantic orientation scores of sentiment words using mutual association between them. In another approach along with polarity identification score was assigned to noun, verb, and adjectives using knowledge of conjunctions and Bayesian computations [12]. A vector concept categorization approach was used to build relation between words and labeled star reviews [13]. A lexicon was constructed from concept category and word frequency for movie and hotel reviews. In another model, experimentation was conducted on five datasets including Twitter data, movie review etc. [14]. Sentiment word polarity variation between datasets is learned using labeled data and a generative model. Sentiment word and document were considered as hierarchical supervision to learn domain-based lexicon. A rule-based unsupervised model included movie review etc. three domains [15]. The dependency graph propagation generated sentiment lexicon based on rules and a few seed words. An autoencoder-meta embedding approach combined pretrained CBOW and GloVe word embedding to create meta-embeddings [16]. The experimentation was conducted on benchmark labeled twitter datasets. The model experimentation involved decouple, concatenated, and average autoencoder meta-embeddings.

Domain transfer-learning/adaptation is one-to-one and multidomain transfer learning. The multidomain transfer learning involves multiple source domain and single or multiple target domains. Sparse rectifier unit stacked denoising autoencoder model taken source domain features from labeled and unlabeled instances [17]. The experiment followed one-to-one domain transfer for all combinations of four domains. Another one-to-one domain transfer research framework [18] constructed combination of multiple embedding. The model concatenated word2vec, doc2vec, and SVD embeddings of source domain and adapted it to target domain. One-to-one domain transfer learning studies lack in defining source and target domains prior to the experimentation. This shortcoming is overcome by diverse multidomain transfer learning approaches. A multidomain approach considered three domains as source and one as target for all possible combinations [19]. The model learns global and domain-specific knowledge from source domains. The most similar domain is identified using graph similarity for domain-specific knowledge. Global knowledge is collected from all source domains considering sentiment-opposite and coherent relations. Similar setup is explored for Hindi language reviews [20]. This n-gram, PMI based model used labeled source and unlabeled target domain corpus to learn lexicon. An adversarial network segregated common features in shared encoder and domain-based features in private encoder [21]. The approach conducted study on four domains with one target and two source domain combinations. Another adversarial neural network study combined domain training and sentiment classification task together [22]. The approach modeled source and target domain data together for joint learning. An attention neural network model explored domain representation to select domain related features [23]. The source knowledge was adapted to target using simultaneous extraction of shared and domain related features.

In-domain supervised approaches are unscalable due to cumbersome labeling task. Unsupervised lexicon learning using seeds or limited labeled data breaks the barrier of requirement of data labeling. Domain transfer learning approaches improve learning scope by transferring the learned knowledge across domains. One-to-one domain transfer learning is inefficient as it demands testing all possible combinations of source-target domains to choose the best. The limitations are handled by multi-to-multi domain transfer learning. It is been studied under different setups and approaches, but most of the approaches use labeled data.

Our unsupervised learning approach do not use any labeled training data. The model uses genre-based polarity seed word knowledge and apply them to the same genre-domains.

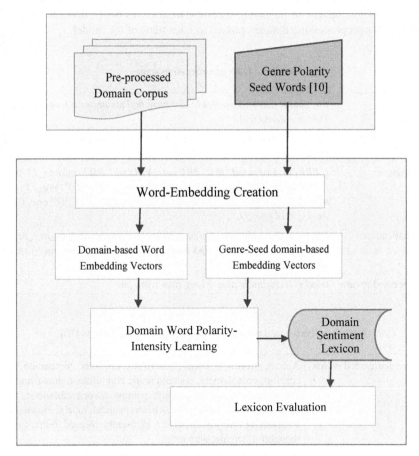

Fig. 1. The proposed model schematic

3 The Proposed Model

The proposed genre-based sentiment lexicon learning model explore usage of different word-embedding approaches at domain level. The model involves four steps, the first step performs data preprocessing, the second step is domain word-embedding vector creation, the third step is domain-based sentiment lexicon learning and, the final step is sentiment lexicon evaluation. The proposed model process is depicted in Fig. 1.

In the first step the data preprocessing is performed in multiple sub-steps. Data are normalized by excluding URLs, non-ASCII, and unwanted characters. Repeating characters are normalized with spell-check. Then the tokenized data are POS tagged, lemmatized [24] and verbs, adverbs, adjectives, and nouns except auxiliary verbs and proper nouns are selected and converted to lowercase. The preprocessing steps illustrating step-wise changes in an example review from Cell Phones domain is given in Table 1. After preprocessing data are passed to later steps of the model.

Table 1. Data preprocessing stages

Raw review	*I'm glad it was still available as I have had my phone a loooong time. This one works fine*
Initial processing	*I'm glad it was still available as I have had my phone a long time. This one works fine*
POS tagging	*I_PRP 'm_VBP glad_JJ it_PRP was_VBD still_RB available_JJ as_IN I_PRP have_VBP had_VBD my_PRP$ phone_NN a_DT long_JJ time_NN This_DT one_CD works_VBZ fine_JJ !_. This_DT one_CD works_VBZ fine_JJ !_*
Lemmatization	*I_prp be_vbp glad_jj it_prp be_vbd still_rb available_jj as_in I_prp have_vbp have_vbd my_prp$ phone_nn a_dt long_jj time_nn ._. this_dt one_cd work_vbz fine_jj !_*
Preprocessed review	*Glad still available phone long time work fine*

Table 2. Genre-based polarity (positive/negative) seed words [10]

Positive genre-seed words	Ample, affordable, bonus, beautifully, beginner, companion, comfort, complement, contemporary, compliment, drawback, detract, easy, excellent, elegant, exciting, favorite, fabulous, fantastic, highly, hesitate, instructor, magical, nicely, organize, outstanding, overjoyed, perfect, pleasantly, pleased, relax, superb, thoughtful, terrific, wonderful,
Negative genre-seed words	Aggravation, ashamed, annoys, awful, badly, crappy, crap, damn, disgusted, defective, donate, garbage, gimmick, horribly, horrible, insult, junk, joke, nonsense, nerve, piss, pathetic, refund, recourse, reimburse, scam, stupid, substandard, trash, torture, terrible, useless, waste, worthless, worst

The proposed model use genre-based polarity seed words listed in Table 2. which were learned in unsupervised setup from research paper by Sanagar and Gupta, 2020 [10]. The genre polarity seed words are learned from source domain corpus where source domains are selected from many domains of same genre. The genre polarity seed words are proved to be effective for consumer review genre and performed very good in unsupervised setup. The model also uses the unlabeled corpus mentioned in the work.

The domain-based preprocessed unlabeled corpus creates unsupervised word-embeddings The proposed model learns domain-based word-embedding using three popular unsupervised learning word-embedding approaches which exemplify three different ways to look at word embeddings. It includes Word2vec Skip-Gram and CBOW, GloVe, and fastText [7–9, 25].

a) Word2Vec Skip-Gram and CBOW

Word2vec is a neural network word-embedding learning model. The word-embeddings are created using a shallow neural network [7] which includes input, hidden, and output layer.

CBOW model predicts the most likely word i.e. target word given its C context words. The model takes one-hot encoded word vectors of the C context words of the vocabulary size V as the initial input. The input vector is multiplied by embedding matrix W_{VxN}. The input contains C context word vectors which are averaged to generate fixed length hidden vector that smooths over the distributional information.

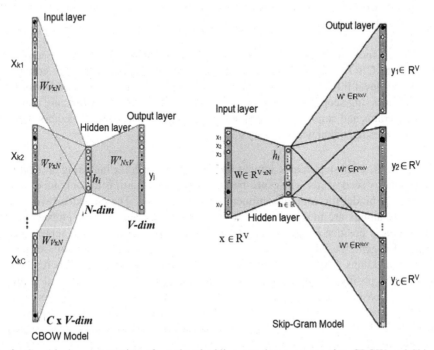

Fig. 2. Graphical representation of word-embedding creation process using CBOW and Skip-Gram models (Source: Google)

A hidden layer forms a hidden vector of size N. From the hidden layer to output layer is weight matrix $W_{N \times V}$, which is obtained by multiplying hidden vector and finally the output layer generates V dimensional output vector. The process is depicted in left portion of Fig. 2.

The skip-gram model predicts the context words given the target word. Skip-gram works well with small amount of data and provides well representation for rare words. It takes input as one-hot encoded target word and work on generating the C context words $y_1, ..., y_C$ words, a reverse process to the CBOW approach. The process is depicted in right portion of Fig. 2. We use negative sampling [8, 26, 27] which has proved to be giving improved results [8]. Negative sampling allows to select just a small number of *negative* words which are ignored and weights for other words are updated. The negative sampling is used with sigmoid for computational efficiency, which learns to differentiate between the actual context words and the noise distribution.

b) GloVe

Glove word embedding approach combines the two approaches, the count-based matrix factorization i.e. global statistics and the local context-based information i.e. local statistics in a single model [9]. Word2vec ignores frequency of occurrence of context word which is addressed by GloVe. The model predicts surrounding words by maximizing probability of context words given the center word using logistic regression. The co-occurrence matrix is the initial input to the model. The vector values for each word are decided by considering co-occurrences of every pair of words. It focuses on leaning ratio of co-occurrence probabilities than the probabilities themselves.

c) fastText

fastText model is considered as an enhanced version of Word2Vec and it is applicable in both CBOW and Skip-Gram setup. fastText learns embedding by conducting deeper level bifurcation of words using n-grams [28]. fastText extends word2vec by improving scope of contextual words to n-gram level. The words are converted to n-grams and skip-gram/CBOW model is applied to learn word vectors. fastText addresses the unknown words by generalization.

The subsequent step creates domain-based words embedding including the contained genre polarity seed words. The genre-based polarity seed words is the only labeled input used in our model for domain sentiment lexicon learning. The embedded words with similar meanings are mapped closer to each other. Our genre-based embedded seed set contains s positive seeds represented as *Psdset* and s negative seeds represented as *Nsdset*. The genre-based seed word embeddings are taken from the domain-based learned word-embeddings. The vocabulary contains n sentiment words, a word is represented as $word_i$. A positive similarity score, *psco* of a sentiment word is calculated by taking average of cosine similarity between sentiment word $word_i$ and positive genre-based seed word psd_s from positive seed word *Psdset* containing s positive seed words as specified in Eq. (1). Similarly, negative similarity score, *nsco* of $word_i$ is calculated considering negative genre-based s seed words from set *Nsdset* using Eq. (2). The final score of $word_i$ is calculated by subtracting positive score from the negative score using Eq. (3) and the sentiment word with final score is added to domain sentiment lexicon.

$$psco(word_i) = \frac{1}{|Psdset|} \sum_{\forall s,\ psd_s 33 Psdset} \frac{\overrightarrow{word_i}\ \overrightarrow{psd}_s}{\|\overrightarrow{word_i}\|\ \|\overrightarrow{psd}_s\|} \qquad (1)$$

$$nsco(word_i) = \frac{1}{|Nsdset|} \sum_{\forall s, nsd_s \in Nsdset} \frac{\overrightarrow{word_i}\ \overrightarrow{nsd}_s}{\|\overrightarrow{word_i}\|\ \|\overrightarrow{nsd}_s\|} \qquad (2)$$

$$Sco(word_i) = psco(word_i) - nsco(word_i), \forall i, i = 1, \ldots, n \qquad (3)$$

The domain-based learned sentiment lexicon is evaluated on domain test set using linear classification [29]. Domain-based word-embedding creation and evaluation is conducted independent of other domains.

4 Datasets, Experimental Setup, Evaluation Metrics and Baselines

This section describes the datasets, experimental setup of domain-based word-embedding creation, lexicon evaluation metrics, and domain-level as well as model-level result comparison baselines.

The proposed work uses two datasets. The first dataset is Amazon consumer product reviews dataset for 18 domains (e.g., Amazon Instant Video, Cell Phones, Electronics, Toys & Games, etc.) and Movie domain for model comparison experiment [30, 31]. The data contains reviews with no overlap between training and test sets. Each domain contains 80,000 unlabeled reviews in training set, 20,000 balanced labeled reviews in test set. The second dataset is Blitzer et al., 2007 [32] dataset used for model comparison. This dataset contains domains belonging to same genre used in the proposed model. Each domain from second dataset contains 1000 positive and 1000 negative test samples of Apparel, Electronics Products, Kitchen, Health Care, and Movie domains.

The proposed model experiments involve creating word-embedding using different approaches which use different hyper parameters. In all the models, minimum frequency of words is set to 5 and window size to maximum review length at domain-level to consider review-level context. CBOW training used embedding size 100, epochs 100, learning rate 0.001, negative samples' (noise words) is set to 5. The initial results of Skip-gram model are observed promising which led to further tuning of those parameters. Skip-gram training used embedding size 100, epochs are varied from 50 to 300 with increment of 50, learning rate 0.0001, negative samples is set to 10. GloVe training used vector size of 100, epochs 50, and other optimal default parameters. fastText training used embedding size of 100, epochs 50, skip-gram with 10 negative samples and 0.001 learning rate.

Each word-embedding model learns different embedding vectors and it reflects the basic learning mechanism of word embedding technique. A comparative listing of highest similar sentiment words from Beauty Products domain learned by different word-embedding model for genre-seed word "superb", "excellent", "garbage", and "waste" are in Table 3. The CBOW and Skip-Gram models have a lot of overlapping similar words. Fast-Text model is based on n-gram technique and is observed in the table where most similar words overlap characters partially such as first four characters "exec" from "excellent" overlap with most of the highest similar words.

The experiments are developed using python3.6, NLTK [34], Stanford Tagger [24], Gensim [35] library, Stanford GloVe [9] embedding creation code.

Sentiment lexicon evaluation uses linear binary classification for model and baseline experiments. A review is assigned the sum of scores of all sentiment words in review with reference to scores from the domain-based lexicon. A zero score is assigned to missing words. The aggregate positive or zero score a review classifies the review as positive and aggregate negative score classifies it as negative. The model and baseline sentiment lexicon in this work are evaluated using standard evaluation metrics in Natural Language Processing used for binary classification. The evaluation metrics includes *precision, recall, F1 score,* and *accuracy* which are calculated based on values from confusion matrix in Table 4. The class-wise metrics are calculated for positive and negative reviews separately. The *Actual class* values represent the ground-truth and the *Target class* represent the model generated values. *precision* is depicted in Eq. (4) which is the fraction of correctly labelled reviews among the total number of labelled reviews. *recall* is depicted in Eq. (5) which is fraction of correctly labelled reviews to the actual number of reviews with correct label. F1 score is give in Eq. (6) and is hormonic mean of values of *precision* and *recall. accuracy* is calculated using Eq. (7) and represents total number of correctly classified reviews.

$$precision = \frac{true\_positive}{true\_positive + false\_positive} \tag{4}$$

$$recall = \frac{true\_positive}{true\_positive + false\_negative} \tag{5}$$

$$F1\ score = 2 * \frac{precision * recall}{precision + recall} \tag{6}$$

$$Accuracy = \frac{true\_positive + true\_negative}{true\_positive + false\_positive + true\_negative + false\_negative} \tag{7}$$

The proposed genre-based model compares 18 domain results of sentiment lexicons created by four word-embeddings. The 18 domain results are also compared to existing research work results that is based on genre-based multidomain sentiment lexicon learning and uses LSA for lexicon leaning [10].

Another results comparison is conducted with two recent research work [10, 33]. We have evaluated the corresponding domain lexicons on Blitzer et al., 2007 [32] test dataset using linear binary classification method mentioned in this section. Movie domain is not part of 18 domains, so its lexicon is created using Skip-Gram approach for model result comparison.

- Xing et al., 2019 [33] is cognitive inspired approach based on SenticNet lexicon and heuristic rules. The learning process propagated back the error as feedback to the

Table 3. Highest similar words learned by different word-embedding models for a few genre-seed words

Genre-seed words	Model	Highest similar words from Beauty Product domain
"superb"	CBOW	Exquisite, outstanding, excellent, superbly, originate, namesake, aforementioned, specification, refine, finest
	GloVe	Overrate, speedy, par, realty, terrific, hugely, sincerely, endorse, fatal, magical
	fastText	Superbly, superlative, supervisor, impeccable, supertape, underestimate, superglue, heartbeat, exceptional, guilty
	Skip-Gram	Finest, pristine, beautifully, brilliant, excellent, fantastic, outstanding, connoisseur, visitor, impeccable
"excellent"	CBOW	Impeccable, outstanding, great, reasonable, superb, exceptional, fantastic, prompt, specification, satisfied
	GloVe	Great, good, pleased, highly, job, wonderful, value, price, delivery, best
	fastText	Excellently, excellence, exceptional, exceed, great, fashionable, exceptionally, exception, exceedingly, appreciable
	Skip-Gram	Great, satisfied, pleased, reasonable, perfect, recommend, best, highly, good, fantastic
"garbage"	CBOW	Trash, junk, away, disgust, horrible, rubbish, crap, nasty, awful, recycle
	GloVe	Trash, throw, toss, crap, waste, junk, money, piece, away, chuck
	fastText	Trash, ashamed, crappy, awfull, stupidly, trashy, plunk, trunk, crap, thrash
	Skip-Gram	Horrible, trash, throw, crap, awful, waste, worst, money, terrible, even
"waste"	CBOW	Save, spend, waist, spending, shell, waisted, worth, replay, drain, fork
	GloVe	Money, total, save, spend, nothing, basically, disappointed, throw, worth, complete
	fastText	Wasteful, haste, spend, spending, waisted, basically, garbage, save, expend, worthless
	Skip-Gram	Money, spend, save, total, nothing, complete, even, buy, disappointed, throw

iterative process for correction that used a few labeled samples. The model experiments were conducted on six diverse domains including Apparel, Electronics, Kitchen,

Table 4. Confusion matrix

Classes		Predicted	
		Positive class	*Negative* class
Actual	*Positive* class	*true_positive*	*false_negative*
	Negative class	*false_positive*	*true_negative*

Health Care, and Movie. The sixth is finance domain which is unrelated to genre-based domains hence excluded from results.

- Sanagar and Gupta, 2020 [10] is a genre-based unsupervised polarity seed transfer learning approach for sentiment lexicon learning. The model used domain clustering to segregate source and target domains and involves source domains in the iterative genre-based polarity seed word learning process from corpus. The target domain learns sentiment lexicon using seed-transfer learning combined with LSA approach.

The proposed model multiple experimental results including domain-wise and model results comparison are presented in the subsequent section.

5   Experimental Result and Comparisons

The following section describes results and comparisons as follows.

- Word-embedding models and existing baseline model results comparisons across 18 domains. Elaborate results and analysis of best performing model.
- Statistical significance test of best performing model
- Result comparison with existing research work from literature [10, 33]

The first part is experimental accuracy results comparison of different word-embedding sentiment lexicon along with the baseline Sanagar and Gupta (2020) [10] for 18 domains. These results are presented in Table 5. The best result at domain level is highlighted. The results indicate that Word2Vec Skip-Gram model has performed well compared with other models and Sanagar & Gupta (2020) baseline. The Skip-Gram model has achieved highest accuracy in 8 out of 18 domains, Sanagar & Gupta (2020) model as well as Glove model have secured highest accuracy in 5 domains. Skip-Gram model secured highest accuracy scores in majority domains and performed second highest with fractional dip in four domains that includes Amazon Instant Video, Health Personal Care, Toys & Games, and Video Game domains. The Skip-Gram model has achieved accuracies above 80% in eight domains. The Sanagar & Gupta (2020) model performed comparative to Skip-Gram. CBOW model can be ranked as third in the accuracy performance measurement. The average results indicate that Skip-Gram has performed best among the other word-embedding based sentiment lexicon learning models. Hence, Skip-Gram model is considered as outcome of the proposed approach and used in further experimentations and results analysis.

Table 5. The model accuracy results of domain sentiment lexicons using different word-embeddings and baseline model

SL. No	Domain/model	Sanagar & Gupta (2020)	CBOW	GloVe	fastText	Skip-gram
1	Amazon Instant Video	75.14	75.81	**78.50**	67.02	78.34
2	Automotive	77.72	75.65	74.75	60.73	**78.04**
3	Beauty Products	80.14	78.09	64.14	77.62	**81.07**
4	Book	**77.84**	73.30	67.47	74.18	73.63
5	Cell Phone	77.30	75.75	64.16	74.47	**78.09**
6	Clothe Shoe Jewel	79.22	76.28	56.69	74.82	**80.50**
7	Digital Music	77.78	72.84	73.48	68.71	**82.03**
8	Electronics	78.44	78.53	**81.17**	77.12	77.32
9	Grocery & Gourmet Food	**79.28**	78.99	63.64	65.72	75.56
10	Home & Kitchen	82.12	83.16	81.27	83.59	**84.40**
11	Health & Personal Care	**76.78**	74.37	74.65	59.97	76.38
12	Musical Instrument	80.42	80.76	74.48	71.45	**81.67**
13	Office Products	77.56	79.63	**82.12**	76.99	76.58
14	Pet Supplies	74.25	73.43	**75.42**	60.29	74.11
15	Sports & Outdoor	78.75	77.55	70.58	75.75	**80.53**
16	Tools Home	80.03	78.28	**81.62**	78.03	78.64
17	Toys & Games	**86.89**	81.66	80.94	80.34	86.32
18	Video Game	**81.76**	78.43	76.30	70.25	81.04
	Average	78.97	77.36	72.06	73.41	**79.13**

Skip-Gram model learned lexicon statistics are presented in Table 6, which displays domain-wise polarity sentiment word count. Table 6 statistics indicate that the count of positive sentiment words is more compared with the count of negative sentiment words across all the 18 domains. Elaborate polarity class-wise precision, recall, and F1 score results of Skip-Gram model are depicted in Fig. 3. The unsupervised model has achieved balanced results using precision, recall, and F1 score evaluation metrics in Amazon Instant Video, Beauty products, Cell Phones, Musical Instruments, Pet Supplies, and Sports Outdoor domains. Some domains display little higher on negative side as the consumer tend to be more descriptive while complaining and more precise in positive responses. Average number of positive and negative sentiment words are 23.4 and 32.5 respectively in test data per review across all the 18 domains.

We conducted statistical significance test using Single Factor ANOVA Test on accuracy results. The test determines significant difference in accuracy among the models

Table 6. Skip-Gram model domain-wise sentiment word polarity statistics

SL. No.	Domain	#Positive sentiment words	#Negative sentiment words
1	Amazon Instant Video	7164	4083
2	Automotive	4695	4588
3	Beauty Products	4557	3717
4	Book	6783	6826
5	Cell Phone	3828	3049
6	Clothe Shoe Jewel	3799	4350
7	Digital Music	6047	4925
8	Electronics	4238	4274
9	Grocery & Gourmet Food	5076	3753
10	Home & Kitchen	4472	4143
11	Health & Personal Care	7453	3645
12	Musical Instrument	5361	4141
13	Office Products	4238	4094
14	Pet Supplies	5038	4051
15	Sports & Outdoor	5186	4304
16	Tools Home	4383	4307
17	Toys & Games	5587	3915
18	Video Game	6103	3211

across the various domains. The ANOVA test generated p-value of less than 5% ($F_{(4, 85)} = 7.15$, p = 0.0001), which indicates that there is a significant difference among the models. The detailed pair-wise comparison is carried out using Tukey's post-hoc test to understand honest significant difference between groups. The test results at 95% confidence level is tabulated in Table 7. Results indicate that the proposed skip-gram lexicon learning model is statistically significant in comparison with all the other models under study.

The proposed model shows a statistically significant increase in mean compared to CBOW, fastText and Glove models, and slight increase compared to Sanagar & Gupta (2020) model.

In the third part of the experimental results, the Skip-Gram model lexicons are evaluated and compared with two recent research work by Xing et al. (2019) [33] and Sanagar and Gupta (2020) [10]. The comparative results are given in Table 8. Skip-Gram model has performed highest in Apparel, Kitchen, and Movies domains. The Sanagar and Gupta [10] model has performed highest in Electronics and Health Care domains. The Skip-Gram model has displayed improvement of 5 to 10.75 points and average of 7.9 points over Xing et al. (2019) model. The table displays average improvement of

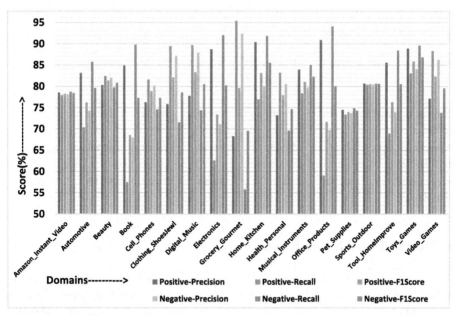

Fig. 3. Skip-Gram model experimental results of 18 domain sentiment lexicon for polarity class-wise precision, recall, F1 score

Table 7. Accuracy results comparison of the Skip-Gram model and Other models listed in column 1 on using Tukey's post-hoc analysis test.

SL. No.	Skip-gram vs. other models	Difference in mean	Std. err. of difference	t-value	Adjusted p-value	95% conf. interval
1	Sanagar & Gupta(2020)	0.157	1.724	0.090	1.000	−4.648 to 4.963
2	CBOW	1.763	1.724	1.020	0.844	−3.042 to 6.568
3	GloVe	5.715	1.724	3.310	0.011	0.909 to 10.520
4	fastText	7.067	1.724	4.100	0.001	2.261 to 11.872

0.36 points over Sanagar and Gupta (2020) model, although results of both models are almost similar.

Table 8. Comparison of accuracy results of Skip-Gram model, Xing et al. (2019) [33] model, and Sanagar and Gupta (2020) [10] model

Models\Domains	Apparel domain	Electronics domain	Kitchen domain	Health care domain	Movie domain	Average
Xing et al. (2019) [33]	74.70	69.20	69.30	65.70	77.90	71.36
Sanagar & Gupta (2020) [10]	79.20	**77.65**	76.45	**78.40**	82.80	78.90
Proposed Model Skip-Gram	**81.90**	74.20	**79.60**	76.45	**84.15**	**79.26**

6   Result Analysis and Discussion

This section presents deeper analysis of domain-based word embeddings and domain relevance of sentiment words learned by domain sentiment lexicons across domains using Skip-Gram model. Analysis is divided into two parts; the first part elaborates on the importance of domain-specific word-embedding and the second part presents analysis of sentiment words from 18 domain sentiment lexicons. The domain-specific word-embeddings carry domain-based context and it also reflects in learned sentiment lexicon. This analysis provides details of how results and sentiment word polarity and intensity diverge from domain to domain.

The proposed model learns domain-based embeddings that preserve domain-specific characteristics. We analyze the most similar words to one positive and one negative randomly selected words. Table 9 presents results for 18 domains. Table 9 listed top 10 most similar sentiment words to positive sentiment word "affordable" and negative sentiment word "junk". The most similar words are listed in descending order of similarity intensity scores. There is an overlap of a few sentiment words between different domains such as "great", "best", "reasonable", "price", "crap", "garbage", "shit", "trash", "cheap", "crappy", "worthless" etc. which are most similar to the selected words. There are interesting domain-relevant words which are most similar such as "income" in Automotive domain is second-most similar, as it correlates to income is proportional to automotive products people purchase. Another sentiment word "ti" is abbreviation for "technical information" which also reflects to how technical details are important and decide "price" that makes a product "affordable". Fourth similar sentiment word in Grocery & Gourmet Food domain is "autoship", which indicates automatic shipment of product which seems synonymous in the context. Most common sentiment word "junk" has social-media reinvented meaning which is synonymous to "worthless". Tenth most similar sentiment word "munchy" in Grocery & Gourmet Food domain is highly similar in context of food. In Video Games domain, sixth most similar sentiment word "breakable" indicates if a videogame breaks it is useless.

The sentiment word polarity and score/intensity divergence are depicted in Fig. 4 for randomly selected 10 sentiment words. Sentiment word "terrific" is highly positive

Table 9. Skip-Gram word-embedding top 10 most similar sentiment words to *'affordable'* and *'junk'* in descending order of similarity across domains

SL. No.	Domains	Top 10 most similar sentiment words to word 'affordable'
1	Amazon Instant Video	convenience, separately, pricey, splurge, hassle, bundle, leisure, cheapest, perk, advert
2	Automotive	great, income, reasonable, reasonably, ti, good, price, qualm, happy, unbeatable
3	Beauty Products	beat, reasonable, budget, reasonably, fantastic, steep, terrific, pricy, fantastically, great
4	Book	module, resale, renovate, storage, courteous, saver, subscription, lifesaver, autographed, adaptable
5	Cell Phone	fantastic, fabulous, great, wonderful, recommend, effeminately, verse, terrific, definably, esp
6	Clothe Shoe Jewel	unbeatable, reasonable, budget, contemporary, amazingly, disappoint, surpass, incredible, timeless, casually
7	Digital Music	xma, inexpensive, locally, spruce, manhattan, deter, availability, approx, alway, convenience
8	Electronics	reasonably, value, great, price, best, excellent, especially, well, pleased, perfect
9	Grocery & Gourmet Food	unsurpassed, brainier, superb, autoship, budget, caliber, competitive, reasonably, simplicity, reliably
10	Home & Kitchen	price, definitely, especially, value, exceptional, best, surpass, competitive, happier, budget
11	Health & Personal Care	choice, excellent, reasonable, great, happy, pleased, especially, value, good, budget
12	Musical Instrument	inexpensive, choice, definitely, great, reasonable, fraction, price, budget, good, satisfied
13	Office Products	pricy, great, happier, reasonable, best, economically, freelance, glad, pleased, conserve
14	Pet Supplies	expensive, budget, bank, traditionally, comparable, ween, lesser, economical, reasonably, find
15	Sports & Outdoor	great, fantastic, durable, price, budget, excellent, well, beat, incredibly, reasonably
16	Tools Home	reasonable, definitely, best, expensive, great, budget, comparably, outrageously, fixer, recommend
17	Toys & Games	happier, reasonable, reasonably, luxury, bargain, unbeatable, exorbitant, compromise, ideal, typical
18	Video Game	inexpensive, competitively, reasonable, happier, leery, fraction, reasonably, savings, recreational, splurge

SL. No.	Domains	Top 10 most similar sentiment words to word 'junk'
1	Amazon Instant Video	crap, garbage, rubbish, trash, dashiki, pile, mtv, crud, fool, shit
2	Automotive	pure, garbage, piece, crap, rubbish, worthless, absolute, worst, total, dumpster
3	Beauty Products	crap, worthless, garbage, crappy, piece, ashamed, useless, ripoff, fool, pathetic
4	Book	trash, garbage, rubbish, pile, grub, unadulterated, paperweight, ounce, throw, dung
5	Cell Phone	crap, pure, hunk, shit, absolute, ashamed, piece, garbage, worthless, trash
6	Clothe Shoe Jewel	crap, garbage, worthless, trash, total, crappy, lousy, pathetic, dollar, utterly
7	Digital Music	ashamed, hack, crap, talentless, garbage, excuse, shat, ripoff, exec, crappy
8	Electronics	crap, garbage, piece, worthless, trash, joke, absolute, ashamed, money, pile
9	Grocery & Gourmet Food	unhealthy, load, bus, tide, grad, isle, goldfish, campus, pronounce, munchy
10	Home & Kitchen	crap, worthless, worst, garbage, total, joke, useless, waste, cheap, money
11	Health & Personal Care	crap, worthless, cheap, piece, money, crappy, ashamed, shit, lousy, useless
12	Musical Instrument	crap, garbage, trash, hunk, shit, ashamed, worthless, crappy, cheaply, employee
13	Office Products	garbage, hunk, crap, worthless, piece, ashamed, worst, curse, landfill, trash
14	Pet Supplies	crap, cheap, garbage, crappy, waste, money, worst, flimsiest, worthless, earn
15	Sports & Outdoor	crap, garbage, trash, piece, worthless, shit, ashamed, waste, hunk, rubbish
16	Tools Home	crap, garbage, absolute, shit, ashamed, worthless, waste, cheap, crappy, piece
17	Toys & Games	crap, hunk, utter, cheapest, cheap, landfill, ashamed, worthless, total, waste
18	Video Game	garbage, crap, piece, trash, worthless, breakable, cheap, landfill, shit, hunk

across all the 18 domains and highly positive in Grocery & Gourmet domain. Similarly, sentiment word "classic" is positive in all domains but less relevant in Toys & Games domain. Another sentiment word "durable" is highly positive in Cell Phones, Electronics, Home & Kitchen, Sports & Outdoor, and other domains, as consumer considers longer the lifespan of product better. But it has lowest relevance in Beauty Products and Book domain, as durability is not relevant. Sentiment word "thin" is mostly a negative polarity word but is positive in Cell Phone domain as thin cell phone is preferred consumer choice. Sentiment word "expire" is mostly used in negative polarity context, it is most negative and relevant in Beauty Products domain to check usability of product and almost neutral in Amazon Instant Videos domain as it is not relevant to this product.

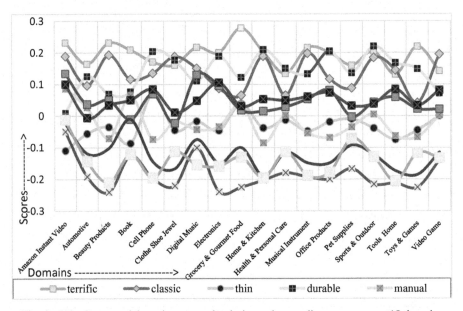

Fig. 4. Skip-Gram model sentiment word polarity and score divergence across 18 domains

The analysis shows that domain-based word embeddings reflect domain-relevance. The domain-based lexicon learns domain-specific scores and polarity and displays domain relevant quality and good results.

7 Conclusions

The proposed work presents unsupervised genre-based sentiment lexicon learning app-roach for multiple domains. The experiments involve 18 domains of the same genre. The domain-based sentiment lexicon learning model experimentation involved differ-ent word-embedding models to create domain-based word-embeddings. The proposed work creates word-embeddings using four approaches that includes Word2Vec CBOW, Skip-Gram, GloVe, and fastText models. The proposed work compares sentiment lexi-con results of 18 domains for all word-embedding models and a LSA-based Sanagar & Gupta (2020) baseline model. The results proved that the Skip-Gram word-embedding lexicon learning model has performed the best among other models, and the second-best model is Sanagar & Gupta (2020). The Skip-Gram word-embeddings gives the best contextual representation.

As a future direction the classification results can be improved to overcome limitations of lexicon by considering additional features along with learned genre sentiment lexicon. Another future direction to improve lexicon quality by exploration with neural-net based models.

References

1. Kumar, S.S., Kumar, M.A., Soman, K.P., Poornachandran, P.: Dynamic mode-based feature with random mapping for sentiment analysis. In: Thampi, S. et al. (eds.) Intelligent Systems, Technologies and Applications, Singapore, vol. 910, p. 15 (2020). https://doi.org/10.1007/978-981-13-6095-4_1
2. Shalini, K., Ganesh, H.B., Kumar, M.A., Soman, K.P.: Sentiment analysis for code-mixed Indian social media text with distributed representation. In: 2018 International Conference on Advances in Computing, Communications and Informatics (ICACCI), pp. 1126–1131. IEEE (2018)
3. Sanagar, S., Gupta, D.: Adaptation of multi-domain corpus learned seeds and polarity lexicon for sentiment analysis. In: Proceedings of the International Conference on Computing and Network Communications, pp. 60–68. IEEE (2015)
4. Fares, M., Moufarrej, A., Jreij, E., Tekli, J., Grosky, W.: Unsupervised word-level affect analysis and propagation in a lexical knowledge graph. Knowl.-Based Syst. **165**, 432–459 (2019)
5. Sanagar, S., Gupta, D.: Roadmap for polarity Lexicon learning and resources: A survey. In: Rodriguez, J.M.C., Mitra, S., Thampi, S.M., El-Alfy, E.-S. (eds.) Intelligent Systems Technologies and Applications 2016, pp. 647–663. Springer, Cham (2016). https://doi.org/10.1007/978-3-319-47952-1_52
6. Tang, D., Wei, F., Qin, B., Yang, N., Liu, T., Zhou, M.: Sentiment embeddings with applications to sentiment analysis. IEEE Trans. Knowl. Data Eng. **28**(2), 496–509 (2015)
7. Mikolov, T., Sutskever, I., Chen, K., Corrado, G.S., Dean, J.: Distributed representations of words and phrases and their compositionality. In: Advances in Neural Information Processing Systems, pp. 3111–3119 (2013)
8. Mikolov, T., Chen, K., Corrado, G., Dean, J.: Efficient estimation of word representations in vector space, arXiv preprint arXiv:1301.3781 (2013)
9. Pennington, J., Socher, R., Manning, C.D.: Glove: global vectors for word representation. In: Proceedings of the 2014 Conference on Empirical Methods in Natural Language Processing (EMNLP), pp. 1532–1543 (2014)
10. Sanagar, S., Gupta, D.: Unsupervised genre-based multidomain sentiment lexicon learning using corpus-generated polarity seed words. IEEE Access **8**, 118050–118071 (2020)
11. Turney, P.D., Littman, M.L.: Measuring praise and criticism: Inference of semantic orientation from association. ACM Trans. Inf. Syst. **21**(4), 315–346 (2003)
12. Xia, Y., Cambria, E., Hussain, A., Zhao, H.: Word polarity disambiguation using Bayesian model and opinion-level features. Cogn. Comput. **7**(3), 369–380 (2015)
13. Hung, C.: Word of mouth quality classification based on contextual sentiment lexicons. Inf. Process. Manag. **53**(4), 751–763 (2017)
14. Deng, D., Jing, L., Yu, J., Sun, S., Ng, M.K.: Sentiment lexicon construction with hierarchical supervision topic model. IEEE/ACM Trans. Audio Speech Lang. Process. **27**(4), 704–718 (2019)

15. Fernández-Gavilanes, M., Álvarez-López, T., Juncal-Martínez, J., Costa-Montenegro, E., González-Castaño, F.J.: Unsupervised method for sentiment analysis in online texts. Expert Syst. Appl. **58**, 57–75 (2016)
16. Wenpeng Y., Schütze H.: Learning word meta-embeddings. In: Proceedings of the 54th Annual Meeting of the Association for Computational Linguistics, vol. 1, pp. 1351–1360 (2016)
17. Glorot, X., Bordes, A., Bengio, Y.: Domain adaption for large-scale sentiment classification: a deep learning approach. In: Proceedings of the International Conference on Machine Learning, ICML (2011)
18. Shinnou, H., Zhao, X., Komiya, K.: Domain adaptation using a combination of multiple embeddings for sentiment analysis. In: Proceedings of the 32nd Pacific Asia Conference on Language, Information and Computation (2018)
19. Wu, F., Huang, Y.: Sentiment domain adaptation with multiple sources. In: ACL, pp. 301–310 (2016)
20. Jha, V., Savitha, R., Shenoy, P.D., Venugopal, K.R., Sangaiah, A.K.: A novel sentiment aware dictionary for multi-domain sentiment classification. Comput. Electr. Eng. **69**, 585–597 (2018)
21. Ding, X., Shi, V., Cai, B., Liu, T., Zhao, Y., Ye, Q.: Learning multi-domain adversarial neural networks for text classification. IEEE Access **7**, 40323–40332 (2019)
22. Zheng, L., Zhang, Y., Wei, Y., Wu, Y., Yang, Q.: End-to-end adversarial memory network for cross-domain sentiment classification. In: Proceedings of the International Joint Conference on Artificial Intelligence (2017)
23. Yuan, Z., Wu, S., Wu, F., Liu, J., Huang, Y.: Domain attention model for multi-domain sentiment classification. Knowl.-Based Syst. **155**, 1–0 (2018)
24. Toutanova, K., Klein, D., Manning, C.D., Singer, Y.: Feature-rich part-of-speech tagging with a cyclic dependency network. In: Proceedings of the 2003 Conference of the North American Chapter of the Association for Computations Linguistics on Human Language Technology, pp. 173–180 (2003)
25. Çano, E., Morisio, M.: Word embeddings for sentiment analysis: a comprehensive empirical survey. arXiv preprint arXiv:1902.00753 (2019)
26. Goldberg, Y., Levy, O.: Word2Vec Explained: deriving Mikolov et al.'s negative-sampling word-embedding method. arXiv preprint arXiv:1402.3722 (2014)
27. Rong, X.: Word2Vec parameter learning explained. arXiv preprint arXiv:1411.2738 (2014)
28. Joulin, A., Grave, E., Bojanowski, P., Mikolov, T.: Bag of tricks for efficient text classification. arXiv preprint arXiv:1607.01759 (2016)
29. Sanagar, S., Gupta, D.: Automated genre-based multi-domain sentiment lexicon adaptation using unlabeled data. J. Intell. Fuzzy Syst. **38**(5), 6223–6234 (2020)
30. McAuley, J., Leskovec, J.: Hidden factors and hidden topics: understanding rating dimensions with review text. RecSys (2013)
31. He, R., McAuley, J.: Ups and downs: modeling the visual evolution of fashion trends with one-class collaborative filtering. In: Proceedings of the 25th International Conference on World Wide Web WWW, pp. 507–517 (2016)
32. Blitzer, J., Dredze, M., Pereira, F.: Biographies, Bollywood, boom-boxes and blenders: domain adaptation for sentiment classification. In: Proceedings of the 45th Annual Meeting of the Association of Computational Linguistics, pp. 440–447 (2007)
33. Xing, F.Z., Pallucchini, F., Cambria, E.: Cognitive-inspired domain adaptation of sentiment lexicons. Inf. Process. Manag. **56**(3), 554–564 (2019)
34. NLTK3.09 Library. https://www.nltk.org/
35. Řehůřek, R., Sojka, P.: Software frame-work for topic modelling with large corpora. In: Proceedings of the LREC 2010 Workshop on New Challenges for NLP Frameworks, pp. 45–50 (2010)

Deep Learning Based Question Generation Using T5 Transformer

Khushnuma Grover$^{(\boxtimes)}$, Katinder Kaur, Kartikey Tiwari, Rupali, and Parteek Kumar

Thapar Institute of Engineering and Technology, Patiala 147004, Punjab, India
khushnumagrover@gmail.com, katinder08@gmail.com,
kartikeytiwari37@gmail.com, rupaligoyal.cs@gmail.com,
parteek.bhatia@thapar.edu
http://www.thapar.edu

Abstract. Manual construction of questions is a tedious and complicated process. Automatic Question Generation (AQG) methods work towards diminishing these costs and to fulfil the requirement for a persistent supply of new questions. Current AQG techniques utilize complicated architectures, that require intensive computational resources as well as a deeper understanding of the subject. In this paper we propose an end-to-end AQG system that utilises the power of a recently introduced transformer, the Text-to-Text Transfer Transformer (T5). We use the pre-trained T5 model and fine-tune it for our down-stream task of question generation. Our model performs very well on unseen data and generates well-formed and grammatically correct questions. These questions can be used directly by students, to examine their own level of understanding, and teachers, to quickly reinforce key concepts whenever required. The model has also been deployed in the form of a web application for public access. This application serves as an educational tool using which any individual can assess their knowledge and identify areas of improvement.

Keywords: Question generation · Deep learning · Transformers · NLP

1 Introduction

Asking questions is an inherent action that humans rely upon for acquiring new information. It is a tool collectively accepted across all the cultures for information exchange. Questions are also used as effective tools for assessment of an individual's understanding of a concept.

Traditional classrooms involve the use of periodic tests, quizzes and exams along with the impromptu questions asked by the instructor during or after every session. This enables the learner to gauge their understanding and the instructor to gauge the effectiveness of their lessons. But creation and selection of questions is a time consuming task. Creating good quality questions is a complex process that requires training and experience [11].

© Springer Nature Singapore Pte Ltd. 2021
D. Garg et al. (Eds.): IACC 2020, CCIS 1367, pp. 243–255, 2021.
https://doi.org/10.1007/978-981-16-0401-0_18

Also due to the unprecedented convenience of MOOCs, a large number of students have shifted to this self-learning paradigm of education to learn new concepts or to aid their classroom courses, but most online classrooms lack relevant and sufficient number of exercises to test the students, which is again due to paucity of time on the creator's side.

Questions are not only limited to educational environments but also make up an integral part of a multitude of intelligent machine activities. As the data becomes abundant and machines are becoming more intelligent, and are expected to learn by themselves, they are automatically expected to learn to question. Machines can work as truly autonomous units only if they learn to question their learnings and ask (or query) for more or relevant data to suffice understanding of a particular concept (or user's queries). Therefore, learning to frame questions from existing knowledge is an important milestone for intelligent machines.

To facilitate these tasks, a separate subset of content generation tasks, Question Generation (QG) [15], was recognised. Question Generation has been defined as "the task of automatically generating questions from some form of input" [16].

In this study we explore and experiment with T5 transformer [13] for the Question Generation task. We introduce a NLG pipeline that uses the pre-trained 't5-small' architecture to generate questions. As will shown in the performance evaluation, the T5-QG model shows performance at par with the other existing models.

Key Contributions. In this paper, we explore the utilization of the pre-trained T5 model for QG tasks. As T5 model performs greatly on standard NLP tasks, we proposed a system where we used T5 model specifically for the purpose of question generation from text without answer supervision.

We also implemented a user-friendly web application to provide users with the functionality of generating questions on any text required.

Several experiments have been performed using the benchmark dataset SQuAD, and the results of these experiments clearly depict the effectiveness of our QG model. Our model is able to generate well-formed and grammatically correct questions from the input context.

The remaining of the paper is organized as follows, Sect. 2 discusses some notable work in the field of Question Generation. In Sect. 3, a brief review of the T5 model is provided. In Sect. 4, architecture and other details of our QG model are discussed, and Sect. 5 provides the results of our research. In Sect. 6, conclusions are drawn and the future scope of the paper is also discussed.

2   Related Work

Question generation and more loosely content generation has been long deemed to be a complex computational task since generation of any kind of content requires understanding of natural language as well as knowledge of the world.

Very first attempts at the content generation task included basic rule-based techniques. For generating questions similar rule based methods were suggested to which several improvements were made in subsequent years [3, 6, 11]. These methods work by recognising anchors (domain specific words), which is achieved by identifying recurrent nouns in the text and then fitting them to predefined rules which form questions. Therefore the performance of such systems depend solely upon the quality and number of rules. Then an overgenerate-and-rank approach was introduced which uses the same rule-based approach to generate questions, but it generates multiple questions from a single input sentence and then ranks them using a supervised learning-based ranker [7]. The results are more accurate than a simple rule-based approach but the questions are often too predictable and give away answers in their wording themselves.

With the introduction of RNNs [21], text processing was finally deemed possible through deep learning, which had brought a revolution in other fields like computer vision. RNNs could process sequences [17], and this was a useful feature that could be exploited in text generation. Theoretically, RNNs should be able to handle very long sequences of data, but in practical applications the results are far from expected. Also RNNs suffer from gradient vanishing and exploding problems.

To overcome this problem a novel neural architecture, LSTM was introduced, which is capable of maintaining long term dependencies due to the presence of gated units and thus leads to generation of more meaningful contextual data [8]. Several other improvements to RNNs have also been suggested but these can not be directly used for question generation since the process requires building relationships between context paragraphs and answer phrases. This was realised with Seq2Seq models, which have separate encoder and decoder modules. Inspired by the advances in other NLG fields, an approach to frame the task of question generation as a sequence-to-sequence learning problem was suggested [5]. This approach was fully data-driven and required no manually generated rules like the previous propositions. This was also the first noted use of attention mechanism in question generation and it outperformed the previous rule-based and overgenerate-and-rank state-of-the-art systems. A novel method to generate factoid questions, from given data instead of text to generate questions, was also suggested [18] which included using GRUs as decoder, in the Seq2Seq encoder-decoder architecture.

Further improvements to Seq2Seq QG models also involved usage of reinforcement learning [23], after it proved to be rewarding in other NLG tasks. For every question generated by the standard seq2Seq model, a reward is associated by a Reinforce algorithm, and the model is trained to maximize the expected reward. Several different reward functions were then explored and experimented with to enhance overall performance of existing models [9].

The concept of Attention [20] was only introduced six years ago but since then it has changed the entire scenario of the field of natural language generation. Originally introduced for machine translation, it has been found effective in nearly all NLP tasks. Attention empowers a model by learning to focus upon the relevant parts of the input sequence. It allows the model to create relationships between the different words of the same sequence. It also overcame the problem of short-term memory of RNNs, by providing a virtually infinite reference window, enabling the model to remember the context of the whole generated document. The introduction of attention gave way to transformers, which was suggested in the same paper [20].

The Transformers outperformed the Google Neural Machine Translation model in specific tasks. All previous techniques in NLP required sequential processing, making training a very tedious and time consuming task, but transformers allowed parallelization of tasks by taking the entire sequence as input instead of token by token, this instantly made them popular. Several variations of transformers have been introduced in the past one year. This also popularized the concept of transfer learning in NLP, which has proven to be a game changer in the field of computer vision.

Bidirectional Encoder Representation for Transformers (BERT) [4], introduced the concept of conditioning to both left and right context, generating a better language model. BERT-HLSQG [2] performed better than the seq2seq global attention based model owing to the use of self-attention, bidirectional language learning and change in format of training data.

Table 1. Overview of existing techniques and models for question generation

Method	Ref	Dataset	Results
Rule-based	[3,6,7,11]	N.A	Automatic QG system proves to be faster than manual question construction. The performance of such models depends upon the number and quality of rules used
Seq2Seq	[5,9,18,23]	SQuAD, SimpleQuestions	QG can be successfully framed as a sequence end-to-end task. Reinforcement learning can be further used to enhance the results
BERT	[4]	SQuAD	Pretrained models have scope to perform better than Seq2Seq model. Answer focused models can generate even better results
GPT-2 Transformer	[10]	SQuAD	Successful use of transformer based pretrained model

A more recent work addresses the use of GPT2 [12] transformer for AQG [10], this highlights that transformer-based finetuning techniques can be used to create AQG systems using only a single pretrained language model, without the use of any additional complex components or features to enhance its performance. The major existing QG techniques and model architectures are summarized in Table 1.

The latest innovation in the field of neural text generation is the Text-to-Text Transfer Transformer (T5) [13]. This transformer pretrained upon a newer large text corpus (C4), achieved state-of-the-art results on several NLP tasks. And we aim to utilize it for the QG task.

3   Overview of T5 Transformer

T5 transformer is inherently a simple encoder-decoder model. It is a "unified framework that converts every language problem into a text-to-text format" [13]. It is the latest model in the transformers series introduced by Google and Facebook.

The most notable feature of this model is its "text-to-text" nature. Unlike other transformers which take in natural language data only after converting it to corresponding numerical embeddings, T5 takes in data in the form of text only. And the outputs are also strings of characters, i.e. text again. This text-to-text nature enables the model to learn any NLP task without changing the hyperparameters and loss functions.

Also it is "unified" in the sense that it can perform several NLG tasks simultaneously. It does not require separate output layers for different tasks like other transformers such as BERT and GPT2. Even for regression tasks, the output can be produced as a string of numbers.

It has been trained upon a multi-task mixture of unsupervised and supervised tasks and for which each task is converted into a text-to-text format. For unsupervised training, it is trained on a novel 750 Gigabyte-huge dataset, the Colossal Clean Crawled Corpus(C4) [13], which was created especially for T5. For supervised training, several popular datasets were used for respective tasks.

Due to the above reasons, T5 model has out-performed several other contemporary SOTA architectures in different NLP tasks(at least in twenty different tasks) like text summarization, Question Answering, Sentiment analysis etc.

The input format for T5 is peculiar and consists of prepending a special prefix to the standard input text as shown in Fig. 1. The prefix indicates the task for which the output is sought. For example, for the purpose of translation of a sentence from English to German language, the input should look like:

"translate English to German: That is good."

Here "translate English to German" is the task prefix. These prefixes are selected at the time of fine-tuning. Some other examples of prefixes for pretrained tasks are "summarize" for text summarization task, "cola" for checking grammatical correctness of a sentence and "stsb" for sentence similarity of two different sentences.

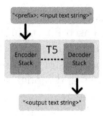

Fig. 1. Input and output formats for T5 model

4   Architecture of T5 Model

The T5 model has an encoder-decoder based transformer architecture which is best suited for the text-to-text approach. The number of parameters is kept same as BERT [4] (which is an encoder only model) by sharing them across decoder and encoder without a significant drop in performance.

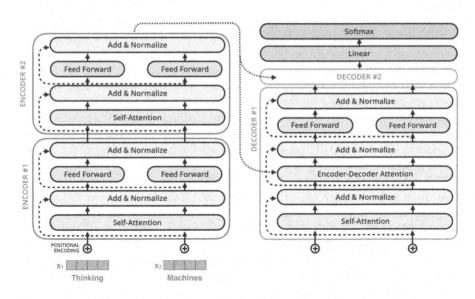

Fig. 2. Architecture of T5. Source: [1]

The architecture of the T5 model is shown in Fig. 2.

The encoder consists of a stack of identical layers. Every layer is composed of two sub-layers. The first sub-layer of each encoder layer is a multi-head self-attention mechanism. The second sub-layer on the other hands is a fully connected position-wise feed-forward network. Residual connections are employed around these sub-layers, each followed by the normalization layer. Similar to the encoder, decoder also consists of a stack of identical layers.

In the decoder, a third sub-layer is also inserted, in addition to the two sub-layers already present in the encoder layer. This third sub-layer performs multi-head attention on the output received by the encoder stack. Here also residual connections are employed around these sub-layers, like that of encoder, each followed by the normalization layer. More details can be referred from the original paper [13].

5   T5 for Question Generation

Owing to the success of the BERT [4] and GPT2 transfer learning QG model, we propose a QG system that utilizes a pre-trained T5 Transformer model. Transfer learning enables the model to learn from abundant data. The pre-trained model can also be applied in the downstream task. Here the pre-trained tasks can be dissimilar from the downstream task. It is especially useful in NLP as labeled data is scarce and valuable while unlabeled data is present in abundance.

The task we will be teaching our T5 model is question generation. Specifically, the model will be tasked with asking relevant questions when given a context. The T5 model is fine-tuned to generate multiple questions simultaneously by just providing the context. The proposed model architecture is shown in Fig. 3.

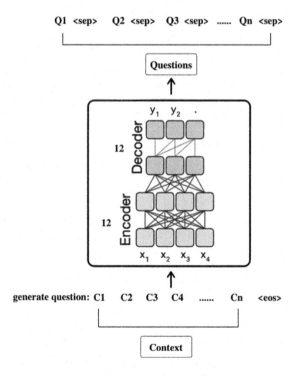

Fig. 3. Model architecture overview for question generation

5.1 Data Preparation

For fine-tuning T5 model we need to convert our question generation task to a text-to-text format and as T5 is trained using teacher forcing method we need to prepare a sequence input and sequence output. For fine-tuning we use the popular Question Answering (QA) dataset, SQuAD v1.1 [14]. We used SQuAD's training and validation sets as our model's training and test sets, as the original test set is hidden. The dataset provides a context, question and answers to each question. For the purpose of training our question generation model, we invert the dataset such that the input is the context paragraph and the target is all the questions posed on the given context. Also, we discarded the answers as we wanted answer-agnostic questions to be generated. A training example fed to the model is formed by an input text and a target corresponding to it. The context forms the input text and all the questions posed on that context form the target, separated by the <sep>. Maximum input length was set to 512 and the maximum target length was set to 128, and examples were truncated or padded accordingly. The process is depicted in Fig. 4. The final training examples feeded to the model are shown in Fig. 5.

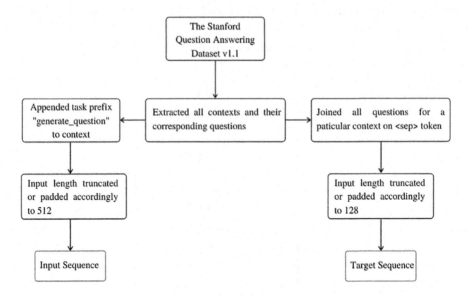

Fig. 4. Preprocessing of training data

5.2 Model Finetuning and Implementation Details

For fine-tuning T5 model for our question generation task, we used Hugging-Face's [22] implementation of t5-small model. The model has 60 million parameters and is the smallest out of the five models proposed in the original paper, the largest having 11 billion parameters.

<table>
<tr><td>

Input Data

Article: Oxygen
Context: "Oxygen is a chemical element with symbol O and atomic number 8. It is a member of the chalcogen group on the periodic table and is a highly reactive nonmetal and oxidizing agent that readily forms compounds (notably oxides) with most elements. By mass, oxygen is the third-most abundant element in the universe, after hydrogen and helium. At standard temperature and pressure, two atoms of the element bind to form dioxygen, a colorless and odorless diatomic gas with the formula O2. Diatomic oxygen gas constitutes 20.8% of the Earth's atmosphere. However, monitoring of atmospheric oxygen levels show a global downward trend, because of fossil-fuel burning. Oxygen is the most abundant element by mass in the Earth's crust as part of oxide compounds such as silicon dioxide, making up almost half of the crust's mass."
Question 1: "What is the atomic number for oxygen?"
Ground Truth Answer: 8
Question 2: "What is the second most abundant element?"
Ground Truth Answer: helium

</td><td>

Processed Data

source_text: "generate question: Oxygen is a chemical element with symbol O and atomic number 8. It is a member of the chalcogen group on the periodic table and is a highly reactive nonmetal and oxidizing agent that readily forms compounds (notably oxides) with most elements. By mass, oxygen is the third-most abundant element in the universe, after hydrogen and helium. At standard temperature and pressure, two atoms of the element bind to form dioxygen, a colorless and odorless diatomic gas with the formula O2. Diatomic oxygen gas constitutes 20.8% of the Earth's atmosphere. However, monitoring of atmospheric oxygen levels show a global downward trend, because of fossil-fuel burning. Oxygen is the most abundant element by mass in the Earth's crust as part of oxide compounds such as silicon dioxide, making up almost half of the crust's mass. </s>"

target_text: "What is the atomic number for oxygen? <sep> What is the second most abundant element? <sep> </s>"

</td></tr>
</table>

Fig. 5. Preprocessed data

The output target is truncated at a length of 128 so that infinite loops and repetition are avoided. The model was trained for 20 epochs, using Adam as optimizer and a learning rate of 1e−4.

For decoding the outputs of model, Beam search with beam size 4 is used with decoding length set to maximum 128.

5.3   Model Evaluation

The trained model generates grammatically sound questions given any context. We use an answer unsupervised model which is more general in nature and can learn to generate questions by itself from any type of context. Also enabling it to look for potential answers on its own.

But since the model is not answer supervised, the questions generated are very different from the SQuAD's human generated questions. Moreover our model generates questions that are not in the target set but are obvious deductions from the input context.

All the current performance evaluation metrics (BLEU, METEOR, ROGUE, etc.) measure similarity of predicted output to the target in different manners. For example, BLEU measures the token-wise similarity, and use of a different token at any position, even with a similar context will result in a diminished BLEU score.

Since our predictions are very different from the training targets, though still sound, the scores on traditional metrics are bound to be low. Also, since it is a general observation that same question can be re-framed in a different manner and still mean the same thing (semantically similar), we believe that these scores do not reflect the performance of our model in totality.

6   Results

In this section we will take a glance at the results achieved by our model.

By the predictions made by our model, it is observed that a T5 transformer can be successfully trained to generate syntactically correct questions from unseen input context paragraphs, even after being trained for just 10 epochs for the task.

Some of the predictions made by our model are listed in Fig. 6. We highlighted the context from where we assume the model predicted the question.

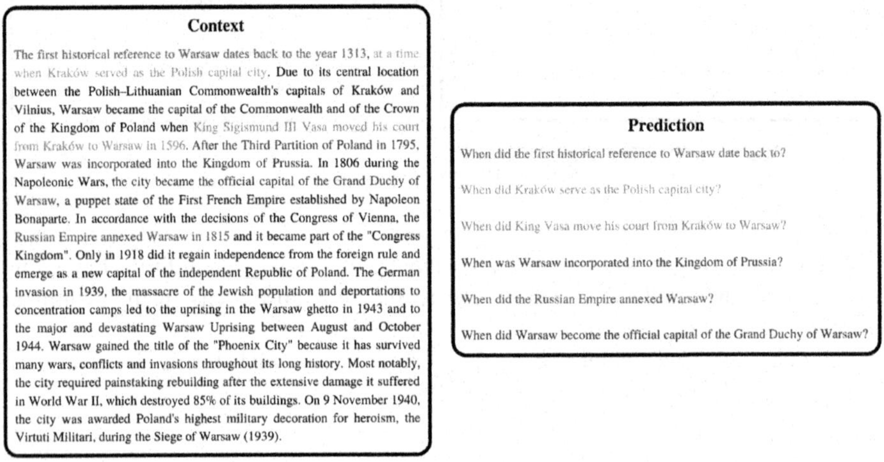

Context

The first historical reference to Warsaw dates back to the year 1313, at a time when Kraków served as the Polish capital city. **Due to its central location between the Polish–Lithuanian Commonwealth's capitals of Kraków and Vilnius, Warsaw became the capital of the Commonwealth and of the Crown of the Kingdom of Poland when** King Sigismund III Vasa moved his court from Kraków to Warsaw in 1596. **After the Third Partition of Poland in 1795, Warsaw was incorporated into the Kingdom of Prussia. In 1806 during the Napoleonic Wars, the city became the official capital of the Grand Duchy of Warsaw, a puppet state of the First French Empire established by Napoleon Bonaparte. In accordance with the decisions of the Congress of Vienna, the Russian Empire annexed Warsaw in 1815 and it became part of the "Congress Kingdom". Only in 1918 did it regain independence from the foreign rule and emerge as a new capital of the independent Republic of Poland. The German invasion in 1939, the massacre of the Jewish population and deportations to concentration camps led to the uprising in the Warsaw ghetto in 1943 and to the major and devastating Warsaw Uprising between August and October 1944. Warsaw gained the title of the "Phoenix City" because it has survived many wars, conflicts and invasions throughout its long history. Most notably, the city required painstaking rebuilding after the extensive damage it suffered in World War II, which destroyed 85% of its buildings. On 9 November 1940, the city was awarded Poland's highest military decoration for heroism, the Virtuti Militari, during the Siege of Warsaw (1939).**

Prediction

When did the first historical reference to Warsaw date back to?

When did Kraków serve as the Polish capital city?

When did King Vasa move his court from Kraków to Warsaw?

When was Warsaw incorporated into the Kingdom of Prussia?

When did the Russian Empire annexed Warsaw?

When did Warsaw become the official capital of the Grand Duchy of Warsaw?

Fig. 6. Prediction results

The generated questions are grammatically sound and context relevant. Though context relevant, some questions generated are also open-ended which is not generally the case in answer focused models.

Also, our model possess the ability to produce multiple questions from given context. The number of questions generated depend upon the beam size selected while making predictions, and therefore it can be adjusted accordingly.

6.1   Web-Interface

We have also made a web interface in order for others to benefit from this work. Generator Q is an application that will allow the user to generate coherent good quality questions from the data input by the user. The question generator will take in a piece of textual data from the user. Accordingly, question and answer pairs will be generated by the system, from the data provided. The PyTorch model is hosted on the web. The website takes in input some text, which can be pasted in the text box provided as shown in Fig. 7. The generated questions are then rendered as shown in Fig. 8. Here is a link to access the website: GeneratorQ.

Fig. 7. Input user interface of the website

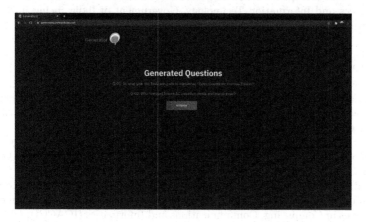

Fig. 8. Output user interface of the website showing questions generated

7   Conclusions and Future Work

Our research primarily focuses on automatic question generation using Transfer Learning on T5 Transformer which was fine-tuned on the SQuAD dataset. As we know manual construction of questions is a complicated and tedious task that requires experience, our model aims to reduce that effort by producing good quality and relevant questions. Our fine-tuned model fulfils this aim.

This can be further extended to generate questions along with answers in a closed setting. Many of the previous techniques utilize a separate module or some additional data to identify key phrases, that can act as answers. Earlier several rule-based answer (or key) extraction modules were suggested. Recent suggestions for this purpose include the use of a seq-to-seq probabilistic model [19]. Another method to address the problem is by highlighting the answer portion in the given context by using different techniques like using <hl> tags [2] and tagging answer start and end locations or pre-mentioning the answer with the context paragraph. This requires additional knowledge and effort.

A problem we faced was the lack of datasets specific to educational setting. More labelled data can be used to further expand this research. Another problem faced by us was the lack of a proper evaluation metric which accurately judges the performance of the model. Since our model is not answer supervised, the questions generated are very different from the SQuAD's human generated questions. More research can be done to produce better evaluation metrics for QG task.

Further better results can we produced by increasing the number of epochs for training and using a powerful GPU.

Acknowledgments. This paper is an outcome of the R&D work undertaken in the Capstone project under Computer Science and Engineering Department of Thapar Institute of Engineering and Technology, and the Visvesvaraya PhD Scheme of Ministry of Electronics and Information Technology, Government of India, being implemented by Digital India Corporation (formerly Media Lab Asia).

References

1. Alammar, J.: The illustrated transformer - jay alammar - visualizing machine learning one concept at a time. http://jalammar.github.io/illustrated-transformer/. Accessed 29 Oct 2020
2. Chan, Y.H., Fan, Y.C.: A recurrent BERT-based model for question generation. In: Proceedings of the 2nd Workshop on Machine Reading for Question Answering (2019). https://doi.org/10.18653/v1/d19-5821
3. Das, R., Ray, A., Mondal, S., Das, D.: A rule based question generation framework to deal with simple and complex sentences. In: 2016 International Conference on Advances in Computing, Communications and Informatics (ICACCI), pp. 542–548 (2016)
4. Devlin, J., Chang, M.W., Lee, K., Toutanova, K.: BERT: pre-training of deep bidirectional transformers for language understanding. In: Proceedings of the 2019 Conference of the North, pp. 4171–4186 (2019). https://doi.org/10.18653/v1/N19-1423. https://www.aclweb.org/anthology/N19-1423
5. Du, X., Shao, J., Cardie, C.: Learning to ask: neural question generation for reading comprehension. CoRR abs/1705.00106 (2017). http://arxiv.org/abs/1705.00106
6. Heilman, M.: Automatic factual question generation from text (2011)
7. Heilman, M., Smith, N.A.: Good question! statistical ranking for question generation. In: Human Language Technologies: The 2010 Annual Conference of the North American Chapter of the Association for Computational Linguistics, pp. 609–617. Association for Computational Linguistics, Los Angeles (2010). https://www.aclweb.org/anthology/N10-1086
8. Hochreiter, S., Schmidhuber, J.: Long short-term memory. Neural Comput. **9**(8), 1735–1780 (1997). https://doi.org/10.1162/neco.1997.9.8.1735
9. Kumar, V., Ramakrishnan, G., Li, Y.F.: Putting the horse before the cart: a generator-evaluator framework for question generation from text (2019)
10. Lopez, L.E., Cruz, D.K., Cruz, J.C.B., Cheng, C.: Transformer-based end-to-end question generation (2020)

11. Mitkov, R.: Computer-aided generation of multiple-choice tests. In: International Conference on Natural Language Processing and Knowledge Engineering, Proceedings, p. 15 (2003)
12. Radford, A., Wu, J., Child, R., Luan, D., Amodei, D., Sutskever, I.: Language models are unsupervised multitask learners. OpenAI blog (2018). https://cdn.openai.com/better-language-models/language_models_are_unsupervised_multitask_learners.pdf
13. Raffel, C., et al.: Exploring the limits of transfer learning with a unified text-to-text transformer (2019)
14. Rajpurkar, P., Zhang, J., Lopyrev, K., Liang, P.: Squad: 100,000+ questions for machine comprehension of text. In: Proceedings of the 2016 Conference on Empirical Methods in Natural Language Processing (2016). https://doi.org/10.18653/v1/d16-1264
15. Rus, V., Cai, Z., Graesser, A.: Question generation: example of a multi-year evaluation campaign. In: Proceedings of WS on the QGSTEC (2008)
16. Rus, V., Wyse, B., Piwek, P., Lintean, M., Stoyanchev, S., Moldovan, C.: The first question generation shared task evaluation challenge (2010). https://www.aclweb.org/anthology/W10-4234
17. Schmidhuber, J.: Deep learning in neural networks: an overview. Neural Netw. **61**, 85–117 (2015). https://doi.org/10.1016/j.neunet.2014.09.003
18. Serban, I.V., et al.: Generating factoid questions with recurrent neural networks: the 30M factoid question-answer corpus (2016). https://doi.org/10.18653/v1/P16-1056. https://www.aclweb.org/anthology/P16-1056
19. Subramanian, S., Wang, T., Yuan, X., Zhang, S., Trischler, A., Bengio, Y.: Neural models for key phrase extraction and question generation. In: Proceedings of the Workshop on Machine Reading for Question Answering (2018). https://doi.org/10.18653/v1/w18-2609
20. Vaswani, A., et al.: Attention is all you need (2017)
21. Vries, B.D., Príncipe, J.: A theory for neural networks with time delays. In: NIPS (1990)
22. Wolf, T., et al.: Huggingface's transformers: state-of-the-art natural language processing (2019)
23. Yuan, X., et al.: Machine comprehension by text-to-text neural question generation (2017). https://doi.org/10.18653/v1/W17-2603. https://www.aclweb.org/anthology/W17-2603

Improving Word Recognition in Speech Transcriptions by Decision-Level Fusion of Stemming and Two-Way Phoneme Pruning

Sunakshi Mehra$^{(\boxtimes)}$ ⓘ and Seba Susan ⓘ

Department of Information Technology, Delhi Technological University, Shahbad Daulatpur,
Main Bawana Road, Delhi 110042, India
mehra.sunakshi623@gmail.com

Abstract. We introduce an unsupervised approach for correcting highly imperfect speech transcriptions based on a decision-level fusion of stemming and two-way phoneme pruning. Transcripts are acquired from videos by extracting audio using Ffmpeg framework and further converting audio to text transcript using Google API. In the benchmark LRW dataset, there are 500 word categories, and 50 videos per class in mp4 format. All videos consist of 29 frames (each 1.16 s long) and the word appears in the middle of the video. In our approach we tried to improve the baseline accuracy from 9.34% by using stemming, phoneme extraction, filtering and pruning. After applying the stemming algorithm to the text transcript and evaluating the results, we achieved 23.34% accuracy in word recognition. To convert words to phonemes we used the Carnegie Mellon University (CMU) pronouncing dictionary that provides a phonetic mapping of English words to their pronunciations. A two-way phoneme pruning is proposed that comprises of the two non-sequential steps: 1) filtering and pruning the phonemes containing vowels and plosives 2) filtering and pruning the phonemes containing vowels and fricatives. After obtaining results of stemming and two-way phoneme pruning, we applied decision-level fusion and that led to an improvement of word recognition rate upto 32.96%.

Keywords: Stemming · Phoneme filtering · Phoneme selection · Decision fusion

1 Introduction

Automatic Speech recognition is the process of transforming speech to recognizable text with the help of computer interface. It is challenging to extract pure text transcript from audio since different speakers may have different styles, different accents, and different voice quality [1]. Speech recognition is not speaker- dependent; recognition of speakers from characteristics of their voices is another line of research [2, 4]. In recent years, a lot of progress has been achieved in the task of spoken text recognition by supervised classification, and less work is focused on unsupervised approaches. Alignment of subset of phonemes on audio track with the sequence of phonemes extracted from the imperfect speech transcript was acknowledged as a challenging task in [5] because of varying

© Springer Nature Singapore Pte Ltd. 2021
D. Garg et al. (Eds.): IACC 2020, CCIS 1367, pp. 256–266, 2021.
https://doi.org/10.1007/978-981-16-0401-0_19

sound/video quality compromised by noise disturbances, different speakers, varying accent and varying style in pronunciation of words. The performance of aligning shows a correct matching of phonemes with 10, 20, 30 error margins when more than 75% of text is aligned correctly within 5 s. Unaligned temporal text is converted to phonemes and the alignment between audio phonemes and text phonemes is done with dynamic programming edit distance transformation [5]. Text to speech synthesizing system based on Grapheme-to-Phoneme conversion resolves problems in rule based approaches [8, 13]. The use of root words or sub-words can be observed in [11, 14, 31, 33, 35] in which the prefix and suffix of every word is stripped off. The idea of grapheme-to-phoneme conversion is extended in [10] that uses the sub-word approach in resolving ambiguity in inflected and compound words. The algorithm segments each word into the main part and the suffix part, and concatenates the pronunciations of the two parts procured separately from two different pronunciation dictionaries. The study shows 6% of the errors are achieved due to inflected or compound words among a total of 8.33%. Recently developed online tools like WinPitchPro perform text-to-speech alignment [23]. Unsupervised acoustic modelling on 100k words of text in [25], measures the effects of weak language models by model training. This method uses word confidences to predict n-gram counts for language modelling by multiplying the word confidences together to get a weighted count which results in better reduction in word error rate. A larger gain might be possible but results improve much more in margin if better estimation techniques are used to identify correct n-grams on small amounts of labelled data [25].

Speech separation can also be used for the classification problem, based on supervised learning [17]. Over the past few decades, speech separation and Weiner filtering make the assumption of background noises which constitutes a major problem in our current system. Deep neural network with multiple hidden layers can perform better than Multilayer Perceptron in speech separation [18]. Morphological parsing may or may not involve stemming. It may just involve searching for a word in its original form as it appears in the sentence [36, 39]. The stemming framework involves two main aspects: first is to expand the sentence selection strategy from the so-called "sentence by phrase" to "list by phrase", and second is to examine different construction methods and component models involved in such a framework [15]. The foremost challenge lies in how the word is pronounced and with how much intensity the person said the word. To map the words to phonemes we used the CMU dictionary which is also called a pronouncing dictionary [40]. In this paper, we use a stemming framework in collaboration with phonemes filtered and pruned in two independent stages for recognizing words and correcting errors in imperfect speech transcripts. The organization of this paper is as follows: Sect. 2 presents the proposed approach, Sect. 3 analyses the experimental results and Sect. 4 states the conclusion.

2 Proposed Approach for Correcting Imperfect Speech Transcription

2.1 Text Pre-processing

The text transcript is of limited size; an example is shown for the word category "signifi-cant" in Fig. 1. The speech transcript normalization is the process of cleaning the data by removing unwanted information- stop words, punctuation, conversion of numeral values to their word form, converting all words to lower case for better reading. Tokenizing of the sentence is performed to read the content properly and distinguish each word separately. Text filtering helps in faster processing and reduces the size of the document.

significance significant null null a significant significance vice president significance
significant significant its significance i am significant significance significant significant
significant significant significant significant significant significant i have significant
significance significance more significant null null significant sunderkand significant

Fig. 1. Text transcription after pre-processing.

Stop words are removed since these have less importance, like "a", "the", "an", "of", "like", "for" that are not of any significance in information retrieval. We have re-phrased commonly used phrases (like "couldn't") with their grammatical form ("could not"). Tokens containing symbols like ".", "!", "#", "$" are converted to word form as per the requirement of the content, are removed, as shown in Fig. 2.

significance significant **null null** a significant significance vice president significance
significant significant **its** significance **i am** significant significance significant significant
significant significant significant significant significant significant **i** have significant
significance significance **more** significant **null null** significant sunderkand significant

Fig. 2. After text normalization (removing all these bold letter words) from a transcription.

2.2 Stemming

In information retrieval and linguistic morphology, stemming is the process of chopping-off suffix from a word and reducing it to its root form also known as the base form. Stemming is used in text and natural language processing. For instance, if the word ends with "ed", "ies", "ing", "ly" the end of the word is removed to obtain its root form or base form. One of the tools used for stemming is Porter stemmer where the stem may not be identical to the morphological root of the words, as observed from the stemmed results in Fig. 3. Stemmer algorithm outlines the process of removing inflectional endings and common morphs from words. It is also used for text normalization in information retrieval systems [7]. Porter stemmer is less aggressive than Lancaster stemmer which trims out most of the valid text. In linguistic morphology, stemming is the process of finding the root or base of the word. However, lemmatization is to find the lemma in a set of lexicons having same word sense. The base or word-form can be derived or inflected. In our LRW dataset, the keyword "absolutely" has lemma as "absolutely" and stem as "absolut". When you go through the text transcription, the occurrence of stem "absolut" is more as compared to the lemma "absolutely". So, the stemmer brings most of the words closer to their respective categories, that would yield higher classification scores than experiments that involve matching words in their original form as in [36] and [37].

signific signific signific signific vice presid signific signific signific signific signific signific signific signific signific signific signific signific signific signific signific signific signific signific signific sunderkand signific

Fig. 3. After applying stemming using Porter stemmer.

2.3 Phoneme Extraction from Text

Phoneme is the smallest unit of speech in linguistics where a sound or group of sounds differ in their pronunciation and meaning, where the pronunciation varies according to the surrounding letters which may affect the letter representation [12]. The word can be sound of speech, including stress, articulation and intonation, for the representation of which we used CMU pronunciation dictionary with over 125k words and their phonetic transcriptions After text normalization, we generated a collection of phonemes from the text aligned transcript. Only the standard detailing pattern of the sound or stress pattern of a syllable, word, and phrase is selected. The phonetic transcription of the word "about" is "AH0 B AW1 T" where 0 represents no stress, 1 represents primary stress and 2 represents secondary stress; all the numerical values are filtered out. Thus the text is first segmented to words and further represented by their phonemes as shown in the example in Fig. 4.

Different speakers contribute to a different pronunciation; searching for a perfect match in transcripts is challenging [22]. CMU pronouncing dictionary follows American English to assume pronunciation of a text. CMU pronouncing dictionary follows the same standard representation as the International phonetic alphabet of sounds in spoken language [40].

Phoneme filtering is the process where the phonemes are filtered on the basis of whether they contain vowels, plosives or fricatives. Phoneme filtering not only reduces the size of the dataset but also improves the category identification as shown from the sequence of phonemes shown in Fig. 5 that are extracted from the normalized text in Fig. 2. Plosives are also known as stop or oral consonant which block the vocal tract so that the flow of air ceases. They include both voiced and voiceless consonants. "b", "d", "g" are voiced plosives and "p", "t", "k" are voiceless or unvoiced plosives. They are also called glottal stop. Fricatives are consonants that are mostly voiced and consist of high energy and amplitude. The example of fricatives is "f", "s", "v", "z". Because of

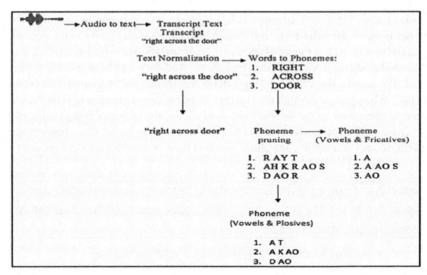

Fig. 4. Overview of phoneme filtering and pruning from a sample phrase. Text phoneme is filtered and pruned to include plosives and vowels and alternatively, to include vowels and fricatives in the same manner.

high amplitude they are easily detected. The International Phonetic alphabet (IPA) aims to transcribe the sounds of all human languages.

The IPA introduced the phonetic chart where each lexical unit is distinguished in the way it is spoken. Consonants are the sounds produced in the vocal tract, more specifically in the oral tract (the mouth and pharynx), where the produced speech is constructed. They are further classified to labials, coronal, radical and dorsal. The vowels contribute to high pitch and amplitude so most of the time they are detected correctly. Based on the manner the speech is formed, if it is sound coming from nose its called as nasal; if it is the sound formed by blocked air flow, then it is called stop, plosive, or oral. Fricatives are consonants such as ("f", "s", "v", "z") produced by placing the lower lip against the upper teeth. Trills are similar to taps and flaps is a sound produced by active and passive articulator [27].

```
S AH G N IH F IH K AH N S  S IH G N IH F IH K AH N T  S IH G N IH F IH K AH N T  S
AH G N IH F IH K AH N S  V AY S  P R EH Z AH D AH N T  S AH G N IH F IH K AH N
S  S IH G N IH F IH K AH N T  S IH G N IH F IH K AH N T  S AH G N IH F IH K AH N S
S IH G N IH F IH K AH N T  S AH G N IH F IH K AH N S  S IH G N IH F IH K AH N T  S
AH G N IH F IH K AH T  S AH G N IH F IH K AH N T  S AH G N IH F IH K AH N T  S
AH G N IH F IH K AH N T  S AH G N IH F IH K AH N T  S AH G N IH F IH K AH N T  S
AH G N IH F IH K AH N T  S AH G N IH F IH K AH N T  S AH G N IH F IH K AH N S  S
AH G N IH F IH K AH N S  S IH G N IH F IH K AH N T  S IH G N IH F IH K AH N T  S
AH N D ER K AH N D  S IH G N IH F IH K AH N T
```

Fig. 5. After phoneme extraction and filtering.

2.4 Decision Fusion of Stemming and Phoneme

After collecting results of pure stemming and phoneme filtering, we pruned each phoneme such that it contains either (i) vowels or plosives or (ii) vowels or fricatives. The pruning was performed in two non-sequential stages. We call the scheme two-way phoneme pruning.

Stage I: Phoneme pruning using Vowels and Plosives
Stage II: Phoneme pruning using Vowels and Fricatives.

In order to combine the goodness of all factors, the outcomes of stemming and Stage I and Stage II of two-way phoneme pruning are combined using a decision level score fusion, by which scheme, if any of the stages (stem, vowel + plosives, vowel + fricatives) identify a given word in the transcript, then the word is considered to be identified.

3 Experimental Results

3.1 Dataset

One of the challenging datasets for speech recognition in the wild is Lip Reading in the wild (LRW) dataset [20]. It is an audio-visual dataset that has motivated various researches in audio-visual speech recognition [9, 21]. In our work, the audio track is extracted and processed for generating the speech transcription. The LRW dataset consists of 500 different classes of words (each class contains 50 samples). We use the testing data alone for the unsupervised experiments. All these videos are in MP4 format and have 29 frames each that are 1.16 s in length, and the word is supposed to occur in the middle of the video. The word length, word details are given in the metadata. To extract audio from the video we used Ffmpeg framework. Ffmpeg is a fast video and audio converter. There is no quality loss while changing the format of multimedia files.

3.2 Results of the Proposed Approach Using Decision-Level Fusion

The experiments were performed in python 3.7.4 on a PC (Intel core i5 with Intel HD Graphics 6000 1536 MB and Mac OS High Sierra with a clock of 1.8 GHz). The computation time for a single audio file is 29 s. In our proposed work, we filtered and pruned the phonemes by selecting vowels and plosives (in Stage 1) and vowels and fricatives (in Stage 2). After applying stemming, the word recognition rate was observed to be 23.34%. Stage 1 of Phoneme pruning yielded a recognition rate of 27.67% while Stage 2 yielded 28.23%. The results of decision-level fusion of stemming and Stage-1 and Stage-2 of phoneme pruning, yielded the word recognition rate of 32.96%, a significant improvement over the baseline method (9.36%) which is explained in the next sub-section. A demonstration of decision-level fusion is shown in Fig. 6 for the word category "significant". All results are summarized in Table 1 with suitable references to the literature regarding the use of the individual components for speech text understanding. We have also compared our approach with two well- known automated spelling correction tools – autocorrect [30] and symspell [6]. The code for both these tools is available online at [32] and [19] respectively.

a) Phoneme pruning using vowels and plosives	b) Phoneme pruning using vowels and fricatives	c) Stemming
A G II K A	S A I F I A S	signific
A G II K A T	S A I F I A	signific
<unk>	<unk>	skiwrd
<unk>	<unk>	signuyt
A G II K A T	S A I F I A	signific
A G II K A	S A I F I A S	signific
A P E A D E T	V A S E Z A E	vice presid
A G II K A	S A I F I A S	signific
A G II K A T	S A I F I A	signific
A G II K A T	S A I F I A	signific
A G II K A	S A I F I A S	signific
A G II K A T	S A I F I A	signific
A G II K A	S A I F I A S	signific
A G II K A T	S A I F I A	signific
A G II K A T	S A I F I A	signific
A G II K A T	S A I F I A	signific
A G II K A T	S A I F I A	signific
A G II K A T	S A I F I A	signific
A G II K A T	S A I F I A	signific
A G II K A T	S A I F I A	signific

Number of significant: 13   Number of significant: 5   Number of significant: 19

After Applying Decision Fusion on Stemming and Phonemes: 1 1 0 0 1 1 0 1 1 1 1 1 1 1 1 1 1 1 1

Occurrence of stem significant: 19

Probability of occurrence of word significant after fusion: 86.36%

Fig. 6. Decision fusion of stemming and two-way phoneme pruning.

Table 1. Comparison of various methodologies on LRW dataset.

Methods	Accuracy
Baseline [29]	**9.34%**
Stemming [28]	**23.34%**
Phoneme pruning (Vowels & Plosives) [3]	**27.67%**
Phoneme pruning (Vowels & Fricatives) [5]	**28.23%**
Autocorrect [30]	**21.50%**
Symspell [6]	**25.16%**
Decision Fusion of Stemming and two-way Phoneme pruning	**32.96%**

3.3 Sliding Text Window-The Baseline Approach

In the baseline approach, we slide a window across the text after tokenizing each word in the sentence. If the category word is found in a sentence, the text window can slide to the next sentence or next line in the text file. After sliding word by word in a sentence and line by line, it determines the number of occurrences of the category word, as shown in Fig. 7. In this way the duplicity and redundancy of the same category in a sentence can be avoided.

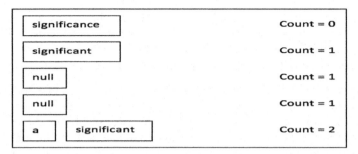

Fig. 7. Sliding text window to search for the keyword "significant" in-text transcription.

3.4 Test Cases

All 500 categories results (averaged) are projected in Table 1. An examination of test cases shows that sometimes stemming performs best, sometimes phonemes (vowels + plosives) performs best, and sometimes phonemes (vowels + fricatives) gives the best results. Our technique combines the best of all three methods and provides the highest accuracy. Some test cases are presented below, that can help us in understanding the role of decision fusion more precisely.

Test Case 1: In some cases, only stem is found sufficient to recognize the word. For instance, in category "announced," the probability of occurrence of the word "announce", which is the root form of the word "announced", is 6%, the probability of occurrence of vowels + plosives is 4%, and the probability of occurrence of vowels + fricatives is 2%. As you can see, in such cases, decision fusion causes the stem to win with a high probability value. After trimming "ed" from the word "announced", the probability of occurrence of stem "announce" increases by 4%. However, in vowels + plosives, the word "announced" is pronounced in CMU dictionary as "AH", "N", "AW", "N", "S", "T". The vowels are- "A" and plosives- "T", the pattern we are looking for in our transcript is "AAT"; the probability of increase in this case is 2%. Moreover, in case of vowels + fricatives, the word "announced" is pronounced in CMU dictionary as "AH", "N", "AW", "N", "S", "T". The vowel is- "A" and fricatives are- "W", "S". The pattern we are looking for in our transcript is "AAWS". The probability of occurrence in this case is same as the baseline. The probability of increase is more in case of stem than other two cases. Hence, stemming performs best for this particular test case.

Test Case 2: Let's take one more example of another category "agreement" where the probability of occurrence of stem is 44%, the probability of occurrence of vowels + plosives is 88% and the probability of occurrence of vowel + fricatives is 92%. In this case, decision fusion causes vowels + fricatives to win with high probability value. In category "agreement", the probability of occurrence of stem "agreement" is same as the baseline. However, in vowels + plosives, the word "agreement" is pronounced in CMU dictionary as "AH", "G", "R", "IY", "M", "AH", "N", "T". The vowels are- "A", "I" and plosives are- "G", "T". The pattern we are looking for in our transcript is "AGIAT", the probability of increase in this case is 22%. However, in case of vowels + fricatives, the word "agreement" is pronounced in CMU dictionary as "AH", "G", "R",

"IY", "M", "AH", "N", "T". The vowels is- "A", "I" and plosives are- none the pattern we are looking for in our transcript is "AI". The probability of increase in this case is 70%. The probability of increase is more in case of vowels + fricatives than the other two cases. Hence, vowels + fricatives perform best in this test case.

Test Case 3: In category "affairs" the probability of occurrence of stem is 4%, the probability of occurrence of vowels + plosives is 20%, and the probability of occurrence of vowels + fricatives is 6%. This is the case in which decision fusion causes vowels + plosives to win with high probability value. After trimming "s" from the word "affairs", the probability of occurrence of stem "affair" is same as the baseline. However, in vowels + plosives, the word "affairs" is pronounced in CMU dictionary as "AH", "F", "EH", "R", "Z". The vowels are- "A", "E" and plosives are- none, the pattern we are looking for in our transcript is "AE". The probability of increase in this case is 16%. However, in case of vowels + fricatives, the word "affairs" is pronounced in CMU dictionary as "AH", "F", "EH", "R", "Z". The vowels are- "A", "E" and fricatives are- "F", "Z", the pattern we are looking for in our transcript is "AFERZ". The probability of increase in this case is 2%. The probability of increase is more in case of vowels + plosives than the other two cases. Hence, vowels + plosives give the best results for this particular test case.

4   Conclusions

We have presented a fusion approach of the best of stemming and two-way phoneme pruning on highly imperfect speech transcription extracted from the LRW dataset which is in mp4 format. After extracting audio samples using Ffmpeg framework, we converted the audio speech to the text transcription using Google API which is publicly available and has various applications in speech adaption, transcribing speech and real-time speech recognition. We have evaluated the baseline results by pure string matching of a word category from a text transcription. The first step is text normalization and speech adaptation by removing stop words which are the most frequent unwanted words from a text file to make text processing faster. After applying stemming on the word, we extracted the most root word and compared it with different categories. At the same time, we converted the word to phonemes using the CMU pronouncing dictionary. After mapping text transcript to phonemes, we applied phoneme filtering on text transcript, where we filtered out the phonemes containing vowels, plosives or fricatives. The phoneme pruning is executed in two non-sequential stages: Stage I: Phoneme pruning using Vowels and Plosives, Stage II: Phoneme pruning using Vowels and Fricatives. Once we got results through the above three methods, we applied decision fusion that confirmed whether the occurrence of the word is detected by any of the three methods. The proposed fusion method outperforms the state of the art and the word recognition accuracy is improved from the baseline accuracy of 9.34% to 32.96% using our fusion method.

References

1. Besacier, L., Barnard, E., Karpov, A., Schultz, T.: Automatic speech recognition for under-resourced languages: a survey. Speech Commun. **56**, 85–100 (2014)

2. Susan, S., Sharma, S.: A fuzzy nearest neighbor classifier for speaker identification. In: 2012 Fourth International Conference on Computational Intelligence and Communication Networks, pp. 842–845. IEEE (2012)
3. Hemakumar, G.: Vowel-plosive of English word recognition using HMM. In: IJCSI (2011)
4. Tripathi, M., Singh, D., Susan, S.: Speaker recognition using SincNet and X-Vector fusion. arXiv preprint arXiv:2004.02219 (2020).
5. Haubold, A., Kender, J.R.: Alignment of speech to highly imperfect text transcriptions. In: 2007 IEEE International Conference on Multimedia and Expo, pp. 224–227. IEEE (2007)
6. Gupta, P.: A context-sensitive real-time spell checker with language adaptability. In: 2020 IEEE 14th International Conference on Semantic Computing (ICSC), pp. 116–122. IEEE (2020)
7. Porter, M.F.: An algorithm for suffix stripping. Program 14(3), 130–137 (1980)
8. Stan, A., Bell, P., King, S.: A grapheme-based method for automatic alignment of speech and text data. In: 2012 IEEE Spoken Language Technology Workshop (SLT), pp. 286–290. IEEE (2012)
9. Haubold, A., Kender, J.R.: Augmented segmentation and visualization for presentation videos. In: Proceedings of the 13th Annual ACM International Conference on Multimedia, pp. 51–60 (2005)
10. Ghosh, K., Sreenivasa Rao, K.: Subword based approach for grapheme-to- phoneme conversion in Bengali text-to-speech synthesis system. In: 2012 National Conference on Communications (NCC), pp. 1–5. IEEE (2012)
11. Wang, W., Zhou, Y., Xiong, C., Socher, R.: An investigation of phone-based subword units for end-to-end speech recognition. arXiv preprint arXiv:2004.04290 (2020)
12. Alsharhan, E., Ramsay, A.: Improved Arabic speech recognition system through the automatic generation of fine-grained phonetic transcriptions. Inf. Process. Manag. 56(2), 343–353 (2019)
13. Gimenes, M., Perret, C., New, B.: Lexique-Infra: Grapheme-phoneme, phoneme-grapheme regularity, consistency, and other sublexical statistics for 137,717 polysyllabic French words. Behav. Res. Methods 52(6), 2480–2488 (2020). https://doi.org/10.3758/s13428-020-01396-2
14. Harwath, D., Glass, J.: Towards visually grounded sub-word speech unit discovery. In: ICASSP 2019–2019 IEEE International Conference on Acoustics, Speech and Signal Processing (ICASSP), pp. 3017–3021. IEEE (2019)
15. Lin, S.-H., Yeh, Y.-M., Chen, B.: Extractive speech summarization- From the view of decision theory. In: Eleventh Annual Conference of the International Speech Communication Association (2010)
16. Siivola, V., Hirsimaki, T., Creutz, M., Kurimo, M.: Unlimited vocabulary speech recognition based on morphs discovered in an unsupervised manner. In: Eighth European Conference on Speech Communication and Technology (2003)
17. Williamson, D.S., Wang, Y., Wang, D.: Complex ratio masking for monaural speech separation. IEEE/ACM Trans. Audio Speech Lang. Process. 24(3), 483–492 (2015)
18. Chen, J., Wang, Y., Wang, D.: A feature study for classification-based speech separation at low signal-to-noise ratios. IEEE/ACM Trans. Audio Speech Lang. Process. 22(12), 1993–2002 (2014)
19. Mamamothb: Python port SymSpell (2019). https://github.com/mammothb/symspellpy
20. Shuang, Y., et al.: LRW-1000: a naturally-distributed large- scale benchmark for lip reading in the wild. In: 2019 14th IEEE International Conference on Automatic Face Gesture Recognition (FG 2019), pp. 1–8. IEEE (2019)
21. Torfi, A., Iranmanesh, S.M., Nasrabadi, N., Dawson, J.: 3d convolutional neural networks for cross audio-visual matching recognition. IEEE Access 5, 22081–22091 (2017)
22. Hazen, T.J.: Automatic alignment and error correction of human generated transcripts for long speech recordings. In: Ninth International Conference on Spoken Language Processing (2006)

23. Martin, P.: WinPitchPro-A tool for text to speech alignment and prosodic analysis. In: Speech Prosody 2004, International Conference (2004)

24. Chen, Y.-C., Shen, C.-H., Huang, S.-F., Lee, H.-Y.: Towards unsupervised automatic speech recognition trained by unaligned speech and text only arXiv preprint arXiv:1803.10952 (2018)

25. Novotney, S., Schwartz, R., Ma, J.: Unsupervised acoustic and language model training with small amounts of labelled data. In: 2009 IEEE International Conference on Acoustics, Speech and Signal Processing, pp. 4297–4300. IEEE (2009)

26. https://github.com/wolfgarbe/SymSpell

27. Schwartz, R., Makhoul, J.: Where the phonemes are: Dealing with ambiguity in acoustic-phonetic recognition. IEEE Trans. Acoust. Speech Signal Process. **23**(1), 50–53 (1975)

28. Mulholland, M., Lopez, M., Evanini, K., Loukina, A., Qian, Y.: A comparison of ASR and human errors for transcription of non-native spontaneous speech. In: 2016 IEEE International Conference on Acoustics, Speech and Signal Processing (ICASSP), pp. 5855–5859. IEEE (2016)

29. Bahl, L., et al.: Some experiments with large-vocabulary isolated-word sentence recognition. In: ICASSP 1984. IEEE International Conference on Acoustics, Speech, and Signal Processing, vol. 9, pp. 395–396. IEEE (1984)

30. Rayson, S.J., Hachamovitch, D.J., Kwatinetz, A.L., Hirsch, S.M.: Autocorrecting text typed into a word processing document. U.S. Patent 5,761,689, issued June 2 (1998)

31. Xu, H., Ding, S., Watanabe, S.: Improving end-to-end speech recognition with pronunciation-assisted sub-word modeling. In: ICASSP 2019–2019 IEEE International Conference on Acoustics, Speech and Signal Processing (ICASSP), pp. 7110- 7114. IEEE (2019)

32. https://github.com/phatpiglet/autocorrect

33. Drexler, J., Glass, J.: Learning a subword inventory jointly with end-to-end automatic speech recognition. In: ICASSP 2020–2020 IEEE International Conference on Acoustics, Speech and Signal Processing (ICASSP), pp. 6439–6443. IEEE (2020)

34. Hermann, E., Kamper, H., Goldwater, S.: Multilingual and unsupervised subword modeling for zero-resource languages. Comput. Speech Lang. **65**, 101098 (2020)

35. Agenbag, W., Niesler, T.: Automatic sub-word unit discovery and pronunciation lexicon induction for ASR with application to under-resourced languages. Comput. Speech Lang. **57**, 20–40 (2019)

36. Susan, S., Kumar, S., Agrawal, R., Yadav, K.: Statistical keyword matching using automata. Int. J. Appl. Res. Inf. Technol. Computing **5**(3), 250–255 (2014)

37. Susan, S., Keshari, J.: Finding significant keywords for document databases by two-phase Maximum Entropy Partitioning. Pattern Recogn. Lett. **125**, 195–205 (2019)

38. Feng, S., Lee, T.: Exploiting cross-lingual speaker and phonetic diversity for unsupervised subword modeling. IEEE/ACM Trans. Audio Speech Lang. Process. **27**(12), 2000–2011 (2019)

39. Ojha, R., Chandra Sekhar, C.: Multi-label classification models for detection of phonetic features in building acoustic models. In: 2019 International Joint Conference on Neural Networks (IJCNN), pp. 1–8. IEEE (2019)

40. CMU Pronouncing Dictionary. www.speech.cs.cmu.edu/cgi-bin/cmudict. Accessed 15 June 2020

MultiDeepFake: Improving Fake News Detection with a Deep Convolutional Neural Network Using a Multimodal Dataset

Rohit Kumar Kaliyar[1(✉)], Arjun Mohnot[1], R. Raghhul[2], V. K. Prathyushaa[2], Anurag Goswami[1], Navya Singh[1], and Palavi Dash[3]

[1] Bennett University, Greater Noida, India
{rk5370,anurag.goswami,ns8558}@bennett.edu.in, arjunmohnot@gmail.com
[2] Sri Ramakrishna Engineering College, Coimbatore, India
raghhulr@gmail.com, prathyushaak2@gmail.com
[3] IIIT Bhubaneswar, Bhubaneswar, India
b317054@iiit-bh.ac.in

Abstract. Nowadays, the news ecosystem has shifted from traditional print media to social media outlets. It has resulted in the inaccuracy and irrelevancy in updating information by people which is commonly known as fake news. Due to the increasing number of users in social media, fake news is quickly publishing by an individual, and its credibility stands compromised, which brings in a need for effective detection of fake news. Since a large proportion of the population uses social media for updating themselves with news, delivering accurate and altruistic information to them is of utmost importance. Fake news detection has recently garnered much attention from researchers and developers alike. This work proposes to detect fake news using various modalities available, such as text, image, and text in the image in an effective manner using Deep Learning algorithms. In this paper, we propose a deep convolutional neural network for handling diverse multi-domain fake news data. Our proposed model (MultiDeepFake) has obtained more accurate results as compared to the existing state-of-the-art benchmarks. Classification results will motivate the researchers to use our proposed model in future for fake news detection.

Keywords: Fake news · Convolutional neural network · Long short-term memo. rumour · Deep learning · Social media

1 Introduction

With the advent of social media and technology [1,2], fake news has become one of the significant problems in the industry today. It has the potential to influence the decisions and opinions of the common public of the society [1]. Fake news is "news articles that are intentionally and verifiably false and could mislead

© Springer Nature Singapore Pte Ltd. 2021
D. Garg et al. (Eds.): IACC 2020, CCIS 1367, pp. 267–279, 2021.
https://doi.org/10.1007/978-981-16-0401-0_20

readers." It is a form of a story that can deceive people for some political and financial benefits [2]. Fake news is often published intentionally or unintentionally due to human neglect or incorrect data extraction and manipulation. It can have severe repercussions if left unattended or undetected. Fake news is usually created by manipulating data in the form of text, image, video, and audio. Hence, there arises the need for a multimodal fake news detection system [3] which effectively detects the correctness and accuracy of the news. Few examples of fake news are shown in Fig. 1.

Fig. 1. Few examples of fake news: Source (Facebook)

As fake news is written to mislead readers, it is a challenging task to detect the actual information using the content of the news only. Various social media platforms are used by people to share news instantly without knowing the fact behind it. Since the news content is diverse in terms of styles, the subject in which it is written, it becomes essential to bring an effective system for the detection. In this paper, we use deep learning models for the classification of fake news. The key benefit of deep learning model over machine learning is that it automatically extracts useful features [3–6]. In machine learning models, the features of the input data to be processed must present explicitly whereas, in deep learning, the model will incrementally learn the high-level features thereby reducing the need of expertise and feature extraction (the key difference is shown in Fig. 2). As we increase the hidden layers in the neural network, our model will be more dense.

In this paper, we propose a deep convolutional neural network (MultiDeep-Fake) having the capability of automatic feature extraction and achieved effective results utilizing multimodal features. For pre-trained word embedding, we used GloVe as our pre-trained word embedding. We have designed our model having four dense layers and in-depth convolutional approach. To validate the results, firstly, we implemented simple CNN model having two dense layers. Then, we have implemented one LSTM model with bi-directional training features. Subsequently, we have implemented our proposed Deep Convolutional Neural Network (MultiDeepFake), which a dense CNN, giving more accurate results compared to the existing state-of-the-art classification methods. The researchers can use our proposed model for significant results.

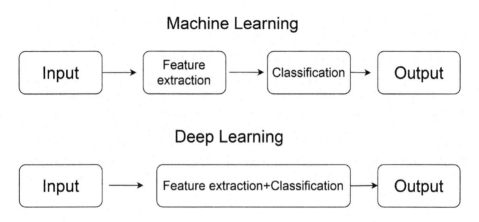

Fig. 2. Machine learning v/s Deep learning

2   Related Work

Conroy et al. [12] have explored several approaches that seem promising towards the aim of correctly classify the misleading articles. They note that simple content-related n-grams and shallow parts-of-speech (POS) tagging have problem insufficient for the classification task, often failing to account for important context information. Feng et al. [13] have used semantic analysis technique by considering object descriptor and contradictions with the text. They have achieved 85%–90% of accuracy with their proposed neural network. One of the researches by Wang [14] in the article "Liar, Liar Pants on Fire", he provided a dataset which can be available publicly. So many researchers are used, we can use natural processing language (NLP) techniques for news outlet stance detection, which can lead to fake news detection. Rubin et al [15] provide an overview of the features of fake news, which contain the style and format of journalistic reporting. Tacchini et al. [16] proposed a professional report on fake news detection using a few machine learning classification models. At first, they have implemented the deep syntax model, and he improved it as semantic analysis technique model. For this fake news detection, some are working on the against of GROVER model, a model which is useful to generate a detect only fake neural news [17]. For news article classification, we can use some models like LSTM by extracting the few LIWC (Linguistic and Word Count) features [18, 19] and combine with the textual content information. Deep Walk is another model for network embedding. In the following model for determining the fake news, they used SVM model after DEEP WALK embeds the news article based on the fake news network structure [20]. By taking the raw text as inputs, they tried to extract some explicit features and was provided as an input to the SVM classification model [21]. They also tested the RNN model, which is based on the textual contents [22]. After applying RNN, they were able to classify the factual news article.

3   Methodology

3.1   Fake News Classification with Deep Learning

Deep learning is a subset of machine learning which contains many useful and efficient algorithms when compared to other learning algorithms [7, 9, 10]. In a deep learning approach, the performance of a classification model is directly proportional to the amount of data (refer Fig. 3 for more details) that is being passed to the model. We designed a deep Convolutional Neural Network having different filters across each convolutional layer and dense layer. We have also implemented a bi-directional Long Short-Term Memory to validate the classification results of our proposed model.

Word Embedding: The text in the dataset is converted into word vectors using a count vectorizer or TF-IDF vectorizer. Here, each sentence consists of words that are converted to vectors using advanced pre-trained embedding techniques [12]. The GloVe uses to obtain a vector representation (for data flow kindly refer Fig. 4) of different length words. It is based on the observation that the ratio of word-word co-occurrences probabilities can be used to encode meaning [11]. It is trained on non-zero word-word occurrence entries which shows how frequently words co-occur with each other.

Convolutional Neural Network: Convolutional Neural Network is a type of Artificial Neural Network that uses perceptron for cognitive tasks in the domain of image processing and natural language processing. It is a class of deep neural networks that are also called as shift-variant or space-variant artificial neural networks. They are a regularized version of a multilayer perceptron in which each node is connected to others in the subsequent layer. In CNN, there is less scope of pre-processing the data required by the filters that are supposed to be hand-engineered are learned by this independently. In this paper, we have used a simple CNN having two dense as well as two convolutional layers.

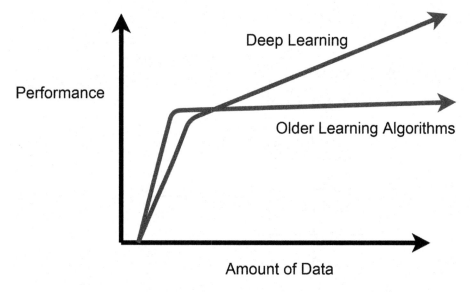

Fig. 3. Performance of deep learning models with large data

Long Short-Term Memory: Long short-term memory is a type of artificial neural network architecture that uses to process multiple data points in images, speech, audio as well as text. It consists of a cell and three gates, namely an input gate, forget gate and output gate. Unlike other architectures, LSTM has connections for feedback which help regulate the information flow through the gates. This architecture designed in such a way that it can remember the long-term dependencies of the data. It could overcome the vanishing gradient problem that arises when using Recurrent Neural Networks. These models can be trained in both supervised and unsupervised method.

MultiDeepFake: In the case of our proposed model (see Fig. 5 for more details), we tried increasing the density of the neural network, with three convolution layers and four dense layers with variable kernel size, and with some changes the hyperparameters to optimize the result further. In our model, initially, we have three convolutional layers with filters 3, 4, 5 respectively, each layer followed by a max-pooling of kernel_size = 5, the activation function used here was the 'relu' function. Subsequently, we had 1 flatten layer with a dropout of 0.1 followed by max-pooling operations, with kerne_size = 5 respectively. Finally, after concatenation, at the end of the model, four dense layers were added to make the model more deep and powerful for more accurate feature extraction. We have a dropout of 0.1 for the last dense layer the activation function used was 'softmax' for output function.

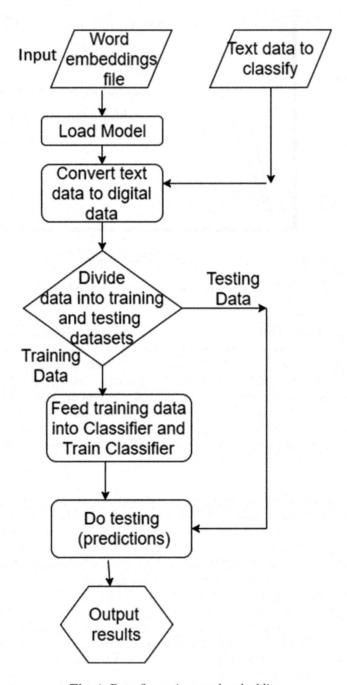

Fig. 4. Data flow using word embedding

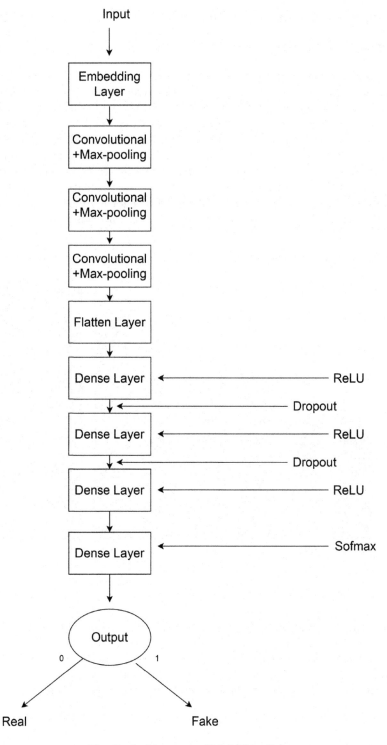

Fig. 5. Architecture of MultiDeepFake

4   Implementation and Results

4.1   Dataset: Fakeddit

Fakeddit is derived from Fake News + Reddit. Fakeddit, a novel dataset comprising of around 800,000 examples from different classifications of fake news. Each example is marked by 2-way, 3-way, and 5-way characterization classes. The dataset contains features like text, clean title, number of upvotes, comments, score, upvote ratio. The dataset containing text is fed into the model in which the words and sentences are converted into vectors and pass through the different layers containing a receding number of nodes to finally get classified as real or fake in the output layer. In this model, we use the feature "clean title" in the dataset as input (refer Table 1 and Figs. 6 to 7 for more details). It consists of 69954 entries of data occurrences for each column in training dataset.

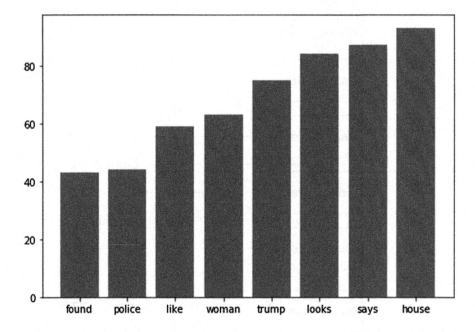

Fig. 6. Top 8 words in real news using Fakeddit

Fakeddit provides a large quantity of text+image samples with multiple labels for various levels of fine-grained classification. With such massive data points in the dataset, it can provide more generic results and helps to identify better credibility of the news. The most frequent words as Real and Fake in the dataset has been plotted to visualize trends whether the given sentence is fake or real.

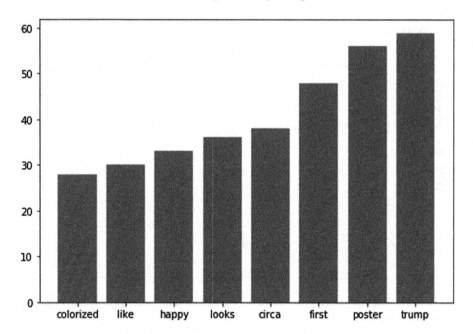

Fig. 7. Top 8 words in fake news using Fakeddit

Table 1. Representation of Fakeddit

Column	Description
ID	Unique value
Author	Provides the name author
Domain	Which domain the news belongs
has_the_image	It is a image or not
Num_comments Neutral	Number of comments
score	Provides score
Title	Title of news
clean title	Cleaned title after pre-processing
upvote_ratio	Voting ratio of news
Output Class	2 way, 3 way or 5 way

4.2   Results

We have implemented different deep learning models (CNN, LSTM, and Mul-tiDeepFake) for the detection of fake news. To train our dataset in an effective manner, we used GloVe as a pre-trained word-embedded vector model. GloVe is a word-embedded vector which contains around 400000 words mapped with 100-dimensional vector each. For CNN, we trained our model for every post,

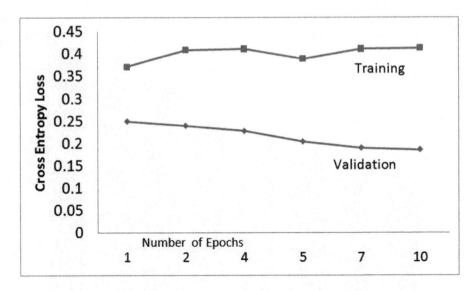

Fig. 8. Cross Entropy Loss with no. of epoch for Training and Validation for LSTM (Color figure online)

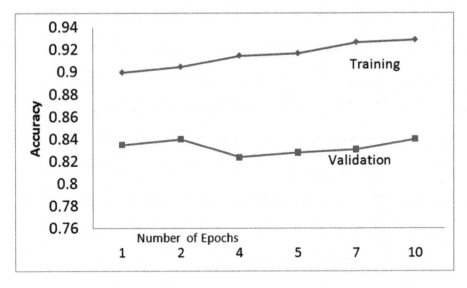

Fig. 9. Accuracy with no. of epoch for Training and Validation for LSTM (Color figure online)

splitting 20% of training dataset for testing, for 10 epochs and got a training accuracy of 91.62%. And for testing, got an accuracy of 83.78% using Fakeddit. For LSTM, we have designed a bi-directional LSTM model. This model was trained only for news data concatenating source of news by their replies.

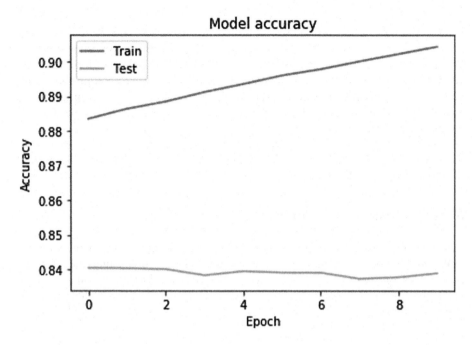

Fig. 10. Cross Entropy Loss with number of epoch using CNN (Color figure online)

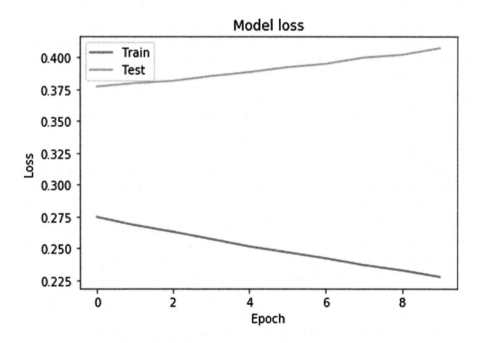

Fig. 11. Accuracy with number of epoch using CNN (Color figure online)

Since our dataset is large, our LSTM model performed better than the CNN model. We have achieved 84.20% in validation accuracy and 92.70% training accuracy. The results for LSTM, CNN, and MultiDeepFake are shown below. We found that LSTM outperforms CNN. The Graphs below (refer Figs. 8, 9, 10 and 11) are for the first nine epochs. For LSTM, dark red colour shows validation accuracy and blue colour shows training accuracy. With our proposed model (MultiDeepFake), we have achieved 97.20% training accuracy and 92.16% validation accuracy, which is highest among all deep learning implementations. Our proposed deep learning model provided more accurate results because of its capabilities like: automatically extracts useful features, fit for a large and unstructured dataset, and high accuracy.

5   Conclusion and Future Scope

In this paper, we have implemented a deep convolutional neural network for multi-modal fake news dataset with the accuracy of more than 95% for the training set and more than 90% for the validation set. In this digital age where hoax news is present everywhere in digital platforms, our model has achieved state-of-the-art results. In future, we will implement temporal and graph features for effective fake news detection.

References

1. AlRubaian, M., Al-Qurishi, M., Al-Rakhami, M., Rahman, S.M.M., Alamri, A.: A multistage credibility analysis model for microblogs. In: 2015 IEEE/ACM International Conference on Advances in Social Networks Analysis and Mining (ASONAM), pp. 1434–1440. IEEE (2015)
2. Abdul-Mageed, M., Diab, M., Kübler, S.: SAMAR: subjectivity and sentiment analysis for Arabic social media. Comput. Speech Lang. **28**(1), 20–37 (2014)
3. Allcott, H., Gentzkow, M.: Social media and fake news in the 2016 election. J. Econ. Perspect. **31**(2), 211–36 (2017)
4. Rubin, V.L., Chen, Y., Conroy, N.K.: Deception detection for news: three types of fakes. Proc. Assoc. Inf. Sci. Technol. **52**(1), 1–4 (2015)
5. Xiao, C., Freeman, D.M., Hwa, T.: Detecting clusters of fake accounts in online social networks. In: Proceedings of the 8th ACM Workshop on Artificial Intelligence and Security, pp. 91–101 (2015)
6. Chen, Y., Conroy, N.J., Rubin, V.L.: Misleading online content: recognizing clickbait as "false news". In: Proceedings of the 2015 ACM on workshop on multimodal deception detection, pp. 15–19 (2015)
7. Using algorithms to detect fake news - The state of the art (2017)
8. Aphiwongsophon, S., Chongstitvatana, P.: Detecting fake news with machine learning method. In: 2018 15th International Conference on Electrical Engineering/Electronics, Computer, Telecommunications and Information Technology (ECTI-CON), pp. 528–531. IEEE (2018)
9. Singhal, S., Shah, R.R., Chakraborty, T., Kumaraguru, P., Satoh, S.I.: SpotFake: a multi-modal framework for fake news detection. In: 2019 IEEE Fifth International Conference on Multimedia Big Data (BigMM), pp. 39–47. IEEE (2019)

10. Zubiaga, A., Aker, A., Bontcheva, K., Liakata, M., Procter, R.: Detection and resolution of rumours in social media: a survey. ACM Comput. Surv. (CSUR) **51**(2), 1–36 (2018)
11. Li, X., Wu, X.: Constructing long short-term memory based deep recurrent neural networks for large vocabulary speech recognition. In: 2015 IEEE International Conference on Acoustics, Speech and Signal Processing (ICASSP), pp. 4520–4524. IEEE (2015)
12. Conroy, N.J., Rubin, V.L., Chen, Y.: Automatic deception detection: methods for finding fake news. Proc. Assoc. Inf. Sci. Technol. **52**(1), 1–4 (2015)
13. Feng, S., Banerjee, R., Choi, Y.: Syntactic stylometry for deception detection. In: Proceedings of the 50th Annual Meeting of the Association for Computational Linguistics: Short Papers, vol. 2, pp. 171–175. Association for Computational Linguistics (2012)
14. Wang, W.Y.: "Liar, liar pants on fire": a new benchmark dataset for fake news detection. In: Proceedings of the 55th Annual Meeting of the Association for Computational Linguistics (vol. 2: Short Papers), pp. 422–426 (2017)
15. Rubin, V.L., Conroy, N., Chen, Y., Cornwell, S.: Fake news or truth? Using satirical cues to detect potentially misleading news. In: Proceedings of the Second Workshop on Computational Approaches to Deception Detection, pp. 7–17 (2016)
16. Tacchini, E., Ballarin, G., Della Vedova, M.L., Moret, S., de Alfaro, L.: Some like it hoax: automated fake news detection in social networks. arXiv preprint arXiv:1704.07506 (2017)
17. Rashkin, H., Choi, E., Jang, J.Y., Volkova, S., Choi, Y.: Truth of varying shades: analyzing language in fake news and political fact-checking. In: Proceedings of the 2017 Conference on Empirical Methods in Natural Language Processing, pp. 2931–2937 (2017)
18. Perozzi, B., Al-Rfou, R., Skiena, S.: Deepwalk: online learning of social representations. In: Proceedings of the 20th ACM SIGKDD International Conference on Knowledge Discovery and Data Mining, pp. 701–710 (2014)
19. Chang, C.-C., Lin, C.J.: LIBSVM: a library for support vector machines. ACM Trans. Intell. Syst. Technol. (TIST) **2**(3), 1–27 (2011)
20. Kombrink, S., Mikolov, T., Karafiát, M., Burget, L.: Recurrent neural network based language modeling in meeting recognition. In: Twelfth Annual Conference of the International Speech Communication Association (2011)
21. Dong, B., Zhang, J., Zhang, C., Yang, Y., Philip, S.Y.: Missing entity synergistic completion across multiple isomeric online knowledge libraries. In: 2019 International Joint Conference on Neural Networks (IJCNN), pp. 1–8. IEEE (2019)
22. Reis, J.C.S., Correia, A., Murai, F., Veloso, A., Benevenuto, F.: Supervised learning for fake news detection. IEEE Intell. Syst. **34**(2), 76–81 (2019)

English-Marathi Neural Machine Translation Using Local Attention

K. Adi Narayana Reddy[1(✉)], G. Shyam Chandra Prasad[2], A. Rajashekar Reddy[1], L. Naveen Kumar[1], and Kannaiah[3]

[1] BVRIT HYDERABAD College of Engineering for Women, Hyderabad, India
aadi.iitkgp@gmail.com, rajashekarreddy.a@bvrithyderabd.edu.in,
naveenkumar.1@bvrithyderabad.edu.in
[2] Matrusri Engineering College, Hyderabad, India
gscprasad@gmail.com
[3] HITAM, Hyderabad, India
kannaiah.cse@hitam.org

Abstract. Machine translation, translates sentences from source language text to target language. NMT (Neural Machine Translation) is a machine translation mechanism based on deep learning. It has improved the weakness of the rule-based and statistical machine translation. In this paper, NMT is applied on parallel corpus pair English – Marathi. We're proposing an NMT with a local attention mechanism. It is efficient and overcomes the OOV (Out Of Vocabulary) problem. The model performance is evaluated using the BLEU score. The results from the experiment confirm that the proposed model has outperformed the global attention mechanism and also Google translator.

Keywords: Deep learning · Machine translation · NMT · English-Marathi parallel corpus

1 Introduction

India is a nation of great diversity, with multiple languages. In India, in different regions, people use different languages for communication. People share their knowledge, opinion, facts, and feelings in their regional languages. Globally English is the most preferred language for human communication. Only 20% of people communicate in English but just 0.2% in India [23]. Human translation of different languages is not feasible. We need the mechanism that performs this function with less minimal human effort.

Machine translation is the most efficient mechanism to do this task. Machine translation, translates sentences in natural language/speech computationally from source language to the target language with little human effort. The machine translation generates grammatically correct target language from the source language. Translation of English to the Indian language has challenges due to morphological and structural divergence.

In the early 1950s, machine translation started [1], and it has advanced rapidly since the 1990s as the data availability increased due to the use of the Internet increased, at

© Springer Nature Singapore Pte Ltd. 2021
D. Garg et al. (Eds.): IACC 2020, CCIS 1367, pp. 280–287, 2021.
https://doi.org/10.1007/978-981-16-0401-0_21

the same time the availability of computational resources. The rule-based mechanism [2, 3], knowledge-based mechanism [4, 5], corpus-based mechanism [6], and hybrid mechanism [7] are traditional machine translation techniques. These approaches have both advantages and disadvantages. Statistical Machine Translation (SMT) is another widely used method, which produces better results than traditional mechanisms. In recent times, the use of artificial neural networks in machine translation has become increasingly common. This technique is referred to as Neural Machine Translation (NMT).

Several papers were proposed on machine translation and most of these works on foreign languages and limited on Indian language Hindi such as Patel et al. [8] and Raju and Raju [9] used conventional machine translation techniques. Revanuru et al. [10] used NMT for the translation of sentences of source and target in the Indian language. In this work, we have developed a neural network model based on a coverage mechanism on English-Marathi parallel corpus. The model is tested with an evaluation metric BLEU score. The architecture has two bi-directional LSTMs [11] as encoders and two LSTMs as decoders. Local attention is applied to the top of the encoder [12].

The overview of the literature review is carried out on machine translation in Sect. 2, machine translation using a neural network with attention mechanism fundamentals are carried in Sect. 3. Section 4 covers the evaluation of the model. The result analysis is elaborated in Sect. 5 and the conclusion is carried out in Sect. 6.

2 The Literature on Traditional Machine Translation

Machine Translation, translates source language text to the target language with minimal human intervention. After 1979, a breakthrough came in machine translation where the weather bulletin was translated from English to French [14, 15]. Researchers from IIT Kanpur in 1991 developed a machine translation system called AnglaBharati-I [16, 17]. It was designed specifically for translating domain-specific English to the Hindi language. MANTRA was developed by CDAC in 1999 [16]. This was developed to work on pairs of parallel corpus English-Hindi, English-Gujarati, English-Telugu, and English-Bengali. In 2004, the hybrid machine translation technique upgraded MANTRA to AnglaBharati-II [16, 17]. The AnglaBharati-II outperformed AnglaBharati-I. The details of the traditional techniques are presented in the subsections.

2.1 Rules-Based Machine Translation

Many of the languages that humans interact to obey certain grammar rules. The rules-based translation program uses rules for mapping the source sentences to target sentences. The Indian languages have to use a large number of rules to translate [18].

2.2 Phrase-Based Machine Translation

Machine translation based on phrase uses a phrase table containing a list of translated phrases from a source language to the target language. It also contains additional information about the rearrange of multiple phrases translation, which generates target-language text. The generated target-language text is not able to like human-generated text as it requires all combinations of phrases every time in the model [18].

2.3 Statistical Machine Translation

SMT uses a corpus to translate the source to the target language. It generates translation based on statistical methods. It uses the combination of a translation model with a decoding and language model. It produced [19] better performance comparing with other methods. A little human intervention was involved in this method.

3 Neural Machine Translation

NMT emerged as a novel technique recently in machine translation. NMT uses a neural network and it translates the source text into target text using conditional probability. In tasks such as translating English sentences into French sentences and also English sentences into German sentences, It has outperformed the traditional machine translation methods [13].

3.1 Simple Encoder and Decoder Architecture

A simple NMT consists of encoder and decoder architecture which is presented in Fig. 1. Initially Recurrent Neural Network (RNN) [11] was used in encoder and decoder as it maps sequences to sequences from source language as input and outputs the target language [20].

Let X and Y are the respective source input text and target output text. The source text $x_1, x_2, ...x_n$ is represented as fixed dimensional vector by the encoder and the decoder uses conditional probability and outputs one word at a time.

$$P(Y/X) = P(Y/X_1, X_2, \ldots, X_M) \tag{1}$$

Here $X_1, X_2, \ldots, X_M$ are fixed size encoded vectors. The Eq. (1) is rewritten using chain rule as

$$P(Y/X) = P(y_i/y_0, y_1, \ldots, y_{i-1}; X_1, X_2, \ldots, X_M) \tag{2}$$

The target word is predicted using previously predicted words and the encoder source vector. Each term of the distribution is expressed with a softmax over the vocabulary of words. The RNN's have problems while training long sequences. This is called long term dependency problem. The Long Short-Term Memory (LSTM) [11] is the variant of RNN, which captures the long term dependency. The encoder and decoder network fails to generate words that occur less frequently in the input corpus. The attention mechanism solves this problem.

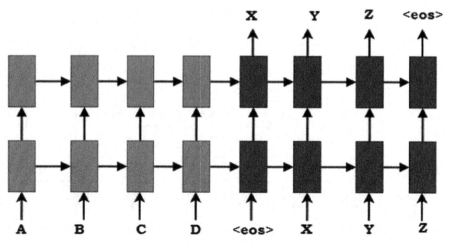

Fig. 1. Encoder and decoder architecture.

3.2 Attention Mechanism

The encoder reads a complete sentence and memorizes it. It is stored in the activation layer. The decoder uses it and generates the translated target sentence. This mechanism supports short sentences and it performances better than the other models but degrades the performance for longer sentences with 30 or 40 words. The encoder-decoder architecture with attention is a solution to handle longer sentences. The attention mechanism catches the dependencies in the input or output without regard to their distance. It translates like human-generated sentences by looking at the parts of the text at a time. The approach determines how much focus should be paid to a specific word during the process of sentence translation. The attention approach is presented in the Fig. 2. The encoder takes the input vector $X_1, X_2, \ldots, X_t$ and generates the attention vector $h_1, h_2, \ldots, h_t$. The context vector C_i is produced by concatenating these vectors for each time step of the input. The decoder generates the target word using context vector, hidden state, and previously predicted word.

3.3 Local Attention

The major drawback of the global attention mechanism is that it considers everyword of the source sentence for each of the target word. It is expensive for longer sequences. A local attention mechanism [12] addresses the deficiency of global attention by choosing a subset of positions from source sentences per target word. It achieves better performance than the global attention. The local attention is presented in the Fig. 3.

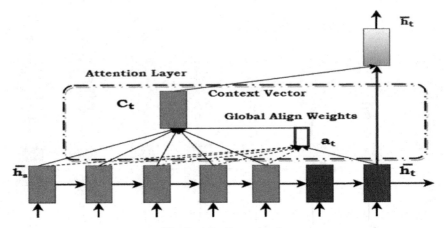

Fig. 2. Attention network

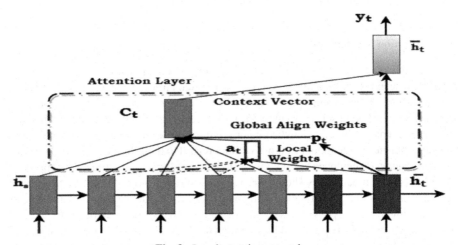

Fig. 3. Local attention network

4 Evaluation

4.1 Evaluation Metric

The BLEU (Bi-Lingual Evaluation Understudy) is the most popular evaluation metric, which measures the difference between human and machine translations [21]. It counts the matching translated text n-gram and referenced text n-grams.

4.2 Dataset

We used the dataset obtained from manythings.org/anki and totaeba.org. The dataset is English – Marathi parallel corpus. The dataset has 38696entries and it is split into train, validation, and test sets. The training has 23977 corpora, each of the testing and validation has 7992 corpora.

4.3 Training Details

We have trained the data on the above-described model. We use Bidirectional LSTMs with 2 layers for encoding and LSTMs with 2 layers for decoding. Each layer consists of 500 cells and 256-dimensional word embedding. We also added a local attention mechanism with window size 3 and 5. It is implemented in Keras and TensorFlow [22]. The results are presented in Table 1.

Table 1. BLEU score

Model	BLEU
Bi LSTM + LSTM + Local Attention with window size 5	31.50
Bi LSTM + LSTM + Local Attention with window size 4	31.49
Bi LSTM + LSTM + Local Attention with window size 3	30.96
LSTM + LSTM + Local Attention with window size 5	30.05
LSTM + LSTM + Local Attention with window size 4	30.05
LSTM + LSTM + Local Attention with window size 3	30.01
Bi LSTM + LSTM + Global Attention	29.75
Google Translator	28.65

5 Results Analysis

To make the comparison impartial, we have used the 20th iteration of the model performance and larger sentences having a word count of more than 25. The results are presented in Table 1.

From Table 1, the architecture with Bi-directional LSTM as encoder and LSTM as decoder with attention added on top of decoder produced better results than the Google translator. The architecture with LSTM as both encoder and decoder with added local attention on top of decoder produced better results than the global attention mechanism. The results show that local attention with window size 4 and 5 are performing better than other window sizes. The architecture with BI-LSTM as encoder and LSTM as decoder with local attention is added on the top of decoder producer even better BLEU score comparing with all other models. The local attention is performed better than the global attention as the local attention focuses only on the small window of the source sentences.

6 Conclusion

The neural machine translation models outperformed the Google translator. The local attention mechanism with Bi-LSTM as encoder and LSTM as decoder outperformed the other models for sentences with more than 25-word length. This is because local attention focuses on the smaller window of source sentences for each target word. In the future, one can explore Generative Adversarial Networks (GAN's) for machine translation on Indian languages. It is also practically applied to legal document translation from English to Marathi.

References

1. Locke, W.N., Booth, A.D.: Machine Translation of Languages: Fourteen Essays. Wiley, Hoboken (1957)
2. Siddhartha, G., Thamke, S., Kalyani, U.R.S.: Translation of Telugu-Marathi and vice-versa using rule based machine translation. Comput. Sci. Inf. Technol. 4 (2014).https://doi.org/10.5121/csit.2014.4501
3. Derek, W., Dong, M., Hu, D.: Machine translation using constraint - based synchronous grammar. Tsinghua Sci. Technol. 11, 295–306 (2006)
4. Tahir, G.R., Asghar, S., Masood, N.: Knowledge based machine translation. In: 2010 International Conference on Information and Emerging Technologies, pp. 1–5 (2010)
5. Wu, W., Li, L.: Automated Chinese-English translation scoring based on answer knowledge base. In: 2013 IEEE 12th International Conference on Cognitive Informatics and Cognitive Computing, New York, NY, pp. 341–346 (2013). https://doi.org/10.1109/icci-cc.2013.6622264
6. Su, J., Wang, Z., Wu, Q., Yao, J., Long, F., Zhang, H.: A topic-triggered translation model for statistical machine translation. Chin. J. Electron. 26(1), 65–72 (2017)
7. Salunkhe, P., Kadam, A.D., Joshi, S., Patil, S., Thakore, D., Jadhav, S.: Hybrid machine translation for English to Marathi: a research evaluation in machine translation: (hybrid translator). In: 2016 International Conference on Electrical, Electronics, and Optimization Techniques (ICEEOT), Chennai, pp. 924–931 (2016). https://doi.org/10.1109/iceeot.2016.7754822
8. Patel, R., Pimpale, P., Sasikumar, M.: Machine translation in Indian languages: challenges and resolution. J. Intell. Syst. (2018). https://doi.org/10.1515/jisys-2018-0014
9. Raju, B.N.V.: Statistical machine translation system for Indian languages (2016). https://doi.org/10.1109/IACC.2016.41
10. Revanuru, K., Turlapaty, K., Rao, S.: Neural machine translation of Indian languages. In: Proceedings of the 10th Annual ACM India Compute Conference (Compute 2017). Association for Computing Machinery, New York, NY, USA, pp. 11–20 (2017). https://doi.org/10.1145/3140107.3140111
11. Hochreiter, S., Schmidhuber, J.: Long short-term memory. Neural Comput. 9(8), 1735–1780 (1997). https://doi.org/10.1162/neco.1997.9.8.1735
12. Luong, M.-T., Pham, H., Manning, C.D.: Effective approaches to attention-based neural machine translation. CoRR abs/1508.04025 (2015). http://arxiv.org/abs/1508.04025
13. Wu, Y., et al.: Google's neural machine translation system: bridging the gapbetween human and machine translation. CoRR, vol. abs/1609.08144 (2016). http://arxiv.org/abs/1609.08144
14. Durand, J., et al.: The eurotra linguistic specifications: an overview. Mach. Transl. 6(2), 103–147 (1991)
15. Lawson, V. (ed.): Practical Experience of Machine Translation. North-Holland Publishing Company (1982)

16. Sitender, S.B.: Survey of indian machine translation systems. IJCST **3**(1) (2012)
17. Dwivedi, S.K., Sukhadeve, P.P.: Machine translation system in Indian perspectives. J. Comput. Sci. **6**(10), 1111 (2010)
18. Naskar, S., Bandyopadhyay, S.: Use of machine translation in India: Current status. In: Proceedings of MT SUMMIT X, Phuket, Thailand, pp. 13–15 (2005)
19. Koehn, P.: Statistical Machine Translation. Cambridge University Press (2010). https://books.google.ch/books?id=4v_Cx1wIMLkC
20. Sutskever, I., Vinyals, O., Le, Q.V.: Sequence to sequence learning with neural networks. In: Advances in Neural Information Processing Systems 27: Annual Conference on Neural Information Processing Systems 2014, 8–13 December 2014, Montreal, Quebec, Canada, pp. 3104–3112 (2014). http://papers.nips.cc/paper/5346-sequence-to-sequence-learning-with-neural-networks
21. Papineni, K., Roukos, S., Ward, T., Zhu, W.-J.: BLEU: a method for automatic evaluation of machine translation. In: Proceedings of the 40th Annual Meeting of the Association for Computational Linguistics, 6–12 July 2002, Philadelphia, PA, USA, pp. 311–318 (2002). http://www.aclweb.org/anthology/P02-1040.pdf
22. Abadi, M., et al.:Tensorflow: large-scale machine learning on heterogeneous distributed systems. arXiv preprint arXiv:1603.04467 (2016)
23. I. Registrar General & Census Commissioner: Abstract of speakers strength of languages and mother tongues 2011 (2011)
24. Jadav, S.A.: Marathi to English neural machine translation with near perfect corpus and transformers. arXiv.2002.116 (2020)

NLP2SQL Using Semi-supervised Learning

H. Vathsala[1]([⊠]) and Shashidhar G. Koolagudi[2]

[1] Centre for Development of Advanced Computing,
Bengaluru, Karnataka, India
vathsala.h@gmail.com
[2] Department of Computer Science and Engineering, NITK,
Mangalore, Karnataka, India

Abstract. Human Computer interaction has been moving towards Natural language in the modern age. SQL (Structured Query Language) is the chief database query language used today. There are many flavors of SQL but all of them have the same basic underlying structure. This paper attempts to use the Natural Language inputs to query the databases, which is achieved by translating the natural language (which in our case is English) input into the SQL (specific to MySQL database) query language. Here we use a semi-supervised learning with Memory augmented policy optimization approach to solve this problem. This method uses the context of the natural language questions through database schema, and hence its not just generation of SQL code. We have used the WikiSQL dataset for all our experiments. The proposed method gives a 2.3% higher accuracy than the state of the art semi-supervised method on an average.

Keywords: NLP (Natural Language Processing) · SQL (Structured Query Language) · MAPO (Memory Augmented Policy Optimization) · NLP2SQL

1 Introduction

Natural Language Processing has been in existence for more than 50 years. As computers continue to become more and more affordable and accessible, the importance of user interfaces that are effective, robust, unobtrusive and user-friendly become more pronounced. Since natural language usually is the preferred mode for human-human interaction, it is only sensible to adopt it in Human Computer interaction also. Hence there has been a major move towards incorporating Natural Language Processing (NLP) into the Human Computer Interaction.

A large swathes of information is stored in the form of relational databases (RDBMS). Relational databases are becoming increasingly important in actual applications and Web sites. They are often used by people who do not have great

© Springer Nature Singapore Pte Ltd. 2021
D. Garg et al. (Eds.): IACC 2020, CCIS 1367, pp. 288–299, 2021.
https://doi.org/10.1007/978-981-16-0401-0_22

competence in this domain and who do not know exactly their structure. The only way to efficiently access, manage and manipulate the data in the databases is through the use of the Structure Query Language (SQL). This is why translators from natural language to SQL queries are being developed.

These translators will prove to be intelligent interfaces for interaction with the data. A lot of approaches have been used to tackle the problem including the traditional sequence to sequence model [19] which is pretty generalized and doesn't make use of the full structure of the SQL queries. Hence a new approach which uses sequence to set along with column attention was proposed to address the previous problems. We solve this problem using a reinforcement learning algorithm (vanilla policy gradient) coupled with off-policy experience replay.

The chief contributions of this paper include

- Use of GloVe [13], a pre-trained word embedding.
- Apart from storing the high positive trajectories, poorly performing trajectories have also been used for training.
- Hyper-parameter tuning with respect to the architecture of internal nodes in every LSTM, dimension of GloVe [13].
- Use of Epsilon Greedy strategy for systematic exploration.
- Use of Bidirectional LSTM [6].

The following section provides details of, (i) Literature review done during the research process (Sect. 2) (ii) The proposed algorithm (Sect. 3) (iii) Implementation Experimentation and results (Sect. 4)

2   Literature Review

This section describes the literature review performed during the research process.

2.1   MAPO

Memory Augmented Policy Optimization (MAPO) [7] reduces the variance in the policy gradient estimates and improves the sampling efficiency with the help of a high trajectory memory buffer. Memory clipping alleviates cold start of policy gradients and an efficient search algorithm is used to explore the memory buffers, for which bloom filters are used. For calculation of Expected rewards from the large memory buffers, sampling is employed. Distributed actor-learner (with 30 actors) is used to quicken the training process. This technique was first employed in [12].

2.2   Coarse2Fine

This algorithm is analogous to 3-step machine translation. It uses attention mechanisms [1] in both encoder and decoder. A rough sketch a is first generated, and this is used to guide the final decoding. The rough sketch is devoid of argument-names, variable-names (replaced with it's datatype), and all other lower level details. All the components of input x, rough sketch a and final output y are treated as sequences. Hence, this becomes a seq2seq problem [20]. GloVe vectors are used to encode the input. The training objective maximizes the joint probability of the final meaning representation and that of the intermediate rough sketch also. During preprocessing of the data, 10-dimensional PoS tag embeddings are appended to the embeddings of the words in the natural language question. This novel idea was presented in [5]. Parent feeding technique is employed in the current work. The authors of this paper have not mentioned how this work is better than that of Yin and Neubig [18] which uses a generic system of abstract syntax trees(AST).

2.3   Gated Convolution Neural Network (G-CNN)

This work aims to perform language modeling using Gated CNNs. This is the first non recurrent approach to language modeling, and the paper achieves substantial accuracy results on large-context datasets also. The main unique selling proposition (USP) is that the CNN units can be parallelized and hence this model is more faster than LSTM based models, only during inference, not necessarily during training. It uses stacked convolutions which increases the number of operations per context to $O(nk)$ (per kernel), where n is the context size and k is the kernel width. Causal convolutions are used, i.e., the kernel can only see the previous words and not the future words. This ensures that the model does not cheat.

The initial part of the sentence is padded with $(k-1)$ tokens, where k is the width of the kernel. Comparison between Gated Linear Unit (GLU) and Gated Tanh Unit has been performed. GLU is better than the latter, because it handles the vanishing gradient problem better. RNNs are parallelized over different sequences while training, and CNNs can be parallelized over different contexts or tokens. The model uses residual activation blocks and the gradients have been clipped to $[-5, 5]$. Kaiming initialization, Momentum and weight normalization are some of the techniques that help in faster convergence even with large learning rates $= 1$. Adaptive softmax is used, instead of the conventional softmax. This is less expensive but approximately gives the same results. It is empirically found that a context size of 40 tokens is sufficient to obtain high accuracy. Similarly, it is sufficient to limit the backpropagation to 40 time steps (instead of the theoretical infinite limits).

Although this work provided better results theoretically, we found it hard to reproduce similar results in our paper when we replaced LSTMs/RNNs with G-CNNs.

2.4   DeepFix

The model trains a neural network for fixing the syntactic (non-semantic) programming errors in the C language. The authors train a GRU with attention to achieve 60% accuracy. The literals are given a fixed vector representation (as they do not affect the syntax) and all the identifiers are given a similar fixed representation. The initial weights of the GRU is drawn from a uniform distribution within the range $(-0.07, 0.07)$. Both encoder and decoder have 4 layers, 300 cells each. The model performs the error localization upto 80% accuracy.

Certain types of errors might never be suitable for LSTMs. For instance, assignment of an array into another is not allowed in the C language (unlike Python). The solution to this is to use a for loop and index through all the elements of the array. It might be impossible to enable an LSTM to generate such solutions.

It is not entirely clear if the vanilla attention mechanism is adding value to the process. The model is stopped from continuing if one of it's proposed corrections is rejected by the oracle(during iterative repair). If this bound is reduced to 3/4 it might give the model more chances to take corrective actions, because a single line might contain multiple fixes(at different positions) which are required to eliminate a single error message.

Eliminating bias has not been argued comprehensively in the paper because real-world data might also have a similar distribution of the types of errors. By forcing equal representation, we could be losing the information regarding the priority of errors.

The mutations in the data set (seeded) were performed manually by the authors. This might have introduced bias and might be a reason for the poor performance. The authors select only one erroneous program per student for every programming task citing the concern of bias. But since syntactic errors are independent of the semantic nature of the program, this leads to wastage of training data. It is true that there may be some correlation between the programming task and the syntax errors and a specific student, but it will be useful if a comparison had been provided.

2.5 SQLNet

The paper proposes a sketch-based model for SQL generation. The contents of the sketch is filled with the help of neural networks. Column attention is used extensively in three different steps. A sql2set model is used in the paper, as the order of the conditions are to be considered only during evaluation in SQL. This technique is very similar to the approach of generating Abstract Syntax Tree (AST) and filling in the slots. To decide whether or not to include a column name in the WHERE condition, binary classification is performed. The mechanism of predicting the column names for SELECT and WHERE clauses are identical. But the weights of the trainable matrices cannot be shared, because the column in either of SELECT or WHERE need not be present in the other also (in fact it might not be present in most of the cases). In predicting columns for WHERE condition, the authors do not share weights between the bi-LSTMs used for encoding the column names and the question. They propose that this ensures independence of the decisions made. But this is a tradeoff, because the current methodology requires a large number of trainable parameters. Apart from this, the WikiSQL dataset does not contain examples of self-join where a single table is involved.

2.6   Execution Guided Decoding (EGD)

EGD uses the partially generated queries and weeds out the incorrect SQL statements(those that produce a runtime error) and queries that do not match any records. Some of the questions may not have any suitable records in the table. The authors hypothesize that this could be because the decoder generated an overly-restrictive where condition. EGD is performed only during inference, and not during training. Using EGD during training may potentially improve the model performance. EGD is model-agnostic and is useful in a variety of auto-regressive tasks. It is difficult to use EGD in pure seq2seq models, because it's hard to know what stage the partial programs are executable. Execution guidance only tries to reduce the number of execution errors. As a by product, the accuracy increases by a small value (because the number of erroneous programs decreases). This increases the number of semantically meaningful programs, but not necessarily the number of semantically correct programs.

The authors make an impoprtant observation that many queries in WikiSQL are grammatically wrong. This might hinder possible approaches like that of GANs. It is not clear whether the beam-size plays an important role in determining the accuracy.

The paper does not use the Teacher-Forcing method while training of LSTMs. We have incorporated this methodology in our proposed algorithm.

Execution guidance only tries to reduce the number of execution errors. As a by product, the accuracy increases by a small value (because the number of erroneous programs decreases). This increases the number of semantically meaningful programs, but not necessarily the number of semantically correct programs

It's not possible to implement EGD for all auto-regressive tasks. Example, for tasks like music generation, there are no standard set of rules to determine if an audio piece is syntactically and semantically correct (except for systems like Carnatic/Hindustani music).

2.7   SQLova

It is very similar in structure to SQLNet [17], but has three important contributions.

- It uses BERT word representations instead of GloVe [13].
- It uses Sequence to sequence (Seq2Seq) model
- It uses Execution Guided Decoding [15]

NLQ is concatenated with the table headers. Every token consists of token, position and segment embedding(see BERT for more details). It is not entirely clear if this ordering of the input had any effect on the accuracy metric. (This is because this paper largely borrows from SQLNet, and SQLNet does not impose such restrictions on ordering of input). [17] predict the where-value using pointer-networks (Vinyals). But this paper follows [5] and predicts the start and the end token for the where-val instead of going for a seq2seq approach. Also, where-val is conditioned on where-col and where-op. The order of where conditions is ignored in measuring logical form accuracy in the model. The final output of where-clause will be that one which has the highest joint probability with respect to all the four where predictors.

The authors claim that SQLNet conditions the where-val only on the where-col. But this is not true. It conditions the where-val on NLQ, column_name, and the partially generated query. This probability is calculated for every column and softmax is used to choose the one with the highest probability.

2.8   XSQL

This work brings in a fresh set of fine-tuning of the results by leveraging recent strides in natural language processing like the MT-DNN algorithm [11] over BERT [3]

- It Uses MT-DNN instead of BERT to encode the question and to generate a new structural representation for schema
- The [EMPTY] token is appended to every table schema to account for cases where there are no WHERE conditions.
- KL-Divergence is used as an objective only for predicting the WHERE condition column name.
- The ground truth Q in predicting the WHERE column name is calculated as follows:
- If there is no where clause, Q[EMPTY] receives probability mass 1 for special column [EMPTY]
- For $n \geq 1$ where clauses, each where column receives probability mass of $1/n$
  Although this paper shows improvements in predicting the individual slots of the SQL query, it would behave been fair playing ground if the authors presented the test and dev accuracy that is prevalent in the NL2SQL research community.

3   Proposed Algorithm

The current work proposes to generate the SQL statements by using the policy gradient [14] algorithm. The algorithm has been developed on top of Memory Augmented Policy Optimization [10]. Similar to MAPO, the memory buffers have also been used to store both the high reward trajectories and the low reward trajectories. Sampling and training periodically from these buffers ensure that the agent/model does not forget the high/low-reward trajectories.

The low-reward trajectories are also included in the memory buffer because agent has equal opportunity to learn from both the high-reward and low reward trajectory. The usage of policy gradient makes it all the more important to reinforce both positive and negative reward trajectories.

The authors of MAPO [10] have not made use of pretrained word embeddings, but they have used random word embeddings. This work alleviates those lacunas by using GloVe word embeddings [13]. This ensures that the inductive priors from the unsupervised training of GloVe word embeddings are leveraged in the proposed NLP2SQL model.

Similar to the original MAPO paper, the epsilon greedy strategy to ensure systematic exploration of the search space has been retained. This step uses bloom filters in order to store billions of patterns to ensure that no programs are missed out.

We have also performed hyper parameter tuning with respect to the size of the pretrained word embeddings and we realized that the optimal value is 300 dimensions. Apart from these, bidirectional LSTM in both encoder and decoder has also been used.

4   Implementation, Experiments and Results

The algorithm has been implemented using Python 3.6, Tensorflow 1.7, gensim 3.2.0, nltk 3.3, Babel 2.5.3, bloom-filter 1.3. The model is tested against the WikiSQL dataset [19] in the Linux environment over a cluster of 2 Nvidia K40 GPUs. Tensorflow GPU optimizations have also been used.

The reinforcement learning agent has been allowed to train for a maximum of 15000 training steps in the environment. We have used the standard baselines from OpenAI [4] for comparison with the vanilla policy gradient algorithm.

4.1   Dataset

WikiSQL [19] is a large database built mainly for the development of interfaces for the natural language processing for relational databases. Annotated with SQL queries, the dataset primarily consists of entries from Wikipedia and other common sources of information. In comparison with other question-answer datasets (like WikiTableQuestions), WikiSQL has simple semantics as the SQL queries have simpler structure and fewer operators. While most of the state-of-the-art models are dependent on the question-program pairs as the data for the supervised learning, we will be using the question-answer pairs for semi-supervised learning.

4.2   Model Architecture

As mentioned earlier, the model proposed in this paper is an improvement over the Memory-Augmented Policy Optimisation(MAPO) [10] model. Neural Symbolic Machine (NSM) [9] framework has been used the implementation of the model, with a bi-directional LSTM as the encoder and two-layer LSTM for both encoder and decoder. The ability of LSTM in assigning credit from high-dimensional and/or continuous actions based on backpropagation and its learning from long-term temporal dependencies to infer states in partially observable tasks makes it one of the best models to be used in the current scenario [2].

4.3   Results

The results from the experiment can be visualised in Table 1 and Table 2, and in the Fig. 1 shown below.

Table 1 is the compilation of the measurement of the accuracy of each feature in the model. As more features are added over the vanilla MAPO implementation, the dev accuracy and the test accuracy increases. Finally, after the inclusion of all the features, dev accuracy of **76.8%** and test accuracy of **77.6%** is achieved.

Table 1. Measurement of accuracy of each feature in the model.

Features	Dev accuracy (%)	Test accuracy (%)
MAPO	72.4	74.9
GloVe Word Embeddings	75.1	76.7
Word Embeddings of Dimension 300	76.9	77.7
Bidirectional LSTM	75.3	75.6
Epsilon greedy exploration	77.3	78.0
Training with extremely good bad performances	77.3	77.9
All the above changes	**79.3**	**78.7**

Figure 1 is a line graph of the dev accuracy of the model against the training steps (epochs). The dev accuracy grows slowly over the epochs, from 62.5% for very small epochs up to 76% for large epochs. The accuracy saturates to 76.8%, which is recorded as the performance of the model proposed.

Table 2 is a comparison of the performance of the model with other state-of-the-art supervised and semi-supervised learning models in terms of dev accuracy and test accuracy. The accuracy of the proposed model is significantly larger than the state-of-the-art semi-supervised learning models (models proposed in [15, 17,19] and [8]), and is close to the accuracy of the supervised learning model (proposed in [5]).

4.4   Discussion

Analysis of the dev accuracy and test accuracy results of the model, and comparison of its performance with various state-of-the-art models can be concluded as follows:

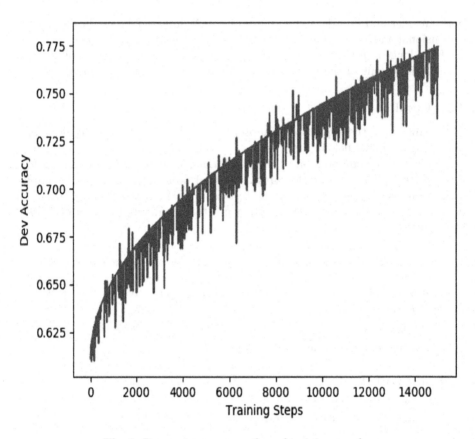

Fig. 1. Dev accuracy vs number of training epochs.

Table 2. Comparison with the previous works in supervised and weakly-supervised setting

Fully supervised	Dev accuracy (%)	Test accuracy (%)
[19]	60.8	59.4
[15]	67.1	66.8
[17]	69.8	68.0
[8]	68.3	68.0
[5]	79.0	78.5
Semi supervised	Dev accuracy (%)	Test accuracy (%)
MAPO	72.4	72.6
MAPO (mean of 5 runs)	72.2	72.1
MAPO (std of 5 runs)	0.2	0.3
MAPO (ensemble of 10)	–	74.9
Current algorithm	**79.3**	**78.7**

- Addition of various features (like GloVe embeddings and epsilon greedy exploration) over vanilla MAPO has resulted in the increase in dev accuracy and test accuracy of the model
- The dev accuracy curve is of positive slope but negative curvature with respect to the training epochs. This implies that the dev accuracy increases with increase in epochs, but there is a drop in the rate of increase of the accuracy. Also, the accuracy peaks to a value of 76.8%
- The performance of the model proposed is better than vanilla MAPO model and the current state-of-the-art semi-supervised models, and is on par with the current state-of-the-art supervised models.

We also explored the option of incorporating recent policy gradient algorithms like Proximal Policy Optimization(PPO) and Trust Region Policy Optimization(TRPO). But these algorithms are substantially different from that considered in the MAPO research paper. The major unique selling point of these algorithms over policy gradient is that they use different objective functions like KL-Divergence and Clipping respectively, to ensure that the newer policy is not significantly different from the old policy. This is done to ensure that the agent is robust and is not brittle.

The baseline paper that we have chosen is MAPO, which makes use of replay buffers to *remember* high trajectory rewards. Although Actor-Critic Experience Replay (ACER) [16] algorithm resembles this setup, the ACER algorithm does not specifically address the usage of high-reward trajectories. More specifically, we could not find theoretic justification with respect to the convergence properties in this modified algorithm.

We also considered the possibility of pure Q-learning algorithms like Deep Q Learning(DQN), Double DQN and Duelling DQN. We faced substantial difficulty in framing this problem in a manner that is amenable to Q-learning in particular. More importantly, historically Q-learning has not been applied to search problems with such a large search space.

5   Conclusion

We have attempted to solve the problem of "NLP2SQL" using policy gradients. We have used cutting edge techniques from program repair machine translation and question-answering to solve this problem. This method gives 2.3% higher accuracy than the state of the art on an average.

As future work, the theoretical underpinnings of this algorithm need to be verified. More specifically, it is necessary to obtain convergence proofs for this algorithm so that it can be applied to other problem areas like robotic control and natural language understanding. Another line of thought worth exploring would be the, although tangential to the topic of this paper, is optimal tuning of hyperparameters. Such tuning techniques would be extremely useful in generating provably optimal model architectures.

Acknowledgements. We thank Chenna Keshava B.S, Rithesh K and H.L Praveen Raj, Department of Computer Science and Engineering, National Institute of Technology Karnataka, India for programming the said concepts during the current work.

References

1. Bahdanau, D., Chorowski, J., Serdyuk, D., Brakel, P., Bengio, Y.: End-to-end attention-based large vocabulary speech recognition. CoRR abs/1508.04395 (2015), http://arxiv.org/abs/1508.04395
2. Bakker, B.: Reinforcement learning by backpropagation through an LSTM model/critic. In: 2007 IEEE International Symposium on Approximate Dynamic Programming and Reinforcement Learning, Honolulu, HI, 2007 (2007)
3. Devlin, J., Chang, M., Lee, K., Toutanova, K.: BERT: pre-training of deep bidirectional transformers for language understanding. CoRR abs/1810.04805 (2018), http://arxiv.org/abs/1810.04805
4. Dhariwal, P., et al.: Openai baselines. GitHub, GitHub repository (2017)
5. Dong, L., Lapata, M.: Coarse-to-fine decoding for neural semantic parsing. CoRR abs/1805.04793 (2018), http://arxiv.org/abs/1805.04793
6. Greff, K., Srivastava, R.K., Koutník, J., Steunebrink, B.R., Schmidhuber, J.: LSTM: a search space odyssey. CoRR abs/1503.04069 (2015), http://arxiv.org/abs/1503.04069
7. Gupta, R., Pal, S., Kanade, A., Shevade, S.: Deepfix: fixing common c language errors by deep learning. In: Proceedings of the Thirty-First AAAI Conference on Artificial Intelligence, AAAI 2017, pp. 1345–1351. AAAI Press (2017). http://dl.acm.org/citation.cfm?id=3298239.3298436
8. Hwang, W., Yim, J., Park, S., Seo, M.: A comprehensive exploration on wikisql with table-aware word contextualization. CoRR abs/1902.01069 (2019), http://arxiv.org/abs/1902.01069
9. Liang, C., Berant, J., Le, Q.V., Forbus, K.D., Lao, N.: Neural symbolic machines: learning semantic parsers on freebase with weak supervision. CoRR abs/1611.00020 (2016), http://arxiv.org/abs/1611.00020
10. Liang, C., Norouzi, M., Berant, J., Le, Q.V., Lao, N.: Memory augmented policy optimization for program synthesis with generalization. CoRR abs/1807.02322 (2018), http://arxiv.org/abs/1807.02322
11. Liu, X., He, P., Chen, W., Gao, J.: Multi-task deep neural networks for natural language understanding. CoRR abs/1901.11504 (2019), http://arxiv.org/abs/1901.11504
12. Mnih, V., et al.: Playing atari with deep reinforcement learning. CoRR abs/1312.5602 (2013), http://arxiv.org/abs/1312.5602
13. Pennington, J., Socher, R., Manning, C.: Glove: global vectors for word representation. In: Proceedings of the 2014 Conference on Empirical Methods In Natural Language Processing (EMNLP), pp. 1532–1543 (2014)
14. Sutton, R.S., McAllester, D.A., Singh, S.P., Mansour, Y.: Policy gradient methods for reinforcement learning with function approximation. In: Advances in Neural Information Processing Systems, pp. 1057–1063 (2000)
15. Wang, C., Huang, P.S., Polozov, A., Brockschmidt, M., Singh, R.: Execution-guided neural program decoding. arXiv preprint arXiv:1807.03100 (2018)
16. Wang, Z., et al.: Sample efficient actor-critic with experience replay. arXiv preprint arXiv:1611.01224 (2016)

17. Xu, X., Liu, C., Song, D.: Sqlnet: generating structured queries from natural language without reinforcement learning. arXiv preprint arXiv:1711.04436 (2017)
18. Yin, P., Neubig, G.: A syntactic neural model for general-purpose code generation. arXiv preprint arXiv:1704.01696 (2017)
19. Zhong, V., Xiong, C., Socher, R.: Seq2sql: generating structured queries from natural language using reinforcement learning. arXiv preprint arXiv:1709.00103 (2017)
20. Ziqiang, C., Chuwei, L., Wenjie, L., Li., S.: Joint copying and restricted generation for paraphrase. In: AAAI (2017)

RumEval2020-An Effective Approach for Rumour Detection with a Deep Hybrid C-LSTM Model

Rohit Kumar Kaliyar[1]($\boxtimes$), Rajbeer Singh[1], Sai N. Laya[2],
M. Sujay Sudharshan[3], Anurag Goswami[1], and Deepak Garg[1]

[1] Bennett University, Greater Noida, India
{rk5370,rb5096,anurag.goswami,deepak.garg}@bennett.edu.in
[2] Sagi Rama Krishnam Raju Engineering College, Bhimavaram, India
layanallaparaju3@gmail.com
[3] Sri Ramakrishna Engineering College, Coimbatore, India
sujaysudharshan@gmail.com

Abstract. For the online and offline world, the widespread rumours on social media have created a tremendous effect on society. In this paper, our primary focus to develop a useful deep learning model for the classification multi-class and real-world rumour dataset. In existing investigations, RumourEval17 have released by the research community, which mainly interest in automated validation of fake content has escalated. After some time, as the insecurity imposed by "fake news" has become a mainstream concern. However, automatic support for rumour verification system remains in its preliminary stage. Subsequently, the main aim of introducing RumourEval-2019 (SemEval 2019) was to determine the veracity of rumours. In this paper, we have designed our proposed deep learning model for classification of rumours using real-world multi-class rumours dataset: Twitter and Reddit. Classification results demonstrate that our proposed model provides state-of-the-art results as compared to existing benchmarks. We have achieved an accuracy of 82.40% for subtask A and 81.04% for subtask B. Our classification results are better as compared to previous RumourEval studies using twitter & Reddit dataset. Classification results motivate the researchers to use our proposed model for future research in the filed of rumour detection.

Keywords: Rumour · Deep learning · Social media · Machine learning · Neural network

1 Introduction

After the first Rumour Eval shared task in 2017 [1], the demand for an automated model for detection of rumours has only deepened, as experiments have exhibited the potential effect of fake assertions on highly significant socio-political consequences [1,19]. Living in a "post-truth world", in which perceived truth can matter more than fact [2,5,8], the jeopardy of unbridled market forces and unauthorized platforms, alongside often poor discernment on the part of the reader, is perceptible. For example, the need to educate young people about critical reading is increasingly recognized. Simultaneously, exploration in the prediction of instance and assembling systems to comprehend and estimate rumours expressed in written context have made some advancements over fountainhead. Still, a detailed interpretation of the relation between stance and veracity and a more extensive dataset is required to explore in broader aspects. Few examples are shown with the help of Fig. 1.

Fig. 1. Few examples of rumours: Source (Facebook)

Subsequently, RumourEval-2019 [4,24] is a competition consists mainly of two tasks. Task A, in which replies of each post classifies followed by SQDC process: Support, Deny, Query, and Deny. Task B [7,8], in which posts are classified for veracity as (True, False or Unverified). The dataset of RumourEval 2017 contained posts of Twitter while RumourEval 2019 contains posts of Twitter as well as Reddit which provide heterogeneity in the types of users, more focused discussions and longer posts. The aim for Task A is to identify how other users on the micro-blogging website respond to the rumour by replying to the post that holds the rumoured statement or the source post. In Reddit dataset, a tweet is defined by the message that has initiated the conversation, and the replies from a nested discussion. The objective was to categorize each of the tweets in the thread as either querying, supporting, commenting or denying for Task A and as true, false or unverified for Task B on the rumour instigated by the rootage tweet.

In this paper, we have designed a valuable and effective deep CNN-LSTM model for multiclass real-world rumour dataset. In our model, we have considered different kernel-sizes convolutional layers with a bi-directional LSTM network. To make our model deep in nature, we have considered six dense layers. Our model is capable of handling different sized input length vectors for better feature representation. For better learning of our CNN model, we have used GloVe with 100-dimensional size as effective word embedding for the text classification task. With our proposed model, we have achieved remarkable results. Firstly, we have converted the existing dataset into the .csv format and applied deep learning models. We have achieved an accuracy of more than 4.5% as compared to existing benchmarks. It demonstrates that results using our model are promising.

2   Background

Zubiaga et al. [1] have presented a survey for the detection and resolution of Rumours in Social Media. They have explored the problem using the power of natural language processing to detect the rumours. They have investigated various strategies in the rumour dataset collection. Their investigation was based on a four-step rumour classification method which is detection, tracking, stance classification, veracity classification.

Pamungkas et al. [8] have proposed their solution for detecting stances in different social media rumours using Twitter dataset. In their investigation, the authors have explored a method to develop a model that extracts the stylistic and structural features categorizing the colloquial language of the micro-blogging website. Additionally, they propose to take advantage of conversational-based features by making the most of the distinguished tree structure of the dataset and inspected the usage of effective based feature by extracting relevant information from affective resources including dialogue-inspire features.

Fajcik et al. [12] have proposed a solution for RumourEval 2019 utilizing a pre-trained Deep Bidirectional Transformers. In their approach, they have explored a method based on recent improvements integrated into language representation architectures. They fine-tuned the model with the pre-trained comprehensive Bidirectional Encoder Representations from Transformers (BERT) model, while using the discussion's source post, target's previous post and the target post itself as inputs to determine the appropriate stance assigned to the target post.

Gorrell et al. [20] have proposed the solution of the RumourEval 2019 for detecting Rumour Veracity and Support. They have explored a method to solve two sub-tasks simultaneously, subtask A: which is the SDQC (support, deny, comment or query) support classification and Subtask B: which is the veracity prediction of rumours.

Baris et al. [10] have proposed a solution for RumourEval 2019 utilizinf a ConvoLving ELMo method Against Rumors. They have presented their approach: CLEARumor (ConvoLving ELMo Against Rumors) for solving both sub-tasks and provide empirical results and ablation experiments of their architecture. They made PyTorch-based implementation and trained their models. After preprocessing the rumour post and embedding with ELMo, the architecture for Task A passes the embedded text through a convolutional neural network (CNN) block, adds additional features, and uses a multilayer perceptron (MLP) block for estimating class membership. These estimates are combined with other supplementary features and fed into an MLP block for the classification for Task B.

Li et al. [25] have proposed a solution for rumour detection on Twitter with tree-structured Recursive Neural Networks. They have used neural rumour detection approach based on Recursive Neural Networks (RvNN) to bridge the content semantics and propagation clues. They proposed two architectures which are established on the recursive nature of neural networks, called the bottom-up and a top-down tree-structured model for rumour detection on Twitter. The inherent nature of recursive models allows them using propagation tree to guide the learning of representations from tweets content, such as embedding various indicative signals hidden in the structure, for better-identifying rumours.

3   Implementation and Results

3.1   Dataset

The dataset used for the implementation of our proposed deep learning model is a collection of Twitter and Reddit conversational threads that are correlated to the rumours that are present in various news headlines. The collection of events includes 325 Twitter conversational threads [6,12,14] comprising of 5568 underlying tweets and 40 Reddit conversational threads containing 1134 fundamental tweets, annotated for stance categorization at tweet level. Individual thread encompasses an origin tweet that initiates the conversation and nests responding tweets, that have either been answered regarding the source tweet or related replied tweets (for more details about dataset refer Table 1).

Table 1. The number of labelled instances for the subtask(A) of the RumourEval 2019 dataset.

SUBTASK A	Twitter	S	Q	D	C	Total
(Train)	Reddit	910	358	344	2907	5217
		15	37	34	612	
SUBTASK A	Twitter	S	Q	D	C	Total
(Dev)	Reddit	94	106	71	778	1485
		8	14	11	403	
SUBTASK A	Twitter	S	Q	D	C	Total
(Test)	Reddit	141	14	11	771	1827
		16	62	92	705	
Total		1184	608	561	6176	8529

RumourEval 2019 (SemEval 2019 Task 7): It is a task from the codalab, dealing with the rumour evaluation based on the veracity. RumourEval 2019, has two subtasks: Task A and Task B.

– Task A is the classification of the rumours according to the veracity available online.
– Task B is the classification of the sentences for veracity and accuracy.

Task A: The first subtask Task A [1,2,8,9] is the classification of the rumours according to the available veracity on social media. This is basically to tackle the rumour's statement with the replies that are commented on that particular rumour's source post. It has an SDQC process (support, deny, comment or

Table 2. The number of labelled instances for the subtask(B) of the RumourEval 2019 dataset.

SUBTASK B	Twitter	True	False	Unverified	Total
(Train)	Reddit	137	62	98	327
		7	17	06	
SUBTASK B	Twitter	True	False	Unverified	Total
(Dev)	Reddit	8	12	08	38
		2	07	01	
SUBTASK B	Twitter	True	False	Unverified	Total
(Test)	Reddit	22	30	04	81
		09	10	06	
Total		185	138	133	456

query) form of classification, where the corresponding comments are categorized according to the respective terms. SDQC process (see Fig. 2 for SQDC process) are:

- Support: the user commenting to the reaction supports the truthfulness of the rumours post.
- Deny: the user commenting to the reaction opposes the truthfulness of the rumours post.
- Query: the user commenting to the reaction enquires for additional authentication in relation to the truthfulness of the rumours post.
- Comment: the user commenting to the reaction makes their own observation without a transparent contribution to evaluating the truthfulness of the rumours post.

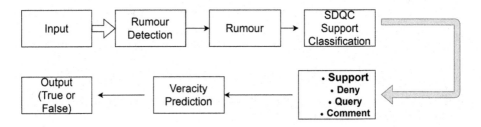

Fig. 2. An example of Twitter thread with SQDC labels for each rumour post

Task B: The second subtask Task B [12, 15–17] is the classification of the sentences for veracity. The task aims to establish a label describing the rumour in two categories true or false. The validation is established by the journalist or an expert's team from any trustworthy source. For task B, our model returns a confidence value falling in the range of 0 to 1 for each false content. If the content is unverifiable, the confidence of 0 is to be returned (refer Table 2 for more details about number of instances).

3.2   Pre-processing

At first step of implementation, we converted the existing dataset (RumourEval 2019) from .json to .csv format for more accurate processing. We have investigated the scope to implement a suitable deep learning model using real-world dataset. In the process of converting the given dataset to .csv format, each post is marked as a source or reply post. Subsequently, we have labelled the dataset for both the subtasks. We used special tokens to pre-process text in the dataset. In the pre-processing of data, we have replaced URLs, mentions, hashtags, and emojis as URL, MENTION, HASHTAG and EMOJI. We used the tweet-pre_processor (as a tokenize value), which is a pre-processing library for tweet data in python. Columns in the real world Twitter Dataset (.csv) are: type, id, in_replyto_status_id, text, favorite_count, retweet_count, label a, label b. Subsequently, columns in Reddit Dataset (.csv) are type, id, text, ups, downs, label a, and label b.

3.3   Deep Learning over Traditional Machine Learning

The primary reason to use Deep Learning over traditional Machine Learning is that the performance increases with as the scale of data raises. Deep Learning algorithms do perform well with large datasets as the architectures are expected to require a burdensome infrastructure in order to train in a reasonable amount of time. In the case of composite problems such as classification of images, natural language processing and recognition of speech, deep learning has outperformed the classical machine learning techniques. A Deep learning methodology aims to solve the problem of rumour detection from end to end, in machine learning, the problem statement is fractionated into different parts, and their individual results are combined in the final stage. When it comes to large datasets, classical machine learning architectures are showing less accurate results. Deep learning models give more accurate results for both structure as well as unstructured datasets. The drawback observed in traditional machine learning technique, is the need of domain expert for applied feature identification, for a reduction in the complexity of data and pattern recognition that can enable efficient learning by the algorithm. Deep learning provides a structured solution to this problem by learning high-level feature extraction from data in an incremental process. This advantage helps in eliminating the need for domain expertise and handcrafted feature extraction.

To execute any Deep Learning model, it has become essential to possess high-end machines such as GPU, contrary to traditional Machine Learning algorithms. Due to a large number of trainable parameters in the system, Deep Learning algorithms take an adequate amount of time to train (training cost is high in deep learning). In our approach, we consider following process:

– Understanding of the research problem
– Collection the dataset
– Design our proposed model
– Validate the performance of our model as compared to others model

3.4   Deep Learning Models Used for RumourEval 2019

Convolutional Neural Network (CNN): A CNN is an advanced version of an artificial neural network that employs a supervised machine learning algorithm called perceptron to analyse the data. CNN's can be employed for various cognitive applications, including image recognition and language processing. For our implementation, we have used a simple CNN having two convolutional and two dense layers. We have used Google Glove 6B vector 100d for training the model.

Vector Representation Using GloVe: As our convolutional neural network helps in the extraction of the features, it is difficult for the system to find the dependence of the words that form meaningful sequences. The GloVe helps in obtaining vector representations of these words that enables to map the global word-word co-occurrence statistics in a word vector space. This vector space results in linear substructure representations.

Recurrent Neural Network (RNN): In RNN's, the connected nodes of the neural network form a directed graph that enables it to showcase dynamic temporal performance for a time sequence. In addition to the RNN model from the previous model, knowledge from an embedding layer can enhance the precision in the classification results. It integrates new information and characteristics associated (lexical and semantic) with the words, a piece of knowledge that has been trained and refined on a massive corpus of text-based data. The pre-trained embedding that will be applying for our model is GloVe (Global Vectors for word representation).

Deep C-LSTM: Long short-term memory (LSTM) is an artificial RNN architecture used in the fields of deep learning. It can process not only single data points but also entire sequences of data. For example, LSTM applies to tasks such as unsegmented, connected handwriting recognition or speech recognition. LSTM unit comprises of a unique cell, and three gates called the input, output and forget gate. In comparison to a conventional artificial neural network, LTSM architectures are highly efficient in processing, classifying and making predictions concerned to time-series data. In our proposed model, we have used the power of automatic feature extraction and passes the entire sequence of data for better prognosis. In our architecture (see Fig. 4 and Table 3 for more details about deep neural network), we have taken three convolutional layers with max-pooling and six dense layers for design our CNN Model deep in nature (see

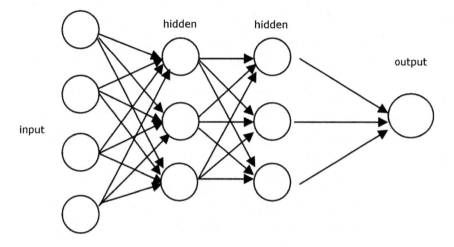

Fig. 3. Hidden nodes or layers in a neural network

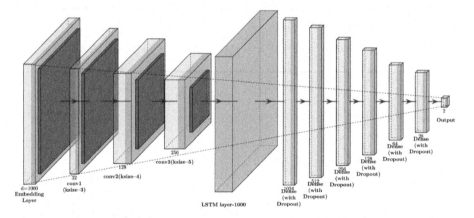

Fig. 4. Architecture of deep C-LSTM network

Fig. 3 for more details). Subsequently, the input from the combined flatten layer passed to a bi-directional LSTM layer following six dense layers with different filters. The method of our proposed model is lucrative towards any real-world rumour dataset. We have used Cross-entropy loss as our loss measure function which measures the performance of a classification model whose output is a probability value between 0 and 1. Cross-entropy loss increases as the predicted probability diverges from the actual label. In binary classification, where the number of classes M equals 2, cross-entropy can be calculated as:

$$L = -\,(y log(p) + (1 - y) log(1 - p)) \tag{1}$$

Table 3. Hyperparameters for our C-LSTM

Hyperparameter	Description or value
No. of convolution layers	3
No. of max pooling layers	3
No. of dense layers	6
Kernel-sizes	3,4,5
Dropout rate	0.1
Optimizer	Adam
Activation function	Relu
Loss function	Binary-crossentropy
Number of epochs	20
Batch size	64

Here, M - number of classes, log - the natural log, y - binary indicator (0 or 1), p - predicted probability

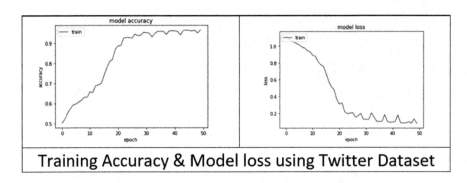

Fig. 5. Training accuracy and model loss using CNN (Twitter Dataset)

3.5   Results

Firstly, we have implemented a simple CNN model using real-world rumour dataset. For word embeddings, we used a pre-trained word-embedded vector-Glove. The glove is a word-embedded vector which contains around 400000 words mapped with 100-dimensional vector each. For subtask A, we trained our model for every post, splitting 20% of training dataset for testing, for 50 epochs and got a training accuracy of 97.62% for Twitter and 97.47% for Reddit (see Fig. 5 and Fig. 6 for more details). The cross entropy loss is also shown for the same. Subsequently, we have implemented our proposed Deep C-LSTM (Long Short

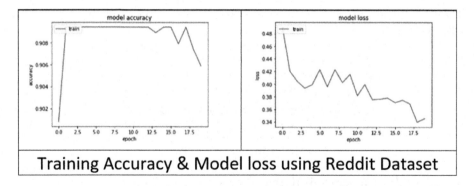

Fig. 6. Training accuracy and model loss using CNN (Reddit Dataset)

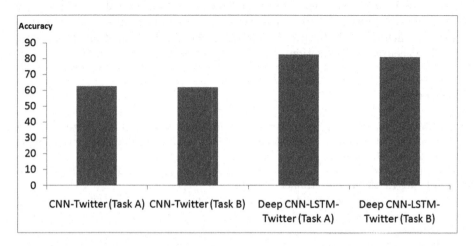

Fig. 7. Accuracy and model loss using CNN and Deep CNN-LSTM (Reddit Dataset)

Term Memory) model with the hyperparameters (refer Table 3 for more details) to train and test the real-world dataset. Using our proposed model, we have achieved a validation accuracy of 82,40% for task A and 81.04% for Reddit-task B. For subtask B; we created implemented the same two models. CNN model was trained only for source tweets, neglecting their replies, and our proposed model was trained on concatenating source tweets by their responses. Since our dataset is not too large, our proposed model performed better than the simple CNN model having two dense layers. Figure 7 clearly indicates that using our proposed model, we have achieved the highest accuracy for both the sub-tasks. A comparison with existing benchmarks and our proposed model is shown in Table 4 utilizing Reddit and Twitter dataset.

Table 4. Comparison with existing benchmark results using Twitter and Redditt dataset

Task and model	Accuracy(%)
SemiEval19 (Subtask-A)	81.50
SemiEval19 (Subtask-B)	75.50
Our Proposed Model-Subtask-A	**82.40**
Our Proposed Model-Subtask-B	**81.04**

4   Conclusion and Future Work

In this paper, we have presented the performance of our proposed C-LSTM model for rumour detection. We have achieved state-of-the-art results as compared to existing benchmarks. In future, we will use graph-based information of fake news for more accurate classification.

References

1. Zubiaga, A., Aker, A., Bontcheva, K., Liakata, M., Procter, R.: Detection and resolution of rumours in social media: a survey. ACM Comput. Surv. (CSUR) **51**(2), 32 (2018)
2. Baris, I., Schmelzeisen, L., Staab, S.: CLEARumor at SemEval-2019 Task 7: ConvoLving ELMo Against Rumors (2019)
3. Eason, G., Noble, B., Sneddon, I.N.: On certain integrals of Lipschitz-Hankel type involving products of Bessel functions. Philos. Trans. Roy. Soc. London **A247**, 529–551 (1955)
4. Jacobs, I.S., Bean, C.P.: Fine particles, thin films and exchange anisotropy. In: Rado, G.T., Suhl, H. (eds.) Magnetism, vol. III, pp. 271–350. Academic, New York (1963)
5. Yorozu, Y., Hirano, M., Oka, K., Tagawa, Y.: Electron spectroscopy studies on magneto-optical media and plastic substrate interface. IEEE Trans. J. Magn. Jpn **2**, 740–741 (1987). [Digests 9th Annual Conf. Magnetics Japan, p. 301, 1982]
6. Young, M.: The Technical Writer's Handbook. University Science, Mill Valley (1989)
7. Gorrell, G., et al.: SemEval-2019 Task 7: RumourEval, determining rumour veracity and support for rumours. In: Proceedings of the 13th International Workshop on Semantic Evaluation, pp. 845–854 (2019)
8. Pamungkas, E.W., Basile, V., Patti, V.: Stance Classification for Rumour Analysis in Twitter: Exploiting Affective Information and Conversation Structure. arXiv preprint arXiv:1901.01911 (2019)
9. Gorrell, G., Bontcheva, K., Derczynski, L., Kochkina, E., Liakata, M., Zubiaga, A.: RumourEval 2019: determining rumour veracity and support for rumours. arXiv preprint arXiv:1809.06683 (2018)
10. Baris, I., Schmelzeisen, L., Staab, S.: CLEARumor at SemEval-2019 Task 7: ConvoLving ELMo Against Rumors. arXiv preprint arXiv:1904.03084 (2019)

11. Liu, Z., Goel, S., Raghuprasad, M.Y., Muresan, S.: Columbia at SemEval-2019 task 7: multi-task learning for stance classification and rumour verification. In: Proceedings of the 13th International Workshop on Semantic Evaluation, pp. 1110–1114 (2019)

12. Fajcik, M., Burget, L., Smrz, P.: BUT-FIT at SemEval-2019 Task 7: Determining the Rumour Stance with Pre-Trained Deep Bidirectional Transformers. arXiv preprint arXiv:1902.10126 (2019)

13. Janchevski, A., Gievska, S.: AndrejJan at SemEval-2019 task 7: a fusion approach for exploring the key factors pertaining to rumour analysis. In: Proceedings of the 13th International Workshop on Semantic Evaluation, pp. 1083–1089 (2019)

14. Yang, R., Xie, W., Liu, C., Yu, D.: BLCU-NLP at SemEval−2019 task 7: an inference chain-based GPT model for rumour evaluation. In: Proceedings of the 13th International Workshop on Semantic Evaluation, pp. 1090–1096 (2019)

15. Li, Q., Zhang, Q., Si, L.: eventAI at SemEval-2019 task 7: rumor detection on social media by exploiting content, user credibility and propagation information. In: Proceedings of the 13th International Workshop on Semantic Evaluation, pp. 855–859 (2019)

16. Ghanem, B., Cignarella, A.T., Bosco, C., Rosso, P., Pardo, F.M.R.: UPV-28-UNITO at SemEval-2019 task 7: exploiting post's nesting and syntax information for rumor stance classification. In: Proceedings of the 13th International Workshop on Semantic Evaluation, pp. 1125–1131 (2019)

17. García-Cumbreras, M.A., Jiménez-Zafra, S.M., Montejo-Ráez, A., Díaz-Galiano, M.C., Saquete, E.: SINAI-DL at SemEval-2019 task 7: data augmentation and temporal expressions. In: Proceedings of the 13th International Workshop on Semantic Evaluation, pp. 1120–1124 (2019)

18. García-Cumbreras, M.A., Jiménez-Zafra, S.M., Montejo-Ráez, A., Díaz-Galiano, M.C., Saquete, E.: T SINAI-DL at SemEval-2019 Task 7: Data Augmentation and Temporal Expressions (2019)

19. Enayet, O., El-Beltagy, S.R.: Niletmrg at SemEval-2017 task 8: determining rumour and veracity support for rumours on twitter. In: Proceedings of the 11th International Workshop on Semantic Evaluation (SemEval-2017), pp. 470– 474 (2017)

20. Gorrell, G., et al.: SemEval-2019 Task 7: rumoureval: determining rumour veracity and support for rumours. In: Proceedings of SemEval. ACL (2019)

21. Kochkina, E., Liakata, M., Augenstein, I.: Turing at semeval-2017 task 8: Sequential approach to rumour stance classification with branch-LSTM. arXiv preprint arXiv:1704.07221 (2017)

22. Wang, F., Lan, M., Wu, Y.: ECNU at SemEval-2017 task 8: rumour evaluation using effective features and supervised ensemble models. In: Proceedings of the 11th International Workshop on Semantic Evaluation (SemEval-2017), pp. 491–496 (2017)

23. Bahuleyan, H., Vechtomova, O.: UWaterloo at SemEval-2017 task 8: detecting stance towards rumours with topic independent features. In: Proceedings of the 11th International Workshop on Semantic Evaluation (SemEval-2017), pp. 461–464 (2017)

24. Veyseh, A.P.B., Ebrahimi, J., Dou, D., Lowd, D.: A temporal attentional model for rumor stance classification. In: Proceedings of the 2017 ACM on Conference on Information and Knowledge Management, pp. 2335–2338. ACM (2017)

25. Li, D., Ma, J., Tian, Z., Zhu, H.: An evolutionary game for the diffusion of rumor in complex networks. Phys. A: Stat. Mech. Appl. **433**, 51–58 (2015)

26. Gorrell, G., Bontcheva, K., Derczynski, L., Kochkina, E., Liakata, M., Zubiaga, A.: RumourEval 2019: determining rumour veracity and support for rumours. arXiv (2018)
27. Zampieri, M., Malmasi, S., Nakov, P., Rosenthal, S., Farra, N., Kumar, R.: SemEval-2019 task 6: identifying and categorizing offensive language in social media (OffensEval). In: Proceedings of the 13th International Workshop on Semantic Evaluation, pp. 75–86 (2019)

Speech2Image: Generating Images from Speech Using Pix2Pix Model

Ankit Raj Ojha, Abhilash Gunasegaran$^{(\boxtimes)}$, Aruna Maurya, and Spriha Mandal

Department of Computer Science and Engineering,
Amrita Vishwa Vidyapeetham, Coimbatore, India
{ankitojha,abhilashg,arunamaurya,spriha27}@am.students.amrita.edu

Abstract. Generating images from speech is a fundamental problem that has numerous applications which include art generation, computer-aided design, enhancing learning capabilities in children among others. We present an audio-conditioned image generation model that transfers features from the speech descriptions (source) to respective image (target) domain. To accomplish this, we have used the Caltech-UCSD Birds-200-2011 (CUB-200-2011) dataset as target images and then we generated high-quality speech descriptions of birds to prepare custom dataset for training. We further verified the generated images using the images of birds provided in the CUB-200-2011 dataset. The model is trained and tested on three types of speech representations, i.e Spectrograms, ConstantQ Transforms and Short Time Fourier Transforms the results of which are discussed in subsequent sections. Unlike conventional approaches for speech to image conversions, which rely on a different intermediary domain such as text to realize this transition, our novel approach relies on an intermediate image transition, effectively restricting the number of domains involved in this process.

Keywords: Pix2Pix · Speech to image · Spectrograms

1 Introduction

Generating images directly from speech is a problem that has applications such as art generation, computer-aided design and enhanced learning capabilities in children by allowing them to generate images directly from speech. Recent work in the field of image generation from text as source has devised ways to generate images from speech descriptions, i.e speech is first converted to an intermediate form(text) and then this text is converted to an image using traditional image generation models. The aforementioned method transitions the source speech through two domains first text and then to image. This may, at times lead to a loss of semantic meaning. Instead, we propose a method which involves an image-to-image translation. We use the Pix2Pix [6] model, commonly known for image to image translation, through which the speech(audio) is translated into its target image by using image to image translational technique.

© Springer Nature Singapore Pte Ltd. 2021
D. Garg et al. (Eds.): IACC 2020, CCIS 1367, pp. 313–322, 2021.
https://doi.org/10.1007/978-981-16-0401-0_24

Generative Adversarial Nets (GANs) were introduced to train generative models. Our work explores how GANs conditioned by audio features can be employed to generate images of birds. To accomplish our above-said experiment, we have used the Caltech-UCSD Birds-200-2011 (CUB-200-2011) [13] dataset for target images and also generated high-quality speech descriptions(audio samples) for bird images from textual descriptions [20]. These audio samples are then converted to their respective spectrograms using Librosa, a Python package for audio analysis. Finally, a custom dataset is created by pairing each of these spectrogram images with their target image. After the first step (dataset creation), the generated data is fed to the Pix2Pix model which facilitates the generation of images based on the given input. The composite model is trained on a new dataset generated from scratch with the help of the CUB dataset and can create pictures of birds close to the speech description given as input (Fig. 1).

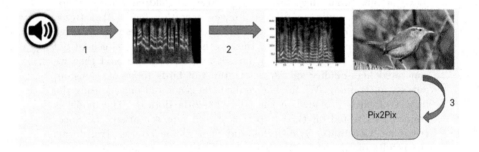

Fig. 1. Overview of speech to image generation

Our work here focuses on generating images from speech using Pix2Pix. Major contributions include:

1. Using an image to image translational model to reconstruct images from their visual descriptions.
2. Creating a comprehensive collection of audio files from preprocessed textual description [20]. This collection consists of ten different descriptions for one target image.
3. Compare the performance of three types of representations, i.e Spectrograms [16], Constant Q Transforms [14] and Short-time Fourier transform (STFT) [15] by calculating the Frechet Inception Distance (FID) score [5].

The rest of the paper is organized as follows: Sect. 2 talks about the related works, Sect. 3 discusses the approach and methodology used, Sect. 4 contains our results obtained and Sect. 5 contains conclusion and future work.

2   Related Works

In the area of **Generative Adversarial Networks** or **GAN**, [3] is a seminal paper in the history of image synthesis. Introduction of GAN opened up avenues of using these adversarial nets for unique applications such as(eg. [1,6,9]). The simple yet elegant architecture of GAN paved way for several other architectures with slight variations in structure. A new class of CNNs having certain architectural constraints called Deep Convolutional Generative Adversarial networks (DCGANs) [11] was developed. While DCGAN proposed and evaluated a large number of constraints on the architecture of CGAN's [12], the problem of image generation that was conditioned by an extra input largely remained unexplored. Conditional Generative Adversarial Nets [10] proved to be a groundbreaking research paper in the domain of conditional image generation. It showed how providing extra conditioning information to the model on this additional information, makes it possible to simplify the data generation process. As described in [10], this conditioning could be any auxiliary information such as class labels or data from other sources. This additional layer acts as an input to both the generator and the discriminator.

Generating images from text has been a subject of extensive research [19, 22,23] where a text is fed as an input to a different kind of GANs (Attentional GAN, Stack GAN and Stack GAN++) to generate images from it. Gruss et al. [4] in his paper developed a trivial way of generating images from speech by first converting speech to text using language translation and then with the help of AttnGAN [19] generating images from text. Though this work forms the basis of our work, our effort has been to avoid the need for the intermediate step of speech to text translation; and instead directly generate images from speech. [2] research brought about image style transfer, inspired by the logic of convolution neural networks (CNNs). Originally created for extracting images,"Neural Style Transfer" used a CNN model for generating a new image which incorporated the style of one image but the content of another image and shed light on how two images could be encoded and style could be actually "understood" by the model.

The problem of image to image translation remained unexplored until Pix2Pix [6] was developed. The **Pix2Pix** model was the first implemented model to shed light on image to image translation. Most adaptations on how one image domain can be transferred to another took place in the feature space. The Pix2Pix model on the other hand directly produces target images by transferring information from a source domain to a target domain while bridging the semantic gap between the two domains. In order to make the transferred image look lifelike and to preserve the semantic meaning and interpretation, an encoder and decoder were wrapped into the converter. The pixel-level domain converter is composed of an encoder for the semantic embedding of a source and a decoder to produce a target image. Pix2Pix was followed by the many variants along the same lines of image to image transfer which included [8,18,24].

GAN is being used in a many areas which include but are not limited to science, art, medicine and technology. The ground breaking research of the Pix2Pix model paved way for newer methods to understand cross domain relationships between objects to perform style transfer, while maintaining key features [7]. Latest work in the field also include Unpaired Image-to-Image Translation using

Cycle-Consistent Adversarial Networks [25]. GAN has also been used to develop innovative solutions for Image-Inpainting [21] and Image-Blending [17].

3   Methodology

3.1   Visual Representation of Speech

The current image generation models generate images from speech (audio) in a two-step fashion, first by converting speech to text and then generating an image from that text. We propose a novel approach in which the image is directly generated from speech. In this approach, we have taken a total of 2750 speech descriptions for a few of the bird species in the CUB dataset. After that spectral images were generated for each of the speech descriptions. We represented images of speech descriptions (audio) in three types: Spectrograms, Constant Q Transform and STFT. These visual representations of speech descriptions (audio) were created using the Librosa Python package (Fig. 2).

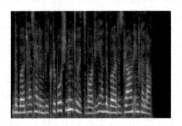 

Fig. 2. Representing speech description *The bird has head and beak proportional to its body and the bird is brown in color* in Spectrogram (Color figure online)

3.2   Custom Dataset Generation

Our work explores how GANs when conditioned by audio features can be employed to generate images of birds. To achieve our goal, we created a custom dataset of speech descriptions and bird images. First, text descriptions of bird images in the CUB dataset were converted to their corresponding speech descriptions. These descriptions were then used to create corresponding audio samples which were in turn converted to their respective visual represention, i.e Spectrograms, Constant QTransforms and STFT using Librosa, a Python package for audio analysis. Next, image pairing is done which involves pairing each of these spectrogram images with their target image(actual image of the bird from the CUB dataset). After this (dataset creation), the generated data is fed to the Pix2Pix model which facilitates the generation of images based on the given input. Our composite model is trained on a new dataset generated from

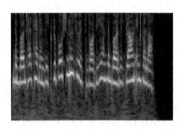 

Fig. 3. Representing speech description *The bird has head and beak proportional to its body and the bird is brown in color* in Constant Q Transform (Color figure online)

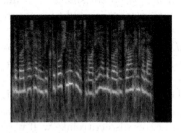 

Fig. 4. Representing speech description *The bird has head and beak proportional to its body and the bird is brown in color* in STFT (Color figure online)

scratch with the help of the CUB dataset and can create pictures of birds close to the speech description given as input. Input for the image-to-image translation model is a concatenated image, the first half of the image being the spectrogram and the second half of the image being the target image (Figs. 3 and 4).

3.3 Image-to-Image Translational Model

Image-to-image translation forms the core of the idea, of image generation from visual representations of audio. The Pix2Pix network consists of a generator which is an encode-decoder model with a U-Net architecture, a domain discriminator and a generic discriminator to assess whether the generated image is close to the original image. This allows the network to learn not just an input-output mapping but a loss function to train this mapping. This makes the network flexible and hence can be modeled for different types of applications. One such application was that of speech2image where we use spectrograms as input to reconstruct the original image. The network is trained on 2750 different spectral images and was used to generate three different models, one for each of these representation: Spectrogram, ConstantQ Transform and Short Time

Fourier Transform. These models were then tested on 1000 spectral images and the FID score was generated and performance compared.

4   Results

This paper aims to throw light on the idea of generating speech conditioned images instead of the usual two-step domain conversion method. Results acquired from comparison of images generated by Spectrograms, Constant Q Transforms, Short Time Fourier transforms (STFT) will help in determining which spectral image holds the most important information and can be used for better image translation. The performance of these networks is usually measured in relative to how well the generative model or the discriminative model is doing with respect to its opponent. Image quality might not necessarily give a satisfactory means of understanding its performance. Therefore, Inception score is used to measure its performance.

But according to *Martin Heusel, et al.* [5], *"Drawback of the Inception Score is that the statistics of real-world samples are not used and compared to the statistics of synthetic samples."*

So, a new metric called Frechet Inception Distance score (also called FID score) was developed. Lower scores indicate greater similarity between the two groups of images or more similar statistics. Lower scores also correlate well with higher quality of images. For the calculation of FID score, the Inception v3 model is used, eliminating the last pooling layer before the classification of images as output. Calculations of the activations for the generated and real images are done and summarized into a multivariate Gaussian, made by computing mean and covariance of these images. The distance between the two distributions is then computed using the Frechet or Wasserstein-2 distance.

We use FID score as the metric for measuring the performance of our model. Each model was trained on 2750 bird images from 150 birds species and then tested on 1000 images to calculate the FID score. Figure 5, 6, 7 and 8 shows some of the images generated by our model.

Formula to compute FID between the real images x and generated images g where μ is mean and $\sum$ is the covariance of a multivariate Gaussian distribution (Table 1).

$$\mathrm{FID}(x, g) = ||\mu_x - \mu_g||_2^2 + \mathrm{Tr}(\Sigma_x + \Sigma_g - 2(\Sigma_x \Sigma_g)^{\frac{1}{2}}),$$

Table 1. Table comparing FID scores between different models

Models	Spectrogram	ConstantQ Transform	STFT
FID scores	51.771	55.175	53.893

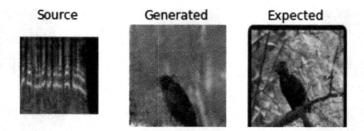

Fig. 5. Image generated from the model showing source spectrogram on left expected image on right and generated image at middle.

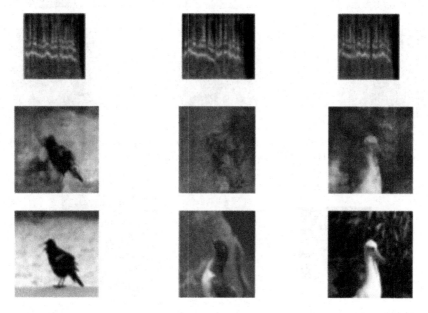

Fig. 6. Images generated from the model showing source spectrogram on top, followed by the generated and then the expected image at the bottom

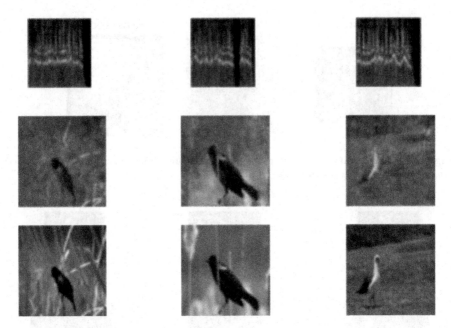

Fig. 7. Images generated from the model showing source spectrogram on top, followed by the generated and then the expected image at the bottom

Fig. 8. Images generated from the model showing source spectrogram on left expected image on right and generated image at middle.

5   Conclusion

The results from this paper highlight the method of generating images by extracting relevant features from the visual representation of a speech sample. A detailed examination and thorough testing clearly shows that Constant QTransforms perform relatively better than its two counterparts, Spectrograms and STFT's as indicated by their respective FID scores. In fact this novel approach introduces the use of a translational model for generation and can be used in a variety of other settings for deriving semantic insights from a spectrogram.

Following are some of the suggested improvements to further the scope of this project:

1. It can be extended to other languages. For example Hindi, Malayalam, Tamil, etc.
2. Train the model to solve a generic problem like the identification and construction of everyday objects by training it on a larger dataset.
3. Improve the neural architecture to achieve higher accuracy and a better image resolution.
4. Condition the project to incorporate sign language for the benefit of specially-abled.
5. Improve the neural net to generate high resolution images.

Acknowledgement. The authors would like to express their thanks and gratitude to **Dr. Vivek Menon** from Amrita Vishwa Vidyapeetham, Amritapuri for his valuable guidance and expertise for our work.

References

1. Brock, A., Lim, T., Ritchie, J.M., Weston, N.: Neural photo editing with introspective adversarial networks (2016)
2. Gatys, L.A., Ecker, A.S., Bethge, M.: Image style transfer using convolutional neural networks. In: 2016 IEEE Conference on Computer Vision and Pattern Recognition (CVPR), pp. 2414–2423 (2016)
3. Goodfellow, I.J., et al.: Generative adversarial networks (2014)
4. Gruss, E., Sapirshtein, A., Heruti, V.: Pictures of jap girls in synthesis, pp. 461–465, June 2019. https://doi.org/10.1145/3325480.3329183
5. Heusel, M., Ramsauer, H., Unterthiner, T., Nessler, B., Hochreiter, S.: GANs trained by a two time-scale update rule converge to a local nash equilibrium (2017)
6. Isola, P., Zhu, J.Y., Zhou, T., Efros, A.A.: Image-to-image translation with conditional adversarial networks (2016)
7. Kim, T., Cha, M., Kim, H., Lee, J.K., Kim, J.: Learning to discover cross-domain relations with generative adversarial networks (2017)
8. Luan, F., Paris, S., Shechtman, E., Bala, K.: Deep photo style transfer (2017)
9. Ma, L., Jia, X., Sun, Q., Schiele, B., Tuytelaars, T., Gool, L.V.: Pose guided person image generation (2017)
10. Mirza, M., Osindero, S.: Conditional generative adversarial nets (2014)
11. Radford, A., Metz, L., Chintala, S.: Unsupervised representation learning with deep convolutional generative adversarial networks (2015)
12. Sagong, M.C., Shin, Y.G., Yeo, Y.J., Park, S., Ko, S.J.: cGANs with conditional convolution layer (2019)
13. Welinder, P., et al.: Caltech-UCSD Birds 200. Technical Report CNS-TR-2010-001, California Institute of Technology (2010)
14. Wikipedia contributors: Constant-q transform – Wikipedia, the free encyclopedia (2020). https://en.wikipedia.org/wiki/Constant-Q_transform. Accessed 5 May 2020
15. Wikipedia contributors: Short-time fourier transform – Wikipedia, the free encyclopedia (2020). https://en.wikipedia.org/wiki/Short-time_Fourier_transform. Accessed 5 May 2020

16. Wikipedia contributors: Spectrogram – Wikipedia, the free encyclopedia (2020). https://en.wikipedia.org/wiki/Spectrogram. Accessed 5 May 2020
17. Wu, H., Zheng, S., Zhang, J., Huang, K.: Gp-gan: towards realistic high-resolution image blending (2019)
18. Xian, W., et al: Texturegan: Controlling deep image synthesis with texture patches (2017)
19. Xu, T., et al.: Attngan: fine-grained text to image generation with attentional generative adversarial networks (2017)
20. Xu, T., et al.: Attngan: fine-grained text to image generation with attentional generative adversarial networks. https://github.com/taoxugit/AttnGAN (2018)
21. Yeh, R.A., Chen, C., Lim, T.Y., Schwing, A.G., Hasegawa-Johnson, M., Do, M.N.: Semantic image inpainting with deep generative models (2017)
22. Zhang, H., et al.: Stackgan: text to photo-realistic image synthesis with stacked generative adversarial networks (2016)
23. Zhang, H., et al.: Stackgan++: Realistic image synthesis with stacked generative adversarial networks (2017)
24. Zhu, J.Y., Park, T., Isola, P., Efros, A.A.: Unpaired image-to-image translation using cycle-consistent adversarial networks (2017)
25. Zhu, J.Y., Park, T., Isola, P., Efros, A.A.: Unpaired image-to-image translation using cycle-consistent adversarial networks (2020)

SQL Query from Portuguese Language Using Natural Language Processing

Carlos Fernando Mulessiua da Silva[(✉)] [iD] and Rajni Jindal

Computer Science and Engineering Department, Delhi Technological University,
New Delhi 110042, India
mulessiua@gmail.com

Abstract. Nowadays, there is a great challenge to make information technology transparent so the end-user can have a good user experience. We are proposing a Natural Language Interface Model in which the user introduces the phrase through a text box in the local natural language, preferably in the Portuguese language. The system will read these words and separate them into a list of tokens, which will be analyzed, and if unnecessary words are found, they will be removed. The system will make a combination of the user's request. In the end, it will arrive until the generation of SQL Query and basics MongoDB Query as well ready to be executed directly in the Database. The model has an average accuracy of 70.27%. A morphological analysis will understand the meaning of the user's sentence ending in a friendly interface.

Keywords: Natural Language Processing · SQL query · Portuguese language · Natural language interface for database · MongoDB query

1 Introduction

Modern databases are made for easy access to information when talking about Natural Language Processing. What comes into mind is Artificial Intelligence. There is a severe difficulty for people who speak the Portuguese language to manipulate the Database's data. Since the language is used to create queries in the English Language, this is becoming more and more abundant as only ten countries have English as official languages.

Currently, non-experienced or non-technical users have difficulties in accessing the Database. This becomes increasingly one reason people escape from the database area and end up choosing other areas. As a result, this area is little explored. There are increasing difficulties in the relationship between the user and the Database. Consequently, the access of people who do not speak the English Language has been infrequent.

There is currently some software created for converting Natural Language into SQL Query, and many of them use only the English Language. These applications were not developed for the creation of very complex queries. Many users have difficulties in formulating syntax for manipulating the Database.

© Springer Nature Singapore Pte Ltd. 2021
D. Garg et al. (Eds.): IACC 2020, CCIS 1367, pp. 323–335, 2021.
https://doi.org/10.1007/978-981-16-0401-0_25

A relational database consists of some operations such as SELECT, UPDATE, DELETE, and INSERT. In this research, only the SELECT operation was used to facilitate access to information in the Database. Subsequently, the rest of the operations will be implemented.

Generally, the process of transforming Natural Language into SQL Query follows the following Algorithm (Fig. 1):

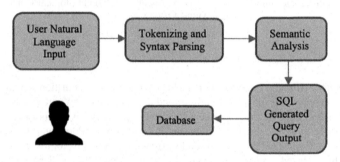

Fig. 1. Algorithm flowchart

This Algorithm is used in several applications that do this process. This type of system can provide people with no technical knowledge access to the Database very quickly. It also provides easy perception from the user's data through the application's interface without any English language knowledge (Fig. 2).

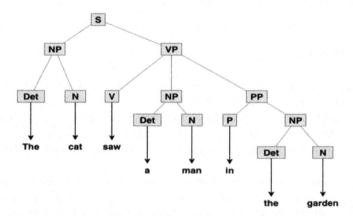

Fig. 2. Syntax tree

2   Related Work

[1] Presented a Natural Language Interface Database, composed in two parts, Linguistic and Database component. In the first part, the input is a Hind sentence, and this will be

processed, will be done the morphological analysis, the word group will be analyzed, tags will be generated, and will be mapped. In the second component, the Query will be generated after passing through the database management system, a response will be generated, and the output will be given.

In this research, [2] a system has been proposed which the user introduces a sentence in his natural language, and the system translates the sentence and turns it into some SQL queries which can be used to access the Database through a DBMS [3]. The process is done as follows: The input is given in natural language and then goes through the translation module. After that goes to Levenshtein distance, and a SQL Query is created, and finally, the Query is sent to Database.

H. Baius and M. Machkour [4] developed an Arabic Language Interface to be used in XML Databases based on previous works. They built a database knowledge module that works together with a linguistic module. The Arabic sentence is given as input, and the user can choose SQL or Xpath or both. After the parse tree is done, the output is generated according to the previous user choice. It is essential to mention that this is a long process because first, the Arabic sentence must be converted into an English sentence, and then the remaining steps are done.

In this approach, a study has been conducted to find the Impact of IntelliSense caused by a Natural Language Interface Database [5]. Was proposed a Graphic User Interface in which the user writes the input, and the system gives some suggestions of words to be filled according to the best sentence formulation. Whatever the user writes the correct sentence or not, the system will provide an output. A set of IF-ELSE is verified in the Algorithm. The highest accuracy was 96%. In a total of 500 queries, 300 were correct, and 200 were incorrect.

Another system was developed to work with yes or no questions. According to the authors, the architecture is based on the user interface, question analyzer, query generator, ontology builder, and database interface. After formulating the user's question, the system responds with a series of suggestions and some yes or no questions that enable the user to make decisions based on his request. According to the authors, with this system, it is also possible to work with unit conversion [6].

A good option for non-expert users of the Database would be to accept that the user enters a sentence in English. The system will first transform the user's words into SQL Queries through the user's sentence. After that, a mapping is done from the Query, it will be executed, and then the output will be given. It is important to note that the system works as an intelligent system that manages queries and facilitates non-technical users. The architecture used goes through the following phases: Semantic Building, the Generation of MR, and the Generation of Queries [7]. This study is based on a mathematical model.

A different application that uses the Matrix Technique can be a great option. The user fills in using the natural language. The system identifies the keywords and does the parsing; after that, the words are modified to resemble a matrix. Then the semantic interpretation is performed, which depends on a network of words already assigned. An SQL Query is then formulated and performed. Furthermore, the output is shown directly to the user through a friendly interface [8]. It should be noted that a simple Query, which uses a logical condition and Query with an aggregate function, were tested.

In paper [9], they propose a model that removes information from the MongoDB database through natural language. The user writes a sentence containing a question in the English Language, and the model returns a result that has the intervention of non-structural Language (NoSQL). In this model, the user is not restricted from entering any specific Query, as long as it meets the requirements for it to work. In this paper, they propose an interface that provides the user, through a search field, to obtain results without technical knowledge of the MongoDB database.

3 Proposed Model

We propose a system that can get phrases in the Portuguese Language [10], convert into SQL Query, and send a query into a database to show information through an available interface to the user [11]. We are proposing an approach that will facilitate the user with less experience in accessing the Database.

It is essential to mention that the system will only work with one sentence at a time. If the user wants to make more than one request, he is requested to do the flowchart again.

In the first phase, the system will only work with a database previously defined by the System Administrator.

System Architecture
For the proposed system to be functional, it is divided into three (3) components:

Natural Language Processing
This is an essential component of the system because most of the Business Logic of our application happens.

1. Tokenizer
   This phase is where the words entered by the user are separated, and each word is represented as a token so that it can be stored, and a specific list can be processed later in the next phases.
2. Lexical Analysis
   After creating the list of tokens from the words separated in the previous phase, this list of tokens will be mapped with an existing dictionary. Unnecessary words or tokens will be discarded.
   After that, the words will be replaced with specific words from a database, which will proceed to the next phase. It should be noted that the words the system replaced are pre-chosen to facilitate the process of identifying verbs, names, and others.
3. Syntactic and Semantic Analysis
   In this phase, the system will identify the names of tables that must be selected, the attributes, and the existing keywords. Based on the dictionary, each token will be mapped. In Semantic Analysis, based on the same dictionary, the words containing conditions will be selected to facilitate the final Query formulation. These conditions are replaced by some symbols like ($\geq$, $\leq$, $<$, $>$).

4. Mapping

In this Mapping phase, a combination of the existing words is made with possible fields in the Database, such as table names, attribute names, if there are any values, if any specific conditions which requested by the user, if there has any order request, if it needs to be grouped and if it has any operations among others. Any other words which are not required will be discarded. After that, all the requirements for creating SQL Query will have been met, and the system will be ready to proceed to the next phase.

Database Component

In this component are the steps related to the Database. This means that the Mapping interaction generated in the last phase of Natural Language Processing begins to be executed.

1. SQL Query Generator

In this phase, the SQL Query is created through mapping, which was done in the previous step. The Query is generated from an existing standard to facilitate syntax, and the tokens are compared to create this Query.

2. MongoDB Query Generator

In this phase, the MongoDB Query is created through mapping, which was done in the previous step. The Query is generated from an existing standard to facilitate syntax, and the tokens are compared to create this Query.

3. Query Ready to be Executed

After getting the SQL and MongoDB Query ready, it is time to deliver the Query to the final user, ready to be executed.

Conversion Component

Finally, in this component, the main one, the translation between the Portuguese and English languages, occurs [12].

1. Conversion to the English Language

After the user has entered his Query in the text box in natural language at this phase, the system will translate the sentence from Portuguese to English. It is essential to mention that this translation works as a conversion so that the system can proceed with the English Language (Fig. 3).

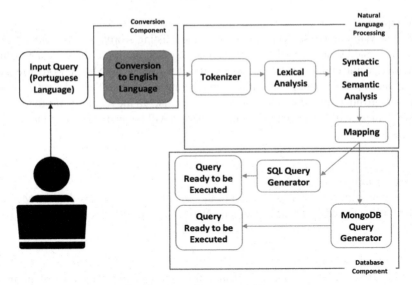

Fig. 3. Proposed system architecture

4 Proposed Algorithm

First step: After opening the system, the user will enter his Portuguese sentence in the text box. Remember that this sentence must follow some questioning patterns.
Let us consider the following sentence entered by the user in Portuguese (Query):

> *"Mostra todos dados dos estudantes do departamento de ciência da computação com a idade maior de 18 anos e notas maiores de 90 e ordenar de forma crescente."*

Second step: The Query must be translated into the English language to be manipulated since the database access key words (SELECT, FROM, WHERE, ORDER, GROUP, DESCENDING,…) are all in the English Language.

> *"Show all data from students in the computer science department which age greater than 18 and marks greater than 90 ascending order."*

Third step: The query moves to the Tokenizer phase, where all words in the sentence considering the spaces between the sentences must be separated and stored as a list of tokens.

> *"Show, all, data, from, students, in, the, computer, science, department, which, age, greater, than, 18 and marks, greater, than, 90, ascending, order."*

Fourth step: Next, the word list (tokens) will be compared with an existing word list, and unnecessary or ignored tokens will be discarded.

Unnecessary list: data, in, the, which than, and, then.

"Show, all, from, students, computer, science, department, age, greater, 18, marks, greater, 90, ascending, order."

Fifth step: After the unnecessary tokens are discarded, go through the process of replacing the tokens with words similar to the word list, such as table name, attribute name, keyword, and values will be attached.

"SELECT (action), * (keyword), students (table-name), WHERE (clause), computer science (value), department (att-name), age (att-name), greater 18 (value), marks (att-name), greater 90 (value), ORDER BY (clause), ASC".

Sixth step: After going through the previous process, now it is time to select the action (SELECT) that will be taken according to the (action) previously entered by the user. These can be several words that will give the same SELECT action such as Show, find, identify,…).

– If the SELECT action were chosen, the FROM keyword would be added before the table name.

It is essential to say that this system works only with the action (SELECT).

"SELECT (action) * FROM students (table-name) WHERE (clause) computer science (value) department (att-name) age (att-name) greater 18 (value) marks (att-name) greater 90 (value) ORDER BY (clause) ASC".

Seventh step: This step is where the conditions found in the tokens entered by the user are replaced. If no token contains comparison words, it will be ignored and will proceed to the next step.

The condition will be inserted according to the keyword WHERE inside the Query ($\geq, \leq, <, >$).

The sign of logical operation and comparison will be added after the name of the attribute in question (age > 18).

Considering the ORDER BY at the end of the Query, an attribute name will be added after this keyword meets the query requirements.

"SELECT (action) * FROM students (table-name) WHERE (clause) computer science (value) department (att-name) age (att-name) > 18 (value) marks (att-name) > 90 (value), ORDER BY (clause) (att-name) ASC".

Eighth step: Here, the complete Query is generated and is executed in the Database and will follow the next steps (Fig. 4 and Table 1).

"SELECT * FROM students WHERE department = 'computer science' and age > 18 and marks > 90 ORDER BY name ASC".

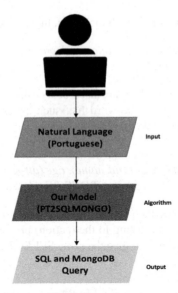

Fig. 4. Flowchart

Table 1. Questions types

No.	Type	Features
1	Question Type A1	['mostrar, 'visualizar']
2	Question Type A2	['o que', 'qual', 'quem']
3	Question Type A3	['maximo', 'minimo']
4	Question Type A4	['somar', 'quantos são']
5	Question Type A5	['contar', 'media']
6	Question Type A6	['ordenar', 'agrupar']
7	Question Type A7	['igual', 'contem']
8	Question Type A8	['juntar', 'separar']
9	Question Type A9	['maior que', 'menor que']

For this model, nine types of questions were structured, organized into different types ranging from "Q. Type A1" to "Q. Type A9". Each type corresponds to a set of rules specifically assigned to it. For each type of question, there are some features associated with it. Whether in an inserted sentence, it contains a word that corresponds to a specific type of question, the flowchart will be redirected to that type of question.

5 Discussion of Results

The model has been developed using the Python programming language because it has more affinities with natural language processing and needs to adapt to the model. This model was developed for integration with the SELECT function in this first phase. For future work, we hope to advance with the following functions DELETE, UPDATE and INSERT. This model is not entirely developed to work with complex queries so far, so some features are not functional (Fig. 5). A Dataset was used to train the model that is present in Fig. 6.

Fig. 5. Model interface

This is the interface that the user sees when opening the model. The user enters the phrase or question in the Portuguese Language, then clicks the button to do the translation. The system will translate the sentence into the English language using the "googletrans" API, and the user can change it whether he thinks something is missing. Further down, he must choose an SQL dump he intends to interact with to allow the model and have access to data that will be used. Then, the user must choose the language setting so that the model recognizes some special characters. He is not obliged to work with the Portuguese language as a configuration; he can select his configuration.

He can select the outputs he wants the model to show between SQL Query and MongoDB Query (NoSQL) [13], thus leaving the user interface cleaner and more selectable. Then he submits. If the system finds any fault in the user's phrase, it will return the error (Table 2).

Table 2. Accuracy of question types

No.	Proposed model	Accuracy (%)
1	Question Type A1	86.7
2	Question Type A2	84.3
3	Question Type A3	77.5
4	Question Type A4	74.1
5	Question Type A5	83.6
6	Question Type A6	65.8
7	Question Type A7	84.0
8	Question Type A8	61.2
9	Question Type A9	85.5

In this model, we have nine types of questions with different types of characteristics, from which we have different results. We highlight the average accuracy, which was **70.27%**. Among them, we find "Q. Type A1" with the highest accuracy of 86.7%, and the lowest accuracy was "Q. Type A8" with 61.2%.

The "Q. Type A1" had the highest accuracy due to the characteristics of considering more possibilities in the formulation of prefixes of the questions involving SELECT Query such as: "mostrar", "dizer", "visualizar", "apresentar", "revelar", (mostrar todos estudantes…, mostrar nome dos estudantes…, visualizar os estudantes…, visualizar idade dos estudantes…, dizer os nomes dos estudantes…, revelar a idade dos estudantes…, apresentar nomes dos estudantes…).

The "Q. Type A8" presented the lowest accuracy because, due to the JOIN function's poor performance, the model currently works only with INNER JOIN. LEFT OUTER, RIGHT OUTER, CROSS, and FULL OUTER have not yet been implemented.

Some queries such as: "mostrar os estudantes que tem o professor de matematica com media superior" and "mostrar todas disciplinas que o estudante silva frequenta" are present in "Q. Type A8" (Table 3).

In this model, 45200 data were trained using Google Colab [14], between "Q. Type A1" up to "Q. Type A9". "Q. Type A7" presents the most trained type with 5800 dues to the wide variation of possibilities which we have at this point, such as "igual" and "contem". The least trained types were "Q. Type A3", "Q. Type A6", "Q. Type A8" and "Q. Type A9" with 4700 data due to the few possibilities of variations available in these such as "maximo", "minimo" for "Q. Type A3", "ordenar" and "agrupar" for "Q. Type

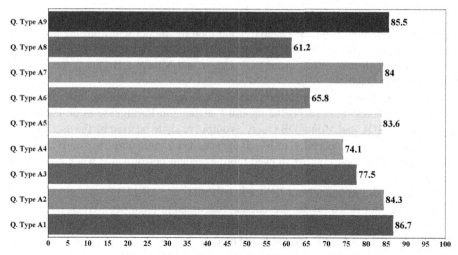

Fig. 6. Accuracy of question types graphically

Table 3. Data trained

No	Proposed model (type questions)	Data trained
1	Question Type A1	5000
2	Question Type A2	5000
3	Question Type A3	4700
4	Question Type A4	5300
5	Question Type A5	5300
6	Question Type A6	4700
7	Question Type A7	5800
8	Question Type A8	4700
9	Question Type A9	4700

A6", "juntar" and "separar" for "Q. Type A8" and finally "maior que" and "menor que" for "Q. Type A9".

6 Conclusion and Future Work

Many new kinds of research have proposed a solution to the artificial intelligence of a different approach. That allows users with little knowledge to have access to them, as is the example of NLP.

Natural Language Processing brought humans a solution from the problems currently encountered by inexperienced users who want to access the Database. This system will benefit mainly people who are not familiar with the English Language and will allow more fluent interaction and better interpretation of the data.

The system will allow the user to input a sentence in the Portuguese language. He wants to retrieve data from the Database, and then the model will translate the words according to get a sequence of tokens, which can be understood by the system. Moreover, that will end with the generation of SQL Query and Mongo DB Query, ready to be executed in the Database.

The model showed a good performance and managed to achieve the main objective, developing a model that accepts the natural Language in Portuguese as an input field and generates SQL and MongoDB Query as output ready to be used by the user. Having an average of 70.27% accuracy, in which the sentences containing the words "mostrar and visualizar" in their context showed more excellent performance when comparing the others.

We intend to implement the INSERT, UPDATE and DELETE operations for the future, so the four functions are present and functional in the model. We also intend to develop more possibilities and make the components LEFT OUTER, RIGHT OUTER, CROSS and FULL OUTER present in the model.

One of the most severe difficulties was generating MongoDB Query since it has a different syntax than SQL.

References

1. Kate, A., Kamble, S., Bodkhe, A., Joshi, M.: Conversion of natural language query to SQL query. In: Proceedings of the 2nd International Conference on Electronics, Communication and Aerospace Technology, ICECA 2018, pp. 488–491. Institute of Electrical and Electronics Engineers Inc. (2018). https://doi.org/10.1109/ICECA.2018.8474639
2. Mohite, A., Bhojane, V.: Natural language interface to database using modified co-occurrence matrix technique. In: 2015 International Conference on Pervasive Computing: Advance Communication Technology and Application for Society, ICPC 2015. Institute of Electrical and Electronics Engineers Inc. (2015). https://doi.org/10.1109/PERVASIVE.2015.7087045
3. Badhya, S., Prasad, A., Rohan, S., Yashwanth, S., Deepamala, N., Shobha, G.: Natural language to structured query language using elasticsearch for descriptive columns. In: CSITSS 2019 - 2019 4th International Conference on Computational Systems and Information Technology for Sustainable Solution, Proceedings (2019). https://doi.org/10.1109/CSITSS47250.2019.9031030
4. Reinaldha, F., Widagdo, E.: Natural language interfaces to database (NLIDB): question handling and unit conversion. In: Proceedings of 2014 International Conference on Data and Software Engineering, ICODSE 2014. Institute of Electrical and Electronics Engineers Inc. (2014). https://doi.org/10.1109/ICODSE.2014.7062663
5. Bais, H., Machkour, M.: Arabic language interface for xml databases. In: Proceedings of 2019 IEEE World Conference on Complex Systems, WCCS 2019. Institute of Electrical and Electronics Engineers Inc. (2019). https://doi.org/10.1109/ICoCS.2019.8930803
6. Choudhary, N., Gore, S.: Impact of intellisense on the accuracy of natural language interface to database. In: 2015 4th International Conference on Reliability, Infocom Technologies and Optimization: Trends and Future Directions, ICRITO 2015. Institute of Electrical and Electronics Engineers Inc. (2015). https://doi.org/https://doi.org/10.1109/ICRITO.2015.7359310
7. Gupta, P., Goswami, A., Koul, S., Sartape, K.: IQS-intelligent querying system using natural language processing. In: Proceedings of the International Conference on Electronics, Communication and Aerospace Technology, ICECA 2017, pp. 410–413. Institute of Electrical and Electronics Engineers Inc. (January 2017). https://doi.org/10.1109/ICECA.2017.8212846

8. Kumar, R., Dua, M.: Translating controlled natural language query into SQL query using pattern matching technique. In: 2014 International Conference for Convergence of Technology, I2CT 2014. Institute of Electrical and Electronics Engineers Inc. (2014). https://doi.org/10.1109/I2CT.2014.7092161

9. Pradeep, T., Rafeeque, P.C., Murali, R.: Natural language to NoSQL query conversion using deep learning, SSRN Electron. J. (2019). https://doi.org/10.2139/ssrn.3436631

10. Pinheiro, V., Pequeno, T., Furtado, V., Franco, W.: InferenceNet.Br: expression of inferentialist semantic content of the Portuguese language. In: Pardo, T.A.S., Branco, A., Klautau, A., Vieira, R., de Lima, V.L.S. (eds.) PROPOR 2010. LNCS (LNAI), vol. 6001, pp. 90–99. Springer, Heidelberg (2010). https://doi.org/10.1007/978-3-642-12320-7_12

11. Posevkin, R., Bessmertny, I.: Multilanguage natural user interface to database. In: Application of Information and Communication Technologies AICT 2016 - Conference Proceedings, Institute of Electrical and Electronics Engineers Inc. (2017). https://doi.org/10.1109/ICAICT.2016.7991706

12. Ribeiro Afonso, A.: Brazilian Portuguese text clustering based on evolutionary computing. IEEE Latin Am. Trans. **14**, 3370–3377 (2016). https://doi.org/10.1109/TLA.2016.7587644

13. Mondal, S., Mukherjee, P., Chakraborty, B., Bashar, R.: Natural language query to NoSQL generation using query-response model. In: Proceedings - International Conference on Machine Learning and Data Engineering, iCMLDE 2019, pp. 85–90. Institute of Electrical and Electronics Engineers Inc. (2019). https://doi.org/10.1109/iCMLDE49015.2019.00026

14. Parvat, A., Chavan, J., Kadam, S., Dev, S., Pathak, V.: A survey of deep-learning frameworks. In: Proceedings of the International Conference on Inventive Systems and Control, ICISC 2017, Institute of Electrical and Electronics Engineers Inc. (2017). https://doi.org/10.1109/ICISC.2017.8068684

Misogynous Text Classification Using SVM and LSTM

Maibam Debina Devi[(✉)] and Navanath Saharia

Indian Institute of Information Technology Senapati, Senapati, Manipur, India
{debina,nsaharia}@iiitmanipur.ac.in

Abstract. Discrimination and manipulation are becoming predominant in social network activities. Comments bearing attitudes, such as distress, hate, and aggression in Social Networking Sites (SNS) add fuel to the process of discrimination. This research aims to classify texts, which are misogynous in nature using Support Vector Machine (SVM) and Long-Short Term Memory (LSTM) for user-generated texts of English and Hindi languages written using the Roman script. Approximately 87% accuracy was achieved while SVM was trained with Term Frequency-Inverse Document Frequency (TF-IDF) feature and for Hindi comments approximately 93.43% accuracy was achieved for English using Bidirectional LSTM (Bi-LSTM).

Keywords: Text classification · Misogyny · SVM · LSTM

1 Introduction

Misogyny, a characteristic that emerged from oppressive patriarchy, reflecting an attitude of animosity towards women [22] that ends up generating a gender gap. Consequences of a misogynistic action have been considered as a matter of public safety [25] and contemplated as a crime [27]. It has become easy to taunt and perpetuate hate with the advent of the Internet and SNS. Pieces of evidence toward cyberhate have become a high threat to society. Implementation of techniques such as automatic detection of abusive language [32,35], hate speech [13,15,34], aggression [33], cyber-bullying [36] in platforms, like Twitter and Facebook are critically required as 76% women under the age of 30 experienced online harrasement[1]. Recently, a number of shared tasks was addressing the issue of automatic detection of abusive language[2,3] aggression[4], and misogyny[5] in texts. Classification of text is an important component for many NLP

---

[1] https://www.cnet.com/news/not-just-words-online-harassment-of-women-epidemic-norton-research; accessed date: 10 July 2020.

[2] https://sites.google.com/site/offensevalsharedtask/home; accessed on 10 July 2020.

[3] https://www.workshoponlineabuse.com/cfp/woah-shared-exploration; accessed on 15 July 2020.

[4] https://sites.google.com/view/trac2/shared-task?authuser=0; accessed on 01 June 2020.

[5] https://amievalita2020.github.io; accessed on 15 July 2020.

ⓒ Springer Nature Singapore Pte Ltd. 2021
D. Garg et al. (Eds.): IACC 2020, CCIS 1367, pp. 336–348, 2021.
https://doi.org/10.1007/978-981-16-0401-0_26

applications including web search [11], filtering [23,30], indexing [28], and opinion mining [10]. Various methods have been introduced ranging from rule-based to neural network-based as a solution to the text classification problem with pros and cons over the last few decades. Neural network-based methods are gaining attention due to the higher accuracy [7,12], whereas, linear classifiers are still considered as strong baselines [1,17,20].

In this research, we focused on the classification of misogynous text using SVM as a representative of the linear classification model and LSTM as a representative of the neural network-based model. We have a set of comments $C = \{c_1, c_2, c_3, \ldots, c_n\}$, a youtube based comments. Each comment c_i is associated with label l_j, where $i = 1, 2, 3, \ldots, n$ and $j = \{0, 1\}$. Problem of the misogynous text classification can be defined as a binary decision-making module to test, whether, c_i belongs to l_0 or l_1. We moved towards a supervised learning approach to design the decision-making module as the success rate of supervised learning is predominant over unsupervised. Therefore, the C is split into a training set TR_C and test set TS_C. TR_C is used to build the prototype for classification. The prototype then applied to TS_C to test, whether or not the $c_i \in TS_C$ has the property of l_1. The discriminative classifiers, SVM, and LSTM are used to build the prototype for the classification of the misogynous text of Hindi and English languages using the dataset of TRAC shared tasks [8]. Contribution of this work lies in performing misogynous text classification using SVM with TF-IDF and $N-gram$ as a feature, and LSTM and its variations with GloVe for Hindi and English languages. We also examined, the stability of these approaches with an unbalanced class label ratio. As the input text for Hindi is code-mixed [14,29] and written in the Roman script we employed pre-trained GloVe[6] with LSTM to train the classifier.

The organisation of this paper is as follows. Section 2 discusses about the related work on misogynous text classification. Dataset and experimental details are discussed in Sect. 3. Obtained result is analyse in Sect. 4. Section 5 describe the conclusion with direction towards future work.

2   Related Work

Venue, such as, IberEval, TRAC, SemEval, and AMI have organised a number of shared tasks related to misogynous texts and other event/action identification on SNS texts. Logistic regression [2,31], SVM [2,31], Random Forest [31], Gradient Boosting and Stochastic Gradient Descent [2], and Naive Bayes [31] are among the used techniques to classify misogynous text. A study by Shushkevich and Cardiff [31] highlighted the work on misogynous text identification using SVM, NB, RF, and LR.

Introduction to a multi SVM approach for solving hate speech detection problems is seen in [26]. Using multi-view SVM as a classifier, with unigram as a feature over linear SVM classifier and creating a view classifier, then combination with another SVM is perform to build a meta-classifier. The result is analysis

---

[6] https://nlp.stanford.edu/projects/glove/.

with a technique like BERT. With the TRAC19 dataset proposed model mSVM (multi-SVM) give an accuracy score with 61.2%.

Classifier combination techniques adopted in [24] experiment, SVM & RF, SVM & GBT, and RF & GBT are combined using algebraic fusion where each class obtained probabilities are taken by average. Of which obtained scores are as follows 0.624, 0.247, and 0.623 respectively. Experiments like [18] give weightage on lexical and stylistic features. Words with high intensity of being misogynous are extracted and information gain is calculated. Collective features like n-gram of words, TF-IDF, and stylistic features are used. With SVM as a classifier, this experiment yields an accuracy score of 0.74 to 0.89 with a different dataset. Gives the idea that features like bigram and trigram perform better than the unigram. Subject features identification on multilingual content of twitter data is seen in [6] shared task report of which machine learning and neural network approaches are the adapted approaches. Trained with 5000 and 10000 tweets for Spanish and English language, 3000 and 1600 as test samples for respective languages. Used techniques include SVM, CNN, LSTM, and BiGRU and embeddings google's Universal Sentence Encode. For which the SVM with RBF kernel obtained the highest score with 0.651 and Google's Universal Sentence Encoder using sentence embeddings as features technique also outperformed then others. CNN and LSTM also report with good scores next to SVM.

SVM as baseline and CNN, LSTM, and FastText with different embedding techniques was explored in [5] where using SVM with TF-IDF as a baseline gives an accuracy of 0.81. Upon it, feed different embedding techniques to neural network architectures [5] and summarise that deep neural network-based learning outperforms the identification of hate speech. Beside Tweets, work like [25] has implemented misogynous text detection using an urban dictionary. A deep learning model like Bi-LSTM and Bi-GRU outperformed the resulting accuracy score of 92.08% compared to Naive-Bayes, Logistic Regression, and Random Forest model.

Misogynous identification using neural network by [19] has highlighted with promising results. With the use of English and Spanish tweets and the Bi-LSTM technique have obtained good results with scores of 78.9% and 76.8%respectively. Another experiment by [3] emphasizes the impact of using Adam optimizer and obtain an F1 score as 0.8199 under the English dataset.

Misogynous text analysis has become a focus area under Natural Language Processing. Reported work so far highlight different approaches related to machine learning and deep learning to perform classification. From it, this experiment consider the two promising model reported SVM and LSTM as base model. And to aim to perform classification with different feature engineering for SVM and LSTM and its variants.

3   Experiment

User-generated texts of SNS quite often attract researchers because of their unstructured, uncensored [32], and spontaneous nature [21]. This research aims to develop an automatic misogynous text identification system using conventional and deep learning approaches. The data-set used in this experiment is taken from TRAC20[7] shared task [9]. The data-set comprised of 5329 English language comments and 4981 Hindi language comments written using Roman script collected from various Youtube videos. For SVM, 4263 and 3984 comments of English and Hindi datasets were used for training. Out of which, ratio distribution is likely unbalanced with 3339 are marked as NGEN (not based on gender, i. e. non-misogynous comments) and 645 are GEN (based on gender i. e. misogynous comments) for Hindi likewise 3963 and 300 as NGEN and GEN respectively for English dataset. Looking forward to the LSTM model, the ratio distribution is 3323 and 661 for Hindi and 3954 and 309 respectively for the English dataset. Table 1 tabulated the basic statistics of the used data-set. Precisely data distribution for training and testing is done with the division of dataset in a ratio of 0.8 and 0.2 respectively.

Table 1. Data-set statistics

Class	TR_{SVM}	TS_{SVM}	TR_{LSTM}	TS_{LSTM}	Total[a]
Hindi.NGEN	3339	829	3323	845	4168
Hindi.GEN	645	168	661	152	813
English.NGEN	3963	984	3954	993	4947
English.GEN	300	82	309	73	382

[a]$(TR_{SVM} + TS_{SVM})$ or $(TR_{LSTM} + TS_{LSTM})$

During the experiment, we extracted only texts and corresponding labels from the data-set, whereas the original data-set comprised of four columns. As the dataset (cf. Table 1) is unbalanced in nature and mixture of language (cf. Fig. 2), it will be worth to note the response of the learning models during the examination. Handling unbalance data with feature, experiment by [16] gives key idea for performing classification. Figure 1 depicted the experimental flow for our experiment.

No solid answer has been claimed on deciding better feature technique between embedding or pre-trained word embedding. Considering this intention for this experiment, we have used an embedding layer and pre-trained GloVe for LSTM. Besides using the embedding layer, it is observed in the Hindi dataset consisting of Hindi-English code mixed comments. Table 2 gives the idea of observed English words that carries rich semantic nature and found useful for this classification task. LSTM is trained with pre-trained GloVe word embedding to observe the weightage and response.

For both languages, the experiment started with cleaning the comments which are referred to as preprocessing steps mentioned in Fig. 1. It starts with the tokenization, lemmatization which remove inflectional endings, elimination of

---

[7] TRAC 2020 dataset. https://sites.google.com/view/trac2/home; July 17, 2020.

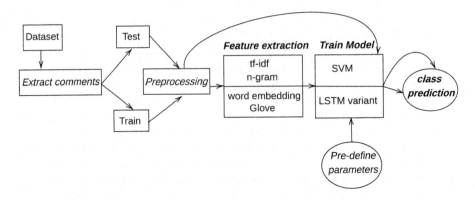

Fig. 1. System architecture

Table 2. Sample comments from Hindi dataset

ID	Text	Class
C7.1810	\<movie-name\> jasy ***** baaji film ki vajah s bollyhood ki ma **** rahy h	GEN
C7.2145	Amazing sir, Feminist irritate krti hai bewajah ki baate krke,	NGEN
C4.2134.2	**** mera sensible... Moral h vdo ka - don't take movies seriously... Just watch for entertainment purpose.... Hollywood v majority level pei chutiyapa hi dikhata h	GEN
C4.1356	Are Bhai agar Bollywood influence Ni krti real life mein to fir ye feminists ko problem Kyu hori h movie se? That clearly means Bollywood Jo khila ra h vo tum khare ho aur ye tumko Ni pachra h to ulti kree ho	NGEN

tokens like punctuation, html tags and stops words. For english dataset perform all steps of preprocessing whereas for Hindi we skip the process of lemmatization and stop words removal. As it is a Youtube based dataset, users tend to give comments in a casual and mixed format. For Hindi dataset which is a code-mixed of hindi and english languages and written form in roman script possesses a word that does not contribute to defining the sensitivity of texts. Such words are discarded under the preprocessing step using nlkt based stop word list. After it passes to the mentioned classifiers for identification purposes.

3.1 SVM

SVM follows a supervised manner applicable both in regression and classification. It has remained as a state-of-the-art model for classification methods. By generating the best possible hyper-plane among the classes. Hyper-planes act as the line of segregation among the classes. For this experiment, we consider SVM as the classifier and TF-IDF (Term frequency-inverse document frequency) as a feature extraction technique to perform misogynous text classification. This feature extraction technique does not maintain word order. Measures the relative values of a term (token) for a text within the entire corpus by giving the relative score.

Two types of input are used during the experiment - the TF-IDF scores that represents word level features and the bi-gram scores in the form of a matrix that represents word-sequence or phrase level information.

For both the cases, it starts with obtaining the frequency count and created a vocabulary size of 9338 and 14850, which contain all unique words for the English and Hindi datasets respectively. Out of which, we considered the top 500 words as `max_features` ordered based on term-frequency. In the first case, both the language words are trained with the TF-IDF score using the sklearn linear SVC of the SVM model and giving accuracy with 92% and 88% for the respective dataset. For the second case, the TF-IDF score of bi-gram is generated as a feature and trained with SVM result accuracy with 92% and 83% respectively. Table 3 tabulated the obtained result for SVM with TF-IDF and $N-gram$. The class column consists of GEN (comments, which are based on gender, misogynous class) and NGEN (comments, which are not based on gender, non-misogynous class) for both the languages.

Table 3. Accuracy of SVM with TF-IDF and N-gram

Class	TF-IDF			N-gram		
	Precision	Recall	F-score	Precision	Recall	F-score
Hindi.NGEN	0.89	0.97	0.93	0.83	0.96	0.89
Hindi.GEN	0.72	0.39	0.50	0.17	0.04	0.07
English.NGEN	0.94	0.99	0.96	0.92	1.00	0.96
English.GEN	0.59	0.23	0.33	0.00	0.00	0.00

3.2 LSTM

LSTM is a variation of Recurrent neural networks, consisting of unit cells for the accumulation of state information. The unit cell is operated using three gates which monitor the flow of information, namely i/p gate, o/p gate, and forget gate. For any new input, information to accumulate to the unit cell depends on the input gate activation. It can process input sequences with the utilization of internal memory. It can capture long term dependencies that help in the detection of misogynous text. Previous information on data can be ignored by activating forget gates through an activation function. Unlike, a one-way/one-directional approach to collect information, Bi-directional LSTM processes in both directions, forward and backward for input sequences with two hidden layers separately. Output of the forward and backward processing is combined together and transferred to the next hidden layer.

Few parameters are predefined before passing it to the model as shown in Table 4. It includes the vocab size of 5000, max_length as 100, and embedding dimension considered as 64. For the input tokens, words that are out of the vocabulary are assigned with special token OOV and padding done with max_length size. The sequential model is then generated with embedding as the first layer where it converts the words into meaningful vectors by taking vocabulary size with embedding dimension as 64 as its arguments. Then it is trained with LSTM with $ReLu$ as input activation function. Then adding a dense layer of 6 units and $softmax$ as the output activation function. Finally, the model is compiled with $sparse\_categorical\_crossentropy$ loss function which gives a good response over computation time and memory and also which gives a better result than binary_crossentropy and $Adam$ as an optimizer. And obtain accuracy scores with 93% and 84% for English and Hindi respectively.

Table 4. Predefined parameters of LSTM

Parameter	Value
Vocabulary size	5000
Max_length	100
Embedding dimension	64
input activation function	ReLu
output activation function	Softmax
Loss function	sparse_categorical_crossentropy
Optimizer	Adam

3.3   Bi-directional LSTM

Bidirectional LSTM is a promising model for text analysis [4]. We conduct classification for bidirectional LSTM with Keras having Tensorflow2.0 backbone for the above-mentioned dataset. Dataset is splitted into two sets in a ratio of `corpus_word_count * 0.8` for training and remaining for the testing, which results approximately 80% for training and 20% for the testing. These partition shows slight differences in the normal split performed in SVM (cf. Table 1). The model is trained with 5000 most common unique words, which is predefined as per the hyperparameters. As texts/comments are of not of equal length, padding with fixed size are used to make them equal. Normally the size can be set based on the maximum length of text for all training sets. For this experiment, the minimum word length for a cell is 2 and the max is 678. Considering this into account, the `max_length` is defined as 100 and padding is performed by adding zeros at the end. Hyperparameter is fitted to the sequential model. For each word, we store a single vector while embedding. Words which find similar meaning often have similar vectors. The LSTM layer with the bidirectional wrapper is used. ReLu activation function with 6 units of dense layer and softmax as output activation. For loss function we have used Sparse categorical cross-entropy, optimization function as ADAM, and train with 10 epochs. The model learns well with 0.64 loss with the first epoch and after 10 iteration decrease to 0.016 and resulting accuracy of 87% for the Hindi dataset and English with 93%.

3.4 LSTM with GloVe

Word embedding is a representation of words with dense vectors. Within a vector space, the word position is assigned with help of a word and its neighboring words. Using a pre-trained embedding model word embedding can be generated. For this experiment, we used `glove.6B.100d` as our pre-trained embedding module and embedding_matrix of length 10992 and 15204 for English and Hindi respectively. Study by Badjatiya et al. [5] showed that GloVe with classifiers for Hindi texts written using Roman script may be worth to adapt for the detection of hate speech. The reported accuracy is 85% and 93% for Hindi and English language respectively using GloVe over LSTM for this dataset. This also showed that despite Hindi based script and code-mixed nature using a single base language pretrained GloVe showed the positive outcome. For it, a sequential LSTM model with input as vocabulary and embedding dimension equal to 100 is passed. To decrease over-fitting we add a dropout layer of 20%. It is passed to a Keras LSTM having 64 units and dense of 6 units. The model is trained considering activation function as *softmax, sparse_categorical_crossentropy* as loss function and *Adam* Optimizer.

It is observed, in the model applying suitable features technique plays an important role in the classification method. With variation in features technique the best capability of the model differs. This experiment gives a strong point that besides linguistic knowledge as a feature and maintaining the originality of data by performing only basic need pre-processing phase. The model can still give a promising result for both the conventional and the long term short dependency model. With an accuracy of 82% to 93% as baseline accuracy for this TRAC dataset. The relative performance of the deep learning approaches for English and Hindi dataset with its accuracy graphs are shown in Fig. 2.

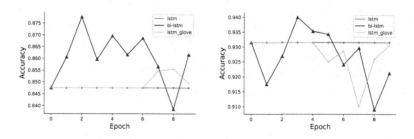

Fig. 2. LSTM variant accuracy graph for Hindi and English dataset

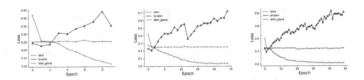

Fig. 3. Loss response of model over multiple epochs for English dataset

3.5   Performance Measure

The F-score is used for the accuracy evaluation. F-score is a known and widely used technique for binary classification. It is computed based on precision and recall for test data. Precision refers positive predictive value and is computed by considering instances of relevant retrieved. Whereas recall measures relevant instances retrieved. Considering each comment in the dataset as c_i with T as true labels set i.e misogynous and non-misogynous class and S define the predicted label set. The equation below 1 shows the used formula for the calculation of the F-score.

$$F - Score(c_i) = \frac{2P(c_i)R(c_i)}{(P(c_i) + R(c_i))} \tag{1}$$

where P = Precision, R = Recall

$$P(c_i) = \frac{|T \cap S|}{|S|} \tag{2}$$

$$R(c_i) = \frac{|T \cap S|}{|T|} \tag{3}$$

In view of deep learning approaches the shown Fig. 2 is based on 10 epochs. In order to select the best fit epoch size, this experiment also went through implementation of 10, 25 and 50 size epochs. Figure 3 explain the loss response of the model over an increase in epochs size for the English dataset. It shows that with increase in size of epochs the LSTM tends to show balanced response, Bi-LSTM clearly shows the negative impact and for LSTM with GloVe gives desirable response to it. Considering the learning effect in each epochs this experiment consider 10 as desirable for execution. Likewise for the Hindi dataset, with an increase in epoch size, the obtained loss and accuracy for both training and testing tend to decrease performances. With consideration, this experiment tends to deliver its implementation taking epochs size 10.

4   Analysis

The $F1$ score is tabulated in Table 3 for both feature extraction techniques of SVM. It is observed that for feature extraction, using TF-IDF with unigram shows better performances compared to bigram. Table 5 tabulated consolidated results for all the classifiers with label HIN for the Hindi dataset and ENG for the English dataset. Among the classifiers SVM with TF-IDF gives the highest accuracy for Hindi and the performance of the variant of LSTM is almost equal on the English dataset of which Bi-LSTM with embedding layer gives the highest accuracy with 93.4%.

Bi-LSTM is capable of capturing syntactic and semantic text features automatically. Learning information techniques in both sequences and direction of text help in making an effective opinion about the category. Moreover, it encodes dependencies between text for long sequences that provide good performance in terms of the prediction task. Having larger vocab results to assign rules to words with rare occurrences that may find useful for the class. As per the distribution of category, it is found that around 1/5 of the total train is a misogynous class only. Embedding methods consider hidden representation information which carries a strong pattern considering unnecessary information. Most comments comprise words less than 50 which also find it easy for the model to attend optimal conditions by obtaining high accuracy for both the language.

SVM follows different feature engineering techniques from embedding. Using TF-IDF as a feature extraction method creates a sparse vector with the weight of words normalizing it by numbers of occurrences. It violates word relationships among each other as TF-IDF makes use of all available words and gains information. This technique gives a good response for the Hindi dataset with a score of 87% running hand with Bi-LSTM. It shows using simple Bi-LSTM with embedding surpass for both the dataset securing the highest accuracy. The bidirectional information learning capability and its long-range dependency handling feature offer superior results for both the dataset. In the future, we aim to study intensity level of misogynous text which comes under sentiment analysis.

Table 5. Accuracy Score for different models

Approaches	Accuracy [HIN]	Accuracy [ENG]
SVM + TF-IDF	**0.871**	0.928
SVM + N-gram	0.831	0.923
LSTM	0.847	0.931
Bi-LSTM	**0.870**	**0.934**
LSTM + GloVe	0.853	0.933

5   Conclusion and Future Work

For this study, performed misogynous text classification with SVM and LSTM its variations for Hindi and English languages. We obtained approximately 87% accuracy for Hindi comments using SVM+TF-IDF and BiLSTM and 93% accuracy for English comments using BiLSTM and LSTM+GloVe. The obtained result is comparable to the state-of-the-art misogynous text classification. We have successfully applied SVM+TF-IDF and SVM+Bi-gram in word level to enhance the accuracy. We observed that despite a small and unbalanced dataset Bi-LSTM outperforms over all the variants of SVM and LSTM. We will further explore the misogynous text classification and intensity level detection by embedding linguistic features.

References

1. Aggarwal, C.C., Zhai, C.: A survey of text classification algorithms. In: Aggarwal, C., Zhai, C. (eds.) Mining Text Data. Springer, Boston (2012). https://doi.org/10.1007/978-1-4614-3223-4_6
2. Ahluwalia, R., Shcherbinina, E., Callow, E., Nascimento, A.C., De Cock, M.: Detecting misogynous tweets. In: IberEval@ SEPLN, pp. 242–248 (2018)
3. Altın, L.S.M., Bravo, A., Saggion, H.: LaSTUS/TALN at TRAC-2020 trolling, aggression and cyberbullying. In: Proceedings of the Second Workshop on Trolling, Aggression and Cyberbullying, pp. 83–86 (2020)
4. Arras, L., Montavon, G.G., Müller, K.R., Samek, W.: Explaining recurrent neural network predictions in sentiment analysis. arXiv preprint arXiv:1706.07206 (2017)
5. Badjatiya, P., Gupta, S., Gupta, M., Varma, V.: Deep learning for hate speech detection in tweets. In: Proceedings of the 26th International Conference on World Wide Web Companion, pp. 759–760 (2017)
6. Basile, V., et al.: SemEval-2019 task 5: multilingual detection of hate speech against immigrants and women in twitter. In: Proceedings of the 13th International Workshop on Semantic Evaluation, pp. 54–63 (2019)
7. Beltagy, I., Lo, K., Cohan, A.: SciBERT: a pretrained language model for scientific text. In: Proceedings of the 2019 Conference on Empirical Methods in Natural Language Processing and the 9th International Joint Conference on Natural Language Processing (EMNLP-IJCNLP), pp. 3606–3611 (2019)
8. Bhattacharya, S., et al.: Developing a multilingual annotated corpus of misogyny and aggression. arXiv preprint arXiv:2003.07428 (2020)
9. Bhattacharya, S., et al.: Developing a multilingual annotated corpus of misogyny and aggression. In: Proceedings of the Second Workshop on Trolling, Aggression and Cyberbullying, pp. 158–168. European Language Resources Association (ELRA), Marseille (May 2020). https://www.aclweb.org/anthology/2020.trac2-1.25
10. Charton, E., Meurs, M.J., Jean-Louis, L., Gagnon, M.: Using collaborative tagging for text classification: from text classification to opinion mining. In: Informatics, vol. 1, pp. 32–51. Multidisciplinary Digital Publishing Institute (2014)
11. Chekuri, C., Goldwasser, M.H., Raghavan, P., Upfal, E.: Web search using automatic classification. In: Proceedings of the Sixth International Conference on the World Wide Web (1997)
12. Conneau, A., Schwenk, H., Barrault, L., Lecun, Y.: Very deep convolutional networks for text classification. In: Proceedings of the 15th Conference of the European Chapter of the Association for Computational Linguistics, Long Papers, vol. 1, pp. 1107–1116 (2017)
13. Corazza, M., Menini, S., Cabrio, E., Tonelli, S., Villata, S.: A multilingual evaluation for online hate speech detection. ACM Trans. Internet Technol. (TOIT) **20**(2), 1–22 (2020)

14. Das, A., Gambäck, B.: Code-mixing in social media text: the last language identification frontier? (2015)
15. Davidson, T., Warmsley, D., Macy, M., Weber, I.: Automated hate speech detection and the problem of offensive language. In: Eleventh International AAAI Conference on Web and Social Media (2017)
16. Devi, M.D., Saharia, N.: Learning adaptable approach to classify sentiment with incremental datasets. Procedia Comput. Sci. **171**, 2426–2434 (2020)
17. Fan, R.E., Chang, K.W., Hsieh, C.J., Wang, X.R., Lin, C.J.: LIBLINEAR: a library for large linear classification. J. Mach. Learn. Res. **9**, 1871–1874 (2008)
18. Frenda, S., Ghanem, B., Montes-y Gómez, M., Rosso, P.: Online hate speech against women: automatic identification of misogyny and sexism on Twitter. J. Intell. Fuzzy Syst. **36**(5), 4743–4752 (2019)
19. Goenaga, I., et al.: Automatic misogyny identification using neural networks. In: IberEval@ SEPLN, pp. 249–254 (2018)
20. Joulin, A., Grave, É., Bojanowski, P., Mikolov, T.: Bag of tricks for efficient text classification. In: Proceedings of the 15th Conference of the European Chapter of the Association for Computational Linguistics, Short Papers, vol. 2, pp. 427–431 (2017)
21. Kim, J.: User-generated content (UGC) revolution?: critique of the promise of Youtube. Ph.D. thesis, University of Iowa (2010)
22. Kim, J.: # iamafeminist as the "mother tag": feminist identification and activism against misogyny on Twitter in South Korea. Fem. Media Stud. **17**(5), 804–820 (2017)
23. Kim, Y., Nam, T.: An efficient text filter for adult web documents. In: 2006 8th International Conference Advanced Communication Technology, vol. 1, pp. 3-pp. IEEE (2006)
24. Liu, H., Chiroma, F., Cocea, M.: Identification and classification of misogynous tweets using multi-classifier fusion. In: IberEval@ SEPLN, pp. 268–273 (2018)
25. Lynn, T., Endo, P.T., Rosati, P., Silva, I., Santos, G.L., Ging, D.: A comparison of machine learning approaches for detecting misogynistic speech in urban dictionary. In: 2019 International Conference on Cyber Situational Awareness, Data Analytics And Assessment (CyberSA), pp. 1–8. IEEE (2019)
26. MacAvaney, S., Yao, H.R., Yang, E., Russell, K., Goharian, N., Frieder, O.: Hate speech detection: challenges and solutions. PloS One **14**(8), e0221152 (2019)
27. Mullany, L., Trickett, L.: Misogyny hate crime evaluation report (2018)
28. Percannella, G., Sorrentino, D., Vento, M.: Automatic indexing of news videos through text classification techniques. In: Singh, S., Singh, M., Apte, C., Perner, P. (eds.) ICAPR 2005. LNCS, vol. 3687, pp. 512–521. Springer, Heidelberg (2005). https://doi.org/10.1007/11552499_57
29. Saharia, N.: Phone-based identification of language in code-mixed social network data. J. Stat. Manag. Syst. **20**(4), 565–574 (2017)
30. Schmidt, S., Schnitzer, S., Rensing, C.: Text classification based filters for a domain-specific search engine. Comput. Ind. **78**, 70–79 (2016)
31. Shushkevich, E., Cardiff, J.: Automatic misogyny detection in social media: a survey. Computación y Sistemas **23**(4) (2019)
32. Teodorescu, H.N., Saharia, N.: An internet slang annotated dictionary and its use in assessing message attitude and sentiments. In: 2015 International Conference on Speech Technology and Human-Computer Dialogue (SpeD), pp. 1–8. IEEE (2015)
33. Teodorescu, H.N., Saharia, N.: A semantic analyzer for detecting attitudes on SNs. In: 2016 International Conference on Communications (COMM), pp. 47–50. IEEE (2016)

34. Waseem, Z., Hovy, D.: Hateful symbols or hateful people? Predictive features for hate speech detection on Twitter. In: Proceedings of the NAACL Student Research Workshop, pp. 88–93 (2016)
35. Wiegand, M., Ruppenhofer, J., Kleinbauer, T.: Detection of abusive language: the problem of biased datasets. In: Proceedings of the 2019 Conference of the North American Chapter of the Association for Computational Linguistics: Human Language Technologies (Long and Short Papers), vol. 1, pp. 602–608 (2019)
36. Yao, M., Chelmis, C., Zois, D.S.: Cyberbullying ends here: towards robust detection of cyberbullying in social media. In: The World Wide Web Conference, pp. 3427–3433 (2019)

Active Learning Enhanced Sequence Labeling for Aspect Term Extraction in Review Data

K. Shyam Sundar$^{(\boxtimes)}$ and Deepa Gupta

Department of Computer Science and Engineering, Amrita School of Engineering, Bengaluru,
Amrita Vishwa Vidyapeetham, Bengaluru, India
sundarshyam030@gmail.com, g_deepa@blr.amrita.edu

Abstract. Analyzing reviews with respect to each aspect gives better understanding as compared to overall opinions and this requires the aspect terms and their corresponding opinions to be extracted. Supervised models for aspect term extraction require large amount of labeled data. Aspect annotated data is scarcely available for use and the cost of manual annotation of the entire data is huge. This study proposes a way of using Active Learning to select a highly informative subset of the data that needs to be labeled, to train the supervised model. The identification of aspect terms is defined as a sequence labelling problem with the help of BiLSTM network and CRF. The model is trained on publicly available SemEval (2014–16) datasets for restaurant and laptop reviews. The results show a 36% and 42% reduction in annotation cost for restaurants and laptops respectively, with negligible effect on the model's performance. A significant difference in cost is observed between active learning guided sampling and random sampling approaches.

Keywords: Active learning · Reinforcement learning · Actor-critic · WMD

1 Introduction

A review is an evaluation provided by the user or a critic based on their opinion. A review usually consists of several lines of text (review) and a numerical evaluation (rating). It tells us how good a product or a service is received by its customers. A survey in 2014 by Myles Anderson showed that 88% of the consumers trust online reviews as much as personal recommendations [1]. Thus, these reviews have high impact on the business. Usually, a company will gather these reviews analyze them together to extract useful information. In order to understand the impact of the product or service with respect to different consumers, we need to perform the analysis on the actual review. This requires extracting of features from the reviews and analyzing the opinions (sentiment) on each feature individually. This process is called Aspect Term Extraction (ATE) [2]. The aspect term refers to the feature present in the review, *i.e.*, the characteristic of the product on which the review provides information. For example, in the review *"The phone has a good resolution but has a very short battery life."*, the terms *"phone"*, *"resolution"* and *"battery life"* are the aspect terms. The aspect term *"resolution"* has a positive

© Springer Nature Singapore Pte Ltd. 2021
D. Garg et al. (Eds.): IACC 2020, CCIS 1367, pp. 349–361, 2021.
https://doi.org/10.1007/978-981-16-0401-0_27

connotation whereas the aspect term *"battery life"* has a negative connotation. The term *"phone"*, on the other hand, has contradictory connation.

In Machine Leaning, supervised models are preferred over unsupervised or rule-based models [3]. This is because there is not specific way of identifying where and in what form is an aspect term present in the sentence. Hence without a target value for the algorithm (unsupervised), the labeling of these aspects will become more difficult. Hence, supervised models which have a specific goal provides a better solution. But the training data required by a supervised model is very high. If we can reduce the amount of training data to be annotated by the user, we can attain a significant cost reduction in model the problem. One way to overcome this is sampling the dataset which reduces the load. But we have no way to identify whether the resulting sample of data is good enough for training the model. This arises the need to identify the usefulness of each record in the resulting sample. Active Learning (AL) provides a solution for this problem. Active Learning is the process in which a highly informative subset of the data is chosen among the entire dataset such that the resulting subset can act as a representative of the original dataset [4]. Active Learning is also known as machine learning with a human in the loop. This is because the model actively queries the user whether a particular sample is to be kept in the final dataset or discarded. This human in the loop is also highly prone to errors and will be biased towards his opinions. But having more than one human to normalize this problem defeats the purpose of reducing labor cost. A possible solution is by automating the active learning process using Reinforcement Learning. Reinforcement Learning (RL) is a process in which a sequence of actions is taken so that reward obtained in following that sequence is maximized [5]. We use a Reinforcement Learning environment as a substitute for the human in the loop to reduce any possible error and reduce the decision making faster and more efficient.

The rest of the article is organized as follows—Sect. 2 provides an outlook on different researches and theories put forth related to this study. Section 3 provides a description of the dataset used in the study. Section 4 describes the proposed architecture and Sect. 5 presents the experimental results. Section 6 presents the conclusion and possible future approaches to the problem.

2 Literature Review

2.1 Aspect Term Extraction (Sequence Labelling)

Machine Learning vs Deep Learning for ATE

Sentiment analysis is a process that is highly dependent on the opinions and responses provided by the consumers. The range and diversity of the consumer base varies from product to product. Hence, the reviews provided by different types of people will be different whether in terms of language, veracity or the depth of information. This implies that the data gathered from these reviews are not consistent with each other, nor are they all good enough to be considered a sample. Extracting aspect term from one of these sentences will be completely different from extracting from another sentence and Machine Learning algorithms have difficulty in processing the data when it contains highly inconsistent features [6]. This problem has been efficiently overcome when Deep

Neural Networks (DNNs) were introduced. Studies in the field of aspect term extraction have provided significant contribution to the society. A variety of approaches have been introduced for extracting sequences from textual data like Conditional Random Field, Autoencoders, Bi-LSTM, etc. Some models incorporate a hybrid approach by using more than one model in sequence, to attain better results.

Unsupervised and Semi-supervised Approaches
With the scarcity of labeled data available for train supervised models, Bagheri et al. [7] proposes an unsupervised approach for detection of aspect terms for sentiment analysis. The model contains a generalized method for detecting multi-worded aspects followed by a set of heuristic rules and a metric (A-Score Metric) based on mutual information and aspect frequency. The model is tested on dataset mention in [8], which contains reviews on different electronic products. The proposed model has a dramatic increase in accuracy of 13.9% as compared to standard MEM and other models. Other studies in the area put forth hybrid theories by using a combination of models to make up for the uncertainty in labeling text sequence with unsupervised models. Studies like [9] and [10] proposes using Attention Model, for dealing with aspect term recognition. The study in [11] uses multiple Word-Embedding method to support cross domain aspect term extraction. The study in [12] uses Bidirectional Long Short-Term Memory network and Conditional Random Field in an unsupervised manner. Semi supervised approach like in [13], have also been tried in this field, where the solution is modeled using variational autoencoders.

Supervised Approaches
Some studies, despite the lack of training data available, are opting for supervised approach in the case of text analysis tasks like sentiment analysis, aspect term extraction, named entity recognition, etc. This is because supervised models are better at making decisions as compared to unsupervised models [14], in this case, deciding whether a term in aspect or not. Xiang *et al.* [15] proposes model using CRF and Multi Feature Embedding (MFE). The model is compared with standard CRF approaches as base line and shows good improvement as compared to the latter. The study by Li *et al.* [16], uses history attention and selective transformation that exploits opinion summary and aspect detection history for better decision-making purpose. It contains a Truncated History Attention (THA) module and a Selective Transformation Network (STN) module for capturing aspect detection history and opinion summary respectively. The model achieved 5.0%, 1.6%, 1.4% and 1.3% gain in F1 score for Laptop-2014, Restaurant-2014, Restaurant -2015 and Restaurant-2016 respectively as compared to standard CRF baselines. Studies in [17–23] also use a supervised approach with different supporting features like Convolution Neural Networks, rule-based approach or alternate gated neural networks, etc.

2.2 Active Learning Strategies in Different Domains

The above studies have clearly established the lack of aspect-annotated reviews. Similarly, in other domains, there exist cases like this where there is a scarcity in labelled data. To overcome this problem, Active Learning strategies have emerged in recent years that provide a solution by reducing the amount of data that needs to manually annotated in the dataset. The study by Viet-Vu et al. [4], proposes a semi-supervised KNN graph structure with Active Learning to select the samples. The approach aims to identify interesting dense regions in the data space using constrained clustering approach. The results show that the S-kNN-G model, that is proposed, show better results as compared to previous models (5–7% increase over different datasets). Karthik et al. in [24], proposed an improvement in the application of RL by collecting external evidence in the design of information extraction systems. The results of the proposed architecture are 11.4% more accurate than the existing Maxent and NumKilled extractors that operate on the same datasets. Studies in [25–28] also provide few approaches on using Active Learning in the field of Natural Language Processing like Named Entity Recognition, Text Classification and other fields.

Research Purpose
Over the years, the concept of Active Learning has been used in different fields of research like medical research, image analysis and in different fields of Natura Language Processing like Named Entity Recognition, semantic segmentation, etc. In the case of Aspect Term Extraction for review data, few have tried to tackle the problem of scarcity in aspect labeled dataset. In this study we propose an automated Active Learning strategy with the help of Reinforcement Learning to overcome this problem. This study helps to identify instances of an unlabeled dataset that are highly informative that can be labeled to aid the supervised models, thereby reducing the cost and time spent on creating a suitable annotated dataset. This study uses a Bidirectional Long Short-Term Memory Network (Bi-LSTM) coupled with Conditional Random Fields (CRF) for sequence labeling model and Self Attention RNN for Active Learning agent.

3   Data Description

The data used is taken from SemEval ABSA task [16], 2014–16 for laptops and restaurants. The data contains reviews that are split into individual sentences. In each sentence, the aspect words are annotated with their corresponding opinions. The sequence labeling model is evaluated only on 2014 datasets for restaurants and laptops as laptop data is not labeled in the 2015 and 2016 datasets. This is to provide a fair comparison of our model with respect to varying aspect terms. The datasets consist of reviews split into individual sentences with each aspect term tagged separately.

4   Proposed Architecture

The purpose of this study is to tackle the problem of having scarce amount of labelled training data available for sequence labeling task. So, we propose an Active Learning strategy that is able to work on unlabeled dataset, *i.e.*, an unsupervised sample selection process. This means that there is no target for the agent to aim for. So, we provide a starting point for the agent to work from, to optimize the agent for selection of samples, that are useful for the sequence labeling model. We propose a three phased architecture to achieve this purpose. Figure 1 represents the overview of the Active Learning enhanced Sequence Labeling process. The proposed architecture comprises of the following phases:

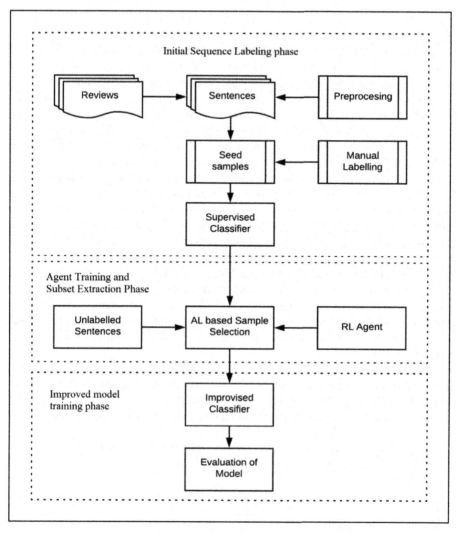

Fig. 1. Proposed architecture

1. Initial sequence labeling
2. Agent *training and subset* extraction.
3. Improved model training.

4.1 Phase 1: Initial Sequence Labelling Phase

Sequence Labeling Architecture

Deep Neural Networks do not work with data in their raw format. Instead they work on numerical vector representation of the data. This enables the model to work on datasets that are inconsistent in nature, that contain missing data or any other form of discrepancies [29]. They can also extract implicit features present in the data during the training process and discover the structure of huge datasets with the help of their backpropagation process [30]. A type of neural networks called Recurrent Neural Networks (RNNs) have shown better performance when dealing with textual data which are mostly sequential. This is because RNNs are neural networks with a memory. They are able to retain information for a certain number of instances which make it easier when dealing with sequential data (sentences → sequence of words). But as we increase the size of memory, it encounters the vanishing gradient problem thus significantly affecting the training process. Hence RNNs, though use for processing sequences, are not suitable for processing longer sequences, *e.g.*, reviews [31]. To overcome the problem of vanishing gradients, the Long Short-Term Memory (LSTM) network was introduced. LSTM is modified version of the RNN with additional control signals. This helps to control the network by only remembering only significant terms in a sequence and discarding the rest, reducing the load on the memory and the probability of encountering a vanishing gradient [32]. Since we are dealing with not only aspects that contains a single term but also multiple terms, we use the Bidirectional Long Short-Term Memory (Bi-LSTM) network for processing the text. BiLSTM is useful in this case because, it retains information on past and future instances, since the network runs from both sides (input and output). This provides additional context information that can assist the labeling process. Once the features are chosen by the BiLSTM network, they are passed to the Conditional Random Field (CRF) annotator.

Since the Bi-LSTM network uses vector representation of the data, we have used GloVe word vector representation for the words. It is available in four different embeddings sizes—50, 100, 200 and 300. The end result of the sequence labeling model is that each term in the sentence according to BIO tagging method where the labels is:

1. **B**—Beginning (Single word aspect / initial word of a multi word aspect)
2. **I**—Inside (Remaining words of a multi word aspect)
3. **O**—Outside (Non aspect terms).

Initial Sequence Labeling Task

To provide a starting point of the agent, we create a **seed model** of the sequence labeling model. This seed model is trained on small random sample set and the final state of this seed model is fed to the active learning agent as its initial state. This is to make sure that the active learning agent is able to select informative subset that is optimal to the sequence labeling task. Here, the final state represents the weight matrix of the Bi-LSTM network obtained at the end of the last epoch.

4.2 Phase 2: Agent Training and Subset Extraction Phase

Active Learning for Sample Selection

The idea of active learning is that the machine learning model can achieve better results with lesser effort if the model is allowed to choose the data from which it learns [33]. The active learner poses a *query* in the form of unlabeled instances of the data, and the *oracle* (usually a human annotator), provides decision making support to keep or discard the instance, and then label the required set of instances. Active learning is good motivation in fields where there is an abundance in raw data, but scarcity in labeled ones. In this study we use an approach called multiple instance Active Learning [34], where the quality of the instances is judged in groups of instances (bags) instead of individual instances. In this method, several different bags with differing number of instances is formed and the bag with the best set of instances is selected to be annotated. The reason for using this is that, the model is going to learning unsupervised, and grouping the instances will give the model an idea on what to compare to aid in the decision-making process.

Reinforcement Learning for Automating Active Learning

Any decision-making process can be defined as a Reinforcement Learning (RL) problem [6]. The decision making of the Active Learning process involves a human in the loop, which leads to an increase in latency of decision-making process and increase in error prone or biased decisions. But this can be defined as a Reinforcement Learning problem in which the decision-making can be redefined as a Markov Decision Process (MDP).

An MDP requires that the future state depends only on the current state. Since the method of multiple instance active learning works on the basis of bags of instances, during the process of adding instances to the bag, the MDP can decide whether the next instance is to be added or discarded based on the current state of the bag. This decision is based on a rewards system where the RL model tries to maximize this reward, *i.e.*, if a new instance is to picked into the bag, the effect produce should be an increase in the reward after adding the instance into the bag. If there is a decrease in the reward, the corresponding instance is then discarded from the bag. Hence, the final set of instances in the bag will be the most suitable set of samples for training the sequence labeling model since the active learning model is initialize with the internal state of a sequence labeling model.

Actor-Critic Model with Self Attention RNN

Monte Carlo approach to an MDP is not suitable because of its high entropic nature and having a high estimated variance. This will cripple our model because, having a high variance will result in a bad decision-making process. Monte Carlo approach also calculates the reward at the end of each episode, since it assumes that the output is dependent on all the instances. This is disadvantageous for our model, because we need to make decisions for each of instances instantly. The Actor Critic model [35] over comes this by employing two different components—the *Actor*, or the policy gradient function; and the *Critic*, the advantage function (*e.g.*, Q value). This allows the actor critic to be more efficient by allowing learning updates at each step instead of each episode, because the values of the actor and critic are dependent only on the current state and the next state, *i.e.*, they will only depend upon the current state of the bag and the state of the upcoming instance. The actor critic agent is implemented as a Self-Attention RNN [14]. It is represented as a tuple (S, A, R) where,

1. S—The current state of the agent
2. A—The possible set of actions
3. R—The calculated reward.

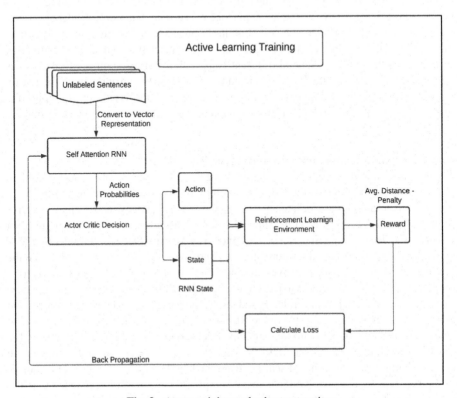

Fig. 2. Agent training and subset extraction

Agent Training and Subset Extraction

Figure 2 shows the active learning process used to extract the samples. For each instance, the actor critic is presented with possible actions—**0**, add instance to the bag; **1**, discard instance; and **2**, end episode (replace the bag of instances). Two different outputs are extracted after each step. The first output is in the form of [1 × 3] vector, where each unit determines the probability of the action to be taken. The second output is the value (Q-value) derived from the action probabilities through linear compression. The reward is calculated after every action is taken by the agent. The reward is dependent on two values—the average distance between each instance in the bag, and the size of the bag. The distance is calculate using the Word Mover Distance method [36]. The reward takes a positive effect from the distances, with the assumption that a set of instances that are far away from each other will probably contain information that are exclusive to that instance. The size of the bag negatively affects the reward because, in the end we are trying to minimize the training cost by reducing the required amount of training data. After each step, the loss is calculated based on the state value, action and reward of that particular instance and it is back-propagated to the network. This process is repeated for a fixed number of epochs over the given dataset to improve the agent. Thus, the agent learns over a period to include only better documents. Once the agent is trained, the support data is passed through the agent model, from which the list of most informative records is extracted used to extract informative samples.

4.3 Phase 3: Improved Model Training Phase

The sample set chosen by the active learning agent is added to the initial seed set, the sequence labeling model is retrained. The loss is calculated as the difference between the Viterbi path score (predicted labels) and score of the Gold Standard path (actual labels). The loss is non-negative and zero when the labeling is correct. The training is continued until an acceptable loss value is reached. The model is also compared with a model trained on randomly selected samples instead of Active learning guided sampling. The comparison is made after taking an average of 10 repetitions to normalize the entropy of the randomly selected samples. The model is then used on the test dataset and the results are evaluated using F1-score because it provides equal importance to precision and recall values and also helps in dealing with class imbalance in the dataset.

5 Experimental Results

Four different models are created for restaurant and laptop datasets respectively, using the different embedding (word vector) sizes available. Higher embedding size implies more amount of context information present in the vector. This helps to identify the optimal amount of contextual information that is sufficient can aid in the sequence labeling task. Too much context information can also confuse the model because of the number of dimensions required to be processed. The four models in each case are compared for better understanding of this process.

The seed model is set to trained on the seed set, which contains 10% of the training data selected using random sampling. The remainder of the 90% is named as the support data from which the agent extracts the informative samples. The initial seed can also be created manually, and not selected from the dataset, or selecting using some rules. Table 1 provides the data distribution after the seed-support split after cleaning the data and removing empty sentences.

Table 1. Seed-support data split

Domain	Data distribution		
	Seed data (10%)	Support data (90%)	Total (100%)
Restaurant (2014)	303	2736	3039
Laptop (2014)	304	2738	3042

Once the seed set is selected, the seed model is created and trained over the seed set for 10 epochs. At the end of the last epoch, the hidden state weight matrix of the Bi-LSTM network is stored (seed state). The seed state of the model is used to initialize the Self Attention network in the agent. The combined data of 2015 and 2016 datasets have been taken for training the agent. Each sentence in the agent data is passed through the network which provides the probability distribution for the actions and the state value. The reward is calculated followed by the loss and backpropagation. If the action taken is 2 (reset the bag), the episode is stopped and the state of the network is reinitialized to the seed state. This helps to keep the objective of the agent to select samples useful for the sequence labeling task. This process is then repeated over 10000 iterations (can be stopped at a suitable time based on the loss value).

Table 2. F1-scores for model with active learning based sampling and random sampling

Domain	Test data	Embed size	Results (F1-Scores) in %	
			Model with AL based sampling	Model with Random sampling
Restaurant	800	50	86.19	84.79
		100	89.25	88.95
		200	89.13	87.54
		300	**90.23**	88.24
Laptop	800	50	87.91	86.65
		100	89.01	89.45
		200	89.83	87.93
		300	**89.81**	88.33

Once trained, the agent is passed over the support dataset. This time, the agent is passed repeatedly for the number of instances present in the support data. This is to ensure a fair probability for each instance to be chosen into the bag. The difference in the subset extraction process is that, the agent is not reinitialized to the when the action taken is 2. Instead the bag containing the documents is carried forward to further episodes. Table 3 shows the number of samples selected for each model by the agent.

After the training data is finalized the proposed model is created and trained. Subsequently, the model on randomly selected samples is also trained. Each model is then used on the test dataset and evaluated. Table 2 lists the corresponding F1-scores of the models.

From the table, we can see the difference between the models where data is chosen randomly or using Active learning agent. The results of random model is obtained by averaging results of 10 iterations to normalize the entropy. Hence, we need at least 10 times the cost for training with random sampling as compared to Active Leaning method to attain similar results. The best results for both domains are obtained using GloVe 300 vectors with a cost reduction of 36.26% and 42.14% for restaurants and laptops respectively. Compared to the model trained on the complete dataset, there is a maximum of ~3% drop in F1 across all the models which is an acceptable loss. Table 3 shows the improvement obtained in our study as compared to previous researches done on Asepect Term Extraction.

Table 3. Comparison of F1-scores on aspect term extraction with previous models

Model	Results (F1-scores) in %	
	Restaurants	Laptops
CRF1 [16] (2018)	79.72	72.77
CRF2 [16] (2018)	82.33	74.01
HTSA [16] (2018)	85.61	79.52
CRF3 [15] (2018)	84.33	76.53
Wo-BiLSTM-CRF [22] (2019)	84.97	81.08
WoCh-BiLSTM-CRF [22] (2019)	86.05	79.21
Proposed model (Active Learning + BiLSTM-CRF)	**90.23**	**89.81**

6 Conclusion and Future Work

Active Learning based selection of training samples is has proved to be a better method as compared to random sampling. Using Reinforcement Learning to automate the Active Learning process has shown its usefulness in terms of training time. The use of DNNs for labeling with the help of word embeddings eliminates the problem of encountering unseen words during the testing process and eliminated the need for feature selection. The Active Learning strategy aims to reduce the amount of data required to train a model, thereby reducing the cost and time taken. This scalability also accounts to the advantages of using Active Learning to select training samples. Active Learning does not require labeled datasets. Hence, an agent can be easily trained over the abundance of unlabeled data available for use. With sufficient amount of data, the agent will be able to select the best set of samples required to labeled for any kind of process. We have achieved a total of 4.18% and 8.73% increase in F1-scores for restaurants and laptops respectively, compared to the best results achieved so far in this field. The performance of the Active Learning aided model is constantly better that the random sampled model in all cases.

The model can be further enhanced by using target specific embeddings instead of pre-trained models like Glove. This ensures better transformation of words into vectors such that the vectors contain context information with respect to that specific domain. Active Learning can also be generalized to an entire domain on which the agent is trained. An agent trained over a single dataset can be used on any similar datasets within the same context. A cross agent analysis with different data on same domain can done. Multiple instance active learning has been used in this study. Branching to other strategies can be considered based on what kind of model will be used on the sampled dataset.

References

1. Search Engine Land. https://searchengineland.com/88-consumers-trust-online-reviews-much-personal-recommendations-195803. Accessed 14 July 2017
2. Pavlopoulos, J., Androustsopoulos, I.: Aspect term extraction for sentiment analysis: new datasets, new evaluation measures and improved unsupervised method. In: Proceedings of the 5th Workshop on Language Analysis for Social Media, pp. 44–52. Association for Computational Linguistics, Gothenburg (2014)
3. Kholgi, M.: Active learning for concept extraction from clinical free text. Ph.D. thesis, Queensland University of Technology (2017)
4. Vu, V., Labroche, N.: Active seed selection for constrained clustering. Intell. Syst. **21**, 537–552 (2017)
5. Ishwaran, H., et al.: Random survival forests. Ann. Appl. Stat. **2**(3), 841–860 (2008)
6. Sutton, R.S., Barto, A.G.: Reinforcement Learning, 2nd edn. MIT Press, London (2018)
7. Bagheri, A., Saraee, M., de Jong, F.: An unsupervised aspect detection model for sentiment analysis of reviews. In: Métais, E., Meziane, F., Saraee, M., Sugumaran, V., Vadera, S. (eds.) NLDB 2013. LNCS, vol. 7934, pp. 140–151. Springer, Heidelberg (2013). https://doi.org/10.1007/978-3-642-38824-8_12
8. Liu, B., Hu, M.: Opinion mining, sentiment analysis, and opinion spam detection dataset (2004)
9. He, R., Lee, W.S., Ng, H.T., Dahlmeier, D.: An unsupervised neural attention model for aspect extraction. In: Proceedings of the 55th Annual Meeting of the Association for Computational Linguistics, ACL, Vancouver, pp. 388–397 (2017)
10. Luo, L., et al.: Unsupervised neural aspect extraction with sememes. In: Proceedings of the 28th International Joint Conference on Artificial Intelligence, IJCAI, Macao, China, pp. 5123–5129 (2019)
11. Chauhan, G.S., et al.: An unsupervised multiple word-embedding method with attention model for cross domain aspect term extraction. In: 3rd International Conference on Emerging Technologies in Computer Engineering, pp. 110–116. IEEE, Jaipur (2020)
12. Giannakopoulos, A., et al.: Unsupervised aspect term extraction with Bi-LSTM & CRF using automatically labeled datasets. In: Proceedings of the 8th Workshop on Computational Approaches to Subjectivity, Sentiment and Social Media Analysis, pp. 180–188. Association for Computational Linguistics, Copenhagen (2017)
13. Fu, X., et al.: Semi-supervised aspect-level sentiment classification model based on variational autoencoder. Knowl. Based Syst. **171**, 81–92 (2019)
14. Tandra, S., Nautiyal, A., Gupta, D.: An efficient text labeling framework using active learning model. In: Thampi, S.M. (ed.) Intelligent Systems, Technologies and Applications. AISC, vol. 1148, pp. 141–155. Springer, Singapore (2020). https://doi.org/10.1007/978-981-15-3914-5_11
15. Xiang, Y., He, H., Zheng, J.: Aspect term extraction based on MFE-CRF. Information **9**, 198 (2018)
16. Li, X., et al.: Aspect term extraction with history attention and selective transformation. In: Proceedings of 27th International Joint Conference on Artificial Intelligence, IJCAI, Stockholm, Sweden, pp. 4194–4200 (2018)
17. Dalal, H., Gao, G.: Aspect extraction from reviews using conditional random fields. In: The Sixth International Conference on Data Analytics, pp. 158–167, Data Analytics, Barcelona, Spain (2015)
18. Cahyadi, A., Khodra, M.L.: Aspect-based sentiment analysis using convolution neural networks and bidirectional long short-term memory. In: Proceedings of the 5th International Conference on Advanced Informatics: Concept Theory and Applications, pp. 124–129. IEEE, Krabi (2018)

19. Dai, H.L., Song, Y.Q.: Neural aspect and opinion term extraction with mined rules as weak supervision. In: Proceedings of the 57th Annual Meeting of Association for Computational Linguistics, ACL, Florence, Italy, pp. 5268–5277 (2019)
20. Query ID="Q4" Text="Kindly provide the page range for Ref. [20], if possible." Ray, P., Chakrabarti, A.: A mixed approach of deep learning method and rule-based method to improve aspect level sentiment analysis. Appl. Comput. Inform. 15(1) (2019)
21. Ning, L., Bo, S.: Aspect-based sentiment analysis with gated alternate neural network. Knowl.-Based Syst. 188, 105010 (2019)
22. Augustyniak, L., Kajdanowicz, T., Kazienko, P.: Comprehensive analysis of aspect term extraction methods using various text embeddings. arXiv (2019)
23. Venugopalan, M., Gupta, D.: An unsupervised hierarchical rule based model for aspect term extraction augmented with pruning strategies. Procedia Comput. Sci. 171, 22–31 (2020)
24. Narasimhan, K., Yala, A., Barzilay, R.: Improving information extraction by acquiring external evidence with reinforcement learning. In: Proceedings of the 2016 Conference on Empirical Methods in Natural Language Processing, pp. 2355–2365. ACL, Austin (2016)
25. Meng, F., Yuan, L., Cohn, T.: Learning how to active learn: a deep reinforcement learning approach. In: Proceedings of the 2017 Conference on Empirical Methods in Natural Language Processing, pp. 595–605. ACL, Copenhagen (2017)
26. Diligach, D., Palmer, M.: Good seed makes a good crop: accelerating active learning using language modelling. In: Proceedings of 49th Annual Meeting of the Association of Computational Linguistics, pp. 6–10. ACM, Portland (2011)
27. Chairi, I., Alaoui, S., Lyhyaouier, A.: Sample selection based active learning for imbalanced data. In: Proceedings of the 10th International Conference on Signal-Image Technology & Internet-Based Systems, pp. 645–651. IEEE, Marrakech (2014)
28. Yang, B., et al.: Effective multi-label active learning for text classification. In: Proceedings of the 15th ACM SIGKDD International Conference on Knowledge Discovery and Data Mining, pp. 917–926. ACM, Paris (2009)
29. Li, H.: Deep learning for natural language processing: advantages and challenges. Natl. Sci. Rev. 5(1), 24–26 (2017)
30. Wick, C.: Deep learning. Informatik-Spektrum 40(1), 103–107 (2016). https://doi.org/10.1007/s00287-016-1013-2
31. Sherstinsky, A.: Fundamentals of recurrent neural network (RNN) and long short-term memory (LSTM) network. Phys. D: Nonlinear Phenom. 404, 132306 (2020)
32. Greff, K., et al.: LSTM: a search space odessy. IEEE Trans. Neural Netw. Learn. Syst. 28(10), 2222–2232 (2017)
33. Settles, B.: Active learning literature survey. Computer Sciences Technical Report 1648. University of Wisconsin–Madison (2009)
34. Settles, B., Craven, M., Ray, S.: Multiple-instance active learning. In: Proceedings of the 20th International Conference on Neural Information Processing Systems, pp. 1289–1296. Curran Associated Inc., Red Hook (2007)
35. Understanding Actor Critic Methods and A2C. https://towardsdatascience.com/understanding-actor-critic-methods-931b97b6df3f. Accessed 16 Feb 2019
36. Word Mover's Distance for Text Similarity. https://towardsdatascience.com/word-movers-distance-for-text-similarity-7492aeca71b0. Accessed 26 Aug 2019

Using Different Neural Network Architectures for Interesting Applications

Intuitive Feature Engineering and Machine Learning Performance Improvement in the Banking Domain

S. Teja$^{(\boxtimes)}$ ⓘ, B. Chandrashekhar, Eswar Reddy, Hrishikesh Jha,
K. Nageswara, Mathew Joseph, Jaideep Matto, and Richard K. Bururu

Centre of Advanced Analytics and Training (CATD) Bangalore, CIMB Bank,
Bengaluru, India
tejas.nitr@gmail.com

Abstract. Performance tuning of the machine learning models is very important, especially in the banking domain. In line with the new age, they are moving away from their conventional methods to target customers for credit cards, loans, etc. products. The transactional data, customer information, which was collected over the years, have a huge scope of applying data mining techniques to extract useful information for maximizing the return on investment, cost optimization and fraud detection. For a successful deployment of a machine learning model multiple out of time validations are performed and stability is strictly evaluated. Here, we propose a cardinal method for intuitive use case related feature engineering, tuning the hyper parameters, best model selection and diagnosing the model for further improvements. The stability of a model plays a huge factor, as we expect the deployed model to work well for the next 6–8 months, then up for re-tuning based on the data distribution and model performance. Statistical and data driven methods are used to develop sophisticated features and achieved minimal accuracy variation across time periods. Implementation of our methods for the use cases like customer attrition from the bank in the next 6 months and detection of the in-bound calls from the customer to the call centre to enquire about balance, transaction details, etc. are discussed. Achieved 47% & 55% recall score in the top 2 deciles respectively for the use cases.

Keywords: Banking domain · Customer attrition · In-Bound call detection · Machine learning · Imbalanced dataset · SMOTE · Supervised learning · Feature engineering · Hyperparameter tuning · Modelling flow and diagnosis

1 Introduction

Earlier, banks used to target customers using personalized marketing by creating different clusters based on the demographic information, transactions, etc. which

CIMB Bank.

are being quickly replaced by hyper-personalized marketing, analyzing the real time customer information. In the era, when deep learning is scaling off quickly with large data sets to achieve higher accuracies, using machine learning models to score similar accuracies can be often underwhelming. But, it may not be always feasible to build a deep learning model with the limited server capacity for every business problem which could take hours/days for training and tuning the network.

Customer attrition is a real challenge which every bank is faced with. In general, the marketing team spends 8 to 10 times to attain a new customer for the bank compared to the spend on retaining an existing customer. Hence, leading to a substantial cost saving for the bank. Also, identifying the to be attrited customers at an early stage can help understand and address the reason behind it. There could be varied reasons like the bank may not be the primary account of the holder, loan/savings account in different banks or due to change in employment of the payroll customers, etc. Predicting such customers before 6 months would help the bank to reach out and offer lucrative incentives to further continue the association with bank. If the customer opts for balance transfer of credit card/loan from another bank, which in turn increases the port folio of the customer with the bank. But the major challenge is the imbalanced dataset.

Detecting the in-bound calls to the customer call centre is another such case. In the age when mobile technology is booming, still a larger audience is dependent on the traditional interactive voice response and customer support based systems to do the balance enquiry, check transaction related information, report an incident, etc. Hence, CIMB Clicks app has been launched a few years back to create a one stop shop for all product services, enquiries and for rolling out hyper-personalized offers to the customers. Targeting these customers using various marketing techniques will help drive the bank in the digital age and provide ease of access to a much larger customer base. Strategies include scheduling a short weekly summary of the transactions as a text message with link to open the digital app, etc.

Model performance improvement techniques are roughly categorized into 3 aspects:

- *Data*: Add more training data, perform feature engineering, etc.
- *Modelling*: Fine-tuning the hyperparameter of the model, using ensemble models, etc.
- *Model Diagnosis*: Using various data driven methods and evaluation criteria to fine tuning the model for further improvement.

Adding more data doesn't necessarily improve the machine learning model performance after a certain point. But, feature engineering using the business knowledge and statistical methods is critical to tune the model performance which is detailed in the Sect. 2.3.

2   Methodology

In this study, we explore intuitive ways of ideation and use of statistical methods to derive self explanatory feature variables and a structured modelling flow for performance improvement. We present the methodological underpinnings of the techniques in this section and the criteria used to evaluate the performance.

2.1   Data Preparation

In this section we present how to identify the positive class customers for the use cases as below:

Customer Attrition. The customers who opt to close their account voluntarily are far fewer than the ones who gradually stop using it. Thus, identify the customers who have been inactive for at least 6 months continuously from a time period in the past 2 years to get sufficient positive class customers for model building. To select the negative class training points, stratified under-sampling was performed by occupation and time period in the last 2 years. Since, the data was highly imbalance, the under-sampling was done in such a way that the ratio of positive class was at least 5–10%.

In-Bound Call Detection. Segregated the in-bound calls mainly into two categories as follows:

- Queries related to *Savings/Current account* balance enquiries, debit card transaction details, incident reporting, etc.
- *Credit card* related enquiries like outstanding balance, payment due date, amount due, bill generation date, overdue interest rates, etc.

Concluded to predict the customers who might call in the next one week for such queries based on various permutations. The time period and the customers were extracted from a 6 month period for the positive labeled customers whereas for the negative labeled, stratified under-sampling was performed by occupation and time period of the customers who have totally not called. The data distribution is maintained at 10% for the positive class.

2.2   Feature Engineering

In this section we present intuitive ways to perform feature engineering for the use cases as below:

Algorithm 1: Deriving trend features

    Input   : **data** variable, list of data points of the variable in the last 6
                  Months (N = 6 data points) sorted on the ascending time period.
    Output : Trend value of the variable in the last 6 months.
    Initialize: counter = 0.

    for $i \leftarrow 1$ **to** $N - 1$ **do**
        for $j \leftarrow i$ **to** N **do**
            if $data[j] > data[i]$ **then**
                counter = counter + 1
            else if $data[j] < data[i]$ **then**
                counter = counter - 1
            else
                counter = counter + 0

    Evaluate: $\frac{counter}{\frac{N * (N - 1)}{2}}$

Customer Attrition. Decoding the pattern behind customer behavior is important. To incorporate such pattern as a feature variable, developed an enhanced version of the Mann Kendall Trend algorithm which is used in the detection of trend for the time series data. Thus, created a feature variable which outputs a scaled value between $[-1, 1]$. This shows the decreasing trend when the value is closer to -1, whereas a closer to $+1$ indicates an increasing trend of the variable.

The data was sorted in the ascending time period, Algorithm 1 depicts the flow for trend feature engineering.

Example 1.1: As shown in the Fig. 1 the trend feature variable was calculated for the Customer C on the count of transactions over time, which was found to be -0.86 shows the decreasing trend of the variable.

Similarly, trend feature variables are calculated for various features like total no. of credit and debit transactions, money inflow and outflow, balance, etc. of the last 6 months. Apart from these, traditional variables like mean and standard deviation were also calculated for similar variables.

In addition to these variables, Coefficient of Variation (CV) which measures the dispersion of data points around the mean was also added as a feature variable to the model. It was calculated using the Eq. (1).

$$CV = \frac{\sigma}{\mu} \tag{1}$$

where σ is the standard deviation and μ is the mean. The Coefficient of Variation feature variable helps to capture the variability of various features and provides a scaled value which can be compared across all the training points.

Example 1.2: For customers A and B the Fig. 2 and 3 shows the variation of savings account balance over a 6 month period.

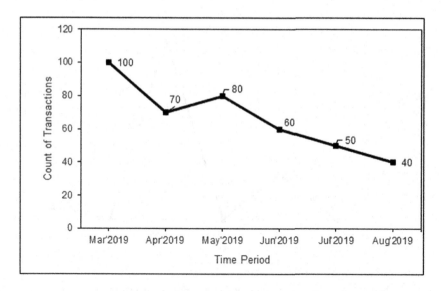

Fig. 1. Trend feature calculation

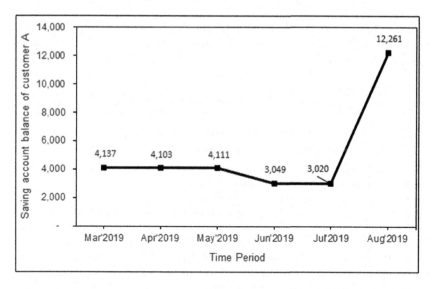

Fig. 2. Customer A Saving account balance variation over time

– CV of Customer A was found to be 0.63.
– CV of Customer B was found to be 1.62.

The customer balances are operating at different scales but the CV feature variable is a scaled value which can be compared across multiple customers with similar variation in the balances.

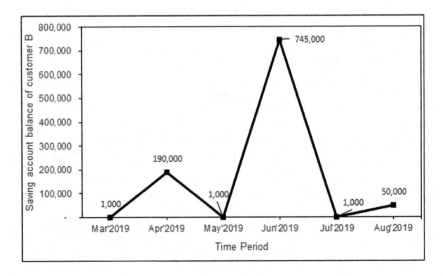

Fig. 3. Customer B Saving account balance variation over time

In-Bound Call Detection. Feature engineering is all about capturing the pattern of the positive class customers using business knowledge. Below traditional features were created:

- Count of prior calls.
- Age, demographics, monthly income and tenure of the customer with the bank.
- Credit card outstanding balance and percentage utilization.
- No. of days before payment is due, amount due.
- Savings/Current account balance.
- Count and amount of debit transactions.
- Count and amount of credit transactions.
- Count and amount of debit/credit card transactions at point of sale machines (POS).

Features created would help distinguish the customers who are likely to call from the rest. But it is also important to capture when they are going to call, since we are predicting the customers who are likely to call in the next 1 week. To address that, the pattern of recurrence had to captured. Hence, below features were created in accordance to that:

- Week number of the month and no. of days of the month in week 1.
- No. of debit and credit transactions done in the week of month to be predicted of last 1 month, 2 months, 3 months and 6 months.
- Similarly, for the amount of debit and credit transactions.

2.3 Feature Selection

Various data driven methods were used for feature engineering. It is possible that many features, which were created in the feature engineering section are correlated, like the debit transactions in the last 1 month, 2 months, 3 months, etc. Hence, feature selection is an important aspect of modelling. Since, the total no. of features present will directly effect the time taken for training the model and variance of the model. Principal component analysis (PCA), an unsupervised learning model could be used for feature transformation to remove the multicollinearity among the variables. But it would result in loss of a business explanation to quantify the effect of top variables in the model, since the variables are transformed into eigen vectors. After train and test split, feature scaling was performed on the training data set using the Min Max Scaler algorithm. The Eq. (2) depicts the algorithm to perform the scaling.

$$X_{\text{new}} = \frac{X_{\text{i}} - minimum(X)}{maximum(X) - minimum(X)} \tag{2}$$

After performing the scaling operation on all independent variables. Devised Algorithm 2 for initial phase of feature selection to select one variable among the correlated variables which the has maximum variance.

Algorithm 2: Feature selection among correlated variables

    Input   : *training_data*, independent continuous variables of the training data.

    Output : List of columns to subset from the complete training data for which are partly uncorrelated features.

    Calculate: Variance of all feature variables.

    Calculate: Correlation matrix of all feature variables.

    Initialize : *variable_names* = List of column names of the training data.

    Initialize : *subset_columns* = [], Empty

    Initialize : *correlation_threshold* = 0.7

    while *variable_names is not empty* **do**

1   *do_column* = variable_names[1] ;
      // Extract the 1st variable name from all the variables.

2   *corr_columns* = Extract the list of variables from the correlation matrix whose absolute value is greater than the *correlation_threshold* value for the variable *do_column*;

3   *select_column* = Select one variable with the maximum variance from *corr_columns*;

4   *subset_columns.append(select_column)*;
      // Append the select_column to create a new list of variables

5   *variable_names* = set{*variable_names*} - set{*corr_columns*};
      // Remove the subset of columns from the base list.

    end

    Evaluate : Use the *subset_columns* variable to subset the feature variables from the train and test data;

Then, embedded method of feature selection was used in the next phase of dimensionality reduction to derive the important features by training a machine learning model. To derive the feature importance, Random Forest model was used to train on the training data set and selected the features which contribute to 98% of the total importance.

2.4   Handling the Imbalanced Data

Imbalance of the data set was a real challenge which could be overcome by using various sampling techniques like stratified undersampling of the negative class or by oversampling of the positive class. But these techniques have various disadvantages like by under sampling the negative class there could be a potential loss of data and by over sampling of the positive class the model could likely overfit.

Hence, to overcome such challenges Synthetic Minority Oversampling Technique (SMOTE) has been introduced which over samples the positive class by creating new synthetic samples using the K nearest neighbors of the original positive class training points. Oversampling by SMOTE is highly advisable when the modelling objective is to achieve higher precision scores. But it wouldn't necessarily achieve higher recall scores. Since, SMOTE creates the samples based on existing positive class samples which in turn increases more pure samples. But to achieve higher recall scores it is important to classify the borderline samples accurately. To achieve that, Borderline-SMOTE has been introduced to oversample the borderline training points using the K nearest neighbors of the positive class and the M nearest neighbors of the negative class to determine if a positive class training point is in the border line.

In this paper SVM-SMOTE algorithm was used to generate the synthetic minority samples. Initially, this algorithm trains an SVM model and then uses the support vectors to construct the borderline area to interpolate new samples.

2.5   Evaluation Criteria

In this study, we use Logarithmic loss (Log loss), Receiver Operating Characteristic (ROC) curve and Decile Analysis for best hyperparameter selection and for model performance evaluation. The goal is to minimize the log loss error, minimize the variation in ROC curve during the multi fold cross-validation and to maximize the recall score. Decile Analysis was performed using Algorithm 3.

Table 1 shows the decile analysis of the model. Minimum probability ranges at the decile level can be used to evaluate F1 score, precision and recall scores. The count of target customers captured at each decile level was in the decreasing order which is a good indication that the model is a good fit.

Algorithm 3: Decile Analysis

Input	: **Data frame object**, With Customer ID, Predicted Probability and Target label as column values).
Output	: Decile Analysis of the data.

- Split the data frame object into 10 equal sized bins on percentile based distribution of the predicted probability data.
- Aggregate the data at each bins level and calculate the following:
  - I Minimum and maximum probability for each bin.
  - II Sort the decile summary in the descending order on probability.
  - III Count of total customers in each bin.
  - IV Count of the target customers in each bin.
  - V % captured of target customers in each bin with respect to the total.
  - VI Cumulative % captured of the target customers shows the recall score at each bin level on the minimum probability.
  - VII Cumulative Lift captured is the cumulative % captured divided by total sample rate till that bin.

Table 1. Decile analysis

Decile	Min probability	Max probability	Count of total ID's	Count of target ID's	Target % captured	Recall	Cum lift
1	0.87	0.98	25680	17719	35%	35%	3.46
2	0.81	0.87	25680	10270	20%	55%	2.73
3	0.73	0.81	25680	6919	14%	68%	2.27
4	0.61	0.73	25680	5519	11%	79%	1.97
5	0.55	0.61	25679	3911	8%	87%	1.73
6	0.49	0.55	25680	2381	5%	91%	1.52
7	0.37	0.49	25680	1705	3%	95%	1.35
8	0.24	0.37	25680	1365	3%	97%	1.22
9	0.12	0.24	25680	912	2%	99%	1.10
10	0.03	0.12	25681	480	1%	100%	1.00

2.6   Modelling Structure

Supervised machine learning models are strictly divided into 2 types:

- *Parametric Models*: Logistic Regression, Linear Regression, etc.
  Challenges:
  - The data should satisfy a series of assumptions.
  - Models may under fit the data when excess features are present in the model.
- *Non-Parametric Models*: Decision Tree, Random Forest, Gradient Boosting, XGBoost, etc.

Challenges:

- Would require lots of data.
- Model training time is more.
- Model may over fit the data. Hence, the hyperparameters must be tuned using the bias variance trade-off.

The Algorithm 4 was coined for a systematic approach to model building, followed by the Sect. 2.7 for hyperparameter tuning of the models.

Algorithm 4: Modelling Flow

    Input   : **Model training data**, output from the Algorithm 2.
    Output   : Decile analysis of the data.
    Modelling: Build a logistic regression model with lasso/ridge penalty.
    Evaluate : Calculate and access the following steps:

1 Predict for both train (*excluding the synthetic samples*) and test data.
2 Median predicted probability of the training data.
3 ROC curve, decile analysis and F1, recall, precision scores using the median probability for both train and test.
4 **Check**: The count of target customers attained in each bin should be in the decreasing order as shown in the Table 1 for both train and test.

    Modelling: Build and tune the hyperparameters of the Random Forest
                       Model as discussed in the Section 2.7.
    Evaluate : Perform the evaluation steps from line 1 to 4.
    Modelling: Build and tune the hyperparameters of the XGBoost Model as
                       discussed in the Section 2.7.
    Evaluate : Perform the evaluation steps from line 1 to 4.

    Compare and select the best model.

2.7   Hyperparameter Tuning

Predominantly, the hyperparameters define the model architecture. In this section, we explore important hyperparameters to tune for Random Forest and XGBoost models, as they are prone to overfitting (Fig. 4).

Number of Tree to Build. Refers to the number of trees built in a forest for model learning. Building less number of trees can result in high variance of the model which would be due to the randomness. It may show high accuracy when the forest has less than 10 trees, but when cross-validation was performed, the error would be unnaturally high on the validation sets. Saturation was attained after a building certain number trees in the forest. Figure 5 shows the log loss of train and test data with incremental growth in the number of trees of the model.

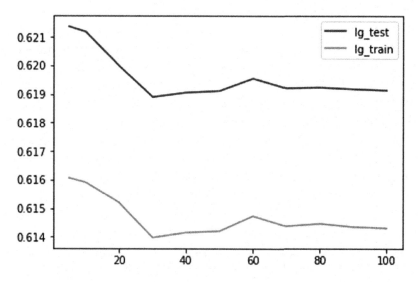

Fig. 4. Log loss vs No. of Trees built

Maximum Depth of the Tree. Maximum depth refers to the level of node splitting of a tree, while building the forest of trees. Too low a depth may result in underfitting of the model and too high a depth would result in overfitting. Figure 5 shows the log loss of train and test data with incremental growth in the depth of trees built in the model.

Class Weight. It refers to the weights which are to be associated with each label of the data to calculate the error, it is mainly categorized into 2 parts:

– Balanced
– Imbalanced

Balanced is used when the distribution of positive and negative class training points are equal. For *imbalanced* data distribution, compute the class weights using the Eq. (3) and update the hyperparameter.

$$W_j = \frac{n}{k * n_j} \tag{3}$$

where W_j is the weight of the class j, n is the total no. of observations, n_j is the total no. of observations of class j and k is the total no. of classes.

It is important to note that class weight has to be updated as per the data distribution, since it is not likely that in every use case the data distribution of each class is equal. Then, the Weighted Cross Entropy of the constructed tree was calculated using the Eq. (4).

$$\text{Weighted Cross Entropy} = -w_0 y \log p - w_1 (1 - y) \ \log(1 - p) \tag{4}$$

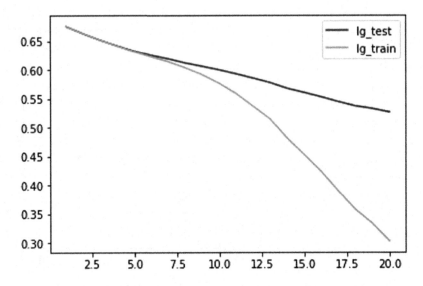

Fig. 5. Log loss vs Depth of the Tree

Tuning such parameter with higher class weights of the positive class would seem like the recall score is improving. But it would only boost the predicted probability (median shifts towards 1), which doesn't necessarily increase the prediction accuracy.

Apart from these hyperparamters, minimum sample in the leaves could be optimized to further constraint the learning of the model.

Stability of the parameters needs to be evaluated by performing multi fold cross-validation using the ROC curve as shown in the Fig. 6.

3   Empirical Study

We applied the proposed method to the real-world database. The data was extracted from the bank's big data platform to implement and deploy the customer attrition and in-bound calls use cases. The data manipulation was done using Hive and Python (Version 3.6) was used for data pre-processing, model building and deployment. All types transactions, demographics and account related information was used to derive the features as discussed in the Sect. 2.2. For customer attrition modelling, the total samples were 256800 as model train and test dataset and a out of time period of 6 months was used for the final model validation. Similarly for in-bound calls, a total of 410300 samples were considered for training and testing. And a out of time validation of 4 weekly prediction was performed.

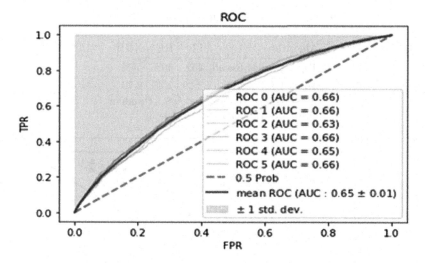

Fig. 6. ROC Curve variation over Cross-Validation

4   Results

The aforementioned methods are applied for feature engineering and model tuning for customer attrition and in-bound calls prediction. The total no. of trees and max depth parameters are tuned for Random Forest and XGBoost model using Log loss metric. Cross-Validation was performed on the selected parameters and stability was evaluated using the ROC Curve as shown in the Fig. 6.

Customer Attrition and In-Bound Calls detection model validation comparison results are shown in Table 2 and 3 respectively. Incremental uplift in recall and lift is achieved with the proposed modelling flow as discussed in the Sect. 2.6. XGBoost achieved the best recall in top 2 deciles. Performance of the validation data is evaluated using ROC curve and decile analysis.

Table 2. Customer Attrition experimental results

Algorithm	LR	RF	XGB
Top 2 Deciles Recall	39%	44%	47%
Top 2 Deciles Lift	1.96	2.18	2.34

LR: Logistic Regression; RF: Random Forest; XGB: XGBoost Model

Figure 7 shows the cumulative captured of attrited customers with each deciles and 29% of it is captured in the top decile. Similarly, Fig. 8 shows the in-bound calls captured at decile level and 35% of it is captured in the top decile.

Table 3. In-Bound Calls experimental results

Algorithm	LR	RF	XGB
Top 2 Deciles Recall	46%	49%	55%
Top 2 Deciles Lift	2.29	2.47	2.73

LR: Logistic Regression; RF: Random
Forest; XGB: XGBoost Model

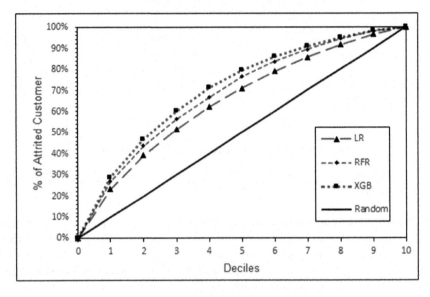

Fig. 7. Recall of Attrited Customers captured vs Deciles

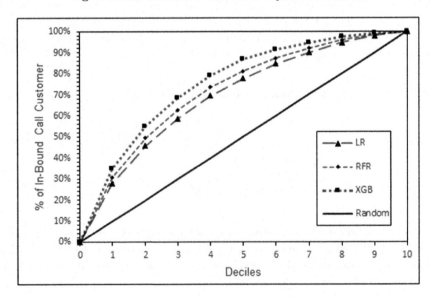

Fig. 8. Recall of In-Bound Calls captured vs Deciles

5   Conclusion and Future Work

In this paper, we have presented the state of the art statistical methods for feature engineering and machine learning model performance enhancement techniques to predict the customer attrition and in-bound calls in the banking domain. Model results show that our methods produce better accuracies than a random model. The imbalance of the data set is a real challenge which we overcame by using SVM-SMOTE and slightly enhanced the minority sample for model training. Accurate predictions is critical in retaining the customers and to increase the digital base of the bank.

Experimental results shows that the stages of modelling improve the performance and the algorithm to tune the hyper-parameters resulted in a stable Random Forest and XGBoost Model. Hence, captured 47% of the total attrited customers in the top 2 deciles. Similarly, 55% of the total calls made to the customer care centre were captured in the top 2 deciles.

Future work includes model diagnosis using various data driven methods, business knowledge and to continue research on more statistical methods for feature engineering in order to capture the inherent pattern. For In-Bound call detection there is a huge potential in the variables varying with time, will continue exploring such features.

Acknowledgment. The complete list of the cross functional team which has worked in these projects are: Ang E Mei, Megan Azreen Ehsan, NG Wai Keat, Abhishek Prakash, Anoop Sharma, Ashish Chauhan, Gajanan Thenge, Ganapathy K, Hylish James, Rajeev Reddy, Saikat Kumar, Shaik Imran, Shilpana Sathyanarayana, Suraj Shukla, Somnath Ojha, Ujjwal Gupta, Uttam Kumar Kushwaha, Varsha Vishwakarma, [†]Decision Management, [†]Consumer Banking.
[†]Organization & Team.

References

1. Adhikari, N.C.D., et al.: An intelligent approach to demand forecasting. In: Smys, S., Bestak, R., Chen, J.I.-Z., Kotuliak, I. (eds.) ICCNCT 2018. LNDECT, vol. 15, pp. 167–183. Springer, Singapore (2019). https://doi.org/10.1007/978-981-10-8681-6_17

2. Ahmad, A.K., Jafar, A., Aljoumaa, K.: Customer churn prediction in telecom using machine learning in big data platform. J. Big Data **6**(1), 1–24 (2019). https://doi.org/10.1186/s40537-019-0191-6

3. Kendall, M.G.: Rank Correlation Methods, 4th edn. Charles Griffin, London (1975)

4. Wang, Q., Luo, Z.: A Novel Ensemble Method for Imbalanced Data Learning: Bagging of Extrapolation-SMOTE SVM (2017)

5. Hirsch, R.M., Slack, J.R., Smith, R.A.: Techniques of trend analysis for monthly water quality data. Water Resour. Res. **18**(1), 107–121 (1982)

6. Coussement, K., Van den Poel, D.: Churn prediction in subscription services: an application of support vector machines while comparing two parameter-selection techniques. Expert Syst. Appl. **34**(1), 313–327 (2008)

7. Saghir, M., et al.: Churn prediction using neural network based individual and ensemble models. In: 2019 16th International Bhurban Conference on Applied Sciences and Technology (IBCAST), pp. 634–639 (2019)

8. Vafeiadis, T., Diamantaras, K.I., Sarigiannidis, G., Chatzisavvas, K.Ch.: A comparison of machine learning techniques for customer churn prediction. Simul. Model. Pract. Theory **55**, 1–9 (2015). ISSN 1569-190X

9. Coussement, K., Benoit, D.F., Van den Poel, D.: Improved marketing decision making in a customer churn prediction context using generalized additive models. Expert Syst. Appl. **37**(3), 2132–2143 (2010). ISSN 0957-4174

10. Xie, Y., Li, X., Ngai, E.W.T., Ying, W.: Customer churn prediction using improved balanced random forests. Expert Syst. Appl. **36**(3), Part 1, 5445–5449 (2009). ISSN 0957-4174

11. Burez, J., Van den Poel, D.: Handling class imbalance in customer churn prediction. Expert Syst. Appl. **36**(3), Part 1, 4626–4636 (2009). ISSN 0957-4174

12. Tang, Y., Zhang, Y., Chawla, N.V., Krasser, S.: SVMs modeling for highly imbalanced classification. IEEE Trans. Syst. Man Cybern. Part B (Cybern.) **39**(1), 281–288 (2009). https://doi.org/10.1109/TSMCB.2008.2002909

13. Wang, H.: Combination approach of SMOTE and biased-SVM for imbalanced datasets. In: 2008 IEEE International Joint Conference on Neural Networks (IEEE World Congress on Computational Intelligence), Hong Kong, pp. 228–231 (2008). https://doi.org/10.1109/IJCNN.2008.4633794

14. Han, H., Wang, W.-Y., Mao, B.-H.: Borderline-SMOTE: a new over-sampling method in imbalanced data sets learning. In: Huang, D.-S., Zhang, X.-P., Huang, G.-B. (eds.) ICIC 2005. LNCS, vol. 3644, pp. 878–887. Springer, Heidelberg (2005). https://doi.org/10.1007/11538059_91

15. Batuwita, R., Palade, V.: Class imbalance learning methods for support vector machines. In: Imbalanced Learning: Foundations, Algorithms, and Applications, pp. 83–99. Wiley, Berlin (2013)

16. Chen, T., Guestrin, C.: XGBoost: a scalable tree boosting system. In: Proceedings of the 22nd ACM SIGKDD International Conference on Knowledge Discovery and Data Mining (KDD 2016), pp. 785–794. Association for Computing Machinery, New York (2016)

17. Chapelle, O., Chang, Y.: Yahoo! learning to rank challenge overview. J. Mach. Learn. Res. - W & CP **14**, 1–24 (2011)

18. Sabbeh, S.: Machine-learning techniques for customer retention: a comparative study. Int. J. Adv. Comput. Sci. Appl. (2018)

19. Alkhatib, K., Abualigah, S.: Predictive model for cutting customers migration from banks: based on machine learning classification algorithms. In: 2020 11th International Conference on Information and Communication Systems (2020)

20. Ahmed, A., Linen, D.M.: A review and analysis of churn prediction methods for customer retention in telecom industries. In: 2017 4th International Conference on Advanced Computing and Communication Systems (ICACCS), Coimbatore, pp. 1–7 (2017). https://doi.org/10.1109/ICACCS.2017.8014605

A Weighted Ensemble Approach to Real-Time Prediction of Suspended Particulate Matter

Tushar Saini[1]([⊠]) [iD], Gagandeep Tomar[1] [iD], Duni Chand Rana[2] [iD], Suresh Attri[2] [iD], and Varun Dutt[1] [iD]

[1] Indian Institute of Technology, Mandi, India
tushar.saini1285@gmail.com
[2] Department of Environment, Science and Technology, Government of Himachal Pradesh, Shimla, India

Abstract. Given the widespread health effects of air pollution, it is imperative to predict air pollution ahead of time. A number of time-series forecasting models have been developed to predict air-pollution. However, an evaluation of individual and ensemble models for real-time air pollution forecasting lacks in the literature. The primary objective of this research is to develop and test individual and ensemble time-series forecasting models for real-time forecasting of air pollution ahead in time. Air pollution data of suspended particulate matter ($PM_{2.5}$) over 5-years from Beijing, China was used for model comparisons. The $PM_{2.5}$-time-series was split as the first 80% for training and the latter 20% for testing time-series forecasting models. Five individual time-series forecasting models, namely, Multilayer Perceptron (MLP), Convolution Neural Network (CNN), Long-Short Term Memory (LSTM), and Seasonal Autoregressive Integrated Moving Average (SARIMA) were developed. Also, a new weighted ensemble model of these individual models was developed. Among the individual models, results revealed that both during training and test, the CNN performed the best, and this model was followed by the LSTM, MLP, and SARIMA models. Furthermore, the weighted ensemble model performed the best among all models. We highlight the potential of using the weighted ensemble approach for real-time forecasting of suspended particulate matter.

Keywords: PM2.5 · MLP · LSTM · CNN · SARIMA · Weighted ensemble model

1 Introduction

Various serious health issues can be associated with air pollution [22]. It was estimated that around 4.2 million premature deaths worldwide in both rural and urban areas were caused by air pollution in 2016 [22]. Among these deaths, a large number of deaths occurred in densely populated regions of China and India with high concentrations of particulate matter of 2.5 microns or smaller ($PM_{2.5}$) [14]. Certain studies have shown that prolonged exposure to $PM_{2.5}$ or PM_{10} can cause short-term and long-term pulmonary and cardiovascular health effects [14, 23]. In fact, the particulate matter of size less than

D. Garg et al. (Eds.): IACC 2020, CCIS 1367, pp. 381–394, 2021.
https://doi.org/10.1007/978-981-16-0401-0_29

10 microns can penetrate deep inside the lungs. In comparison, particulate matter of size less than 2.5 microns can penetrate the lung barrier and can even enter the blood system. The air quality index of million-plus cities in India shows that more than 50 percent of cities have moderate to poor air quality [23]. In recent years, the problem has only been made severe. The major cause of ever-increasing air-pollution can be attributed to industrialization, vehicular emissions, crop burning, and other activities like burning crackers. As per a study based on 2016 data, at least 140 million people in India breathes air that is ten times more over the WHO safe limit. Additionally, air pollution also incurs economic costs [14]; according to the report by Greenpeace Southeast Asia [14], India is estimated to bear 10.7 lakh crore rupees or a loss of 3.39 lakh rupees per second. Also, according to The Economic Consequences of Outdoor Air pollution report, it was reported that global healthcare costs associated with air pollution were expected to rise from USD 21 billion in 2015 to USD 176 billion in 2060 [14]. It was also projected that the market impacts of outdoor air pollution, including effects on labor productivity, health spending, and crop yields, will lead to economic costs that will steadily rise to 1% of global GDP by 2060 [14].

Given the health effects and increasing costs, it is imperative to have some mechanism that can not only monitor the air pollution in real-time and but also forecast future air pollution values. It is of utmost importance that we develop forecasting models that can predict the values with high accuracy. This forecasting of air pollution may likely help policymakers in making informed decisions about opening new industries, starting mining activity, etc. Various decisions like issuance of permits to set up new industries, vehicle permits, or setting up new policies for sectors can be based on the forecast. It will also help individuals to have some degree of awareness about their surroundings. They can use the forecasts to plan their daily routines. It will help them to avoid areas that may have a higher concentration of pollution, which can be detrimental to their health.

Various researchers have proposed a number of machine-learning approaches for the prediction of particulate matter. For example, reference [12] proposed a hybrid of the Convolutional Neural Network-Long-Short-Term-Memory (CNN-LSTM) model for forecasting $PM_{2.5}$. Reference [4] employed a multilayer perceptron (MLP) based model for predicting fine particulate matter (PM_{10} and $PM_{2.5}$). Reference [5] even used an ensemble of three methods, namely Gradient Boosting, Neural Network, and Random forest, for prediction of $PM_{2.5}$. Although prior research has considered certain ensemble models, a comprehensive evaluation of ensemble models via calibration of model parameters has been less explored. Furthermore, an evaluation of an ensemble model's performance against individual statistical and machine-learning models is yet to be undertaken.

The primary objective of this research is to overcome these gaps in the literature and to propose a comprehensive evaluation of an ensemble model for particulate matter prediction against individual statistical models (e.g., seasonal autoregressive integrated moving average or SARIMA) as well as machine learning models (MLP, LSTM, and CNN). The ensemble model is built by combining a weighted average of individual statistical and machine learning models using a weighted average and a grid-search method. The main novelty in this work is that it considers individual and ensemble models, where ensembling is done by considering both statistical and machine learning models on a larger air pollution dataset. An application of the developed models is to provide the policymakers with highly accurate forecasting of air-pollution concentrations so that proactive measures can be taken to curb the pollution before it occurs. In what follows, Sects. 2 describes the background of models for forecasting air pollution data. Next, we have described the air pollution dataset that was used and different models calibrated on the dataset. Furthermore, we detail the method of calibrating different model hyperparameters. Finally, we detail the results and discussion of forecasting air pollution via ensemble and individual models.

2   Related Work

Reference [4] proposed an MLP prediction model for forecasting of $PM_{2.5}$ levels. However, the dataset selected for model training and testing was limited to only two years. The parameters were varied in the MLP model over smaller variable ranges, and other machine learning, statistical, and ensemble models were not investigated. Reference [23] also proposed an MLP and stack ensemble model. The data used for the training purpose was 2350 samples, which was collected for 2.5 months. Again, the hyperparameters of the models were not optimized over a defined range.

Reference [20] proposed an LSTM model for forecasting air pollutants. The data used was retrieved from the EPA of Taiwan between the years 2012 and 2017. However, only the lookback period and activation function were varied. Other parameters, like the number of nodes per layer and the number of hidden layers, were kept constant. There were no benchmarking or comparisons with other models. Reference [3] investigated the use of the vanilla LSTM model for the prediction. The dataset used was the Beijing dataset from the UCI Machine Learning Repository. However, again there was no comparison or benchmarking with other machine learning or statistical models. Reference [16] investigated the use of Stacked Autoencoder LSTM (SAE-LSTM) for the prediction of $PM_{2.5}$ and compared the results with six other models, namely, BP, SAE-BP, SAE-BiLSTM, SAE-ELM, LSTM, ELM. However, the dataset size was smaller, and only 1610 samples were used for training and testing purposes, and only a subset of parameters of LSTM was optimized over a small range. Also, no ensemble model was developed for forecasting purposes.

Reference [12] proposed a deep CNN-LSTM model for the prediction of $PM_{2.5}$. The dataset used was the Beijing dataset from the UCI Machine Learning Repository. Here, CNN was used for feature extraction, and LSTM was used for forecasting. However, the hyperparameters of the models were not optimized and were set to some constant. The model results were compared with other models like SVM, MLP, CNN, and LSTM, but no statistical model was used for comparison. Also, the use of the ensembling process was absent. Reference [7] proposed a CNN-LSTM model for the prediction of $PM_{2.5}$. The data used was the Shanghai data set for the year 2015 to 2017. Again, a subset of hyperparameters was optimized over a short-range. The CNN was used for feature extraction while LSTM was used for obtaining the final prediction. The result was compared with the RNN, CNN, and LSTM models. However, the ensemble model was not investigated.

Reference [15] proposed the SARIMA forecasting method for the Brazilian city, Sao Paulo. The data consisted of 2190 samples. The parameters of SARIMA were optimized using the grid search method. However, the comparison was limited to another statistical method, called Holt-Winters. Also, no machine learning and ensemble models were investigated.

Reference [24] proposed an ensemble framework-based LSTM model. An ensemble empirical mode decomposition (EEMD) model was used for modal transformation from single to multi-mode. Then, LSTM was employed for model's feature learning, and lastly, an inverse EEMD computation was performed to integrate multi-modal learning. The data used was for Beijing, China, for the duration of 1st Jan 2016 to 31st Dec 2016. The results were compared with a feedforward neural network and vanilla LSTM model. However, the hyperparameters were not optimized and were kept constant. Also, no statistical or other ensemble models were investigated.

3   Methodology

3.1   Data

The data used in this experimentation were collected at the US Embassy in Beijing and were provided by the UCI Machine Learning Repository [13]. The data comprises hourly logged data of the pollutant and weather parameters. For this experimentation, we only considered the pollutant variable, which represents $PM_{2.5}$ concentration in the air, in the units $\mu g/m^3$. The data were collected over five years, between 1st Jan 2010 to 31st Dec 2014, and it consisted of 43,824 data points with 1-hourly air pollution values. Dataset was split (without shuffling) into two; 80% of data were used for training (calibrating) models and the remaining 20% for testing the calibrated models. So, nearly four-year data, i.e., from 1st Jan 2010 to 31st Dec 2013, was used for model training; and one-year data, i.e., from 1st Jan 2013 to 31st Dec 2014, was used for model testing. As plotting all 43,824 data points in one graph made it cluttered, we only plotted 800 data points from the dataset to visualize data observations and model predictions. Out of these 800 data points, the first 600 data points are the first 600 training data points, and the remaining 200 data points are the first 200 testing data points. Figure 1 shows the plot of 800 data points of $PM_{2.5}$ concentration from the dataset (the vertical line indicates the split between training and test data points).

3.2   Data Pre-processing

The time-series data were logged at different timesteps. All machine-learning models followed a supervised learning approach, where a set of predictors forecast the dependent variable of interest. To apply a supervised machine learning algorithm, we had to transform the time-series data into a supervised format. Thus, a time series $y_t, y_{t-1}, y_{t-2}, y_{t-3}, \ldots, y_{t-n}$ was transformed into a supervised format in the following form:

$$y_t = f(y_{t-1}, y_{t-2}, y_{t-3}, \ldots, y_{t-n})$$

where y_t is the variable value to be predicted and $y_{t-1}, y_{t-2}, y_{t-3}, \ldots, y_{t-n}$ are the values of the predicted lag-observations of the variable on n prior timesteps. Here, y_t represents the $PM_{2.5}$ concentration at time t. The number of lag-observations n used to predict

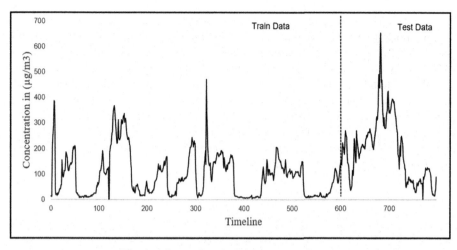

Fig. 1. Time-series plot of the Beijing dataset.

the observation at the current timestep was treated as the lookback period in different machine learning algorithms. So, the models used n prior observations to predict the next time step $PM_{2.5}$ concentration.

3.3 Models and Algorithms

Multilayer Perceptron (MLP): MLPs or feedforward artificial neural networks are machine learning models, having at least three layers of nodes: an input layer, a hidden layer, and an output layer [17]. The MLP models may contain several hidden layers having a number of nodes. These nodes take input from the prior layer, multiply it with weights, and return the output to the forward layer after adding a bias [17]. The backpropagation technique is used for training the models [11]. Backpropagation works by approximating the non-linear input-output relationship by internally changing the values of the weights [11]. The algorithm consists of two steps: feedforward and backpropagation. In the feedforward step, inputs (predictors) are applied to the input layer, and the output is generated after passing through the hidden layers at the output layer. The expected output is compared to the generated output, and an error is calculated [11]. This error is then backpropagated to subsequent layers, and the weights of nodes of the MLP are updated [11]. In our experiment, the MLP possessed three free variables, namely, lookback period, number of hidden layers, and the number of nodes per layer. These variables were optimized using a grid-search procedure (more details ahead in this paper).

Long-Short Term Memory (LSTM): An LSTM model is an artificial recurrent neural network (RNN) architecture used in machine learning. LSTM has feedback connections, unlike normal feedforward neural networks [19]. A standard LSTM unit comprises a cell and three gates: an input gate, an output gate, and a forget gate ([9]; see Fig. 2). At arbitrary time periods, the cell has some values, and the three gates control the flow of information into and out of the cell. The forget gate filters out the data from the previous cell state [9]. The input gate uses the sigmoid or tanh activation functions with point-wise multiplication to control the flow of information in the cell [9]. Finally, the output gate decides which data is passed on to the next cell state [9]. Based on time-series data, LSTMs are well-suited for classifying, analyzing, and making predictions as there can be lags of uncertain length between essential events in a time series. These networks learn the relationship between the lagged data and the current data by introducing the concept of memory [6]. In our experiments, LSTMs possessed three free variables, namely lookback period, number of layers, and nodes per layers. The x_t in Fig. 2 represents the input at time t, h_t is the output value of the cell, and C_t represents the cell state. The subscript t $-$ 1 represents a value at time step t $-$ 1.

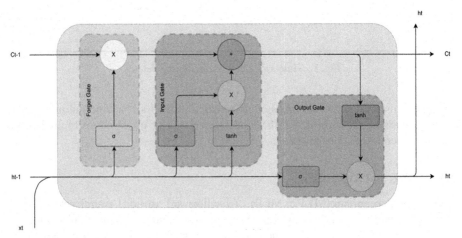

Fig. 2. A cell of LSTM containing three gates, forget gate, input gate, and output gate.

Convolution Neural Network (CNN): CNNs are a class of networks that try to learn the local spatial relationships between data [8]. CNNs were developed with the idea of local connectivity. Each node in the input is only connected to the local region [21]. The spatial scale of such a connection is referred to as the node's receptive field [21]. Local connectivity is accomplished by substituting convolutions for the weighted sums in the neural network. In the layer of the convolutionary neural network, the input is transformed to construct a feature map with the weight matrix (also called the filter) [21]. In other words, the weight matrix slides over the input and computes the Hadamard (dot) product between the input and the weight matrix [21]. CNNs' local networking and shared weights minimize the overall number of parameters that must be trained, resulting in more effective training [21]. Applications of CNNs have been generally in data having spatial aspects (e.g., images) [23]; however, we considered this model to encapsulate the hidden information between the subsequent data-points in a time series. In our experiment, we optimized five hyperparameters of CNN, namely, lookback period, number of layers, number of nodes per layer, kernel size, and number of filters in the CNN models.

Seasonal Auto-Regressive Integrated Moving-Average (SARIMA): is a statistical forecasting model used for univariate time-series data and is best suited for data having trend and seasonal components. It forecasts the time-series by describing the autocorrelations in data [1].

Stationarity: In the SARIMA model, the time-series data must be stationary. A stationary time-series has the property in which the mean, variance, and autocorrelation remain constant over time. A time-series that is not stationary can be made approximately stationary using differencing [1].

Auto-regressive: AR part of the SARIMA model predicts a parameter by passing the past values of the same parameter to the model. Thus, the AR part can be defined as:

$$y_t = c + \Phi_1\, y_{t-1} + \Phi_2\, y_{t-2} + \ldots\ldots + \Phi_p\, y_{p-1} + \epsilon_t \tag{1}$$

in Eq. (1), p is the AR trend parameter, ϵ_t is the white noise and y_{t-1}, y_{t-2}, and so on denotes the pollutant concentration.

Moving-Average: MA part of the SARIMA model uses the current and past values of stochastic (imperfectly predictable) term, which is given by Eq. (2):

$$y_t = c + \epsilon_t + \theta_1\, \epsilon_{t-1} + \theta_2\, \epsilon_{t-2} + \ldots\ldots + \theta_q\, \epsilon_{t-q} \tag{2}$$

in Eq. (2) q is the MA trend parameter, ϵ_t is the white noise and ϵ_{t-1}, ϵ_{t-2}, to ϵ_t are the error terms at previous timestamps.

   If we combine auto-regression (AR), i.e., Eq. (1) and a moving average (MA), i.e., Eq. (2) on stationary data, we obtain a non-seasonal ARIMA model, which is defined by Eq. (3):

$$y_t' = c + \Phi_1\, y_{t-1}' + \ldots\ldots + \Phi_p\, y_{t-p}' + \theta_1\, \epsilon_{t-1} + \ldots\ldots + \theta_q\, \epsilon_{t-q} + \epsilon_t \tag{3}$$

   SARIMA is an ARIMA, having a seasonal component. The standard SARIMA model has various hyperparameters, such as (p, d, q), (P, D, Q), and m. where p is the non-seasonal auto-regressive (AR) order; d is the non-seasonal differencing order; q is the non-seasonal moving average (MA) order; P is the seasonal AR order; D is the seasonal differencing; Q is the seasonal MA order; and m is the seasonality (a time span of repeating seasonal pattern In this experimentation, we had optimized all seven parameters mentioned above using the grid-search technique.

Ensemble Model: Ensemble modeling is a technique where multiple models are used to predict an outcome [10]. In this experiment, we ensembled the above-mentioned individual models (namely MLP, LSTM, CNN, and SARIMA) using a weighted average method [2]. The weighted average method assigns weights to each model, defining the importance of each model in the prediction. Thus, in the novel ensemble model approach, first, the grid search method was used to find the optimized hyperparameters of each model, and then the grid search method was used again to find the weights for the ensemble model. The weights which provided the least error for the ensemble model in training data were chosen as the final weights in the model for testing. Equation 3 shows how the prediction is computed in the ensemble model by using weights and their respective model predictions. The y'_t is the predicted value of the ensemble model, which is computed by taking a weighted sum of the individual model predictions in the following manner:

$$y'_t = w_{MLP}\, m_{MLP} + w_{LSTM}\, m_{LSTM} + w_{CNN}\, m_{CNN} + w_{SARIMA}\, m_{SARIMA} \qquad (4)$$

where, w_{MLP}, w_{LSTM}, w_{CNN}, and w_{SARIMA} were the 4 weights in the range [0, 1] representing the weight of each model, MLP (m_{MLP}), LSTM (m_{LSTM}), CNN (m_{CNN}), and SARIMA (m_{SARIMA}), respectively. Figure 3 shows the architecture of the ensemble model.

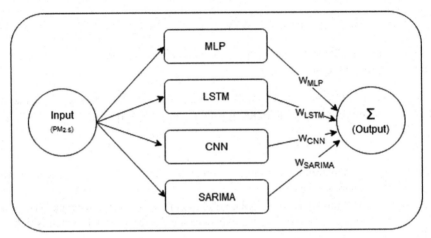

Fig. 3. The architecture of the ensemble model.

3.4   Optimization of Model Parameters

We implemented a grid search procedure for finding the hyperparameters of different models [2]. Grid search is a technique where we take into consideration all the relevant values of each parameter of the model, and we choose those parameters which perform best on the data. We varied each parameter in a range and step size in combination with other parameters in their ranges and step sizes. Thus, all possible combinations of parameter values were run in the grid search procedure in a model. The objective in the model was to accurately forecast the next 1-hourly PM$_{2.5}$ value given the values on prior timesteps. The performance of the time-series model was evaluated by calculating the error between the actual and the predicted values. In this research, Root Mean Square Error (RMSE) was used for evaluating the performance of a model [2]. Hence, the parameter configuration for which the RMSE came out to be minimum was considered as the best configuration. We did some preprocessing to convert PM$_{2.5}$ hourly data into time series data before inputting it into the models. The models predict the concentration of PM$_{2.5}$ for the next hour by taking prior values of PM$_{2.5}$ in the time series. Table 1 shows the combinations of hyperparameters that were used in the grid search to find the optimized hyperparameters for which models best fitted $PM_{2.5}$ data. Although the epochs and the batch size could also be varied in the machine learning models; however, we fixed them to a reasonably high value to reduce the combinatorial complexity (batch-size and epochs were fixed to 1 and 100, respectively). The hyperparameters for MLP were varied in following ranges: lookback period (1, 3, 5, 7); number of hidden layers (1, 2, 4, 6, 8, 16, 32, 64); and, nodes per layer (1, 3, 6, 12, 25, 50, 75). For LSTM, the hyperparameters were varied as: lookback period (1, 3, 5, 7); number of hidden layers (1, 2, 4, 6, 8, 16); and, nodes per layer (25, 50, 75, 100). For CNN, the hyperparameters were varied as: lookback period (1, 3, 5, 7); number of hidden layers (1, 2, 4, 6, 8, 16); nodes per layer (25, 50, 75, 100); filters (2, 4, 8, 16); and, kernel size (1, 2, 3, 4). Lastly, for SARIMA, the hyperparameters were varied as: p (0, 1, 2); d(0, 1); q(0, 1, 2); P(0, 1, 2, 4, 8, 16, 32); D(0, 1, 2); Q(0, 1, 2); and, m(1, 2, 4, 12, 24). These variations in the hyperparameters across models were based upon prior literature.

Table 1. Hyperparameters range used for the models.

Model	Parameter	Range of values
MLP	Look Back Period	1, 3, 5, 7
	Layers	1, 2, 4, 6, 8, 16, 32, 64
	Nodes Per Layer	1, 3, 6, 12, 25, 50, 75
LSTM	Look Back Period	1, 3, 5, 7
	Layers	1, 2, 4, 6, 8, 16
	Nodes Per Layer	25, 50, 75, 100, 125
CNN	Look Back Period	1, 3, 5, 7
	Layers	1, 2, 4, 6, 8, 16
	Nodes Per Layer	25, 50, 75, 100
	Filters	2, 4, 8, 16, 32
	Kernel Size	1, 2, 3, 4
SARIMA	p – AR Order	0, 1, 2
	d – Difference Order	0, 1
	q – MA Order	0, 1, 2
	P – Seasonal AR Order	0, 1, 2, 4, 8, 16, 32
	Q – Seasonal Difference Order	0, 1, 2
	D – Seasonal MA Order	0, 1, 2
	m – Seasonality	1, 2, 4, 12, 24
Ensemble	w_{MLP}	[0, 1] in steps of 0.01
	w_{LSTM}	[0, 1] in steps of 0.01
	w_{CNN}	[0, 1] in steps of 0.01
	w_{SARIMA}	[0, 1] in steps of 0.01

4 Results

Table 2 shows the optimized hyperparameter values that best fitted the data found using the grid search method in each model. As shown in Table 2, the optimized parameters for MLP were lookback period: 1, number of hidden layers: 6, and the number of nodes per layer: 32. For LSTM, the optimized parameters were lookback period: 5, number of hidden layers: 8, and number of nodes per layer: 100. For CNN, the optimized parameters were lookback period: 5, number of hidden layers: 4, number of nodes per layer: 25, filter: 16, and kernel size: 3. For SARIMA, the optimized parameters were p: 0, d: 0, q: 1, P: 4, D: 0, Q: 1, and m: 2. For the ensemble model, the weights obtained from the grid search were w_{MLP}: 0.06, w_{LSTM}: 0.36, w_{CNN}: 0.58, and w_{SARIMA}: 0.00. Thus, the SARIMA model did not enter the ensemble model.

Table 2. Optimized value of parameters in different models.

Model	Optimized value of parameter
MLP	lookback Period: 1, number of layers: 6, nodes per layer: 32
LSTM	lookback Period: 5, number of layers: 8, nodes per layer: 100
CNN	lookback period: 5, number of layers: 4, nodes per layer: 25, filters: 16, kernel size: 3
SARIMA	p: 0, d: 0, q: 1, P: 4, D: 0, Q: 1, m: 2
Ensemble Model	w_{MLP}: 0.06, w_{LSTM}: 0.36, w_{CNN}: 0.58, w_{SARIMA}: 0.00

Table 3 shows the RMSE values of the developed models in the training dataset, where the models possessed the calibrated hyperparameters. The lowest RMSE was obtained for the ensemble model, which was 24.68 $\mu g/m^3$. In contrast to the ensemble, the CNN model performed the second-best having an RMSE of 26.49 $\mu g/m^3$. Furthermore, LSTM and MLP models had RMSEs of 27.28 $\mu g/m^3$ and 28.25 $\mu g/m^3$, respectively. The SARIMA model performed the worst, having an RMSE of 32.47 $\mu g/m^3$.

Table 3. The RMSE of different models in the training dataset.

Models	RMSE for the training dataset ($\mu g/m^3$)
Multilayer Perceptron	28.25
Long Short-Term Memory	27.28
Convolution Neural Network	26.49
SARIMA	32.47
Ensemble Model	24.68

Table 4 shows the RMSE values from different models in the test dataset. Again, the lowest RMSE was obtained for the ensemble model, which was 23.45 $\mu g/m^3$. The CNN model performed the second-best having an RMSE of 23.49 $\mu g/m^3$. The LSTM and MLP models had RMSEs of 24.96 $\mu g/m^3$ and 24.51 $\mu g/m^3$, respectively. Furthermore, the SARIMA again performed the worst, having an RMSE of 30.73 $\mu g/m^3$.

Table 4. The RMSE of different models in the test dataset.

Models	RMSE for the test dataset ($\mu g/m^3$)
Multilayer Perceptron	24.51
Long Short-Term Memory	24.96
Convolution Neural Network	23.49
SARIMA	30.73
Ensemble Model	23.45

Figure 4 shows the forecast graph of the ensemble model against the PM$_{2.5}$ observations in training and test datasets (the two datasets are divided by the vertical dotted line). The forecast was computed by taking the weighted sum of MLP, LSTM, CNN, and SARIMA model predictions using the optimized weights found in Table 2. For the ensemble model, the RMSE on train data was 24.68 $\mu g/m^3$, and on the test data, it was 23.45 $\mu g/m^3$. As can be observed from the figure, the blue line shows the actual PM$_{2.5}$ concentration, and the red line shows the predicted PM$_{2.5}$ concentration. Both lines near-perfectly superimpose on each other. The ensemble model was also able to capture the peaks and troughs in the PM$_{2.5}$ values.

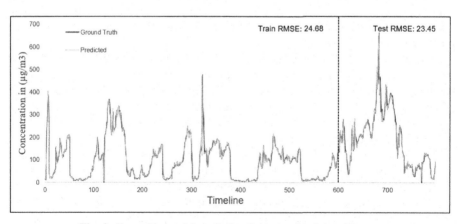

Fig. 4. Ensemble model prediction for test and training data set.

Using the same UCI Beijing PM$_{2.5}$ dataset, reference [3] trained a Vanilla LSTM model for forecasting PM$_{2.5}$ concentration. The RMSE obtained using Vanilla LSTM was 24.37 $\mu g/m^3$. Thus, the RMSE obtained by the ensemble model (23.45 $\mu g/m^3$) was less than that of the best model in the literature.

5 Discussion and Conclusion

Air pollution is detrimental to health, and it may cause pulmonary and cardiovascular diseases among human beings [22]. In fact, the effects of $PM_{2.5}$ exposure are severe and long-term exposure may cause diseases like lung cancer [22]. Air pollution also inflicts heavy economic losses due to the loss of lives and health expenditures [14]. Thus, it is crucial to monitor and forecast air pollution. The primary objective of this research was to develop ensemble forecasting models, which could combine the predictions of individual machine learning and forecast particulate matter concentrations with a high degree of accuracy. For the purpose of model training and testing, we utilized the large Beijing air pollution data set provided by the UCI machine learning repository [13]. Our results revealed that all the developed and optimized models, i.e., MLP, LSTM, CNN, SARIMA models, were able to perform $PM_{2.5}$ forecasting with high accuracy. Furthermore, a weighted ensemble model, which combined the individual prediction models, performed the best both in the training and testing datasets. The RMSEs for both the training and testing datasets were quite low in the ensemble model. Also, the ensemble model was able to capture the peaks and troughs in the $PM_{2.5}$ data. Also, the best RMSE value obtained in this research was better than the one cited in the literature on these data [3].

First, we found that the machine learning models (e.g., MLP, LSTM, and CNN) performed better compared to the statistical models (e.g., SARIMA). A likely reason for this result could be that the machine learning models have memory capabilities (LSTMs) and spatial capabilities (CNNs), and these capabilities allow these models to learn better the relationships between the current air pollution values and prior air pollution values. These findings are consistent with prior literature [15, 16, 21], where also machine learning models like MLPs, LSTMs, and CNNs have been developed to predict air pollution values.

Second, we found that the weighted ensemble model performed better than all other individual models, including individual machine learning models. A likely reason for this finding could be that the ensemble model takes the best out of the forecasts of the individual models by weighting different individual predictions. Again, these findings agree with prior research [18, 24], where ensemble models have been shown to perform well for forecasting air pollution data.

This work has a number of implications for the real world. For example, using the ensemble model developed, one could timely warn policymakers and citizens 1-h ahead of time if the $PM_{2.5}$ values exceed predefined thresholds. This timely warning may help policymakers evacuate people from polluted areas before the problem causes pulmonary problems. Also, the timely warning may help policymakers to take steps to reduce vehicular traffic and other sources of pollution in an area to reduce the predicted effects of air pollution. Furthermore, the developed models can be deployed at air quality monitoring stations with minimal cost, where air quality is measured manually or using real-time methods. Future research may build upon this work and develop and compare multivariate models to forecast air pollution. In such models, values of weather variables (like wind speed and direction, temperature, and relative humidity) may be used along with prior values of pollutants ($PM_{2.5}$) to arrive at superior forecasts. Here, the developed individual and ensemble multivariate models may be compared with univariate individual and ensemble models. Another aspect is to consider classical machine learning models like decision trees, support vector machines, and k-nearest neighbor approach alongside connectionist models (like MLPs, LSTMs, and CNNs) for forecasting air pollution. Still, another focus could be in developing longer-term forecasts of pollution values that are several hours ahead in time. Some of these ideas form the immediate next steps in our program concerning monitoring, warning, and prediction of air pollution.

Acknowledgment. This research work was made possible by a grant provided by the Department of Environment Science and Technology, Government of Himachal Pradesh, on the project IITM/DST-HP/VD/240 to Dr. Varun Dutt and Er. Pratik Chaturvedi. We are also grateful for the computational support provided by the Indian Institute of Technology Mandi, HP, India.

References

1. Asteriou, D., Hall, S.G.: ARIMA models and the Box–Jenkins methodology. Appl. Econom. **2**(2), 265–286 (2011)
2. Busemeyer, R.J., et al.: Cognitive Modeling. SAGE Publications, Inc. (2009)
3. Ferlito, S., Bosso, F., De Vito, S., Esposito, E., Di Francia, G.: LSTM networks for particulate matter concentration forecasting. In: Di Francia, G., et al. (eds.) AISEM 2019. LNEE, vol. 629, pp. 409–415. Springer, Cham (2020). https://doi.org/10.1007/978-3-030-37558-4_61
4. Feng, R., et al.: Analysis and accurate prediction of ambient $PM_{2.5}$ in China using multi-layer perceptron. Atmos. Environ. **232**, 117534 (2020)
5. Ganesh, S.S., et al.: Prediction of $PM_{2.5}$ using an ensemble of artificial neural networks and regression models. J. Ambient Intell. Humaniz. Comput., 1–11 (2018)
6. Haşim, S., et al.: Long short-term memory based recurrent neural network architectures for large vocabulary speech recognition. arXiv preprint arXiv:1402.1128 (2014)
7. Huang, C.J., et al.: A deep CNN-LSTM model for particulate matter ($PM_{2.5}$) forecasting in smart cities. Sensors. Article no. 18, 2220 (2018)
8. Jiuxiang, G., et al.: Recent advances in convolutional neural networks. Pattern Recogn. **77**, 354–377 (2018)
9. Kaushik, S., et al.: AI in healthcare: time-series forecasting using statistical, neural, and ensemble architectures. Front. Big Data **3** (2020). https://doi.org/10.3389/fdata.2020.00004
10. Kotu, V., et al:. Data Science, 2nd edn, pp. 19–37 (2019)
11. Leung, H., et al.: The complex backpropagation algorithm. IEEE Trans. Signal Process. **39**, 2101–2104 (1991)
12. Li, T., et al.: A hybrid CNN-LSTM model for forecasting particulate matter ($PM_{2.5}$). IEEE Access **8**, 26933–26940 (2020). https://doi.org/10.1109/ACCESS.2020.2971348
13. Liang, X., et al.: Assessing Beijing's $PM_{2.5}$ pollution: severity, weather impact, APEC and winter heating. Proc. R. Soc. A **471**, 20150257 (2015)
14. OECD: The economic consequences of outdoor air pollution. https://www.oecd.org/env ironment/indicators-modelling-outlooks/Policy-Highlights-Economic-Consequences-of-out door-air-pollution-web.pdf
15. Pozza, S.A., et al.: Time series analysis of PM2.5 and PM10− 2.5 mass concentration in the city of Sao Carlos, Brazil. Int. J. Environ. Pollut. **41**(1–2), 90–108 (2010)

16. Qiao, W., et al.: The forecasting of PM2. 5 using a hybrid model based on wavelet transform and an improved deep learning algorithm. IEEE Access **7** (2019)
17. Ramchoun, H., et al.: Multilayer perceptron: architecture optimization and training. IJIMAI **4**(1), 26–30 (2016)
18. Sharma, R., et al.: An online low-cost system for air quality monitoring, prediction, and warning. In: Hung, D.V., D'Souza, M. (eds.) ICDCIT 2020. LNCS, vol. 11969, pp. 311–324. Springer, Cham (2020). https://doi.org/10.1007/978-3-030-36987-3_20
19. Sepp, H., Schmidhuber, J.: Long short-term memory. Neural Comput. **9**(8), 1735–1780 (1997)
20. Tsai, Y., et al.: Air pollution forecasting using RNN with LSTM. In: IEEE 16th International Conference on Dependable, Autonomic and Secure Computing, 16th International Conference on Pervasive Intelligence and Computing, 4th International Conference on Big Data Intelligence and Computing and Cyber Science and Technology Congress, Athens, pp. 1074–1079 (2018)
21. Wang, J., et al.: CNN-RNN: a unified framework for multi-label image classification. In: Proceedings of the IEEE Conference on Computer Vision and Pattern Recognition (2016)
22. WHO: Ambient (Outdoor) Air Pollution. https://www.who.int/news-room/fact-sheets/detail/ambient-(outdoor)-air-quality-and-health
23. Yamashita, R., Nishio, M., Do, R.K.G., Togashi, K.: Convolutional neural networks: an overview and application in radiology. Insights Imaging **9**(4), 611–629 (2018). https://doi.org/10.1007/s13244-018-0639-9
24. Zhou, Q., et al.: A hybrid model for PM2.5 forecasting based on ensemble empirical mode decomposition and a general regression neural network. Sci. Total Environ. **496**, 264–274 (2014)

DualPrune: A Dual Purpose Pruning of Convolutional Neural Networks for Resource-Constrained Devices

Tejalal Choudhary, Vipul Mishra$^{(\boxtimes)}$, and Anurag Goswami

Department of Computer Science and Engineering, Bennett University,
Greater Noida 201310, India
tejalal.choudhary@gmail.com, {vipul.mishra,
anurag.goswami}@bennett.edu.in

Abstract. Many successful applications of deep learning have been witnessed in various domains. However, the use of deep learning models in edge-devices is still limited. Deploying a large model onto small devices for real-time inference requires an adequate amount of resources. In the last couple of years, pruning has evolved as an important and widely used technique to reduce the inference cost and compress the storage-intensive deep learning models for small devices. In this paper, we proposed a novel dual-purpose pruning approach to accelerate the model performance and reduce the storage requirement of the model. The experiments on the CIFAR10 dataset with AlexNet and VGG16 models show that our proposed approach is effective and can be used to make the deployment of the trained model easier for edge-devices with marginal loss of accuracy. For the VGG16 experiment, our approach reduces parameters from 14.98M to 3.7M resulting in a 74.73% reduction in floating-point operations with only 0.8% loss in the accuracy.

Keywords: Deep Neural Network · Pruning · Model acceleration and compression · Resource-constrained devices

1 Introduction

Deep Neural Networks (DNNs) are getting popular in various domains, and have shown significant improvement in their ability to work well on a variety of data such as text, audio, video, and image. One of the popular variants of the DNNs is the convolutional neural network (CNN). CNNs have achieved state-of-the-art accuracies in various vision-based applications such as segmentation, detection, classification, image generation to name a few. Over the years, CNN architecture has expanded in their depth (increased number of hidden layers) and width (increased nodes/filters in each layer) from a 5 layer LeNet-5 [19] to 152 layers ResNets [11]. The large number of parameters helps DNN during training to converge faster and generalize. At the same time, the over-parameterized model leads to over-fitting [30]. Moreover, the introduction of graphics processing units

© Springer Nature Singapore Pte Ltd. 2021
D. Garg et al. (Eds.): IACC 2020, CCIS 1367, pp. 395–406, 2021.
https://doi.org/10.1007/978-981-16-0401-0_30

(GPUs) has solved the problem of training the DNN model with millions of parameters up to some extent, and it is a onetime process.

Nowadays resource-constrained devices such as Smartphone's and other IoT based-devices are increasing year by year. Bringing the power of DNNs in edge-devices can open dozens of possibilities for real-time on-node inference. However, DNN models generally have millions of parameters which consume large memory, energy, and require high processing power. There are many applications that require on-demand human-like decision-making abilities, for example, a driverless car must detect various objects on road in real-time such as animals, pedestrians, traffic signals, and other vehicles to make them successful. For real-time applications, DNN needs to be deployed in end-devices rather than relying on cloud or web-based solutions.

One of the important constrains that limits the deployment of the trained model in edge-devices is that the edge-devices cannot run DNNs with millions of parameters due to the lack of computational and battery power required to run the large DNNs, limited memory is another contraint. In addition, DNNs perform a lot of FLOPs while operating on input data. Each FLOP consumes some amount of battery power [13]. In short, the deployment of DNNs on resource-constrained devices is hindered by their limited resources availability. The storage requirement of the DNNs can be lowered by reducing the number of learnable parameters from the dense layers, while the inference performance can be improved by reducing parameters/filters from convolutional layers [4].

Inference with deeper networks with a large number of parameters takes more time. It has been found in earlier research that once the training is over, DNNs do not need a large number of parameters during inference. Hence, eliminating unimportant connections would lead to a better model and also reduce storage and computational cost. Eliminating the parameters will result in removing unwanted/unimportant connections which will improve the performance of the DNN.

There exists various methods to find the unimportant weight parameters and eliminate them. The main motive behind the elimination of unimportant parameters is to compress the size of the model and also lower the time taking FLOPs to accelerate the inference performance [9]. However, removal of these parameters should least affect the performance of the network.

Out of the many compression and acceleration techniques such as weight quantization and sharing, knowledge distillation (KD), low-rank approximation, pruning is a widely used technique to remove the unimportant/redundant parameters from the network. In pruning, the parameters are either set to zero or completely removed from the network [9]. Pruning can be applied at different levels i.e. individual weight connections [9], a complete neuron [29], filter [22], or layer [2]. Pruning DNN makes model smaller in size, inference efficient, and it also solves the issue of over-fitting.

The main idea of the paper is to compress and accelerate the performance of the DNN model so that it can run under the constraints of the target device. To achieve the compression and acceleration, we proposed to prune unimportant weight parameters from the dense layers and filters from the convolutional layers respectively. Pruning dense layer will help to reduce the model size whereas pruning filters will reduce the number of FLOPs that directly affects the inference time.

This paper has been organized into various sections. The existing contribution made by the researchers in the field of model compression and acceleration has been discussed in Sect. 2. Section 3 explains the proposed methodology. The experiments performed on the pre-trained models and results are included in Sect. 4 and 5 respectively. Finally, the conclusion is summarized in Sect. 6.

2 Related Work

Model compression and acceleration has become a popular research area in the deep learning community, and significant improvements have been seen in the last couple of years. There are several techniques to compress and accelerate the model performance such as pruning, quantization and weight sharing, knowledge distillation, and low-rank approximation. Each of these techniques solves a different purpose. In this section, we have discussed the existing contribution made in the field of model compression and acceleration.

Pruning is a well-known method to remove unimportant parameters of the model and improve inference performance. The early works on pruning were based on removing connections based on the saliency of the parameters [10,20]. In one of the research [9], the authors proposed to remove small magnitude parameters from the network. Specifically, the authors proposed training, pruning, and fine-tuning pipeline. [29] found in their research that removing individual weight connections is a time-consuming process, the authors proposed to remove complete neuron if it is redundant. The authors relate it with the popular Hebbian rule which says "neuron that fire together wire together". Before removing the neuron, the activation of the removed neuron is transferred to another neuron. In another research [22], it is found that removal of the parameters from the dense layers only makes model smaller, to accelerate the actual performance of the model, the authors proposed to prune complete filter from the layer based on the L1-norm. There are other research work in which the authors proposed to remove filters based on batch-normalization parameters [24], the influence of the filters on the next layer [25]. In another research [32], the authors proposed to prune network layers based on their power consumption. From a very DNN, pruning of a complete layer is also proposed by [2].

The existing pruning methods only perform one particular type of pruning either i.e. individual weight or filter pruning. We have proposed to prune individual weight connections from the dense layer, and also the pruning of filters which not important from the convolutional layer. This helps in reducing the size of the model as well as in improving the inference performance.

Quantization is another popular techniques to make DNNs efficient. In quantization weights are represented with smaller bits instead of 32-bit precision [3,21]. The weights of the DNN can be quantized to sixteen bit, eight bit, or even less. Other than the weights, gradient and activations can also be quantized [14]. Another popular form of the quantization is known as weight binarization where the weights are represented with 1-bit [5,23]. The weights of the DNN can be quantized during or after the training.

The use of low-rank approximation methods is also explored to represent the large weight matrix with smaller matrices. Singular value decomposition (SVD) is a well known approach to factorize the large matrices into smaller matrices [8,33]. [31] proposes a sparse-low rank (SLR) approach in which the authors first make the weigh matrix sparse and to make the model smaller uses low-rank representation for resulting dense layer sparse matrix.

Knowledge distillation (KD) is another popular way of reducing the model size and computational required. In KD, a smaller student model is trained by the large teacher model [4,12]. There are many research works [1,18,27] which addressed KD in different ways. For a more detailed study of various compression and acceleration techniques, the readers are suggested to refer to recent surveys [4].

3   Methodology

In this section, we discuss the proposed convolutional and dense layer pruning approach. In each convolutional layer l, a set of filters is applied that works as a feature extractor and generates one feature map which is given as input to the next $l+1$ layer. The convolutional layer is followed by another kind of layers such as batch normalization, pooling, and non-linearity. Figure 1 shows the pruning of filters from the convolutional layer and pruning of weight connections from the dense layer before and after pruning. In Fig. 1, the unimportant filters are shown as a dotted line and dense layer weight connections are shown as a red dotted line. In the lower part of Fig. 1, the pruned filters and its corresponding feature map is highlighted with the red color. Similarly, the unimportant weight connections from the dense layer are removed.

The earlier methods of model compression and acceleration do not solve both purposes. Some methods are designed to only reduce the storage while others bring acceleration. In CNN, the storage required by the model is dominated by the dense layers, while the convolutional layers are responsible for consuming more than 90% computational time [7]. We target to achieve both goals keeping in mind that for edge-devices a model not only needs to be fast but also smaller in size. We proposed a dual-purpose pruning approach to compress and accelerate the trained CNN. Our proposed approach takes the trained model as an input and removes the unimportant filters from the convolutional layer and weight connections from the dense layers. Figure 2 shows our proposed dual-purpose pruning and fine-tuning approach. It takes an original train model M as input and finally generates accelerated and compressed model M_p. The whole approach can be divided into two main sub-blocks. First is the acceleration block in which we prune unimportant filters and second is the compression block, where the accelerated model is compressed to make it smaller in size.

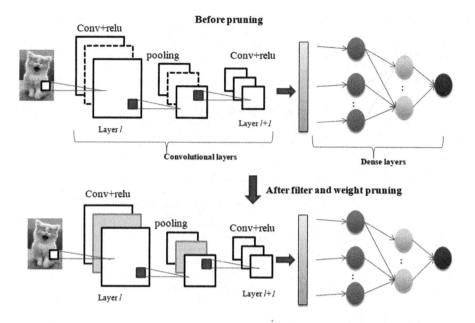

Fig. 1. CNN before and after pruning. (Color figure online)

3.1 Acceleration Block

In CNNs, the feature extraction part is done by the convolutional layer filters. Each filter applies to the input to generate the feature map. In each convolutional layer, there are few filters that are unimportant compared to the other filters and do not contain useful information. In our proposed acceleration block, we used the absolute sum of each filter to identify these unimportant filters. All the filters are ranked by their absolute sum and a given percentage of low ranking filters are pruned. Figure 2 shows the overall steps followed to accelerate the model after training. We locally prune the least important X% filters in each layer. The selection of the X is done empirically. After removing the filters and their activations, the numbers of input channels are also reduced in the next layer. Once the unimportant filters are pruned, a new network architecture is created with remaining filters and the weights of the remaining filters are copied into the new model.

3.2 Compression Block

The working of the compression block is shown in the lower part of Fig. 2. After pruning of convolutional filters, dense layer weights are examined to identify weight connections that are less important and can be removed. It has been shown in earlier research that weights with smaller values do not contribute more to improve the network performance and reduce the error. Hence, the selection of the weight connections for pruning is done based on their magnitudes. In

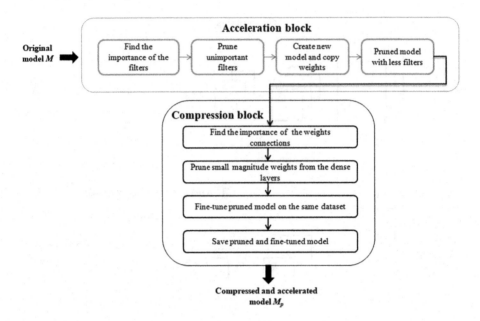

Fig. 2. Proposed 'DualPrune' acceleration and compression framework.

the compression block, the accelerated model is given as input where the small magnitude weights are ranked as per their magnitudes, and pruned. Finally, the resulting network is re-trained to recover the accuracy loss.

4   Experiments

This section details the experiments performed on the AlexNet [17], VGG16 [28] model, and CIFAR10 [16] dataset to validate the generalization and effectiveness of the proposed method. All the experiments are performed on a single GPU of NVIDIA DGX V100 supercomputer with 16GB RAM. The next subsections provide the details of the convolutional architecture and dataset used in the experiments.

4.1   Convolutional Models Used

The initial sets of experiments are performed with AlexNet [17] architecture. Original AlexNet architecture has 5 convolutional layers and 3 dense layers. It was trained on ImageNet [6] dataset, and won the ILSVRC challenge in 2012. In our experiments, we used a modified version of the original AlexNet [15], and make some changes to the dense layers to have 512 neurons in the first two dense layers instead of 4096. Finally, a softmax output layer is added with 10 classes.

We further extend our experiments to a more popular VGG16 convolutional architecture. VGG16 has shown its importance on various computer vision tasks. It has 13 convolutional layers and 3 dense layers, and it was trained on the ImageNet dataset. It has 138M parameters and 30.97B FLOPs. Our experiments use a variation of the original model in which convolutional layers are the same, however, has one dense layer with 512 nodes and one softmax output layer. The number of nodes in the softmax layer is equal to the number of classes in the CIFAR10 dataset. VGG16 is trained from scratch. One reason behind reducing the number of dense layers is that the CIFAR10 is a comparatively small dataset than ImageNet which has 1000 classes.

4.2 Dataset

CIFAR10 is a widely used classification dataset. It has 60,000 color images of 32 * 32 pixel size divided into 10 classes. The 10 different classes are truck, ship, horse, airplane, frog, dog, deer, cat, automobile, and bird. Five training batches contain exactly 10,000 images each, and one testing batch has exactly 10,000 images. Following are the common steps involved while performing experiments

- Train AlexNet, VGG16 model on CIFAR10 dataset, and save the trained models.
- Use the proposed approach to prune the trained model for the desired percentage.
- Finally, re-train the pruned model for more epochs to recover the accuracy loss.

4.3 Training the Base Models

AlexNet base model is trained for 100 epochs on the CIFAR10 dataset with ReLu non-linearity. VGG16 model is trained on CIFAR10 datasets for 160 epochs. No changes are made to the training and testing data distribution, the default data splits are used. An SGD optimizer with momentum is used to optimize the network during training. The learning rate was set to 0.1 during training and it is decayed by 10 after every 30 epochs. Weight decay was set to 1e-4. PyTorch [26] deep learning framework is used for the implementation. In each case, the model with the best accuracy is saved and used for pruning.

4.4 Pruning

The filters from the convolutional layer are pruned based on their absolute sum. The absolute sum is calculated for all the layers and a given percentage of filters are pruned from each layer. During pruning of the filters, their corresponding activation maps are also pruned. Pruning filter and its feature map reduces the input channels for the next layer, hence, after pruning the number of input channels in the next layer is also reduced. We tested our approach with different pruning percentages for convolutional as well as for the dense layer. For the dense layer pruning, all the weight connections are ranked as per their magnitude and the desired percentage of connections are pruned.

4.5   Fine-Tuning

Pruning trained model brings some degradation in the accuracy. It is necessary to re-train the resulting pruned model on the same dataset for few more epochs. We fine-tuned AlexNet and VGG16 pruned model for 50 & 80 epochs respectively to recover from the accuracy loss. The same hyper-parameters are used that we used while training the base models excepting the learning rate. Since the model was already trained and does not require higher learning rates. Keeping this in mind, during fine-tuning the learning rate is reduced to 0.001 from 0.1. We do not make any other changes to the training parameters while fine-tuning the pruned model.

Table 1. Summary of the various experiments performed on the AlexNet model and CIFAR10 dataset. DLPP: dense layer parameters pruned

Exp no	Pruning%	#Para	DLPP	FLOPs	Acc drop
1	Conv:50, Dense:50	958506	166401	4458506	−1.8
2	Conv:50, Dense:30	958506	99841	4458506	−2.1
3	Conv:50, Dense:50 First conv layer:25	1002762	166401	5447690	−0.9
4	Conv:60, Dense:60 First conv layer:0	810181	191693	5164338	−0.7
5	**Conv:60, Dense:60 First conv layer:25**	**773525**	**191693**	**4296754**	**−0.7**
6	Conv:60, Dense:60	723123	191693	3103826	−2.7

5   Results

AlexNet: Table 1 shows the summary of the various experiments performed on the AlexNet model and the CIFAR10 dataset. In Table 1 DLPP is the dense layer parameters pruned. It can be seen from Table 1 that the best pruned model is achieved when the pruning percentage is 60% for both convolutional layer as well as dense layer, however, the first layer is more sensitive to pruning, in that case, the pruning percentage for the first layer was 25%. This pruning configuration results in reducing model parameters from 2.87M to 0.72M. Also, the FLOPs are reduced from 15.38M to 4.2M with a marginal loss of accuracy. The best accuracy is achieved during fine-tuning at 45th epoch.

VGG16: For the VGG16 model, multiple experiments are performed with different pruning configuration and the best results are achieved when the pruning configuration for the convolutional and dense layer was 50 and 30 percent

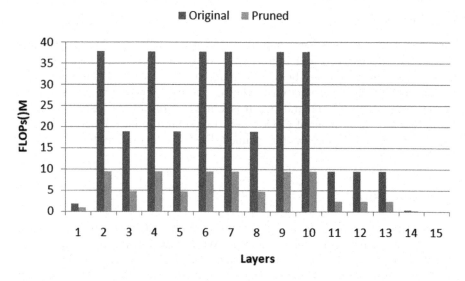

Fig. 3. The layer-wise number of FLOPs in the original vs best pruned VGG16 model

Table 2. Comparison with other methods (VGG16 model)

Method	#Parameter left	FLOP reduction	Accuracy drop
[22]	5.4M	34.2%	0.15
[34]	3.92M	39.1%	−0.07
Ours	**3.7M**	**74.73%**	**−0.8**

respectively. The model parameters are pruned from 14.98M to 3.7M. The time-consuming FLOPs are also reduced from 313M to 79.07M with only 0.8% loss in the top1 accuracy after fine-tuning. Figure 3 shows the FLOPs of the original vs best pruned model. It can be seen from Fig. 3 that the convolutional layers contain a significant number of unimportant filters and a large number of filters can be removed from the layers that brings the acceleration in the model performance.

The experiments on the AlexNet and VGG16 model show the importance and effectiveness of the proposed dual-purpose pruning approach. However, the dataset onto which the experiments are carried out is very small. To test the generalization ability of the proposed approach, experiments needs to be performed on the large scale dataset. ImageNet is one such dataset which has 1.2M training images. In the future, more experiments will be performed with different convolutional architectures and the ImageNet dataset.

5.1 Comparison

The initial sets of experiments are performed with AlexNet and CIFAR10 dataset to test the effectiveness and applicability of the proposed method. We compare our method with other best performing methods on VGG16 and CIFAR10 dataset. Table 2 shows the details of the comparative study. The proposed approach is compared with [22] and [34]. It is found that our method is superior than [22] in terms of the number of FLOPs reduction. Our approach is also superior to [34] in both number of parameters pruned, FLOP reduction, and also improved accuracy.

6 Conclusion

In this paper, we proposed a dual-purpose pruning approach to make DNNs efficient for resource-constrained devices. We tested our approach on two different popular convolutional networks and CIFAR10 dataset. For the VGG16 experiment, our approach reduces parameters from 14.98M to 3.7M resulting in a 74.73% reduction in floating-point operations with only 0.8% loss in the accuracy. The experimental results suggest show that our method is able to reduce the number of learnable parameters and also time-consuming FLOPs of the model. Resulting pruned model is efficient for deployment in edge-devices where the adequate resources required to run DNNs are not available. In the future, we will test the applicability and generalization ability of our approach to distinct convolutional architecture and large-scale ImageNet dataset.

References

1. Xiang, L., Ding, G., Han, J.: Learning from multiple experts: self-paced knowledge distillation for long-tailed classification. In: Vedaldi, A., Bischof, H., Brox, T., Frahm, J.-M. (eds.) ECCV 2020, Part V. LNCS, vol. 12350, pp. 247–263. Springer, Cham (2020). https://doi.org/10.1007/978-3-030-58558-7_15
2. Chen, S., Zhao, Q.: Shallowing deep networks: layer-wise pruning based on feature representations. IEEE Trans. Pattern Aanal. Mach. Intell. **41**, 3048–3056 (2018)
3. Cheng, J., Wu, J., Leng, C., Wang, Y., Hu, Q.: Quantized CNN: a unified approach to accelerate and compress convolutional networks. IEEE Trans. Neural Netw. Learn. Syst. **29**, 4730–4743 (2017)
4. Choudhary, T., Mishra, V., Goswami, A., Sarangapani, J.: A comprehensive survey on model compression and acceleration. Artif. Intell. Rev. 1–43 (2020)
5. Courbariaux, M., Bengio, Y., David, J.P.: Binaryconnect: training deep neural networks with binary weights during propagations. In: Advances in Neural Information Processing Systems, pp. 3123–3131 (2015)
6. Deng, J., Dong, W., Socher, R., Li, L.J., Li, K., Fei-Fei, L.: Imagenet: a large-scale hierarchical image database. In: IEEE Conference on Computer Vision and Pattern Recognition, pp. 248–255. IEEE (2009)
7. Denil, M., Shakibi, B., Dinh, L., De Freitas, N., et al.: Predicting parameters in deep learning. In: Advances in Neural Information Processing Systems, pp. 2148–2156 (2013)

8. Denton, E.L., Zaremba, W., Bruna, J., LeCun, Y., Fergus, R.: Exploiting linear structure within convolutional networks for efficient evaluation. In: Advances in Neural Information Processing Systems, pp. 1269–1277 (2014)
9. Han, S., Pool, J., Tran, J., Dally, W.: Learning both weights and connections for efficient neural network. In: Advances in Neural Information Processing Systems, pp. 1135–1143 (2015)
10. Hassibi, B., Stork, D.G.: Second order derivatives for network pruning: Optimal brain surgeon. In: Advances in Neural Information Processing Systems, pp. 164–171 (1993)
11. He, K., Zhang, X., Ren, S., Sun, J.: Deep residual learning for image recognition. In: Proceedings of the IEEE Conference on Computer Vision and Pattern Recognition, pp. 770–778 (2016)
12. Hinton, G.E., Vinyals, O., Dean, J.: Distilling the knowledge in a neural network. CoRR abs/1503.02531 (2015)
13. Horowitz, M.: 1.1 computing's energy problem (and what we can do about it). In: 2014 IEEE International Solid-State Circuits Conference Digest of Technical Papers (ISSCC), pp. 10–14. IEEE (2014)
14. Hubara, I., Courbariaux, M., Soudry, D., El-Yaniv, R., Bengio, Y.: Quantized neural networks: training neural networks with low precision weights and activations. J. Mach. Learn. Rese. **18**(1), 6869–6898 (2017)
15. Krizhevsky, A.: One weird trick for parallelizing convolutional neural networks. arXiv preprint arXiv:1404.5997 (2014)
16. Krizhevsky, A., Hinton, G.: Learning multiple layers of features from tiny images. Technical report, Citeseer (2009)
17. Krizhevsky, A., Sutskever, I., Hinton, G.E.: Imagenet classification with deep convolutional neural networks. In: Advances in Neural Information Processing Systems, pp. 1097–1105 (2012)
18. Lan, X., Zhu, X., Gong, S.: Knowledge distillation by on-the-fly native ensemble. In: Proceedings of the 32nd International Conference on Neural Information Processing Systems, pp. 7528–7538. Curran Associates Inc. (2018)
19. LeCun, Y., Bottou, L., Bengio, Y., Haffner, P.: Gradient-based learning applied to document recognition. Proc. IEEE **86**(11), 2278–2324 (1998)
20. LeCun, Y., Denker, J.S., Solla, S.A.: Optimal brain damage. In: Advances in Neural Information Processing Systems, pp. 598–605 (1990)
21. Li, F., Liu, B.: Ternary weight networks. In: 30th Conference on Neural Information Processing Systems (NIPS), Barcelona, Spain (2016)
22. Li, H., Kadav, A., Durdanovic, I., Samet, H., Graf, H.P.: Pruning filters for efficient convnets. Published as a conference paper at ICLR (2017)
23. Lin, Z., Courbariaux, M., Memisevic, R., Bengio, Y.: Neural networks with few multiplications. Published as a conference paper at ICLR (2016)
24. Liu, Z., Li, J., Shen, Z., Huang, G., Yan, S., Zhang, C.: Learning efficient convolutional networks through network slimming. In: Proceedings of the IEEE International Conference on Computer Vision, pp. 2736–2744 (2017)
25. Luo, J.H., Zhang, H., Zhou, H.Y., Xie, C.W., Wu, J., Lin, W.: Thinet: Pruning CNN filters for a thinner net. IEEE Trans. Pattern Anal. Mach. Intel. **41**, 2525–2538 (2018)
26. Paszke, A., et al.: Automatic differentiation in pytorch (2017)
27. Shen, J., Vesdapunt, N., Boddeti, V.N., Kitani, K.M.: In teacher we trust: Learning compressed models for pedestrian detection. arXiv preprint arXiv:1612.00478 (2016)

28. Simonyan, K., Zisserman, A.: Very deep convolutional networks for large-scale image recognition. In: Published as a Conference Paper at ICLR (2015)
29. Srinivas, S., Babu, R.V.: Data-free parameter pruning for deep neural networks. arXiv preprint arXiv:1507.06149 (2015)
30. Srivastava, N., Hinton, G., Krizhevsky, A., Sutskever, I., Salakhutdinov, R.: Dropout: a simple way to prevent neural networks from overfitting. J. Mach. Learn. Res. 15(1), 1929–1958 (2014)
31. Swaminathan, S., Garg, D., Kannan, R., Andres, F.: Sparse low rank factorization for deep neural network compression. Neurocomputing (2020)
32. Yang, T.J., Chen, Y.H., Sze, V.: Designing energy-efficient convolutional neural networks using energy-aware pruning. In: Proceedings of the IEEE Conference on Computer Vision and Pattern Recognition. pp. 5687–5695 (2017)
33. Zhang, X., Zou, J., He, K., Sun, J.: Accelerating very deep convolutional networks for classification and detection. IEEE Trans. Pattern Anal. Mach. Intell. 38(10), 1943–1955 (2016)
34. Zhao, C., Ni, B., Zhang, J., Zhao, Q., Zhang, W., Tian, Q.: Variational convolutional neural network pruning. In: Proceedings of the IEEE Conference on Computer Vision and Pattern Recognition, pp. 2780–2789 (2019)

Incremental Ensemble of One Class Classifier for Data Streams with Concept Drift Adaption

Shubhangi Suryawanshi[1,2]([✉]), Anurag Goswami[1], and Pramod Patil[2]

[1] Bennett University, Greater Noida, India
{ss5683,anurag.goswami}@bennett.edu.in
[2] Pune University, Pune, India
shubhangi.suryawanshi@raisoni.net, pdpatiljune@gmail.com

Abstract. Due to the digital era, and recent development in software and hardware technology uses enormous applications like e-commerce, mailing system, social media, fraud detection, weather and network application. These applications generate a huge amount of continuous, sequenced, temporarily ordered and infinite data called as a data stream. There is a need to manage such data streams with real-time responses and sufficient memory requirements. Data streams lead to a problem of changing data distribution of the target variable is called as the concept drift. The Learning model performance degrades if the concept drift is not addressed, so there is a need for a learning model that adapts the concept drift by retaining the good performance of the model. One-class classification is a promising research area in the field of data streams classification. In the One-class classification, only the positive samples are considered to address the class imbalance and drift detection problem by not considering their counterparts. In this paper, an Incremental One-class Ensemble classifier is used to adapt the concept drift problem in streaming data. Model is evaluated with the Spam and Electricity real-world datasets and the model is used to address Gradual and sudden drift with 82.30% and 81.50% accuracy.

Keywords: Data stream · Drift · Data distribution · Incremental ensemble classifier · One class classification

1 Introduction

Due to the recent advancement in technology, an infinite amount of continuous Streaming data are evolving which leads to a change in the data distribution over time. This change is known as a concept drift that is affecting the accuracy of the learning model [1,2]. Many applications which are facing the problem of concept drift [1], few are Emailing System, Weather, Energy Consumption, Fraud Detection, E-commerce. Consider the example of the buying preferences of customers, which are changing and depending on many factors like a month,

© Springer Nature Singapore Pte Ltd. 2021
D. Garg et al. (Eds.): IACC 2020, CCIS 1367, pp. 407–416, 2021.
https://doi.org/10.1007/978-981-16-0401-0_31

day of the week, seasons, Fashion trends, rate of inflation that may not be the features of the dataset, as the customer's interest changes over time depending upon above parameters, and it affects the prediction of the learning model . In this example, the seasons are recurrently appearing every year.

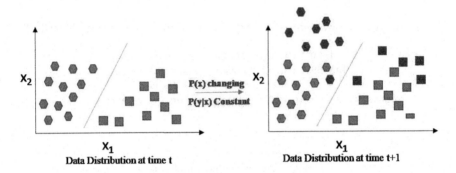

Fig. 1. Virtual drift

Concept drift is categorized into Virtual and the Real drift. Consider a source S generating the data streams $S = (x_1, y_1), (x_2, y_2), \ldots, (x_n, y_n)$. In virtual drift as shown in Fig. 1 the $P(x)$, the input variable's data distribution is changing but it is not affecting the class boundary, and the posterior probability the target variable remains constant [1]. This category of the drift is not affecting the accuracy of the classifier [3].

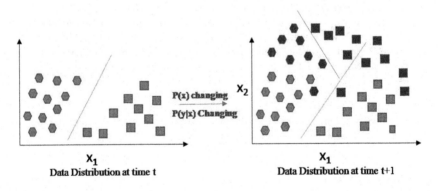

Fig. 2. Real drift

In the second category of the drift i.e. Real drift as shown in Fig. 2, the $P(x)$, the data distribution of the input variable is changing or sometimes remains constant but it is affecting the class boundary, and with changing the posterior probability of the target variable. This category of the drift is affecting the accuracy of the classifier [3]. Following is shown an example of the real drift.

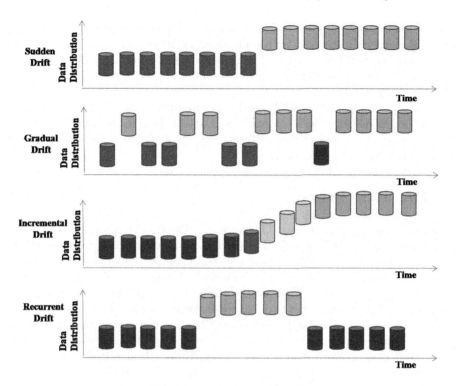

Fig. 3. Types of concept drift

1.1   Concept Drift Types

There are four types of concept drift Sudden, Gradual, Incremental, and recurrent drift [1,2] shown in Fig. 3.

- In the sudden drift, suddenly the data distribution is changing, and it never goes back to previous distribution. It is a permanent change. e.g.. consider a sensor, if it suddenly gives the faulty reading [1,2].
- In Gradual Drift continuously the data distribution is changing according to a particular timestamp, but it will become more noticeable over time. After a long time, the change will be identified [2].
- In the Incremental drift incrementally, changes are accruing in data distribution, it is noticeable after a long time [2].

There is a need for a learning model to identify the different types of concept drift and to differentiate different drift with noise. Many algorithms can be applied to adapt to drift without compromising the learning accuracy.

One-class classification [4,5] is a promising research direction in the area of Concept Drift adaption in data streams. It can be applied for the binary classification, Detection of Outlier, and identification of novel class. One-class classification can be applied to Non-stationary data streams to adapt to drifts by considering only the positive samples and not its counterparts.

The objective of this paper is to increase the learning accuracy of an ensemble of a One-class classifier with incremental learning. It gives promising results than a single classifier.

The paper is organized as follows: Literature Survey, Next Section is Experimental Design describe the Research Goal, Dataset, Independent and Dependent Variables and Experiment Steps. Result and its analysis is presented in next Section. Last section is Conclusion.

2 Literature Survey

This section details the different One-class classification algorithms and how one class classification can be applied to detect and adapt the concept drift problem.

In the research article [2] the data stream classification, as well as the data stream classification Challenges are discussed. The problem of classification i.e., the evolving data streams faces the problem of Concept drift. The changes in data distribution of the target variable are discussed to address the issue different techniques are discussed like One-class classification where only training data of positive samples are considered but for the negative class is available. In one class classification can't preserve the old data. Ensemble algorithm is applied for the concept of drift detection it can work well with the recurrent drifts. Decision tree-based algorithms are also discussed for the drift adaption.

In another research [3], authors have discussed the different data streams classification algorithms and their capability to address the concept drifts, Different categories of the concept drift and its types are explained. different concept drift datasets and the research direction in this field are discussed.

The integrated One-class classification [4] is used to address the concept drift issue by considering both positive and negative samples. They have performed the experiments on the text document dataset. The stacking of SVM is used to adapt the change in the concept that occurred due to the users changing interest rate. Achieved a maximum accuracy of 63.2% and addressed gradual and sudden drifts.

Weighted One class SVM classifier [5] employed for the gradual concept drift in the real-world dataset. One class classifier can be applied for binary classification. SVM is used with Incremental learning which can identify the hyperplane boundaries that can easily distinguish the change in the data distribution. Performed the experiments on Electricity and airline dataset with 72.04 and 66.14% accuracy.

New Random Forest Method for One-class Classification [6] in this paper they have used the one class classifier with random forest on the UC Irvine repository. In the random forest, they have used l = 200 tress. Compared the result with One class SVM (OCSVM). Random Forest's performance is outperformed than another classifier with 91% accuracy.

A Survey on One-class Classification [7] in this paper different ensemble methods for drift detection are discussed. AdaBoost and Bagging classifiers [13] are discussed for the dataset which is improperly sampled into positive and negative classes. For generating the prediction, the voting rule is used.

The ensemble approach is more popular in the concept of drift adaption in data stream processing [10,12]. In an ensemble approach, the heterogeneous classifier or same classifier with different parameters are combined. Drift detection based incremental classifier [8,9], explicit drift detection technique is used to detect the drift. It used an ensemble of hoeffding tree, for the drift detection in data streams. Many estimators of hoeffding trees are used old data is preserved by using the ensemble model.

A Survey on Supervised Classification on Data Streams [14,15] in this paper different algorithms like Naïve Bayes [11]. Hoeffding tree, very fast decision tree (VFDT), and the ensemble classifier for the data stream classification are discussed and how they are adapting the concept drift with or without drift detectors are discussed.

So based on this literature, we were motivated to apply the Ensemble of One-class classifier to detect and adapt the concept drift in evolving data streams.

3 Experiment Design

The motivation of this experiment was to provide evidence-based experimentation performed on the real-world data stream dataset, by using the ensemble of One-class classifiers and the results are compared with One-class SVM and One-class Naïve Bayes algorithm. Scikit-learn and Scikit-Multiflow framework used for experimentation. The Experimentation is performed in a computer with Core i3 Processor, 12 GB of main memory.

3.1 Research Goal

This research has the primary goal to analyze the efficiency of an ensemble of One-class classifiers to adapt the concept drift in the evolving data streams.

3.2 Dataset

- Electricity Dataset contains total number of 48,312 instances, attributes are 8 and with 2 classes. Real world Electricity dataset from Australian Electricity Market is used. The rise (UP) or a fall (DOWN) predicted by classifiers in electricity dataset.
  https://moa.cms.waikato.ac.nz/datasets/
- Spam Dataset is real word streaming dataset. Which is having 500 attributes with 9, 324 instances. Two class labels are considered spam and legitimate. This dataset is with gradual drift.
  http://spamassassin.apache.org/

3.3   Independent and Dependent Variables

The one class classification dependent variable is drift count and the independent variable features data distribution. Drift detection is depending on the change in data distribution of the features. If there is a change in the data distribution there will be a drift its value will be 1 otherwise the value will be 0.

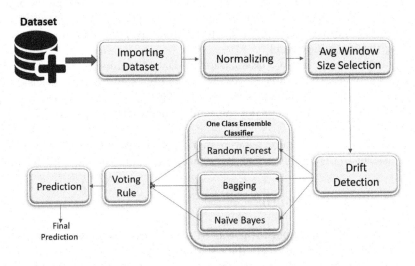

Fig. 4. Ensemble of One-class classifier for drift detection

3.4   Experiment Steps

The Experimentation steps (also shown in Fig. 4) are as follows:

Step 1 **Importing & Normalizing Dataset**
  Dataset is imported and converted into Panda's data frames.for the Normalization of Dataset MinMaxScaler is used for rescaling and for handling missing values. After converting it into data frames for the conversion of the features data, MinMaxScaler () is used. Which converts the data into the range of 0 to1, for missing values NaN is used.

Step 2 **Window Selection**
  For processing the data streams, the data stream is added into the window with a specified size. Optimal Window size is selected by performing Experiments with different window sizes. By appropriate selection of windows, the data distribution of that specific window size is checked.

Step 3 **Drift detection**

For drift detection, the data distribution of the incoming data streams is checked with previous data streams from the previous window if the data distribution is changing that point is identified as drift.

Step 4 **One-class Ensemble classifier and Voting Rule**

In this Ensemble of One-class Classifier, the group of different classifiers is combined and trained incrementally for prediction, the hard voting is considered. In hard voting, the rule of majority voting is applied for the prediction of outcome.

clf = Voting Classifier (estimators = [('RandomForest Classifier', clf1), ('Bagging Classifier', clf2), ('Multinomial NB', clf3)], voting = 'hard',weights = [2, 2, 1])

for the classifier, weights are assigned as [2, 2, 1] and the majority voted rule is applied.

Step 5 **Prediction**

for the prediction classifiers-based classifier hoeffding tree is used, to predict the new instance the Ensemble classifier is used. If the classifier misclassifies the incoming instance, then the model is updated incrementally with the incoming data instances.

The Experimentation performed by considering three classifiers One-class SVM, One-class Naïve Bayes, and Ensemble of One-class Classifier on Spam and Electricity dataset the results are as follows.

Step 6 **Result**

The Experimentation performed by considering three classifiers One-class SVM, One-class Naïve Bayes, and Ensemble of One-class Classifier on Spam and Electricity dataset the results are as follows (Table 1).

Table 1. Result with the real-world dataset and drift detected window size = 500

Sr. No	Classifiers	Dataset	Accuracy	Drift detected
1	One Class SVM	Spam Dataset	79.44	5
2	One Class Multinomial Naive Bayes		81.20	23
3	Ensemble of One class Classifiers		82.30	1
1	One Class SVM	Electricity Dataset	78.17	6
2	One Class Multinomial Naive Bayes		81.30	219
3	Ensemble of One class Classifiers		81.50	254

4 Analysis and Results

Experimentation is performed with different window sizes 50, 100, 500, 1000, 1500. It is observed that, 500 window size gives the optimal result. After performing the experimentation on the Spam and Electricity dataset by using One-class

SVM, One-class Naïve Bayes and Ensemble of One-class classifier. It is observed that the Ensemble of One-class is efficiently detected the drifts in One-class classification.

Total Number of Drift Detected 1
Parameters: Window Size 500,
Final Ensemble of One Class Classifier accuracy: 82.3004,
Elapsed time: 116.5569

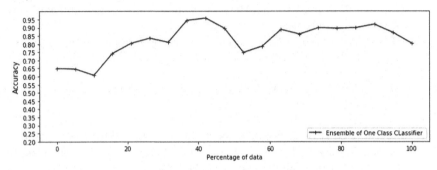

Fig. 5. One class ensemble classifier with electricity dataset

Total Number of Drift Detected 254
Parameters: Window Size 500,
Final Ensemble of One Class Classifier accuracy: 81.5023,
Elapsed time: 1009.2637

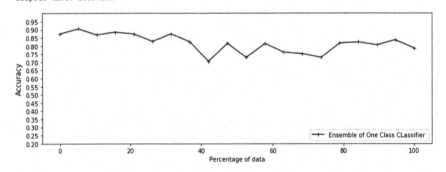

Fig. 6. One class ensemble classifier with spam dataset

In the Fig. 5 & Fig. 6 Graph is Shown, with Spam and Electricity dataset. In this graph, the blue line shows the accuracy measure across all batches (window). Y-axis shows the data instances, and the X-axis shows the accuracy measure. The variation or fluctuation across the different batch of data instances is shown in the graph and finally, the mean of the accuracy is calculated as output. The comparison of accuracy on the Spam and Electricity dataset is as shown below in Fig. 7.

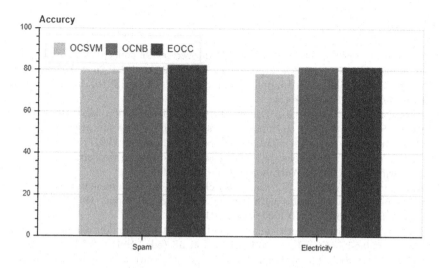

Fig. 7. Comparison of accuracy on spam and electricity dataset

The Incremental One-class Ensemble Classifier is adapting to the concept of drift and incrementally classifying the incoming instances. Drift detection methods are used to detect gradual and sudden drifts in a given dataset, and the ensemble One-class classifier adapts to drifts without compromising learning accuracy.

5   Conclusion and Future Scope

In this paper, the different One class Classifier algorithms are compared on the real dataset concept drift dataset. Our results show that the performance One-class Classifier in the drifting dataset depends on the appropriate window size which depends on the size of the dataset. In predefined norms, it shows that One-class SVM gives promising results in addressing Concept Drift in the data stream. In this paper, it is observed that the Ensemble classifier with heterogeneous learning model outperforms than other classifiers to address gradual and sudden drift.

In our experiment, we have used the change in the data distribution for detecting the drifts without differentiating with outlier maybe by considering the counterparts i.e. the negative samples affect the accuracy of the classifier.

In the future, One-class Classification can be applied to address the recurrent and incremental drift detection and adaption.

References

1. Žliobaitė, I., Pechenizkiy, M., Gama, J.: An overview of concept drift applications. In: Japkowicz, N., Stefanowski, J. (eds.) Big Data Analysis: New Algorithms for a New Society. SBD, vol. 16, pp. 91–114. Springer, Cham (2016). https://doi.org/10.1007/978-3-319-26989-4_4

2. Aggarwal, C.C.: Chapter 9 A Survey of Stream Classification Algorithms (2015)

3. Mehta, S.: Science direct concept drift in streaming data classification: algorithms, platforms and issues. Procedia Comput. Sci. **122**, 804–811 (2017)

4. Zhang, Y., Li, X., Orlowska, M.: One class classification of text streams with concept drift. In: ICDMW Workshop, pp. 116–125 (2008)

5. Krawczyk, B., Woźniak, M.: One-class classifiers with incremental learning and forgetting for data streams with concept drift. Soft Comput. **19**(12), 3387–3400 (2014). https://doi.org/10.1007/s00500-014-1492-5

6. Désir, C., Bernard, S., Petitjean, C., Heutte, L.: A new random forest method for one-class classification. In: Gimel'farb, G., et al. (eds.) SSPR /SPR 2012. LNCS, vol. 7626, pp. 282–290. Springer, Heidelberg (2012). https://doi.org/10.1007/978-3-642-34166-3_31

7. Bhatt, Y., Patel, N.S.: A survey on one-class classification using ensembles method. IJIRST **1**, 19–23 (2014)

8. Li, Z., Y. Xiong, Y., Huang, W.: Drift-detection based incremental ensemble for reacting to different kinds of concept drift. In: 2019 5th International Conference on Big Data Computing and Communications, pp. 107–114 (2019)

9. Krawczyk, B.: Diversity in ensembles for one-class classification. In: Pechenizkiy, M., Wojciechowski, M. (eds.) New Trends in Databases and Information Systems. AISC, vol. 185. Springer, Heidelberg (2013). https://doi.org/10.1007/978-3-642-32518-2_12

10. Krawczyk, B., Cyganek, B.: Selecting locally specialised classifiers for one-class classification ensembles. Pattern Anal. Appl. **20**(2), 427–439 (2015). https://doi.org/10.1007/s10044-015-0505-z

11. Sahami, M., Dumais, S., Heckerman, D., Horvitz, E.: A Bayesian approach to filtering junk e-mail. In: Learning for Text Categorization, Papers from the 1998 Workshop, vol. 62, pp. 98–105, July 1998

12. Krawczyk, B., Minku, L.L., Gama, J., Stefanowski, J., Wozniak, M.: Ensemble learning for data stream analysis: a survey. Inf. Fusion **37**, 132–156 (2017)

13. Trivedi, S.K., Dey, S.: Interplay between probabilistic classifiers and boosting algorithms for detecting complex unsolicited emails. J. Adv. Comput. Netw. **1**, 132–136 (2013)

14. Lemaire, V., Salperwyck, C., Bondu, A.: A survey on supervised classification on data streams. In: Zimányi, E., Kutsche, R.-D. (eds.) eBISS 2014. LNBIP, vol. 205, pp. 88–125. Springer, Cham (2015). https://doi.org/10.1007/978-3-319-17551-5_4

15. Nguyen, H.-L., Woon, Y.-K., Ng, W.-K.: A survey on data stream clustering and classification. Knowl. Inf. Syst. **45**(3), 535–569 (2014). https://doi.org/10.1007/s10115-014-0808-1

Detection of Ransomware on Windows System Using Machine Learning Technique: Experimental Results

Laxmi B. Bhagwat and Balaji M. Patil[✉]

School of Computer Science Engineering and Technology, Dr. Vishwanath Karad World Peace University, Kothrud, Pune, India
{laxmi.bhagwat,balaji.patil}@mitwpu.edu.in

Abstract. Recent statistics show that malware attacks have been increased by over 97% in the past two years. Among these, a large portion is due to Ransomware, a subset of malware. Ransomware codes are easily available as Ransomware as-a-service (RaaS). Because of it, there is a significant threat to the world, as this is a malware which generates high revenues and is creating a viable criminal business model. Because of this the systems of private companies, individuals, or public service providers are at stake and can suffer a severe disruption and financial loss. There are two methods for the detection and analysis to be done for the detection of ransomware. One is the Static detection approach and the other is the Dynamic detection approach. We have done the detection using the Dynamic approach. This paper focuses on detection of ransomware and benign applications using machine learning algorithms for dynamic detection of ransomware. Our experimentation results show that high accuracy is obtained using the KNN algorithm.

Keywords: Malware · Ransomware families · Encryption · File systems · Machine learning

1 Introduction

In today's world digitization is increasing professionally, socially, and financially in various sectors such as government, military, education, business [5], and health. These sectors rely more on the computer systems for their smooth operations. So these sectors are becoming targets of the cyber attackers. The attackers do attacks using malware. Malware is the malignant code used to perform malicious actions in digital devices like mobiles, tablets, and computers. Typical names of malware are viruses, worms, Trojans,etc. They are designed with different components and have various functionalities. This malware is spread across the world through internet. The Internet is a carrier for this malware and they enter the system by various techniques such as system vulnerabilities, drive-by download, attachments, and social engineering, etc. It becomes very important to just find a way to detect the malicious activity in the system. We have used the Machine Learning technique to detect the behavior of the Ransomware. As per the literature survey for detection of ransomware using dynamic approach we have used

© Springer Nature Singapore Pte Ltd. 2021
D. Garg et al. (Eds.): IACC 2020, CCIS 1367, pp. 417–423, 2021.
https://doi.org/10.1007/978-981-16-0401-0_32

KNN (K- Nearest Neighbors Classifier), SVM (Support Vector Machine), Random Forest and Logistic Regression as machine learning algorithms. We have used wrapper RFE (Recursive Feature Elimination) method and Extra Trees Classifier for feature selection. We have found the intersection of few features which were highly ranked by these two feature selection methods. Some features which were not common we saw the ranking of them and selected the highly ranked among them.

2   Related Work

Hajredin Daku et al. [4] used machine learning to identify new variants of Ransomware. They have used three ML algorithms for the detection of Ransomware. They have used 150 samples from 10 different families of Ransomware. They also have given the benefits of using dynamic analysis using machine learning over static analysis of Ransomware. In another study that is done by Zhi-Guo Chen et al.[3] tells how we can overcome the disadvantage of signature based and static analysis. They have done dynamic detection of Ransomware using Random Forest (RF), Support Vector Machine (SVM), Simple Logistic (SL), and Naive Bayes (NB) ML algorithms. They have used API calls and control flow graphs for the detection of Ransomware dynamically analysis technique. Daniele Sgandurra et al. [6] implemented EldeRan, an ML approach that detects Ransomware by dynamic analysis technique. EldeRan checks for the sign of Ransomware by monitoring the set of actions performed by an application. They have achieved a ROC curve of 0.995 in their implementation. Monika et al. [7] had their main understanding of how the evolution of ransomware occurs under the Windows and Android platforms. They had chosen ransomware variants from ransomware families in windows and Android environments. Their analysis after experimentation is there can be a significant improvement in the techniques used for encryption while performing ransomware attacks. The detection was done by monitoring the registry actions and file system actions. Yu-Lun Wan [8] et al. used Argus for labeling merging and packet preprocessing for the network traffic. They have combined six feature selection methods to obtain high accuracy while at the time of classification. A decision tree algorithm was used by them to improve the intrusion detection system. Ahmad O. Almashhadani et al. [11] have done the behavioral analysis of crypto-ransomware recording the activities that take place in the network. They have implemented an intrusion detection system by simultaneously recording the packet and flow levels.

3   Overall Process of Proposed System

The ransomware attack is mainly on the file system of the computer system. As shown in Fig. 1 for overall processing there are three main components: System/Virtual Machine with Windows OS platforms, Ransomware detection phase, and Classification phase. The system/virtual machine runs the application exe files in the sandbox. The sandbox generates the report in various formats. These reports generated were used for the generation of the data set. They were also used to find the required attributes from the generated data set values. From these data set some instances were used for training and some were used for testing. The models were trained using the training data sets and then the test data set were used for the detection of benign or ransomware.

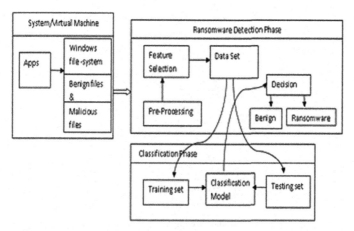

Fig. 1. Overall process of Proposed System

4   Ransomware Data Set Collection

4.1   System Overview

The data set collection process is as shown in Fig. 2. We created our data set from the ransomware sample files and benign application files. Ransomware and benign files samples were given to the cuckoo sandbox for analysis and report generation. The cuckoo sandbox [9] produced a detailed report for the samples provided in different formats. As we have decided on a dynamic analysis of Ransomware, we required the behavioral analysis category in the report that was generated by the Cuckoo sandbox. The report generated by the cuckoo sandbox was in the JSON file format. As we got the results in JSON format, we had written the parser to parse the contents of the file and extracted the keyword features relating to file access, processes, registry changes, etc. Data that was related to the extracted features were stored in a CSV file format to do further analysis. When extracting different features we have maintained the count for each feature that was affected or altered by the ransomware samples. After creating the CSV file we got 262 features on which we applied feature selection methods to select the most important and relevant features for the detection of ransomware. The machine learning classifier was the final stage that performed the task of detecting if a file is benign or ransomware.

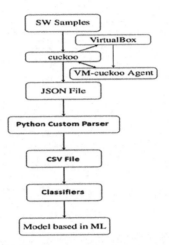

Fig. 2. Data set collection process

5   Feature Selection

5.1   Feature Selection Methods Used

As mentioned in the previous section we got 262 features from the behavioural report that was produced by Cuckoo sand box. Feature selection was the most important part of our implementation. From 262 we obtained 45 top ranking features using the following methods. From 45 we selected 15 best and top features. How the feature selection was done is explained further.

The dataset that we obtained had many redundant attributes, which had less contribution towards the detection of ransomware. There are many methods than can be used for feature selection. Some of them are Filter methods, Wrapper methods and Embedded methods. We have used used two methods for the selection of attributes. First method that was used was wrapper RFE (Recursive Feature Elimination) method. Recursive Feature Elimination with cross validation was used for better results. It uses greedy technique which finds the best performing features from the set of features. It repeatedly creates models and removes the weakest feature at each iteration. It constructs the next model with the left out features, until all the features are exhausted. It then ranks the features based on the order of their elimination. However, for this method we had to specify the number of features that we want. Recursive feature elimination with cross-validation on the other hand, add Cross-validation into the mix. The calculation of score for feature importance is done based on the validation data only. This can be a more resource consuming process depending on the size of the data and the estimator used. Using this we found that the best results were obtained by selecting the best 15 features which were highly ranked by this method.

Second method that was used was Extra Trees Classifier - Extra Trees is like Random Forest, in that it builds multiple trees and splits nodes using random subsets of features. It uses Gini Index for finding the importance of the feature. To perform feature selection, each feature is ordered in descending order of Gini importance. The user has to select the value of k,which is the no. of top k features. We selected k as 15 from which top 15 features were selected according to the ranking done by Extra Trees Classifier.

As mentioned in the introduction section we have found the intersection of a few features which were highly ranked by these two feature extraction methods. Some features which were not in common for them we saw the ranking of them and extracted the highly ranked features.

Hence we got our 15 behavioral attributes using above methods. This was a novel part of our research as till now there has been a debate on what can be the number of features that can give the best accuracy for detection. The various behavioral features for dynamic analysis that we have obtained were related to file system, process related, processes memory and registry operations. There are four features which are not mentioned earlier in any of the research done earlier [4, 5, 8].

6 Experimental Results

The experiments were conducted on a 32-bit Windows-7 system with no additional software installed other than python. We used windows-7 32 bit in an oracle virtual box for an isolated environment. The virtual machine (VM) that was running in the sandboxed environment was Windows 7 and had network connectivity. Every time a new analysis was done on VM it was reverted to the original clean or safe state before each new analysis. The samples of benign and ransomware files were analyzed in the Sandbox. We had network connectivity to the VM, and PCAP traces were collected, but our focus was on the analysis of host-based and stand-alone features only. The results that were obtained were in the json format. As described in the previous section we had written a parser in python to create a csv file for the analysis and detection to be done. Collecting malware was an important part of our research. We have referred to many online sources. We gathered most of our samples from Virus Total [10], and we captured the remaining by manually browsing through security forums and some researchers database. Andrea Continella [1] et al. provided the database for all ransomware files. This was the only initial state of our research.

6.1 Classification Results

Cross-validation To evaluate the performance of our system we have used the k-fold cross-validation technique [1, 3]. In this technique, it divides the data samples into an equal number of groups depending upon the value of k specified. It keeps one group of samples for testing and another group of samples for training. This step is repeated k-times. We used this technique so that we can have the effectiveness of the machine learning models that we have selected for the detection and analysis. After selecting the relevant attributes for the classification to be done we had selected KNN (K- Nearest Neighbors Classifier) the value for k we selected was 5, SVM (Support Vector Machine), Random Forest, and Logistic Regression as machine learning algorithms [2] for the detection of the samples collected as ransomware or not. The following table gives the results of the evaluation metrics True Positive rate, True Negative rate, and Accuracy.

Table 1. Results of classification algorithms for True Positive rate, True Negative rate, and Accuracy.

Sr. No	ML Algorithm	TP rate	TN rate	Accuracy
1	Logistic Regression	89.06%	100%	94%
2	SVM (Support Vector Machine)	92.15%	100%	92.45%
3	KNN (K- Nearest Neighbors Classifier)	100%	60%	96.22%
4	Random Forest	90.47%	0	90.47%

The above-mentioned algorithms were evaluated on the 15 features that we had obtained using feature selection methods as explained in Sect. 5.1.

From Table 1, it is clear that KNN performs well as compared to other algorithms used for classification. We have used total 260 data set samples for benign and ransomware applications of different ransomware families. The output that will be displayed to the user of our implemented system is '1' when the software/application given as input to our system is malicious or '0' if it is a benign software/application.

6.2 Comparison of Results

From above table KNN performed exceptionally well in our experimentation done giving a TP rate of 100% as compared to the TP rate of 95.30% as achieved by Alhawi O.M.K et al. [2]. Also in our experimentation we achieved a accuracy of 96.22% as compared to the accuracy of 77.33% for KNN mentioned in the research by Hajredin Daku et al. [4].

7 Conclusion

From the results obtained it is clear that the accuracy by KNN was very high for the detection of ransomware files. Hence the features that were selected using the feature selection algorithms gave a good accuracy for the detection of ransomware.

Thus, dynamic (behavior) analysis in conjunction with machine learning gave good results and hence are capable of zero-day ransomware detection.

Acknowledgments. We would acknowledge and thank Aditya, Anagha, Mrunmai, and Shradhha for their assistance with the feature extraction process and experimentation to be done. They were very sincere and helpful at the time of implementation to be done. We are also thankful to Andrea Continella et al. for providing us the vast collection of malicious files to be used for our research.

References

1. Continella, A., et al.: ShieldFS: a self-healing, ransomware-aware filesystem. In: ACSAC 2016: Proceedings of the 32nd Annual Conference on Computer Security Applications, pp. 336–347, December 2016
2. Alhawi, O.M.K., Baldwin, J., Dehghantanha, A.: Leveraging Machine Learning Techniques for Windows Ransomware Network Traffic Detection. In: Dehghantanha, A., Conti, M., Dargahi, T. (eds.) Cyber Threat Intelligence. AIS, vol. 70, pp. 93–106. Springer, Cham (2018). https://doi.org/10.1007/978-3-319-73951-9_5
3. Chen, Z.-G., Kang, H.-S., Yin, S.-N., Kim, S.-R.: Automatic ransomware detection and analysis based on dynamic API calls flow graph. In: RACS 2017, pp. 20–23. Association for Computing Machinery, September 2017
4. Daku, H., Zavarsky, P., Yasir Malik, K..: Behavioral-based classification and identification of ransomware variants using machine learning. In: 17th IEEE International Conference on Trust, Security and Privacy. In: Computing and Communications/12th IEEE International Conference on Big Data Science and Engineering (2018)
5. Kesselman, D.N.: A behavioural-based approach to ransomware detection. In: MWR Labs Whitepaper
6. Sgandurra, D., Muñoz-González, L., Mohsen, R., Lupu, E.C.: Automated Dynamic Analysis of Ransomware: Benefits, Limitations and use for Detection. arXiv:1609.03020v1
7. Monika, P.Z., Dale, L.: Experimental analysis of ransomware on windows and Android platforms: evolution and characterization. In: 2nd International Workshop on Future Information Security, Privacy & Forensics for Complex Systems (FISP 2016) (2016)
8. Wan, Y.-L., Chang, J.-C., Chen, R.-J., Wang, S.-J.: Feature-selection-based ransomware detection with machine learning of data analysis. In: 3rd International Conference on Computer and Communication Systems (2018)
9. Cuckoo Sandbox. https://www.cuckoosandbox.org/
10. Virus Total - Intelligence Search Engine. https://www.virustotal.com
11. Almashhadani, A.O., Kaiiali, M., Sezer, S., O'Kane, P.: A multi-classifier network-based crypto ransomware detection system: A case study of locky ransomware. IEEE Access 7, 47053–47067 (2019)

Leading Athlete Following UAV Using Transfer Learning Approach

Shanmukha Sai Sumanth Yenneti[1]([⊠]), Riti Kushwaha[2], Smita Naval[2], and Gaurav Singal[1]

[1] Bennett University, Greater Noida, India
shanmukha.yenneti@gmail.com, gauravsingal789@gmail.com
[2] MNIT Jaipur, Jaipur, India
riti.kushwaha07@gmail.com, smita.cse@mnit.ac.in

Abstract. Nowadays Unmanned Aerial Vehicles (UAVs) have tremendous applications to make human life easier or to automate the process, similar to other technologies. In this paper we are developing a vision-based navigation system for UAVs, so that a UAV can follow a human athlete autonomously. This work involves two sub tasks 1) To detect and mark the leading athlete and 2) To navigate the UAV in such a way that it follows this marked athlete and continuously changes its position with respect to the person which has been marked. Since detecting the person in the video is one of the important tasks while tracking an athlete, we need a model which gives quick and reliable outputs in low resource-constraint environment. We will perform person detection on live video and one of the most popular models for this purpose is MobileNet with SSD, object detection with convolutional neural network-based characteristics because using SSD (Single Shot Detector) makes detecting objects much faster compared to 2 shot detectors like Faster R-CNN. A control algorithm uses the bounding box position to change the UAV flight parameters in order to keep the runner in the field of centre view. When this model has been tested on 100 images of side view of various running races, 95% of the time the athlete in the lead was marked correctly.

Keywords: Convolutional neural networks · Object detection · MobileNet · SSD · UAV

1 Introduction

Recently, human monitoring and object detection [6] are seen as the main factors for smart-city surveillance, which can be used to improve digital society security. For several research areas, an unmanned aerial vehicle, called a drone, has been developed. It can be operated by a person, or a system built to fly the task automatically. Such as military services, disaster relief services, forestry, and transport. This will contribute to the development of the UAV smart system, which is easy to monitor. UAVs that are programmable for a user to operate have lots of noteworthy applications. For instance, a drone/UAV [8] could track an athlete or even actors, working as a "private camera man."

© Springer Nature Singapore Pte Ltd. 2021
D. Garg et al. (Eds.): IACC 2020, CCIS 1367, pp. 424–433, 2021.
https://doi.org/10.1007/978-981-16-0401-0_33

The subsequent video recorded could be used for entertainment (a cricket game filmed from the viewpoint of the leg umpire or to record bloopers made by actors), analysing performance by athletes (recording the dribbles and field position of a soccer player), etc.

A drone may be flying over a first responder or fireman in search and rescue or fire-fighting, offering an enhanced view of the scene. It may be trailing an elderly person in the sense of assisted living, creating an alarm if the person is in a dangerous situation or if the person falls down [10]. Finally, a drone may be escorting a child to or from school in a child safety scenario [12]. As drones reduce in size, many of these applications, e.g. by fly-sized UAVs, could be introduced almost seamlessly. Currently, only tracking user coordinates with GPS and mobile phones helps the individual to follow. In addition to the widely known fallibility of this solution indoors and in calamity assistance situations, the above applications involve meticulous control of drone and subject relative positions being monitored. Often the drone must be kept in front, often behind and sometimes above. In each case, you may need to remain aligned directly with the person, e.g. immediately above the rescue team, or at an angle, e.g. 30 above the swimmer, and monitor the person of interest from far or near. For instance, the "private cameraman" should remain close to the technique of recording football dribbling, and far from recording the positioning of each player. Such precision in controlling its location allows the UAV to identify the location of the athlete precisely in the scene, to comprehend how the athlete is confronted etc. [11].

Although these objectives could, in theory, be accomplished by equipping drones/UAV's with computer vision applications, earlier robotic vision work stressed on autonomy, explicitly a self-governing navigation system based on synchronized localization and mapping, visual odometry, and obstacle evasion; However, these are not key criteria for the above applications where, rather than complete independence, the goal is to strongly obey an individual, regardless of the person's pose, time of day, etc. Similarly, intricate user experiences, such as gesture or emotional recognition, are not important for robotics that follow a human [15]. In this sense, robot-human communication comes down to simple "drone behaviour software design" instructions, such as defining whether to capture video from behind an individual or in front of him/her, the distance and angle that follows the individual, and simple "virtual barrier" commands that prevent drone movements in constrained zones. This program can be made possible by tampering simple visual patterns.

Through this paper we want to put forward a method that we developed to extend the use cases of drones/ UAV's to sports activities, especially during running races using transfer learning [13] which is a quick way to deploy a vision-based navigation system for a drone into action. We provide a way to use a lightweight model to achieve the best trade off between performance and speed for object detection and applied computer vision techniques to mark the leading athlete and navigate the UAV according to this athlete's movements.

In the next section we discuss about the related work done to solve similar tasks using various methods. Section 3 explains the approach we have implemented to solve this task. And Sect. 4 explains the experimental setup which we have used to carry out our experiments and approach. The results of our work are also discussed in Sect. 4. Finally, we make a conclusion about our work and its extension in Sect. 5.

2   Literature Review

For this work we have referred many researches works of other people which share a similar aim and methodology [14], all of which are mentioned in the acknowledgement section of this paper. Primarily there are a few papers that tackle a similar problem using various computer vision techniques while others have used machine learning and deep learning methods. These methods include the usage of HOG feature vectors to identify the human like structures in an image and implement the k-means clustering algorithm [1], together which detected humans and their direction of motion in the frame. This is critical for reidentification of individuals which is another active research problem.

A research [2] using computer vision techniques is usage of skpexels - a spatiotemporal depiction for skeleton sequences to fully utilize the "local" correlations between joints using the 2D convolution filters of Convolution Neural Networks. They converted skeleton videos into Skepxel-based images of flexible dimensions and develop a CNN-based structure for efficient human action recognition using the skpexel images.

Due to its robustness and high accuracy the method of deep learning was extensively used in object detection. For the task of human recognition, the current state of the art is Retina Net. Retina Net provides the greatest accuracy of human detection among all the deep learning approaches (Lin, Goyal, Girshick, He, & Piotr Dollar, 2018). In the paper [3], the images temporal relation has been used to enhance the human detection accuracy. Their task has been broken down into two sub tasks – firstly to detect if there are any humans in the image and next to identify their locations in the image. When a series of images is employed, the model accuracy of human detection has increased by 21.4% as compared to making use of only one image.

Another method known as Hierarchical Extreme Learning Machine (H-ELM) [4], which is one of the unsupervised feature learning methods, uses sparse auto encoders to deliver more strong features that adapt to data variations without pre-processing. These deep neural models have proven to be skilled in human and non-human classification. Yet another research work approaches the task of face discovery using frames from the video and applied to the approval of the face detection, is a Haar-cascade classifier and max-margin object detection with CNN based features because they have high accuracy [5]. To develop an obstacle detection system, Colour discovery system has been used, which only focuses on the colour of bodies and thereby detects the impediments in the way of drone.

In another work, a self-governing drone having person detection and tracking framework which utilizes a static wide-edge camera and a lower-edge camera mounted on a pivoting turret, has been exhibited [9]. To utilize memory and time productively, they have proposed a joined multi-outline profound learning location procedure, where the casing coming from the zoomed camera on the turret is overlaid on the wide-edge static camera's casing. With this methodology, we can assemble an effective pipeline where the underlying discovery of little measured flying interlopers on the fundamental picture plane and their location on the zoomed picture plane is performed at the same time, limiting the expense of asset thorough recognition calculation. Using YOLO algorithm and CNN on NVIDIA GPU to train a deep learning model to detect humans/ persons or other objects on the frame. Now programming the drone movements, to follow the object in whichever direction it moves. Their future work included the detection of possible collisions.

3   Methodology

In existing literature as per our best knowledge, no one has explored the similar use case with UAVs. This technique will make the process automatic and reduce the requirements of multiple cameras for tracking the athlete that is leading in a running race.

3.1   Approach

A the main aim of this work is to make a UAV that can identify the leading athlete and follow that person on the racetrack. This task can be broken down into two parts – firstly, identifying the leading athlete [7] and getting the locations of that person. Secondly, we must program the drone in such a way that the drone always follows the leading athlete only.

Preparing a model to recognize humans form scratch without any training would take a great many training data and hours or long stretches of training time. To speed this up, we can utilize Transfer learning – a process where we use the weights of the model that has been trained on a large amount of data to perform a analogous task. And then fine tune the layers in the way we want our results. Many models are available which we can use which have been trained to distinguish a wide variety of objects in images. From these trained models we can use checkpoints of their training phase and then apply them to our own task of detection. Transfer learning helps not only in cutting down the time required for training a model, but one can also improve the model's accuracy by training the layers further on different data.

We decided to use MobileNet as it has a lightweight architecture. It uses depth wise separable convolutions which essentially means it performs a single convolution on each colour channel instead of blending all three and flattening it. This has the consequence of filtering the input channels. This architecture also needs very low maintenance hence it performs well with high speeds. SSD layers are added to the last DSC layer to replicate the architecture we have used.

For detecting the athlete in each frame of a live stream video obtained from the drone, we are using COCO SSD MobileNet_V1, a MobileNet neural network trained on the COCO dataset. MobileNet is an efficient Convolutional Neural Network for Mobile Vision Applications, Howard et al., 2017. COCO is a large object discovery and segmentation dataset. That has over 66 thousand instances of humans at various poses and under diverse lighting conditions. COCO expands to common objects in context, like the name says the images are taken from everyday scenes. The authors of the MobileNet demonstrated that ReLU6 is better than regular ReLU when we use low precision computation. Single shot detector (SSD) generates anchors and selects the topmost convolutional feature map and at a lower level it selects a feature map having higher resolution.

After that it adds a sequence of convolutional layers with spatial resolution with a specified configuration (decay rate for instance) Using this architecture and pretrained weights on COCO we can obtain the locations of every person in the image and using coordinates we are able to mark a bounding box around each individual. Using these coordinates and computer vision techniques we can identify the individuals at the extreme ends of each frame. Depending on the direction of the race the drone will select either individual as the leading athlete.

Now, the second task of following the athlete throughout the race, begins. We tackle this task by measuring the relative position of the centre of the bounding box with respect to the centre of the frame of video stream. We will move the drone/ UAV in such a way that these two points always overlap each other. Once the UAV has detected a leading athlete, it returns the four coordinates of the bounding box: its top-left corner symbolized by $(x1, y1)$ and its bottom right corner denoted by $(x2, y2)$. Given these, we will compute the centre of the box and its area. To compute the area, we compute the width as $(x2 - x1)$ and the height as $(y2 - y1)$ and multiply them. While the centre, is calculated as $(x2 + x1)/2$ and $(y2 + y1)/2$.

The total flow of the activities is as follows, first the UAV captures live video feed through its camera, then the video that is captured is broken down to frames which are processed one after the other. After which each processed frame is sent as an input to the SSD MobileNet model to detect the no. of persons. Then using the coordinates of each person, we locate the athlete at the extreme ends of the frame and mark that person. This bounding box over the marked person will act a s an input to the drone navigation control which will command the drone to move in a way that the bounding box is always at the centre of the frame.

A pseudocode of the flight parameters to enable the UAV to follow the. Athlete marked is shown in below Fig. 1.

A person detection platform has been created using Python 3 and TensorFlow version 1.15.2 and recreated the model architecture to load the weights. The model has been downloaded from TensorFlow model zoo which is publicly available. A pipeline of different processes at each stage was created. Initially the videos are captured and processed frame by frame and each frame has been resized before being converted to an array of pixels and sent to the model as input. After which the TensorFlow graphs are loaded and the model makes a prediction. Then the model returns the coordinates of the bounding boxes (in the format [ymin. xmin. ymax, xmax]) which are used to calculate the position of each person identified in the frame. With these coordinates the leading athlete can be detected by calculating the position of each bounding box with respect to the centre of the frame. The person at the extreme ends is marked as the leading athlete and a bounding box is drawn over the leading athlete only as shown in Fig. 2.

```
Drone_Control((x1,y1), (x2,y2)):

    turn = ""
    move = ""
    rise = ""
    box_area, center = calculate_area_and_center((x1,y1), (x2, y2))
    #Normalize the X center so that it is between 0.0 and 1.0
    norm_center[x] = center[x] / image.width
    #Normalize the Y center so that it is between 0.0 and 1.0
    norm_center[y] = center[y] / image.width
    if norm_center[x] > 0.6 :
        turn = "right"
    elif norm_center[x] < 0.4 :
        turn = "left"
    if norm_center[y] > 0.6 :
      rise = "up"
    elif norm_center[y] < 0.4 :
      rise = "down"
    #if the area of the bounding box is too big move backwards
    if box_area > 150 :
      move = "back"
    elif box_area < 110 :
      move = "forward"
    return turn, move, rise
```

Fig. 1. Pseudocode of the flight control applied on UAV

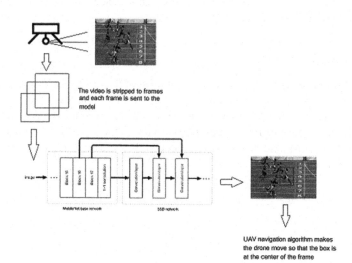

Fig. 2. Workflow of the approach which includes several steps. 1 - The gimbal captures the video footage of the race from the side, 2 - this video is broken down into frames and each frame is sent to the model as an input after which the leading athlete is marked with computer vision and finally 3 - the UAV navigation algorithm commands the UAV to move accordingly

4 Experiment and Results

This section shows the results and configuration of a UAV that has been used for implementation of the work.

4.1 Experimental Setup

The drone setup includes standard propellers – a pair of 1045 propellers to help pull the drone through air, with clockwise rotation. And pusher propellers at the back rotating counter clockwise. Brushless motors (Model: A2212 1000KV), which are better than a brushed motor, are used. Since we have a gimbal at the bottom it is mandatory to have ground clearance, for this purpose 4 pieces of tall landing skid gear legs are mounted. To control the speed of motors an electronic speed controller is used (30A ESC). The flight controller on the drone is a pixhawk 2.4.6 32bit ARM RC flight controller. A gimbal and gimbal controller board are used for capturing live feed through the drone and to send commands to the gimbal on the drone respectively. An RC receiver transmitter set (Fly Sky FSi6 2.4G 6 channels AFHDS RC transmitter and a FS-iA6B receiver is used) to communicate with the drone and to transmit the video to the ground control. Collision avoidance sensor (TINY LIDAR Laser Ranging Sensor VL53L0X having 2 m range), although not mandatory, helps from damaging the drone due to any obstacles during the flight. And a battery 7.4 V, 2200 mAh is needed to power up the drone and keep all the components running. To make room for all these components, while making sure it is light weight, the frame of the drone acts like a hub to place all these parts, so a frame model: F450 HJ450 DJI is used.

4.2 Result Analysis

As seen in Fig. 3, the model was able to detect most of the test cases. A few misclassifications happened due to the image quality and the form of athletes in the picture/video streams. The classification accuracy among the test images taken from internet containing 100 random images of races from the side view came out to be 94.9 percent. The usage of SSD with Mobile-Net version produced the best accuracy trade-off with the performance speed.

Fig. 3. In the above two instances the leading athlete is marked by a green bounding box while the trailing athlete is marked in red. The UAV will follow the green box in such a way that the centre of the box is at the centre of the frame. While the last image was used to detect the leading athlete when the race direction is configured (Color figure online).

The model accuracy when trained on COCO dataset over all the classes is shown in Fig. 4. Single shot detector when used with MobileNet has achieved the highest mAP among all other advanced models when tested for real time processing, which explains its balance between speed and accuracy.

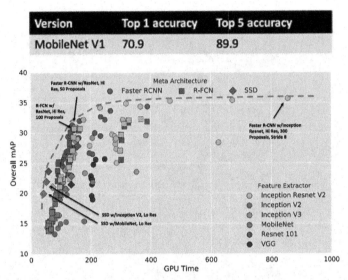

Version	Top 1 accuracy	Top 5 accuracy
MobileNet V1	70.9	89.9

Fig. 4. The performance of the pretrained model on the coco dataset. The image on top shows the comparison between MobileNet and other popular architectures. Due to its light architecture (lesser parameters) the model performs very quickly compared to most state-of-the-art architectures while not compromising the accuracy. The comparison between the models with respect to GPU times is made by a Google research. (Source: Google research)

5   Conclusion

Here, we would like to point out that usage of transfer learning for tasks like athlete following UAV, which needs to be quick at handling the frames and detecting humans, is useful because it removes the training phase while deploying a drone into a required activity. Using transfer learning in the new domains, having inadequate data or compute power for a model to train is useful to implement many advanced neural networks that have been trained on a large amount data and have state of the art performance. We also want to mention that Mobile Net SSD trained on COCO is a fast and robust model for this task since it only has a footprint of around 1 GB in memory. Today most of the drones are being used for various tasks like aerial photography, security and surveillance and other military activities. This work introduced a way to put UAV's into work in sports domain. After this paper we would like to improve our current workflow to maximize the efficiency and reduce latency issues. In future we want to extend our work into other activities, especially in sports, where usage of drones may give us a better perspective in that domain.

References

1. Huang, C.-P., Hsieh, C.-H., Lai, K.-T., Huang, W.-Y.: Human Action Recognition Using Histogram of Oriented Gradient of Motion History Image (2011). https://doi.org/10.1109/IMCCC.2011.95

2. Liu, J., Akhtar, N., Mian, A.: Skepxels: spatio-temporal image representation of human skeleton joints for action recognition. In: CVPR Workshops (2019)
3. Lin, T., Goyal, P., Girshick, R., He, K., Dollár, P.: Focal loss for dense object detection. IEEE Trans. Pattern Anal. Mach. Intell. **42**(2), 318–327 (2020). https://doi.org/10.1109/TPAMI.2018.2858826
4. Zhu, W., Miao, J., Qing, L., Huang, G.-B.: Hierarchical extreme learning machine for unsupervised representation learning. In: IJCNN (2015)
5. King, D.E.: Max-margin object detection. arXiv preprint (2015)
6. Girshick, R., Donahue, J., Darrell, T., Malik, J.: Rich feature hierarchies for accurate object detection and semantic segmentation. In: Proceedings of IEEE Conference on Computer Vision and Pattern Recognition, pp. 580–587 (2014)
7. Pareek, B., Gupta, P., Singal, G., Kushwaha, R.: Person identification using autonomous drone through resource constraint devices. In: 2019 Sixth International Conference on Internet of Things: Systems, Management and Security, pp. 124–129. IEEE (2019)
8. Singal, G., Laxmi, V., Gaur, M.S., Rao, D.V., Kushwaha, R.: UAVs reliable transmission for multicast protocols in FANETs. In: 2019 Sixth IEEE International Conference on Internet of Things: Systems, Management and Security, pp. 130–135 (2019)
9. Aulinas, J., Petillot, Y.R., Salvi, J., Llado, X.: The SLAM problem: a survey. In: Proceedings of the 11th International Conference of the Catalan Association for Artificial Intelligence, pp. 363–371 (2008)
10. UCSanDiego, Person-following UAVs. https://www.svcl.ucsd.edu/projects/dronefollow/. Accessed 23 July 2020
11. Bertrand, O.J., Lindemann, J.P., Egelhaaf, M.: A bio-inspired collision avoidance model based on spatial information derived from motion detectors leads to common routes. PLoS Comput. Biol. **11**, e1004339 (2015)
12. Andert, F., Adolf, F.: Online world modeling and path planning for an unmanned helicopter. Auton. Robots **27**(3), 147–164 (2009)
13. Pan, S., Yang, Q.: A survey on transfer learning. IEEE Trans. Knowl. Data Eng. **22**, 1345–1359 (2010)
14. Girshick, R.: Fast R-CNN. In: Proceedings of International Conference on Computer Vision, pp. 1440–1448 (2015)
15. Dalal, N., Triggs, B.: Histograms of oriented gradients for human detection. In: Proceedings of IEEE Conference on Computer Vision and Pattern Recognition, pp. 886–893 (2005)

Image Forgery Detection & Localization Using Regularized U-Net

Mohammed Murtuza Qureshi[1]([✉]) [ID] and Mohammed Ghalib Qureshi[2]([✉]) [ID]

[1] Information Technology, Storytech Private Limited, Hyderabad, India
mdmurtuza1237@gmail.com
[2] Information Technology, Xeta Analytics Private Limited, Hyderabad, India
ghalib.qureshi@hotmail.com

Abstract. With the rise in digital media and popular image sharing platforms there has been an increase in the manipulation of images through image editing software. Image editing has never been easier because of the readily available and easy-to-use software. This has led to a wave of tampered images flooding the Internet. Traditionally, the human eye could distinguish between an original image and a tampered one, but with editing software developed recently, it has become significantly harder. Broadly Image Forgery can be either Copy-Move, where a region of an image is copied and pasted on another location in the same Image or Image Splicing, here, a section within a specific region of the image is copied and pasted on another region in a different Image. Most of the current methods and algorithms for Image Forgery detection use manually chosen features to identify and localize manipulated portions of the image with some moving towards Deep Learning models. We followed a deep learning approach of using a modified version of the Image Segmentation Model U-Net. The U-Net model was modified by adding regularization. The results were promising with an F1 score of 0.96 on the validation and test sets with the model able to detect and localize forged sections.

Keywords: Image forgery · Image manipulation · Image segmentation · Regularization · Deep learning · Artificial intelligence · Neural networks

1 Introduction

Photographs are the recording of an event in the past, these images were definitive recordings which could be used as evidence, as they were tamper proof. Although a lot has changed since the first photographs were invented, methods to tamper with real photographs emerged. A similar path was followed with digital images, several developments in the world of digital editing of images has led to images being modified [1]. This has in turn led to massive increase in tampered images being circulated on various social media platforms such as Facebook, Instagram, Baidu and Twitter.

Forgery of an Image can be done using various techniques, among them the most prominent techniques are Copy-Move and Image Splicing we will briefly go through each of them:

© Springer Nature Singapore Pte Ltd. 2021
D. Garg et al. (Eds.): IACC 2020, CCIS 1367, pp. 434–442, 2021.
https://doi.org/10.1007/978-981-16-0401-0_34

Copy-Move is a method of image tampering where a small region within the image is copied and added to another location in the same image. This can generally be done to increase the counts of a certain item in an Image or to hide something in the Image or to create similarity between two different items in the Image.

Image Splicing is an image forgery technique where a region in an Image is copied and pasted on another location in a different Image. This can be done to add things which are not already present in an Image and thus create a False impression of their existence in the first place.

Image forgery and manipulation is one of the major reasons for the spread of fake news in this digital media era when the focus is shifting from textual information to more visual information. The consumption of images has increased manifold with popular social media platforms like Instagram which are predominantly image based making it ever important to check the authenticity of images. Add to this, is the easy availability of professional editing software on computers and even on mobile devices. Detecting Image forgery is a crucial step in spreading fake news and preventing many unwanted misconceptions in the minds of people. To this end, there has been very active research in this area [2].

We took the approach of using a modified version of the very successful image segmentation model U-Net. The original U-net was developed to segment medical Images. Our experiment and research involved trying variations and finally rounding off to using a Regularized version of the U-Net to reduce the model complexity which proved to be effective.

2 Previous Related Works

There are multiple machine learning approaches to detect image forgery, these algorithms work on the principle of identifying pixel-wise differences to detect and localize tampered sections of the image. One of the first methods widely used for forgery detection was Error Level Analysis (ELA), first developed by Jonas Wagner. Wagner [3] describes ELA as a method to identify differences between original and recompressed versions of the image. This enables the user to identify any manipulated regions as they can vary in brightness. ELA as mentioned by [4], is based on the process of identifying different compression levels in an image which marks the manipulated regions.

Popescu and Farid discuss in their article [9], most techniques proposed to recognize tampering were based on detecting resampling on digital images, mostly performed using linear or cubic interpolation. They proposed that resampling techniques produce considerable statistical correlations, and these can be identified using an Expectation-Maximization (EM) algorithm. However, this approach was very susceptible to images with JPEG quality factor (QF) of 95 or lower. This method was later improved by [8] by adding a Radon transform and derivative filter-based approach to detect tampering on images with JPEG QF lower than 95. Bunk et al. in [5] use this Radon transform method to build a feature extraction that detects manipulated regions in the image. They blended this method with deep learning models to detect tampering in images.

As most digital images are stored in the JPEG format, most of the machine learning techniques are based on the detection of anomalies in JPEG compression levels due to smoothing and/or resampling of forged parts of the image. However, constant research and development in the field of deep learning has since enabled a lot of different approaches that were applied to Image Forgery Detection. With recent advances in computer vision, the deep learning models display great efficiency in visual detection functions such as image classification and image segmentation [5].

Long et al. [7] propose that the strides of development done with convolutional networks are driving huge advances in visual recognition. In the article, they discuss that fully convolutional networks which are trained end-to-end, on each pixel to perform semantic segmentation outperform all previous works.

Beste Ustubioglu et al. [13] used DCT-phase terms for restricting the range of the feature vector elements' and Benford's generalized law to determine the compression history of the image under test.

In [12], the authors propose a CNN model for detecting image splicing based on weight combination strategy, the algorithm extracts three different types of features which include YCbCr features, edge features and PRNU (photo response nonuniformity) features. The model is trained until the best combination of these weights is obtained.

3   Research Methodology

While most of the previous works focus on using different manual techniques and rules to learn features and differentiate the forged part from the original image, our focus was more on using a Deep Learning approach. Deep Learning has been proven effective in solving a lot of complex problems in computer vision and by building an appropriate neural network we can allow the model to find complex hidden patterns in the data which can differentiate the forged part from the original image.

Since our research involved detecting & then localizing the forged part in an Image, we decided on using the Deep Learning technique of Image Segmentation where the goal is to classify each pixel of an Image to a certain class. We decided on using a Segmentation Model, specifically we used a modified/regularized version of the U-Net model, a popular segmentation network developed for use in Medical Images Segmentation. U-net integrates the location information of the pixel with contextual information to acquire a common information by merging localization and context. The main reason for regularizing our neural network was to reduce its complexity to control the number of parameters present in the model which can lead to overfitting on the training data.

3.1   Base Model Framework

The network consists of a contracting path (which acts as an encoder) and an expansive path (a decoder), which gives the architecture its U-shape. U-Net learns segmentation in an end-to-end setting. Like most other convolutional networks, it is based on processing many convolutional operations. The input image is supplied, and the data is propagated through the U-Net with the output segmentation coming out at the end [11] (Fig. 1).

It is an end-to-end fully convolutional network (FCN). It does not contain any Dense layer and only contains Convolutional layers and because of which it can accept any image size.

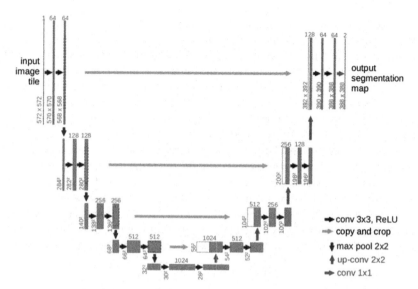

Fig. 1. Original U-Net segmentation model architecture

After every cycle of convolution, only the applicable portion of the convolution is carried forward by the network, therefore, for every 3×3 convolution, a one-pixel row is lost on all sides. This allows compression or reduction in size of large images. It is followed by a max pooling layer (Max Pooling) which further reduces the size of the image. After the network performs max pooling operations, the total number of feature channels are increased by a scale of 2x. This sequence of convolutions and max pooling results in the increase of feature channels and at the same time cause spatial contraction, thus increasing the "What" and decreasing the "Where".

Mapping of all features to a single vector is done with the Standard classification ending here. Apart from the contracting path, U-Net creates a high-resolution segmentation map using an extra expansion path. This additional expansion path consists of up-convolutions and concatenations with high resolution features from the contracting path. The expansion path, also referred to as the decoder is used to enable precise localization.

Up-convolution: A learned kernel is used to output a segmentation map which has two channels one for the background and one for the foreground. The kernel maps each feature vector to the 2×2 pixel output window subsequently by a nonlinear activation function.

To summarize, U-net combines spatial and feature information, simply put the location information and the contextual information are extracted by the U-net to finally obtain general information which is needed to predict a good segmentation map.

3.2 Modifying/Regularizing the U-Net

Overfitting refers when a machine learning model or a neural network follows the training data closely and builds a perfect model around it but fails to generalize on new unseen data. It is generally caused by noise in the data it is being trained on, the models pick up the noise which is usually specific to that dataset.

This happens because the complexity of the network is too high. This could be because of two reasons: 1. If we increase the number of hidden layers then the neural network complexity increases. 2. When there are too many hidden layers the number of parameters increases. Deep neural networks in general have an extremely large number of parameters compared to the traditional statistical models. U-Net specifically has a total number of parameters of 61.4×10^6.

To make sure that the model does not overfit to the training data and captures more of generalized features we introduced regularization. Since the variation can be huge in the new data and if the model overfits the training data, it can tend to fail while segmenting the new images, we decided on the method of L2 Regularization of weights.

Also, called Ridge Regression or weight decay, L2 Regularization. The loss function used in the neural network is extended by a regularization term denoted by Ω, which is the sum over all squared weight values of a weight matrix, defined as the L2 norm.

$$\Omega(W) = \|W\|_2^2 = \sum_i \sum_j w_{ij}^2$$

So as the weights go up the loss increases. By adding this term, the model tries to minimize the weights. A method to keep the coefficients of the model small because as the weights go up the loss increases and, in turn, the model becomes less complex.

To control, how much of the weights affect the model there is an additional hyper-parameter introduced in the neural network, Alpha. Alpha is sometimes called the regularization rate. Thus, in general terms, alpha defines how much the model needs to be regularized.

Here, if Alpha is zero then we aren't penalizing or making any change to the loss function. However, if Alpha is very large then it will add too much weight and it will lead to under-fitting. It's important how we choose Alpha (Fig. 2).

$$\hat{\mathcal{L}}(W) = \frac{\alpha}{2}\|W\|_2^2 + \mathcal{L}(W) = \frac{\alpha}{2}\sum_i \sum_j w_{ij}^2 + \mathcal{L}(W)$$

3.3 Dataset

The dataset used for the experiment was developed from the Casia V2.0 Dataset for Image Splicing by [6]. The dataset primarily consists of 7200 original untampered images, which were then morphed using splicing or copy-move techniques. The total number of edited images numbered 5123. Each edited image was paired with a mask image which represented the manipulated region, which was used as the y-label for training the model.

3.4 Data Augmentation

To increase the amount of data available for training and testing purposes we used the strategy of augmenting the available data. Data Augmentation is a strategy through which one significantly improves the amount of data available, without collecting data, by augmenting or transforming the data we already have. There are various techniques which include cropping, flipping, padding etc. (Fig. 3).

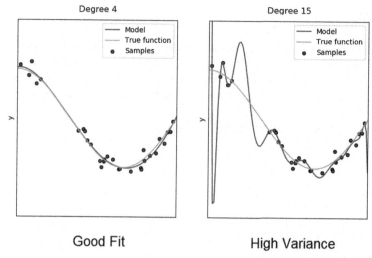

Good Fit   **High Variance**

Fig. 2. Example of a model with good fit and high variance.

We used the following techniques for augmenting our data:

- Horizontal Flipping: Reversing the entire rows and columns of an image pixels (Fig. 4(i)).
- Transpose: Transpose the input by swapping rows and columns (Fig. 4(ii)).
- Rotate: Randomly rotate the input by 90 degrees zero or more times (Fig. 4(iii)).
- Elastic: deformation of images as described in [10] (with modifications) (Fig. 4(iv)).

Fig. 3. Tampered image and corresponding mask

i   ii   iii   iv

Fig. 4. Augmented images

4   Results

The regularized network was trained for 20 epochs on the augmented data with the
L2 regularization with a learning rate (alpha) of 0.0001 which provided the following
results. The F1 score, which is the harmonic mean of precision and recall, provides a
better metric to understand the output of the model. The loss function used in the model
was binary cross entropy (Fig. 5).

A detailed list of Parameters & Hyperparameters used:

- Batch size: 8
- Steps per Epoch: 64
- Epochs: 20
- Learning Rate: 0.0001
- Regularizer: L2 Loss
- Regularization Type: Kernel
- Loss: Binary Cross Entropy
- Optimization Algorithm: Adam
- Metric: F1 Score
- Input Size: 512*512*3
- Training Set Size: 3277
- Validation Set Size: 820
- Test Set Size: 1025
- Data Augmentation Techniques: Horizontal Flipping, Transpose, Rotation, Elastic
  transform

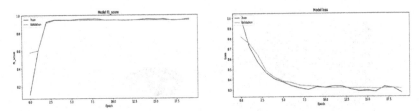

Fig. 5. Graphical representation of model loss & F1 score for each epoch

As the model was loaded with pretrained 'Imagenet' weights, the training F1 score
reached a figure above 0.90 after initial few epochs, the highest F1 score recorded was
0.9614 during epoch 9, the model ended with an F1 score of 0.9604. The validation F1
score also reached above 0.90 very quickly then stabilized at around 0.9486 till the end
of training.

The loss figures instead took a very gradual decline, the training loss bottoming out
at 0.2701 while the validation loss was floating around 0.31 after the 10th epoch.

The test results show some promising performance in identifying and localizing
the tampered sections of the image, as shown in Fig. 6. In the first example, it can be
noticed that the model has performed really well, segmenting the tampered region from

the background, whereas in the second and third examples, we can notice that there are relatively high amounts of pixels/regions being identified as tampered when compared to the first example, even though the identification of non-tampered regions as tampered is sparse,. This can be attributed to the fact when the background region and tampered region pixels are having similar RGB pixel values.

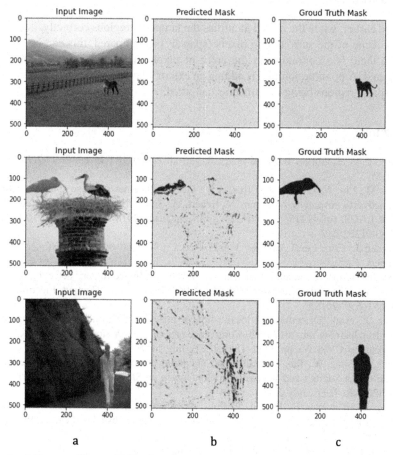

a   b   c

Fig. 6. a) Tampered Image, b) Predicted manipulated region, c) Actual manipulated region

5 Conclusion

In this paper, we tried to identify image tampering using a U-Net model which was regularized and modified using L2 regularization to reduce the total parameters used in the model which improved the overall accuracy and F1 score of the model by avoiding overfitting. Our experiments results were quite promising and since the model is not constrained by type of the input image unlike few of the previous works the deep learning model can be further improved by adding layers and filters which can help in identifying the forged region. Further research can involve adding layers which can help in image compression irrespective of image type like Discrete Cosine Transform which has been previously used in detecting Forgery.

6   Limitations

As noted earlier, while the model identifies the tampered regions correctly, it also tends to mark some of the surrounding pixels (sparsely) as tampered, this can be attributed to when there is a continuity in the color of pixels of the tampered region and the background. A possible solution is adding an external layer which can filter/remove out all the sparse regions being identified as tampered.

References

1. Qazi, T., et al.: Survey on blind image forgery detection. IET Image Proc. **7**(7), 660–670 (2013)
2. Huh, M., Liu, A., Owens, A., Efros, A.A.: Fighting fake news: image splice detection via learned self-consistency. In: Ferrari, V., Hebert, M., Sminchisescu, C., Weiss, Y. (eds.) ECCV 2018. LNCS, vol. 11215, pp. 106–124. Springer, Cham (2018). https://doi.org/10.1007/978-3-030-01252-6_7
3. Wagner, J.: Error Level Analysis. FotoForensics (2012). https://fotoforensics.com/tutorial-ela.php
4. Sudiatmika, I.B., Rahman, F.J., Trisno, T., Suyoto, S.: Image forgery detection using error level analysis and deep learning. TELKOMNIKA Telecommun. Comput. Electron. Control **17**, 653–659 (2018)
5. Bunk, J., et al.: Detection and localization of image forgeries using resampling features and deep learning. In: 2017 IEEE Conference on Computer Vision and Pattern Recognition Workshops (CVPRW), pp. 1881–1889. IEEE, July 2017
6. Dong, J., Wang, W., Tan, T.: Casia image tampering detection evaluation database. In: 2013 IEEE China Summit and International Conference on Signal and Information Processing, pp. 422–426. IEEE, July 2013
7. Long, J., Shelhamer, E., Darrell, T.: Fully convolutional networks for semantic segmentation. In: Proceedings of the IEEE Conference on Computer Vision and Pattern Recognition, pp. 3431–3440 (2015)
8. Mahdian, B., Saic, S.: Blind authentication using periodic properties of interpolation. IEEE Trans. Inf. Forensics Secur. **3**(3), 529–538 (2008)
9. Popescu, A.C., Farid, H.: Exposing digital forgeries by detecting traces of resampling. IEEE Trans. Signal Process. **53**(2), 758–767 (2005)
10. Simard, P.Y., Steinkraus, D., Platt, J.C.: Best practices for convolutional neural networks applied to visual document analysis. In: ICDAR, vol. 3, no. 2003, August 2003
11. Ronneberger, O., Fischer, P., Brox, T.: U-Net: Convolutional Networks for Biomedical Image Segmentation. arXiv:1505.04597 [cs.CV] (2015)
12. Wang, J., Ni, Q., Liu, G., Luo, X., Jha, S.K.: Image splicing detection based on convolutional neural network with weight combination strategy. J. Inf. Secur. Appl. **54**, 102523 (2020)
13. Ustubioglu, B., Ulutas, G., Ulutas, M., Nabiyev, V.V.: A new copy move forgery detection technique with automatic threshold determination. AEU-Int. J. Electron. Commun. **70**(8), 1076–1087 (2016)

Incorporating Domain Knowledge in Machine Learning for Satellite Image Processing

Ambily Pankajakshan[(✉)], Malay Kumar Nema, and Rituraj Kumar

Centre for Artificial Intelligence and Robotics, DRDO, Bangalore, India
{ambily,malay,rituraj}@cair.drdo.in

Abstract. This paper highlights the need for incorporation of domain knowledge in the context of satellite image processing. We take an application area of satellite image processing and make our assertion for incorporation of human domain knowledge. Traditionally, a machine learning based approach do not take general human intelligence into account for training and classification. We suggest to apply general human intelligence through suitable domain knowledge filters on the outcome of a deep classifier network. The results of processing become more suitable for human understanding and decision making after they pass through the domain knowledge-based filters. We devise intuitive filters (not an exhaustive set) and demonstrate the utility of incorporation of domain knowledge with the example of air traffic infrastructure.

Keywords: Deep learning · Domain knowledge · Satellite image processing · Object classification · Object detection · Airstrip detection

1 Introduction and Prior Work

Deep learning algorithms [1] in association with suitable hardware [2, 3] have been proven as an enabling tool for big data exploitation. So far, this powerful tool has been performing exceptionally well in various application areas. The application areas are ranging from image object classification and detection [4], video action/activity recognition [5–7], face recognition [8], medical diagnosis [9], weather prediction [10] etc. The area has been investigated for applications related to generative adversarial network [11] as well. Despite the fact that the deep learning stack has been thoroughly explained [12, 13], it was pointed out that the results are not understood/explainable. This is largely attributed to the fact that traditionally the deep learning based methods do not provide any means of capturing the domain knowledge as part of learning. To assist in this situation explainable AI [14] was developed which can coarsely be defined as a method which provisions a better understanding of the results to users. In this paper we take this approach and try to come up with results which are more meaningful for human understanding.

1.1 Satellite Image Processing

Satellite imagery provides a lot of coverage of features like clear/turbid water, dense forest, grass/shrubs, barren land, built up areas and other man-made structures etc. These features help in development planning. Collecting this much detail from alternate sources is an effort intensive as well as time-consuming exercise. Assessing these features for any changes with the help of satellite imagery is a faster and easier exercise.

Challenges of Satellite Image Processing

Satellite imagery comes with its own set of challenges which can primarily be divided into two categories (i) data availability and handling and (ii) data processing and its interpretation. If we consider data availability and handling, the availability of data is dependent on access to appropriate data pertaining to the location of interest. Data handling is largely associated with the availability of required storage and suitable hardware. Most of the challenges associated to data availability and handling are nearly solved, hence large volume of data is already available with the necessary storage capacity and processing capabilities.

Challenges related to automated processing and its interpretation without human in the loop are still being pursued. In the context of deep learning-based approaches, relevant data collection, correct labeling and interpretation of satellite imagery are the main challenges to be addressed in order to develop a system. Prior works on satellite imagery have reported results in object detection in satellite images [15–17]. The article [18] submits that satellite imagery cannot be used for prediction of development markers reliably but we tend to differ. While existing work stops at object detection on the input imagery, we extend the processing by adding one post processing filter. This filter captures the human domain knowledge related to the intended detection.

In this paper we take airports/airstrips as an indicator of developmental possibilities. Processing of satellite imagery for finding airports is susceptible to give segments of express highways, toll booths, bridges, long fields as output because these objects, though semantically different, possess largely overlapping features. Also, it can be noted that sensors in satellites do not capture domain knowledge as part of imagery. We address these challenges and assert that satellite imagery can be leveraged for assessment of regional development. In Sect. 2 we give outline of our approach and introduce our filtering logic. The filters are used for capturing the domain knowledge which otherwise is not part of satellite imagery. In Sect. 3 we give the implementation details for our approach and provide result and conclusions in Sect. 4.

2 Proposed Method

Regional development was always assumed to be predicated on the availability of railways. Nowadays, the development of a region gets a boost the moment an airstrip is operational. Therefore, our work is focused on identifying airstrips which can later be used as an indicator of developmental activities.

2.1 Data Collection

For the purpose of capturing varying types of airstrips/airports we chose to select satellite imagery of developing countries. The imagery was collected from open domain. General awareness towards developed airports and developing airports was used to select the satellite imagery of the areas. Airstrip/airport images with large variance in their development were selected for the purpose of training and testing. A set of 1000 images were taken for this task.

2.2 Post Detection Filtering (Capturing Domain Knowledge)

In this section we deliberate on the filters (not an exhaustive set) for assessment of development and elaborate the specific case of airstrips/airport. These filters capture the domain knowledge and can help in effective decision making about assessment of regional development. For example, let us denote a geographical region by G, urban areas by U, cultivated area by C and barren land by B as detected by the deep learning methods then the ratios of U/G can be a good assessment of urbanization; C/G will be an indicator of agricultural development, and B/G gives a fair idea about the availability of land where new development can start. These values can be reconciled with the surveyed values. In case of any mismatch between these values and domain knowledge about the area (generally available through surveys) a suitable correction to achieve a realistic assessment can be obtained. This can be summarized by the block diagram given in Fig. 1 below. The outcome of the object detection is subjected to a post detection calculation and filtering based on domain knowledge. This step applies a threshold on the outcome parameters from the deep network followed by application of human domain knowledge filters. Application of the domain knowledge-based filtering leads to results with enhanced precision.

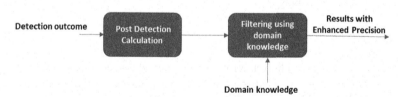

Fig. 1. Schematic diagram of post detection filtering process

Here we make a point that the post detection calculations are not limited to the suggested ratios. The key idea is to apply domain knowledge on these calculations. The approach can be generalized as follows.

Let O be the outcome (set of objects) from deep learning classifier, M be the metric set related to the data and D be the set of metrics from the domain knowledge then

$$O \Rightarrow S \text{ iff } M(O) \in D \tag{1}$$

Where S is the set of objects selected as the desirable object set.

Otherwise

$$O => V \qquad (2)$$

Where V is the set for review by experts for further correction if required. It is to be noted that the number of elements in M and the details they capture is an important aspect of domain knowledge filtering concept.

Application to Airstrip/Airport Detection

The accuracy of the learning-based classifiers is predicated largely on the quality of labeled data on which it is trained. It can be observed from the structure of deep learning framework that the features are analyzed to great details at different resolution levels. Similar structures which may not be semantically airports but possess the same/similar/overlapping feature set comes up as the deep network output. While this outcome cannot be attributed as incorrect labeling or incorrect performance of deep learning algorithm, the outcome is not usable as it is. To a certain level, application of a threshold on the detection accuracy helps. Still a large number of similar objects pass through it. Our approach plans to capture the domain knowledge to filter the detection done by the deep learning method. In this we apply the knowledge about airstrip dimensions which are measurable through images and locations which are available as part of the metadata of the satellite imagery.

3   Our Implementation

We used YOLO V4 [19] based on CSPdarknet-53 as the backbone for our implementation. We further subdivided the airports/airstrips into two subclasses, namely (i) developed-airport and (ii) undeveloped-airstrips. Following are the implementation details of training and testing.

3.1   Training

In our implementation we chose the following hyperparameters of the network. These are mainly driven by the knowledge of the input data dimensions, number of images in the data set and capability of the available hardware (Table 1).

Table 1. Chosen hyper parameters

Batch	64	Channels	3
Subdivisions	32	Max batch	6000
Width	608	Steps	4800,5400
Height	608	Filters	21

In order to reap benefits of transfer learning, convolutional weights that are pre-trained on Imagenet on darknet53 model were used as starting point. Our training set had 732 images which were labeled into the two classes as mentioned above. We used NVIDIA K-80, 12 GB GPU for training and testing. The focus of our work is to introduce the human domain knowledge filtering post detection. Therefore, the data was not augmented with techniques like adversarial training, generative adversarial training etc.

3.2 Testing

The trained model was tested for performance using the test data set. The images in the test data were the images which were not used for training purpose. For the performance metric we chose to use the mean average precision (mAP) at 6000 iterations. The mAP for the developed-airport class was 52.35% and for undeveloped-airstrips class, the mAP obtained was 45.56%. Finally, for the full training the mean average precision (mAP@0.50) is 0.489525, or 48.95%.

3.3 Post Detection Filter (Capturing Domain Knowledge)

In this section we give details of domain filtering implementation specific for airstrip/airport. Our post processing filter is based on a few filtering parameters which may not be easily provided to the deep network for training. However, these parameters are part of domain knowledge for a person of civil infrastructure development team. These parameters are size and location. In other words, the set M in case of airstrips consist of size and lat-long. Typically, a runway has to cater for a length that allows safe take-off and landing by an aircraft. This length is further dependent on the type of aircraft, altitude etc. The analysis for obtaining the runway length is out of scope of the present paper and we take this as given knowledge. If the runway is denoted by R then R_{min} and R_{max} are the minimum and maximum lengths for the desirable runway length. A filtering on this parameter will avoid small construction areas, long and medium expressway segments etc. Further, if the location (latitude-longitude) of the object is denoted by $L_{[lat, long]}$ then the knowledge of runway location within the land mass will lead to reliable detection and hence will avoid objects like large ships, speed-boats and their wake. In other words the set D consists of R_{min}, R_{max} and $L_{[lat, long]}$. Let any object as given in the outcome of the deep learning classifier be O then the object with the measurement of dimensions be O_d and the object with lat-long meta data be O_L.

Let A be the desirable set of airstrips then

$$A = O_{[d, L]} : R_{min} \leq d \leq R_{max} \text{ and } L_{[lat, long]} \in G \qquad (3)$$

Where G is a geographical region known to be bounded with valid lat-long. For our implementation we had chosen R_{min} and R_{max} as 1.5 km and 5.0 km respectively.

4   Results and Conclusion

In this section we report the results from two perspectives. The first one is confirming the correctness of the object detection from deep network. The correctness of the detection

Fig. 2. Three objects of type developed airport detected with 99% confidence score. This result is part of experiment for confirming the correctness of detection. This image is not part of satellite data set of Sri Lanka.

Fig. 3. Object of type developed airport detected with 99% confidence score. This result is part of experiment for confirming the correctness of detection. This image is from the satellite data set of Sri Lanka.

can be observed in the results as given in Fig. 2, Fig. 3 and Fig. 4. The second perspective is for our contribution i.e. post detection filtering.

After assurance of good training of the deep learning network, we continued the experimentation on validation data of 1000 satellite images. For the purpose of covering a self-sufficient region, we chose open source satellite imagery of Sri Lanka. The deep

Fig. 4. Object of type undeveloped airstrip detected with 85% confidence score. This result is part of experiment for confirming the correctness of detection. This image is not from the satellite data set of Sri Lanka.

network detected 213 objects with 3 false negatives. These numbers were reduced to 65 airport objects after application of accuracy threshold of 0.55. When the object detector was run on the chosen set of images, the outcome O was not only the airports. Upon examination it was found that the output consists of all the objects which maps to a similar feature set as airport. These objects were typically long straight stretches like segments of express highways, tollbooths at highways, long field etc. As a classifier, the machine has done the correct job but these objects are not semantically airstrip or airport. A lot of spurious objects were dropped when we applied the threshold on the confidence score. Still a lot of objects remained in the outcome as airport. One such result detecting a road segment as an airport is given in Fig. 5. This type of results needs to be reduced/eliminated in order to improve the detection.

The detection outcome which consisted of True Positives (like the ones in Fig. 2, Fig. 3, and Fig. 4) and False Positives (like the one given in Fig. 5) was then subjected to our filtering logic for further refinement of the results.

Result After Application of Domain Knowledge Filtering
Our filtering logic as defined in Sec 3.3 provided a reliable outcome. After the application of filter, the resultant objects reduced to 20 including 8 False Positives. The number of objects after filtering was far less than the initial estimate by the deep learning classifier. In other words, it can be stated that the application of domain knowledge filter has resulted in better quality of outcome both from the perspective of accuracy as well as human understanding. The results are summarized in Table 2.

Effectively, the precision improved to 0.60 from the original value of 0.056 after application of post classification filter. The proposed filtering method is not exhaustive. The parameters in the filter can still be increased by many other elements such as terrain information. Inclusion of a greater number of relevant filtering elements can lead to a generalized domain filter and hence a better performance on a variety of terrain. As concluding remark, it can be stated that an exercise containing good quality data, accurate labeling and well-trained classifier/detector can still result in an outcome which may not

Fig. 5. Segment of road detected as undeveloped airstrip with 95% confidence score. Elimination of false positives like this using the domain knowledge filtering is the aim of this paper.

Table 2. Outcomes before and after application of domain knowledge filter

	Before application of domain filter	After application of domain filter
True positives	12	12
False positives	201	**8**
Precision	0.056	**0.6**
Recall	0.8	0.8

be qualitatively up to the mark. We again make assertion for capturing of general human intelligence in the form of domain knowledge filter for improving the quality of the results.

References

1. Pouyanfar, S., et al.: A survey on deep learning: algorithms, techniques, and applications. ACM Comput. Surv. **5**(51), 1–36 (2018)
2. Chen, Y., Xie, Y., Song, L., Chen, F., Tang, T.: A Survey of accelerator architectures for deep neural networks. Engineering **6**(3), 264–274 (2020)
3. Capra, M., Bussolino, B., Marchisio, A., Shafique, M., Masera, G., Martina, M.: An updated survey of efficient hardware architectures for accelerating deep convolutional neural networks. Future Internet **12**, 113 (2020)
4. Druzhkov, P.N., Kustikova, V.D.: A survey of deep learning methods and software tools for image classification and object detection. Pattern Recogn. Image Anal. **26**(1), 9–15 (2016). https://doi.org/10.1134/S1054661816010065

5. Feichtenhofer, C., Pinz, A., Wildes, R.P.: Spatiotemporal multiplier networks for video action recognition. In: Proceedings of the IEEE Conference on Computer Vision and Pattern Recognition (CVPR), July 2017

6. Feichtenhofer, C., Pinz, A., Zisserman, A.: Convolutional two-stream network fusion for video action recognition. In: Proceedings of the IEEE Conference on Computer Vision and Pattern Recognition, June 2016

7. Singh, T., Vishwakarma, D.: Human activity recognition in video benchmarks: a survey. In: Rawat, B.S., Trivedi, A., Manhas, S., Karwal, V. (eds.) Advances in Signal Processing and Communication. LNEE, vol. 526, pp. 247–259. Springer, Singapore (2019). https://doi.org/10.1007/978-981-13-2553-3_24

8. Zhao, B., Feng, J., Wu, X., Yan, S.: A survey on deep learning-based fine-grained object classification and semantic segmentation. Int. J. Autom. Comput. **14**(2), 119–135 (2017). https://doi.org/10.1007/s11633-017-1053-3

9. Xu, J., Xue, K., Zhang, K.: Current status and future trends of clinical diagnoses via image-based deep learning. Theranostics **9**(25), 7556–7565 (2019). https://doi.org/10.7150/thno.38065

10. Reichstein, M., Camps-Valls, G., Stevens, B., et al.: Deep learning and process understanding for data-driven earth system science. Nature **566**, 195–204 (2019)

11. Pan, Z., Yu, W., Yi, X., Khan, A., Yuan, F., Zheng, Y.: Recent progress on generative adversarial networks (GANs): a survey. IEEE Access **7**, 333622–336333 (2019)

12. Srinivas, S., Sarvadevabhatla, R.K., Mopuri, K.R., Prabhu, N., Kruthiventi, S.S., Babu, R.V.: A taxonomy of deep convolutional neural nets for computer vision. Front. Robot. AI **2**, 36 (2016)

13. Montavon, G., Samek, W., Müller, K.R.: Methods for interpreting and understanding deep neural networks. Digital Signal Process. **73**, 1–15 (2018)

14. Samek, W., Montavon, G., Vedaldi, A., Hansen, L.K., Müller, K.-R.: Explainable AI: Interpreting, Explaining and Visualizing Deep Learning, 1st edn. Springer, Cham (2019)

15. Li, K., Wan, G., Cheng, G., Meng, L., Han, J.: Object detection in optical remote sensing images: A survey and a new benchmark. ISPRS J. Photogram. Remote Sens. **159**, 296–307 (2020)

16. Ball, J.E., Anderson, D.T., Chan, C.S.: Comprehensive survey of deep learning in remote sensing: theories, tools, and challenges for the community. J. Appl. Remote Sens. **11**(4), 042609 (2017)

17. Daqui, L., Bo, C., Chin, T.-J., Rutten, M.: topological Sweep for Multi-Target Detection of Geostationary Space Objects. IEEE Trans. Signal Process. **68**, 5166–5177 (2020)

18. Vota, W.: Oops ! Satellite Imagery cannot predict Human Development Indicators. https://www.ictworks.org/satellite-imagery-human-development/

19. Bochkovskiy, A., Wang, C.-Y., Liao, H.-Y.M.: YOLOV4: optimal speed and accuracy of object detection (2020)

Enabling Oil Production Forecasting Using Machine Learning

Bikash Kumar Parhi[(✉)] [iD] and Samarth D. Patwardhan [iD]

Maharashtra Institute of Technology (WPU), Pune 411038, MH, India
bikashparhi@gmail.com

Abstract. Machine learning is defined as an application of artificial intelligence where available information is used through algorithms to process or assist the processing of any set of data. There is growing evidence of machine learning being used in many oil and gas industry operations for better predictions, right from facies identification to pipeline maintenance, thereby enhancing safety significantly. The rate of a production well decreases with time and this relationship is known as the decline curve. Decline curve analysis is a graphical method used for analyzing oil and gas production rates and forecasting future performance, thereby assisting in overall field performance management. Arp's decline curve analysis is usually the most common method which includes a comprehensive set of equations defining the exponential, harmonic and hyperbolic declines which can only be applied in case of a stabilized production trend. This paper focuses on predicting the decline curve by using appropriately designed neural networks and machine learning algorithms irrespective of production trend. The feature vectors are geological location of the well, production data, pressure data, and operating constraints. Fine tuning these parameters lead us to predict the performance of a well with reasonable certainty.

Keywords: Machine learning · Decline curve · Oil and gas production · Neural network

1 Introduction – A Brief About Oil and Gas

Petroleum is a naturally occurring black organic substance found in geological formations beneath earth's crust. Petroleum engineering is a study which includes survey and planning of a field which is termed as a 'Reservoir' followed by drilling and at last completion for production from the well. There can be oil wells, gas wells or a combination of two depending on the subsurface conditions of temperature and pressure. After production from a well, crude or gas are stored in facilities from where they are sent to refineries where they are processed, and are then supplied to industries or sent in cargo to various depots and petrol pumps. From surveying for oil till its production, the process is termed as "upstream" and from refinery till consumption the process is termed "downstream". Figure 1 shows a schematic of oil reservoir. A reservoir is always formed when a porous rock is encountered in-between overlying and underlying layers of impermeable rock. The reservoir itself is highly porous and permeable which is

© Springer Nature Singapore Pte Ltd. 2021
D. Garg et al. (Eds.): IACC 2020, CCIS 1367, pp. 452–464, 2021.
https://doi.org/10.1007/978-981-16-0401-0_36

said to have been trapped inside geological formations like folds, faults, anticlines. The overlying layer is known as cap rock as it forms a seal for any further movement of hydrocarbon.

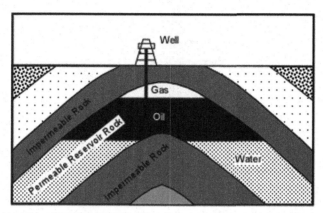

Fig. 1. Schematic of reservoir (earth & environmental sciences 1110 physical geology by Prof. Stephen A. Nelson, Tulane University)

Figure 2 shown below is a schematic of a petroleum well under production with various surface and sub surface units. Christmas tree is the main component attached above surface equipment which regulates the flow and helps in shutting off the main flow during testing operation as well as while performing well activation and stimulation jobs. Other main components are the 'subsurface casings', 'packers' which are used to hold the production tube in position and for zone isolation. Perforations as shown in the schematic as carried out with help of perforating guns after casing is run and cemented.

A petroleum reservoir (oil and gas) is a subsurface pool of hydrocarbons contained in porous or fractured rock formations. Geological and geophysical survey is the first step in the development of any field. This helps us in estimating the crude hydrocarbon volume as well as the size of the reservoir. The total volume estimate of hydrocarbon crude is known as OOIP (Original oil in place) which is a function of porosity and water saturation of the reservoir. Only after the survey is carried out and interpreted, further development of the field is done only if the volume estimate is productive enough to carry out huge investments in drilling and completion. Post surveying operation, drilling plans are made which constitute hydraulics design, drill bit design, casing and cementing plans. Drilling and casing are carried out as per the plan. Completion of the well is followed up with the use of various surface and subsurface production equipment like Christmas tree, subsurface valves, gas sleeves, etc. Perforations are done in the casing at the required depth with help of detonators and shaped charges which act as the passage for flow of crude from reservoir to the wellbore.

Once a well starts to produce, the production rate is maximum initially and gradually decreases with time over years due to various factors. The main factor is because the reservoir pressure gradually decreases as crude comes out of the reservoir over time.

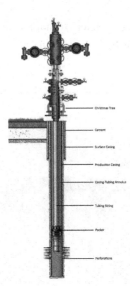

Fig. 2. Well schematic under production phase after completion with casings and perforations (https://www.researchgate.net/publication/309088198_Methods_in_Oil_Recovery_Proces ses_and_Reservoir_Simulation)

Various other factors which leads to drop in production rate are due to scale and asphaltene formation inside the wellbore, blocking of the rock pores or fluid paths through which crude flows inside formation. There are treatments and remedies like fracking (hydraulic and mechanical both) which are used for well activation or well stimulation, in order to bypass the created damage.

1.1 Machine Learning in Oil and Gas

Machine learning methods are being increasingly deployed across various oil and gas industry operations. These methods are frequently performed to expedite/automate operations or to assist with laborious assignments, many a times enhancing safety of the crew. The benefits of employing machine learning methods include increased speed of execution, reproducibility, and consistency, thereby providing an overall cost advantage to the operator.

Application of these methods in the oil and gas industry are diverse and some have been studied while carrying out literature review. Some very efficient and useful applications that have been successfully carried out using Machine learning are - Shale discrimination using AI (André et al. 2013), Screening of EOR/IOR techniques using ML (Alvarado et al. 2002), Prediction of PVT parameters using ML (Ramirez et al. 2007), ML used for production performance optimization (Bowie et al. 2018), ML for improved directional drilling survey (Pollock et al. 2018), Modeling ETR in unconventional reservoir using ML (Vyas et al. 2017), Detecting failures and optimizing performance in Artificial Lift using ML (Pennel et al. 2018). From all of these application, the most important aspect is that it is a fast, reliable process and gives a prediction which is comparable with the original results from predefined equations and industry benchmarked software tools. Thus ML can be used to increase the efficiency of operations without any risk. These methods have also been evaluated for petro physical and geo-technical analyses and interpretations, which are commonly performed by human experts on the basis of log data and, when available, seismic and core data.

Some other general applications of machine learning in oil and gas industry are smarter maintenance, predictive analysis, health and performance optimization, and smarter operations. Smarter Maintenance is the approach or applications that help in a smarter maintenance of field and personnel with very low downtime. Reactive Maintenance (RM) is the most basic approach which involves letting an asset run until failure. It is suitable for non-critical assets that have little to no immediate impact on safety and have minimal repair or replacement costs so that they do not warrant an investment in advanced technology. Preventative Maintenance (PM) approach is implemented in hopes that an asset will not reach the point of failure. The preventative maintenance strategy can be formulated on a: fixed time schedule or operational statistics and manufacturer/industry recommendations of good practice. Condition-Based Maintenance (CBM) is a proactive approach that focuses on the physical condition of equipment and how it is operating. CBM is ideal when measurable parameters are good indicators of impending problems. Predictive Maintenance (PdM) is implemented for more complex and critical assets. It relies on the continuous monitoring of asset performance through sensor data and prediction engines to provide advanced warning of equipment problems and failures. Risk-Based Maintenance (RBM) enables comprehensive decision making to plant operations and maintenance personnel using PdM, CBM and PM outcomes. Predictive analytics together with PdM can lead to the identification of issues that may not have been found otherwise. Predictive analytics software keeps a track of historical operational signatures of each asset and compares it to real-time operating data to detect even the precise changes in equipment behavior. With Predictive asset analytics software solutions, oil and gas organizations get early warning notifications of equipment issues and potential failures which help them to take corrective measures and improve overall performance which Health and Performance Optimization of ML. For Smarter Operations with the help of predictive analytics, they can ascertain and comprehend actual and expected performance for an asset's current ambient, loading and operating conditions.

1.2 Production Trend and Decline Curve

After a well is completed (cased, cemented, perforated), the well is ready to start production. Production from well starts generally at a high rate and decreases continuously with time. There may be only oil production, only gas or combination of both which depends on the temperature and pressure in the subsurface. Water is also accompanied in production along with the hydrocarbons. The graph between production rate and time is known as the decline curve. The decline curve shows the production trend of the well for that period of time. This graph can be extrapolated to get the Estimated Ultimate Recovery (EUR) of the well, which is the maximum hydrocarbons which can be recovered with feasible commercials. Some remaining crude is always left out in the subsurface which is known as Irreducible Oil (IR) and can be recovered partially with Enhanced Oil Recovery or Improved Oil Recovery (EOR/IOR) methods. The trend also gives a future estimate about the life of the well by determining the EUR. It is also used in production forecasting which can be used by extrapolating the trend line to the required time (or date).

1.3 Decline Curve Analysis (DCA)

This is a graphical method used for analysis of declining production rates and forecasting future performance of oil and gas wells. Prediction of future oil well or gas well production is done based on the concept of "history match" of the past production history.

As shown in Fig. 3 below, the production rate vs time is a declining curve primarily due to the loss of reservoir pressure, and changing relative volumes of the produced fluids. The red line indicates the decline curve trend.

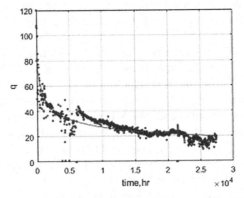

Fig. 3. The graph illustrates a production vs time curve from an oil well (Fetkovich et al. 1996)

Arp's Decline Curve. This analysis is usually the most common empirical method for performing a decline curve analysis. This includes a comprehensive set of equations defining the exponential, harmonic and hyperbolic declines. Stabilized production trend is a criteria which needs to be satisfied while using Arp's decline curve analysis.

Arp's general equation of decline is given in Eq. (1). q (t) is the flow rate at any time 't', qi is the initial flow rate of the well, 'b' decline constant or co-efficient which values range between 0 and 1, Di is the initial rate of decline.

$$q(t) = \frac{q_i}{(1 + bD_it)^{1/b}} \tag{1}$$

As per Arp's decline analysis, the value of b = 0 for exponential, b = 1 for harmonic and 0 < b < 1 for hyperbolic decline trends. The respective equations for flow rate in the three types of decline trend is given in Eq. (2), (3), (4).

$$q(t) = q_i e^{-dt} \tag{2}$$

$$q(t) = \frac{q_i}{(1 + D_i t)} \qquad (3)$$

$$q(t) = \frac{q_i}{(1 + bD_i t)^{1/b}} \qquad (4)$$

Figure 4 below depicts typical empirical decline curves used in the upstream oil and gas industry, to match and forecast the production till a well's economic ultimate recovery (EUR).

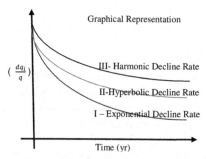

Fig. 4. Production vs time graph for three types of decline curve trend as per Arp's DCA (Arp's et al. 1944)

2 Objectives, Methodology and Workflows

In this work, a machine learning technique is applied on a set of data to first match the existing production history, and further predict the production, leading to an assessment of how much oil/gas can be produced from the existing well. This prediction helps in managing the field, from an operational standpoint. The dataset includes typical values of parameters from oil and gas fields i.e., production history, pressure values, and well logs. Artificial Neural Network (ANN) is the type of machine learning algorithm which is employed in this work for the prediction of the decline curve. Data sets for training of the algorithm are obtained from wells drilled in previously worked fields. A sigmoid activation function is used and proper regression is applied to the data sets for obtaining the decline curve trend. These trends are then compared with previously generated decline curves from the actual field production data, and the model is further trained. It is seen that with successful training of the algorithm, a reasonable accuracy from a decline curve perspective is obtained.

2.1 Data Sets Acquisition

Data sets are procured from previously worked oil and gas fields for the purpose of successful training of the machine learning algorithm. Sufficient sets of data are required for a successful training of algorithm to ensure a high level of accuracy between the match and the actual data. A well-trained algorithm will assist in predicting the curve, for the operators to be able to analyze the field performance, and make critical investment decisions regarding further drilling of new wells, or re-completion of existing wells. The parameters included in the dataset include production history, wellhead pressure data, and operational constraints.

The first set of data include production history of 5 oil wells within the same reservoir with 17 years data. The production process is even accompanied with well activation or activation methods which can be visible in the graphs plotted in this paper.

The second set of data includes production history of a well producing only gas for 5 years. The production trend in this case is a stabilized trend. Both sets of data are used for training and testing of our designed model.

2.2 Neural Network Model Design

In the design of a typical neural network architecture, the number of hidden layers and nodes in each layer play significant role in determining the performance of the algorithm and hence, the final result. There is no rule as such and it depends on how effectively we can choose our model so as to not over-fit any data and/or under-fit the results. The network model that has been designed for this work is based on the availability of the data sets. As we have two cases for oil and gas wells, the architecture is designed as follows:

Case 1: For oil wells, sufficient data was available and thus the neural network architecture constitutes of 3 layers with 1 input layer, 1 output layer and 1 hidden layer with 3 nodes in the hidden layer, as shown in Fig. 5 below.

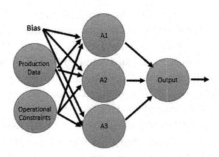

Fig. 5. Model representation 1 for oil wells

Case 2: For a gas well, the architecture comprised of a simple neural network of 2 layer with one input layer and one output layer, as shown in Fig. 6 below.

In this case, a hidden layer is not used as it was in earlier case. The reason is due to the data sets which were included in training of the algorithm. For Gas well, a hidden layer was added at first which lead to slow convergence of our cost function and the predicted curve obtained was showing overfitting of the data. Thus to reduce this variance and for

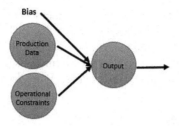

Fig. 6. Model representation 2 for gas wells

fast execution, a simple neural network with no hidden layer was used in case for gas well.

While training the model, in the step for forward propagation of our network we use the following function:

$$H\,(\theta,\,x,\,b) = \theta_{ho}G(\theta_{ih}.x + b_{ih}) + b_{ho} \tag{5}$$

Where H $(\theta,\,x,\,b)$ is the hypothesis function of our ANN obtained by adjusting the weights/parameters (θ) and bias (b) from the training examples or input 'x'. The subscripts 'ih' and 'ho' represents the input to hidden and hidden to output terms respectively.

The activation function used is a sigmoid function:

$$G(x) = 1/(1 + e^{-x}) \tag{6}$$

During the learning phase, for effective training of the neural networks, a squared sum function (Eq. (7)) is used as the cost function for efficient learning of weights (θ) and bias (b) respectively:

$$J\,(\theta,\,b) = \sum_{i=1}^{n}\left((H(\theta,\,x,\,b))^2 - Y_i^2\right) + a\,(\theta^2) \tag{7}$$

Where n = no of training examples, Y_i = Actual Output, a = learning rate or decay rate of cost function J.

An effective and efficient method of 1st order Gradient descent is applied with respect to 'θ' and 'b' for obtaining the parameters/weights 'θ'. Learning rate (a) is optimized so as to obtain the best fit for our curve which is done by iterative selection method. The obtained value found is 0.01 which is used as the learning or decay rate 'a' for our algorithms.

The methodology applied for learning of the neural network model is called the Back-propagation algorithm. At the start, all the weights/parameters are assigned with random values. The neural network algorithm is activated with these randomly assigned values of weights and tested for each input in the training dataset. The output obtained from hypothesis is noted and compared with the actual output values. The difference between the actual and the obtained output is compared and noted as error. This error value is propagated back to the previous layer of the output and similarly further backwards until the input layer. The error in each layer is noted and the randomly assigned values of weights/parameters are adjusted as per the error values. This step goes to repeat until the error obtained in output is minimal and our results of hypothesis matches with the actual results/inputs. Once the above algorithm terminates, we obtain a trained/learned neural network model which can now be used for future prediction.

3   Testing and Results

For training of the neural network, 70% of the data sets were used and the remaining 30% are used for testing of the model. As shown in Fig. 7, the blue dots represents the actual production data from well logs and past production history (70% of the data) and was used for training. The red curve represents the trend line obtained from hypothesis of our neural network model. The trend line obtained is refined by adjusting the parameters and bias of our algorithm which is achieved by proper selection of decay rate. Though it can be observed that the trend line accurately cannot predict the deviation which are caused by certain well activation or any other factor but the average prediction is good and this further can be extrapolated to obtain the ultimate recovery and life of the well. Remaining 30% of the data was used for testing purposes. The trailing part of the curve shown in green is the result obtained and it can be seen that the model displays an accurate fit as per the trend line. The accuracy of any model depends on how well we choose the number of layers in neural networks and also on the decay rate which in turn determines the weights or parameters of the model. Once a good trend line was obtained using the developed neural architecture, the testing results were accurate fit to the trend line and the real data set.

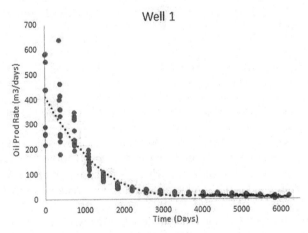

Fig. 7. Production rate vs time graph for an oil well 1.

The neural network model design is same for all the oil wells shown below that are taken up for study. The difference in each of the cases is the proper optimization of the cost junction J (Eq. (3)) so as to obtain the proper weights or parameters and bias.

As shown in Fig. 8(a) for well 2, the production trend obtained is giving an average fit to maximum sets of data and the final result obtained by using the testing data set is shown in the trailing part of the graph in green which shows an accurate fit to the trend line. The production trend is declining in a regular manner.

In Well 3 and Well 4, as shown in Fig. 8(b) and Fig. 8(d), it can be observed that it is showing a very irregular production pattern. It is showing very high rate in certain days which are mainly triggered due to the activation of well. The actual trend is both increasing and decreasing. It was a challenge to get a good fit but with various iterations for obtaining the appropriate decay rate, it was finally possible to get the appropriate values of weights and bias and it can be inferred from the end parts (in green) of the graph which shows the testing results which is very accurately fitting with the actual data and trend line. Having a good hypothesis is a must in order for the model to obtain the final results. Good hypothesis is obtained which is a function of proper selection of neural network design, sufficient training set data so as to efficiently train our algorithm and proper selection of decay rate for our cost function to help efficiently minimize the critical parameters as well as bias.

In well 5 as shown in Fig. 8(c), the production data shows very steep decline during initial years of production but the rate stabilizes after some years. The trend line as can be seen doesn't fit accurately with various initial data sets but the overall performance of the function is good as it can predict the future values accurately when testing was carried out with the last 30% of the datasets. Green part denotes the results of testing.

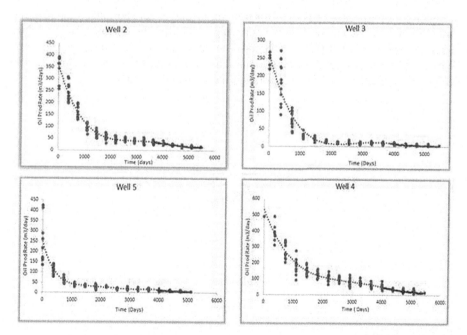

Fig. 8. From top left to bottom right the graphs are (a) for well 2, (b) for well 3, (c) for well 5, (d) for well 4 showing the production rate vs time for each respectively. (Color figure online)

The graph shown below in Fig. (9) below is between cumulative oil production and time in days for well 1. The same model was used as shown in Fig. (5) for obtaining the desired trend. As before, 70% of the data was used for training while the remaining 30% of the inputs were used to obtain the predictions. As it can be shown our model is perfectly trained and a perfect match to the original cumulative production is obtained.

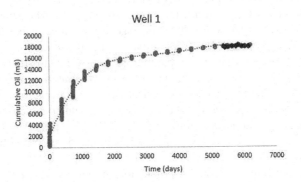

Fig. 9. Cumulative oil production vs time for well

Result from Gas Well

A different neural network structure was used for the gas well model design. As shown in Fig. 10, first 70% data was used for training of the model and remaining 30% for testing purposes. The gas well shown is having a stabilized production trend and thus hypothesis was a good fit to the actual trend. The test results are shown in green and it can be observed how accurate the prediction is. This well is showing a regular production decline trend and thus our model to actual is a significantly good match.

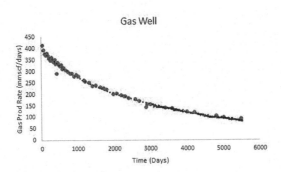

Fig. 10. Production vs time graph obtained from gas well under study

4 Conclusion

As the oil and gas industry is adopting the machine learning techniques to better understand and interpret data, this work is focused on proposing a new and efficient approach for predicting the decline curve or the production trend by using appropriately designed neural network algorithms. The variables for input are production history, operational constraints, and by adjusting the parameters of weight and bias of our neural network model, it is observed and concluded that a proper decline curve trend has been obtained for any well within the reservoir or field of study. Analysis of the decline curve help us determine the life of a well and also used for reserve estimation purpose. In short, how much oil/gas is down there in the reservoir, and how much of it has been produced, and how much remains to be produced still.

There are even certain limitations of machine learning approach, for e.g. finding patterns is sometimes difficult and more often the availability of enough dataset for training purpose is a major issue. Because of these issues, many ML algorithms do not give the required output/result as expected. Other limitations of ML are biased dataset where in the data used for training and validation is itself not in proper order or format due to which the output is not correct as the programmer expects.

The proposed ANN method is a fast and reliable method for production forecasting which can be employed in oil and gas production operations. Sufficient data set acquisition and proper training of the neural network are the two important factors which determine the efficiency of the designed ANN model. For the available data at our disposal, we were able to accurately match the data and forecast it with reasonable accuracy. This will help the operators in planning their field exploitation strategies with optimum efficiency.

References

Arps, J.J.: Analysis of decline curves. Trans. AIME **160**(01), 228–247 (1945). https://doi.org/10.2118/945228-G

Cao, Q., Banerjee, R., Gupta, S., Li, J., Zhou, W., Jeyachandra, B.: Data driven production forecasting using machine learning. In: SPE 2016. Schlumberger (2016)

Hoeink, T., Zambrano, C.: Shale discrimination with machine learning methods. Baker Hughes, Houston (2017)

Crumpton, H.: Well Control for Completions and Interventions (2018)

Alvarado, V., et al.: Selection of EOR/IOR opportunities based on machine learning (2002)

Sneed, J.: Predicting ESP lifespan with machine learning. Devon Energy (2017)

Bowie, B.: Machine learning applied to optimize Duvernay well performance. Apache Constructions (2018)

Ramirez, A.M., Valle, G.A., Romero, F., Jaimes, M.: Prediction of PVT properties in crude oil using machine learning techniques MLT (2017)

Fetkovich, M.J., Fetkovich, E.J., Fetkovich, M.D.: Useful concepts for decline curve forecasting, reserve estimation, and analysis. SPE Reserv. Eng. **11**(01), 13–22 (1996). SPE-28628-PA

Ilk, D., Rushing, J.A., Perego, A.D., Blasingame, T.A.: Exponential vs. hyperbolic decline in tight gas sands: understanding the origin and implications for reserve estimates using Arps' decline curves (2008). https://doi.org/10.2118/116731-MS

Valko, P.P., Lee, W.J.: A better way to forecast production from unconventional gas wells (2010). https://doi.org/10.2118/134231-MS

Shelley, R.F., Grieser, W.V.: Artificial neural network enhanced completions improve well economics (1999). https://doi.org/10.2118/52959-MS

Cunningham, C.F., Cooley, L., Wozniak, G., Pancake, J.: Using multiple linear regression to model EURs of horizontal marcellus wells (2012). https://doi.org/10.2118/161343-MS

Snøtun, H.: Using machine learning to create data. AGR Software (2018). https://doi.org/10.4043/28587-MS

Kalu-Ulu, T.C., Andrawus, J.A., George, I.P.S.: Modelling system failures of electric submersible pumps in sand producing wells (2011). https://doi.org/10.2118/151011-MS

Westphal, H., Bornholdt, S.: Lithofacies prediction from wireline logs with genetic algorithms and neural networks. Zeitschrift der DGG **147**, 465–474 (1996)

Udie, A.C., Nwakaudu, M.S., Aguta, R.M., Obah, B.: Estimation of oil and gas reserves in place using production decline trend analysis (2013)

Ani, M., Oluyemi, G., Petrovski, A., Rezaei-Gomari, S.: Reservoir uncertainty analysis: the trends from probability to algorithms and machine learning (2016). https://doi.org/10.2118/181049-MS

White, A.C., Molnar, D., Aminian, K., Mohaghegh, S., Ameri, S., Esposito, P.: The application of ANN for zone identification in a complex reservoir (1995). https://doi.org/10.2118/30977-MS

Maniar, H., Ryali, S., Kulkarni, M.S., Abubakar, A.: Machine-learning methods in geoscience (2018). IDSEG-2018–2997218

Vyas, A., Datta-Gupta, A., Mishra, S.: Modeling early time rate decline in unconventional reservoirs using machine learning techniques (2017). https://doi.org/10.2118/188231-MS

Pennel, M., Hsiung, J., Putcha, V.B.: Detecting failures and optimizing performance in artificial lift using machine learning models (2018). https://doi.org/10.2118/190090-MS

Li, Y., Han, Y.: Decline curve analysis for production forecasting based on machine learning (2017). IDSPE-189205-MS. https://doi.org/10.2118/189205-MS

Shale Mohaghegh, S.D.: Shale analytics. In: Shale Analytics. Springer, Cham (2017). https://doi.org/10.1007/978-3-319-48753-3_3

Qazi, N., Yeung, H.: Modeling of gas–liquid separation through stacked neural network. Asia-Pac. J. Chem. Eng. **9**(4), 490–497 (2014)

Dindoruk, B., Ratnakar, R.R., He, J.: Review of recent advances in petroleum fluid properties and their representation. J. Nat. Gas Sci. Eng. **83**, 103541 (2020)

Sandham, W., Leggett, M. (eds.): Geophysical Applications of Artificial Neural Networks and Fuzzy Logic. Springer, Heidelberg (2003). https://doi.org/10.1007/978-94-017-0271-3

Daniel, A., Isehunwa, S.O.: Estimation of developed reserves in gas lifted wells (2009). https://doi.org/10.2118/128892-MS

Website References:

https://www.onepetro.org
https://en.unionpedia.org
https://valiancesolutions.com

TABot – A Distributed Deep Learning Framework for Classifying Price Chart Images

Matthew Siper[(⊠)], Kyle Makinen, and Raman Kanan

CS6513 CSE NYU Tandon School of Engineering, New York University,
Brooklyn, NY 11201, USA
ms12010@nyu.edu

Abstract. In this work, we propose a framework called *TABot*, a distributed deep learning (DL) framework for classifying price chart images. The deep learning engine we outline consists of an ensemble of convolutional neural networks employed for classifying price chart images. We present three workflows that compose our framework. The first is the data sourcing workflow: a distributed asynchronous pipeline to collect price data and programmatically generate candlestick charts. We measure the processing times of our distributed solution relative to a synchronous analog to identify a nominal processing time differential between the two solutions. The second is the model training workflow. We again leverage a distributed asynchronous pipeline to train each convolutional neural network in a parallel fashion. We measure the processing time of our parallel solution and compare to a synchronous analog. The third is the prediction workflow. We introduce a simple scheme for collecting the prediction output of each component model in an ensemble network model. Our results support the viability of convolutional neural networks to classify price chart images. The TAbot architecture additionally highlights the benefit of utilizing elastic computing environments to manage computational and data persistence costs incurred by deep learning frameworks.

Keywords: Deep learning · Convolutional neural network · Distributed pipeline orchestration

1 Introduction

Recent breakthroughs in deep learning and elastic computing have increased access to the compute machinery necessary to persist and train models performant on complex tasks. Many deep learning techniques have been applied to financial time series data as a means of forecasting for financial assets. A recurrent neural network is an example architecture that is often implemented for this purpose. However, such implementations require vast amounts of price data to effectively meet forecasting objectives.

By contrast, one benefit we see to leveraging a convolutional neural network architecture is no price data in the underlying security is required to make predictions. Instead, the convolutional neural network requires only images of price charts for model training and pattern prediction. In this work, we train an ensemble model consisting of several convolution neural networks using computer-generated candlestick charts produced

© Springer Nature Singapore Pte Ltd. 2021
D. Garg et al. (Eds.): IACC 2020, CCIS 1367, pp. 465–473, 2021.
https://doi.org/10.1007/978-981-16-0401-0_37

by the TABot data sourcing workflow. We use the prediction accuracy achieved on a validation set of images to measure model quality.

This paper is structured as follows. Section 2 describes related work of deep learning applications to financial domains and a discussion of pipeline architectures implemented in nonfinancial domains. In Sect. 3, we introduce the three workflows that compose TABot: data sourcing, training, and prediction. In Sect. 4, we explain the experiments conducted to measure model quality and processing performance of the data sourcing and training workflows relative to respective synchronous analogs and present our results. Section 5 includes our concluding remarks and suggestions for future work.

2 Related Work

Applying deep learning models to time series data is not a new technique. Deep learning applicability to price forecasting is particularly relevant for financial instruments. For example, Sreelekshmy et al. [1] leverage deep learning and various linear models (e.g. AR, ARMA, ARIMA) to predict future price values in the NSE index. Devadoss et al. [2] use a multilayer perceptron implementation to forecast price values. Each of these techniques involves fitting a deep learning model to predict a continuous value. To achieve high model quality with such implementations requires large amounts of continuous price data for model training.

Our implementation differs in that we train an ensemble model of convolutional neural networks to classify price patterns of stocks. This architecture requires labeled images of price patterns for model training in lieu of actual price data. This distinction suggests that less complex normalization techniques may be required to achieve model generality compared to techniques that are common amongst multivariate regression problems.

Distributed pipeline architectures are used in many domains where big data is prevalent for which there is an abundance of research and data available. For example, Dean et al. [3] propose a large scaled distributed deep learning software framework called *DistBelief*, whereby the authors introduce several novel distributed optimization strategies that allowed for faster training across CPU cluster versus GPU hardware. Gupta et al. [4] proposes *Rudra*, a server architecture for training large-scale deep neural networks that would assist with scaling TABot image patterns and batch sizes. Akiba et al. [5] and Tokui et al. [6] introduce a distributed deep learning framenwork called *ChainerMN* and show state of the art parallelization efficiency when the framework is employed across a cluster of GPUs. Dai et al. [7] introduce a deep learning framework called *BigDL* that provides distributed training support directly on top of a functional compute model of existing big data systems. Jacob et al. [8] leverage a RabbitMQ pipeline architecture for processing real-time ECG data from patients. Moreno-Schneider et al. [9] build a similar pipeline architecture for NLP and content curation processing workflows. Robertsen et al. [10] propose a pipeline architecture for mapping and processing marine mategenomic sequence data. In this work, we propose analogous pipeline architectures that constitute the data sourcing and training workflows of TABot, respectively.

3   Method

3.1   Data Sourcing Workflow

The data sourcing workflow is responsible for generating the training data required to fit our ensemble network (see Fig. 1). The workflow is distributed across three independent work paths. Each work path consists of two distributed asynchronous queues. Disjoint subsets of tickers, where each subset represents a distinct pattern label, are dispatched to their target path by a *Processor* object. The execution path details of the data sourcing process are summarized below.

Step 1. The Processor object publishes a disjoint set of tickers in the form of messages to its write queue.
Step 2. The ChartBuilderWorker reads a message from its queue and extracts the ticker and the pattern from the message. The worker then uses the ticker value and makes an API call to Yahoo to retrieve price data for the last 120 days (this value represents a default parameter that is overridden by a lookback period variable). The worker uses this data to construct a candlestick chart using the Matplotlib library. The resultant chart is saved as a JPEG file in the designated pattern directory. Finally, the worker publishes a message to its write queue. This message contains the absolute file path of the locally persisted image.
Step 3. The UploaderWorker reads the published message from its read queue and extracts the absolute file path for the given image. The worker then increments its internal message counter variable and checks whether it is greater than the preconfigured threshold. If it is, then the worker issues a bulk upload command to copy the locally persisted images to their designated S3 bucket in AWS. Finally, the worker deletes the images from the local file directory and resets its internal counter to zero.

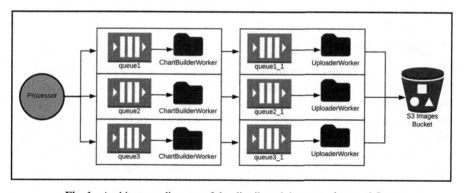

Fig. 1. Architecture diagram of the distributed data sourcing workflow.

3.2   Training Workflow

The training workflow is responsible for model fitting (see Fig. 3). Model fitting is done in a distributed asynchronous pipeline analogous to the data sourcing workflow.

The training workflow is parallelized across three independent work paths. Each work path consists of a queue and a corresponding *ModelWorker* object. A *Processor* object dispatches a *training message*, which contains the key-value pairs that collectively define how the training process will be executed by a ModelWorker upon its read operation. The training process carried out by each distributed ModelWorker is summarized below.

Step 1. The ModelWorker reads the training message from its queue and extracts the key-value pairs that collectively define the training instruction to be executed. One such item in the message is the model_configuration_value key that maps to a config-uration object defined within the TABot framework. The configuration object con-tains the parameters used to configure the model (e.g. the shape of each convolutional layer or the pooling scheme to use), and hyperparameter tuning instructions, if any.

Step 2. The worker checks its local data, validation, and model directories to see if the expected file hierarchies exist. If the file does not exist, then the ModelWorker creates them.

Step 3. The worker downloads the S3 image directories to its local data directory.

Step 4. The worker collects ten twenty percent of the image files from each pattern label and moves each image to its corresponding pattern directory under the validation root directory.

Step 5. The worker checks if a model file exists in its model directory. If a model file exists, then the worker loads it in and begins fitting the model. If no such model exists, or if the *from_scratch* key from the training message was set to true, then the worker constructs a new model from scratch according to the mapped configuration object. If the *tune* key in the training message was set to true, then the training process consists of the hyper tuning algorithm outlined in Fig. 2 below.

Step 6. After the worker has finished its training process, the model is saved to its corresponding model directory and the worker waits for the next training message to arrive at its queue.

3.3 Prediction Workflow

The prediction workflow is responsible for fetching the predicted label and probability from each component-model and mapping predictions based on an ensemble scheme. Since the focus of our work was to evaluate the viability of using a convolutional neural network architecture for price pattern classification, we opted for a logical and simple ensemble scheme.

The scheme consists of two rules that map the set of component-model predictions to one ensemble prediction. The first rule is to search for the most common label in a set of component-model outputs. If such a label is identified in the prediction set, then we compute the confidence for this prediction as the average of all the confidence intervals in the prediction set that correspond to the predicted label. The second rule is if no common label exists in the prediction set, then the label with the highest confidence is selected.

Step 1. A ChartBuilderWorker object uses the ticker value selected by the user via the dropdown event to make an API call to Yahoo to fetch price data for the last 120 days (this

```
function TRAIN-OPTIMAL-MODEL
    max_pooling_sizes ← [(2,2), (3,3), (4,4)]
    convolution_sizes ← [16, 32, 64]
    dropout_factors ← [0, 0.25, 0.5]
    activation_functions ← ['relu']
    optimizers ← ['rmsprop', 'adam']
    epochs ← [5, 16, 32]
    steps_per_epoch_options ← [1, 2, 4]

    training_parameters ←GENERATE-PARAMETERS-COMBINATIONS(...)
    for each parameter_combination in training_parameters do
        model ← model.COMPILE(parameter_combination)
        model.FIT(training_data)
        current_accuracy ← model.PREDICT(test_data)
        if current_accuracy > optimal_accuracy then optimal_parameters ← pa-
        rameter_combination

    model.SAVE(optimal_parameters)
```

Fig. 2. Hyper-parameter tuning algorithm pseudo-code.

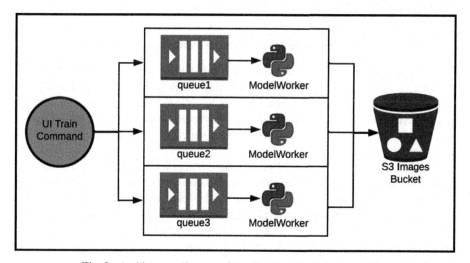

Fig. 3. Architecture diagram of the distributed training workflow.

value represents a default parameter that is overridden by a lookback period variable). The worker uses this data to construct a candlestick chart using the Mat-plotlib library. The resultant chart is saved as a JPEG file in the live-cache local directory.
Step 2. The candlestick chart is rendered in the UI.

Step 3. The locally persisted JPEG file is read and converted into to a 300×300 matrix of triplets, whereby each triplet represents the scalar values of red, blue, and green, respectively, present in the corresponding pixel.

Step 4. The pixel matrix is iteratively fed to each component-model and the subsequent prediction output is appended to a results dictionary.

Step 5. The ensemble scheme is applied to the results dictionary to compute the ensemble model prediction. The ensemble prediction is then appended to the results dictionary.

Step 6. The contents of the results dictionary, which contains the prediction output of the ensemble model and the prediction outputs of each component-model are rendered in a table within the client UI.

4   Empirical Evidence

This work seeks to answer three questions. The first is whether a convolutional neural network architecture can be used to classify price chart images. The second is what performance gains can be realized by distributing data sourcing workflow relative to a synchronous analog? Similarly, the third is what performance gains can be realized by distributing the training workflow relative to its synchronous analog? We will address questions two and three in Sect. 4.1 and 4.2 below followed by Sect. 4.3 where we draw conclusions on our primary experiment of interest to test the viability of convolutional neural networks to identify chart patterns.

4.1   Experiment 1 – Measuring Data Sourcing Workflow Performance

In this section, we describe the experiment conducted to answer question two: what performance gains can be realized by distributing the data sourcing workflow relative to its synchronous analogs? The first step was to collect 300 tickers from each of the price pattern labels (wedgeup, wedgedown, horizontal, and no pattern). These tickers were sourced from the FinViz screener tool and stored in a variable locally scoped to the Processor object.

Next, we defined two additional processing environments of varying synchronicity. In the first environment, which we labeled the *Synchronous* environment, all processing was executed in a continuous single-threaded block of code using one locally instantiated ChartBuilderWorker and one UploaderWorker instance. The second environment, which we refer to as the One_work_path environment, consisted of one work path (i.e. two asynchronous queues), as oppose to the three independent work paths present in the Distributed workflow (see Fig. 4).

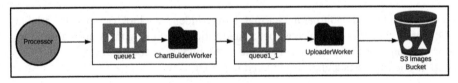

Fig. 4. Schematic of the *One_work_path workflow.*

Each environment executed the data sourcing workflow ten times. Their respective nominal processing times were recorded. The results, listed in Table 1 below, confirm that the Distributed environment was significantly faster than both the Synchronous and One_work_path environments, respectively.

Table 1. Average processing time of the data sourcing workflow per environment.

Environment	Average runtime (s)
Synchronous	~ 50000
One_work_path	547
Distributed	298

4.2 Experiment 2 – Measuring Training Workflow Performance

In this section, we describe the experiment conducted to answer question three: what performance gains can be realized by distributing the training workflow relative to its synchronous analog? Each component-model was trained using the data sourced from Experiment 1. Specifically, the first 100 images from each pattern directory were migrated to a target directory created for this experiment. We evaluated the nominal runtime of the distributed training workflow and compared runtimes to the synchronous environment. The synchronous environment executed the training of each component-model iteratively within a single-threaded continuous block of code. The resultant runtimes, listed in Table 2 below, show that the synchronous environment was unexpectedly faster than the distributed environment. We attributed much of this runtime differential to network overhead and relatively small batch sizes.

Table 2. Average processing time of the training workflow per environment.

Environment	Average runtime (s)
Synchronous	225.4
Distributed	365.7

4.3 Experiment 3 – Measuring Model Quality

In this section, we describe the experiment conducted to answer our primary question of interest: how viable is a convolutional neural network architecture in the classification of price chart images? To answer this question, we trained the ensemble model using four different pattern labels. The labels we used were wedgeup, wedgedown, horizontal, and no_pattern. The training data consisted of 600 images for each pattern. The labeled tickers were sourced from the FinViz screener tool. To source differentiable images across pattern types, we set the pattern filter in the screener tool to 'strong' to minimize weak pattern formations in the training data.

To source tickers for the no_pattern label, we selected 150 weak formations for each of the other pattern labels in the label set. The remaining 150 tickers were selected randomly from other patterns not represented in the label set. In order to increase model robustness, each component-model was configured with a distinct lookback parameter. This allowed for each-component model to learn periodicities, scales, and pattern locations unique to each lookback period. Component-model 1 was configured with a lookback period of 40 bars. Component-models 2 and 3 were configured with lookback periods of 80 bars and 120 bars, respectively.

Twenty percent of the training data for each label was moved to a corresponding validation directory. This validation set was used to measure model accuracy. The classification accuracies produced by the ensemble, as well as, each component-model are presented in Table 3 below.

Table 3. Ensemble and component-model performance.

Model	Accuracy
Component-model 1	72.6%
Component-model 2	79.7%
Component-model 3	76.3%
Ensemble Model	80.3%

5   Conclusion

In this work, we presented a framework called TABot, a distributed deep learning framework for classifying price chart images. We sought to test convolutional neural network viability for predicting chart patterns and the benefits of synchronous versus asynchronous workflows. We showed that utilizing a distributed asynchronous architecture for data sourcing was significantly faster than both the One_work_path and Synchronous workflows, respectively. For model training, we found the distributed training workflow was unexpectedly slower than its synchronous analog. We attributed this slowdown to the costs incurred by network overhead and relatively small batch sizes.

As for convolutional neural network viability for chart pattern recognition, the accuracy achieved by our ensemble network was 80.3%. This performance confirms convolutional neural network architectures can be employed to classify price chart images. Future work to enhance the ensemble model and extend its practicality includes techniques that measure variations within chart pattern labels to increase model robustness. Key sources of variability include pattern size, coloring and orientation, all of which are instrumental to producing actionable models.

References

1. Sreelekshmy, S., Vinayakumar, R., Vijay, K., Soman, K.: Stock price prediction using LSTM. Centre for Computation Engineering and Networking, Amitra, RNN and CNN-sliding window model. In (2018)
2. Devadoss, A., Ligori, A.: Forecasting of stock prices using multi layer perceptron. Int. J. Comput. Algorithm **2**, 440–449 (2013)
3. Dean, J., et al.: Large scale distributed deep networks. In: Advances in Neural Information Processing Systems, Mountain View (2012)
4. Gupta, S., Zhang, W., Wang, F.: Model accuracy and runtime tradeoff in distributed deep learning: A systematic study. IBM Watson Research Center. Weill Cornell Medical College, New York (2016)
5. Akiba, T., Fukuda, K., Suzuki, S.: ChainerMN: scalable distributed deep learning framework. In: Proceedings of Workshop on ML Systems in The Thirty-first Annual Conference on Neural Information Processing Systems (NIPS), Vancouver (2017)
6. Tokui, S., et al.: Chainer: A Deep Learning Framework for Accelerating the Research Cycle. Preferred Networks, Inc., Japan (2019)
7. Dai, J., Shi, D., Lu, Q., Huang, K., Song, G.: BigDL: a distributed deep learning framework for big data. In: Symposium of Cloud Computing (SoCC), Santa Cruz (2019)
8. Jacob, S., Mahajan, R., Akbilgic, O., Kamaleswaran, R.: PhysOnline: an online feature extraction and machine learning pipeline for real-time analysis of streaming physiological data. IEEE J. Biomed. Health Inform. **23**(1), 59 (2018)
9. Moreno-Schneider, J., Bourgonje, P., Kintzel, F., Rehm, G.: A workflow manager for complex NLP content curation pipelines. In: Proceedings of the 1st International Workshop on Language Technology Platforms, pp. 73–80. European Language Resources Association, Marseille (2016)
10. Robertsen, E., et al.: META-pipe - Pipeline Annotation. Analysis and Visualization of Marine Metagenomic Sequence Data, Norway (2016)

Multi-class Emotion Classification Using EEG Signals

Divya Acharya[1]([⊠]), Riddhi Jain[2], Siba Smarak Panigrahi[3], Rahul Sahni[4], Siddhi Jain[4], Sanika Prashant Deshmukh[5], and Arpit Bhardwaj[1]

[1] Bennett University, Greater Noida, India
{da9642,arpit.bhardwaj}@bennett.edu.in
[2] Jaipur Engineering College and Research Centre, Jaipur, India
riddhi.ten.jain@gmail.com
[3] Indian Institute of Technology Kharagpur, Kharagpur, India
sibasmarak.p@iitkgp.ac.in
[4] Dr. B. R. Ambedkar National Institute of Technology Jalandhar, Jalandhar, India
rsahni9785@gmail.com, siddhi.ten@gmail.com
[5] Fr. C. Rodrigues Institute of Technology, Navi Mumbai, India
dsanika0@gmail.com

Abstract. Recently, the availability of large EEG datasets, advancements in Brain-Computer interface (BCI) systems and Machine Learning have led to the implementation of deep learning architectures, especially in the analysis of emotions using EEG signals. These signals can be generated by the user while performing various mental, emotional and physical tasks thus, reflecting the brain functionality. Extracting the important feature values from these unprocessed signals remain a vital step in the deployment. Fast Fourier Transformation proves to be better than the traditional feature extraction techniques. In this paper we have compared the deep learning models namely Long Short-term Memory (LSTM) and Convolutional Neural Network (CNN) on 80–20 and 75–25 Train-Test splits. The best result was obtained from LSTM classifier with an accuracy of 88.6% on the liking emotion. CNN also gave a good accuracy of 87.72% due to its capability to extract spatial feature from the input signals. Thus, both these models are quite beneficial in this context.

Keywords: Emotion recognition · EEG · Convolutional neural network · Long short-term memory networks · Deep learning

1 Introduction

Electroencephalography (EEG) signals track and record brain activities with small metal discs with thin wires (electrodes) placed on the scalp. Analysis of EEG signals help researchers, doctors to assess and diagnose brain and mental diseases. Due to complex nature, noise, artefacts in EEG signals, and data from many patients making the EEG signal analysis process time-consuming and may not always be accurate. Careful analysis of EEG with computer algorithms provides valuable insights and helps better

© Springer Nature Singapore Pte Ltd. 2021
D. Garg et al. (Eds.): IACC 2020, CCIS 1367, pp. 474–491, 2021.
https://doi.org/10.1007/978-981-16-0401-0_38

understanding of diseases like Stroke Diagnosis, Epilepsy Diagnosis, Autism Diagnosis, Sleep Disorder Diagnosis, Dementia Diagnosis, Alcoholism Diagnosis, Anesthesia Monitoring, Coma and Brain Death, Brain Tumor Diagnosis [1]. The new and emerging Brain-Computer Interfaces (BCIs) technology captures EEG signals and analyses and translates it into the command to carry out the desirable tasks. Different researchers have used different Machine Learning algorithms for improvement in the study of EEG signals.

Emotions play a significant role in human beings as these are associated with the brain and bring neurophysiological changes in thoughts, feelings, behavioral responses, and a degree of pleasure or displeasure.

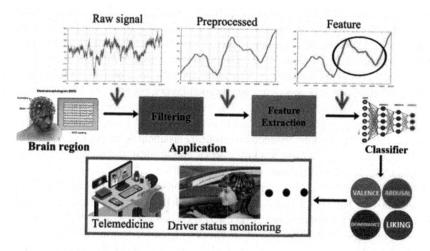

Fig. 1. Proposed model architecture for emotion recognition using EEG signal processing

Emotions are complex in nature as they involve various components like subjective experience, cognitive processes, psychophysiological changes, and instrumental and expressive behavior. Everyday interaction between humans like facial expression, voice, the text provides primary data to researchers to identify human emotion, but it may not be exactly how they are feeling but rather as they feel others would respond. EEG signals to aid in identifying emotions as it gives a better understanding of participant's underlying responses captured at the time of observation [2]. As shown in Fig. 1, signals are captured using electrodes. These signals are then filtered by removing the noises and artifacts, which can be done by bandpass filtering. Removal of artifacts entirely is not possible, as removal of artifacts entirely may result in the loss of some valuable information. After filtering data, necessary features are extracted and shaped correctly to fit into a classifying model for the analysis of several emotions. Once the model is implemented successfully, it can be used to deploy various applications. Therefore, it offers high accuracy for recognition of emotions as compared to voice or facial expression. Various researchers worked on EEG data to classify emotional states using machine learning algorithms like random forest [3], Naive Bayes [4], KNN [5], SVM with RBF kernel function [6]. But very few researchers used deep learning algorithms like CNN [7] and RNN [8] to analyze EEG signals.

In this paper, we are proposing a distinct comparison between two deep learning architecture LSTM (Long Short-term Memory) & CNN (Convolution Neural Network), in which we have split the pre-processed DEAP data into two splits, i.e., 75–25 and 80–20 where we received a good result. We are using LSTM as sequences tasks as they can capture more dependency and predicts the sequence of data. The data used in this paper is not continuous but is sequential, so LSTM offers excellent results. For CNN, the prediction is much faster and is done in computationally efficient manner, that is why CNN is in this research paper.

2 Related Work

S Tripathy et al. (2017) [9] explored Deep Neural Network (DNN) and Convolutional Neural Network (CNN) for emotion classification on DEAP dataset. The proposed architecture of their DNN model is an input layer of 4040 units followed by 5000, 500 and 1000 hidden units in three hidden layers. The output layer is a 2 or 3 class softmax (Dunne and Campbell (1997) [10]) classifier depending upon the requirement. Further the proposed architecture of CNN was two convolutional layers, followed by Maxpooling and Dropout layers, which connects to Fully Connected layers to provide the output. They achieve an accuracy of 75.78% and 73.125% for DNN and 81.406% and 73.36% for CNN in 2 class (high and low) valence and arousal classification respectively. For 3 class classification (high, normal and low) of valence and arousal, the accuracy achieved is 58.44% and 55.70% for DNN and 66.79% and 57.58% for CNN.

W. Liu et al. (2016) [11] extract features by the Bimodal Deep Auto-encoder (BDAE). They design two Restricted Boltzmann Machine (RBM), one for EEG (EEG RBM) and other for eye movement features (eye RBM). They concatenate the hidden layers and obtain an upper RBM. The BDAE network is used for feature selection and they train linear SVM classifier on the high-level features extracted. The mean accuracies achieved with the BDAE network are respectively 91.01% and 83.25% on SEED and DEAP datasets.

S. Alhagry et al. (2017) [12] proposed 2-layer stacked LSTM architecture for emotion recognition on DEAP dataset. The first LSTM layer consists of 64 units with ReLU activation function, followed by a dropout layer with 0.2 probability. Second layer consists of 32 neurons with sigmoid activation function connected finally to a dense layer again with sigmoid activation. They divide valence, arousal, and liking to high/low class and respectively obtain an average accuracy of 85.65%, 85.45%, and 87.99% on DEAP dataset.

J. Zhang et al. (2016) [13] obtain average classification accuracy of 81.21% and 81.26% on valence and arousal respectively. They use Probabilistic Neural Networks (PNNs), which consists of four layers including the input layer, and the output layer. The second layer is termed as Pattern layer and the third layer is termed as Summation layer.

P. Zhong et al. (2020) [14] propose a Regularized Graph Neural Network (RGNN) for EEG based emotion recognition, in addition to two regularizers to make their model robust, node-wise domain adversarial training (NodeDAT) and emotion-aware distribution learning (EmotionDL). They beat the state-of-the-art results of bi-hemispheric discrepancy model (BiHDM) (Y.Li et al. (2019) [15]) with the average accuracies of 94.24%

and 79.37% for subject-dependent classification accuracy on SEED and SEED-IV (all-bands), while the BiHDM achieved average accuracies of 93.12% and 74.35% respectively. Further in case of subject-independent classification, RGNN obtained 85.30% and 73.84% mean accuracy respectively.

D. Acharya et al. (2020) [16] provide LSTM architecture for negative emotion classification and also briefly examines the human behavior in different age groups and gender. Their LSTM model, for four class negative emotion classification obtains classification accuracy of 81.63%, 84.64%, 89.73%, and 92.84% for 50–50, 60–40, 70–30 split of data, and 10-fold cross-validation. The models have been evaluated on both DEAP and SEED datasets.

A. Bhardwaj et al. (2014) [17] provide a novel Genetic Programming approach with hill-climbing integrated constructive crossover and mutation operators. They have estimated their classification accuracy to be 98.69%.

Another novel Genetic Programming approach with provision of a technique for hybrid crossover, intron deletion and mutation operation has been proposed in H. Bhardwaj et al. (2019) [18], which increases the accuracy of classification and also leads to a decrease in time complexity. This further suggests the possibility of a real-time Genetic Programming classifier for detection of epileptic seizures.

A new fitness function termed as Gap score (G score) has been proposed in D. Acharya et al. (2020) [19] to address imbalance in dataset. They propose a framework termed as GGP, a Genetic programming framework with G score fitness function. Their GGP framework provides 87.61% classification accuracy using EEG signals.

3 Methodology

In this section dataset description, feature extraction technique used, model architecture, and hyperparameter used for training the classifier including description of implementation tools are described next.

3.1 Dataset Description

The collection of the original DEAP dataset [20] was done in 2 parts. The first part was the online self-assessment where 14–16 subjects rated 120 YouTube music videos each of 1-min extract based on valence, arousal, dominance, likeness and familiarity all listed in online ratings.csv or.xls file. The second part involves physiological recordings and participant ratings of 32 volunteers. These unprocessed physiological clips were in BioSemi.bdf format. Out of 120 videos 40 were shown to each of them. Frontal face clips were also recorded for 22 subjects and could be downloaded from face_video.zip file. Apart from these, the dataset also had list and links of YouTube music videos and a participant questionnaire file containing all the answers given by each participant to the questions asked before the experiment. Original 512 Hz EEG signal were pre-processed to 128 Hz after down sampling, filtering, segmenting and removing all the artefacts like eyes blinking, muscle movements etc. They were present in MATLAB.mat and Python.dat format.

In each of these 32.dat files corresponding to each participant there were 2 arrays: Data and labels. Data was of 40 × 40 × 8064 dimensions. There were 40 channels in each video which in turn had 8064 EEG signal data that forms 322560 in total. The labels had 40 × 4 shape where 4 signifies valence, arousal, dominance and liking (Table 1). Python NumPy arrays is used and loaded.dat files using cPickle library and encoding latin1.

Table 1. Pre-processed dataset description

Data	40 × 40 × 8064 (video × channel × data)
Labels	40 × 4 video × label (Valence, Arousal, Liking, Dominance)
No. of participants	32
Sampling rate	128 Hz

3.2 Feature Extraction

Fast Fourier transformation was performed for feature extraction reducing it to final dimensions of (58560,70) from (40,40,8064) hence resulting in faster training as well as giving better accuracy.

These extracted features comprise of five frequency bands: Delta-δ (1–4 Hz), Theta-θ (4–8 Hz), Alpha-α (8–14 Hz), Beta-β (14–31 Hz), and Gamma-γ (31–50 Hz), shown in Fig. 2. Extracted 70 features in total and have used PyEEG python library.

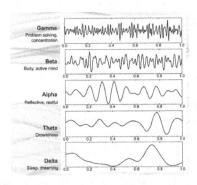

Fig. 2. Brain wave samples for different waveforms [21]

FFT is used to change the Signal domain that is the x-axis from time to frequency. It works on the principle of computing the discrete Fourier transform (DFT) of time Series in an efficient way. It makes the calculations easier by calculating the coefficients of the DFT in an iterative manner, which results in the reduction of computational time as well as computational complexity. It also reduces round-off errors associated with the computations.

As shown in Table 2, 14 channels and 5 bands for our model is selected. The window size was chosen 256 which averages the band power to 2 s. The step size is 16 which means that each 0.125 s update once.

Table 2. FFT parameters description

Channel	1, 2, 3, 4, 6, 11, 13, 17, 19, 20, 21, 25, 29, 31
Bands	4, 8, 12, 16, 25, 45
Window size	256
Step size	16

3.3 Model Architecture

Two deep learning Architectures for our research, Long Short-Term Memory Networks (LSTMs) and Convolutional Neural Networks (CNNs). The dataset used is the python pre-processed version of DEAP dataset. The models were trained for each emotion-arousal, valence, dominance and liking- separately classifying them on a scale of 0 to 9 with varying train-test splits. Both the models were implemented using Keras (Chollet (2015) [22]) and described below:

3.3.1 Long Short-Term Memory (LSTMs)

Long Short-Term Memory Networks (LSTMs) introduced by Hochreiter and Schmidhuber in 1997 [23] are special kind of Recurrent neural networks (RNN). LSTM's were created as a solution to the short-term memory. They have internal mechanisms called gates which can learn which data in a sequence is important to keep or throw away. Hence stores both short- and long-term input units. This is the major reason why we use LSTM in our research.

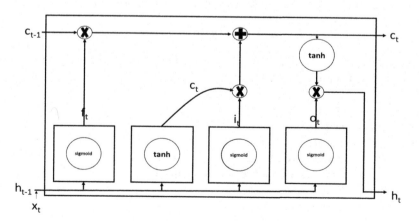

Fig. 3. LSTM cell

A common LSTM unit in Fig. 3 is made of a cell, an input gate, an output gate and a forget gate. The cell remembers values over time and the three gates are used to regulate the flow of information into and out of the cell.

The Sigmoid Activation function helps us to classify if the neuron is active or not. The Sigmoid function transforms a real value to a value ranging from 0 to 1. Consider 0.5 as the threshold value, if the value ranges between 0–0.5 then it is considered not activated, if the value ranges between 0.5–1 then it is considered activated.

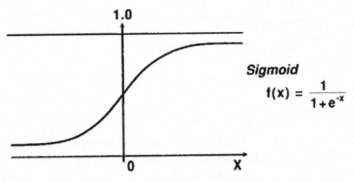

Fig. 4. Sigmoid function [27]

All the three gates use sigmoid function because the gates must give only positive values. The equations for the gates are given:

$$i_t = \sigma \left(\omega_i \left[h_{t-1}, x_t \right] + b_i \right) \tag{1}$$

The first equation is for input gate which tells use what new information will be stored in the cell state.

$$f_t = \sigma \left(\omega_f \left[h_{t-1}, x_t \right] + b_f \right) \tag{2}$$

This second equation is for forget gate; it tells what information to throw away.

$$o_t = \sigma \left(\omega_0 \left[h_{t-1}, x \right] + b_0 \right) \tag{3}$$

Third equation is for output gate which is used to provide the activation to the final output of LSTM at t timestamp.

i_t: represents input gate
f_t: represents forget gate
o_t: represents output gate
w_x: weight for the respective gate(x)
h_{t-1}: output of previous LSTM block at timestamp t-1
x_t: input at current timestamp
b_x: biases for the respective gate(x)

The next three equations are used for calculation of cell state, candidate cell and the final output.

$$\widetilde{c_t} = \tanh\left(\omega_c\left[h_{t-1}, x_t\right] + b_c\right) \tag{4}$$

$$c_t = f_t * c_{t-1} + i_t * \widetilde{c_t} \tag{5}$$

$$h_t = o_t * tanh(c_t) \tag{6}$$

c_t: cell state (memory) at time stamp(t).
$\widetilde{c_t}$: represents candidate for cell state at timestamp(t).
$*$: represents the element wise multiplication of the vectors.

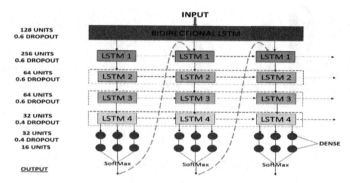

Fig. 5. Proposed LSTM architecture

In our proposed approach one bi-direction LSTM layer, four LSTM layers and two dense layers in the model architecture as shown in the Fig. 4. The first bi-directional LSTM layer has 128 units (in total 256). It involves duplicating the first LSTM layer in the network so that there are two layers side by side. It provides the input sequence as input to the first and a reverse copy of it to the second. Followed by this is the dropout layer with a probability of 0.6. This helps in preventing overfitting by randomly setting inputs to 0 according to the rate during training.

The next layer is a LSTM layer of 256 neurons, followed by dropout layer of 0.6. The next 4 layers are 2 LSTM layers of 64 neurons each followed by a dropout layer. The dropout rates being 0.6 and 0.4 respectively. The final LSTM layer is of 32 neurons followed by dropout layer of 0.4. Then a dense layer of 16 units is used. The activation used for the same is ReLU. Then a dense layer of 10 classes is used with the SoftMax activation function. It results in a multiclass probability distribution over our 10 classes. Knowing the probabilities of all the classes, use of argmax to find the class output is done.

3.3.2   Convolutional Neural Network (CNN)

CNNs are very effective models for Image Processing and classifications. The best thing with the CNN architecture is that there is no need of external feature extraction. The network employs a mathematical operation called convolution. It is a special type of linear equation. Instead of the general matrix multiplication, it uses convolution of data and filters to generate various features which are then passes to the next layer. It is used for its excellent capability to extract spatial features from the data.

$$Z = X * f \tag{7}$$

With X as input, f as filters and $*$ as convolution.

Convolution Neural Network Model Architecture

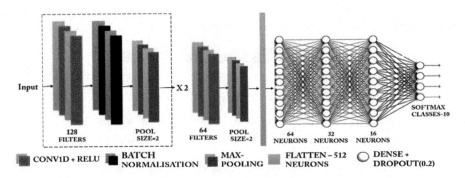

Fig. 6. Proposed CNN architecture

In our proposed model three conv1D, three fully connected dense layers and a dense layer with SoftMax activation for 10 classes in the end as seen in the model architecture in the Fig. 5.

The first convolution layer uses Rectified linear unit (ReLU) as activation function and 128 filters with kernel size of 3. The accurate no. of filters and size of filters is found after a lot of hyperparameter tuning using Grid Search and manual changes. The input passed to the first layer of conv1D is of shape (70,1) and same padding and stride of 1 is used.

The outputs of the first layer are standardized that is having a mean of zero and standard deviation of one using a Batch Normalized layer. The next layer is Max pooling 1D layer of pool size 2 for down sampling the input by taking the maximum value over window size of 2. The padding and strides are set to default i.e. "valid" and "none" respectively. The resulting output has a shape of:

$$n_{out} = \frac{n_{in} + 2p - k}{s} + 1 \tag{8}$$

n_{in}: number of input features
n_{out}: number of output features

k: convolution kernel size
p: convolution padding size
s: convolution stride size

The next Convolution layer is same as the first one followed by batch normalization and max pooling layers. Then Flatten the shape to form a 1-dimensional layer and feed it to a fully connected layer of 64 neurons and TanHyperbolic (tanh) as the activation function. Dropout on the outputs of dense layer is used to reduce the overfitting of the network, with a dropout probability of 0.2. This is followed by 1 dense layer of 32 neurons, tanh activation and dropout layer of 0.2 and another dense layer of 16 neuron with activation function as ReLU and dropout probability of 0.2.

Finally, a Dense layer of 10 neurons with activation function as SoftMax is used to give the output of the network.

3.4 Hyperparameter Tuning

A lot of hyperparameter tuning was carried out while finalizing the Network parameters. Due to the problems like vanishing and exploding gradients Recurrent neural networks (RNNs) is not opted for this. However, one layer of Gated recurrent units (GRU) was tried instead of the Bidirectional LSTM as the first layer, but results were not satisfactory.

In the CNN architecture, Conv1D layers are used because it is most suitable for time series data. Both Max pooling and average pooling was tried but, max pool gave better results as expected from the literature.

Other parameters like the number of epochs, batch size, optimizer, loss function, activation functions and learning rates were finalized using the Grid Search.

Table 3. Network parameters for CNN and LSTM

Parameters	Chosen values
Epoch	200
Batch size	256
Loss function	Categorical cross entropy
Optimizer	Adam
Metrics	Accuracy

The epoch size finalized for the CNN and LSTM architecture is 200 with batch size of 256. The models are trained on various train test splits like 80–20 and 75–25 and K-fold cross validation with 10 folds is also used for finding the most appropriate metrics-accuracy. The loss function used by them for updating the weights during back-propagation is categorical cross entropy and the optimizer used is Adam. And activation function for the last layer is SoftMax for both.

Parameters like no. of layers, number of hidden units, filter size, number of filters and pool size for CNN model and number of hidden neurons, dropout rates and layers for LSTM model were finalized separately, parameters detailed in Table 3. This was done through both Grid search and manual testing.

3.5 Implementation Tools

The environment used for the computation of CNN and LSTM classifiers is Google Collaboratory which is a hosted Jupyter notebook service that requires no setup to use while providing free access to computing resources including GPUs. The python version is Python (3.6.9). The TensorFlow version is 2.2.0. The code is executed in a virtual machine. The GPUs available in CoLab often include Nvidia K80s, T4s, P4s and P100s.

4   Experimental Results

In this section discussion on the experimental results and conclusions attained from the above proposed methodology is done. Created various models with different model architectures and also varying the train test split into different ratios. As Table 4 illustrates that LSTM model architecture which is proposed gives best test accuracy of 88.6% with 75–25 train test split, whereas CNN model architecture gives best accuracy of 87.72 with 80–20 train test split.

Table 4. Comparison between model results on the basis of splits

Classifier	Train-test split	
	75–25	80–20
CNN	87.45%	87.72%
LSTM	88.6%	85.74%

Table 5. Both model's performance on all the four emotions

Classifier	Emotion	Train-test split	
		75–25	80–20
LSTM	Arousal	81.91%	85.07%
	Valence	84.39%	83.83%
	Dominance	69.69%	81.43%
	Liking	88.60%	85.74%
CNN	Arousal	84.77%	85.48%
	Valence	85.01%	82.59%
	Dominance	85.50%	83.61%
	Liking	87.45%	87.72%

The above results are for the liking emotion. Trained these models on all the four emotions individually and got impressive results. Our models were generalizing results very well as they have achieved above 80% accuracy while classifying each emotion. Categorical cross entropy is used as the loss function.

As illustrated in Table 5 both CNN and LSTM model test accuracies are found out for each emotion using both the train test splits and table helps to summarize the results for each emotion. As inferred from the table both the model architectures generalize results very well for all four emotions.

The change in train-test split hardly changes the model performance as the model generalizes results pretty well for both the splits. However, after analyzing the results here this can be concluded that CNN model results are quite précised for each emotion whereas LSTM model results vary with dominance emotion classified with only 69.69% whereas Liking emotion classified with 88.6%.

After training a lot these hyper tuning parameters are finalized to obtain these results. Initially simple LSTM layers are used but the model accuracy was not improving above 65%. Trained model consisting of GRU units but the results were not convincing. Batch size does not have a strong impact on the model results. Dropout and batch normalization layers have significant impact on model's accuracy, dropout helped to avoid overfitting on training data which helped to improve model's results. Categorical cross entropy is used as loss function.

As illustrated in Fig. 6 Similar output are obtained for all the four emotions where least number signifies that emotion present is least and maximum number signifies that the amount of emotion is maximum.

Table 6. Test loss for both models using different train test split

Classifier	Train-test split	
	75–25	80–20
CNN	0.474	0.459
LSTM	0.399	0.503

As illustrated in Table 6. It is found that here LSTM model with data split in 75–25 ratio provided the lowest classification loss of 0.399. Ideal value for categorical cross entropy loss should be equal to zero but practically loss under 1 is considered that the model generalizes results on unseen data pretty well. Both the models reported the value of loss less than 1, which is what we expect as referred to literature. Various learning curves for both the models are also plotted.

All the curves follow the expected pattern as referred to literature, the train and test accuracy for both the models increases with the increase in the number of epochs as shown in Fig. 7. (a) (b). Both the train and test loss decrease with the increase in the number of epochs. Third set of curves is plotted between test accuracy and test loss here. Observed a slight difference between curve of LSTM and CNN as illustrated in Fig. 7. (b), (e). LSTM starts learning a little later than the CNN model and also loss reaches to

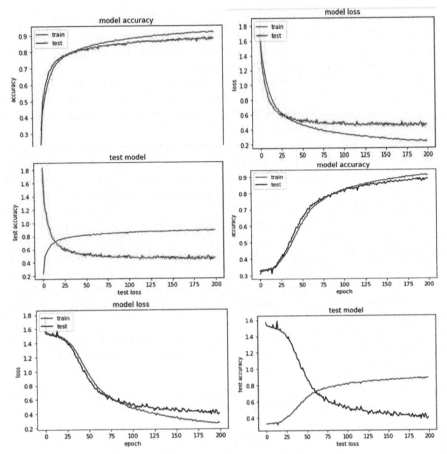

Fig. 7. Row 1: (Left-Right) (a) accuracy vs epoch (CNN), (b) loss vs epoch (CNN) **Row 2: (Left-Right)** (c) test accuracy vs test loss (CNN) (d) accuracy vs epoch (LSTM) **Row 3: (Left-Right)** (e) loss vs epoch (LSTM) (f) test accuracy vs test loss (LSTM)

minimum or stable point after around 40 epochs for CNN whereas it took around 120 epochs to do so for LSTM model.

The comparison between our proposed models and previous works accuracy for different type of emotion is shown in Table 7. The results provided by the proposed method has been compared with four different methods which all used DEAP dataset. The proposed models i.e. our CNN model has attained 87.72% for liking class and also LSTM model has attained 88.6% for the same which is better than the previously attained best accuracy of 87.9% by LSTM model [12] and 81.46% by CNN model [9]. Our proposed models have generalized very well as they are getting above 80% on all classes of emotions. The method proposed by S. Alhagry [12] have managed to get better accuracy than our models for two classes i.e. Arousal and Valence but our proposed models give more finer results i.e. on the scale of 0 to 9 as shown in Fig. 8 for each emotion as compared to S. Alhagry [12] i.e. High or low. This proves that though the accuracy sees a little less, still our model is better capable of classifying the emotions on a finer range.

Table 7. Comparison with other State-of-the-art methods

	Arousal	Valence	Dominance	Liking
Choi et al. [24]	74.65%	78%	-	-
Naser et al. [25]	66.2%	64.3%	-	70.2%
Rozgic et al. [26]	76.9%	68.4%	-	-
S Alhagry et al. [12]	85.65%	85.45%	-	87.9%
Our CNN	84.7%	85.01%	85.5%	87.72%
Our LSTM	81.91%	84.39%	69.7%	88.6%

Figure 8 compares the mean accuracy comparison with other State-of-the-art results. We have compared our results with best results known to us in two (high/low) or three class (high/normal/low) classification of EEG signals on the Arousal, Valence, Dominance, and Liking in Table 7 and Fig. 8.

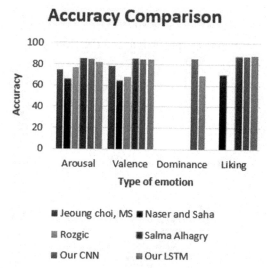

Fig. 8. Mean accuracy comparison with other State-of-the-art results

Confusion matrix is a good technique to measure the performance of classifier for multiclass classification. It is always drawn between true and predicted label. Findings stated that both the classifier algorithms perform similarly for all the classes with classes 4 and 5 being predicted with highest scores. On comparing scores from both Fig. 9 and Fig. 10 the confusion matrix it can be reported that LSTM model scores are better than the CNN model for all the classes except for classes 0 and 7. This also justifies why LSTM architecture is performing better on unseen data (88.6%) than CNN architecture (87.45%).

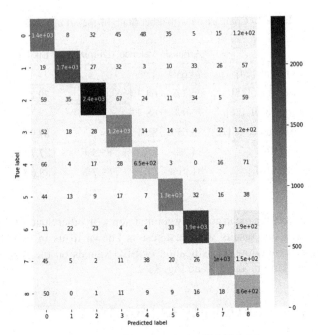

Fig. 9. Confusion matrix for CNN Model

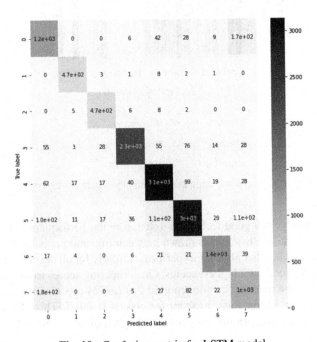

Fig. 10. Confusion matrix for LSTM model

5   Conclusion, Limitation and Future Scope

In this research paper the comparison between CNN and LSTM models on 80–20 and 75–25 Train-Test splits for the classification of EEG signals for emotion analysis is performed successfully. The best result achieved is with the LSTM model using one Bidirectional layer. It has enhanced the performance of the model on this sequence classification problem as compared to the previous papers due to Bi-LSTM's ability to preserve information from future to past as well from past to future. FFT for feature extraction has also contributed in the hike of accuracy as compared to traditional feature extraction techniques. CNN also gave a good accuracy due to its capability to extract spatial features from the input signals.

Still some of the limitations lead to setback in integrating real-life emotion analysis systems like collecting emotion data in a convenient and reliable way such that the signal to noise ratio is increased. Also sometimes decoding the affective state consistently and accurately pose problems. Real-Time online analysis systems also require timely output of the EEG data computation, imposing constraints on the computation speed. The collection of EEG data with the help of EEG headsets with either dry or wet electrodes pose real problems including discomfort to the users especially with long hair, its weight on the head, etc. Sometimes decoding the affective state consistently and accurately pose problems.

In future our team would like to work on Multi-task cascaded-hybrid models of LSTM and CNN to combine their power and thus increase the accuracy of the emotion recognition system. The emotion detection system can be very effective in eliminating the gap between human emotions and computational technology, thus, enabling robots and computers to receive natural emotional feedback and improve human experiences. Even this system can be used by therapist to better evaluate their patients and find ways to predict and prevent depression before there are any clear outward signs of it.

Acknowledgment. This research work is performed under the nation wise initiative leadingindia.ai and Bennett University, India. They have supported us with lab and equipment during the experiments.

References

1. Acharya, D., et al.: An enhanced fitness function to recognize unbalanced human emotions data. Expert Syst. Appl. **166**, 114011 (2020)
2. Acharya, D., Billimoria, A., Srivastava, N., Goel, S., Bhardwaj, A.: Emotion recognition using fourier transform and genetic programming. Appl. Acoust. **164**, 107260 (2020)
3. Bairavi, K., Sundhara, K.K.: EEG based emotion recognition system for special children. In: Proceedings of the 2018 International Conference on Communication Engineering and Technology, pp. 1–4, February 2018
4. Dabas, H., Sethi, C., Dua, C., Dalawat, M., Sethia, D.: Emotion classification using EEG signals. In: Proceedings of the 2018 2nd International Conference on Computer Science and Artificial Intelligence, pp. 380–384, December 2018
5. Li, Y., Hu, B., Zheng, X., Li, X.: EEG-based mild depressive detection using differential evolution. IEEE Access **7**, 7814–7822 (2018)

6. Li, X., Yan, J.Z., Chen, J.H.: Channel division based multiple classifiers fusion for emotion recognition using EEG signals. In: ITM Web of Conferences, vol. 11, p. 07006. EDP Sciences (2017)

7. Donmez, H., Ozkurt, N.: Emotion classification from EEG signals in convolutional neural networks. In: 2019 Innovations in Intelligent Systems and Applications Conference (ASYU), pp. 1–6. IEEE (2019)

8. Yang, Y., Wu, Q., Qiu, M., Wang, Y., Chen, X.: Emotion recognition from multi-channel EEG through parallel convolutional recurrent neural network. In: 2018 International Joint Conference on Neural Networks (IJCNN), pp. 1–7. IEEE, July 2018

9. Tripathi, S., Acharya, S., Sharma, R.D., Mittal, S., Bhattacharya, S.: Using deep and convolutional neural networks for accurate emotion classification on DEAP dataset. In: Proceedings of the Thirty-First AAAI Conference on Artificial Intelligence, pp. 4746–4752, February 2017

10. Dunne, R.A., Campbell, N.A.: On the pairing of the softmax activation and cross-entropy penalty functions and the derivation of the softmax activation function. In: Proceedings of 8th Australian Conference on the Neural Networks, Melbourne, vol. 181, p. 185. Citeseer, June 1997

11. Liu, W., Zheng, W.-L., Bao-Liang, L.: Emotion recognition using multimodal deep learning. In: Hirose, A., Ozawa, S., Doya, K., Ikeda, K., Lee, M., Liu, D. (eds.) Neural information processing, pp. 521–529. Springer, Cham (2016). https://doi.org/10.1007/978-3-319-46672-9_58

12. Alhagry, S., Fahmy, A.A., El-Khoribi, R.A.: Emotion recognition based on EEG using LSTM recurrent neural network. Emotion 8(10), 355–358 (2017)

13. Zhang, J., Chen, M., Hu, S., Cao, Y., Kozma, R.: PNN for EEG-based emotion recognition. In: 2016 IEEE International Conference on Systems, Man, and Cybernetics (SMC), pp. 002319–002323. IEEE, October 2016

14. Zhong, P., Wang, D., Miao, C.: EEG-based emotion recognition using regularized graph neural networks. IEEE Trans. Affect. Comput. (2020)

15. Li, Y., et al.: A novel bi-hemispheric discrepancy model for EEG emotion recognition. IEEE Trans. Cogn. Dev. Syst. (2020)

16. Acharya, D., Goel, S., Bhardwaj, H., Sakalle, A., Bhardwaj, A.: A long short term memory deep learning network for the classification of negative emotions using EEG signals. In: 2020 International Joint Conference on Neural Networks (IJCNN), Glasgow, United Kingdom, pp. 1–8 (2020). https://doi.org/10.1109/IJCNN48605.2020.9207280

17. Bhardwaj, A., Tiwari, A., Varma, M.V., Krishna, M.R.: Classification of EEG signals using a novel genetic programming approach. In: Proceedings of the Companion Publication of the 2014 Annual Conference on Genetic and Evolutionary Computation (GECCO Comp 2014), pp. 1297–1304. Association for Computing Machinery, New York (2014). https://doi.org/10.1145/2598394.2609851

18. Bhardwaj, H., Sakalle, A., Bhardwaj, A., Tiwari, A.: Classification of electroencephalogram signal for the detection of epilepsy using Innovative Genetic Programming. Expert Syst. 36, e12338 (2019). https://doi.org/10.1111/exsy.12338

19. Acharya, D., Goel, S., Asthana, R., Bhardwaj, A.: A Novel fitness function in genetic programming to handle unbalanced emotion recognition data. Pattern Recogn. Lett. 133, 272–279 (2020). https://doi.org/10.1016/j.patrec.2020.03.005

20. https://www.eecs.qmul.ac.uk/mmv/datasets/deap/readme.html

21. Abhang, P.A., Mehrotra, S.C.: Introduction to EEG- and Speech-Based Emotion Recognition. Chapter 2 - Technological Basics of EEG Recording and Operation of Apparatus (2016)

22. Chollet, F. (2017). Keras (2015)

23. Hochreiter, S., Schmidhuber, J.: LSTM can solve hard long time lag problems. In: Advances in Neural Information Processing Systems, pp. 473–479 (1997)

24. Choi, E.J., Kim, D.K.: Arousal and valence classification model based on long short-term memory and deap data for mental healthcare management. Healthc. Inf. Res. **24**(4), 309–316 (2018)
25. Naser, D.S., Saha, G.: Recognition of emotions induced by music videos using DT-CWPT. In: 2013 Indian Conference on Medical Informatics and Telemedicine (ICMIT), Kharagpur, pp. 53–57 (2013). https://doi.org/10.1109/IndianCMIT.2013.6529408
26. Rozgić, V., Vitaladevuni, S.N., Prasad, R.: Robust EEG emotion classification using segment level decision fusion. In: 2013 IEEE International Conference on Acoustics, Speech and Signal Processing, Vancouver, BC, pp. 1286–1290 (2013). https://doi.org/10.1109/ICASSP. 2013.6637858
27. Næs, T., Kvaal, K., Isaksson, T., Miller, C.: Artificial neural networks in multivariate calibration. J. Near Infrared Spectrosc. **1**(1), 1–1 (1993). https://doi.org/10.1255/jnirs.1

MaskNet: Detecting Different Kinds of Face Mask for Indian Ethnicity

Abhinav Gola[1]([✉]) [iD], Sonia Panesar[2], Aradhna Sharma[3], Gayathri Ananthakrishnan[4],
Gaurav Singal[5] [iD], and Debajyoti Mukhopadhyay[5] [iD]

[1] National Institute of Technology, New Delhi, New Delhi, India
abhinavgola@gmail.com
[2] Babaria Institute of Technology, Vadodara, Gujarat, India
leosonia@gmail.com
[3] Maharaja Surajmal Institute of Technology, Delhi, India
aradhna.7sharma@gmail.com
[4] Vidya Academy of Science and Technology, Thrissur, Kerala, India
gaya3ananthakrishnan@gmail.com
[5] Bennett University, Greater Noida, Uttar Pradesh, India
gauravsingal789@gmail.com, debajyoti.mukhopadhyay@gmail.com

Abstract. The COVID-19 pandemic has rendered social distancing and use of face masks as an absolute necessity today. Coming out of the epidemic, we're going to see this as the new normal and therefore most workplaces will require an identification system to permit employees based on the compliance of protocols. To ensure minimal contact and security, automatic entrance systems need to be employed in workplaces and institutions. For the implementation of such systems, we have investigated the performance of three object detection algorithms, namely SSD MobileNet V2, YOLO v3 and YOLO v4 in the context of real-time face mask detection. We conducted training and testing of these algorithms on our dataset focusing on various type of masks in the Indian community. We have exhibited in this paper that YOLOv4 transcends both YOLO v3 and SSD MobileNet V2 in sensitivity and precision and thus has a major use case in building AI identification systems.

Keywords: Covid-19 · Face mask · Detection · Convolutional neural networks · YOLO · SSD MobileNet V2 · Object detection · Object recognition

1 Introduction

SARS-CoV-2 commonly known as Coronavirus has been wreaking havoc in more than 200 countries since December 2019. As of late October 2020, atleast 52 million people have been diagnosed with the virus with a total of more than 1 million deaths worldwide.

This has raised a grave need to improve fundamental public health measures and minimize the social and economic damage caused by this pandemic. Furthermore, many organisations have made it mandatory to allow their staff and/or customers to enter

D. Garg et al. (Eds.): IACC 2020, CCIS 1367, pp. 492–503, 2021.
https://doi.org/10.1007/978-981-16-0401-0_39

their premises only if they wear masks, which requires placement of either manual or automatic mask detection systems.

This can be achieved by using artificial intelligence techniques which are currently state-of-the-art methodologies and are being progressively involved in the detection of specific objects in images and videos. We focused on the object detection application of this field for the task of face mask detection. It is a two-step process to understand - first is to detect whether a mask is present in the image or not; in more technical terms this part is called object localization [18] where the model identifies all the predefined classes present in an image and then draws bounding boxes around each of them. The second step is to assign class labels to these bounding boxes which in our case refers to classifying whether the faces detected in an image are wearing a mask or not.

This was done with the use of Region-Based Convolutional Neural Networks, or R-CNNs, which address tasks of object localization and recognition. You Only Look Once, (YOLO) is another technique for object recognition in real-time. These type of face recogniser systems which are developed using machine learning make use of a large amount of data to learn. Also, this can't be done only for a single type of mask. There are different types of masks available like disposable masks, non-disposable masks which consist of surgical masks, non -surgical masks, clothed face masks and respirators with filtering features like N95 masks etc. Other protective equipment like face shields, medical goggles are sometimes used along with face masks. In India especially, as there is no examination on disinfecting and reusing fabric veils, as of May 2020 [1], people do not use standard surgical face masks and instead rely on covering their faces by their hands or other types of veils like a clothed face mask. These types of masks vary in style and type – a scarf around the face or a tied handkerchief on the mouth etc.

As far as we are aware, there are no publicly available datasets covering such variety of masks, and therefore this work proposes a dataset focused on specific types of masks used in India. We present this dataset in 2 formats – YOLO and Pascal VOC for which two types of annotations were carried out on the dataset. Various pre-processing algorithms were applied to the dataset which included adding noise, rotating, flipping, cropping and resizing of the image. The dataset has been made public and can be found at [9]. We also propose a novel face mask detector based on the state-of-the-art object detection model YOLO v4. To the best of our knowledge, the proposed system is the first such detection system dedicated to the Indian society.

The rest of the paper is composed as follows. We discuss previous works related to face mask detection in Sect. 2. Methodology and datasets are expressed in Sect. 3. Then, the final results are displayed in Sect. 4 with the conclusion and future work in Sect. 5.

2 Related Work

The authors of [4] investigated the impacts and workings related to Coronavirus in their paper on February 20, 2020. This study is being used as a basis for a source of information for every research related to Covid-19. Approaching our specific task, studies conducted for masked face detection and/or recognition are quite sparse. This work was initiated by the authors of [2], who realised that the existing facial recognition systems which were employed for the tasks of security checking, automation of attendance etc. were giving poor performance because of increased use of masks in this pandemic. In the paper, they've explained various practical applications of face detection and recognition and have also produced three datasets for such tasks.

Building on the previous research, the authors of [3] have proposed a feature pyramid network (FPN) to build a one-stage detector. Their cross-class object removal algorithm which rejects low-confidence and high intersection of union (IoU) predictions achieved good results for precision and recall metrics. Daniell Chiang with AIZOOTech implemented a mask detecting algorithm with 5 major deep learning frameworks – PyTorch, TensorFlow, Keras, MXNet and Caffe. Their algorithm which was based on SSD Lite was trained on the dataset which they created using images from WIDER Face and MAFA [16]. All of their models along with the dataset have been open-sourced for anyone to use.

Xiaobin Li and Shengjin Wang in their paper [5], have proposed a concise and efficient framework of two eight-layer CNNs [17] for object localisation in remote sensing images. They have achieved great results in detecting inshore ships using Google Earth images. They have also proposed a new cropping method of trapezium shape instead of rectangular shape for doing the pre-processing of sample images which can be used for object detection tasks where conventional cropping methods are not possible to implement.

Joseph Redmon and Anelia Angelova in [6], have explored the real-time approach to robotic grasp detection using single-stage regression as an alternative to 'sliding window' and regional proposal techniques. Their model has shown good results while running at 13 FPS on a GPU. It can simultaneously perform detection of an object and assigning a bounding box to it in a single step. Also, in [7] Toshanlal Meenpal, Ashutosh Balakrishnan and Amit Verma have proposed a binate face classifier which can detect randomly aligned faces in input images. They used a pre-trained VGG-16 model to expedite their training time while using Binomial Cross-Entropy as their loss metric. Using post-processing techniques on the outputs from the model, they were able to detect multiple sideways aligned faces too. The authors of [8] have proposed an end-to-end trainable model for extracting face masks from video frames. They used a combination of convolutional LSTM networks and FCNs with a loss function that they introduced named as segmentation loss, optimising the IOU outputs. Their study shows a significant improvement over the baseline FCN network.

Currently, all of the models which are being used for real-time face mask detection are trained on datasets primarily containing images of people of Chinese and in other cases, western ethnicity. Due to this, they fail to perform when tested on datasets with people of other countries. India, currently the second-worst country to be hit by this pandemic can't rely on these existing models. Therefore, there was a critical need to develop a system specifically trained on images of people of Indian ethnicity.

Additionally, current SOTA models are trained to detect only standard surgical masks and thus, do not recognise makeshift masks like handkerchiefs, dupatta etc. Especially in India, where people use different types of veils like scarves or chunnis around their head and neck, these types of clothing can confuse an artificial model unless it's previously trained to recognise and discard them. We overcome these challenges by first constructing a data set consisting of all the nuances of the Indian culture. We included images with people wearing the various type of garments such as turbans and stoles to wrap their bodies. Therefore, training our model on such a dataset helped it in understanding the myriad of situations that it might face in real-world scenarios.

3 Methodology

In this paper, we compare and evaluate the performance of three object detection methodologies – SSD MobileNet V2, YOLO v3 and YOLO v4 when applied for the task of real-time face mask detection, in terms of accuracy and precision. Figure 1 represents the procedure to implement these three end-to-end trainable models.

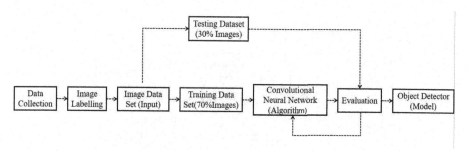

Fig. 1. Methodology flowchart

3.1 Architectures and Algorithms

SSD MobileNet V2: MobileNet uses bottleneck residual blocks consisting of 3 convolutional layers as shown in Fig. 2. Each layer uses batch normalisation and,ReLu6 as an activation function to introduce non-linearity to the data flowing through them except the last layer which doesn't use an activation function. Using an activation function in the last layer destroys useful information obtained from it as it outputs a low dimensional data. First one is the 1×1 convolution expansion layer which is named so as it boosts the numbers of channels in the input data. The output coming from the 1st layer is *filtered* by the depth-wise convolution layer. It involves edge detection, colour filtering, and so on.

The last layer in the model is the linear projection layer that outputs a low dimensional tensor which was projected from a high dimensional data. It serves as the bottleneck layer as it is responsible for narrowing down of the data flowing through the network. It operates much as in ResNet, and aids with gradient flow through the network. Stacking 17 of such blocks in series and then following them by a traditional 1×1 convolution, a pooling and a classification layer results in the complete MobileNet V2 structure. To use SSD with MobileNet we take the outputs of the last layers of MobileNet and feed them into the SSD layers.

YOLO v3: It was introduced as an upgrade over its predecessors: YOLO v1 and YOLO v2. Unlike YOLO v1 which had 24 convolutional layers followed by 2 fully connected layers and YOLO v2 which used a custom deep architecture darknet-19, v3 uses a variant of Darknet, adding 53 more layers to the initial structure for the detection function, and thereby giving us a 106-layer convolutional network.

The newer architecture incorporates what YOLO v2's architecture was lacking - residual blocks, skip connections and upsampling. Detections being done at three distinct ratios using detection kernels is one of the most significant features of the v3. The shape of the detection kernel is:

$$1 \times 1 \times (B \times (5 + C)) \tag{1}$$

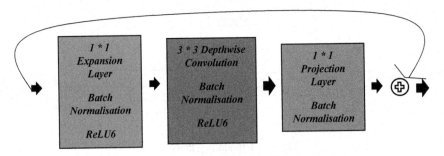

Fig. 2. Bottleneck residue block of MobileNet V2

Here, B represents number of bounding boxes and the number of classes is given by C. Also, YOLO v3 now allows multilabel classification for detected objects by using logistic regression instead of softmaxing the classes. YOLO algorithms use 2 primary evaluation metrics for object detection. First is the Intersection Over Union (IOU) which is calculated by dividing the area which is common in both boxes with the total area of the two boxes. Its value lies between 0 and 1.

When an object detection model predicts a bounding box, it initially calculates the IOU between the predicted bounding box and the ground truth box and if the IOU value [11] is above the threshold only then the bounding box is considered.

$$IOU = \frac{Area\ of\ Intersection}{Area\ of\ Union} \tag{2}$$

The second metric used by YOLO algorithms is Non-Max Suppression which keeps track that the algorithm detects an object only once. It will look for the probability of detection of each bounding box. The most confident detection will be the one having the highest probability and the metric will then suppress the other boxes.

YOLOv4: *YOLOv4 Backbone Network – Feature Extraction*: It compresses features down through a convolutional neural network backbone. Based on their intuition and experimental results, the final YOLOv4 network implements CSPDarknet53 for the backbone network and based on DenseNet. Its main function is to eliminate computational bottlenecks in the DenseNet and providing an unchanged feature map as its output to facilitate learning.

YOLOv4 Neck - Feature Aggregation: The combination of backbone feature layers happens in the neck. YOLOv4 chooses PANet for the feature aggregation of the network. Additionally, YOLOv4 adds a SPP block after CSPDarknet53 which improves the receptive field and sorts out relevant features from the backbone.

YOLOv4 Head - The Detection Step: YOLOv4 deploys the same YOLO head as YOLOv3 for detection with the anchor-based detection steps, and three levels of detection granularity. CIoU loss is used as it gives an improved performace over MSE, IoU and GIoU loss as a result of faster convergence. [12] The integrated architecture of YOLO V4 is shown in Fig. 3.

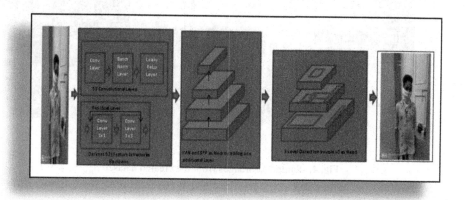

Fig. 3. YOLO v4 architecture diagram

3.2 Generation/Fabrication of Dataset

Most of the datasets available for the face mask detection problem pertained to either Western countries or China. Therefore, there was a necessity of a dataset centred towards the Indian community where alongside standard surgical masks, images of people wearing other types of home-made veils like dupattas and handkerchiefs must also be included. Also, cases like cloth or a turban covering the head need to be included to help the models learn better.

Table 1. Dataset size

Model	Train	Valid.	Test
Size of dataset	1700	200	100

We tackled this challenge by generating our dataset including the above-mentioned categories of images. For this task, we used Sony IMX 519 with pixel size 1.22 um, Samsung Isocell GW1 with pixel size 0.8 um and Sony IMX 586 with pixel size 1.75 um sensors. With each sensor, we collected 800 images with different angles and backgrounds. This dataset was then pre-processed which included splitting it into training, validation, and testing folders and performing resizing, orienting and colour corrections. The ratio of train:valid:test images was kept 1700:200:100. The dataset was then converted into 2 formats -YOLO [For v3 and v4] and Pascal VOC [For SSD MobileNet V2]. This was done using the open-sourced software -LabelImg [10]. The final dataset has been uploaded on the Mendeley Data repository for future uses. Some samples of the images created are displayed in Fig. 4 and the dataset size is mentioned in Table 1.

Fig. 4. Sample of images from the created dataset

3.3 Experimental Setup and Model Training

Transfer Learning: In order to train faster and maximise our accuracy more efficiently with our limited face mask dataset, we used transfer learning. The idea is to first train a model on an extensive and broad dataset. Then, the feature maps learned by this model can be customized for a targeted task. All three models were trained in Google Colab with Nvidia Tesla K80 GPU chip and 12 GB RAM to recognise two classes – 'masked and 'without mask'. Also, before feeding the dataset into the networks we used data augmentation techniques like flipping, rotating, cropping, adding noise and occluding portions of the images to improve the downstream performance of our model.

SSD + MobileNet V2: We used SSD MobileNet V2 as our base model. After preprocessing, we had two.csv files that contained the images' filename and the label/box position respectively. We also had a.pbtxt file that carried a label map for each class. TFRecords file was created for the test and train labels as we're working on TensorFlow and it takes input in the form of data.record file.

Our next step was selecting the pre-trained model, ssd_mobilenet_v2 from the TensorFlow object detection API. Necessary changes were made to the configuration file and saved. The initial learning rate was set to 0.003 and both the momentum and weight decay value were set to 0.9. The model was then trained for 200k steps. The training process was visualized using the TensorBoard. Finally, the model was evaluated on the test set.

YOLO v3: We trained the YOLO v3 model on Darknet framework. First, we configured v3's GPU environment on Google Colab by installing cuDNN on top of Colab's GPU drivers. We added the paths to our images and annotations to the Darknet folder. Then we customized the.confg file according to our dataset. Batch size was set to 32 and subdivisions to 8. The momentum value for stochastic gradient descent and the weight decay had values of 0.9 and 0.0005 respectively. The size of input images was set at height $= 608$ and width $= 608$ and the initial learning rate at 0.001. The threshold value was kept at 0.3. Finally, the model was evaluated on the test set.

YOLO v4: The YOLO v4 model was also trained on the Darknet framework. Again, the configuration of v3's GPU environment on Google Colab was done by the installation of cuDNN on top of Colab's GPU drivers. The paths to our images and annotations and the file containing the names of our cases (obj.names) were added to the Darknet folder. Then we customized the.confg file by setting the batch size to 64 and subdivisions to 12. The momentum value for stochastic gradient descent and the weight decay were put as 0.949 and 0.0005 respectively. The size of input images was set at height $= 416$ and width $= 416$ and the initial learning rate at 0.001. The threshold value was again kept at 0.3. Finally, the model was evaluated on the test set.

4 Experimental Results

We initially tested each of the three models on our own test data. They were also tested on the task of detecting face masks in video sequences using the method presented in Fig. 5.

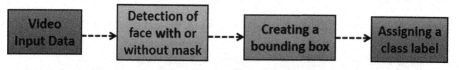

Fig. 5. Stages of detection

4.1 Metrics Used

Performance evaluation for all the three algorithms was done using four parameters (Precision, Recall, F1 Score and Mean Average Precision). These are defined as follows:

$$Precision = \frac{True\ Positives}{True\ Positives + False\ Positives} \tag{3}$$

$$Recall = \frac{True\ Positives}{True\ Positives + False\ Negatives} \tag{4}$$

$$\text{F1 Score} = 2 \cdot \frac{\text{Precision} * \text{Recall}}{\text{Precision} + \text{Recall}} \tag{5}$$

where True Positives are the number of times our classes were successfully detected by the model while False Positives are the number of times our classes were falsely detected by it. Furthermore, False Negative tell us the number of times our model failed to recognize any of the classes in the image. YOLO uses the Mean Average Precision criterium as defined in the PASCAL VOC 2010 challenge. Broadly, it can be defined as the area under the precision-recall curve.

4.2   Performance Evaluation

Samples of the images used to test our models are demonstrated in Fig. 6 with their corresponding results in Fig. 7. Table 2 displays the values of the chosen evaluation metrics for each model. We can observe from the table that all three of the algorithms have a high precision rate (99.34% for SSD MobileNet V2 vs 99.59% for YOLOv3 vs 99.88% for YOLO v4). Therefore, the probability of a class being right when detected is very high. We also observe that YOLOv4 outperforms both YOLO v3 and SSD MobileNet V2 in the comparison of recall values 99.21% for YOLO v4 versus 99.03% for YOLOv3 and 86.70% for SSD MobileNet V2. The plots for loss curves for each model are shown in Fig. 8.

Fig. 6. Sample of images used for testing

Fig. 7. Detection results

Because of the high *recall* values, YOLOv4 has a higher F1 score than the other two models with a value of *99.54%*. Comparing the mean average precision score for each, we notice that YOLO v4 again surpasses the others with an mAP of *88%* while V3 and SSD have respective values of *85%* and *79%*.

Table 2: Evaluation metrics used

Metric	SSD MobileNet V2	YOLO v3	YOLO v4
Precision (TPR)	99.34%	99.59%	**99.88%**
Sensitivity (recall)	86.70%	99.03%	**99.21%**
F1 Score	92.59%	99.30%	**99.54%**
mAP	79%	85%	**88%**

4.3   Result Comparison with Related Works

For this dataset [9], there is no reported accuracy as this is a novel dataset which we have proposed during our study. We report F1 scores of 92.59%, 99.3% and 99.54% on our 3 models. For the sake of comparison, we reproduced the research of authors of [13] by employing ResNet50 as a feature extractor and with decision trees, SVM and ensemble as classifiers. We trained this hybrid model on RMFD [2], SMFD [15] and LFW [14] datasets and they produced F1 scores ranging from 45% to 60%. We believe the poor performance of these hybrid models on our test dataset is due to them being trained on datasets disparate from the Indian milieu and with no understanding of various makeshift masks used by Indian citizens.

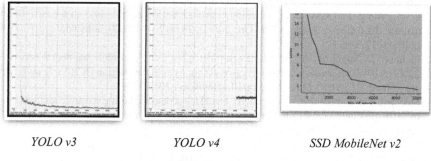

YOLO v3   YOLO v4   SSD MobileNet v2

Fig. 8. Loss curves

5   Conclusion and Future Work

Three object detection pipelines were implemented and analysed for our task of real-time face mask detection – SSD MobileNet V2, YOLO v3 and YOLO v4. We first described the architectural structure and working of each model. Then, we specified the procedure for creating a face mask detection dataset specifically focused towards India. All the three models were trained and tested on this captured dataset. Based on the higher values of the evaluation metrics obtained in case of YOLO v4, we infer that for the future purposes of object detection tasks, it should be set as the paragon model against which other models can be contrasted.

This research serves as a guideline for systems that plan to use AI for face mask monitoring. Though it demonstrates that YOLO v4 is the apropos go-to model for the subsequent tasks, it also provides experimental information to serve as a basis for other researchers to determine the algorithms suitable for their tasks. A minor limitation of the proposed model is that it struggles with small-sized objects and variance in aspects and ratios. Still, YOLO v3 and YOLO v4 are a huge improvement over the earlier versions. Ideally, the model should be able to detect objects at multiple scales and ratios but it struggles when encountering a wide range of sizes and aspect ratios. Our study can be expanded for detection of masks specific to other local regions. Also, to make the entrance validation system more efficient, the detection of thermal imaging can be added as a filter for healthiness.

References

1. Garcia Godoy, L.R., Jones, A.E., Anderson, T.N., et al.: Facial protection for healthcare workers during pandemics: a scoping review. BMJ Glob Health. **5**(5), e002553 (2020). https://doi.org/10.1136/bmjgh-2020-002553
2. Wang, Z., et al.: Masked face recognition dataset and application, arXiv preprint arXiv:2003.09093 (2020)
3. Jiang, M., Fan, X.: RetinaMask: A Face Mask detector. arXiv preprint arXiv:2005.03950 (2020)
4. Zhu, N., et al.: China Novel Coronavirus Investigating and Research Team: A Novel Coronavirus from Patients with Pneumonia in China (2019)
5. Li, X., Wang, S.: Object detection using convolutional neural networks in a coarse-to-fine manner. IEEE Geosci. Remote Sens. Lett. **14**(11), 2037–2041 (2017). https://doi.org/10.1109/LGRS.2017.2749478
6. Redmon, J., Angelova, A.: Real-time grasp detection using convolutional neural networks. In: 2015 IEEE International Conference on Robotics and Automation (ICRA), Seattle, WA, pp. 1316–1322 (2015). https://doi.org/10.1109/ICRA.2015.7139361
7. Meenpal, T., Balakrishnan, A., Verma, A.: Facial mask detection using semantic segmentation. In: 2019 4th International Conference on Computing, Communications and Security (ICCCS) (2019). https://doi.org/10.1109/ICCCS46555
8. Wang, Y., Luo, B., Shen, J., Pantic, M.: Face mask extraction in video sequence. Int. J. Comput. Vision **127**(6–7), 625–641 (2018). https://doi.org/10.1007/s11263-018-1130-2
9. Ananthakrishnan, G., Gola, A., Panesar, S., Sharma, A., Singal, G.: Indian Facemasks Detection Dataset. Mendeley Data, V2 (2020). https://doi.org/10.17632/xz5hbd6zds.2
10. https://github.com/tzutalin/labelImg. Accessed 22 Oct 2020
11. Yu, J., Jiang, Y., Wang, Z., Cao, Z., Huang, T.: UnitBox: an advanced object detection network. In: Proceedings of the 24th ACM International Conference on Multimedia (2016). https://doi.org/10.1145/2964284.2967274
12. Rezatofighi, H., Tsoi, N., Gwak, J., Sadeghian, A., Reid, I., Savarese, S.: Generalized intersection over union: a metric and a loss for bounding box regression. In: 2019 IEEE/CVF Conference on Computer Vision and Pattern Recognition (CVPR), Long Beach, CA, USA, pp. 658–666 (2019). https://doi.org/10.1109/CVPR.2019.00075
13. Loey, M., Manogaran, G., Taha, M.H.N., Khalifa, N.E.M.: A hybrid deep transfer learning model with machine learning methods for face mask detection in the era of the COVID-19 pandemic. **167**, 108288 (2021). https://doi.org/10.1016/j.measurement.2020.108288

14. Learned-Miller, E., Huang, G.B., RoyChowdhury, A., Li, H., Hua, G.: Labeled faces in the wild: a survey. In: Michal Kawulok, M., Celebi, E., Smolka, B. (eds.) Advances in Face Detection and Facial Image Analysis, pp. 189–248. Springer, Cham (2016). https://doi.org/10.1007/978-3-319-25958-1_8

15. prajnasb: observations. observations. https://github.com/prajnasb/observations. Accessed 21 May 2020

16. Kushwaha, R., Singal, G., Nain, N.: A texture feature based approach for person verification using footprint bio-metric. Artif. Intell. Rev. (2020). https://doi.org/10.1007/s10462-020-098 87-6

17. Veeramsetty, V., Singal, G., Badal, T.: CoinNet: platform independent application to recognize indian currency notes using deep learning techniques. Multimedia Tools Appl. **79**(31–32), 22569–22594 (2020). https://doi.org/10.1007/s11042-020-09031-0

18. Pareek, B., Gupta, P., Singal, G., Kushwaha, R.: Person identification using autonomous drone through resource constraint devices. In: Sixth International Conference on Internet of Things: Systems, Management and Security (IOTSMS), p. 124. IEEE (2019)

Author Index

Printed in the United States
By Bookmasters